CHEMICALLY DEPENDENT ANONYMOUS

Copyright © 1990 by
CDA COMMUNICATIONS, INC. GENERAL SERVICES OFFICE
All rights reserved.

The Twelve Steps and Twelve Traditions
are reprinted and adapted with permission of
Alcoholics Anonymous World Services, Inc.

Permission to reprint and adapt the Twelve Steps and Twelve Traditions does not mean that A.A. has reviewed or approved the contents of this publication or that A.A. agrees with the views expressed herein. A.A. is a program of recovery from alcoholism. Use of the Twelve Steps and Twelve Traditions in connection with programs and activities that are patterned after A.A. but which address other problems does not imply otherwise.

The first and last paragraphs of Chapter 6, CDA's Twelve Steps, are reprinted and adapted with permission of Narcotics Anonymous World Service, Inc.

CDA FOR THE NEWCOMER is copyrighted
© by CDA Communications, Inc.

Adaptation of the last paragraph of the introduction to the questions, the first ten questions and the final paragraph of Chapter 11 are reprinted here with permission. CDA's Twelve Steps and Twelve Traditions are also reprinted here with permission.

Library of Congress Catalog Card Number 90-81598

ISBN 978-0-9778506-2-4

First Printing 1990
Second Printing 1997
Third Printing 2002
Fourth Printing 2007
Revised Fifth Printing 2012
(revised "The Fellowship," "Why CDA," "The CDA Gifts")
Printed in the United States of America

CHEMICALLY DEPENDENT ANONYMOUS

CDA COMMUNICATIONS, INC.

GENERAL SERVICE OFFICE
P.O. Box 423
Severna Park, MD 21146-0423

1-888-CDA-HOPE

CONTENTS

FOREWORD VII
ACKNOWLEDGEMENT IX
TESTIMONIALS XI

PART I 1

1. THE FELLOWSHIP 3
2. WHY CDA? 5
3. LET'S REDEFINE "ADDICT" AND "ADDICTION" 7
4. THE ESSENTIAL ELEMENTS 13
5. CDA ROOTS 17
6. CDA'S TWELVE STEPS 21
   - *Step 1* 23
   - *Step 2* 26
   - *Step 3* 31
   - *Step 4* 35
   - *Step 5* 41
   - *Step 6* 44
   - *Step 7* 46
   - *Step 8* 48
   - *Step 9* 51
   - *Step 10* 56
   - *Step 11* 59
   - *Step 12* 63
7. CDA'S TWELVE TRADITIONS 69
   - *First Tradition* 71
   - *Second Tradition* 71
   - *Third Tradition* 73
   - *Fourth Tradition* 73
   - *Fifth Tradition* 75
   - *Sixth Tradition* 75
   - *Seventh Tradition* 76
   - *Eighth Tradition* 78
   - *Ninth Tradition* 80
   - *Tenth Tradition* 82
   - *Eleventh Tradition* 83
   - *Twelfth Tradition* 84
8. THE CDA GIFTS 87
9. H.O.W. 89

	Honesty	*89*
	Open-mindedness	*91*
	Willingness to Try	*92*
10	LOW SELF-ESTEEM	95
11	QUESTIONS: CDA FOR THE NEWCOMER	97
12	A CDA JOURNAL	103
13	FUN IN RECOVERY	117
14	EPILOGUE: THE FUTURE	121

PART II **123**

15	I FINALLY FOUND MY NICHE	127
16	THY WILL BE DONE	131
17	OUT OF THE CRACK HOUSE	135
18	THINGS I MUST EARN	149
19	RECOVERED, NOT CURED	153
20	DREAMS COME TRUE	159
21	RITES OF PASSAGE	167
22	DARKNESS DISPELLED	173
23	GOING TO ANY LENGTH!	183
24	GOD DOESN'T MAKE JUNK	187
25	I AM	197
26	MY LOVE FOR CDA	201
27	IN GOD'S OWN GOOD TIME	215
28	LOVE SET ME FREE	229
29	MISERABLE MIKE	239
30	A SIXTIES IDEALIST	249
31	EVENING THE ODDS	259
32	HAPPINESS TOO IS INEVITABLE	273
33	I COULDN'T KNOCK THE LOVE	285
34	A MEDICAL MIRACLE	299
35	NO MORE EXCUSES	313
36	KEEP AN OPEN MIND: SOMETHING MAY FALL IN	325
37	A LOVE STORY	339
	APPENDIX A	357
	APPENDIX B	359

Foreword

This is the first attempt of the Fellowship of Chemically Dependent Anonymous to share its history, philosophical underpinnings and program with others in our own book. We have based our program on one proven successful for over half a century by Alcoholics Anonymous in helping alcoholics find the road to recovery and a new way of life. As the focus of our program, we have adapted A.A.'s Twelve Steps and Twelve Traditions, changing them only as they refer to chemical dependency in its entirety rather than alcohol abuse alone. We are grateful to A.A. for pointing the way for us as it has for many other anonymous groups.

The CDA First Edition Committee consisting of four members of the Fellowship first met in May 1986 at Thanksgiving Farm in Harwood, Maryland to discuss the possibility of publishing a book for CDA. We delegated various committees such as the Steps Committee, the Traditions Committee and the H.O.W. Committee to begin work on enlarging upon the fundamental principles of our program. We found a lawyer to advise us on the legalities connected with our literary endeavor.

We then made several announcements to the general membership over a period of three years requesting personal story contributions to the book. We found editors who compiled our materials and prepared it for publication. We incorporated our publishing division, CDA COMMUNICATIONS, INC., General Service Office, in

October 1989. At long last, our dreams have come to fruition as we present *Chemically Dependent Anonymous* to the world.

The First Edition Committee wishes to thank all the individuals and committees who generously contributed their time and ideas and those who gathered or submitted material for this volume. Special thanks go to the 23 courageous recovering men and women who have been willing to share their personal stories about their addictions, their attempts at recovery and their successes in combating many varieties of substance abuse. The stories have been kept as close to their exact words as possible. Only those who have been there can so eloquently explain how they have been able to rebuild their lives. These CDA members want to give hope to others that they too may find freedom from their addictions through CDA's own time-tested program of recovery.

The CDA First Edition Committee dedicates this book to you, the reader, with our sincere wishes that what you find herein will help you or those you are helping discover the new life of health, sanity and sobriety that CDA has to offer. May God (as you understand Him) guide you on your way.

Acknowledgement

We are grateful to those in the mental health field, members of other anonymous organizations, business people, the clergy and the public in general for their support and recognition of our efforts to continue carrying our message of hope for recovery to others.

Testimonials

SLIGO CREEK PSYCHOLOGICAL SERVICES
1420 Woodman Avenue
Silver Spring, Maryland 20902

Dear CDA Members,

I am very pleased that the Chemically Dependent Anonymous (CDA) meetings are now available to younger teenage clients and other young-adult residents of Montgomery County, Maryland, and that they are encouraged, confronted and supported by others of this peer group in their efforts to become free of chemicals. I know that the therapists of this and other private practices, as well as public services for adolescent day treatment, family therapy and adult addictions, have been deeply inspired by the supportive work of CDA. The attendance of voluntary and mandatory clients and the high volume of participation at these meetings speak very well for the dedication and sincerity of involvement by their leaders. The resulting changes in attitude, lifestyle and school grades of CDA adolescents and young adults have been very encouraging.

Thank you for your continued efforts in the collaborative support of private and public programs here in Montgomery County. I wish continued success to your Fellowship in its endeavors to provide a program for those who seek recovery from drug and alcohol dependence. I strongly endorse your twelve-step method as a viable process for achieving recovery from substance abuse.

Sincerely,

*Thomas W. Summers, Ph.D. Psychologist,
Clinical Director*

To Whom It May Concern:

Years ago, my life was utterly hopeless because of a drinking problem. Then I got "trapped" into attending Alcoholics Anonymous meetings and gradually started working the Program. That saved my life and showed me a way to personal freedom. Indeed, I have seen the miracle of A.A. work for countless others in our country and around the world.

Along with A.A.'s success has come a profound change in the public's attitude. People now recognize alcoholism, once thought to be a moral deficiency, as a health problem. This conversion is having a beneficial effect on the prospects for still-suffering alcoholics.

Alcoholics can help other alcoholics because they understand each other and are unified by their common problem. This wholeness however has suffered in recent years because of changes in society and the way drugs are used today. Many newcomers to A.A. now have other drug problems along with their alcoholism and a small number are not alcoholics at all.

This inconsistency has been lessened in our area of the country because of the influence of Chemically Dependent Anonymous, an organization that began in

Annapolis, Maryland in 1980. CDA is open to anyone who is dependent on mind-altering chemicals of any sort. Although not allied with A.A., CDA closely follows the model provided by Alcoholics Anonymous. Having both programs available, newcomers can decide whether they properly belong in CDA, A.A. or both. And, as a result, both fellowships have become healthier and more complete.

I was initially attracted to CDA because a family member had recovered from cocaine addiction by participating in that program. I started attending CDA meetings too and I now consider myself eligible for membership because of my chemical dependency to alcohol.

I believe that in working together (though still independently), CDA and A.A. will strengthen both fellowships and offer greater hope and opportunity for recovery to those enslaved by drugs. Eventually, the myths and hysteria about drug addiction will slip away and the public will become more understanding and supportive. And I think that in the 21st Century, Chemically Dependent Anonymous will do for the drug addict what A.A. has done for the alcoholic in the 20th Century.

Bob R. (an active member of A.A. for over 30 years)

To Whom It May Concern:

In 1981, I had the good fortune of meeting a young man who was a member of CDA. After many conversations and interviews, and being fully aware of his background as a chemical dependent, I offered him a contract as a New York Life Sales Representative. To this day, I am very glad that I made that decision. Not only has this employee become a strong force and successful sales representative in my office, but he is also one of the top agents in the entire company.

In the years I have known him, I have had the opportunity to become acquainted with many others who are also part of the CDA Program. Some of these people we have hired and some we've rejected from a job application standpoint. However, I have been very impressed with the personal programs each one of these individuals has established. Although some of them were unable to become successful as sales representatives with New York Life, I think that everyone who departed the company left with a better understanding of sales and went on to be successful in other fields.

Through CDA, these people have been able to establish new lives for themselves with a commitment not often found in others. Until seven years ago, I had no idea of the impact CDA had on its members, but I can assure you I am most impressed. Today, I do not hesitate to talk to any members of CDA who have established programs of their own.

Sincerely,
James E. Adkins, CLU, ChFC General Manager

My Dear Friends,

By the grace of God and through His gift to me, the blessed Fellowship of Alcoholics Anonymous, I am a grateful recovering alcoholic. At this writing, I have been sober in Alcoholics Anonymous for 13½ years (since November 17, 1973). A miracle - believe me!

I am a religious brother who has been a member of a Roman Catholic order for the past 37 years. Currently, I am the order's chief financial officer and its corporate treasurer.

On a daily basis, I am actively involved in Alcoholics Anonymous. I attend meetings, conduct twelve-step oriented retreats for members of Alcoholics Anonymous and Al-Anon, sponsor or serve as spiritual advisor to approximately 40 men, do one-on-one counseling and serve part time on the staff of an alcoholic treatment facility in this geographical area of Maryland.

I acknowledge without reservation that my sobriety is a gift that I received from God, as I understand Him, bestowed upon me through the Program of Alcoholics Anonymous. I further acknowledge that my continued sobriety is contingent upon my fidelity to the principles of Alcoholics Anonymous' Twelve-Step Program, to my continuing to practice these principles in all my affairs and to my continued participation in A.A. meetings on a regular basis.

I have come to know that alcoholism and drug abuse are diseases - fatal diseases - and that the compulsive addiction to the substance abused is the overriding characteristic of these illnesses. Truly, diseases of addiction!

My first encounter with the Fellowship of Chemically Dependent Anonymous (CDA) was in 1980 in the Annapolis, Bowie and Rockville areas of Maryland. CDA publicly acknowledges in its literature its indebtedness and gratitude "... to the co-founders of Alcoholics Anonymous for the 'Twelve Steps' and 'Twelve Traditions' which are the basis of our program." Many Chemically Dependent Anonymous members who are alcoholics attend A.A. meetings. It was in this setting that I first met members of CDA.

Immediately, I was deeply impressed by individual recovering addicts I met, and I agreed to share my experience, strength and hope at a Chemically Dependent Anonymous meeting. Later, I agreed to lead discussions on the Twelve Steps, especially the Third and Eleventh Steps. I was privileged to conduct the first CDA-oriented retreat. To demonstrate my support, great esteem and deep affection for the members of Chemically Dependent Anonymous, I attend CDA meetings where individuals are celebrating periods of being "clean and sober."

Chemically Dependent Anonymous deals with the disease of addiction without making any distinction as to the substance being abused. CDA calls for total abstinence from any mood-changing chemical.

In my judgment, based upon personal association and experience with CDA members, that fellowship's program of recovery from the disease of addiction is viable. It works! "By their fruits you shall know them" (Luke 6, 44). Could it be otherwise? No! At least not when an individual unconditionally surrenders to the Twelve-Step Program of CDA. The Fellowship of Alcoholics Anonymous has fifty years of undeniable success of its members who have lived lives based upon that program's Twelve Steps. These approximately 200 words of inspired wisdom, wisdom that transcends human wisdom, are the keys to sanity and sanctity, to wholeness and holiness. The Twelve Steps are what Father Al G. once described as: "A master plan for living more accurately, the Master's plan for living."

Chemically Dependent Anonymous is rapidly developing its own undeniable record of success! Men and women are coming to this program in increasing numbers and are recovering - becoming, and remaining, clean and sober. They are happy people living useful and *productive lives, loving and serving God as each understands Him. They have learned to love and serve God in the person of His creatures, especially other suffering addicts (their "brothers" and "sisters"). Each enthusiastically carries the message of hope and the conviction which is based upon personal experience: "It can be done, with God's help!"*

I have observed that the members of Chemically Dependent Anonymous are bonded together, merrily traveling the road to freedom. They do not limit their association with one another simply to "meeting times," but have expanded their times of togetherness to include many other dimensions of life which enriches their fellowship and provides an even greater measure of support.

I am pleased and honored to humbly but enthusiastically endorse and recommend the goals of Chemically Dependent Anonymous and the means that fellowship recommends to achieve those goals.

To the newcomer: "Sursum corda!" – "Lift up your hearts!" God wills your recovery. You do what you can.

Study this book! Work the Twelve Steps! Go to meetings! Live the CDA Program as best you can! Then, God will do for you what you have not been able to do for yourself. Promise!

Friend, keep comin' back!

B.A.N.

PART I
CHEMICALLY DEPENDENT ANONYMOUS

1   The Fellowship

Chemically Dependent Anonymous is a 12-step fellowship for anyone seeking freedom from drug and alcohol addiction. We of CDA do not make distinctions in the recovery process based on a particular substance. The basis of our program is abstinence from all mood-changing and mind-altering chemicals, including street-type drugs, alcohol and unnecessary medication.

The primary purpose of CDA as a whole is to remain clean and to help others like us gain recovery. By sharing our Experience, Strength and Hope with each other, we solve our common problem and help others recover from chemical dependence which has made their lives unmanageable.

CDA is not affiliated with any political, religious, or commercial organizations or institutions.

CDA remains grateful to the co-founders and Fellowship of Alcoholics Anonymous for the Twelve Steps and Twelve Traditions which are the basis of our program.

2   Why CDA?

There is nothing more powerful than an idea whose time has come. This has been amply demonstrated by the Program and the Fellowship of Chemically Dependent Anonymous. The concept behind CDA is not original by any means. It is based on the principle of simplicity that Alcoholics Anonymous developed in a time-proven format designed to give direction to those suffering from addiction to alcohol.

This concept has been at the core of hundreds of other self-help groups that share the Twelve Steps and Twelve Traditions. The only difference between the groups is the altering of the group's primary purpose and the requirements for membership. The formula shared by all twelve-step groups is the common bond of experience and hope from its individual members. This is what makes miracles happen.

But why CDA? Why start a new organization when A.A. and N.A. already exist? If these groups are working well, it would seem that there is no need to change anything. However, society, and many professionals in the recovery field, realize that there is the addict who shows no real preference for any single drug of choice. There is also the addict who primarily uses drugs and uses alcohol only to enhance the drugs, thus not seeing alcohol as a problem. The simplicity of CDA is that it covers all the bases by not distinguishing between drugs and alcohol. This is clearly stated in CDA's Third Tradition which states: "The only requirement for membership is a desire to abstain from all mood-changing and mind-altering chemicals, including street-type drugs, alcohol and unnecessary medication."

Alcoholics Anonymous has been lovingly tolerant of addicts, many of whom have felt that A.A. has been the beginning point of new lives for them. But A.A. and other fellowships narrow the identification process to just alcohol or sometimes a specific drug rather than the addiction itself. And rightly so, since the "singleness of purpose" in A.A., for example, is to carry the message to the alcoholic who still suffers. In CDA, we believe that speaking about the full, unedited story of our drug and alcohol addiction is critical to those wanting to remain clean and sober.

CDA members are encouraged to come from other fellowships and no one is restricted from mentioning any recovery literature they read or how they identify themselves in the meetings. CDA also has its own recovery readings, including Step guides, a meditation book and this book, Chemically Dependent Anonymous (its version of the A.A. "Big Book").

Many who were skeptical about attending a new fellowship have continued coming to CDA and celebrate many clean and sober anniversaries. The Fellowship is still unique in its approach to addiction and offers the same direction and hope as it did in the beginning. CDA is indeed an idea whose time has come!

3 Let's Redefine "Addict" and "Addiction"

All too often communication, especially in the English language, gets scrambled because of what is known as semantics. This is when a word or phrase involved in conversation or the written word will mean something different to each person receiving the message. Each one of us brings his own mental images and understanding to words as they are presented to him. Even a solid dictionary definition of a concept does not cover all that the word conjures up in the brain because of the differing backgrounds and experiences of those hearing or seeing that word and the ways in which they therefore relate to it.

A word may bear a stigma that takes it so far from its meaning that it loses its original definition. In order to eliminate confusion, it is necessary to return to the original definition to regain its proper meaning. Words such as "addict" or "addiction" are cases in point. *Webster's New World Dictionary of the American Language*, Second College Edition, defines an "addict" as "a person addicted to some habit, esp. to the use of a narcotic drug." It defines "addiction" as "the condition of being addicted (to a habit), specif., the habitual use of narcotic drugs."

These words will have different meanings for those who have had some experiences, however indirect, with them: those who work in the fields designed to deal with the addict; those who have had only direct, negative experiences with addiction; those who are actually addicted at this time. Despite the literal descriptions of these people and their problems, we each hold different pictures in our minds of the drug addict and have different feelings about addiction. But in order to understand the concept behind Chemically Dependent Anonymous, it is necessary to drop all those images of what these words mean to us, including *Webster's* version, in order to consider the drug addict's own definition of an addict and of his addiction.

Who has a greater right to redefine these words than the people who have been so defined? Surely those who have won that right have looked into the meaning of the words "addict" and "addiction" from a very personal standpoint. They have made an honest attempt to reach a deeper understanding of what they truly are and what their problems are. Sorry *Webster's*. And no stigmas are acceptable here either.

The most common conception of a drug addict is that of the desperate, emaciated pincushion junkie in a dark, dingy apartment with an eyedropper and a rusty syringe, nodding and puking between armed robberies and drugstore holdups. It cannot be denied that this picture does apply in some cases. But most addicts who once fit this bill and are now recovering useful lifestyles will quickly assert that their addictions began long before their world got that ugly. In fact, the self-proclaimed drug addicts who are finding recovery in the self-help movements and who stopped before they reached the above-described stage, readily agree that their addiction patterns were present long before they arrived at whatever junctures turned them to the path of recovery.

However, those who fit this latter definition of an addict know that if they begin to use again, they will probably end up qualifying for the worst-case description even though they never reached that point previously. And in some cases, they had never become as truly addicted physically as the dictionary definition would seem to imply before they came for help. Sorry again *Webster's*.

As CDA sees it, alcoholism is simply one form of addiction. Effective professionals who work with addicts agree with this viewpoint as well. Many other people acknowledge this fact too but are also quick to make at least an unspoken distinction between the alcoholic and the dope fiend. Even the dictionary seems to do so by omitting alcohol as an addictive substance. However, as far as the important aspects of the recovery process are concerned, CDA refuses to make such a distinction.

The young person who commits repetitive acts of problem behavior while using any type of chemical, including alcohol, is not just a "problem child" in the opinion of the addict who has run this course. To him, that youngster is already an addict even if it's only the early stages of addiction. We are not certain whether preventative measures, if forced on such a person, would work or not. All we know about prevention is that it did not work for us and we find it to be futile for the ones who have reached such a point. It is too much like the story of the boy trying to plug the dike with his finger unless the one in question is willing to take preventative action on his own. He can only avert a further progression of his disease by totally abstaining from all drugs.

However, we must acknowledge the existence of the social drug user who never seems to have problems with using chemicals. Hats off to him! We cannot understand that phenomenon, nor can the professionals in the field of addiction. And we lose some members when they begin to believe that they are in that fortunate category. Their thinking gets twisted and they forget where they have come from. Somehow they think that recreational drug use will be all right for them. That happens most often when addicts drift away from meetings and the support groups that had been saving their lives. The terrible problem with addiction is that it is a disease that can convince the addict he does not have a disease should he drop his defenses at any time. It can happen to any one of us, and does all too often.

Our redefinition is not complete unless we include our fellows who have been on the pharmacy circuit for too long with the aid of often well-meaning, undereducated physicians. These drug addicts travel day after day from one doctor to another, filling "script" after "script" in order to stay within the "legal" limits of their drugs of choice. They are protected from reaching their "bottoms" by doctors as well as their families and society at large. They frequently die without ever wearing the label of "addict" or being called "chemically dependent." That identification might have given them the opportunity to be pointed toward recovery. Instead, they are allowed to remain hidden behind the enabling walls of their homes, communities and society. Stigmas can kill.

It used to be that way for the alcoholic before Alcoholics Anonymous came along and suggested to society that it ought to reconsider its original definition of the drunk. That organization proved that an alcoholic *can* recover: Take Uncle Bill out of the attic, get him into A.A. and miracles may happen. He can be changed into a responsible member of his community who is a loving, giving and spiritually-oriented human being. People might say, "It's a good thing he wasn't a *drug* addict or he wouldn't have had a chance." Get the point?

However, we are seeing a change in the medical profession's viewpoint about drugs and addiction. Slowly, it is taking place as the truly dedicated people in the field begin to understand there is such a thing as unnecessary medication. Medical and psychological workers are now detecting the disease pattern of addiction much earlier. Probable addicts are usually directed to self-help groups much sooner as statistics have begun to indicate that the most effective medicine addicts can ever receive is found there.

Remember that we are using the term "unnecessary" medications here, only seeing these as the possibly abusive elements. CDA cannot denounce the use of pain-killing drugs or even sedatives if they are truly needed. We have members who have had to undergo surgery, painful dental procedures and other such treatments that necessitated the administering of addictive substances. These members have proved that the CDA Program is effective by withstanding periods of use of *necessary* chemicals without reinstituting self-destructive patterns of usage or increasing dosages without physicians' orders.

How did they do this? They clung to the Program like epoxy. Their fellow members showed them love and support throughout the process. They remained clean and free as if they had never broken the pattern of abstinence. Their desire to *live* the Program was stronger than the chemicals that had formerly enslaved them. They represent one more example of the effectiveness of a program that prefers not to limit its understanding of addiction to any one substance. Addiction is addiction is addiction.

Obvious social and sometimes moral issues arise when such a diverse group of addicted people gathers in the CDA setting. The Valium-eating homemaker has existed in a much different world from that of the motorcycle-riding junkie or the paranoid speed freak. And if we were to emphasize these differences in this setting, endless possibilities for confusion and dissension might arise.

But even as our diversity makes us unique, our addiction makes us all one and the same. In CDA, the emphasis is placed on **this** common ground. We each had different types and degrees of addiction but we all want help in recovery. So let us work together to gain new understanding about the differing aspects of this disease of addiction that we have endured, seeing each as a piece of the much larger puzzle to be solved. Through the past experiences and the resulting valuable insights of every person in our Fellowship, we can learn to avoid mistakes in areas we never would have thought of as problematic.

If you are reading this and think you may need help, try on our redefinition of addiction for size. It could lead you to CDA to seek the answers you have been looking for. If you don't believe that your identity fits the descriptions of the addict you have seen here, try to make use of this new understanding of our disease in your everyday living. It might save someone else's life someday, maybe even your own.

4 The Essential Elements

One question that is frequently raised when outsiders show an interest in Chemically Dependent Anonymous is, "What was the main thing that got you started in the direction of recovery?" The answer is as varied as the number of addicts in the world. We each had a different "bottom." Sure, the stories are often similar and sometimes run nearly parallel. But in CDA, the entire spectrum of addiction types is accepted. Therefore, there exists a wide range of circumstances leading up to each member's entry into the Program.

But no matter what the physical descriptions are (drug, place, age, duration of usage), the universal effects were deep, desperate fear and paralysis of the spirit. It seemed that there was nowhere left to turn for help. The drug of choice no longer worked as it had at first. Our friends and families had given up on us. We were living in isolated shells of confusion and anxiety, experiencing feelings of guilt, self-pity, resentment and the whole gamut of negative emotions.

For many of us, the worst emotion of all was tremendous self-hatred. We had become trapped within the enemy's walls. But the enemy was "self." We were living lives that only permitted enough room in the center of the universe for our own selves. Everything, everybody, everyplace circled around our feeble existence and our relentless need to reinforce the right to use our drug of choice. That requirement was of the utmost priority. The final act of being left alone in the center of the universe with nothing but a habit that no longer worked for us was Hell on Earth (an extremely understated description of the state in which we finally found ourselves).

We were at the crossroads. As we stood on the tracks watching the oncoming freight train, the decision we had to make was whether to get off the track and stay off or let the damn train hit us. It sounds like an easy choice. Why is it then that so many choose to stay and take the full force of the impact? No one knows for sure.

It is true that many just do not believe it will happen to them. They feel that they are different. It is denial to the bitter end. For others, it is because of plain old fear of the unknown. In their cases, the problem is obvious even to them but the rocky roadbed is at least a familiar one. Although it keeps getting worse, they believe that it is easier and safer than taking the risk of getting off the long, old track and trying a new way of life.

These explanations are mere speculation however. Most of us were given opportunities for insight into our problems many times before we finally took the plunge and "got honest" with ourselves. It was not just a matter of a second chance. Sometimes it was the hundredth chance. An odds maker would be baffled at this news. We were extremely fortunate to live through all of these risks and be able to make it into recovery.

But most of us who can now look back on our former lives from a relatively calm perspective do not think it was luck at all. We believe that, for one reason or another, a force of a positive nature that we call our Higher Power guided us here to CDA. We know this might sound mystical, supernatural or even religious. It seems even stranger to us.

After all, weren't we our own centers of the universe at one time? Weren't we the ones who cursed God when we thought there was the remotest possibility that such a Being might exist out there somewhere? We even cursed our own existence because "that God" was just out there to make our lives miserable. Most of us really did believe that. And, now there is this change of tune about a higher power? It doesn't make sense!

Our new track records show that, although it may not make sense or even seem reasonable, this adjustment in our spiritual attitude is one of the characteristics or essentials of "getting" the Program. If you are reading this book with the idea of getting help from CDA, however, rest assured that we are not a religious movement or a fanatical group. Should you be turned off by the very thought of joining such a fellowship, you have nothing to fear. The essentials for belonging are simply these, as encompassed in the Twelve Steps and the Twelve Traditions: reaching our own "bottoms" and the eventual grasping of a spiritual understanding that fits our individual needs.

It must be added that at the time most CDA members first sought help, a conscious spiritual recognition was absent or very cloudy at best in most cases. It was not until later that we could look back at our recovery and realize how our Higher Power had led us into the Program and guided us ever since. As He did for us, your Higher Power will work for you. He has brought you this far. Just give us a chance and leave the rest to Him.

5 CDA Roots

Chemically Dependent Anonymous is a fellowship that was created in the Annapolis, Maryland area by some younger members of Alcoholics Anonymous to fill a perceived need. In 1976–1980, we founders of CDA were people who had bottomed out on alcohol in our late twenties. Yet we also had extensive histories of using other drugs. We had used alcohol in the last stages of our active addictions and so A.A. had seemed the logical place to come for recovery.

In working with individuals who used drugs other than alcohol, in addition to alcohol or whose primary drug of choice was something other than alcohol, we began to see that some of these newcomers were not getting the message in A.A. that all mood-changing and mind-altering drugs were part of their problem of addiction. Alcohol was not the sole obstacle to recovery for them. Even more important was the fact that earlier A.A. members seemed uncomfortable when these people shared their experiences about using drugs. Members new to the Program felt alienated within the Fellowship. Clearly, something had to be done to help them.

One of us, Ric R., attempted to start Narcotics Anonymous in the Annapolis area but it did not succeed there. And because of its very name, N.A. shared its parent organization's problem of *seeming* to disqualify from membership those addicted to other substances. We wanted to found another group that would resolve that problem; one that was still based on the principles of A.A., whose structure was time-tested and God-given. Their program had been designed by a group of alcoholics in the 1930's. Through trial and error, they had managed to come up with the idea of a fellowship that had proven itself successful for over 50 years for people addicted to alcohol. We wanted to be a similarly anonymous organization based on the Twelve Steps and Twelve Traditions of Alcoholics Anonymous.

But we also wanted to choose a name containing no words that could lead a prospective member to believe that we would exclude any particular type of addict or addiction. Previously existing literature from the Hazelden Foundation in Center City, Minnesota gave us our name. There, we also found verification for the truths we had lived.

Twelve people attended the first meeting of CDA on August 17, 1980. It was held at the home of Ric R. and Elin H. in Annapolis, Maryland. That night, we decided on our name and purpose. For the next few months, we continued to hold meetings at their house on Fridays at 6:30 p.m. As CDA steadily expanded, these Friday meetings were moved to St. Anne's Church in downtown Annapolis. Within six months, there were three meetings a week attended regularly by about 25 members. Soon, groups were meeting in church halls, church basements and schools all over the Annapolis area.

The only requirement for CDA membership is a desire to abstain from all mood-changing and mind-altering chemicals, including street-type drugs, alcohol and unnecessary medication. There are no dues or fees for membership. We are self-supporting through our own voluntary contributions. We neither endorse nor oppose any causes and we do not wish to engage in controversies of any type.

Our program was designed for the still-suffering, chemically-dependent person who would otherwise have nowhere to turn. Because of the all-inclusive nature of our organization, we can open the door to recovery for anyone who has a sincere desire to be free from self-destructive chemical usage. We hope that our fellowship will continue to expand and serve the needs of all tormented addicts whose numbers are currently at an epidemic level.

Using CDA as an alternative to or in conjunction with the other anonymous groups offers members of all these programs and the millions of people who still suffer a better chance for recovery. CDA does not attempt to replace A.A. or N.A. for those of us also finding recovery there.

In starting the CDA Fellowship, we can never forget the many beautiful A.A. role models who have been supportive and an example of courage for us. Nor should we forget what their program has taught us about being responsible to the practicing addict who wants help. In order to keep what we have, we must give it away. We are confident that this book will aid in that cause.

6   CDA's Twelve Steps

If you want what we have and are willing to make the effort necessary, then you are ready to take certain steps. Here are the Steps that we took which have made our recovery possible:*

1. We admitted we were powerless over mood-changing and mind-altering chemicals and that our lives had become unmanageable.

2. We came to believe that a Power greater than ourselves could restore us to sanity.

3. We made a decision to turn our will and our lives over to the care of God as we understood Him.

4. We made a searching and fearless moral inventory of ourselves.

5. We admitted to God, to ourselves, and to another human being the exact nature of our wrongs.

6. We were entirely ready to have God remove all these defects of character.

7. We humbly asked Him to remove our shortcomings.

---

* Reprinted and adapted with permission of Narcotics Anonymous World Services, Inc.

8. We made a list of all persons we had harmed and became willing to make amends to them all.

9. We made direct amends to such people wherever possible, except when to do so would injure them or others.

10. We continued to take personal inventory and when we were wrong promptly admitted it.

11. We sought through prayer and meditation to improve our conscious contact with God as we understood Him, praying only for the knowledge of His will for us and the power to carry that out.

12. Having had a spiritual awakening as the result of these Steps, we tried to carry this message to other chemically dependent persons and to practice these principles in all our affairs.*

There is one thing more than anything else that will defeat us in our recovery. This is an attitude of indifference or intolerance towards spiritual principles. Although there are no musts in CDA, there are three things that seem indispensable. These are HONESTY, OPEN-MINDEDNESS and WILLINGNESS to try. With these we are well on our way.**

---

* Reprinted and adapted with permission of Alcoholics Anonymous World Services, Inc.
** Reprinted and adapted with permission of Narcotics Anonymous World Services, Inc.

Step 1

WE ADMITTED WE WERE POWERLESS OVER MOOD-CHANGING AND MIND-ALTERING CHEMICALS AND THAT OUR LIVES HAD BECOME UNMANAGEABLE.

We who are recovering from dependency upon mood-changing and mind-altering chemicals are generally able to pinpoint the moment at which we finally said, "That's it. I can't take any more. Chemicals are in control of my life; I cannot stop on my own. I need help." We call this moment our "bottom" for we have seen that with recovery we need never sink to the depths to which our chemical dependency took us. We have also seen that without this admission of powerlessness, we have little hope of such recovery.

Why the need for this admission of powerlessness? Surely chemicals have beaten us down enough. Why make it worse by talking about how hopeless we are? Besides, there are those of us who were not always powerless. Early in using and from time to time later on, some of us could control our use of chemicals and its consequences. Why not simply say, "Sure, I've got a problem with chemicals," and leave it at that?

Step One comes first because it is the foundation upon which chemical-free lives are built. We need to admit our powerlessness so that we may become willing to do whatever is necessary to recover. The process of recovery is found in the Twelve Steps. However, while simple, the Steps are not easy. It is our experience that those who have some reservation, who hold onto the belief that they may be able to use chemicals safely someday, will not be honest, open or willing enough to walk the difficult but essential path of the remaining eleven Steps.

When we do take an honest look at our use of chemicals, we begin to see our powerlessness. How many times did we say, "I'll just have one drink, toke, shot, line or hit," yet found ourselves loaded again? How many times did we set out to control our use, yet days, weeks or months later realized we were worse than ever? How many times did we hurt others and ourselves as a result of using, yet turned around and used once more? We even tried using, combining or eliminating different chemicals in an effort to convince ourselves that we were not chemically dependent. Inevitably, these efforts failed.

To most of us, this powerless was not as obvious in our early days of using. Whatever our reasons for using chemicals—to enjoy ourselves, to go along with our crowd, to mask our pain, to build our self-confidence—we generally got what we wanted out of chemicals. We could use or not use, and the price of using was not too high. However, this was the beginning of a fatal progression. As it continued, we used more chemicals more often to less effect. The worse our dependency became, the harder it was to stop. In the end, we were left with no power whatsoever.

We now believe that this progression into utter powerlessness is the result and the sign of the disease of chemical dependency. We believe it to be a physical disease that consumes every part of us. Our bodies react to chemicals by craving more. Our minds are warped into denial and sick thinking that support our continued use. Our spirits are dulled, damaged and eventually crushed by the punishment exacted in our lives from the consequences of continued use. We have no more power over our chemical dependency than the blind have over sightlessness. We are powerless, whether the chemicals involved are street-type drugs, alcohol, unnecessary medications, or any combination of these.

When we admit that we are powerless over chemicals, we also need to admit that our disease has made our lives unmanageable. We have seen that we can no longer determine what, when, where, how much or with whom we use. We need to see that our actions and attitudes are out of control. The getting and using of chemicals became our number one priority regardless of the consequences. This pursuit took us to places we never would have gone had it not been for our using. Our skid row or shooting gallery may have been an actual physical place or the emotional equivalent within us. When we have been horrified by our actions to the point of despair, we are ready to admit the unmanageability of our addiction.

Many of us have balked at this, believing that we were "not that bad." Some of us had lost all. However, many of us still had some or all of our outward lives intact. We may have hoped that we could clear up this little chemical problem and then move on. We had to become fully honest with ourselves about the effects that our chemical dependency had on our lives, whether outwardly or inwardly.

Unmanageability may show itself in any facet of our lives. We may have lost our jobs, our ability to work, our families, our lovers, our possessions. Perhaps we still had these things but there were problems between us and the boss, the teacher, the spouse, the lover, the creditor, the police officer or the judge. There may have been no visible threat in these areas, yet we were restless or worried. Most of us, regardless of the state of our outward lives, suffered inwardly. We knew that we were not meeting our responsibilities or living up to our potential and our self-respect was going or gone. Our ability to deal with life on a daily basis was compromised. Our behavior was generally erratic, immature and self-centered to the extreme. We alternated between heights of egotistical folly and depths of self-hating remorse. Materially intact or not, we were emotionally confused and out of control. We needed to admit that our lives were unmanageable to whatever degree due to our chemical dependency.

Often it was the unmanageability in our lives that brought us to the point of seeking help. We knew that something or everything was going wrong and we finally admitted that this was due to our use of chemicals. However difficult this admission, it opens the door to a new way of life. We are not responsible for the disease but we are responsible for our recovery. How well we say, "I cannot do it alone but I alone can do it." Once we are willing to take responsibility for our recovery, we are able to seek and receive the necessary help.

Having admitted our powerlessness and unmanageability due to the use of chemicals and the disease of chemical dependency, what next? We have given up the idea that we can use without losing control. We have taken the difficult but necessary step of asking for help. In active dependency, if we are powerless over chemicals and our lives are unmanageable, our own power is insufficient to recover. We have come to CDA to find a power that will suffice. If we have truly taken Step One, then we are ready for Step Two.

Step 2
WE CAME TO BELIEVE THAT A POWER GREATER THAN OURSELVES COULD RESTORE US TO SANITY.

Powerlessness and unmanageability were not easy to admit but we could not deny the evidence in our own lives. Chemical dependency, which we had tried again and again to control on our own, had brought us to the point of desperation. The pain in our lives was now great enough for us to admit defeat. From this point, we looked to CDA for help. What would it take to get and stay chemical-free?

To those of us accustomed to instant gratification and quick chemical cures, Step Two is dismaying to say the least. A power greater than ourselves? Restore us to sanity? What's going on here? We want a way out of chemical dependency, we say, not a religion or cult to join. What does this Step have to do with anything?

What was it we admitted in Step One? Powerlessness and unmanageability. What is it we are offered in Step Two? A power greater than ourselves. If our own power is not sufficient, then we can only conclude that a higher power is necessary. The alternative to denying this power is insanity and death.

Insanity, we say. Yes, it could have reached that point. We could have used until we utterly destroyed our minds as well as our bodies. At least we didn't have to go that far.

Step Two, however, does not talk about being relieved from some possibility of insanity in the future. It states that anyone who accepts Step One must next accept the need to be restored to sanity. In other words, our chemical dependency has already resulted in some kind of insanity.

Even those of us who have spent time in psychiatric hospitals or in some form of counseling would have trouble describing themselves as insane. How much stronger then is the denial of those who have not experienced this much? Are we really crazy?

In Step One we looked at examples of our powerlessness. We were dismayed to realize how many times we had told ourselves that we could control our use: by trying to limit the amount; by trying to behave differently while under the influence. Yet we found ourselves using more and hurting ourselves and others worse than ever. We believed it would be different "this time," even though it had never been different before. We believed we could repeat the same actions and get different results in spite of more evidence to the contrary. Is this the work of a sound mind?

We also looked at the unmanageability in our lives. We saw loss or impending loss of those things that give life stability and rationality—the ability to work and be responsible, the ability to love and have positive relationships of all sorts, the ability to respect ourselves. We knew that we had lost or were losing these things due to our actions under the influence. How sane were these actions? Did it make sense to go to work loaded or skip work altogether when we knew our bosses were ready to let us go? Did it make sense to keep pushing our loved ones to their limit? Did it make sense to attempt to fill the emptiness inside of us with that which was destroying us? Are these sound actions?

Unsound in mind, unsound in action—what better definition of insanity?

"Okay, okay," we cry. "We're powerless over chemicals, our lives are unmanageable. We have not been thinking, acting or living sanely. Now the only way out is religion? We're sunk!"

Relax. CDA is not a religion nor does it require any specific belief of its members. We state the obvious: *If our own power is not enough, we need a greater power.* The beauty of it is that each of us has chosen our own concept of a higher power. All we had to do is believe that it could do what we could not.

It does not take a great leap into an organized belief system to accomplish this. It takes only a little bit of faith. We can make a beginning by saying, "Yes, it's possible I am not the most powerful being in the universe. There must be something or someone greater and I must begin to put my trust in it."

Even at this simple beginning, many of us found ourselves blocked. We had spent too much time ignoring, criticizing or misusing faith. It was not easy to give up these old ways; we had become comfortable with them. CDA told us we had to change old ways if we were to live chemical-free lives.

Many of us ignored faith. It just didn't fit into our lives. We could put our trust in the ethics of our parents, in the value of the sciences or simply in the evidence of our senses. That was enough. We were startled to realize that by placing trust in these things, we were already operating on a kind of faith. If it worked with that which we could see and feel, wouldn't it work with that which was beyond sight and touch? If we had faith in the familiar or scientific, couldn't we have faith in the spiritual? We could and we do! Our desperation made short work of all our rationalizations.

There are many others of us who criticized faith. Not only did it not work in our lives, we said, but those who claimed it did work in their lives often acted in ways we found destructive. The truth was that we were critical because our expectations had not been met. Disappointed and disillusioned by our experiences with faith, we lashed out in anger and judged all such experiences harshly. We did not leave room for new ideas about faith until we had no other choice.

The misuse of faith was difficult for still others who believed that they had faith that was not working. Indeed, some of us had already asked a greater power to take away our chemical dependency. However, we were taking things out of order. We were asking to have the destruction in our lives removed but we were not ready to admit our powerlessness over chemicals. We wanted what WE wanted rather than what our Higher Power wanted for us.

As we attended more and more meetings, we heard it said time and again, "It's time to let go of old ideas." When we were ready to give up the use of chemicals, we also had to be ready to give up the beliefs and behaviors that went with our use. We were ready for a faith that works.

When we got past the old ideas (the blocks to faith), we discovered that we were not being asked so much. We expected to be trapped in a narrow hallway but we found ourselves walking on a broad highway. We were not told to believe in this or that Supreme Being; it was suggested to us that there was a power greater than ourselves. If we had faith, our Higher Power could do for us what we could not do for ourselves. To make a beginning, all we needed was an open mind. We simply needed to look around us and see, without judgment.

When we opened our eyes and our minds in meetings, we saw the most amazing things. We saw chemically dependent people who were no longer using chemicals and who were able to live life day to day. They were not toughing it out, grimly determined to resist the urge to use. They were free from chemicals, free and happy for perhaps the first time. Oh, surely they experienced difficulties. Yet, they believed that they would make it through such times, even grow from them, and so they did—without using. We knew how powerful chemicals were in our lives, yet these folks could live, and live happily, without them. There was a greater power at work in their lives. Indeed, for many of us, it was beginning enough to have faith in the Fellowship itself as we could clearly see the miracles being worked within it.

At this stage, we found it helpful to make small attempts at a conscious contact with this Higher Power. We could do this in a number of ways: sharing at meetings, listening to the voice of conscience, speaking out loud to an invisible listener, meditating, praying. We often started saying "please" and "thank you" (each morning asking our Higher Power for a day without using and each evening thanking that power for another chemical-free day). With open-mindedness and such small efforts, we began to find our own faith.

Thus it was that we came to believe that a power greater than ourselves could restore us to sanity. We accept our insanity and we accept that there is a higher power that can bring sanity into our lives. How do we let that power work in us? If we have come this far, with open-mindedness and willingness, we are ready for Step Three.

Step 3
WE MADE A DECISION TO TURN OUR WILL AND OUR LIVES OVER TO THE CARE OF GOD AS WE UNDERSTOOD HIM.

In CDA meetings, we often hear recovering people speak of Step Three as the pivot of the Program. When we look at the words of the Step, many of us find this statement frightening. We came to CDA because of our lack of control over chemicals and the resulting consequences in our lives. We hoped to find control. Instead, we had to admit our powerlessness and unmanageability and accept that we need a power greater than our own. The next step forward is to surrender ourselves to that power. However, most of us find control difficult to surrender.

We need to remember that we have a disease, one that warps our bodies, minds and spirits. CDA members often say, "Don't pick up. Go to meetings. Work the Steps." As we don't pick up, our bodies begin to heal. As we go to meetings, our minds begin to heal and we replace sick thinking with recovery thinking. As we work the Steps, our spirits begin to heal and we develop a relationship with a higher power. Mental and spiritual healing is a slow process. In Step Two, our acceptance that neither our thinking nor our actions while using was sane must be reexamined in recovery.

This is one of the most humbling experiences in the recovery journey. We realize that our self-centeredness and self-will continue to drive us. We may be hardheaded or softhearted. We may care only about ourselves or we may truly believe that we want only what's best for others. It doesn't matter! The point is that it is OUR will that we pursue. Whether by force, cunning, manipulation or cajoling, we are still trying to control. In the meantime, the fear upon which self-centeredness is based eats at us internally. We wonder what we're doing wrong and may even wonder if being chemical-free is worth it. In short, just as in our using days, our efforts at control are doing us much more harm than good.

We have an alternative to misery in active addiction and misery in recovery. Our alternative is to work the Twelve Steps. We need not be pushed to the brink or beyond before we give Step Three a chance. As with the first two Steps and anything else in CDA we take it one day—or one bit—at a time.

We hear many members talk about "letting go" or "turning it over." We see that we've already made a beginning with Step Three by turning our chemical dependency over to a higher power whether that is our home group, CDA as a whole or the God of our understanding. As we weary of other apparently unsolvable problems in our lives, we try turning these over to a higher power. An amazing thing happens: Either the problems are solved or they simply aren't problems anymore. Our experiences begin to match the wonders we see in the lives of others in the meetings. We begin to let go of the desire to control. We begin to trust God.

For some, surrender (the ultimate act of trust) comes in a single, overwhelming experience. The realization that this higher power loves us and is working in our lives fills us. For most, however, this is a gradual process. Trust does not come easily. In Step Two, we looked at the blocks to faith and came to see those blocks as layers of defensiveness. Now we can look beneath these defenses and see our pain and fear. We may be hurting from betrayal of trust, our own or others. We may have closed off our capacity to trust while living the lifestyle that accompanied our chemical usage. We may have lost it long before we picked up. Growing up in chemically dependent or otherwise abusive families, we are fearful. In our caution, we give God a little bit at a time. And it works—it works!

As time goes on, we are reminded once more that "half measures availed us nothing." Testing the waters is all well and good for a time but sooner or later we have to dive in. By that time, fortunately, we have begun to learn some wonderful things about our Higher Power. As Tradition Two tells us, we realize that our God is a loving God. We find that this is not the limited and conditional thing that we sometimes call love. Rather, it is unconditional and beyond our imagination. Unlike chemicals and any single human being, God always and unfailingly gives us what is truly best for us. Slowly, as we allow the God of our understanding to be revealed to us, we understand that God patiently awaits our decision.

Regardless, this decision must come from within. Herein lies the beauty of Step Three. After our desire for control has taken us in so many destructive directions, we are offered the opportunity to do something healthy and life giving with it. This decision is not and CANNOT be made by chemicals, by another person, by a group of people or by circumstances. It is our decision.

How surprised and delighted we are to discover that Step Three means strength rather than weakness! WE make the decision to give ourselves completely to that which has our best interests at heart at every moment.

We are not plunging into harmful dependence; we are being freed from it. We are finally free to be who we really are.

And it is simply a decision. Those who told us that Step Three is the pivot of the Program meant exactly that. Steps One and Two get us to it and Steps Four through Twelve allow us to live it. In a sense, the decision in Step Three is the agreement to work the remaining Steps. We are expressing our willingness to do whatever is necessary so that we can live the kind of lives we really want to live.

With whatever help we need from those who understand, such as our sponsors, we make the decision and act on it. We say to our Higher Power whatever words we wish to say. We may invoke our God by whatever name we see fit and say something like, "Take my will and my life into your care. I give it to you completely, without any reservation. I accept whatever you have to give me knowing that it will be what is best for me. Your guidance, your power and your love will meet my every need and will work through me to help others. I will to will your will."

The action does not stop here, yet already we begin to feel the results. We feel a lessening of the fear that has consumed our lives and know the beginnings of real freedom. For some, this means being released from worry or sleeplessness; for others, it means some break in our obsessive anger, guilt or depression; for others, it means being able to function on a day-to-day basis; and, for others, it means the beginning of taking healthy, growth-enhancing risks. In all cases, these freedoms bring us a new sense of peace. Slowly, one day at a time, we start to understand the concept of serenity that is expressed by so many in CDA.

Again, the action does not stop here. If we try to sit back and bask in the pleasant feelings that most of us experience when initially working Step Three, we will lose them. Our sponsors remind us that we have now agreed to work the remaining Steps. To stop here as though we have arrived is to court disaster. We are told that many have relapsed by seeing the first three Steps alone as sufficient tools in recovery. There is much healing and, therefore, much work to be done. If we have truly begun to turn our will and our lives over, we need to walk the course that our Higher Power has laid out for us. Willingness, enhanced now by surrender and commitment to our God, takes us on to Step Four.

Step 4
WE MADE A SEARCHING AND FEARLESS MORAL INVENTORY OF OURSELVES.

Action! That's what our sponsors keep telling us. Either take positive action and move forward or sit around and be drawn backwards. Having taken the action of turning our will and our lives over to the care of God, we were ready to take the action of looking closely at ourselves. So why didn't we FEEL ready?

Some of us look at Step Four with dread, believing it is that fateful time when we reveal all the ugliness in our past to someone else. Others of us are so filled with self-hatred that we cannot stand to examine our lives. Some of us view this Step as unnecessary since we're "back to normal" now that the chemicals are gone, irrelevant as our difficulties are not of our own making or awe-inspiring because it sounds like some mystical inner quest. Many of us, seemingly blind to the fact that we have shortcomings, regard Step Four with disdain. What's the point really? Who needs it?

WE need it! In Steps Two and Three, we accepted some uncomfortable truths—not only about our chemical use but also our need to heal our sick bodies, minds and spirits from the disease of chemical dependency. If we are making excuses or otherwise avoiding Step Four, we are forgetting Step Three and falling back into self-centered fear. We are taking our will back from our Higher Power (or we never turned it over in the first place) and trying to run the show again.

Self-centered fear shows itself in many ways. It may be anxiety about whether our needs will be met through this process, dread of revealing our past to another or worry that we will stir up memories that will cause us to relapse. We may tell ourselves that we cannot do the Step unless we do it completely and perfectly. It is often pride which assures us that our thoughts are always good and our actions always justifiable. It is just as often self-hatred (pride in reverse) which says we have no redeeming qualities whatsoever. It may surface as anger over being told that we need to examine ourselves when we would rather catalog the harms done to us by others, thus enabling us to sink back into resentment and self-pity. It may even exhibit itself as apathy, allowing us to push away any action.

What a powerful spiritual sickness, this self-centered fear. However, we now have something in our lives that is much more powerful—a God of our understanding and the decision we made to turn our will and our lives over to the care of that God. As we renew that decision, we realize we have what it takes to move through the feelings and take action. Our inventory can be fearless because our Higher Power replaces our fear with faith, bringing all excuses to naught. We are taking stock of who we are, not making a record of ugly incidents. We are taking responsibility, not drowning in blame and shame. We are acting out of the love our Higher Power gives us, not beating ourselves up. In the words of one CDA member:

"As I grew increasingly more aware in my recovery—it was around the nine-month mark—I realized that there was a pattern in my life that was the source of my troubles. Generally, it was that I never wanted to grow up and take responsibility for my life. I thought the world owed me …. I knew enough about the Steps to see that it was time for a searching and fearless moral inventory. I needed to write it down to see clearly what was causing the pain in my life. I was so full of anger, hurt and fear that I just started writing. Emotions poured onto the page; I had found a constructive outlet for my confused feelings."

Taking an honest look at our feelings, attitudes and actions is the work of Step Four. At the outset, it is important that we do not make moral judgments about our feelings. Experiencing emotion is part of being human and emotions themselves are neither good nor bad. However, they manifest in healthy or unhealthy ways. As we recover, we let go of unhealthy, destructive attitudes and behaviors and make room for healthy, life-giving ones. It is these that we acknowledge and inventory.

how do we go about it? We could waste a lot of time and energy worrying or intellectualizing about methods. We need to see that HOW we do it is not as important as THAT we do it. And we do it, as with any Step, with the guidance of other recovering chemically dependent people. In particular, we need the experience, feedback and stability of a sponsor. Trying to "go it alone" with Step Four is as fruitless as our one-time efforts to stay free of chemicals without help. We remember that we have taken Step Three and we trust our Higher Power to work through others and give us the help we need as we answer some pretty tough questions about ourselves:

Pride

Where does my PRIDE hurt others and me? Do I believe that I am better or worse than everyone else? Do I expect myself to be perfect? Do I set a perfectionist's standards for others or assume that things work out best when done my way? Am I arrogant? Do I insist on handling everything on my own? Do I feel like a failure if I ask for help? Do I present a false front to the world or perhaps a different one for each situation? Do I lie to puff up my ego? Do I secretly wallow in shame?

Humility

How am I growing in HUMILITY? Do I take a realistic appraisal of my abilities and feel confident in them? Am I willing to accept my mistakes and the mistakes of others as part of being human? Do I let others see me as I really am? Do I ask for, accept and return help? Do I offer empathy rather than criticism to those in need?

Selfishness

Where does my SELFISHNESS hurt others and me? Do I constantly put my wants before the needs of others? Am I greedy or stingy with money, possessions, affection or time? Do I insist upon having my sexual desires gratified regardless of who might get hurt in the process? Do I take people and things for granted? Am I consumed with self-pity when life is not as I wish? Do I envy those who have what I want? When my desires are not fulfilled, do I resort to immature behavior? Do I take everything personally?

Caring

How am I growing in CARING? Am I warm? Do I demonstrate acceptance of others and myself? Do I take responsibility for my own needs? Do I make sufficient time and effort to eat, sleep, work, play, talk, listen, pray, meditate and get to meetings? Do I appreciate the good people and things in my life? Do I honor my friends? Do I treat my spouse or sex partner with dignity and respect? Am I grateful for recovery?

Anger
Where does my misdirected ANGER hurt others and me? Do I rage, subjecting others or myself to physical, emotional, sexual or verbal violence? Do I carry resentments? Do I hold grudges or seek revenge? Am I impatient when things do not go my way or intolerant of those who are different from me? Am I overly sensitive, reacting to the slightest perception of disagreement or rejection?

Acceptance
How am I growing in ACCEPTANCE? Am I making an effort to vent my rage without hurting anyone? Do I accept help with this from a neutral party (a sponsor, counselor, or clergy)? Do I try to understand others? Am I becoming more patient and tolerant? Am I willing to wait? Am I willing to see both sides of an issue? Do I set aside my insistence on being right all the time? Am I able to stand up for myself without putting down another? Do I demonstrate compassion? Am I willing to forgive?

Dishonesty
Where does my DISHONESTY hurt others and me? Do I lie to others or myself? Does what I gain by lying really balance out the integrity I lose? Do I persist in rationalizations, alibis or excuses? Am I cheating or stealing? Am I lying to or cheating on my spouse or sex partner? Do I pretend that there is nothing wrong with failing to live up to my responsibilities?

Honesty
How am I growing in HONESTY? Am I getting honest with myself? Am I making an effort to tell the truth? Do I accept responsibility for my own feelings? Do I own my attitudes? Do I accept the consequences of my actions? Do I pay my

bills? Do I earn my way rather than trying to get ahead by conning and manipulating? Is my word worth something? Do I honor my commitments? Am I honest with my sex partners, especially about my history and the possibility of disease? Do I share honestly in meetings rather than trying to sound good?

Fear

Where does my FEAR hurt others and me? Am I constantly afraid? Do I have a sense of impending doom? Do I insist on carrying around a heavy burden of guilt? Do I persist in anxiety and worry? Do I continue to think and act like a victim? Am I obsessively caught up in negative thinking? Do I isolate, fearing what others will think if they "really" know me? Do I procrastinate? Am I still trying to control my chemical dependency, other people or circumstances?

Trust

How am I growing in TRUST? Am I opening up to my Higher Power's will for me? Do I let other people get to know me? Do I have self-respect? Am I cultivating positive thinking? Am I willing to let go? Do I have hope? Do I take positive action in my life as I am guided to do so? Am I loving and accepting of love?

It is important that we do our inventory in writing. As we answer these questions, we use examples. Often, our sponsors suggest that we include a list of people and institutions that we resent. In doing so, we have the opportunity to let go of blame, examine our own emotions and attitudes, and take responsibility for our part. This brings up past incidents and actions that we need to acknowledge. We may not want to get them out, but we can look forward to the freedom of letting go of the past.

The Steps that follow will carry this work further so it is good to begin it here. Also, we balance our inventory by acknowledging our strengths and our healing. If we see only the sickness, our work is incomplete. Done as morose self-punishment, Step Four could be avoided or used as an excuse to relapse. Done as honest self-appraisal, however, it can only further our recovery.

Is this an uncomfortable process? Certainly! Each Step requires honesty and thoroughness and often involves pain. However, it also involves joy. With a sense of wonder, we see patterns emerge, giving us a new sense of ourselves and our responses to the world. In any case, we need not be overwhelmed. If we have worked the preceding Steps, we have help that is more than sufficient. Indeed, this is one place where we can feel the interdependence of the Steps. The work that we did in Step Three gives us the strength to complete Step Four. At the same time, doing the Fourth Step is a demonstration that we are carrying out that Third Step commitment.

Indeed, each Step helps us grow in our relationship with the God of our understanding. However, throughout the process of working Step Four, we focus on this Step without concern for the next. We are not writing for an audience; we are writing for ourselves. It is only after completing this work that we begin to think about sharing it with another. Only after we have been searching and fearless to the best of our ability are we ready to move on to Step Five.

Step 5
WE ADMITTED TO GOD, TO OURSELVES, AND TO ANOTHER HUMAN BEING THE EXACT NATURE OF OUR WRONGS.

In Step Four, we talked a great deal about fear. We saw that we could, through self-centered fear, block our relationship with a higher power and bring our positive action to a halt. We understood that we could always go back to the Third Step, renew our commitment and move through the fear. Most of us need to remember this work and continue it as we move on to Step Five.

The problem with our fear is not that it's wrong to feel it. In fact, it is pretty human to do so. But it is dangerous to allow fear to run our lives. CDA experience shows that this is particularly true. When we come to Step Five, many of us want to hold back some of the negative truths about ourselves. Putting them on paper in Step Four was hard enough; the idea of sharing them seems almost impossible. Why tell God? Doesn't God already know? Why tell ourselves? Didn't we do that by completing our inventory? Why tell another human being? Why risk our newfound sense of freedom and belonging by letting someone else know how terrible we really can be?

In meetings, we hear recovering people say, "I'm as sick as my secrets." When we hold onto the secrets, we hold onto the sickness. We perpetuate the sense of shame that characterized our active chemical dependency and made it so difficult to accept help in the first place. We become, in short, a relapse waiting to happen. Many a CDA member has returned to the use of chemicals because of hiding away and denying the importance of some part of the past or present. Even the professionals now tell us that it is in this return to denial that we set ourselves up to relapse.

This does not mean that we indiscriminately race off and tell everyone all there is to know about us. We use care in choosing the person with whom we will complete our Fifth Step. We avoid the cop-out of picking a family member or a program buddy who has less experience with the Steps than we have ourselves. Those folks don't have that all-important ingredient of objectivity. We need to know that the person understands our purpose and will listen without judgment. For this reason, many of us decide to ask our sponsors to hear us out. Similarly, we may choose someone else in the Program that has completed a Fifth Step and feels trustworthy to us. A compassionate and confidential friend may fit the bill. If we find ourselves unable to share our entire inventory with such a person, we may choose to share the rest with a member of the clergy or perhaps a professional counselor.

However we go about it, our watchword is thoroughness. In prayer, we make our admissions to God. In quiet time with ourselves, we acknowledge the truth of all that we have written in our inventory. We then meet with the person of our choosing, at a comfortable place and with plenty of time, and share all we have to share. But if we're wondering if we have completed the first and second parts of this process, we can rest assured! By speaking our inventory aloud to another human being, we affirm that we have also admitted it to God and to ourselves.

The last of our fear disappears as our listener responds without criticism or rejection. If we have chosen a sponsor or other recovering person, we often hear experiences that match or surpass ours. Had we forgotten that this person has also walked the road of active chemical dependence with all of its consequences? We remember now and we can be grateful for the identification and feedback we receive.

The completion of Step Five has brought various reactions from CDA members. Many simply feel relief as the anxiety falls away and the job is done. Some experience a lessening of isolation and loneliness and feel more a part of the Fellowship and the human race. Others gain a new level of self-acceptance when the response to their sharing is compassion rather than judgment. And there are those who are conscious of a powerful or subtle spiritual experience. The light is let into the dark places within and the presence of God is felt.

The important reward of Step Five however is not a feeling. It is the fundamental change that has taken place in our behavior. We let go of our fear, believed in our program and our Higher Power and shared ourselves fully with that higher power and another person. These actions are utterly contrary to our using behaviors; they express and affirm our recovery work. In short, they declare that we are not who we were and open the door to the person we are meant to be. To continue this process, we move directly into Step Six.

Step 6
WE WERE ENTIRELY READY TO HAVE GOD REMOVE ALL THESE DEFECTS OF CHARACTER.

Take a look in the mirror. Is this the same person, who out of fear and desperation, began to work Step One by attending a CDA meeting for the first time? No, it can't be. That old person was not capable of leaving chemicals alone. The person in the mirror has done that—and much more—for some time! This new person has experienced levels of self-honesty, willingness and trust that were simply impossible in active addiction. The image in the mirror slowly shakes its head. Yes, there has been change but surely it is not enough. Surely there could be more sincerity, greater risk-taking, deeper belief and less indulgence in character defects. This person is hardly perfect. Maybe with some harder work ...

No, this person is not perfect. And no, exerting self-will is not the answer. Did that work with chemicals? Of course not. A limited ability to affect when or how much one used created an illusion of control. But, in the end it invariably failed. Having accepted that truth in Step One, it became necessary to accept many more in the Steps that followed: the need for a loving higher power; surrender to that power; a thorough self-examination; and, the sharing of what it revealed.

In that process, fundamental changes took place. It became clear that powerlessness applied to a lot more than chemicals. It extended to people, places, things, situations, circumstances and events. In short, everything outside the self was added to the list. Again, a limited ability to affect the outside world was twisted by the disease into an illusion of control. And again, it inevitably failed as things did not turn out as planned. That this control was attempted over and over, despite the negative result was simply more evidence of the insanity of the disease.

The Steps have taken the focus from chemicals, people and situations. They have placed the emphasis where it belongs—on the person in the mirror. This person has had to give up the illusion of control in order to survive.

Step Six offers an opportunity to go beyond that. It says, "Good work so far. Now take a hard look at the old way of life and the new. Which one do you want? You can have the old one back anytime—just pick up a chemical or go back to 'self-will run riot.' The new way though offers more than survival. Now you have a chance to thrive. All you need to do is become entirely ready to have the destructive attitudes and behaviors removed. How about it?"

The image in the mirror immediately narrows its eyes, trying to figure out how to get rid of the character defects. It seems impossible. Some are too tough to face, while others are too much fun to lose. Such rationalizing is another attempt at control. Guess what? It doesn't work here either. Indeed, a brief review of experience shows that the harder one "works" on what appears to be wrong—a character defect or a shortcoming—the worse it gets. This Step isn't about fighting harder, it's about surrender. As one CDA member declares, "For me, this Step is a reinforcement of Step Three. This is when I really get serious! Am I willing to let my Higher Power be totally in charge? Am I willing to give credit to my Higher Power for everything happening in my life and only take credit for the willingness to work and live the Twelve Steps? If so, then I'm ready to receive the gift of true humility in the Seventh Step."

It's not the job of the person in the mirror to decide what needs to be removed and how to remove it. That is God's job. This person need only become entirely ready.

Look the person in the mirror directly in the eye. Is the readiness there—all the willingness that can be mustered? Is this person, this recovering person, prepared to give up the illusion of control or the need to decide outcomes and to just let the chips fall where they may? If not, it's time to consult a sponsor and finish the work not yet done in the earlier Steps. Otherwise, the disease will have its way once more. If the readiness IS there, Step Six is completed. Give the image in the mirror a smile. It's time for Step Seven.

Step 7
WE HUMBLY ASKED HIM TO REMOVE OUR SHORTCOMINGS.

In working Step Six, we needed to confront the issue of control. It was important to understand that the control we sought was nothing but an illusion. We are powerless over that which is outside ourselves and we need help with the inside work. Step Six was not so much an action as an acceptance—an acceptance of the full reality of our need for a power greater than our own. Step Seven is the action.

The desire to control, like most aspects of the disease, is based on fear. It may show itself as rage, immaturity, manipulation or a hundred other "defects of character," but it is about fear. The belief is: if things are not going our way, then they are going terribly wrong. It has often been suggested that our fears are perceived threats to our survival, whether physical or emotional. This does not mean that our survival instincts are no good. Indeed, they are probably part of what got us into recovery. Rather, it appears that we chemically dependent people carry them too far. For whatever reasons, we seem to be creatures of extremes!

Once again, fear is the ally of the disease. When we give it power, we act in ways that separate us from God. This is where humility comes in.

By the time we reach Step Seven, we have been to many meetings and heard many recovering people talk about humility. We have learned that it is not about being humiliated, or that we are weak or that we should "be doormats." Instead, people in CDA refer to "being teachable." One of the big lessons in Step Six is to accept that we are MUCH better off when we are NOT trying to run the show. Humility is the quality that allows us to accept this. It is, in short, openness to the will of God—in action as well as in prayer.

In Step Six we were asked, "What do you REALLY want?" We decided that we really wanted God to remove our shortcomings, while remembering that it is God's job to determine what they are and how they are to be removed. In Step Seven, we let them go. Repeating the Third Step Prayer, we add words such as these: "Help me to grow in trusting your path for me. Take away any obstacles that I have placed in the way; I release them now. I accept the challenges ahead as opportunities and gifts. Let my gratitude show itself in service to you."

We move forward. When we see our limitations, we do our best to accept them as part of our humanity. When we feel fear, we act anyway. When we grow restless, we remember that this is a progressive Step. And when we need to acknowledge that progress, we get affirmation from others in our lives.

The words of this Step are few and simple, yet their healing effect is profound. It is a healing that we return to time and again because the self-acceptance it fosters must be learned at new levels. In the meantime, that same self-acceptance has made us ready to take a look at our relationships with others. We are ready for Step Eight.

Step 8
WE MADE A LIST OF ALL PERSONS WE HAD HARMED AND BECAME WILLING TO MAKE AMENDS TO THEM ALL.

Picking up a pencil to begin Step Eight is likely to remind us of the writing we did in an earlier Step. This is a timely memory. The Fourth Step inventory will provide the basis for our Eighth Step list. Having already examined our sick characteristics and behaviors, we can see where they have had an impact on others. Simple—but not easy!

Having worked so hard to acknowledge and let go of our shortcomings, we may decide that we've had enough of the past. If we choose to see the work done thus far as sufficient for recovery, we are then likely to use some handy rationalizations to deny the need for Step Eight. We may decide that the harm done to us was worse than what we did to others so we really don't owe anyone anything. We might believe that we never hurt anyone but ourselves while we were out there. Or we could say that we were not truly at fault since we would have never done those things if it hadn't been for our chemical dependency. We might decide that making amends would just reopen old wounds that are starting to heal in our relationships and negate the trust we are rebuilding with people. Or we may be afraid that certain persons are just too dangerous to go to with honesty and humility.

Our rationalizations ignore a few basic facts. First of all, we HAVE hurt others. As the Fourth Step inventory attests, we cannot live a chemically dependent life—full of pride, selfishness, anger, dishonesty and fear—without affecting those around us. Second, we need to be concerned with our own actions and attitudes not those of other people. If we are too arrogant or too afraid to even consider making amends to those we have harmed regardless of their past or possible future actions, then we need to go back to Step Seven and learn a little more about humility. Third, in this Step, as in others, we are not alone. We have the guidance of a higher power, other CDA members and, of course, a sponsor.

Sponsorship is essential to this process. A sponsor has worked the Steps and understands the pitfalls. When we get to Step Nine, we will rely on that understanding to keep from causing undue harm when making amends. In the meantime, our tasks are to make the list and to become willing. We write down the names of all who have experienced injury, pain or loss due to our actions. We include family members, intimate partners, children, friends, associates, employers, colleagues, creditors and crime victims. We include them even if we don't know their whereabouts, even if we don't know their names and even if they are deceased. Our Fourth Step inventory provides a guide and springboard as we strive to list them all:

Pride

Who has been hurt by my PRIDE? Who has experienced injury, pain or loss due to my perfectionist, arrogant, self-absorbed, false-fronted or egotistical behavior?

Selfishness
Who has been hurt by my SELFISHNESS? Who has experienced injury, pain or loss due to my self-centered, greedy, ungrateful, self-pitying, envious, licentious or immature behavior?

Anger
Who has been hurt by my misdirected ANGER? Who has experienced injury, pain or loss due to my raging, abusive, violent, resentful, grudge-holding, vengeful, impatient, intolerant or oversensitive behavior?

Dishonesty
Who has been hurt by my DISHONESTY? Who has experienced injury, pain, or loss due to my self-deceiving, lying, rationalizing, cheating, stealing, unfaithful or irresponsible behavior?

Fear
Who has been hurt by my FEAR? Who has experienced injury, pain or loss due to my guilty, anxious, worried, victim, negative, isolating, procrastinating or controlling behavior?

Thoroughness is important here. It is often easy to list the dramatic injuries and "forget" the small day-to-day events that might not be remembered anyway. Nonetheless, those hurt in small ways belong on our list as much as anyone. The person we insulted privately is as important as the person we humiliated publicly. The acquaintance we stole $10 from is as important as the creditor to whom we owe $10,000. The folks who worried when we isolated are as important as those who were outraged when we acted like bullies. The child we ignored is as important as the child we abused. We ourselves are as important as anyone else we hurt. However difficult these acknowledgements, they are essential to completing this Step.

And our thoroughness has its rewards. As we review the completed list with a sponsor, we begin to feel that we are ready to make amends. This is a willingness born of all our work to date. Just as Steps Two and Three prepared us for Step Four by leading us to a source of strength and caring, so did Steps Six and Seven bring us to Step Eight. We have released all that stood between us and God. We can be rigorously honest in a self-accepting rather than self-punishing way. Now we are ready to practice that acceptance. Where it does not come easily, we simply keep praying for the willingness. As we were reminded in Step Seven, our Higher Power will do the work when we open ourselves and allow it to happen.

It is not difficult to trip over ourselves at this point. On the one hand, we need to remember that this is a deliberate process. If we scribble down a list and race out the door to set everything right, we are still acting out of fear. On the other hand, we may drag our feet when it comes to taking responsibility for our actions. All our rationalizing is denial once again, and this places us back in danger of relapse. When we slow down, receive help, and do the work, we gain the full benefit of Step Eight. We let go of others' actions and take ownership of our part in things. We are preparing to experience the true freedom of being clean and sober. We move forward to Step Nine.

Step 9
WE MADE DIRECT AMENDS TO SUCH PEOPLE WHEREVER POSSIBLE, EXCEPT WHEN TO DO SO WOULD INJURE THEM OR OTHERS.

Willingness. Commitment. Humility. Strange words to find in our vocabularies! Stranger still to realize that they are not just words to us—they have become part of our lives. In active dependency, we were all about Me, Mine and Now. The first eight Steps have worked essential changes in us.

Step Nine does more than affirm our recovery work—it takes us to a new level. Taking our Eighth Step list in one hand and all our willingness, commitment and humility in the other, we go out and make amends. This means accepting responsibility for harms done, taking the consequences of our actions and trying to set things right. In short, it means acting like grown-ups.

This is not a familiar place for a chemically dependent person to be! When we live in the self-centered fear of our disease, we are comfortable in our immaturity. We would rather continue to be big kids or overgrown teenagers; at least we know *how* to do that. Walking into difficult situations with levelheaded maturity is new stuff.

There is no need to detail how our resistance shows itself. We know by now that it's easy to rationalize our way out of doing the hard work of recovery. We also know that rejecting or putting off any part of that work is the beginning of relapse. We have come too far to lose all we've gained. If we are having trouble with the willingness to make certain amends, then we're still on Step Eight. When we are ready for Step Nine, all we need to know is how to go about it.

As always, accepting guidance is a vital part of this process. There are many people in CDA, our sponsors included, who have walked this path ahead of us. They know where the pitfalls are and how to avoid them. We need to trust their experience.

To get started, we sit down with a sponsor. We review our Eighth Step list in detail and explore how we can make amends to each person on the list. We may choose to write down the suggestions so that we can stay clear on what we need to do. At the sponsor's advice, we may talk to others in the Program who have dealt with specific situations similar to our own. Having done these things, we are ready to take action. We have been told by experienced CDA members that amends fall into four basic categories:

The first is the profound and obvious amends that actually began before we reached Step Nine. The people with whom we interact on a daily basis—spouses, lovers, children, parents, friends, employers and business partners—were strongly affected by our chemical dependency and have been affected by our recovery as well. Chances are that we told them what was going on when we first sought help and that they have seen changes in us since that time. The very act of living differently has been the beginning of our reparation to them. It is, however, only a beginning—a time to demonstrate our commitment and to start rebuilding trust. We may tell ourselves that this is enough, but it is not. We cannot live in the Ninth Step while trying to shortchange the people we love and hurt the most. It is time to formalize our amends. At a mutually agreeable time, we sit down with the other person. We talk about our past actions. We explain that they were manifestations of our disease, but we do not *blame* the disease. We take full responsibility for our actions. We describe our recovery work. If the other person is receptive, we talk about the spiritual nature of recovery. Not everyone will be open to this and we do not force it on anyone. We then express our desire to make amends and discuss how we intend to go about it. We avoid grandiose apologies for the past and grandiose promises for the future. The people close to us have heard this far too often. We find realistic, concrete ways that we can make reparation and we practice them one day at a time.

The second category is the amends that require partial disclosures. When we have caused harm through old using associations, nonpayment of bills or the commission of crimes, those harmed do not want to hear our stories. Using buddies want us to pick up again, creditors want their money and the legal system wants to complete appropriate proceedings. In these cases, we must be brief in explaining our situation and willing to take whatever action is necessary. We need only explain the new limits to the old buddies, arrange payment plans with our creditors and live up to our legal obligations.

Third, we need to consider cases where action needs to be deferred. There are people that have been hurt so badly that they refuse to have contact with us. This may be a bitter ex-spouse, a betrayed friend or a terrified crime victim. If these folks cannot be approached without worsening the situation, there is little we can do besides pray. We can offer the individuals and the situations to our Higher Power and stay willing. If appropriate, we will be presented with future opportunities to make amends. We may have a chance encounter with the person or feel that the time is right to express our amends in a letter. We may be able to help a stranger who has been hurt in the same way.

The fourth and final area includes those with whom we are unable to make direct personal contact. There are those that are lost to us through time, anonymity and, of course, death. These amends often give recovering people a lot of trouble but they are not insurmountable. We need to rely on the experience of others and our own imagination. For instance, if we have cheated faceless strangers out of money, we can make reparation by helping those without any money. We could volunteer at a soup kitchen or homeless shelter. Most difficult for some is the thought that a deceased loved one, often a parent, never got to see us clean and sober. We struggle with our powerlessness and our guilt, however, we have an ally—our Higher Power. Often, all we can do is place this issue in God's hands and take comfort in the fact that today we are living differently.

Many of us find it hard not to focus on the responses we might get from others. Sometimes we are encouraged by the thought of congratulations on our hard work and the renewal of damaged relationships. On the other hand, we may become discouraged when we worry about receiving anger or rejection. We cannot allow either to influence our actions. The purpose of making amends is to come clean about our own actions, not to bring about a specific outcome. We leave others' responses to God.

In all our Ninth Step work, we remember the Step's warning: "… except when to do so would injure them or others." *At no time* do we make amends at someone else's expense! Such selfishness is completely contrary to the spiritual aim of this Step. We do not tell our closest using friend about the fling we had with his wife when he has never suspected it. This does further harm to both of them. We do not spend every penny settling old bills when we have children to care for. We see that our family's basic needs are met first, and arrange payments we can afford. We do not turn ourselves in on an old warrant that means imprisonment when others are counting on us. We consult those to whom we have commitments and settle our affairs if necessary.

However, some have taken this warning about "injuring them or others" to mean that we never do anything where *we* might get hurt. The fact is that most of these amends-making situations will be uncomfortable and some will be downright painful. Nonetheless, we proceed. We count on the experience of CDA and the love of God to help us through these tough times. After all they are of our own making.

Standing up and taking the consequences of our own actions is maturity. Now we discover a truth that parents often try to pass on to children, namely, that growing up has its own responsibilities—and its own rewards. As we work Step Nine, we experience the joy of recovery as never before. Our hearts become truly grateful and our spirits finally light. One member speaks of "restored relationships, wrongs set right and freedom from guilt." Another celebrates "giving instead of taking, being thoughtful instead of selfish and breaking down the walls to escape the isolation." Our parent fellowship, Alcoholics Anonymous, tells us of Twelve Promises, among them freedom, happiness, peace and spiritual fulfillment. At last, we are alive.

We have come too far to accept the old ways any longer. However, as we are often reminded, we are not perfect. We need tools to help us maintain this way of life. We move on to Step Ten.

Step 10
WE CONTINUED TO TAKE PERSONAL INVENTORY AND WHEN WE WERE WRONG PROMPTLY ADMITTED IT.

We came to CDA to find relief from active chemical dependency and we found it. By this time, most of us feel that chemicals are neither friend nor enemy. We don't need them and we don't need to fight them off. They are simply no longer central to our lives.

If only we could say the same about our troublesome attitudes and behaviors! However thoroughly we work the Steps, we do not entirely rid ourselves of pride, selfishness, misdirected anger, dishonesty and fear. Indeed, there are times when these familiar traits are quite appealing. The difference today is that we are no longer powerless. We have accepted a higher power in our lives and we can choose to act out of that power rather than out of our disease.

For our disease is not gone. Although mood-altering chemicals are no longer central to us, we still have an illness that is chronic, incurable and patient. Indulging in old behaviors is a sure way to compromise our recovery. Some refer to this as "emotional relapse." It shows itself most clearly in our interactions with others

As human beings, we have many types of relationships. As recovering people, we have had to look closely at all of them. To begin with, in Steps One, Two and Three we needed to examine our relationship with God. We worked on our relationship with ourselves in Steps Four through Seven, and our relationship with others in the Eighth and Ninth Steps. When we see our old behaviors in any of these, we need to take action. The Tenth Step is a potent guide for growth in our relationships with self and others.

The first part of the Step states that we "continue to take personal inventory." This can be done in a number of ways. Many members find it helpful to stop in moments of difficulty or conflict and assess themselves on the spot. Here is one member's experience:

"In the beginning, I had many crazy emotions. Dealing with people was all new to me. From being so into myself, I took comments personally and would feel very hurt and insecure. Of course, I would throw that outward and blame others for my feelings. This, in turn, would cause a lot of resentment. The spot-check inventory helped me to focus more on my own defects rather than on the defects of others."

This experience reminds us that we have learned to take responsibility for our own behaviors, attitudes and feelings. At any time, we can remember this and stop to take stock of our part in the present situation. We see where our behavior is contributing to the difficulty or conflict, how our attitude is affecting our perspective, and what feelings are being triggered. We detach these from the other people involved and usually seek guidance in owning our "stuff" by praying, calling a sponsor, or talking to a friend. We can then respond to the situation with appropriate action.

This same self-inventory can be done on a scheduled basis. Some like to take stock at the end of each day, in weekly meetings with a sponsor, at an annual retreat or in some other set pattern. As with Step Four, the most important thing is not HOW we do it but THAT we do it. Whatever method we use, we focus on our own responsibilities, avoiding both blame and shame.

The ongoing inventory of Step Ten is about more than acknowledging our hurtful actions. We are told that recovery is "progress, not perfection." We see our progress when we affirm healthier behaviors (humility, caring, acceptance, honesty and trust). This balances our ongoing inventory, and provides encouragement during rough times in recovery.

As we continue to look at our own behavior, we find ways in which we affect others. The second part of the Step reminds us that we still have a responsibility to make amends when our actions are harmful. There are times when we bristle at this, seeing our attitudes and behaviors as justified in some way. We suggest, often indignantly, that we "had a right" to do what we did. When this happens, we need to see it as a warning sign. Our guides in CDA tell us that whenever we are disturbed or upset, no matter what the situation, WE have a problem. Whatever that problem is (a hurt feeling, a self-centered attitude, an attempt to force our will, an issue we'd rather ignore) it is not the other person's problem, it is our problem. We need to return to the attitude we adopted in Step Nine and let go of both grandiosity and self-punishment.

As in the Ninth Step, our amends are simple: We acknowledge the reality of our actions, take responsibility for them and let go of the outcome. Simple, however, still does not mean easy. We often need help. Meetings and meditation provide guidance, and sponsorship can be invaluable. By now, our sponsors know us well and can help us see ourselves more clearly. A sponsor also reminds us that the Step says, "When we are wrong, we PROMPTLY admit it." Most recovering people make an effort to clear up their part before the day's end. Where this does not happen, we continue to seek guidance.

There is more to the Tenth Step than trudging along doing the same old thing. Yes, we continue to practice Steps Four through Nine in a more consistent, condensed form. We also get to do much more. We get to live different lives. Having stepped out of our self-centeredness and insanity and replacing these with a more mature way of thinking and living, we get to grow daily in maturity and freedom. We have begun to FEEL that we belong. Now we get to ACT that way!

We are paying attention to our relationships with self and others. We need to also attend to our relationship with God. To continue growing, we move on to Step Eleven.

Step 11
WE SOUGHT THROUGH PRAYER AND MEDITATION TO IMPROVE OUR CONSCIOUS CONTACT WITH GOD AS WE UNDERSTOOD HIM, PRAYING ONLY FOR KNOWLEDGE OF HIS WILL FOR US AND THE POWER TO CARRY THAT OUT.

Much of our growth in the Steps has been growth in our reliance on God. We saw that we could not get and stay chemical-free without daily dependence on a power outside of ourselves. Faced with this reality, we learned, grudgingly at times, to trust that God offers us guidance and strength that we could never have on our own.

In this learning, we found it essential to make deliberate conscious contact with God. In Step Two, we read that there are many ways to do this: sharing at meetings, listening to the voice of conscience, speaking out loud to an invisible listener, praying and meditating. In practicing the Steps we have done some or all of these and possibly much more. Now, Step Eleven focuses our attention on two particular routes to this contact: prayer and meditation.

Why are these worthy of special attention? To answer that, we must first look at the importance of consciously developing and enlarging our relationship with God. As CDA members share their experience on this subject, we hear a common theme:

"As the literature says, I'm an alcoholic and I'm undisciplined. I let God show me discipline through the habit of prayer."

"Frequent efforts at prayer help me maintain emotional balance."

"I must have a relationship with God. Without communication, there can be no relationship."

"After practicing meditation for some time, I came to the realization that my mind had begun to calm down."

"The pain in my life must be offered as a prayer each day. Pain must have a transcendent meaning, otherwise it eats me alive."

"Recovery has more to offer me than simply being chemical-free. This spiritual path gives my life meaning, purpose and joy."

"Without God in my life, I would self-destruct. Through prayer and meditation, I renew my commitment to God daily and He renews my strength. Communion with God gives me peace, hope and confidence."

If we have worked the first ten Steps, we can identify with such experiences or list some of our own. If not, it's time for some reflection. What motivates us to remain chemical-free? Why do we keep coming back to meetings? How do we work Steps Three and Seven on an ongoing basis? If we are not clear about these questions, we may need to spend more time with the Tenth Step, looking clearly at ourselves. If we believe that we have become the greatest power in our own lives, we are not practicing honest self-appraisal.

When we can value our contact with God, we appreciate opportunities to strengthen that contact. Our experiences suggest that prayer and meditation are ways to do so. How, then, do we meditate and pray?

It has often been said that prayer is talking to God and meditation is listening to God. Prayer takes many different forms for different individuals. Some prayers have no formality at all. Some of us look to religious devotion or writings for prayers, while others study spiritual texts, stories from CDA or cultural traditions. There are those who do not use formalized prayers at all, preferring to follow their sponsor's advice or their own intuition. In any case, we generally find it best to have some routine in our practice of prayer. Morning and evening prayer have become vital to the ongoing sobriety and serenity of many CDA members. Time in the morning talking to God puts the day into perspective and gives us a chance to reaffirm that our will and our lives are in God's care for another 24 hours. At the end of the day, prayer can aid us in our Tenth Step review, as well as offer time to acknowledge our gratitude. In between, we have many chances to pause and make contact, however brief. When faced with a confusing or difficult situation, we can ask God for direction and wisdom in that moment. Energy spent on the Serenity Prayer, instead of on resentment or judgment, reminds us of what's most important.

While many choose to keep prayer a private time, others may seek to pray with their sponsor or a small group. It has been said that, "Where two or more are gathered, God is in their midst." We can see this demonstrated through a CDA meeting's group conscience. Spiritual retreats also create an ideal setting for communing with God through prayer and meditation.

Some of us find the word "meditation" rather intimidating. It sounds mystical, far outside our experience. In fact, meditation can be as simple as relaxing. Over time, by practicing for a minute or two at a time, we can learn to quiet the body, mind and spirit, and be open to God's will. However, some of us find quietness as alien as sobriety once was. Many members have found that having a focus is helpful. Anything will do: a candle flame, a flower, a mental image, a favorite prayer. For instance, we may start with the Serenity Prayer, "God grant me serenity to accept the things I cannot change, courage to change the things I can, and wisdom to know the difference." This can be repeated slowly, allowing the meaning of the phrases to reach us. A particular word may catch our attention and we can focus on that word, asking God to reveal its special importance to us this day. By such simple measures, we begin a habit of meditation. With some experience, we may find ourselves able to slip into a calm, meditative state whenever we need a short break.

The final words of this Step teach us a little more about how to pray and meditate. We are instructed to ask for knowledge and power, to whatever degree God sees fit. If we are to receive this guidance and strength, it helps to be still and open; thus, our meditation serves us well here. Whenever we bring a request to God, we remember to add, "if it be your will," then let ourselves be open to that will.

Through practicing Steps Ten and Eleven, we are developing a habit of self-examination, meditation and prayer that allows us to continue to grow in recovery and trusting God. Our spirit is awakened to the reality of God's abiding presence. We see that it is important to be earnest in working these Steps to maintain continuous, contented sobriety. We now have something to share with others especially the CDA newcomer. We are ready for Step Twelve.

Step 12
HAVING HAD A SPIRITUAL AWAKENING AS THE RESULT OF THESE STEPS, WE TRIED TO CARRY THIS MESSAGE TO OTHER CHEMICALLY DEPENDENT PERSONS AND TO PRACTICE THESE PRINCIPLES IN ALL OUR AFFAIRS.

Awakening from sleep is a varied experience. It may come suddenly in response to an alarm or a loud noise. It can be gradual (drifting from a dreamy state, to vague awareness, to full consciousness). Sometimes it comes early, bringing with it the struggle to recapture sleep. Other times, through chance or neglect, it's late, leading to a hurried scramble. Regardless, one eventually reaches the point of being irrevocably awake.

So it is with spiritual awakening. Whether one's experience is sudden or gradual, whether struggled against or hurried along, eventually it just is. One is awake and alive, aware of the world and of one's own participation in it.

There is something different about a spiritual awakening: One never goes back to sleep. A change has taken place, one so fundamental that it will not yield to pain, doubt or denial. Whether one likes it or not, the change in self is here to stay. Even relapse cannot wipe it out completely. That is why it is often said that CDA "ruins your using for you."

The first phrase of this Step reads, "Having had a spiritual awakening as the result of these Steps." Spiritual awakening is what the Twelve Steps are all about. While many opportunities for change come out of the Steps—staying clean and sober, becoming honest and clear, having strong relationships, contributing to the community—they are simply manifestations of this powerful, life-giving process of transformation. As we become spiritually awake and alive, our actions cannot help but reflect our awakening.

Before examining those actions let's take another look at spirituality. We didn't come to CDA to "get spiritual." We came because we were desperate, defeated and hopeless. Many of us weren't sure what all this God talk was about, but we knew we needed something. Others in CDA shared their experience, strength and hope with us. We began to trust them and, more importantly, trust the recovery process. We weren't perfect at it! Sometimes we rebelled and rejected our sponsors' feedback or the guidance offered in the Steps. Still, the recovery process was always there when we needed and accepted it.

And it worked. We saw ourselves and our lives change. While this change would occasionally manifest as a dramatic shift, it usually showed up in a gradual way. Sometimes, we didn't even notice it until it was pointed out to us. However varied our experiences, they had this in common: We could now do what we had never done alone. What made the difference was letting go of all that stood in the way of our relationship with God, with ourselves and with others.

This is the essence of spirituality (a connection with sources of strength and, most of all, with a power greater than ourselves). Steps One through Eleven give us all the tools we need to open up our end of the connection. When we do, all that we need is available to us—ALL that we need. That is why we now place spiritual values first in our lives; when they are attended to, everything else falls into place.

We realize this most fully when we place other concerns ahead of our spiritual principles. For instance, when a relationship or a job takes top priority, we can lose focus on what we've learned about honesty or humility.

When that happens, we tend to slide into old behaviors. We may become more and more demanding, dependent, intolerant or withdrawn (often without even noticing). Whatever the behavior, it threatens the very thing we are trying to preserve. On the other hand, when we consistently attend to a spiritual program, we have "knowledge of God's will for us and the power to carry that out." However imperfect we are, when we are spiritually fit, we bring the best of ourselves to the relationship, the job or whatever our area of concern may be.

One may object to this by saying, "How can spiritual principles come first? At meetings, everyone says that staying clean and sober is the number one priority!" This is true, and it demonstrates beautifully the Twelve Steps in action. In active chemical dependence, we were in a downward spiral—using made us miserable and our misery led to more using. In recovery, we are now in an upward spiral. Being chemically dependent has given us access to a spiritual program and our spirituality allows us to stay free from chemicals. At last we understand what CDA members mean when they describe themselves as "grateful alcoholics and addicts." Were it not for chemical dependence, we may not have found this incredible, fulfilling way of life.

Having said that, let's turn our attention to the actions that flow from spiritual awakening. The rest of the Twelfth Step describes them: "We tried to carry this message to other chemically dependent persons and to practice these principles in all our affairs." CDA is founded on the principle that our common experience of both dependence and recovery provides us with unique opportunities to help others like us. And in the act of helping others, we ourselves stay clean and sober and grow. Therefore, carrying the message is vital.

How do we go about it? Most of us start doing small acts of service early in recovery. Sharing at a meeting or cleaning up afterwards are ways to help ensure that the newcomer to CDA has the same chance we had to hear the message. Some of us want to do much more. We want to tell everyone we know about the gifts of the Program. We are ready to convert all our using buddies to the CDA way! This enthusiasm is generally redirected by a sponsor who has the experience to understand that we cannot carry a message we haven't fully received ourselves. What we are passing on is the possibility of transformed lives through the spiritual program of the Steps. Before offering this to another chemically dependent person, we take the time and do the work needed to experience this transformation ourselves.

Once that has happened, the opportunities are many. A world of service opens up starting at the group level and moving far beyond it. Groups require secretaries, treasurers and other trusted servants. Not only can we take one of these jobs, we can also help start new meetings where they are needed. We can also represent a group at Intergroup where we can help out as officers and committee chairs. Consider how much we are doing to carry the message when chairing a Hospitals and Institutions Committee which allows meetings to be held in hospitals, treatment centers, jails and prisons. Area Assembly and General Service are further levels of service. The pamphlet you are reading was written by the Step Committee of CDA General Service with the input of many members of the Fellowship. The people on this committee were simply recovering chemically dependent individuals with experience in working the Steps and a desire to pass it on.

Service work takes on many other forms. One of the most moving is sponsorship. To sponsor newcomers in CDA is to give back what we've been given many times over. While no one of us has all the answers, our experience can help guide a struggling sponsee along the path to recovery. Another kind of service is being available to those still using and being there when they decide to ask for help. We might answer the phone for the local CDA information line or accompany another member on a Twelfth Step call. And while it may seem that we are doing these things to get the still-suffering person clean and sober, in fact, we are not. All we can do is offer what we have. If it is accepted, fine; if not, we are reminded of the power of the disease and our own powerlessness. Newcomers and sponsees are put in our paths for many reasons, some of which we never know. This Step says that we only try to carry the message. The outcome of these encounters is always left to God.

While we have much to offer in words, often our most profound sharing has to do with who we are rather than what we say. The Steps have brought powerful spiritual principles into our lives: honesty (with ourselves and others), humility, trust, self-examination, self-disclosure, acceptance, making amends, prayer, meditation and caring. When we live these principles, the results are evident to others. They see our calm in troubled times, our willingness to admit when we're wrong and set things right, our compassion for those who still suffer, our ability to live up to our responsibilities and our insistence on enjoying life. There is no stronger declaration of our changed lives!

This is not to say that we have somehow reached perfection. The Twelfth Step is a daily goal not a conclusion. "To practice these principles in all our affairs" is an ideal. We are still human. We will frequently act in ways that are not consistent with our spiritual values, and we will need help in recommitting to those values. Meetings, sponsorship and Steps Ten and Eleven provide that help. Some of us find support in other resources as well, and with the work we have done, we learn much more from them.

Sometimes we really feel stuck. We think we're just not making progress. We may be repeating an unwanted behavior or frequently going into emotional relapse or simply standing still when we want to be moving forward. What then?

Often the answer is as simple as Step Twelve. We ask three questions: Am I paying attention to my spiritual needs? Am I passing on what I've received? Am I living the principles I've come to hold so dear?

If the answer to any of these is "no," then we apply ourselves to the practice of this Step, thus ensuring our sobriety, sanity and serenity. However, if we are doing these things and still feel stuck or if we're thoroughly blocked on doing them, it may be time to return to Step One. At this point the question becomes, "Where am I struggling with powerlessness and unmanageability in my life?"

Part of practicing the principles is knowing that we can begin the Steps again at any time. Whether it's an old issue or a new one, with the help of CDA or another fellowship, and with or without the support of a professional or spiritual guide, the recovery process is still there—and still ours. We need only open ourselves to it.

And this is the miracle. Lives once nearly lost in desperation and degradation are now lived openly, powerfully and joyously. The pain that tore at our souls is transformed into a message of serenity, courage and wisdom. We of CDA reach out to those who seek help. We offer our collective recovery to any who want it. We declare that the possibilities are endless. And as we say in every meeting: KEEP COMING BACK—IT WORKS!!

7   CDA's Twelve Traditions

1. Our common welfare should come first; personal recovery depends upon CDA unity.

2. For our group purpose there is but one ultimate authority—a loving God as He may express Himself in our group conscience. Our leaders are but trusted servants; they do not govern.

3. The only requirement for CDA membership is a desire to abstain from all mood-changing and mind-altering chemicals, including street-type drugs, alcohol and unnecessary medication.

4. Each group should be autonomous except in matters affecting other groups or CDA as a whole.

5. Each group has but one primary purpose—to carry its message to the chemically dependent person who still suffers.

6. A CDA group ought never endorse, finance, or lend the CDA name to any related facility or outside enterprise, lest problems of money, property, and prestige divert us from our primary purpose.

7. Every CDA group ought to be fully self-supporting, declining outside contributions.

8. CDA should remain forever nonprofessional, but our service centers may employ special workers.

9. CDA, as such, ought never be organized but we may create service boards or committees directly responsible to those they serve.

10. CDA has no opinion on outside issues; hence, the CDA name ought never be drawn into public controversy.

11. Our public relations policy is based on attraction rather than promotion; we need always maintain personal anonymity at the level of press, radio, films and social media.

12. Anonymity is the spiritual foundation of all our traditions, ever reminding us to place principles before personalities.*

---

* Reprinted and adapted with permission of Alcoholics Anonymous World Services, Inc.

First Tradition
OUR COMMON WELFARE SHOULD COME FIRST; PERSONAL RECOVERY DEPENDS UPON CDA UNITY.

Unity is the most treasured quality that our Fellowship possesses. Our lives and the lives of those who come after us depend on it. Without unity, there is absolutely no hope. Unless CDA continues to survive, most of us will die.

We believe the individual's service to the group is very important. In addition, individual recovery depends upon the group and the presence of a God-consciousness in that group. However, we are not implying that the group should dominate the individual. There is not another society which is as willing to go to any length to help, love and care for its fellow members as ours. We are an organization that allows its members to act, speak and think as freely as they wish.

The primary problem facing any society is how to survive and then how to continue to grow and prosper. We believe that by placing our common welfare first and remaining unified, we are well on our way. Our lives depend upon obedience to spiritual principles shown to us in the Twelve Traditions.

Second Tradition
FOR OUR GROUP PURPOSE THERE IS BUT ONE ULTIMATE AUTHORITY—A LOVING GOD AS HE MAY EXPRESS HIMSELF IN OUR GROUP CONSCIENCE. OUR LEADERS ARE BUT TRUSTED SERVANTS; THEY DO NOT GOVERN.

CDA has no president or sole individual who governs us nor do we have a so-called board of directors. No CDA member can issue an order to any other member or try to force adherence to his or her own beliefs. In actuality, our Fellowship is a democracy with a loving God as our director as He may express Himself in our group conscience. He is the only authority in CDA. We trust in His presence and guidance.

Each CDA group has a set of elected officers. These individuals are trusted servants of the members. They carry out the groups' responsibilities. Most groups have a program chairman whose duty it is to obtain speakers for the meeting and make sure that the meetings open on time. There is also a treasurer who deposits the money collected in meetings, pays rent and other bills, and gives a periodic report at the group conscience meeting. The secretary of the group opens the meeting and makes sure the literature is displayed there.

Each group has an intergroup representative who attends the Intergroup meeting and reports back to his group about what was discussed there. The intergroup representative also attends the Area Assembly meeting and reports the meeting proceedings to his group. And last, but certainly not least, is the coffeemaker whose responsibility it is to make coffee for the meeting, set up the tables and chairs beforehand and make sure everything is put away at the end of the meeting.

Elected officers cannot give any spiritual advice, issue any directives or judge anyone's conduct. We in CDA believe that gratitude is an action word and that being a trusted servant is a positive way of expressing gratitude and passing on what has been so freely given to us.

Third Tradition
THE ONLY REQUIREMENT FOR CDA MEMBERSHIP IS A DESIRE TO ABSTAIN FROM ALL MOOD-CHANGING AND MIND-ALTERING CHEMICALS, INCLUDING STREET-TYPE DRUGS, ALCOHOL AND UNNECESSARY MEDICATION.

You are a member of CDA the moment you say you are one. No matter what your past has been or whatever other emotional problems you may have, we cannot deny you membership. We welcome you to CDA.

We will not deny anyone membership as long as he or she has a desire to stop using. If someone comes to a meeting under the influence, no one has the right to tell him he is not welcome in our fellowship. The suggested method for handling an individual who is disruptive at a meeting is to take the person outside and talk to him or her alone.

To deny any chemically dependent person a chance would be allowing that individual to die or force him to return to a life of endless torture. We are not judges. God is the only one who has a right to judge for He alone knows the workings of our minds.

It has been our experience that our disease tries to deceive us when it comes to unnecessary medication. Therefore, rigorous honesty with yourself and with your physician is imperative concerning this matter. Consulting your sponsor may also be helpful in this regard.

Fourth Tradition
EACH GROUP SHOULD BE AUTONOMOUS EXCEPT IN MATTERS AFFECTING OTHER GROUPS OR CDA AS A WHOLE.

The Fourth Tradition suggests that each group should take an honest inventory of itself. CDA groups should see the Traditions as a tested guide towards the primary purpose of each group which is to carry the message to the chemically dependent person.

The first part of this Tradition states that "Each group should be autonomous." Autonomy is described as self-government. In CDA, this is the process by which each group handles its own affairs, carefully following the Twelve Traditions as it does so.

Such freedom also requires responsibility. Each group is responsible for its own decisions and the way in which these decisions affect other groups or CDA as a whole. The self-governing process allows groups to be self-sufficient. Tradition Four gives each group the freedom of choice as well as the responsibility that goes along with that freedom.

Though groups may differ greatly, all members suffer from chemical dependency. Each group is a spiritual entity strictly reliant on its group conscience as a guide for direction. A group may be creative in shaping its own personality. However, it is suggested that it keep its creativity within the guidelines of the Traditions and always maintain the primary purpose of recovery as the main goal of the group.

The group should be responsible for electing its own officers, the trusted servants who carry out the duties and responsibilities of the group as described in the Second Tradition. Participation in the service structure eliminates group isolation and program illiteracy. It is important to know what is affecting other groups or CDA as a whole and participation in the service structure creates an awareness of such valuable information.

The Fourth Tradition is known in the circle of anonymous recovery groups as the addict's or alcoholic's loophole. It is sometimes mistaken for the right to do "what I want, how I want and when I want." A group that reflects this attitude will exist in anarchy where self-will becomes dominant. CDA can profit from using the history of Alcoholics Anonymous as a learning tool and guide to proper self-government that allows us to continue to grow and prosper.

Fifth Tradition
EACH GROUP HAS BUT ONE PRIMARY PURPOSE—TO CARRY ITS MESSAGE TO THE CHEMICALLY DEPENDENT PERSON WHO STILL SUFFERS.

The very existence of our Fellowship requires the preservation and practice of this Tradition. Our unity is the support enabling us to carry the message to others. In other areas of society, we may be able to help as individuals but seldom as a group. The history of Alcoholics Anonymous however has shown how important group action is in helping addictive people recover. CDA, as a society working in unity, has proven to be an effective source of recovery for an addict and/or alcoholic who desires to get clean and sober.

We believe that in order to keep sobriety and the better way of life that we have found, it is necessary for us to pass on to the newcomer and other chemically dependent persons what has been so freely given to us. We in CDA believe that our recovery is a gift from God and that the primary purpose of that gift is for us to give it away to those who need it.

Sixth Tradition
A CDA GROUP OUGHT NEVER ENDORSE, FINANCE, OR LEND THE CDA NAME TO ANY RELATED FACILITY OR OUTSIDE ENTERPRISE, LEST PROBLEMS OF MONEY, PROPERTY, AND PRESTIGE DIVERT US FROM OUR PRIMARY PURPOSE.

By related facilities, we mean any organization, group or institution related to the field of addiction. A CDA group should never support such facilities or enterprises. A CDA group can cooperate with anyone but never to the point of connecting itself to or sanctioning any of these facilities or enterprises in any manner.

In the area of property and finances, too many problems may arise where money is involved. Questions of prestige can become very detrimental to our anonymity which is part of the spiritual foundation of our program. We have found it absolutely necessary to separate the material from the spiritual, allowing nothing to divert us from our spiritual goal. We have found that CDA is best served through its primary purpose: carrying "its message to the chemically dependent person who still suffers."

Seventh Tradition
EVERY CDA GROUP OUGHT TO BE FULLY SELF-SUPPORTING, DECLINING OUTSIDE CONTRIBUTIONS.

As recovering individuals, we learn through the Program that not only must we stop using chemicals, we must also begin taking responsibility for ourselves, for our own lives and actions. Among the many pleasures of living a sober life is a growing awareness that we are capable of taking care of ourselves. This awareness comes from doing the daily tasks necessary for our survival. Through the consistent practice of the Program, we learn that we can be the adult men and women we always yearned to be but could never be while using chemicals.

A new sense of self-worth is born in us and, along with it, a sense of responsibility to those around us. We finally become a part of society and start giving back. We gain knowledge and learn many valuable lessons as we become self-supporting, responsible people. Some of us become so for the first time in our lives. Similarly, we mirror the same attitude of responsibility in our groups when we support the Program with our money, time and energy.

The lesson we are learning is the same for each of us: Heretofore, we have been incredibly dependent on drugs and alcohol, other people and social institutions. We must now begin to take care of ourselves if we are to survive and grow in recovery. The Program provides us with the tools and support necessary for us to become *real people*. It is up to us as individuals to grasp the tools and use them. If we continue to allow others to assume responsibility for us, the changes we need to make will never occur.

Consequently, our groups must be run in the same manner, assuming financial responsibility for their own operations and for the survival of the Program. If we allow outside contributions to support our groups instead of paying our own way, we are simply continuing our old behavior. We have been given a second life through the Program and we have the opportunity to support it in return. Being fully self-supporting is necessary to our group's well-being and to the continued growth of each individual member.

Like most of our other Traditions and Steps, there are several sides to being fully self-supporting in our groups. We have one primary purpose: to meet together, share in recovery and spread the message to the still-suffering individual. Only a recovering chemically dependent person can understand the dramatic difference made by the message of recovery. As recovering individuals, we have all heard that message and been given the opportunity to repair our lives. We know through our own experiences that spreading hope and faith is the single most important factor in our program. Our experience tells us that supporting our groups to keep the message available is paramount, not only to ourselves but also to the chemically dependent person who has yet to arrive at our door.

No matter how well intended, no gift is offered free from all commitments between the giver and the receiver. When we accept contributions from each other in our meetings, we are sharing in our collective commitment to keep the Program alive and working for us as well as others yet to come. If we accept contributions from outside, we are made vulnerable to commitments outside of our CDA Program and perhaps even outside of our primary purpose. Therefore, we must share the responsibility for the Fellowship's continued well-being among ourselves. This will ensure that CDA remains healthy and ready to receive the newcomer.

Eighth Tradition
CDA SHOULD REMAIN FOREVER NONPROFESSIONAL, BUT OUR SERVICE CENTERS MAY EMPLOY SPECIAL WORKERS.

This Tradition contributes much to the stability of CDA and helps clarify the relationships between individuals, and between individuals and their groups. It is in this Tradition that we define the differences between service to the still-suffering chemically dependent person, individual service to CDA groups and the role of people performing support services for CDA.

Here, we state clearly that no one among us is a professional specializing in the treatment of chemically dependent persons. In our program, the privilege of helping these people is reserved for individual recovering members who, through their 12-step work, further their own sobriety and spiritual progress while helping others to recover. Because our experience has taught us so strongly that helping another dependent person is not just beneficial but actually crucial to our recovery, we state in this Tradition that CDA must never take credit for the act of reaching out. We will not become nor hire professionals to help recovering and still-suffering persons. We must always remain a group of equals helping equals to attain sobriety through the grace of their Higher Power.

We do not deny the role of professionals in assisting us or working with dependent people outside of CDA. We respect and admire the helping professionals, accepting them as powerful allies. We only state that we ourselves cannot act as professionals because doing so would eliminate much of the unity and equality that has made our program effective.

An individual's service to CDA groups is beneficial to individual recovery, and necessary for the continuation of each group. Coffee always needs to be made; furniture has to be arranged; doors must be opened; newcomers must be made welcome. Many other routine tasks are involved with the opening and closing of our meetings each week and administration of our expenses. This group-level service is the responsibility of individual members and we gladly share the work out of gratitude to the groups that keep us clean and sober.

When we need service work done that will affect all of our groups such as running a full-time area or national service office, we simply cannot rely on volunteers to do the job. These offices or service centers are not actual CDA groups. We do not meet there expressly to discuss sobriety. Rather, they perform essential administrative tasks relating to all our groups: clerical work, telephone reception or making printing arrangements for our literature. These centers can operate best for CDA if we allow them to perform their tasks in as businesslike a fashion as possible. So, as in any business, we allow our service centers to employ workers to perform these tasks, recognizing that these people are doing jobs necessary to the welfare of us all.

We make a clear and sharp distinction between service workers doing essential tasks for all of CDA and professionals reaching out to the still-suffering person. Service workers are responsible to the entire organization of CDA when they work for its benefit. But we do not allow professionals to come inside of CDA to accomplish its basic purpose. This would mean replacing individual 12-step work and removing one of our greatest aids to recovery and individual growth: the benefit derived by one chemically dependent person helping another. While we need to employ service workers to grow as an organization, we will always need individual recovering members of CDA to perform 12-step work. This is how we help one another in CDA. We remain nonprofessional in a spirit of gratitude with the full realization of where we have come from and the acknowledgement of a higher power which has led us to freedom.

Ninth Tradition
CDA, AS SUCH, OUGHT NEVER BE ORGANIZED; BUT WE MAY CREATE SERVICE BOARDS OR COMMITTEES DIRECTLY RESPONSIBLE TO THOSE THEY SERVE.

CDA is an extraordinary organization in that there are no rules governing individual membership and no requirements imposed on groups by our Area Assembly or Intergroups. Even if they did exist, no provisions are in place for the enforcement of such rules or regulations. In CDA, individuals are members "when they say they are" based only on a desire to stop using mood-altering chemicals. There are no requirements imposed by our groups on members and our entire program is stated simply in the form of suggestions. Likewise, groups are free to structure their meetings how they wish and to hold them when they choose. No Intergroup or other Assembly can dictate to a group its format or membership. The rare exception is when a group's decisions would affect other groups or CDA as a whole. Our Traditions, along with many other "traditional" aspects of our program, are also only suggested to our groups.

Such an unstructured approach might spell disaster in other settings, but there is one unique feature of CDA not to be overlooked here: CDA deals entirely with the disease of chemical dependency, a devastating and all-too-frequently fatal problem for the dependent person. In CDA, we have a program consisting of mere suggestions because our collective experience has been that to reject these recommendations is a most dreadful choice for the individual or group. Chemical dependency itself provides sufficient penalty in our lives for our failure to follow the spiritual principles that our program outlines.

Groups as well as individuals can deteriorate and die unless there is approximate conformity to CDA's Twelve Traditions. So we obey the spiritual principles of our program in both our personal and group lives. At first, we do this because we must, but later because we have learned to live again in sobriety. We have all suffered much in active chemical dependency but we have found great freedom in our program. Our experience has been that the Program contains the roots of a greater discipline than any we might impose through formal organizational rules.

Clearly, such an unstructured organization should never have a governing body. Therefore, CDA will have no area or national body centrally "organizing" our groups. This does not mean however that CDA has no need for committees to do service work or boards to assist in administering our collective affairs. There will always be a need for them to assist us in the task of bringing sobriety within the grasp of all who seek it. Just as we elect informal service officers in our groups and intergroup associations for our areas, we create special committees and boards to serve the larger organization for specific needs. It is in the spirit of service, responsive to the people we assist, that we work individually or appoint special committees or boards to aid us in our endeavors.

Tenth Tradition
CDA HAS NO OPINION ON OUTSIDE ISSUES; HENCE THE CDA NAME OUGHT NEVER BE DRAWN INTO PUBLIC CONTROVERSY.

CDA should never take sides or voice any opinions on any outside issues in areas such as drug and alcohol reform, religion, politics or abortion (which crosses religious-political lines). No matter how worthy the cause may be, we do not become involved with it. It is especially important to remember that when we speak on a public level, the opinion we express should be considered merely that of the individual and not the viewpoint of CDA.

History has dictated the importance of tradition in the survival of our fellowship. Engaging in such controversy has destroyed many societies such as ours. One example is that of a local group of alcoholics who had united together to help one another. They were successful for a period of time but soon became involved in outside issues and controversies. This led to disharmony among the group members and the eventual destruction of their organization.

CDA takes only one stand. It is that we have been given and are applying the Twelve Steps and Twelve Traditions in our lives today so that we may recover from chemical dependency. The only issue that we concern ourselves with is the survival and growth of CDA so that the individual member may recover and help others to do so. Concerning ourselves with any outside issues or controversies will only prove fatal to our fellowship and the individuals who depend upon it so much.

Eleventh Tradition

OUR PUBLIC RELATIONS POLICY IS BASED ON ATTRACTION RATHER THAN PROMOTION; WE NEED ALWAYS MAINTAIN PERSONAL ANONYMITY AT THE LEVEL OF PRESS, RADIO, FILMS AND SOCIAL MEDIA.

Most of us knew of the existence of Chemically Dependent Anonymous or about one of the other 12-step organizations prior to getting sober. CDA is not a secret society and we do not try to hide our existence from the public. In order for the "hand of help" to be grasped, those in need must be able to find our rooms and locate sober people who can show them the way back to sanity and health. It is necessary however that those needing help reach us as we ourselves reached sobriety – by seeking it for ourselves at the time our Higher Power decided was best for us rather than by being pushed or cajoled into it.

No amount of outside effort would have prevailed with us until we were ready to accept help. And we have found that no amount of advertising will lead those in need to the Program any faster. By setting a good example through actions taken in our sober lives, we are the Program's best public relations representatives.

People like us who are afflicted with a disease characterized by inflated egos and flagrant behavior patterns are particularly at risk of becoming caught up in any public relations policy that might call for more personal testimony. Furthermore, it would be far too easy for well-intentioned members to put forth their personal beliefs and experiences as a model for sobriety. That would do harm in two ways: damaging CDA by restricting sobriety to only one model, and doing the members a disservice by inflating their importance. Our program must be allowed to remain a broad and gentle one with many diverse members and experiences. We must avoid the self-seeking behavior that has driven us in our past lives.

For our continued personal and group recovery, anonymity is the best possible protection for CDA.

We have found that this quiet public relations policy has brought great rewards. CDA, along with the other 12-step organizations, is well respected by the professional community which continues to refer many prospective members to our rooms. The public at large is generally aware of the existence of CDA and similar groups and knows that we have achieved great success in dealing with the problem of addiction. And we are also able to remain chemical-free and serve as the best possible advertising – caring, sober people whose lives have been changed through the Program.

Twelfth Tradition
ANONYMITY IS THE SPIRITUAL FOUNDATION OF ALL OUR TRADITIONS, EVER REMINDING US TO PLACE PRINCIPLES BEFORE PERSONALITIES.

There are many reasons why we seek to disclaim personal importance in our program: because we have spent our previous non-sober lives in self-seeking behavior; because we stay sober through the continued survival of our groups, not as individuals; and, because we know it is through the work of our Higher Power that we survive at all and not by any effort of our own. For us, anonymity is the acceptance of these spiritual truths and an essential outgrowth of our sobriety. For us, anonymity means reflecting humility in our lives. Sobriety demands this of us.

As individual members, we may disagree with a particular point of view. We may strongly believe that a particular approach to recovery is the best possible one. We may adhere to any of a thousand different ways of living our programs. But in the tradition of anonymity, all of us are equal members of the group. The spiritual principle of anonymity renders all other distinctions meaningless.

There is an all-pervading spiritual quality in the lives of CDA members who are working their program. Experience teaches us that humility is an essential part of this spiritual quality. As CDA members, we lay aside the natural desire for personal distinction when we are with both CDA groups and the public in general. Humility allows us to maintain this anonymity of ourselves and others. Anonymity likewise enhances humility and aids us in our spiritual growth because we are placing principles above personalities.

8 The CDA Gifts

As we work the CDA Program of Recovery, our old ideas are replaced with new ways of thinking and new attitudes. We believe these are gifts of a spiritual nature from our Higher Power. When we follow this path, we become healthy, responsible people and live a life of peace, healing and serenity.

1. We live one day at a time with dignity and self-respect.

2. We replace fear and self-pity with courage and gratitude.

3. We accept the changes in our life with optimism and hope.

4. We learn how to lighten up, laugh often and have fun again.

5. We find that challenges and setbacks become the touchstones of spiritual growth.

6. We discover our talents and gifts and unlock their full potential.

7. We experience freedom as we forgive ourselves and others.

8. We are willing to take risks as we choose growth over fear.

9. We develop healthy relationships as we learn how to communicate with respect and love.

10. We believe that love and service are the foundation of a lifetime of happiness.

As we continue on our journey, the possibilities are endless. Remember: "The Sky's the Limit!"

9 H.O.W.

We have found that the basic concepts of the CDA Program can be broken down into the three major principles of Honesty, Open-mindedness and Willingness to try. This is *H.O.W.* the Program works. With these qualities, we are on our way to recovery.

Honesty

Most of us in CDA can recall that in the last stages of our drinking/drugging, we knew something was wrong with us and we pretty well knew it had to do with our substance abuse. So in spite of our denials, the truth was beginning to surface. We were starting to add two and two together to get four, not five or three we had been accepting as correct answers in the past. Now, there could be no more shortcuts to the truth.

After we had attended one or more meetings, we also had to face the fact that the only way we were going to recover was by first admitting our lives had truly become unbalanced through addiction, and then by gradually understanding we were going to have to live in total abstinence from all drugs and alcohol. At some point, we all got that revelation. We don't think that God says, "Well, I think these few people here are going to get honest." Rather, each of us eventually gets a flash of the truth. Regardless of what we're doing or what the issue of the day might be, we all have to make decisions in every area of our lives.

God gives people the freedom of choice and we must choose at some point to say, "I have had enough of this pain," or we will perish. Making that right choice to finally "get honest" with ourselves may be our first true adult act. We realize that we have to grow up, pull ourselves up by our bootstraps and become responsible for ourselves. We just can't suppress this kind of honesty anymore.

After we enter the Program, we come to understand that honesty is still the single most important ingredient in our recovery. We have to continue evaluating our motives and position on a daily basis and the Twelve Steps are the tools that enable us to rise above our own egos so we can see the truth. The greatest element in the universe is truth and we can only find it by being honest with ourselves. We all have these little places within us that refuse to grow up, but we must do it. We have to constantly work at being "straight" with ourselves. We find a reliable aid in this struggle in the Serenity Prayer: "God grant me the serenity to accept the things I cannot change; courage to change the things I can; and wisdom to know the difference."

That prayer enables us to become grownups. When we can sense what our true course of action must be, even if it is just waiting at that moment to let other circumstances change, we are practicing honesty. We will always know the truth and be able to act on it if we accept the guidance of the Serenity Prayer. What will help us get through most situations is to pause, pray, meditate about what the proper action might be and then do it. This is living honestly.

There is an old saying: "The shortest distance between two points is a straight line." For us, "straight" means that we don't drink and drug but stay true to our consciences. This is the straight life. In the past, we have always tried to find shortcuts but there are none. The straight line – the straight life – *is* the right way. Alcoholics Anonymous has given us a clue about how to live the straight life successfully. They call it the H.O.W. of the Program: Honesty, Open-mindedness and Willingness to try. The letters also stand for "Hang Onto Winners." In CDA, we employ the pure simplicity of such slogans to help us stay on the straight line to success.

Open-mindedness

We of CDA cannot stress enough the importance of open-mindedness. This condition, completely foreign to us when we were practicing addicts, is essential to a healthy recovery. We do not achieve such a virtue all at once however because years of using drugs have left us distrustful of others.

When we first decide that recovery is what we want for ourselves, it is the beginning of a change in our thinking. Based on the positive results we see in other recovering addicts' lives, we put a positive plan of action into our lives. We have begun to trust what others say is possible and that we too can stay away from drugs for long periods of time.

We then become open to the realization that a new way of thinking is not only possible but essential, and that many of our ideas were twisted as a result of our years of drug use. We become willing to listen for the first time to the experiences of others in recovery. And we begin to see more changes in our own lives.

The next step is to select a sponsor. This requires a new move toward open-mindedness because a sponsor is going to direct our lives in our sobriety journey. We have finally come to the point of honesty in our recovery where we know we don't have all the answers and that we need help from one another. We begin to understand how insane our behavior was when we were using and we start to realize that an examination of this behavior is necessary. For the first time in our lives, we are willing to look at our past as honestly and thoroughly as we possibly can and to share our experiences with another person. This is all new to us. We buried our past for many years because of the pain we suffered under the influence of drugs and alcohol.

This step of inventory can come only after we become receptive to the idea that not only do our fellow addicts care about our welfare and recovery, they also truly love us. We have broken down a great barrier when we realize at a gut level that we have finally found people we can trust whose only motive is love. They want to help us and we believe in them.

The only thing remaining to do before we begin to delve into our former lives is open our hearts and minds to the concept of a higher power. At first, this step is very difficult for some of us. But after a while, as we begin to see the miracles in our lives and the lives of others, we do believe in God. With this new force behind us, we can start to rid ourselves of the guilt that has bothered us for years. We share our past with another chemically dependent person, and it is over. We have dealt with the guilt caused by our addiction.

We are now ready to tackle staying straight. We have only come to this point in our recovery because we have broadened our understanding of trust, change and love. We have accepted the higher power concept and have begun to depend on this God to give us more love and the ability to continue to grow in open-mindedness.

Willingness to Try

Most of us can recall the first time we attempted to ride a bike. Even though we were full of apprehension, we got on and gave it our best shot. It wasn't that the fear of falling or the pain of injury had left us. Rather, the desire to learn how and to acquire the benefits that came from riding a bike became stronger. In a word, we became willing to try something new and risky that would improve our lives.

So it is in recovery. In order to take that all-important first step, we have to become willing to do something and to take responsibility for our own reclamation. It's not enough to just admit our dependency. Long before coming to the Program, many admit that they are powerless over chemicals. But it is not until they become willing to do something about it that recovery can begin. The more willing we are to accept the reality of our addiction and take the actions necessary to change, the more likely our recovery process will be successful.

There must be willingness to ask for and accept help from others. Chemically Dependent Anonymous is a "we" program. If recovery could be achieved by ourselves on our own terms, we would not need the Program. In the beginning, we are asked to trust in the idea that there is a way to do together what we could not do alone. Trust, an ability we lost because we couldn't trust ourselves much less another, is the first "risk" we take to improve our lives. It remains a risk until we start to realize its benefits. As we come to believe that CDA is working in our lives, we turn the risk into faith in others, the Program and ourselves.

It is said that if we stay the same, we will use again. Recovery is about change and growth. In order to ensure this continued growth, we need to remain willing to look honestly at ourselves and work at changing the things in us that threaten our sobriety. Getting a sponsor and working the Steps will enable us to make these changes. As long as we remain willing and teachable, we will be able to accept this new way of living and our growth and success will be limited only by our imagination.

10 Low Self-Esteem

There are very few of us who come to Chemically Dependent Anonymous feeling good about ourselves. The things that we did in pursuit of or under the influence of chemicals usually involved hurting someone else. In most cases, we hurt someone we loved or someone who loved *us*. Our broken promises, deceit and, in many cases, immoral actions left us feeling empty inside with a sense of self-loathing. We felt like failures. We had abandoned all that was good in our lives, both people and principles, in order to fill a craving for something we could not control. The need to use had become more important to us than jobs, school, family, God or our own health. The guilt and self-hatred had become so consuming that many of us lost hope entirely and tried to end it all through continued use of chemicals or by more direct means.

For those of us who have been fortunate enough to enter this program, many came in believing CDA was like a prison sentence. We felt unforgivable, unlovable and unworthy of any good in our lives. It was not until we became willing to follow the suggestions we heard in the meetings and started working the Steps that we were able to begin the process of change needed to relieve us of our guilt. We could then open our hearts to a different way.

In starting to sense that a power greater than ourselves is "doing for us what we cannot do for ourselves" and beginning to feel grateful for the chance to rebuild our lives, we begin the process of forgiveness. We wake up and realize that without our Higher Power, we would not have been saved from a life of pain, fear and guilt and that we would have had to live a life full of remorse. In this realization, we begin to get that glimmer of hope that our lives will get better. We must be able to make amends where we can and forgive ourselves. We have to be able to love and trust ourselves. If we can't, we will never be able to extend these benefits to others.

Our Higher Power loves and has forgiven us. He never stopped loving us. All we have to do is reach out and accept and believe that things will work out for the best. If the God of our understanding who is all-loving and all-powerful has forgiven us, who are we to think we are so unique in our sinfulness that we are the only ones that cannot be forgiven? Although genuinely painful, our guilt trips are nothing more than ego trips which allow us to wallow in self-pity rather than do the difficult and painful work of change.

We are all children of God. Our Higher Power wants us to be happy. We are worthy of good things. If we ask for help and let God's plan, timing and will be ours, we can let go of our old ideas. Fear of the future will leave us.

11 Questions: CDA for the Newcomer

Past experiences have shown that upon arriving at the Fellowship of CDA most newcomers are unsure about many areas of the recovery process. Certain questions seem to arise more frequently. Herein we attempt to answer these questions to the best of our ability.

It is unlikely that each and every issue and question that a newcomer might have could be fully answered or satisfied in this space. All we can say is that almost every question seems to answer itself in time. Just "Keep Coming Back!"

1) "What do these people want from me?"

We've been there and we know the pain and suffering caused by this disease. We have found a way out – a new freedom. We no longer feel the desperate "need" to use drugs. Our lives are more our own today than ever before.

In order to keep growing, we have come to believe and understand that we must give back that which we have received freely. We want nothing from you other than the chance to share with you our experience, strength and hope.

2) "What is a 'bottom'?"

Because of the amount of pain caused by our use of chemicals, we reach a place where it becomes necessary to ask for help and get honest about our addiction. This is called reaching a "bottom."

You do not have to lose your house, driver's license, family or years of your life in jails or institutions, although some or all of these things have happened to many of us. Through our own experiences and those of others, we have found that if we continue to use, these things will happen. It is up to you whether or not you become progressively better or continue the downhill slide.

3) "What is 'anonymity'?"

"Anonymity" means that what you hear or who you see at meetings is not discussed outside the meetings themselves. We respect each other's privacy. Whether or not you want someone outside these meetings to know about *your* presence here is a decision left up to you.

Anonymity is the spiritual foundation of our program. For the purpose of unity, we do not ever associate our names with CDA on the public level (i.e., newspapers, radio, film, social media, etc.).

4) "Do I have to stay 'straight' forever?"

Each one of us began by staying "straight" for just one day. We break "forever" down into "one day at a time." The choice of whether or not to use will always be there. After staying straight over several 24-hour periods, we have found that we choose not to use rather than return to the misery which brought us here.

5) "What about prescription medication?"

We realize that some conditions require the use of prescribed medication. On the other hand, a great deal of medication is abused. Our disease tries hard to get us to use again and often the use of prescribed drugs can provide the "excuse" we need to get high. Being honest with yourself and your physician about your chemical dependency is of the utmost importance.

6) "What is a 'compulsion'?"

When the only thing you can think about is the next fix, pill or drink, you are suffering from a "compulsion." Compulsion is what ruled our lives while we were using and what proved so overpowering whenever we tried to stop on our own. Willpower alone cannot overcome our compulsions. From our own experiences in CDA, we can assure you that the compulsion to use will lessen greatly over a period of time.

7) "How many meetings should I go to?"

In the beginning, we suggest that all newcomers aim at going to 90 meetings in 90 days. It's very difficult to stop using at first and most of us have found that we needed all the help we could get. Most often, the compulsion to use is especially strong during the early stage of recovery. We have found that if we can just put off using until we get to a meeting, we can find the support we need to stay clean for one more day.

8) "What is a 'slippery place'?"

If you keep coming back, there is a saying you might hear that goes: "If you hang around the barbershop long enough, eventually you'll get a haircut." This means that if you hang around people, places or things associated with the use of chemicals, you are setting yourself up for a fall.

All too often we have seen newcomers who could not say no when offered a drink or a drug in these "slippery" surroundings. We have found it wise and advisable to question our motives for coming in contact with people who are using chemicals.

9) "What is a sponsor and why do I need one?"

A sponsor is someone who is willing to share his or her own experience, strength and hope with you on a personal level. Having been clean and sober for a while himself, a sponsor will help you to understand the Program. From what we've learned so far, it seems best if men find male sponsors and women find female sponsors. In choosing a sponsor, it is important to look for someone to whom you can talk comfortably. Based on experience, we also believe that it is best to find a suitable sponsor as soon as possible.

10) "What is a 'higher power'?"

When people talk about finding a "higher power," it means finding something greater than ourselves in which to believe. Some people use the group, some the God of their religion and some use nature. Many use the word "God" to describe their Higher Power. As newcomers, many of us had a great deal of difficulty with or were turned off by this idea. We found it necessary to keep an open mind and listen to the ideas of others.

In time we came to understand that a higher power is anything we choose it to be.

11) "What is a Home Group?"

A home group is the name of a member's favorite meeting which he makes a commitment to attend every week. The member does everything in his power to make this the very best meeting in all of CDA and he usually celebrates his yearly anniversary at this meeting.

12) "What is an anniversary?"

A member's annual celebration of his sobriety is called his anniversary. On this day, he either leads the meeting or has someone he really respects lead it for him. The member also receives a birthday cake on his anniversary with candles indicating the number of years since his last drink or drug.

13) "What are 'chips'?"

"Chips" are tokens that symbolize how long a person has been free of chemicals. CDA members cherish these chips and many carry them in their pocket as a reminder that staying free of chemicals is the Number One priority.

14) "What should I read to help me learn how to grow in this program?"

In addition to this book, there is other available CDA literature: *Conscious Contact Meditation Book, Twenty Questions Pamphlet, Newcomer Pamphlet, Sponsorship Pamphlet* and the *CDA Twelve Step Pamphlet Series*. We also recommend reading and studying the Big Book of Alcoholics Anonymous.

15) "How can I contact CDA?"

The contact information for CDA is:

CDA COMMUNICATIONS, INC.
General Service Office
P.O. Box 423
Severna Park, MD 21146-0423
1-888-CDA-HOPE
www.cdaweb.org

12 A CDA Journal

Part I: A WEEK IN THE LIFE OF AN ADDICT

Sunday

    I do not want to wake up. I'm so ashamed of what happened last night, I wish I were dead. When I got home (lucky I made it), I was so drunk I do not remember getting into the apartment. I do remember trying to undress and then falling back on the bed, only to feel a violent spinning. I was completely out of control. I vomited all over the rug and table and my hair stuck to my face. I thought I was finished, got into bed and then it started again. This time, I began vomiting so hard that I started to choke.
    Thinking I would die that way, I became hysterical and crawled on my hands and knees to my neighbor's apartment. I saw light under the door, started pounding and yelling, "Help me please! I'm sick!" My neighbor was away for the weekend and there was an out-of-town friend of hers staying there. He quickly dressed (he was in pajamas) and all but carried me back to my apartment. He was very alarmed, but he stayed with me for two hours watching me cry, scream and vomit. He stayed until the attack was finished and I fell out. Oh I hope he doesn't tell H. about this. She'll never talk to me again.
    But I am alive! I do want to stay alive. I'm stuck in this life and I need to get out. I just don't know how.

Monday

Went to work on time today. That's a first for a Monday. Still feeling regrets about Saturday night. I didn't drink yesterday, just smoked a little and took some pills so I could stop feeling so guilty. I don't want to think about Saturday – I hate that a stranger saw me so weak and pathetic. And now I have to avoid H. so I won't have to see her anger or accept her pity. I'm so sick of having to avoid people. The list steadily grows longer and it's always due to something that happens when I'm high and lose control.

Work dragged on today. I'm always so bored and distracted. It's so hard to get high and enjoy it There are too many perceptive people. I'm supposed to go out tonight but I think I'll cancel. Feel too depressed to be around anyone. I don't feel like pretending that I'm okay. Think I'll just get some wine and stay in and read. But I *can't* get drunk. Tomorrow I have to take an exam in the afternoon.

Ate a little dinner. Wasn't too hungry. Stayed up until about 2 a.m. – and finished the wine.

Tuesday

Bad headache this morning. Took some speed and waited but didn't feel anything. Took some more pills around Noon (should have waited longer) and got crazy. Smoked cigarette after cigarette and cleaned my desk out fifty different ways. At lunchtime, K. approached me and asked me what was wrong. I told her I had a headache. She said, "I'm not stupid. You look awful and you're on something." We almost got into an argument but P. walked by and distracted us for the next hour.

I feel so guilty lying to K. all the time about the drugs and the drinking. She's my best friend and I don't want to lose her. No matter what happens, she has always stuck by me and loved me even at my worst. I hate hurting her with all the lies, but isn't the truth worse? Somehow, I feel acceptable when I'm with her because she's a normal human being who leads a fairly contented, regular life. As sick as I am, I've no idea what she can possibly see in me. K. is an angel; she only looks for the good in people and focuses on that.

Was so wired by 4 p.m. that I couldn't finish the exam. My mind went blank and I forgot a lot of things that I knew. I don't know how I'm going to get out of this one. I'll have to come up with a good excuse.

Went out with K. to her apartment after work. Sat around and talked and drank coffee – took some downers in the bathroom so I'd be able to sleep by the time I got home. Got home by 11 – in bed by Midnight.

Wednesday

Woke up in the middle of the night and couldn't sleep. Got up and took some pills and read for a while. Fell asleep with the light on and the book on my stomach. Got up around 7 a.m. I felt terribly depressed. Called work around 8 a.m., said I was sick and went back to sleep. Got up around one o'clock in the afternoon and felt a little better. Made some lunch and went back to bed. Pulled the plug on the phone. Don't want to talk to anyone today. Back to sleep. Got up again around 6 p.m. It gets dark outside so early now.

Got dressed and walked down to the grocery store. Saw a couple of people I know in the deli and had a cup of coffee. Went and bought some wine and walked home. The sky was so clear tonight and the stars were so bright that I felt there was some hope. Maybe things will be all right one day and I'll be able to live without this terrible shame and depression. Have therapy tomorrow after work. I dread going there lately. Rehashing my past never seems to make me feel better, never seems to improve my present life. But I'm also too afraid not to go, not to work on feeling better.

Made plans with K. and some of the other girls at work to go out Friday night. I *will not* have more than two drinks. I'm just going to get a little buzz, act right and be like *them*.

Drank a little wine and took some pills. Read and fell asleep by Midnight.

Thursday

Back to work. Caught up on a lot of my paperwork. I need to get more motivated, to start caring more about the things I do. Mother called this morning and we had an argument. She claims that I was incoherent when she called on Tuesday night, and she talked about my needing to go into a hospital again. I flew into a rage and said awful things to her to make her feel guilty and force her to take responsibility for how terrible I've become. It seems that we can never talk without arguing and blaming. Something is really wrong here! I can't stand living like this, fighting and hurting the people who love me, the people I want to love. I know by now she's given J. a call. She always has to get the family to take sides against me.

Went to the shrink after work. Talked about my fight with my mother. And for the millionth time, explored my childhood. Don't know why I go there except that I can get some scripts from that doctor. He is so smug – probably thinking about his next vacation (the one I'm helping to pay for) while I'm talking. I'm so sarcastic lately. Seems I don't trust anyone.

Came home and got very high. I just want to sleep and forget all of this…

Friday

Woke up in a pretty good mood. I'm so glad it's the weekend and I can sleep late tomorrow. Really looking forward to going out tonight with the girls. Must be very careful not to drink too much and lose control.

Went shopping after work. Too late to cook dinner when I got home. I'll eat something out later. Have to hurry.

Saturday

Out of control again last night. It was horrible. I never intended to get like that. I only had about four drinks. But not eating all day and taking all of those pills made me so crazy.

All I can clearly recall is meeting K. and R. downtown around 9 p.m. Don't know why but I began to feel very anxious about being around people. On the way there, took some pills to relax. Felt reassured by having my own car so I could leave if I got too uncomfortable.

Vaguely remember making the rounds of the bars with K. and R. I also remember feeling irritated that they could drink one or two drinks, get giggly and have fun. I just sat there wondering how long it had been since my last drink so I could order another without looking too greedy. I wished the girls would disappear so I could drink as much as I wanted. I stayed until I couldn't stay a minute more. K. told me that I was in no shape to drive. That pissed me off, but what really angered me was that wounded look in her eyes – the look that let me know I had screwed up again. At that moment, I hated myself and hated her for arousing those feelings in me so I left. I don't remember driving home or getting home, but I must have fallen on the steps because my back is bruised today.

I don't know what it is about me but I just can't enjoy being around people until I'm drunk or high. I'm so afraid to be *me* around them, whoever "me" is. There's no denying how sick I am and have been all these years. I've always believed that things would somehow get better one day. But nothing's going to change until *I* get better and I don't know how. I really don't know how.

Part II: IN RECOVERY

Sunday

Woke up around 8 a.m. Got to hurry. I'm leaving at nine o'clock for a meeting at Reality. I wish I could rest more today since it's Sunday but I know that once I'm there, I'll be glad I went. Having institution commitments is a Godsend especially when I've been feeling a little down. It's so easy sometimes to forget how hard it was in the beginning and how little hope I had of any recovery then.

Meeting was great. S. always leads a good meeting at Reality. She explains the basics so well. She had everyone's attention. People really got honest in the meeting and shared a lot of the ugliness and pain they had gone through before treatment. One man there spoke of his guilt about the way he's stolen from his mother and taken advantage of her. When I shared, I related the remorse I felt about my mom in my early recovery. And I saw a little of the pain leave his eyes. It's so critical for me to remember the person I was and that using could change me back into that person all over again.

Came home after the meeting and showered. Husband is out watching a football game with some friends. Someone I sponsor is coming over for a visit soon. Will try to exercise before she comes. Uh oh! J. is here now with her baby. I'll have to finish riding my bike later. Sometimes it's so overwhelming. Every minute of the day is accounted for. If you don't fit something in at exactly the right time, it doesn't get done. Being compulsive and rigid as I still am, I have a hard time shifting my schedule and accepting any changes in my routine.

    J. and I talked for a long time and we realized we're experiencing H.A.L.T. (Hungry, Angry, Lonely or Tired). We were absolutely famished so we had sandwiches and fresh strawberries with cream. How wonderful just to share a simple meal and sit and talk with someone you care about! There has been so much growth in J. physically, emotionally and spiritually. There have been times when I felt drained by her constant needs. But I have learned that as a sponsor, I can be honest and ask for some space when that happens. Our relationship has been getting better and J. is becoming a person I'm really proud of.

    This is what the Program is about – helping each other. My own personal growth can only go so far because of the time taken up by my work and other activities. But the real growth comes from my relationships. Having such an enjoyable time with J. has really made the day for me.

    J. left and I finished riding my bike. It's almost time for the meeting. There's an anniversary tonight.

    The meeting was very emotional and touching. Came home around 8:30. Will cook dinner for tomorrow night and refrigerate it. Then it's a bubble bath, some reading and to bed. Tomorrow looks like a full, busy day and I want to be well rested.

Monday

    Restless night. I was up frequently because of troubling dreams. This always seems to happen when I harbor a resentment. It is the last thought on my mind when I retire at night and it enters my mind as soon as I wake up. Part of the problem is my lack of forgiveness towards people in my life. In the Program, they tell me that If I pray for the willingness to pardon others, God will provide it. Sometimes, I wonder if I'm praying the right way because I still cannot arouse that sense of forgiveness within me. But I have to continue to believe that God will intervene with His assistance because I am not able to do it alone. Just as I couldn't stop the drugs and alcohol without His help, I am unable to change my character without it.

Up and dressed and out to a beautiful hotel where a work conference is being held. How easy it is today to greet people, look them in the eye and make conversation. I couldn't do that before without drugs. Even then, drugs wouldn't have controlled my enormous anxiety. I am so grateful that most of the fear and shame is gone and I no longer feel the need to hide.

Took a break for lunch. Found a book that I'd been looking for. The conference has been slow today – too much time to *think*!! Spent the afternoon writing an inventory to explore my resentments. Seems that there's thirty-some years' worth of anger stored up that sometimes gets dumped on the people around me. Many of the resentments result from repressed emotions that are reawakened in me – old wounds from the past.

Came home and went to work out. Warmed up dinner quickly. Got to the meeting a few minutes late which is very unlike me. I'm usually an early bird.

Meeting was good. A lot of young people were there tonight. I really enjoy listening to them share. And I can relate so well to the confusion they feel about everything at that age. I sometimes wonder what my life would have been like if I'd gotten straight at 17 or 18 years of age. But I also believe that I "came to" on the exact day and moment that I was ready to surrender. Getting late now. Time for sleep.

Tuesday

Up around 7 a.m. Slept straight through the night; no dreams that I can recall. Was asked last night to speak at an upcoming function. That created instant anxiety. I haven't confirmed yet that I'll do it. I wanted to pray about it tonight. At first, I wanted to decline but then the "show-off" in me said, "Don't be so hasty. Hold off on saying no." Even though the thought of speaking before such a crowd is frightening, I know that I have to trust in God and confront my fears.

Had the conference again but had company at it today. Talked for a long time with someone I work with who is also in the Program. It was like having our own little meeting, using the language we both understand so well. Through our sharing, we discovered that although our backgrounds are so very different, we have many of the same personality traits, fears and insecurities.

After work, met B. and we went to an eating meeting in Annapolis to try to sell some tickets to a CDA social function. Got lost on the way and we were so famished that we ate half of the food we had brought with us before we got there. We really laughed it up in the car, sharing some old memories of when we would get the "munchies" and what we liked to eat then. After arriving at the meeting, B. was asked to lead a meeting at a nearby rehab center so we left and went there. The rehab was packed with people from the outside. Since I had volunteered B. for the meeting, I thought I might catch some flak from her but she handled the crowd like a real pro and did a super job.

B. and the other women I sponsor are so very important to me. We have become so close this year and have shared a lot of our pain and joy together. I feel a tremendous love and protectiveness toward B. and I am so glad that God placed us in each other's lives. I know that without the people I sponsor I would be thinking about myself nonstop. How boring!!

We got home around 10:45 p.m. I'm so tired that I'm starting to slur my words. Read (the last addiction I have left) until around Midnight, then said a few quick prayers of thanks. Can't wait to close my eyes and drift off into the stillness of the night.

Wednesday

Up around 7 a.m. – feel weak and sick. Throat is sore. This might be the cold I've been fending off for the past two weeks. Made some hot tea with fresh mint and doubled up on my Vitamin C.

Got to work a little late; I just don't feel motivated today. When I get sick, I begin to obsess about how it's going to affect my plans for that day or, if I really want to project into the future, for the entire week. Back to "one day at a time!"

Ate some lunch. Tried to set up some appointments. Still no motivation. I feel too weak. I know from experience that my drive will return. I can even ask God to supply some when I'm empty because that has also worked in the past. "This too shall pass" applies in so many ways during the course of a day. When I first came into the Program, I used to think that a negative attitude would be there forever and that I had no way out of my depression or my moods. I know better now.

Left work early. Came home and canceled a visit with a new girl I have just started to sponsor. Felt guilty about doing it but I have to work the Program the way I would suggest it to someone else. And that means taking care of yourself.

Stayed in and did some paperwork. Read a little, said my prayers and went to bed early.

Thursday

Woke up early. Still feeling ill. Can't decide whether to go to work. The great debate in my head begins:

Voice #1: "Stay home. You're sick. You need a break. You deserve it."
Voice #2: "Faker! You're not that sick. See how you feel after you're up."

Got up, had a cup of hot tea and did feel a little stronger. Compromised with the two voices and decided to go into work but to leave early if I still felt sick after I got there.
Arrived at work and was extremely busy for the next seven hours. Didn't have time to think about "me." Left and went to meet a friend for dinner. Planned on going directly home after that but stopped off at a store and bought some clothes for work. Home by 9 p.m. Read, said prayers and went to bed.

Friday

Up early with my husband. He's going on some out-of-town appointments today. Reset the clock for my wake-up call. When it went off, couldn't get up right away. I skipped some of my morning routine so I could sleep in a little and take care of myself.
Got up later and went to first appointment of the day. Only 10 a.m. and I'm thinking about catching a noon meeting. But I still feel weak and there's a lot of paperwork to do here and calls to make. Sometimes I've

gone to meetings at Noon and let my work slide but not too frequently lately.

Decided against noon meeting since I'm going this evening. Had some lunch and stayed in the office most of the day. Still catching up on work piled up while I was on vacation. Got to take this "one project at a time" so I don't become so overwhelmed that I lose control.

Glad it's Friday. Looking forward to the weekend, primarily just to get some extra sleep. Plans for Sunday with S. to go to a meeting and a fair in town. Saturday, maybe B. and I can just be alone and see a movie in a theater. No telephone and no distractions.

Talked on the phone a lot. So many emotional crises going on. I'm glad I am trusted enough that people feel they can call and share with me. It means so much to me that I can be useful today and perhaps lighten someone's load. I am also glad I've been given the courage to say "I love you" to friends because they need it. When I'm able to do that, I find I lose my own fear of rejection.

Worked out and then home by 5 p.m. Ate a sandwich. J. is picking me up for the seven o'clock meeting. She'll be here by six. Took out five minutes just to sit and relax. What did I ever do with my time before I came into the Program? My life was never full the way it is now. It was just months and years of playing out life as if it were a death sentence.

Saturday

Up at 7 a.m. Tried to sleep longer but was unable to. It seems that once I'm up, my mind begins churning out an agenda of "things to worry about" and I can't fall back to sleep. So I get up and start my day early. What a change from the old days of staying up all night and repeatedly crashing during the day. I'm still not comfortable sleeping late in the day because it reminds me of my using days.

Got up, showered and ate breakfast. Read my meditation books. One idea made a deep impression on me. It stressed how important it is to remember that God makes greater use of the channels that are the most willing and receptive. I have to remember how easy it is to become blocked as a channel if I become stressed out and out of control.

After meditation, exercised and did some chores. Finished by Noon and took some time to relax. Spent the entire afternoon and evening with B. (dinner out and a movie at home). What a blessing and not one phone call during the evening. Glad to have this block of time to ourselves to strengthen our relationship.

To bed early. Lots to do again tomorrow!

13 Fun in Recovery

By now, you have come to the realization that there is much that must be given up in order to be a member of Chemically Dependent Anonymous. However, you will soon see by reading many of the members' stories that there is much more to gain than there is to lose from joining the Fellowship. Yet when it comes to thinking about what life might be like in sobriety, you may be wondering if there is a life after addiction. CDA offers a wide range of activities for all its members. We'll show you some typical examples of life's re-creation in recovery. Herewith, a CDA play-by-play in recovery:

SOFTBALL
   Big Al hits one over the fence for a home run for the CDA Fun Bunch Twelve-Step Team. Coach Mike S. jumps for joy when Tim makes a double play look easy. John throws another pitch. Missy and Kim are both loved by their teammates for getting a hit and making a catch. Metro makes an unbelievable catch once again. Then Rick and Ken make still another catch. As Perry stretches on first base to make another out, Jim and Greg make a pop fly look easy. Amy catches a pop-up ball. As Heidi, Mike B., Marlene and Jeni cheer, the CDA Fun Bunch wins the 1987 Softball Championship.

HORSEBACK RIDING
   Cowboy J.T. can't get his horses to move but finally Mike G. and Arundel get him to follow their horses. The

horses are all glad to see the stables after one hour of hard riding by the crew of CDA.

VOLLEYBALL

Willie sends the ball Ron R.'s way for the slam. Brent taps it over the net for a point. Perry spikes another one. The CDA volleyball team wins it all.

WHITE-WATER RAFTING

Mark R. is swept into the rushing waters. Ron R. falls into the rapids once again. Willie is carried for a long ride. Gary has a close call but keeps on going. The river is fast and thrilling. That night, Tommy has the big fire going for the bonfire meeting. Frank Y. talks about love in the Fellowship. Kevin, Gwinn and Big Rob share their experiences. Brian and Dave put another log on the fire. Lynn smiles and shares about the love she gets in the Program. Roy L. needs help getting his tent set up.

GRATITUDE BREAKFAST

Brent speaks from the heart while Candy, Heidi, Maureen and Marie listen and finish their coffee. Bobbi and Sterling smile and laugh as the speakers share their experience, strength and hope with all of us.

SPIRITUAL RETREAT

The CDA Men's Retreat is very special to us. It's a time to renew our relationship with our Higher Power, to share our God with others and to grow closer to our fellow man. It's also a time for men like Allen to be used by God to serve Him and his brothers. Leaving the retreat is always hard but we know we can come back to Manresa next year. It's good to see the young ones like Paul and Brian praying in the chapel. Kevin and Sparks share their true feelings of joy. As always, the retreat master is a joy to hear.

ANNUAL PICNIC

The CDA picnic is always so much fun. Sterling shares from his heart and speaks in a low-pitched, soft voice as hungry people eat hamburgers. The food is wonderful and there is plenty of it. We have games to play. Ron and Patti throw the water-filled balloons but Missy and Rick are the winners. It's always great to get the volleyball games going. There's fellowship, caring and sharing (the CDA way) at our picnics. Denny enjoys the ride home on his motorcycle after snapping tons of photos of the event. Kevin also enjoys riding his "cycle" on this hot summer day.

NEW YEAR'S EVE DANCE

It's 11:30 p.m., the clock is ticking and the music's playing. Heidi, Bucky and Bev are getting down on the dance floor. Across the room, Lori and Marie kick up their heels. The clock strikes Midnight. The kisses and hugs begin as we say goodbye to the old and welcome in the new year.

14 Epilogue: The Future

Without the slightest doubt, we know that God's will is for our recovery from the disease of addiction. This knowledge is not only based on our solid faith but also on the many chemically dependent people who have come before us and stayed clean. They have done it by finally finding CDA, attending our meetings and ultimately discovering a higher power to rely on in all situations during the recovery process.

Our future as a twelve-step program remains uncertain only in that it is based on God's will for us and not our will. We can set no restrictions or limitations on His decisions. We can only hope and pray that our Higher Power will continue to allow us to be used as instruments to help people still suffering from the disease of alcohol and drug addiction. We believe that this is our mission as individuals and as a recovery fellowship. And we know that our ultimate dream can become a reality with His help.

After ten years of dealing with our personal challenges and those of other chemically dependent people, there is much we still do not know about this disease. But there is much we have learned as a result of our experiences. We will keep coming back. We will keep it simple. We will be ready to help the newcomer. And hopefully, we will continue to grow as chemical-free adults and as a fellowship.

We submit ourselves to the principles of our program and to our Higher Power saying: "Here we are. Show us your will and give us the power to carry it out."

PART II
PERSONAL HISTORIES

To the Reader

These personal histories were not meant to be read all at one sitting. Look through them (some are quite short) and find one that says something to you. Read others at your leisure. All come from the heart in the hopes of reaching out to help you. Each story is being shared by a recovering chemically dependent person with much pain but much more promise. If you are looking for a new, drug-and-alcohol-free way of life, these stories are presented as examples of how that goal can be achieved.

Many of these stories repeat major ideas from the Program of Chemically Dependent Anonymous. They are offered in the words of those whose circumstances may differ but whose major life experiences are often very similar. You will recognize one or more of them. They are you. They are all of us.

15 I Finally Found My Niche

After being brought up in an environment where alcohol use was prevalent and street drugs were used behind closed doors, I could not wait until I was old enough to partake of them. I related chemicals to having a good time. Any time my parents or older sister had a party, booze and other drugs were the main ingredients. I started experimenting with alcohol at a very young age and found that I didn't really like the taste. Every time I tried alcohol, I got drunk, and I would inevitably get sick.

Marijuana, among other drugs, was very popular in my neighborhood, and it was used by just about all the people I hung around with. The first time I smoked pot, I knew I had found my drug of choice. I liked the taste, I loved the feeling, and there was no sickness afterwards. The friends I was running with were the kind that my mother told me not to hang around; but what mom didn't realize was that I had become one of those people. I found much less pressure, a lot more fun, and I felt very accepted in this group of people. I didn't need to be intelligent; I didn't need to be good-looking; I didn't need to do anything or be anything special. All I needed was the honest desire to party hearty. I had found my niche. . .

It wasn't too long before it became a real problem to use when I wanted and how I wanted. By now, I would use anything that changed my mood and the way I felt about myself. My preference was amphetamines. I think that, because I also smoked so much pot, I always felt ragged out. But I found I could drink enormous amounts of alcohol and not pass out or get sick. The problem came with not taking care of responsibilities I had, such as showing up for school—all day, every class. I flunked out of the ninth grade. It became a real job to remember what I told which people. The alibis and excuses were running out. I was constantly in my parents' wallets and my younger brother's piggy bank.

I didn't realize that, after just a short time, I was using to live and living to use. Getting high was all I wanted to do. I might have some extracurricular activity, but I would not think of starting it without a buzz. As a young child, I had watched my family party it up; now they had all hit their bottoms. My parents were ready for divorce. My older sister was in one jackpot after another. I wasn't like them. I didn't have a girl to divorce. I could never get anything together to lose, or have anything in good enough shape to screw up. My situation was pretty hopeless, as well, but I didn't notice, because all the people I ran with were the same, or worse, than me.

But, one by one, my family started attending Alcoholics Anonymous meetings. I was glad for them and thought that my parents were at the age when they should think about doing something about their problems. I was shocked when I found out that my sister was going to A.A., however. I couldn't understand why. I knew about her jackpots, but I had figured she would straighten that out, but not with A.A. I didn't know much about A.A., but I knew that if you went there, you couldn't drink anymore. My sister was only twenty-four years old.

It was not long before I was given this choice: "Either go to A.A., or get out and live on your own." My parents knew that I would never realize I had a problem as long as they continued to let me live at home and behave the way I was doing. They would no longer enable me to live life on my own terms. I didn't know where I was going to live or how I was going to support myself. I was only seventeen. I was still going to high school. I know, today, that my parents saved my life.

I went to A.A. begrudgingly. It was like jail for a whole hour. I felt humiliated. I realized that I seemed to be the only teen-ager around the meetings. I couldn't relate to the horror stories. After all, I had not yet wrecked cars, gone to jail, lost my wife, or ended up in an institution.

I heard about a new program that had just started, called Chemically Dependent Anonymous, so I went there. At that first meeting, I realized I was in the right place, with people just like me. The people in that room were talking about *me*. The majority of them were younger than the A.A. group and were sharing the pain that they had experienced. I remember someone sharing that he had felt like such a loser and had no hope that the future would be any better. But after coming into CDA, all his problems had become challenges. He also said that, because he was not using any drugs and/or alcohol, he was starting to feel like a winner. Someone said, "Good things happen to addicts who don't use."

Someone else grabbed me, after the meeting, and we talked. He told me that all those things that had happened to the others didn't necessarily have to happen to me. But if I stayed chemically dependent, they would. And if I continued to use, I would die. I had a friend who had died from an overdose, and I had seen other friends locked up in jail. I knew that this guy was telling me the truth, and he seemed to care. After all, he had no reason to lie. I had found my niche.

I kept going back to CDA and I didn't get high—one day at a time. One second at a time. I have to say, after being clean and sober for over five years, that I've never experienced a bigger challenge than getting straight. I thought that there would be no life after sobriety, but much to my surprise, I have just started living. I have more material things than I thought could be possible in just five years. But I've found that those things don't, and can't, make me happy for long. My most prized possessions are the relationships I've developed since coming to the Fellowship and working with the Program of Chemically Dependent Anonymous.

The first relationships I had were with other people in CDA who cared for me when I wasn't able to care for myself. The second was the relationship with God, as I understand Him that people in the Program told me I must have if I wanted to ensure my sobriety. Through the people who cared for me, and the God Who, I know, loves me, I have been able to get to know myself. I'm not the terrible, mean, uncaring individual I had feared I was. I found that I actually have the ability to care for another person. I do not try to harm others, mentally or physically. I know, now, that I was never a really bad person, but my behavior as a user was always in contradiction to my true self.

I do not behave like that, anymore. I have a love for life. I look forward to getting up in the morning. I love my job; I don't believe there is a better one in the world. I help people for a living. I enjoy watching, listening, and interacting with people. Today, I am able to go to the new guy in CDA and talk with him. I let him know I care, share with him my story, and tell him what I did, and still do today, to stay clean and sober. And that is:

1. Don't drink or drug (even if my ass falls off).
2. Go to meetings (my friends will screw it back on).
3. Pray.
4. Help another person.

It's very simple—so simple that I almost didn't make it. But I had, and still have, today, a desire for a new way of life.

I've found my niche in CDA.

16 Thy Will Be Done

I first started to use when I was fifteen. I grew up in a household affected by alcoholism (my father is an active alcoholic). So I convinced my parents to send me away to a boarding school for my sophomore year in high school. I was desperate to escape an emotionally chaotic environment. My first set of friends at school consisted of the campus potheads and acid freaks. I had never made many friends as a kid, and I wanted to fit in, to win the acceptance and approval of my new friends. So I did what they did—smoked a lot of dope, dropped a lot of acid. I was tripping every weekend.

The following summer, my father got me a job with his company. Since the job was out-of-town, I lived at the home of one of my classmates. During that time, my whole life revolved around getting high, doing as many drugs as possible, and running around. I'd go in to work high, if I went at all. I was ashamed of myself and how I was living, but I didn't know how to change it. My life was already unmanageable due to drugs.

At the beginning of my last semester at school, I was expelled for smoking dope in my dorm room. I was filled with remorse and guilt and self-pity over this. My parents were pretty easy on me—they knew I was remorseful—but this incident drove a wedge deeper between us. Fortunately, I had already been accepted at college, and I was able to start immediately. I was afraid the school wouldn't take me, but they didn't care about my expulsion.

Drugs weren't prevalent at college. Drinking was more the thing there. So I began to drink. In any case, I knew that I couldn't handle the drugs anymore. They were more powerful than I was. But I thought I could handle drinking. I remember my first hangovers—so mild, compared to the crippling headaches and nausea I would experience later.

After two-and-a-half years, I dropped out of college. I had started working as a waiter in restaurants. It was the perfect life for an alcoholic. So easy: work in the evening, party until three or four in the morning, then sleep it off the next day, and do it all over again! Everyone drank on the job. When I first started coming to meetings, I heard people say that they had become unemployable, and I didn't think those things applied to me. Yet I was always drinking within a couple of hours of waking up. It was okay because it was after noon, I thought. I was certainly incapable of working a responsible nine-to-five job, however. I could never have functioned on that kind of schedule.

I didn't have much self-esteem to begin with, but alcohol robbed me of the little I did have. I was incapable of setting realistic goals and then working a plan to achieve them. All I had were grandiose fantasies, and I was too physically and mentally debilitated by my using to put together a workable plan of action and stick to it. I knew I had some brains and abilities, but I couldn't seem to get out of the rut I was in. I became more and more frustrated by the lack of direction in my life, by my inability to get my life on track. This state of mind led to more self-pity and lower and lower self-opinion. It was a vicious circle.

But it was my blackouts, and a seemingly unstoppable month-long drinking spree, that finally got to me. Almost every night, I drove home from some bar in a blackout. I had become belligerent and vicious when I was drunk, particularly when I blacked out. Finally, one night, I came out of a blackout on the floor of my apartment, and someone I didn't know was kicking me in the face. If my neighbors hadn't intervened, he might have killed me. But I couldn't even remember how it had all come about. The next day, I went to my first meeting.

I was scared when I first came in: scared of going back out, scared of not being able to stay sober and clean, scared of everything. I didn't think I'd be able to make the Program work for me. People who had stayed clean for a year were like gods to me; they were a different order of being from me. I just clung to meetings and to people I met, and I kept coming back. And today, as I write this, I've been clean and sober for over three years.

I've been through several different stages in my recovery. At first, I just operated out of raw fear. I lived from meeting to meeting. I could barely comprehend the Steps or anything else people told me.

Eventually, though, that same fear, along with a desire to have what others in the Program had, compelled me to start trying to work a "program" of my own. I took a written and oral First Step, which helped in clearing away some of the guilt and remorse associated with my using days. I tried to tackle the Second and Third Steps. As I look back, my notions of these Steps, of a higher power and how it could work in my life, were very limited. I wanted to take the Steps because other recovering alcoholics and addicts told me I had to change, in order to stay sober. But I wasn't really willing to surrender to a God. I just didn't trust enough, yet.

In any case, I still wanted to grapple with the emotional garbage of my life, so I started a Fourth Step shortly after my first anniversary. I was as honest as I could be (which was not very), and I was sincere in my effort. I told it all to my sponsor, in my Fifth Step, and he helped me to dig a little deeper, to be more searching and less fearful. The Sixth and Seventh Steps were truly "The Lost Steps" for me, because I hadn't laid the groundwork, in the Second and Third Steps, for the close relationship with my Higher Power that these Steps demand. Finally, I wrote out my Eighth Step list and, over time, have tried to carry out the Ninth Step.

Then I basically stopped practicing the Steps in my life. I went to meetings, I associated very closely with some friends in the Program, and I continued to try to develop my understanding of how the Program worked. I don't mean to discredit my earlier efforts in recovery; I was sincere and earnest in my desire to grow. But mine was a selfish program in the worst sense—I wanted what the Program could offer to *me*. I was only concerned with how it could get me the things I wanted. My own will was still the final arbiter of what I would do in recovery.

What was missing in *my* program was the spiritual: the active presence of a Power greater than me. I hadn't let my God into my life. I guess I just wasn't willing to let go of my own will yet. But I finally became uncomfortable and isolated enough to hit a kind of emotional bottom that led me to reach out—to others in the Program and to my God. That was a gift, His allowing me to reach a point where I was able to see and admit that my way didn't work. Through trying, each day, to surrender my will and my life to His care and by taking the daily action that is part of the letting go of my self-will; my life has been turned around completely in the past few months. The missing element has fallen into place. I've found a real joy in living and in sharing with others. It all goes to show, "Don't 'pick up' before the miracle happens."

17 Out of the Crack House

 This is Vince R. My story is that of an addict and an alcoholic who always felt the need to be accepted. I took my first drink, a beer, when I was about seventeen years old. I was a senior in high school. When I took my first sip of beer, it didn't do anything to me. I don't even remember getting a buzz. But I do know that I began to feel a part of the group. During my final year in high school, I did what it took to graduate. My drinking was not excessive or alcoholic. I drank on rare occasions; if someone was passing around a six-pack and everybody was drinking, I would take a beer and drink it, too.
 But my real, heavier use of alcohol began when I was in college. I went to a black college down South. It was my very first time away from home. I don't remember really wanting to attend this school. I kind of wanted to stay home, close to my family. But my father and his brother had attended this college. And when I was accepted, my father patted me on the back, shook my hand, and said, "Congratulations!" I guess, once again to feel a part of something, I decided to go to that school.
 My freshman year seemed normal. My drinking was confined pretty much to weekends. And it felt good. For the first time in my life, I felt that I belonged. But within a short time, I began associating with people who drank much more than I did. And quickly, without really knowing it, drinking alcohol became a part of my social life. It got to the point where I didn't want to go to a party or a dance, or even to be with a bunch of the guys in a room, just

sitting around shooting the breeze, without having something to drink.

So, my first year in college is when I consider that I started drinking alcoholically, although I wasn't drinking even as much as a pint a day. My drinking was born out of the continuing need to belong. I drank to suppress feelings of loneliness, and inadequacy, and all the problems that come with drinking. Needless to say, my grades, at the end of that year, were a little over a C average. But on the surface, things still seemed to be normal. My drinking did not start affecting me until the second year I was in school.

That second year, I began to associate with a different crowd of people, and I had my first experience with marijuana. It occurred when (again out of the need to belong) I joined a fraternity. I can recall how our fraternity used to march across campus in a line, singing songs. One day, someone at the front of the line had a joint. Since I was over six feet tall, and we'd lined up by height, I was near the back. I remember watching that joint being passed from the person at the front, all the way down that line. When it got to me, I assumed a kind of "Oh, heck, why not?" attitude and took a hit. Again, as with my first drink, I didn't feel any immediate sensation of getting high. It seemed like such a natural thing to do. Nobody made a big deal out of it. It was just part of being in the group.

After that, my drug and alcohol use escalated to the point where, by my third year in college, my grades were quite poor. In fact, I had quit attending classes and had dropped out of school. By this time, I was using THC, mescaline, all kinds of uppers and amphetamines, such as Black Beauties. On top of all that, I was drinking alcohol. At that stage, I really felt lost. I knew that something in my life was not right, but I didn't know what it was. It did not occur to me that using drugs and alcohol had anything to do with it. I was never much of a drinker, but when I found pills, and when I found herb, that was my kind of high. I considered people who got drunk a lot real sloppy, so I would drink just enough to get a little buzz, to mellow off the drugs. The pills and the herb were my drugs of choice.

When I was about twenty-four years old, I married a woman I had met when I was in my second year of college. She had gone to the sister school across from ours. She was the type of person I had always wished I could be, and she still is. She is, and was, very independent, very intelligent, and popular. She knew where she wanted to go, and I knew she was someone I wanted to be around. We fell in love, we got married, and we had three children. By the time our first daughter, who is now nine years old, was born, I had been introduced to cocaine. I was still drinking heavily and using marijuana.

But when that baby girl came into my life, I told myself that I wanted to do things differently. I wanted to change. I wanted to make something of my life for her. Like a lot of other addicts and alcoholics, I had big dreams. I spent a lot of time in bars, thinking about big, big deals that I was going to make. And I had an idea: I wanted to own my own business. So we relocated back down South, leaving my home town, with our young daughter.

My wife's grandfather had owned a paint store for over twenty-five years, and nobody else in the family was interested in it. He was over eighty years old and was ready to give it up. Somehow, I got it in my mind that I could run this little mom-and-pop operation, despite the fact that, during this period of time, I was drinking daily, buying marijuana whenever I could get the money, and using cocaine. I was able to obtain a loan from a bank by persuading my wife's grandfather to co-sign for the loan. For $25,000, I bought the old man and his partner out, and I became a self-employed person. I thought that purchasing my own business was the greatest thing that could happen to me.

But something funny happened. Soon after I bought that store, I realized that I had to go in and open the doors, sell that product, and actually work. Looking back on it now, I realize that I didn't want that. I did it just for the thrill of doing it. When it came time for doing the footwork, the hard work of running the business, I wasn't prepared, at all. In fact, within two years, because of my use of drugs and alcohol, I took a business that had supported a family for more than a quarter of a century and ran it into the ground, robbed it blind. During these two years, I was introduced to other drugs, and I think I used more cocaine than I had during the whole previous time I had been doing drugs. And yet, I still didn't know what was wrong.

Something else happened, though, one day during the latter stages of my owning that business, when it had become clear to me that I didn't want to be there anymore, but that I didn't know what I did want to do. A cousin of mine came into the store. I think there had been one occasion, three or four years earlier, when he and I had gotten high together. He had been to a rehab and had just gotten out. He asked me, "Man, are you still using that cocaine?" I said, "Yeah, every once in a while." And he told me, and I'll never forget this, "You know, that stuff ain't no good for you. I went to rehab, and I kicked it, and I'm trying to get my life together." I looked at him, thinking, "Huh, what does this guy know? He's just somebody who couldn't handle it."

That's what I thought of people who were trying to get help, who were leaving drugs and alcohol. I thought they were weak people. This was a problem—if it was a problem—that I could handle, you see. I didn't feel that I had any problem, though all around me, my life was coming apart: my marriage was becoming strained, my business was folding. But I couldn't see it.

I remember the first time that I knew, or at least I had an inkling, that I had a problem with drugs. I had sold some paint, about $300 or $400 worth of it, to a friend. I took that money and went out and spent every penny of it on drugs, when I should have put it in the cash drawer at the business, to pay the supplier for the paint. I bought all that cocaine and I looked at it and wondered why. I needed that money. How was I going to pay the supplier? I kind of brushed it off. But I think that was when I really began to have a feeling that this drug, cocaine, might be affecting my judgment, to some degree.

Then my business collapsed, and my marriage fell into real turmoil as my wife realized that something was very wrong. When we first met, she had dabbled in drugs, but she did not get into them to the extent that I did, and she was able to stop. Now she came to me and said, "Vince, I've had enough. I want you to do something about this." I had lost the business, and I was unemployed. I had lost my self-respect. I was bankrupt, spiritually and emotionally. But I was in deep denial.

My wife talked to other people about this problem of drug addiction, and what her husband was going through, and what was happening to her marriage, and then she told me, "Unless you get help, you've got to leave." I was more afraid of losing her, I think, than of anything else, because she was my only hold on the world. I had lost everything else. And so, with a great deal of anger and a lot of pain, I enrolled in a treatment program.

This treatment program was at a local hospital. It had been determined that I could go there as an outpatient, that I wasn't so bad that I needed to be hospitalized. I went in with a bad attitude. I really didn't want to quit drinking or using drugs. However, when I did go, I began to hear words like "denial," and people talked about the Twelve Steps, Alcoholics Anonymous, Cocaine Anonymous, and the other twelve-step programs, and I began to want what they were talking about. But there was a part of me, deep, deep down, that still wanted to use. And I did use. We didn't have sessions on the weekends, but we were supposed to go to A.A. meetings, or other Twelve-Step meetings somewhere. I remember using on the weekends, and coming right back to treatment during the week.

Occasionally, we would get so-called "surprise" urinalysis tests. I recall *wanting* to get caught because I did want help. I just didn't know how to get it. One particular time, they did a urinalysis, and a couple of days later, they came back and said, "Somebody in the group has been using." And it was another guy. I thought they were going to finger me. But they didn't and I was pissed. I said to myself, "Why couldn't I get caught?"

A couple of weeks after I went into treatment, my counselor committed suicide. I was just becoming very close to her. I came in one day and learned about her death, and that was another excuse to use. But I made it through the treatment program and went into after-care, even though I used throughout the whole process. I know, now, that I went into treatment for the wrong reason.

When I came out of treatment, I discovered a new drug, a drug that really was what I was born to use. And that was crack. Back when I started doing crack, it was fairly new. It had just kind of hit the scene, and it was cheap. The high was intense. Crack took me places where I had never dreamed I would go. It was different from snorting cocaine powder. Crack was so addictive.

The first time I took a hit of crack, it was in what is called a crack house. That's just a place where addicts get together and use. They cook the crack up, they share pipes, and they sit there for hours and hours, until there's no more left. When I first went there, I went with a so-called friend. I thought I would only try crack a couple of times. I went back, the second time, on my own. I had just received my pay from a job that I'd had for a very short period of time. I went over one evening after work, about four or five o'clock and I did not leave until I had spent every penny I had with me. After that, I was gone. From that point on, crack ruled my life.

Since then, I've been in many crack houses. I was known as "Red" there. I don't know why, maybe because I'm a light-skinned black person; or maybe because I looked kind of red, especially if you were looking at me through rose-colored eyes. In the crack houses, I was known as a person who, if he had money, would spend it all. And if he had none, he would stand around and beg. I begged, many a night, at the crack house.

I've seen people pull guns out at the crack houses. On several occasions, I've seen the police raid other units. The crack houses were not usually detached houses. There were more often apartments. We would see the police out there, and we would refuse to move. I actually had the feeling that if the police came right in where I was, I wouldn't move. They could do anything they wanted to with me. I did not want to take the risk of getting up and leaving that crack house, leaving whatever chance there was for me to get high. It's the worst existence any person could have, being in a crack house.

I smoked crack for about a year. It took only that long for crack to totally destroy whatever was left of my life. My last drug use took place three years ago. By this time, my wife had become pregnant again, and we had just had our second daughter a couple of days earlier. I had no job. I had been stealing money from anywhere I could get it. I was stealing money from my older daughter's purse, from my wife's purse. I was getting money by returning items to stores. I was writing bogus checks. I would do anything to get my hands on crack.

I was going to take my wife home from the hospital the following day, and I had no money. Before I left the hospital that afternoon, my wife gave me a personal check, made out for $50, asking me to cash it so I would have some money to come get her the next day and also pick up a few things we needed. I was due back, later that evening, for a steak dinner the hospital provided for new parents. My wife's father and sister had arrived in town, she had a brother already living there, and they were all with her for the blessed event. I left about four o'clock with that check.

To show you how insidious the disease is, I cashed that check and went straight to the crack house. There had been no question, even as I watched my wife make out that check and hand it to me, what I was going to do. When I left the hospital, I knew right where I was going. I ran through the parking lot to get to my car.

My last drunk was terrible. I took that money and within thirty to forty minutes, it was gone. Fifty dollars' worth of crack was nothing, to me. I proceeded to go back to our home and unplug the stereo and take it to the crack house. At the crack house, you could do anything: You could pawn. You could have sex. You could get high. Sometimes, you could even find a place to sleep, but not many people slept there. I got $20 or $25 for my stereo at the crack house and smoked that up. I went back home, again, and got our only television set and brought it back and pawned that. I had paid almost $600 for that set, a few years before. I got $25 for it and smoked that crack up, too. I was off and running. By midnight, I had nothing left to pawn. And, of course, I was too ashamed to go back to the hospital.

When I arrived back home, I heard the phone ringing, but I knew what they were doing. My wife's family was looking for me. So I didn't answer the phone. I decided I wanted to end it. I felt so low. It's almost impossible to describe, except to another addict or alcoholic. Only they know how bad you feel at that point in your life. I didn't know what was wrong with me. I loved my wife. I loved my daughter and my newborn baby. I knew I did. I did not know why I acted this way, but I felt that I could not live this way, every day, for the rest of my life. I just could not go on.

So I thought I would kill myself, but I was too much of a coward to go through with it. I did take some pills, in a feeble attempt at suicide, but the pills were not really of sufficient strength to even render me unconscious. I did not want to face my wife and family the next day. There was no way I could hide what I had done, with everything missing from our house. So I went up to the attic, lay down on the cold wooden floor, and prayed to God that I would die.

I woke up the next day and went to pick up my wife at the hospital. On the way back, I explained to her how I had pawned all the items in our house. When we got home, she had this look on her face, and I could tell that she had come to a decision, that she had had enough. She told me, "Vince, I've got a newborn baby here, just home from the hospital. I can't take care of her and you, too. You've got to go." And I knew she was right. Something inside of me wanted to beg her to let me stay. But there was also something inside that said, "No. Think of somebody else, for a change." I agreed to leave.

And that day, I packed up and left. At the time, I had a six-year-old daughter, a two-day-old baby girl, and a marriage of almost nine years' duration. I was thirty-two years of age, and I was flying back to my home state to live with my parents. My mother told me, later, that when she saw me get off that airplane, she thought I was a ghost, I looked so pale. I had virtually no clothes, and I had just one bag with me when I arrived. And I had no hope; I didn't see how I was going to be able to live without my wife, my children. I knew I couldn't live with this disease—not here, at home.

So, again, I thought I would commit suicide. I had always been a gun buff; I like to hunt. When I was a young child, my grandfather would take me hunting, and those were some of the most enjoyable times of my life. Fortunately, my father had kept my shotguns at home with him, so they were not at my disposal when I was going through my earlier decision to kill myself, down South. But when I got home, I knew they were there, and I felt that I didn't really see that I could survive here very long. My life was over. There was nothing left for me.

Once I was home again, my father laid down the rules I would have to accept if I wanted to live under his roof. He told me that he wanted me to go to Alcoholics Anonymous meetings, and I said that I would. I didn't have much choice. I don't remember much about the first meetings I went to. All I remember is that somebody got up and said, "Vince, we're going to love you until you love yourself." That was the first time anyone had ever said that to me. I grabbed hold of that.

But it wasn't quite enough to hold on to, so a guy came up to me at my second meeting, after hearing me whine and complain about how I'd lost my whole family and my life was over, and so on, and he said, "You sound like you need a sponsor." And I replied, "Yeah, I guess I do." And he said, "Well, I'm going to be your sponsor." Then he added, "You might need something to do during the day, so I'm going to give you a job, too."

This man not only became my first sponsor, he also became my first boss, in sobriety. He was in construction, and he hung sheet rock. We would go to jobs together, just the two of us, as generally this work, in a house, is just a two-man job. He would pick me up, because I didn't have a car, sometimes as early as five o'clock in the morning, and he would take me to work. We would work together all day, and he would talk about the Program, and he would impart little mottoes, such as "First Things

First," "Easy Does It," "One Day at a Time," and "No relationships for the first year," because, of course, as I began to feel a bit better, I began to want things. And I began to satisfy myself, but he would keep my straight on that. At the same time, he was teaching me a trade, and I loved him.

This went on for about three or four months, and that feeling of doom, and of wanting to commit suicide, began to go away. I still had compulsions to use, but eventually they subsided. I did a 90 in 90 (ninety meetings in ninety days), as it was suggested, and my life started to change. Now, some of these changes that occurred in my life were subtle. But others were drastically, terribly quick.

My sponsor and I split up, as far as the job was concerned. He remained my sponsor, but he got back together with his old partner, and I went on to another job. I was a courier for a while.

I had an idea in my mind, though, something I'd wanted to do, back when I was using, in the banking field. Of course, I had no hope of attaining it. I had no college diploma. I had left school after my second year. But someone in the Program came up to me one day and said, "Vince, this might be something good for you," and set me up with a job interview. That interview led me to the career I am enjoying today.

The way this program works is truly wonderful, and my life continued to change really fast. I began to communicate with my wife, and we even started to talk about getting back together. I had been sober for about eight or nine months and I was starting a new career. I was feeling good about myself and thought that I was accomplishing something.

Around this time, I was introduced to another fellowship, Chemically Dependent Anonymous. I had been going to A.A., but alcohol was not really my drug of choice; crack cocaine was. I remember someone pulling me aside and asking, "Hey, have you ever been to a CDA meeting?" And I hadn't. So later on that week, I went to a meeting of CDA. Man, it is almost impossible to describe my feelings as I sat there and listened to other people talk about their experiences with drugs – their experiences with coke! You see, in A.A., we talked a lot about drinking, and I would have to try to substitute, in my own mind, that word "coke" for "alcohol" when people talked about their experiences. Sometimes I was able to do that, and sometimes I wasn't.

Not until I attended my first CDA meeting did I realize just how much I needed that program. I needed to be somewhere around people I could sit down with and talk about how it *felt* to do drugs, what it was like out there. At my first CDA meeting, I was really uncomfortable because I was hearing the God-honest truth about things. Somebody was telling my story, and it didn't feel very good when they were talking about drugs.

I talked to my sponsor, who had never done drugs (he was an ex-alcoholic), and he said, "Vince, if those people help you like that, it's a program you have to incorporate into your life." I began attending CDA meetings regularly and got involved in the Program. It was good for me because I was a newcomer, and CDA was kind of a new fellowship. As the new kid on the block, it was easy for me to become involved because there were a lot of possibilities for commitment, but not so many people to fulfill them.

If it weren't for those first few commitments in CDA, I don't know that I'd have had the courage to do some of the other things that I've been able to do since I have been in the Program. CDA and A.A. have been lifesavers to me. And the Program, overall, has helped me to come to terms with who I am: that I am an addict and alcoholic, that I have a disease, and that there is something I can do about it today.

I'm happy to be able to share my story about my addiction, about my experience with crack, about my experience with alcohol, now. I'm coming up on my three-year anniversary this month—three years out of the crack house; three years out of hell. I never could have dreamed, in my using-days, that I would be sitting here in a home with my family back together, with a two-week-old son born of the same mother as my first two children. Three years ago, but for the grace of God and the Fellowship, that would not have been possible.

Working the Twelve Steps of the Program; getting involved; doing what I can, has made my life so busy that I often don't have as much time to spend with my family or on the Program as I would like. But this program is the most important thing in my life. Without it, without the God of my understanding, the Twelve Steps, the people in the Fellowship, I would have nothing.

I hope that the few things I have to say here will help someone else. God put me on this earth, and this program is teaching me the reason why I am here. I'm not on this earth to be a success in business, and I don't believe that I've been put here to teach everybody some new way of life. I think that God put me here to live a productive life and to do what I can to help another suffering alcoholic and addict. And if, along the way, He provides me with the things that I need, and throws in a couple of the things that I want, that's just icing on the cake.

Crack cocaine took me to the bottom, and now CDA and A.A. have taken me up, almost to the top. I don't know how far I can go. I just know that I love the way my life is now. I want things to continue to get better. And I know that as long as I stay sober, one day at a time, as long as I don't take a drink or a drug, they will.

18 Things I Must Earn

When I heard the statement, at my first Chemically Dependent Anonymous meeting, "I was sick and tired of being sick and tired," I was startled into my first glimmer of hope. For three years, prior to coming into the rooms, I had suffered from anxiety, fear, bad nerves, diarrhea, loneliness, and despair. I was considering the possibility of suicide, as there seemed no other way out. Doctors had proclaimed me physically sound but suggested I see a psychiatrist. The psychiatrist proclaimed me mentally "loose" and promptly equipped me with medication to calm my nerves. Ironically, my nerves were shattered because of my abuse of drugs and alcohol.

The sedatives I was placed on I took only as prescribed, but I still suffered from fear, anxiety, loneliness, and emptiness. I had stopped doing most drugs, as oftentimes I would experience anxiety attacks from getting high, but I still drank alcohol and used tranquilizers to soothe my shaking insides. I would often hyperventilate, and I had an intense fear of going crazy. Life had ceased to be fun. All the good times were gone. I was just existing, and I wanted so much to feel normal again. I wasn't asking to get high anymore, just to stop hurting. Consequently, when I heard, "I was sick and tired of being sick and tired," I could really relate to that.

I met the people in the rooms, and they told me it didn't have to be that way anymore. They also told me I only had to get sober once. After some time in the Program, I can truthfully say it's a lot easier to stay sober than to get sober. At first, I went through some horrible withdrawals and a lot of emotional pain, but the people in the Fellowship told me to hang in there, that it would get better. And it did. I have wonderful friends in the Program, and my life just keeps getting better. Sobriety is a gift, and I now feel very privileged to be a part of CDA.

In the beginning, I also experienced a lot of denial. Even though I was sick and hurting, I kept listening to the events in the people's stories, not the feelings. I consoled myself by claiming, "I'm not that bad." I had never had a DWI; I had never gone to jail, and so on. Therefore, I had a slip.

When I came back into the Program, my sponsor told me to get honest and made me do a written First Step. I had to look at the unmanageability of my life caused by my use of all of the chemicals. I never got involved in my child's activities, joined P.T.A., or became a den mother because getting high was my top priority. Feeling the guilt, remorse, and anxiety from the "great" time I had the night before was another aspect of this unmanageability.

Spending the family money to party, wetting the bed, and experiencing blackouts were part of this disease, too. My inability to stop using chemicals, even though I wanted to, proved that I was powerless. I had tried jogging, exercise, vitamins, and religion, and I still couldn't stay sober. The Program was the only thing that worked for me.

Today, I am so grateful to CDA for giving me hope and teaching me how to live sober, one day at a time. CDA taught me not to worry about which chemical I was using. It was not what, or even how much, I used. It's what it was doing to me. I thought that I wasn't an alcoholic because I didn't drink every day. But this addiction disease is cunning, baffling, and powerful. For my slip, as it turned out, was on alcohol.

CDA taught me to realize that, even though I wasn't a daily drinker, there wasn't a day that went by that I didn't put some sort of mood-changing chemical into my system. So I have to consider myself chemically dependent. Alcohol, tranquilizers (even medication), pot, and diet pills are all chemicals. In my case, using any kind of chemical is just feeding my addiction. Thank God, I stuck with the winners who were honest enough to tell me the truth about my disease.

Members of the Fellowship also told me that if I wanted what they had, I had to do what they did. They didn't seem to be hurting the way I was. They were even smiling. They told me, "Meeting makers make it," and said that I should get to a meeting every day. Get a sponsor; get a Home Group; get involved: these were other suggestions for recovery. I did all these things because I was willing to go to any length to stop hurting. I was also told to pray to a God of my understanding. I chose a loving, caring God Who speaks through the people in the Program, and my recovery was well on its way.

I would be lying if I said that, because I've been sober for some time now, everything is a bed of roses. However, it's much better than it was. I still go through a great deal of emotional pain, but I'm told that it's part of the growth. I do get glimpses of peace of mind and serenity. And, little by little, I'm beginning to get out of myself. My head still "thinks" too much, but it's not as loud or as frantic as it used to be.

The people in CDA told me that it would take time to get well. I drank and drugged daily for nine years, so I have to be patient about my recovery.

"TIME" stands for "Things I Must Earn," and as long as I trust in God, clean house (Fourth and Tenth Steps), go to meetings, and pray, I can get well.

I also have to pass what I've received on to others, in order to keep it. I must do for the newcomer what was done for me when I came in. And it seems I feel my best when I try to give it away. All in all, I have a great deal of hope for the future because of the Program.

Thank you CDA for giving me back my life and my sanity.

19 Recovered, Not Cured

My name is Bill B., and I am a grateful recovered alcoholic. My father was also an alcoholic and, perhaps because of that, was physically abusive to me when I was a child. When I was seven years old, I made a decision that he would never again make me cry. This does not mean that I didn't use tears to get what I wanted, but I did turn off most of my feelings after that. I did not really cry again until I was thirty-one years of age and had been sober for a whole year.

I took my first drink when I was around nine years old. It was a swallow of whiskey, and it tasted terrible. But it felt great when it got down to my stomach. I took drinks from the bottles in the house over the next three years, but I never got drunk. When I was twelve years old, I took about a half of fifth of rum to school with me. I drank most of it, but I did not get drunk. I just got a good buzz.

One New Year's Eve, I got a pint of whiskey and drank it in about ten or fifteen minutes. This was my first real drunk. I got sick and had a blackout. For the next seventeen years, when I drank, I usually got drunk and sick and had blackouts. When I drank, I usually got into some kind of trouble. I rebelled against all authority. For the next five years, it was great for me, but not so great for my family. My mother finally suggested that I get out of the house. So I joined the Army, also at her suggestion.

In the early sixties, I was sent overseas, and there the party started. I drank almost daily. I also started using drugs. I smoked grass and hash. I took speed while I was on leave, for about fifteen days. I also took a hallucinogen, for the first time, while I was in Europe. Alcohol and drugs made me think I was cool. I almost got kicked out of the Army, but I talked my way out of that, receiving an honorable discharge three years after I'd joined up.

I then moved back in with my mother and told her that I was a changed man. That made two lies. Lie number one: I had not changed. Lie number two: I was still a kid, not a man. For the next three years, I drank and used no drugs. Yet trouble was still with me. I had two auto accidents, caused by excessive drinking, in the same month.

I decided to go to college but quit because school got in the way of my playing. I thought of myself as Peter Pan. I did not want to grow up. I was arrested, many times, for drinking and being drunk in public, for disturbing the peace, and, one time, for trespassing—in a bar. I had been asked to leave and refused to do so. The police were called, and I was put in jail.

A friend bailed me out and took me back to my car. I drove around for about an hour, going seventy to eighty miles per hour most of that time. I really wanted a police officer to pull me over. On the seat next to me was a nine-shot, .32-caliber automatic. I fully intended to shoot any officer who pulled me over, to get even for having been arrested. Luckily, no one stopped me, so I just went home.

The next morning, when I woke up, I remembered what I had done. Of course, I never even considered stopping the drinking, but I did give away the gun. I realize now that I was in total denial that I had any problem with alcohol at that stage of my addiction.

Near the end of the sixties, I took LSD for the first time, and I loved it. I ate LSD, on an almost daily basis, for four years. By now, I had started dealing drugs, too, and I tried just about every one of them. I loved PCP pills, speed, hash, and mushrooms, in addition to the LSD. I did not drink very much during this period. And I never got into needles—probably because my brother was a diabetic, and I had had to give him his shots when I was young. But I became a hippie, during the next year, and started mixing drugs and alcohol.

Then my life really went crazy. I won a court case and received a settlement of about $7,000, and I went on a very long binge. I started using PCP and alcohol daily. I was also snorting cocaine, to mellow me out. I bought the kind of car a teenager would love, although I had just turned thirty. The girls I liked were teenagers, too. They liked money, drugs, alcohol, long hair, and fast cars. I was on top of the world because I had all of those things, and that made me cool.

During the next year, I had a lot of blackouts and woke up in some strange places. I would go to my brother's house and pass out on the couch. He told me that he was afraid he would wake up one morning and find me dead, but it meant so little to me that I didn't ever remember his telling me that until he reminded me later. One morning, I woke up in a house and heard a man asking me what I was doing there. On the table was about a half of a fifth of Scotch, and I was in my underwear. I asked the man for a ride home, but he evidently had no sense of humor.

While I was hitchhiking home, I figured out what had happened. I had been with a friend, and we had gone to a bar and had been invited to a party. I remembered going out to the car to get another bottle of Scotch and taking a drink before going back to the party. I had obviously gone into the wrong ground-floor condo. Sometime during the night, I had taken off my clothes and passed out.

Another time, I came out of a blackout while I was driving and saw a car cutting me off. I went off the road, down a long hill, and stopped, luckily, without hitting anything. While I was walking back up the hill, I slowly realized that the vehicle that had blocked be off was a police car. I asked the officer why he had cut me off, and he told me that I had gone through a tollbooth without paying the toll. He had chased me across the toll bridge, going over eighty miles per hour, and had intercepted me when I still refused to stop. I really must have handed him a good line that night because he only gave me a $17 ticket for my failure to pay the toll. Somehow, he let me drive away, despite the fact that I was wasted.

When I began to realize that I had only $900 left of the $7,000 settlement I had received less than two months before, I decided that I had better find a job. I began looking for sales jobs and, by the end of the month, had received an offer from a carpet wholesaler. The salesman I was to replace had made $35,000 in the previous year, I was told. I thought that this was the best day of my life. I went home, got all my PCP and cocaine, and went out to celebrate. I had almost a full fifth of Scotch in the car, and I bought a case of beer.

I celebrated getting that job from around noon until midnight. During the day, the police pulled me over twice and searched my car, but they let me go. I guess they were looking for drugs, but they never searched *me*, which is where my drugs were hidden. About midnight, I decided that driving home was not such a good idea, so I went for a long walk. When I got back to my car, a couple of hours later, I drove around the parking lot and felt that I was now able to drive. But on the way home, I was pulled over again. I was very upset.

When the police officer asked me to get out of the car, I said, "This is the third time I have been stopped by your police department today, and I don't like this harassment." I felt that I had been driving perfectly fine. The officer asked me, again, to get out of the car. I said, "You tell me why you pulled me over, and then I might get out of the car." I still refused to get out when he ordered me to do so a third time. He then said, "Mr. B., you were going five miles per hour. Now, please get out of the car." He seemed very nervous, so I finally got out. I agreed to take a Breathalyzer test and was taken to the police station.

There, I got into a fight with some police officers and went into a convulsion that was caused by the excess of alcohol and drugs in my system. The police called an ambulance, and I was taken to the hospital. In the next twenty-four hours, my heart stopped beating three times, but the doctors were able to bring me back to life each time. That was fifteen years ago. I have not had a drink of alcohol, or used any drugs not prescribed by a doctor, since that day.

I believe that I made a decision to live, at that time. I went to my first Alcoholics Anonymous meeting five days later, while I was still in the Hospital. I have been trying, to the best of my ability, to work the Twelve Steps of the Program ever since. Very early in A.A., I met a friend there who had drunk and drugged, just as I had. He asked me to identify with those people in A.A., and I did what he suggested.

I know, today, that I must practice the Twelve Steps, each day, if I want to stay sober and enjoy life. I want to have a good life, so I do what I believe my God wants me to do. I now have a house, a good job, a wife, a son, a baby girl, and lots of other *things*. But if we work for them, the Program promises that we will receive even more important gifts: happiness, freedom, peace, selflessness, wisdom, security, and a sense of God's plan for our lives.

I was able to be in the delivery room when my baby girl was born, eight years ago. That birth coincided with the exact date of the seventh anniversary of my sobriety. I could not have made such a coincidence happen. I believe it somehow symbolized how God's plan works in my life.

This past year, a woman I grew up with asked me to take her to some meetings of Chemically Dependent

Anonymous. She was a cocaine addict who had tried A.A. but had gone back to using drugs again. I began taking her to some of the CDA meetings in the area. I thought I was "Twelve Stepping" her, but actually she "Twelve Stepped" *me* into CDA. Although she unfortunately did not stop using, CDA was able to give me new insights into my own behavior.

Not too long ago, I had a spiritual awakening—the educational variety—at a meeting. I realized that the alcoholic part of me could be described as *over*sensitive, while my drug-addict side could best be called *in*sensitive. I have spent thirteen years cleaning up my alcoholic behavior. My Higher Power has now given me CDA so I can work on the drug-addict personality problems that I have been ignoring.

I had never put *myself* on the Eighth-Step list of "persons we had harmed." Because of CDA, I now realize that I definitely belong on that list. I am working the Eighth Step on myself now, so I can better understand the relationship I should be having with myself. I intend to make amends to myself, and I believe that doing this will make me better able to serve God and my fellow human being.

I know that I can only live one day at a time, but as it is my intention to stay sober in A.A., it is also my intention to stay sober in CDA for the rest of my life. I need and want what both fellowships have to offer me.

20 Dreams Come True

As a child, I was accustomed to being the center of attention. I was an A student, involved in music, art, ballet, and horseback riding. Our family had horses, ducks, chickens, gardens, and a vineyard when I was growing up. I was very happy, as I recall, but even then I had unrealistic expectations about life. I lived in a fantasy world. I was totally unaware of any family problems.

My parents sent me away, the summer of my eleventh birthday, to my grandmother's. When I returned, my fantasy world was shattered. Mom and dad had split up and were planning divorce. My father became obsessed with religion and the church, and my mother pursued her career. I was no longer the center of attention. I had to take on additional responsibilities around the house, since mom was gone, and I had less and less time to be a kid.

I started drinking and drugging when I was twelve, not as a rebellious act, but rather to escape myself and my life, and to gain acceptance. I went to great lengths to hide the fact that I was getting high because I knew that if my father found out, I would be severely punished. But I was soon getting high every day, before and after school. I was sneaking booze into my locker and peddling drugs. By the eighth grade, I was hooked. The school knew it and had me seeing a counselor on campus, but my parents were still not informed about my problem.

Dad noticed other things, though. I had changed my friends. I skipped school, was hitchhiking, and was picked up by the police when I was supposed to be spending the night with friends. Finally, my father decided there were certain friends I was not going to see as long as I was under his roof. I moved back with my mother. I was fourteen years old.

A new school, new friends, and a new environment did not change anything. I got worse. In ninth grade, I was asked to attend a private school, in hopes that it would straighten me out. I declined the offer. I was using daily and knew where to get a good supply. THC was my drug of choice at the time, but I did whatever was available. I quit taking care of myself, refused to ride the school bus, and skipped school, again.

My mother was at the school constantly, trying to salvage my academic future. I had special classes, special consideration, and special counseling—none of which worked. I was sent to child psychologists and a Christian youth organization. The only thing I had any interest in at all was my art, and my mother tried desperately to keep that part of me alive. But, eventually, I lost all interest in that, as well. I was only interested in using and whatever it took to ensure that I always had something available.

I don't really remember why I went back to my father. I was getting very "soul sick," and I was trying to get back to the "good times" I recalled from my childhood. I remember riding in the car with my dad one day and thinking that everything would be all right. It was him and me against the world.

But he had found someone else, my stepmother, and I became very jealous of her. It was at this point that I started using as a rebellious act. I wanted to hurt others, and I did this by hurting myself. I got into harder drugs and more trouble. I was expelled from school. My father took me to a girls' ranch, at this point, and tried to convince me to stay. I told him I would run away if I were sent there. We returned home.

Finally, dad could take no more. I constantly broke house rules. I had become defiant and rebellious. He told me to get out, and I did. I didn't need him, or anybody, I thought. I could make it on my own. What did he know about life, anyway?

I moved in with a teenage girl who also drugged. Through her, I was introduced to heroin and the crowd that used it. Still wanting to be accepted, I did as they did. But even though I looked "bad" on the outside, I was scared on the inside. During this time, I attempted to hold down part-time jobs, but failed. I had to have money, though, so I resorted to various methods to get it, all of which I had sworn I'd never do. By now, my values had deteriorated to that point.

I was sixteen. Everything I owned would fit into a grocery bag, and I was strung out. I rarely knew what day it was. I should have died; but, for some reason, God spared me. One day, during all of this, I woke up with no idea where I was, or with whom. I wanted to go home.

I called my mom. She said that she hadn't known if I was dead or alive. She came and got me. This wasn't the end of my problems, however. As soon as I was better, I was at the doctor's office, getting "scripts." Not long after that, I found a dealer and was on the merry-go-round again.

Mom got me back into school. I stayed only long enough to finish drivers' education, and then I dropped out. There were also problems at home. I started coming home drunk, or stoned, all the time. Or else I just didn't go home at all, sometimes for days. I was selling drugs out of the house. Things just came to a head, and I left on my own.

I moved in with a dealer I had met a couple of weeks earlier. It was supposed to be a temporary arrangement, but it turned into three insane years. At least I was off the streets. I got my high school equivalency diploma and started junior college. However, my drug addiction only allowed for one semester of that.

I would do anything for my dealer, to make sure I had an ample supply. I risked my life in numerous ways: the guns, the robberies, the smuggling, the twenty-four-hours-a-day traffic, the junkies who would sell you their souls, the police, and that whole underworld scene. It was scary, and yet I felt a little superior to "ordinary" people because I was living precariously.

Things got hot, though, and my relationship with my dealer was going downhill, since neither of us could pass up a good opportunity. At nineteen, I decided it was time to move on. So, once again, I called my mother. Perhaps this time it would be different, I thought. I moved out-of-state to be with her. I tried to quit drugs entirely, but I never gave much thought to my abuse of alcohol.

At first, it seemed that things might work out. I got a job at a factory, making minimum wage. I met the beer-and-pot crowd. I swore off hard drugs, but soon I met "angel dust," and, very soon after that, my addiction was in full force again. I was on the phone to my dealer, begging him to send me cocaine and take me back. I was drinking more and more and doing crazier and crazier things. I was losing my mother's respect rapidly. She had already bailed me out of jail once. I tried religion to straighten myself out, but that only lasted a few weeks.

Finally, I decided I would go back to my dealer, where I would be safe and taken care of. I rationalized the move back down South by saying I was going to college there because it was cheaper. But when I arrived, my real scheme failed. Someone else had assumed my role as the dealer's girl. I went on a three-day binge over this. The binge resulted in a blackout, during which I threatened the dealer's new girlfriend and broke the windows in his house. After that, most of my blackouts were violent.

Now I needed a place to live. That's how I met my first husband—a tall, handsome guy who needed a roommate and who also drank and drugged. I had no intention of marrying him, at the time. It just worked out that way. Our life was pretty routine: We would sleep late, work, and party all night. I held down various types of jobs as a waitress or bartender, which worked well with our lifestyle.

We had many drunk-and-violent fights. I left my husband three times and divorced him before we had been married a year. I believed *he* was my problem. I wanted to make something of myself, and he was in the way. I had landed a job as a courier with a major corporation and had started attending school again, since the company would reimburse me. I was tired of bailing my husband out of trouble. Of course, once I got rid of him, I had no one else to blame.

I started hitting the bar scene heavily. In the mornings, I ate speed to get going and looked out the window to see whether my car was in the driveway or not. I generally kept last night's last drink next to the bed so I could just roll over and get a little help for getting up the next morning.

One morning, I woke up and felt that horrible sense of impending doom, of going nowhere and just not knowing what's wrong. I hated myself. I called a self-help hot line, and they recommended that I go to the local mental health institution. I was screaming for help, but I could not see that my problem was drugs and alcohol abuse. So the progression continued.

I met my future second husband in a bar, but, as fate would have it, we also worked for the same company. I thought that he was "Mr. Wonderful," that my ship had come in. He would fix all my problems, and we would live happily ever after. He had a job that paid well, a house, and prestige. I decided that I would marry him, and, a year later, I did. He liked me because I was wild. I liked to ride motorcycles, drink, and party. I kept a fairly decent house, so he overlooked my bad blackout sprees.

Once, before we were married, I drove off the road in his pickup truck while I was in a blackout. I blew out two tires and tore up one side of the truck. This episode landed me in jail for the night. I lay in bed most of the next day, feeling sorry for myself. When my husband-to-be phoned me, I explained what happened. He immediately dismissed the incident as if it had never occurred.

There were many similar incidents, in the years to follow, which he similarly ignored. Since my husband was not into drugs, I became a daily drinker and only did drugs when I had easy access to them. He had asked me to give them up, particularly the amphetamines I had been using, daily, when we met.

Soon after we married, we were transferred to a large city up North. I really believed that life would be different there. Six months later, I woke up from another bad drunk, wanting to die. I couldn't stand to live that way, anymore. For the first time in my life, I realized that it wasn't my marriage, the people we hung around with, or the activities we were involved in that were the problem—it was me and my drinking. I really wanted to quit. That was my last drunk, and my bottom.

I admitted myself to a rehab program, which is where I was introduced to the Twelve Steps and the Program. I showed up at my first meeting with a broken nose and a broken spirit. I was ready to listen. I would do whatever I was told because I knew that I did not know how to quit drugs and alcohol on my own. I had tried, several times, in the last fourteen years. I found a sponsor who had been clean and sober for some time. Together, we began working the Steps.

Things did get better, because I was getting better, but there were still major changes to come. When I was sober for eight months, I was still living with a practicing alcoholic. It was getting harder and harder for me to "Let Go and Let God." I felt that if I did not take action, I would drink again. I decided my sobriety was more important than anything else. So I moved out on my own. As time went on, I realized that I had to let go of the relationship entirely. I believe, today, that this was God's will for me, as He has opened up other doors in my life which far replace any void that resulted from this breakup.

I'm also in the process of changing my career. I was never very happy with my profession, but I had never felt I could do anything else. Yet the Program outlined in the Steps of Chemically Dependent Anonymous and the encouragement of individuals in the Fellowship have helped me to reach for my dreams. I'm not afraid, anymore, to try new things. I attend a university where I am taking courses for a degree which will get me one step closer to what I want to do. As long as I stay clean and sober, a day at a time, my goals are within my reach. Without my sobriety, I have nothing.

It has been over two years since I quit using drugs and alcohol. I'm twenty-seven years old now, and I'm living as God intended for me to live, for the first time in my life. I am happy—joyous and free! Throughout my using days I would always say, "I just want to be happy." The problem was that I wanted something outside of myself to make me happy on the inside. Today, I'm truly happy on the inside because I'm comfortable with myself. I could never begin to describe all the blessings which I have received from this new way of life, but they include friends, love, security, and, most of all, peace.

21 Rites of Passage

Hi! My name is Max, and I'm an addict-oholic. I'm powerless over everything but my attitude and my actions. I'm also powerless over pot and hashish.

It has only been a year and nine months since I stopped using pot on a daily basis, and nineteen months since I stopped taking *any* mood-altering substance, except for coffee. My "clean time" has just recently entered a phase which I dare call recovery. I am very grateful to be able to come into the rooms and listen to myself and others share their hope and strength, the wisdom of all our experiences. I have become truly fond of many people in the Fellowship and really feel as if I belong.

A relationship with my Higher Power is the most difficult, and at the same time, most rewarding, part of the Program, or process, of working the Steps. Meetings like these are what I think I have searched for all my life. The subjects we discuss, the level of honesty, are what I always thought meetings should be about. But I never found them until I started coming into these rooms. When I don't get to a meeting for one or two days, I feel very insecure, not necessarily that I'm going to go out and use, but just spiritually "out of practice."

I come to Chemically Dependent Anonymous meetings because I need help. I come to CDA to admit to myself, my sponsor, Sterling S., and the people in the Fellowship of anonymous addicts and alcoholics, that I am powerless against the drugs to which I have become addicted, especially marijuana. My life not only had become unmanageable; it, like my body, was seriously, gravely damaged through years of constant abuse. I have lost at least two jobs (and perhaps as many as ten) and have ruined two marriages and several relationships. I have caused pain to my parents and have very likely inflicted psychological damage on my daughter.

I started drinking, with the old gang of mine, in the tenth grade, when I began trying to get blitzed on malt liquor every weekend. But even before that, there was an incident. When I was fourteen, I stole a quart of bourbon from my father's cellar stash. He had cases of booze stored down there because it was cheaper by the case, and he was frugal. I was very sneaky about the theft of this quart, pouring its contents into a one-quart, aluminum Boy Scout canteen and throwing the bottle away. Then I went with my friends into nearby woods. One of them was coming along to watch and take care of us, in case we got into trouble.

The rest of us, in a puberty rite of passage, guzzled one-third of the quart each, in the manliest way we could muster. Well, we certainly got drunk, and sick, and crazy. I was hanging from tree branches like an orangutan, my friends were puking from other trees, and there were great, melodramatic groans filling the woods. I went out on the road in front of a liquor store and lay down to get run over. It was part of my *macho* merit badge requirement, to prove to my peers that I was suicidal, a rebel without a cause, outrageous and crazy.

The sober friend called my Boy Scout patrol leader and his girlfriend for help. When they dumped my body into the leader's car, I told his girlfriend that I loved her. She screamed, and my patrol leader came running to save her. He was tall, and blond, and very heroic-looking.

When I was seventeen, to impress my peers, I guzzled all of a large pitcher of beer at a bar in a college town. All of a sudden, my eyes got very big, and my face had the unmistakably worried look for someone about to barf. A path opened in the crowd, and I was hurried down the gauntlet into the men's room. I was very proud of *this* rite of passage.

At the age of twenty, I went to a lot of trouble to find pot and smoke it. I finally found some, and it didn't do anything the first couple of times, but I had faith and kept trying. One night, as I was supposed to be performing blues-guitar songs at a now-defunct coffee-house, I smoked some strong pot, and it finally worked. A friend kept asking me what was wrong, as I giggled uncontrollably, my legs writhing spastically. He said "Come on, Max. Let's do the song." "What song?" I asked. "'Stagolee,' like we planned in practice" he said. "Okay," I said. "How does it go?" "Like this," he said with a disgusted look on his face, as he jogged my memory.

When I then had to ask what chord it started with, and how to make that "D" chord, he became more and more angry with me. I was scarcely able to talk, I was giggling so much. But he showed me how to start. "Oh, yeah," I said, "and what was that next chord?" He told me I was disgusting, and I apologized, but my ribs were hurting from laughing so hard. The crowd was spellbound at this display of dopey stupor and helplessness. I staggered to the door, out to the sidewalk, down the street, laughing my head off. "I feel sorry for you, you pathetic dope fiend," my friend shouted down the sidewalk. Of course, I didn't believe, at the time, that I was any such thing. But I was just getting started.

Seventeen years ago, I was foiled by U.S. Customs agents in my first, and last, attempt to bring marijuana into the country. In an absurdly foolish adventure with three other young men, I hiked fourteen miles through the desert, at night, with several kilos in a knapsack on my back. I was brought to trial and convicted of failure to pay the tax on a controlled substance, a felony. The judge sentenced me to three years, twenty-eight days of which I spent in a federal detention center. I was then placed on probation.

In spite of such extremely obvious warning signs, it was not until my own child was born, four years later; that I remorsefully came to realize that marijuana smoking was undeniably and absolutely self-destructive. I then tried, on my own, to break myself of the habit, but was unsuccessful. Shortly before my daughter's third birthday, I began attending a series of individual and group sessions at a pastoral counseling center. That process took four years, and ultimately did prove successful, in that it resulted in a change in my behavior.

I have always wanted to be a writer, I think perhaps because I always enjoyed reading books. In college, I had great ambitions of someday becoming a famous author. During that notorious decade known as the sixties, I was in my twenties, and the ubiquitous presence of all kinds of drugs, and most specifically, marijuana, was not the given fact of life that it is today. It was only in books that I had ever even heard of these exotic substances, and the very idea of partaking of them was extremely remote and confined to literature, as far as I was concerned.

When I was actually invited to try some marijuana, I was not even dimly aware that I was among the first few drops of what was to become a tidal wave of drug users. Back then, it seemed smart to disdain alcohol and prefer the "relatively harmless" and "creativity-enhancing" effects of marijuana. I was, quite honestly, ignorant of the very serious dangers, psychologically, physically, and socially, into which I was placing myself every time I indulged. I imagined that the things I wrote when under the influence of pot were profound, publishable descriptions of the new frontier of the mind. I would not heed the warnings of parents or "straighter" friends; when they urged me not to jeopardize my life; I proceeded obstinately down my own path. I really believed that I knew better than everybody else.

I also used pot to escape having to deal with problems. It enabled me to procrastinate, indefinitely, doing the work on myself I knew needed to be done. It allowed me to tolerate intolerable situations. I was absolutely out of control in my never-ending lust for the pleasure of the high, the escape from responsibility.

But now I am ready to pay the price. I am ready to experience the pain of awareness: that I was mistaken and stupid to waste so much precious time of my life doing drugs, that I may have caused my child to have cerebral palsy, a wrong for which there could never be adequate amends. No matter how horrible I feel, no matter how guilty, I vow to myself, and to my Higher Power, to remain clean in my body and mind, each day, one day at a time. I am willing, wholeheartedly, to try the Twelve Steps to recovery. Just making this statement fills me with hope for myself and the ones around me.

At this moment, I have nearly two years drug free. My old resentments are leaving, fading. I am doing a great deal of reading, have organized a book club, and am trying to get a teaching job. Meanwhile, I am working every day as a trim carpenter for a home builder. I have a terrific fiancée, as well as my marvelous daughter. There is no desire for pot, or for any other drug, today. I feel "high on life" and enjoy each day with gratitude.

My great foe is laziness, spiritual and physical, the deadly sin of sloth. I am more afraid of it, in myself, than the compulsion to go out and use. Truly speaking, one leads to the other, and staying off drugs is the best way for me to combat sloth. Staying off drugs is my number one job, my priority, from now on. I need to remember that every day, to begin life on earth. One toke is no joke.

I pray to my Higher Power to be my guide. As Virgil guided Dante through the inferno, I humbly beseech *my* Guide to lead me out of the hell of marijuana.

22 Darkness Dispelled

My name is Anne L. I'm chemically dependent. And here's my story, as best I can recall it. I was the middle of five children. We moved, as a family, a total of six times by the time I was ten years old. So I didn't have any real close friends, growing up, or else I lost them when we moved. I became used to always being the "new kid." Out of all of the children in our family, I was the quiet, studious one. You never had to worry about Anne, because she pretty much took care of herself. I remember reading and listening to music a lot.

I feel I grew up very quickly, around the age of twelve, because there was so much going on at home. My parents hadn't gotten along well at all for quite a while. There wasn't fighting, as much as silence, around the house. My mother was having emotional difficulties, and she would confide in me. I remember feeling helpless about the whole situation and wishing there were something I could do. Yet it was out of my hands. My mother ended up having a breakdown and going into the hospital. Once she got out, there was talk about divorce and where each one of us children would go. Everything was up in the air.

Shortly after this time, I was introduced to booze. I'll never forget the first time I had "enough," to the point where alcohol had any effect on me. The feeling I had was one of pure joy. I was elated at the tingling in my fingers, the light-headedness, and the good feeling I had from that very first time. It just grabbed hold of me. From then on, I took any chance there was to have a drink. I loved what it did for me. I wasn't shy and withdrawn, anymore. I felt OKAY about me, and it was fun being around people. There was no more discomfort. I was transformed in some way, so I could be a part of things and could feel I belonged. From that point on, booze became a part of my life.

It wasn't too long afterwards that I was introduced to other drugs—to grass, and acid, and uppers and downers, and all the other things that were passed around in the crowd I wound up in. Everybody was doing it, and everybody seemed OKAY, doing it. Drugs were nothing that I thought might harm me. They were just recreation—fun—I owed it to myself!

And so, throughout the rest of high school, and into college, I partied whenever I could. The disease, which I didn't know I had, progressed. Looking back now, I can see that most of the symptoms were there from the beginning. I had blackouts. My tolerance was very high: other people would be stumbling and slurring, but I could handle it. I felt inwardly proud of that fact. But it was a sign. All along, I felt I could handle the drugs, that *I* was the master of *them*—until it turned around. It was a gradual turn, but one that picked up speed very quickly, once it started.

At first, it was quite gradual—shakes in the morning, blackouts where I didn't remember, even vaguely, what had gone on while I was out of it. I'd lose whole evenings; I'd lose whole days and weekends. There were feelings of just wanting to get away, that something was wrong. But I couldn't figure out what it was. So I wound up going to some shrinks. I thought maybe I was having some of my mother's emotional problems. Maybe it was hereditary. There was a discomfort, an unrest, a fear that was building, growing inside of me.

I dropped out of college, during my senior year, because of my growing anxiety and paranoia when I was with people. For the next two years, I had a job in an office where I was alone three days of the week, but I lost that because my performance wasn't getting any better. I moved back home and, after five months, hit bottom.

During those five months, I experienced a deepening depression, a growing hopelessness and helplessness, confusion about what was going on. I really felt I was losing my mind, that the only thing keeping me together was the booze. By this time, I was drinking around the clock, yet it wasn't working anymore. I'd get up—and throw up. I wasn't eating right. I wasn't bathing. I was afraid to be around my mother and sister, and that scared me. I hated sunny days; I'd draw the curtains. I took the phone off the hook. I thought about suicide.

I had no idea what alcoholism or addiction were. I had been so wrapped up in myself for so long that, even if I had known someone (and I surely must have) who had a problem with booze and drugs, I wouldn't have seen it. About the only thing I could see, at the end, was that I was alone; that I needed help and didn't know how to get it. I was too proud to ask. I was too proud to admit what was going on with me.

I didn't like myself very much however, despite my pride. I didn't understand the creature I had turned into. I'd been through the one-night stands, waking up the next day not knowing the person who was lying beside me, not being able to find my car, not wanting to hear people talking about what I had done the night before. I didn't know how to get back to the real world. I wanted some*one*, or some*thing*, to just come along and take me away from the place I'd wound up in.

One night, I took a bunch of pills from the medicine cabinet, but I soon went and told my mother what I had done. She called the hospital and stayed up with me all night. I don't know where my head was when I took those pills. But it was clear that something had to be done with Anne. My family was disgusted with me. So, an appointment was made for me to see another shrink. I felt like a child. I thought, "Here we go with the shrinks, again. They didn't help before. How can they help now?"

The next night, two programs were on TV, back-to-back, that dealt with addiction. My head was clear enough that I could relate to the stories being told. In one of the programs, there was a person who was getting along in life all right until he stumbled across the whole drug scene. Then everything turned into chaos, and he was hurting. Yet, by the end of the show, something had turned things around so his life became OKAY, again. One of the programs also mentioned Alcoholics Anonymous.

That night, evidently in a blackout, I called an A.A. Inter-Group. I don't know whether I reached a person, or a recording, or what. But the next morning, someone called me, and I found out about a meeting that was right up the road from our house. I called a sister to come get me, because I was not able to drive. I was too wired and filled with fear to get behind the wheel of a car. My sister agreed to take me to the meeting.

I don't remember much about that first meeting, other than the fact that I was made to feel welcome. The warmth and caring that I saw in those people's eyes was in such contrast to the looks of disgust and intolerance I'd received from my family. It was like sunshine coming in through the gray fog I had been in, for so long. And the people told me to come back. They told me I would be all right, that they understood what I was going through.

That meant so much to me, when they said that they understood, because I didn't understand, myself. I didn't think anybody could. I left the meeting, and I broke down and cried. My mind wasn't clear enough to analyze anything then, but I was feeling hope. I do remember, too, that I went home and poured out all the booze.

Someone from the group came to pick me up, the next day, for another meeting. There, the A.A. people said, "Don't drink. Just for today, don't drink." And I didn't. I went through the shakes, and the anxiety, with my mind going in all different directions. Yet I didn't even think about drinking. I can see what a real gift that was, now. But, at the time, I wasn't able to realize it. I was still in a fog.

In the beginning, people were driving me around to the meetings, and it was as if I were being *led*. I really didn't know what their program was all about. I just knew I was no longer in that bad place and people were telling me that my life could be different. I wanted so much for that to be true. So I would listen, as best I could. And when they called on me, I would pass.

But I found people who made me feel comfortable talking with them. They came up to *me*, after the meetings. I would ask them what this or that meant, in the Program. They gave me some literature, and they gave me phone numbers to call if I got into trouble or just wanted to talk some more. And they gave me love. Things gradually began to sink in: both what was being said in the meetings and what the Fellowship was all about. I knew I was where I belonged, and I came to understand that I had a disease.

It was so comforting to know I wasn't alone. I wasn't to blame for what had happened, and there was a solution, a better way to live. And I was *there*. I was learning about it and was a part of it. I kept coming back, and I got a sponsor. I began going to Step Meetings and listening to things I didn't really want to hear, listening to talk about a higher power.

I'd shut off God a long time ago—when He hadn't mended my parents' marriage, when I saw that He left

177

children around the world hungry and homeless, when I realized that He let so many innocent people go through suffering and allowed them to be killed. The people in the Program talked about a God *as you understand Him.* I had to admit I didn't understand God, at all. But, by listening, I found out that I wasn't the only one who had that problem. As long as I tried to keep my mind open, was honest with myself, and was willing find another way, I would make it.

And I didn't want to go back out. I was afraid, from the stories people told, that if you didn't work the Steps, if you didn't change, you would end up back out there. I knew what was waiting out there for me, if that happened. The certainty that I was an alcoholic and that I was in the right place, in the Program, has stuck with me ever since then, except for a couple of shaky periods in the beginning where God intervened before I had even admitted that He was there.

Rather than face the darkness, I prayed, and there was always an answer to my prayer. There was always a better feeling, inside, that I was being taken care of. It might not, necessarily, always be in the manner that I would like, but I knew I was being watched over, and no matter how tough the situation or how shaky I might feel, I would be okay. And so I came to understand God, in a small, beginning kind of way, as a Force which would help me and guide me, comfort and strengthen me. God became a friend. He was everywhere. But most of all, He was in the rooms where folks were talking. Because of Him and you, that feeling of "okayness," the feeling that we can fight together whatever the problem, was there.

So I proceeded through the Steps, and I began taking part in some service work: in making coffee, and then in answering the phone, in sharing at meetings, and then in sharing outside of meetings. And the Program became more a part of my life as I practiced praying, in the morning and at night. Even though there were still some things I didn't understand, as long as I sat and listened, and kept that willingness to try, I found I was either able to understand better or able to accept that I didn't have to understand everything, yet.

Now my life is a whole lot better, much richer and fuller. It's not that I've been restored to anything that I was before. I feel I have been restored to so much more than I have ever been. I have learned that this disease I have is three-fold: spiritual, mental, and physical. As I make progress in recovery, I realize that there aren't any real limits, other than those I set on myself, in any of these areas. Through working the Program, growth can be a constant—will be a constant—part of my life.

Although I started out in A.A., a great part of my story lies in Chemically Dependent Anonymous, and in being around and watching its growth, from the very first meeting in one man's house, to the many meetings of this group available today. In A.A., there were some old-timers who frowned upon talk about drugs. They would say that their meetings were for *alcoholics*. One of the first questions I asked, after being in A.A.'s Program not too very long, and I asked it of a younger member, was, "Does this mean I can't have any pills, or smoke any grass, or whatever?" She replied, "I strongly recommend that you don't. Anything affecting you from the neck up is very likely to carry you back out."

The meaning of that was firmly planted in my mind when a fellow who had been secretary of the Young People's Meeting at A.A. shot himself in the head. After I found out what he had done, I went back to the member who had told me to avoid any substance abuse and asked her about this young man, a close friend of hers. She said that he had maintained his sobriety from booze, but he had been smoking grass, and he never really *got* the Program. He couldn't; his mind wasn't clear. The whole thing can't work if you aren't willing to go to any length. It made quite an impression on me.

But there was also a disillusionment that this man had been in what he had thought was the perfect place for help. And, somehow, the message hadn't come across— a message that might have saved his life. The message is that it is not just alcohol that is dangerous. Anything you put into your system that is altering your mind is unsafe.

Rick R. was the one who really got CDA started. He was my sponsor's boyfriend. I remember being at their house when he came home from A.A. meetings and seeing how upset he was that somebody had mentioned drugs and other members had made some derogatory remarks about drug users. I know, in my own case, how important it had been to feel that these people accepted me. If I had felt rejected when I first came into A.A., I might not have come back. Comments about my using drugs other than booze would have made me feel that A.A. was not the right place for me.

Luckily, perhaps, booze was the only substance I was using when I came to A.A., but I could just as easily have been on something else. There were many people who had come to A.A. for help, even though alcohol was not their primary problem, because there wasn't any other program around for them. They wound up back outside those doors because, for some reason, they felt, or were made to feel, that they didn't belong or were not welcome there.

And there were also people in the A.A. Program, including the fellow who had committed suicide, who felt that they were sober as long as they didn't have alcohol inside them. The quality of their sobriety was very questionable. Rick felt, strongly, that you couldn't justify the use of any drug other than prescribed medication, and that you had better be sure you understood the medical need for even that use of drugs before you took them. An addict can't safely use any drug that affects his mind, and even prescriptions have to be monitored carefully.

That is the force behind CDA – to help people who have a problem with addiction regardless of the drug. CDA was formed so these people would have a place where they could come and feel accepted. I decided I wanted to be a part of it, just from what I had seen and learned in the small amount of time I had been around the group. It is amazing how CDA has grown since then, a definite proof that the need was there. I now feel very much a part of both fellowships, since CDA is based upon the same foundations that A.A. has found to be effective.

And I think times have changed. The membership in the Program of A.A. has changed, today, to the point where people are pretty comfortable in going back and forth between both meetings. There are so many potential candidates for either A.A. or CDA out there, now. And, after all, both programs are really proclaiming the good news of the same hope and the same gift from a higher power that is there, no matter what you call that Force, to help people: to help them out of that dark place, to show them a new way of life, and to give them companions along the way. My thanks to all of you in CDA. Good luck and God bless.

23 Going to Any Length!

I believe "GOING TO ANY LENGTH" on a daily basis has been a very important concept in my recovery in Chemically Dependent Anonymous. It involves several factors which I will try to discuss briefly.

Sponsorship has been very important to me. I was scared to ask Danny to be my sponsor but after I did, we talked and I felt much better. I have received good direction and suggestions from him. Having a sponsor has allowed me to let someone know what is going on inside of Brian. It has made me realize that I am not unique and that I am not alone.

When I decided to try to get sober, I had to become willing to let go of friends from my past who were still using. I was very sick and being around those people only increased my chances of getting loaded again. I was not willing to take that chance. Today, I have nothing in common with those people. They don't call and I don't call them. Some have died and some have gone to jail. But I have become physically, mentally and spiritually healthier. I have more friends who love me than I've ever had before in my life.

After first entering the Program, I could not go to bars, stadium events or concerts. I was loaded anytime I had gone to these places in the past. I was afraid that if I went back, the old tapes in my head would start playing and I would start using again. Now, after almost two years clean, I have been to a few clubs and stadiums with program people but I still don't feel really comfortable about it. I have not been to any concerts because of all the drugs that would be there.

In the Program, there is a saying: "Meeting makers make it!" That has been essential in my recovery. In almost two years, I have missed meetings on only four days. In my first six months, I had strong compulsions to use and the meetings saved my life. I would go to a Noon meeting and then to another one at night. Before I knew it, it was Midnight and I had another day of sobriety.

Now, I attend at least one meeting a day. When I can, I attend two or three a day depending on how I feel. I've asked people who relapsed and come back into the Program why they left and every person has told me that when they stopped going to meetings, they slipped. The meetings are where I learn to live clean. I never knew how to function in life without being under the influence. Today, I am finding out how to do that with the help of my fellow addicts.

Another suggestion I heard when I came to CDA was, "Try not to get involved in a relationship for the first year." I did not date anyone for eight months which was hard to do. But I suffered from low self-esteem and knew that I really didn't have anything to offer someone else.

I was sober once before and got into a relationship four months into recovery. The end result was that I got loaded again. I made that person the number one priority in my life. As a result, I slacked up on my meetings, stopped calling my sponsor and ceased communicating with people in the Program. I believe that when I depended on that person to make me feel good, I also gave that person the ability to hurt me. And since I was still in early recovery, I did not accept rejection very well. Picking up that drink and drug was just the final act of the slip.

Today, I know that I cannot give away what I do not have. Since I did not love myself, it was impossible for me to love anyone else. A recovering addict needs time to acquire some self-esteem before he attempts a new relationship.

I did not have a car in early recovery. I believe that was an example of "going to any length." With a car, I probably would have gone back to my old neighborhood to be around my old friends. That might have led to a loss of my sobriety.

I hope that someone reading my story can relate and finds it helpful. I would like others to find what I have. I have been very lucky. If it were not for my Higher Power, the CDA Program and the Fellowship, I would not be clean today.

24 God Doesn't Make Junk

My name is John E. and I'm an alcoholic and drug addict. To qualify that a little bit further, I'm lucky to be alive today. It's only by the grace of God and the Fellowship of Chemically Dependent Anonymous that I *am* alive. I really thank God for the Program. Before CDA, my life was a mess and I felt that there was no place in this world where I belonged. It was one big trial after trial after trial (and most of my trials were criminal ones).

I was basically a good kid growing up. I liked athletics and I played sports of all kinds. I dabbled with alcohol when I was a teenager and it got progressively worse. It is said that addiction is a progressive disease, and I believe that to be very true. I know that my addiction was that way.

I got in trouble at the age of 18 for stealing a car. It was the first time that I'd really been in trouble with the criminal justice system. At that time, I knew nothing about the court system. I went to court the day after I got picked up. The judge found me guilty of the charge and sentenced me to one year in jail. I couldn't believe it.

In that one year in jail, my disease really took over. I got involved with my cell partner who was a drug addict. He used any kind of drug to get high and to change his mood. So I tried it all too.

The first drug I used was a nasal inhalant. When you squeezed the cotton, juice came out. You drew the juice up in a syringe and injected it in your arm. My partner got really high and he told me that it was very good stuff.

Being the crazy person that I was, I said, "Let me try some." I did and I fell in love with it. I started my abuse with doing that drug on a pretty regular basis during my year in jail. I bought that stuff and cocaine also. Along with everything else, there was some heroin that came through so I did that too.

When I got out of jail, I fooled around with heroin for another year. I liked it but I didn't have a physical habit to the point that my body really needed it. Mostly, I used it only on weekends. That type of recreational use was called "chipping." I liked the way it made me feel.

While I was in jail, I learned how to open safes so I thought I was a safecracker. I broke into some places and got caught in one of them. When the police arrived, I was stoned drunk on the floor. I wasn't using drugs that day but I was drinking. I always drank when I wasn't using. I kept going back to alcohol but my drug of choice was DRUGS in general; it didn't matter what they were. I think the main reason I got caught is that when I was drunk I did crazy things. And this time, the thing I did made a lot of noise. I had set the burglar alarm off. The police found me and took me to jail. I got three years.

I made wine in jail the whole time I was there. Homemade wine was called "jump-steady." I stayed drunk on it most of the time. Of course, I got caught. My mother tried to visit me once and was turned away because I was on 90-day lockup. I was in there for breaking the rule which forbade the possession of an alcoholic beverage in jail.

Confined to my cell on lockup, I was allowed out only once a week to take a shower. My jailers brought my food to me. They used to put it underneath the bars and kick it to me as if I was a dog; at least that's the way I felt. Sometimes I used to throw my tray and tell them to open the door to feed me. But what I wanted didn't matter - I was an inmate and they could treat me any way they wanted.

I got off lockup but hadn't learned my lesson. I went right back to making that wine and got sick from drinking so much of it. I did my time and finally got out. The first thing I did after I was released was get married.

I married for all the wrong reasons. Everybody seemed to be getting married at the time. I figured it was the thing to do so I did it too. I don't really have any other explanation for my behavior. The neat thing is that I'm still married to the same woman today after all these years!

Out of jail and married, I kept drinking very heavily and I also began fooling around with different drugs. I experimented with PCP but I didn't like that very much. I couldn't function when I was on it. I couldn't steal or do the other things I was learning how to do. Crime was a big part of my life and, as a result, I spent my entire adult life going in and out of institutions.

The next time I was caught was for breaking into a house for which I got 10 years in prison. I did almost 4 of those 10 years under the influence of all kinds of drugs. I was taking pills, barbiturates and speed. I was mixing everything with drinking. I stayed messed up.

When I got out of jail that time, I went home to my wife. She was hoping I would straighten myself out. But even though I came from a family where no one had broken the law before, I felt that God had created me to be bad. I believed that there was no way I could ever get straight, do good and stay out of prison.

The last time I was incarcerated I was sent to a mental institution for the criminally insane for about three months. That made me all the more certain that there was something fundamentally wrong with me. So when I finished my time, I went right back to the same old drugs and crime.

But this time I started fooling with cocaine. I used it for six or seven months on an almost daily basis. I liked the way it made me feel and the rush it gave me. I liked shooting that dope. Sticking something into your arm that would get you high within a couple of seconds after you pushed it in was like a fantasy. That was a lot better than waiting on alcohol. Alcohol was too slow even though I enjoyed drinking too.

I was a beer drinker when I did drink. I got drunk quite often. Almost every time I drank, I either passed out on the couch, in somebody's car or had blackouts and couldn't remember where I had been or what I had done. My whole life was just insane and I felt that there was no way out. But I didn't want to stop using because I liked what it did for me.

By now, I was also shooting anywhere from six to eight quarters of heroin every day. But I wanted to get off the heroin. I knew that it just made me do bad things. I did some boosting in the stores and other stealing to keep my drug habit going. I couldn't work. How could I hold a job? I didn't even want to *try* to work.

I talked to another addict who told me about a methadone program. He said I should try to go on it and that it would eliminate my heroin addiction. But it didn't stop my addiction. The methadone was a more potent drug than any of the heroin I'd ever been on. There was one good thing about it though. It was free. I went in every day to get my methadone. I was on 50 milligrams for about a year. I couldn't even function the first week I was on the program. I really liked that methadone high.

By this time, there were some outstanding warrants out on me for several different charges. One of them was my second DWI which had never been brought to trial. I couldn't go back to the clinic to get my methadone for fear that the police would be waiting for me. They knew I was a drug addict and that I was on methadone so I was sure they would come pick me up there. I didn't want to go back to jail again. I kept moving all around my local area, to locations within 100 miles of it and then out into the surrounding counties.

I returned home to give my wife some money and the police caught me at the house. In the past, I had been giving her $30 or $40 at a time for child support. My three children were all grown by now but I still wanted to do my part. I later realized that $30 to $40 doesn't buy much but I thought I was doing a good deed. The police just happened to come over the day I was there. They told me that they had an outstanding warrant on me and took me to the courthouse. I wound up doing 30 days on a shoplifting charge.

I also had a second DWI from another county. I was transferred there and the judge sentenced me to one year. I explained to him that this was not the first time I had been put away and that jail was not the answer. I had a problem with alcohol and drugs and I didn't know what to do about it. I said that I would like to get some help.

Even though I had realized much earlier that I was a drug addict and an alcoholic, this was the first time I really surrendered and admitted I had a problem. I had not been ready to stop because I liked the way I felt when drinking and doing drugs. I did not want to take responsibility. I didn't know what responsibility was.

The only things I did know about were the ins and outs of the institutions in which I had been placed for so much of my life. I had put guns in people's faces. I had robbed stores with a pistol. I had broken into many places. I had done insane things under the influence of drugs and alcohol.

When I told the judge that I needed help, he sent a counselor over from a drug-and-alcohol clinic in his county. The counselor told me that I certainly qualified for rehab and I definitely had some kind of problem with drugs and alcohol. He told me that if I really wanted help, it was available for me but it was up to me. The judge signed a court order and gave me a 30-day leave to go to rehab but I would still be under my year's sentence while I was there. I thank God for that program because it taught me how absolutely powerless I am over alcohol and drugs. My track record shows that my past life was absolutely unmanageable. I had been unable to stay out of jail for more than two years at a time.

I think I may have forgotten to mention that I had been in a mental institution during my first jail sentence. I was there for about 40 days and was then sent back to jail to serve out my time. So it had been noticed early on that I needed some kind of help. When I was sent to the rehab this time, I really listened. I kept an open mind about it. For the first time in my life, I was honest about being an alcoholic and a drug addict.

I found out that I would have to go to a lot of meetings when I got out of there. I was told to go to 90 meetings in 90 days, and I did that. But first, I went back and did another month in jail, the judge let me off with time served and put me on probation. I'm still on probation today. But my life is better than it has ever been because of the Fellowship, the meetings I attend and the help of the Higher Power that I choose to call God.

I'm now in contact with God as I pray on a daily basis. I try to help the newcomer and go to a lot of meetings. I have 18 months of sobriety - the best months of my life. I have started to work for myself as a painter. I get more work than I can handle. I try to do a good job, to show up on time and get the work done promptly. I am finally trying to be responsible.

My wife and I are back together again. Although we've been married 23 years, it's all really new for us right now. My wife is in the Fellowship and I love her to death. I have a better relationship with my three children and I'm communicating with them. They understand now and they are so glad that I am in the Program. They know there's an almost unbelievable change in me because I go to the meetings. It's a miracle to me too, especially when I recall that I once had no hope that a person as bad as me, a person born bad, could ever reform. But I found out that God does love me and that He doesn't make any junk.

I'm beginning to notice things that I never paid attention to before. I see flowers blooming, I notice the change in seasons, I realize that there's snow on the ground - all the things I've ignored all these years. For me, life had always been one big, gray day.

Without God's help, my way was destructive. I didn't care who I hurt, what I stole or how I acted. I would go to any length to get money for my addictions. I fed on other people and loved to manipulate them.

I am not that way now. I believe that God has a plan and that's why He spared my life. I was involved in so many situations where I should have been killed. Many times, I barely escaped being shot. In fact, I was shot once. I even shot myself on one occasion when I went to draw my pistol and hit myself in the leg. Today, such things never happen. I don't even own a pistol anymore. The only thing I like to carry is my Bible. I keep it with me and read it daily. Today, my power is God.

I attend CDA meetings now and I really like the Fellowship. I don't feel bad there as I do at some other meetings. I know that I can share about my drug addiction and alcoholism with these people and my problems don't offend anyone. CDA is a good program for me because I know that the people really love me and I surely love them. They have listened to my story and they really do care. They are interested in me.

At one time, I didn't care about you at all. I didn't care about anybody. Money was only for getting high. Now I worry about my next dollar so I can pay my bills and maybe give some of it to others to help them.

People who have more time than I, in CDA, say: "Keep coming back. It keeps getting better;" But I can't imagine that my life could be any better than it is now. Since we've been in the Program, my wife and I have gone to new places and done many new things together. We've gone horse-back riding and I've been whitewater rafting. For the first time ever, I've been to a dance while clean and sober. I have found out that I can actually dance - something I never realized before. It's really neat!

Being clean and sober is the miracle that has happened to me. But I see the same miracles happen to many other people in and out of these rooms. I thank God every day for those miracles of sobriety for myself and others.

If I can say anything to encourage anybody to try the Program, it's that CDA does work. But you've got to want it. I wanted it because I was tired of hurting. I was tired of the institutions. I was just sick and tired of being sick and tired. I decided to give the Program my best shot and I'm going to keep coming back. I hope that the newcomer does the same.

If there was hope for a hopeless case like me, there is hope for you too. My parents were once ashamed of me because I was always in trouble. I left them as soon as I turned 18 and only disgraced them more as I got older. But now, my whole family is proud of me.

I'm straight today because the Program works and because God has been on my side. He has opened a lot of doors in my life. He never left me; I left Him. Now, I just want to get closer to Him. I know that my God is a great and loving God. I just can't say enough about my Higher Power. I asked Christ to come into my life and He has. He has shown me ways to better my life but I still have a long way to go. I have many character defects but I'm working on them. Working the Steps is an important part of my program and a big part of my being where I am today. I am happy to help others because it helps me get and stay better.

I thank you all in CDA so much and, most of all, I am grateful to God for my new happiness. I'm happy to be a husband, I'm happy to be a father and I'm happy to be a child of God.

25 I Am

When I came into the doors of Chemically Dependent Anonymous, I was spiritually dead but had no desire to stay that way. I was finally ready to look inside and find the stranger I never knew. Once the fog began to lift from 11 years of drug and alcohol use, my true feelings started surfacing and they were painful. But CDA not only deals with substance abuse, it deals with these feelings too. The most important thing I did was to make a decision not to go back to the way I had been living. I knew I had that choice. I never had to go through that again. When I realized that, I felt a warmth inside for the first time in a long time.

I never thought I'd find people like myself but CDA is open to all addictive people. In my first few meetings, I saw people of all ages. And they too were looking for a better way of life. They were willing to give living a chance. Their love is what kept me alive for the first month.

Before I came to CDA, I had tried finding a higher power. I would get stoned and try meditating. But there was a fog between my Higher Power and me. Now that I am straight, I feel that power even when I'm down. It's a feeling of calmness I never got from drugs and alcohol.

I still have a strong urge to explain who I was and who I am now. But that's the old tape playing. I recognize that my past is why I'm here today. I accept that I can't change the things I did because they were meant to be. Those past events brought me down so I could look inside.

Today, at times, I feel so strange and confused. It's as if I'm meeting a new person in myself. I'm scared, happy, sad and lost. In my mind, the new person can see what the old person couldn't. It's a different entity from the old one. It's as if I'm being drained of old ways which only leave room for new ones. I know the soul remains constant but it is what I never listened to before. Now it speaks strongly (though not all the time) but my head is still trying to convince me that my soul is wrong.

All my life I searched for the truth outside of myself. Not willing to make my own decisions, I put my world into the hands of others, only to realize I was stagnating when I did so. My relationships led me to self destruction because I'd let people, places and things control my happiness. I had no foundation of self. Once I finally made a decision for myself, however, I discovered that foundation of self and it began to work for me.

Never knowing the self is a spiritual death. That realization was the turning point that brought me to CDA. Now I live my words. I stop to feel the pain because I have no choice. "Myself" has finally caught up with me. But I've found out that I'm o.k. After I go through the pain, I reach the other side which is growth. The only way to understand the mistakes I've made is to see them as part of my growth. Letting go of my past has been worth it.

My old friends and my lover are in some other place in their own journeys. Now I have true friends who go out of their way to help me love myself. I work every day to find the true self within. There are no guidelines that I use to do this other than being honest with myself. Most of all, I try to find that fine line between self-abuse and self-love.

Some days, all I can do is to say the Serenity Prayer over and over. But the most amazing thing happens when I do – the pain goes away. I know I only get what I can handle, even though I sometimes think my Higher Power might be pushing it too far. If I weren't pushed, I wouldn't grow.

I'm here to live day by day and to learn *who I am.* In doing so, I get closer to my Higher Power (who has been with me always). Now, every morning I MAKE A DECISION to work with my Higher Power. Because of CDA, I have a chance to start my life over and to become friends with my Higher Power.

I AM....

26 My Love for CDA

Since I am a garden-variety alcoholic/drug addict, Chemically Dependent Anonymous appealed to me from my first meeting seven years ago. At that time, it had been almost 11 months since my last drink or drug. I had no idea it would be my last because when I joined the Fellowship, I still had desires to use. I had been to some Alcoholics Anonymous meetings four years before when I was in an alcoholic treatment center (which was basically, a halfway house). Before that, I had been committed to various mental hospitals - the last time for almost two years.

By the end of my using, I had been drinking for 30 years and using drugs off and on for 25 years. My addiction reached its peak in the late Sixties/early Seventies. I resigned my job as an assistant VP for a large corporation in public relations & advertising to become a "beach bum" and occasional bouncer in nightclubs. I began to put anything available into my system. This resulted in what I consider to be my death. I was incarcerated on a supposed permanent basis in a state hospital. I really thought I had died and that I was in the eternal living Hell the preachers talked about.

For 23 days, I was in seclusion in a 6 by 8 foot concrete room. My clothes were removed the second day. My rubber mat disappeared on the third. I was refusing all medication and food. My attendants cooperated with my refusals and left me alone except for one elderly white-haired gentleman with a crew cut. He was the only one I wouldn't bite and hit and he brought me water often enough so I didn't die. Somewhere along the line, I started beating my head against the door and wall, knowing only that I wanted to stop thinking. Were you supposed to think when you were dead?

Five years later, I was called upon to "think" when I was offered some vodka and mixer. Although it had been about four months since I had last injected chemicals, very little thought actually went into the process. After only one drink, I was arrested six hours later and escorted to a police cruiser. During the ride to jail, my arrogance caused a police officer to strike me with a blackjack, very neatly removing my left eye.

That arrest turned out to be a tremendous benefit! From jail I was admitted to another mental hospital. I was released two months later and directed to a mental health clinic. There I met strong members of A.A. who became long-time friends. And I eventually heard of CDA, my long-sought-after, beloved fellowship.

I had a good and loving mother and father. However, as a child I showed every sign of becoming a juvenile delinquent. I loved adventure and needed to prove how tough I was. My dealings with the "Men in Blue" included shooting out street lights with a BB gun at the age of 9, and stuffing mud in the gas tanks of city buses when I was ten years old. Somehow I managed to avoid reform school.

In the 5th grade, I overreacted to the experience of moving to a smaller town. On the first day at my new school, I felt compelled to fight it out with the class leader at lunch break. Even though he had been demolishing me when a teacher broke up the fight, he announced "It's a draw" and my reputation was made.

I always knew what alcohol was. My father was a moderate drinker who imbibed only on holidays or special occasions. My mother used liquor sparingly for medicinal purposes - in a hot toddy for colds or flu. And we, like many children, were given a mild version of this remedy for the same illnesses. But neither my environment nor my genetic inheritance led to my disease of alcoholism, and certainly not to my drug addiction. Chemical dependency was, and is, all mine.

My teenage years were spent in a typical small-town middle-class environment with no great trauma or dramatic happenings. But as I examine how I reacted to the events of my life, I see the pattern that was established for my addiction to chemicals. It began when I stole my first bottle of bourbon from our basement. I spent a lot of time during puberty fantasizing in solitude in that basement. My dad who did some carpentry kept liquor locked up in one of his tool chests down there. I thought, "How could the old man miss just one?" It never occurred to me that my dad could count. As a result, no matter what else I have done in my life, I have never stolen that particular brand of bourbon again.

To my friends and me, words like "snow," "grass," "acid," "buzz" and "toot" were familiar. But they had different meanings than those I would later discover. Beer, cigarettes and corn liquor; sniffing glue, gasoline, varnish or shellac; the dizzy kick from aspirins in a soft drink were all we knew in those days. A particular addiction I had as a teenager was to laxatives. It seems that I was always constipated because I didn't want to take the time to go relieve myself. I was too busy having fun (contemplating a high; planning some destruction or a theft). Stealing was another of my addictions. I even stole coins from a wishing well that earmarked its proceeds for charity. This vice continued into adulthood where it took the form of padding expense accounts.

Childhood ended with my high school graduation. As for adulthood, where did that begin? Maybe it began with registering for the draft. Or maybe it was at 18 years old when a group of friends and I proved our manhood by guzzling a quart of beer in less than 20 seconds. With a freshly killed, beer-soaked rabbit roasting on the open flames and a supply of beer and corn liquor, we juvenile neophytes of the adult world were just having innocent fun.

Of course night hunting was illegal. Twenty-one was the legal age for drinking. Since we bought our beer across the state line along with possession of moonshine, bootlegging could have brought the revenuers down on our heads. But laughing at the law was all part of growing up! We loved drag racing and stealing watermelons too.

Being 18 also meant that if we were not going to attend college, we were expected to work on the family farm or get some other legitimate job. I compromised. Hoping to avoid being sent to the Korean conflict, I enrolled in an apprentice program for draftsmen at a shipbuilding company where aircraft carriers and other warships were being built. Unfortunately, no program such as *A.A.* was offered along with the apprenticeship. However, by this time I was really abusing alcohol. None of my friends or family members knew it. And what was even worse, neither did I.

Some of my associates from the year I spent as an apprentice provided guidance and examples that eventually played a significant role in my reentry into the world of the living as well as my successful introduction to A.A. But it is also important to recall that my parents had provided compassionate and strong training as well. They were loving but strict. My disease didn't arise out of a lack of parental love or a reckless, wild childhood unchecked by parents or teachers. My mother was herself a teacher. Helping others was important to her. Dad loved his family and all mankind. I was given a strong foundation by more people than I can count: neighbors, teachers, ministers and employers. I don't think I ever really lost that no matter what I did.

None of these people contributed to my self-inflicted corruptions. They helped give me something to return to when everything else around me had deteriorated. That is an important fact to remember. And I'm bringing it up because I want to convey this message to everyone reading this book: There is much in your life to be grateful for, just as there has been in mine.

My drafting instructor is a case in point. He was as kind and patient a person as I have ever met. Our short association has proven fruitful for me especially in these past few years of attempting sobriety. But while under his guidance, sobering up after heavy drinking was my way of life. My drinking finally got me into real trouble when I got very drunk at my high school class reunion. While trying to "get it together," I was careless and received a facial injury that resulted in a blood clot and hallucinations. My parents and my brother had to admit me to the psychiatric ward of a hospital for several weeks of shock treatments and therapy. Of course, alcohol had nothing to do with it! Afterwards, I went back to work for a few months.

But by then the Korean conflict was winding down so four of my hometown buddies and I decided to volunteer for the draft. I was assigned overseas to the U.S. Army Corps of Engineers' Stock Control Division. My job was to transfer the old wartime stock numbers to a new system, paving the way for yet-to-come computers. I also quickly mastered some other numbers such as the exchange rates on all foreign currencies and became a runner for an Army Department civilian employee who dealt primarily in currency on the Black Market. Running a PX I bought and bartered cigarettes, cameras and small appliances and increased my ability to count quickly.

I spent my earnings, both legitimate and illegal, on beer at the enlisted men's club where a buck and a quarter would buy a scrumptious steak dinner with all the trimmings including a bottle of wine. The price for alcoholic drinks was ridiculously low. Even before my overseas stint, the on-post clubs in the U.S. allowed a soldier to booze it up cheaply. During basic training and a subsequent two months of school, I drank more than I care to remember.

Drugs were also widely available both at home and abroad. During an assignment overseas, an excursion to the country's capital city led me to the streets looking for some action. It wasn't long before a young woman wearing only a raincoat offered me what I wanted. Included in the "transaction" was smoking something called the "steek." It didn't resemble any brand of cigarettes I had ever seen before. But one long drag and I knew I had found wings to fly. That was my first taste of marijuana.

Although I would not want to do it again, I wouldn't take a million dollars in exchange for my experiences of military life. The discipline, the travels and the friendships I acquired are very important to me. I and only I abused my time in the military. My superiors were trying to tell me something when I was hospitalized due to alcohol abuse. But I thought that I had just drunk too much bad wine. I celebrated my release from the hospital by marching right back to the enlisted men's club for shots of bourbon washed down with beer. No more of that rotten wine for me, at least not that night.

I managed to go AWOL several days before I was to ship out back to the States. That cost me a stripe. But before the action made it through the normal red tape, I was able to con my way through the personnel office and to an honorable discharge. That enabled me to spend six years in the inactive reserves and later to receive veteran's benefits which made it possible for me to attend college under the GI Bill.

When I got home, I had money to burn. I hung around the bars, showing up around noon or so each day. My dad gently but firmly suggested to my mom that shoving me out of the house would be a compassionate and necessary act of parenthood. Six children had been brought up within the walls of that home and all of them would make our parents proud and pleased some day one way or the other. I just took a little longer than the rest. Mom was the softy and dad the tough guy. However, my father did give me his old car when I wrecked the beautiful new car my brother and sister-in-law gave me when I came home from the War. It took all of 18 months for me to junk my second gift vehicle.

One of my brothers has always been the towering strength of our family. He was living in a neighboring state, in high-middle-class suburbia. When I said that I was going to enroll in college in that area, he and his wife offered to let me move in with them. I got a part-time job selling books door-to-door. The job was mostly a con, offering books that could have been bought at a much cheaper price at a bookstore. Next, I sought more legitimate employment in the world of finance with a loan company. After about a year, I was promoted to supervisor and sent out of state to initiate a new credit card system in 13 Southeastern states.

No one would have guessed that at the hardened bachelor age of 23 I would meet a Southern belle who would transform my life. She had everything, both physical and internal beauty. Unfortunately for her, I was a self-made rotten con artist. My alcohol intake was astronomical but I could talk almost everyone including myself into believing that it was normal. I'm sure that I didn't fool my girl though because she suggested that it might be a good idea if we both abstained from alcohol, especially since her parents had died from alcoholic complications. I agreed. No problem! I welcomed the thought of a completely new life with her.

My girl had decided that we should get married on the Fourth of July as a symbol of her independence from her wealthy, high-society grandmother. I had met my future wife in a bowling alley. She avoided questions about her background for more than a month after we met. At first I didn't want her to know that I was living at the YMCA. But she was even more fearful that her lifestyle might frighten *me* away as it had so many others. On dates, we would meet at prearranged places or she would pick me up at the "Y" in her car.

When my girl's grandmother became curious as to why she was so secretive about me, she had her ask me to dinner. Not until that night did I discover what I had let myself in for. These people were in a class I never even knew existed. I had been happy to accept the dinner invitation, excited to finally learn the truth about my girl and to shoot down the "princess" fantasy I had built up in my mind about her.

I was overwhelmed from the first moment I saw her grandmother's residence. The old lady had had my background thoroughly checked out and I was not her idea of a good catch. The evening was a nightmare. But if she thought that she could prove to my girl that I was an unacceptable choice, she was sadly mistaken. My girl wanted a more normal life and a regular guy.

After our wedding, we lived comfortably, if not very extravagantly, while I attended school. We were healthy, busy and productive for the first years of our marriage. My wife worked at her chosen profession and we were active in church and civic affairs. We participated in all sorts of volunteer work. I even gave up smoking, cigarettes included, as well as the alcohol. But I didn't attend *A.A.* despite my past record of abuse. That was for winos or those who had a real drinking problem. I know now what a mistake that was.

At the time, I still thought I was *normal.* My father had never believed in mental illness. With his philosophy of hard work, I guess it was difficult to find time to drink, be depressed, become a "schizoid" or be paranoid. Despite his example, I would somehow find the time.

When my oldest brother hanged himself in the early Sixties, it was a complete shock to my family. But my mom was able to accept it as the Lord's will. My brother had been a minister, and a good one at that. He had left a lucrative career and, after 15 years of marriage, packed up his wife and three children to take up a rural pastorate. When he left for a larger city ministry and to further pursue his studies, something went wrong. But seeing this happen didn't help to refocus my life.

I was a lay speaker in my own church and was dry and free of drugs at the time, but far from alright. For a long time, I was unable to speak of my brother's death and the problems resulting from it. His youngest son became close to me but I was incapable of showing him proof of a better way to live. His own life later became one of grief and pain because of drugs. I pray that he can find the light that I have, and that he will be able to overcome his difficulties. I am convinced that my church work was another influence that saved me and later led me to accept the help that I sorely needed.

I wish that I had been more teachable when I attended my wife's *alma mater,* twenty years ago. I managed to graduate through my usual deceptions and con games. I cheated, cut classes, and induced instant recall with the aid of Black Beauties and other little goodies of the day. I also used my office as chapter president of my business fraternity as a lever against professors and deans. It took five years, but with the additional help of the GI Bill and part-time jobs, I got my degree in business management.

After graduation, I worked in a variety of fields. But success was never in the forefront of my mind. Perhaps that was due to the realization that my wife would someday inherit a fortune. While everything appeared to be going well on the surface, our life was not really what it seemed to be. My reentry as a user had begun with an occasional beer at frat parties. I was now spending more time playing golf and drinking gin than I was at working. My wife and I had both become hooked on pills. These were not the street variety I was to sample in future years, but prescribed dope, the upper-class scourge.

During my final semester in school, my wife had had a complete nervous breakdown and had to be hospitalized. Doctors had offered little hope of a cure. I was given medical, legal, and family advice to have her declared mentally incompetent. This was in order to facilitate the settlement of her grandmother's estate, as well as for other business reasons. A lawyer was appointed to handle her affairs.

In the ensuing six months, I really went off the deep end with my carousing. I felt fully justified in doing so because of my loneliness. When my wife finally came home, we attempted to live a normal life again. Before the year was out she had left me. I then moved into my frat house on campus and became a real rogue about town. I went so far off the deep end that I was actually relieved when a year later my wife called and asked to visit my parents. She, too, was hurting. But she could admit it, and I never would. I had graduated and gotten a job so I couldn't stay with her full time but I did spend weekends with her.

On one of these weekend trips, I was offered a job in as the assistant to the vice president for a major tourist attraction. The deal included an apartment in a management-owned motel. My wife and I were offered the additional opportunity to manage it for a year, which we accepted. It was more work than we had bargained for. When my mother died later that year we moved in with my dad for awhile.

The following summer, my wife left me again and returned to her home state. I was able to keep track of her through old friends. Because of the earlier ruling on her mental competency, state law forbade divorce. Although her mental health seemed to improve she remained under a doctor's care. The laws in her state eventually changed, and a divorce decree was issued five years later. She remarried, but, sadly, eventually took her own life.

I kept my job at the tourist attraction even though my vice president was well aware that I "occasionally" drank too much. I even passed out at a travel council annual meeting at nine o'clock in the morning. I hadn't started drinking in the morning, yet; I had simply never stopped from the night before. But I convinced myself that I had just been sleepy because I didn't have any Black Beauties with me on this trip. My boss's wife convinced him that everyone drinks too much once in a while, so I was not fired. In fact, I was given even greater responsibilities.

My job was promoting the tourist attraction and the surrounding area, and much of it entailed traveling. My trips were carefully mapped out by my boss in advance. I would, however, always find some way to manage a side trip to a certain town where an old fraternity brother owned a bar. That "some way" was often by means of a feigned illness, sometimes even requiring a supposed three- or four-day hospitalization. That way I could have my fun, as well as make my calls. And, of course, the best way to entertain business people is with booze. I traveled with a well-stocked portable bar. At least seventy-five percent of its contents was for my own private consumption.

After about three years on the job, I began having "accidents" with company station wagons. I wrecked two cars in two months' time. In the first incident, I rammed three other vehicles waiting at a red light and sent several persons, myself included, to the hospital. Thanks to certain influential help, I was convicted only of failure to keep a vehicle under control and was given a $50 fine. After all, the gas pedal had "stuck" (weighed down by the heavy foot of a driver who had just finished about ten double martinis).

If only I had realized that my life was as out of control as that car had been, I might have avoided my second accident. This time, the car struck a light pole. I had been drinking just about the same amount, of the same substance. I was thrown into the mirror and windshield, receiving a major gash in the side of my head. An unknown Good Samaritan wrapped my head in a towel. Doctors later told me that person's action had kept me from bleeding to death.

But several days of hospitalization had not served as a warning about the growing severity of my disease of alcoholism. In less than two weeks, I was off and running for a winter-weekend funfest filled with eating, fishing, and boozing at the seashore. I think that this was when my dependency on alcohol really took a grave turn for the worse. My badly deteriorating brain thought about booze while I was sleeping, and, I truly believe, even when I had passed out from drinking. Thinking about liquor certainly filled my every waking moment.

My father passed away just after the new year began. And I was roaring drunk at another one of those travel council annual meetings. I was always drunk, no matter where I was or what I was doing. But my dad and I had become so much closer the last four years of his life, that I got even drunker, if possible, the night before his funeral. My sisters were understandably upset and now realized I had a problem. They waited patiently and supportively for several more years until I recognized that fact for myself and more years still until I actually started to do something about it.

The next nine months are still foggy in my memory. My character defects were in full bloom. During Easter week, I abused not only alcohol and drugs, but also many human beings. I persuaded a young woman to spend the weekend at the shore with a sick friend-me. I then conned her into flying off to an island in the Caribbean, where we joined an old fraternity brother of mine in his decadent lifestyle. My chaotic life led me steadily downhill, until I found A.A. and finally CDA.

Chemically Dependent Anonymous made no distinctions, in the recovery process, when I cried out, "But I'm twice as old as most of you;" or "I am a Buddhist, my Higher Power is called 'Gohonzon,' not God" or "I've been to meetings for years, and I can't make it;" or my last resort, "I only have one eye." You people answered "We love you," and "Keep coming back."

Yes, it took me a long time to get to the Twelve Steps, and almost as long to grasp them. With the help of my Higher Power, my sponsor, co-sponsors, spiritual advisors, and the newcomers, I'm here, one day at a time, for the rest of my life.

Now I too, can say, "I love CDA," and "We love *you*. Keep coming back!"

27 In God's Own Good Time

My name is Bobbi and I'm a grateful alcoholic. I couldn't have conceived making that statement until about seven or eight years ago. My life is wonderful today, really beyond my wildest dreams. I know none of this would be a reality without Chemically Dependent Anonymous and Alcoholics Anonymous. CDA wouldn't be part of my life had I not gone through the hell of active alcoholism.

I grew up in New England in an upper middle income family. I certainly never lacked for anything in terms of food, clothing, toys and so forth. Somehow, though, I grew up feeling I was always on the outside looking in. I felt I just didn't fit in. When I was young, my family moved frequently. One of the effects of moving was that it seemed that whenever I started to get comfortable in any place, we were up and gone again. I was always the "new kid on the block" which fueled my feeling of always being an outsider.

I believed that the best was expected of me all the time in athletics, school grades, you name it. I was pretty successful in many ways. I never stopped to take any pride in my achievements because I was off and running to the next thing. I never felt successful and I was constantly afraid of failure, but I kept that feeling to myself. Anyone from the outside would have thought that I was one of the happiest, most well-adjusted and mature kids around. I was pretty good at putting up a front.

I picked up my first drink when I was 14 years old. Normally enough, it was at a party with my boyfriend and his family was there. It was not just a bunch of kids having a rowdy time. I was given a beer and I had no idea about the effects of alcohol or what it could do to you. I'd never thought about it. So I drank the beer that was given to me. When I stood up I had the most wonderful feeling. I really thought this was liquid gold.

Looking back, I now know that I was an active alcoholic from that point on. I had just been waiting for the drink to get in me. I certainly had all the symptoms in terms of personality. From then on, I went to all the parties I could and became a weekend drinker. I drank as much as I could whenever I could.

Externally, my life continued to look pretty good. I still got straight A's in school and participated in activities. So of course nobody suspected anything, least of all me. I wound up skipping my senior year of high school and going right on to college. In retrospect, I realize this may have been ill-advised. While in college and away from family, my alcoholism progressed much more rapidly. All of a sudden I didn't have to conform to parental guidelines. I could set my own. I wasn't wild and crazy, but I wasn't an angel either.

During my first two years of college, I was a math major. By the middle of my 3rd year, I decided I didn't want to do whatever math majors did after they got out of college. As far as I could tell, that was basically confined to teaching or working in an insurance company. I decided that I wanted to be an architect. I liked the results of what architects did. I had no idea how they actually did it though. A university accepted me into their school of architecture and off I went.

I still can't fathom why they let me in. During my first semester there, I realized it was more of an artistic endeavor than I had anticipated and I absolutely didn't have that kind of talent. So, I went trotting off to the engineering school which I'd always figured I'd fall back on if things got too rough. But I had failed at something and my house of cards was beginning to wobble. One of the effects of failing in architecture was that my drinking increased. And my fears increased. Deep down inside, I knew that there was something different about me. I certainly wasn't near a point of admitting to myself that I had a problem with alcohol.

It wasn't just alcohol. I abused other chemicals from time to time. However, alcohol was my drug of choice. If you laid out every drug known to man on the table and alcohol was among them, that's what I would have gone for. I guess it's because I knew what it did. I felt I could control my intake to some extent whereas the drugs frightened me. I always had the feeling that once I put them in my body, I couldn't control where they would take me. If there was no alcohol on the table, I would have picked up something else. I think it would have been marijuana or some sort of sedative-type of drug. I know that I would have substituted something for the alcohol.

In college, my boyfriend had caught on to the fact that I had a drinking problem. I denied it up and down and made excuses all the time. One of the things that helped fool him was that he was going to school in another city so I could hide my drinking much of the time. After he realized how bad things really were, my boyfriend alerted my parents to the fact that I seemed to be drinking too much. When I went home for vacations, they began to watch their bottles and also picked up on my problem. Now, I felt that everyone was on my case and I took it very personally.

I thought that if I was an alcoholic, it was my fault and it indicated that I was very weak of character. That was totally unacceptable in my mind. On the outside, I seemed to always be the strong person. I appeared to be emotionally stable. The truth was that I was a wreck on the inside. Eventually, I got rid of the boyfriend who was on my case for my drinking. I had to in order to keep drinking!

In my last year at the university, my drinking reached a point where it was affecting my schoolwork. I could no longer study. It was also affecting me physically. I was often so sick in the morning that I literally couldn't get out of bed and face the day. I was missing classes and having to catch up with the work later.

I now had a new boyfriend, a classmate and a civil engineer like me. He and all my friends were successful, well-adjusted and stable in life--all the things I wanted to be. For reasons I still don't understand, he really loved me and tried to help me. Were it not for him, I would never have made it through my senior year of college and I would never have graduated.

Some of my professors knew I had a drinking problem but they also knew it was my final year. They just wanted to pass me on and not get involved with my problems. My grades in my senior year were down to C's. But my grade-point average had been so high up until then that I graduated *cum laude.* That's something that still looks good on my resume.

When I left college, I took a job with a consulting firm that is considered a leader in environmental engineering. Without the pressure of schoolwork and having to be someplace from 8 to 5 o'clock, my drinking took off like never before. The physical effects of the alcohol were becoming much worse. I became a binge drinker. When I got too sick, I'd dry myself out and stay straight until I felt I had it under control again. Then I'd go on another binge and once I started I couldn't stop until I was too sick to keep on drinking.

During all this time, I embarrassed myself. I became irresponsible. I couldn't follow through on all the things I wanted to do because I was physically unable. Unless I was in one of my dry periods, my free time was spent drinking. When I was in a dry period, I had to patch up my life from the binge before.

The job lasted two years and then I got fired because of "absenteeism." I don't know if anybody there really knew about my drinking. I expect a few did, but absenteeism was a good enough reason to fire me and not get involved with my alcoholism. I can't blame them.

Somehow, I got another job working for the Department of Transportation back in my home state. I moved back into my parents' house. Since I was living in their home, I couldn't drink the way I wanted to so I was always trying to find someplace else to go. Consequently, I'd wind up driving around and drinking. It is a miracle that I never got into any serious accidents and never killed myself or anyone. I did crash into objects quite a bit, though. My car looked as if it belonged in a demolition derby.

Naturally, my parents noticed that things weren't right. My whole alibi system began to fall apart. The excuses I made up began to sound wild even to me. I can imagine how they sounded to people who were looking at this more objectively and with a clearer mind.

A series of rehabs followed. I went through several rehabs for treatment of chemical dependencies (four to be exact). The first one I went to was renowned on the East Coast for its celebrity clients. My parents thought it had to be good if it attracted people with a lot of money. And I was covered by insurance if I went there. After a few days, once the alcohol was out of my system, I began to feel pretty good again as I had in all my drinking/drying periods. I also began to deny that I was an alcoholic again. Once again I told myself that the next time was going to be different. That is the insanity of this disease– that I did the same thing over and over and over and expected different results every single time. The results were always the same and always devastating.

I got out of that rehab and naturally started drinking again. Within a couple of weeks, I was right back to where I'd started. But this time I was not liking myself a whole lot because I couldn't live up to my ideal of the kind of person I wanted to be. Alcohol really had me. I just couldn't consider living without it. I couldn't imagine what I would do without alcohol. That was something that frightened me to think about–living my life without *ever drinking again.*

I was getting worse physically and mentally. My relationships were all lying in tatters: with my boyfriend (who still kept hanging around); with my parents and with the people at work. I was so ashamed about my behavior that I didn't even bother to try to get close to people. I knew I would somehow embarrass myself and hurt them. It just wasn't worth it. So I became rather isolated.

In my rural home state, female professionals were relatively few. The combination of being a professional in a male-dominated field and being an addict made me feel that I was truly unique. Hiding my addiction was paramount, so I continued to drink by myself. I'd long since stopped going to bars. There was no evidence of alcoholism around me; no one else in my family was an alcoholic. Or so I thought. Since I have been in the Program, however, I have found out that my uncle (my mother's brother) is an alcoholic. He's been recovering for the last five years. When I was younger, there was no role model of addiction for me to play to. I was the only alcoholic I knew: a pioneer–so to speak. I didn't want to be a pioneer in alcoholism. I thought that it was absolutely the worst thing that I could be.

When I was again feeling really sick, my parents convinced me to go to another rehab. This place wasn't quite as ritzy as the first one but the facilities were still pretty good. I went through the same thing again. I started feeling better and I thought that things were going to be different, this time. So I got out and within two months from the time I went in, there I was again–hurting. By this time I wasn't working. Things kept on in this vein. I went to yet another rehab. This one was a state-run facility. It was kind of nice and up in the mountains. When I started feeling good, I was able to go hiking and do some rather enjoyable things there.

I did things a little bit differently after I got out of this latest rehab. One of the biggest consulting engineering firms in northern New England had somehow gotten a hold of my name, given me a call and hired me. It was a very good job in another part of the state. I moved there and stayed sober during this period. Shortly after I found a place to live and became a little settled in my new job, I started drinking again. It was just a matter of weeks before I was even worse than before. The progression of this disease really made itself known to me and I immediately felt the physical effects. I wasn't able to get up to go to work and people at the office took notice.

For some reason, people at this particular company were a little more willing to deal with my problems. They confronted me and I was told, "We know what your problem is. You'd better straighten out or you're going to lose this job." They gave me that chance as a sort of warning shot. So I did the only thing I knew to do which was to go to another rehab. This one was located very close to the office (another state-run facility), but not at all as nice as the last one.

Right before I decided to go, I was out drinking and driving one night across the state line and got picked up for DWI. This wasn't my first such offense. It was in the middle of the night and I was far from home. The police just threw me in jail. No one cared what I said and they weren't going to call anybody. They would let me call, but who the hell would come? The only person I could think of at that point was my father. I couldn't call anyone where I was residing now. I didn't feel I knew anybody well enough to ask them for anything. I hated to phone my dad, but I did it. Of course, he wasn't going to come at one o'clock in the morning. He said that I would have to wait until the next day. So I spent the night in jail.

That was one of the most frightening experiences I have ever had. I was totally alone. I was caged like an animal, and I felt like one. The thing that I had feared the most throughout my life was now happening: I had lost my freedom. This was one reason I had always denied having a drinking problem all those years. I was so afraid that they would take all my alcohol, lock me away somewhere and throw away the key.

I think that was the beginning of the end. Right after I got out of jail, I made the decision to go into rehab. I had reached the point where I was about to lose my job if things didn't work out. My parents had cut me off. They weren't going to help me out of my scrapes anymore (something I now realize they should have done a long time before). My boyfriend had just about left me on my own. He told me that I could call him if I wanted to but he wasn't going out of his way for me anymore. He was now dating other people.

On my own now, I was alone and scared. I was full of remorse and self-loathing, and I had absolutely no self-respect. I had reached a point where I felt the only alternatives were death or getting sober. I didn't believe it was possible to stay sober. I really wanted to die but I lacked the courage to kill myself.

I went into the rehab with this attitude: If it works, fine but if it doesn't, then I *will* kill myself. I decided to turn my life over to the care of the counselors there. I surrendered; I gave up control. I knew I hadn't been doing a very good job on my own. It was with that attitude that a feeling of hope was somehow able to get through. When the counselors introduced me to Alcoholics Anonymous, I listened, and I learned. I did whatever those people told me to do because they were successful at life and I was a failure. They had what I wanted, what I had chased after my whole life, but was never able to attain. I had been miserable all this time. Now I was just surviving a day at a time. But I wasn't drinking anymore.

When I got out of the treatment program, I went back to work but I was never given a clean bill of health by the rehab people. By that, I mean that they were good enough to keep me there on a halfway-house basis. (I was the first one they allowed to do that. To my knowledge, they have never had anybody else since then on such a basis because they are an inpatient center.) I am so grateful because I know that if they had just let me go, I probably would have wound up drinking again as soon as I started feeling better as I had all the previous times. It's so easy to fool ourselves that we're cured when we feel well again. I needed a place to go home to that was clean and safe. So I lived there for three months, and I went to work every day and to meetings every night. I did what everybody told me to do. I even got a sponsor. When I was ready to move into my own apartment after about three months, I still went for weekly counseling.

One thing I've left out is that during all my drinking and up until I went into the rehab that last time, I'd always believed that I was master of my own destiny. I was an agnostic. I had never truly believed that there was a Supreme Being and all that "stuff" I'd been taught in church. I never even gave it a lot of thought. Once in the Program, with the words "Higher Power" and "God" being thrown out in every other sentence, I couldn't ignore these concepts too much longer. And so after about six months, my sponsor pointed out to me that I now had these months of sobriety (something I'd never achieved before). She asked me how I had done it. In all honesty, I knew I could not give myself credit for that; I had not done it under my own power. That was the first step in coming to believe for me.

I realize now that I had turned my will and my life over to the care of a higher power that I didn't understand and I was using the Fellowship as my "Higher Power." Since that time, my concept of a Supreme Being has developed to the point where I have a relationship with a "someone" whom I choose to call God today. And I still don't understand Him! But I pray daily and I don't think my prayers go unheard.

My life improved as I began to live in sobriety. My health improved. I acquired a sense of self-respect that kept growing. I even began to like myself. I also began to have friends, not only in the Program, but healthy relationships outside the Fellowship as well. I became very active in Alcoholics Anonymous.

But my story doesn't really end there. I still had my job with the consulting firm. After I had about four years of sobriety, we got very busy at the office which wasn't unusual. But this time, the busy period lasted about six months. I was working really hard, putting in a lot of overtime and working many weekends. I stopped going to my A.A. meetings. Although I'd missed meetings in the past, I'd never attended meetings sporadically for as long as this.

After approximately half a year, the busy period was over; the work was done. But I didn't start going back to meetings as I had always done before. And I don't know why. I guess it is easy to take sobriety for granted and to forget where our priorities are. Our first and foremost priority should be our recovery and the willingness to go to any length to keep it. Then should come everything else because without our sobriety, we can lose it all.

I gradually removed myself from the Program. At first, people from the Fellowship would ask me what I was up to and how I was doing, but they were pretty much concerned with their own lives as they should be. After a while, they just stopped bothering with me.

About three months before my 5th anniversary, I was no longer going to meetings. I took a new job, one that entailed a move to another state. So there I was again all alone. When the job didn't go as well as I had expected it to and things just weren't as hunky-dory as I wanted them to be, I did what is very natural for any alcoholic to do. I picked up a drink. Within three weeks, I returned to the point where I had left off and was going far beyond it. I was missing work. Physically, I was sick as hell. Emotionally, I was much worse. I kept thinking that I'd thrown away all that recovery time.

I'd only been on the new job a couple of months when a company in the state where I now live called and asked if I was still interested in working for them. (When applying for my current job, I had flooded the market with résumés.) I was more than happy to get out of where I was so I accepted the job offer and moved again. But I was still drinking. I was back to my old pattern of bingeing and drying out. Knowing everything I did, I still told myself all of the old excuses.

When I became established a little bit, the people at the office picked up on the fact that I might have a drinking problem. One day a woman at the office, a member of Alcoholics Anonymous in the local area, confronted me. All of my defenses came down right then and there. I knew I couldn't go on. I knew what lay ahead and that I wouldn't be able to survive it if I kept on going this way. I knew that I needed something more than just going back to the Program so I went to another rehab. And I'm glad I did.

In a lot of ways, I could easily be considered a so-called "high-bottom" drunk. But as an engineer, my chemical dependencies were highly visible. Active alcoholics are easy to spot and they are not well tolerated in my profession. My job required me to be alert all the time. I couldn't be drinking at Noon, come back to the office and get away with it. My colleagues were going to notice when I was drunk, not just because they smelled it on my breath, but because it would be apparent that I was sloppy and not on the ball.

The company I worked for, or at least the people in my branch office, were good enough to work things out for me so I could be gone for a month and not lose my job. I have to point out that my second recovery (I'd only been drinking for five months this time) was the most difficult thing I've ever done–much worse than my first. Statistically, the chances for somebody to recover a second time, after the length of sobriety I experienced, are very, very slim.

When I got to the rehab, there were wonderful people there to help me. What they pointed out was that before I could begin recovering again, I had to forgive myself. That was so difficult. I just couldn't do it. I read all the A.A. literature that was handed to me. I had already read a lot of it before but now it had new meaning. I found the words there that I needed to comfort me. It took a lot of work and most of the month I was there, but I was finally able to forgive myself.

One of the things I learned was that out of all bad can come good, if we're willing to recognize the ways to make that happen. The options and the choices are always there. It's just up to us to do something about them. Thus, my relapse became an important part of my recovery.

When in rehab, I was introduced to local chapters of both Alcoholics Anonymous and Chemically Dependent Anonymous. CDA was a group I had never heard of until then. Although I continue to go to A.A. today, I felt so comfortable with CDA that I have more or less adopted Chemically Dependent Anonymous as my home so to speak. All my close friends are in CDA and my whole social life revolves around that fellowship. I not only get what I need but what I want from their program.

Shortly after I became involved in CDA, I met my future husband. We were married three years ago and my life today really is beyond my wildest expectations. I have a wonderful job (a new one) and my career is going well. My relationships with my family couldn't be better. I have a new family, my husband's, which is now mine, as well. I have so many things to be grateful for, so many blessings. My new life is a real gift from God.

Today, my priorities are in order. Today, my recovery comes first–above my husband, above everything else–because without sobriety, all of this would be gone. I've already proven that to myself once. When I look back on my relapse, now, I see it as a blessing. I guess I needed that and I believe God knew that I would somehow survive it. Since choices are ours to make, He knew that if I wanted to, I would make it through.

I can't think of any way I could improve my life as it is now. It's not that I don't have problems. Of course, there are problems. But the point is that now I am *living* life on life's own terms. I'm dealing with my problems and I'm walking through them. I'm also dealing with the good times and walking through those.

Everything passes, everything changes, and it's just a question of taking it a day at a time. We plan for the future only in such a way that we have direction, some sort of path to follow today. If we do our best today, we'll have a good tomorrow. I know that because it's been happening for me day after day after day.

What I've learned through all that's happened to me is that if I'm not spiritually fulfilled, I won't be happy. If I'm not continuously paying attention to my spiritual health and trying to further develop my relationship with God, all the material things in the world aren't going to matter. I have material things and they improve the physical quality of my life, but they certainly aren't the basis for my life. Without my relationship with my God, I wouldn't have the contentment that I always feel, the deep-down faith that no matter what, everything's going to be all right. I have peace of mind and that's what I never had before. I never dreamed I would ever achieve it. That's what I'm truly grateful for today.

28 Love Set Me Free

I had seen drugs around my neighborhood for a couple of years, but I was nearly 11 years old when drugs first began to interest me. I saw big-shot guys around town smoking dope, laughing and having a good time, and I wanted to do that too. I tried to talk them into giving me some dope but none of them would. After a while though, they finally decided to let me try it.

They let me smoke pot and drink wine. It got to the point where it was a little entertaining for them. When I'd get high, I'd play around and make a fool of myself. But I was having fun, and I liked that and the attention. I started smoking pot and hash and I would do just about anything to look cool. I wanted to be someone who was looked up to by other people as being cool.

As a kid, I always did badly in school. My goals were not to be a straight-A student or to be a very successful businessman and get rich. I was the class clown. I liked getting into trouble and being a smart aleck. When I found drugs and the world that drug people are involved in, I said, "Man, this is it!" There are a lot of people who say they didn't want to become addicts and they didn't want everything that went with the drug scene. But once I got into that world, it was exactly what I wanted – to get loaded every day. I thought I was going to make my money selling drugs and become a big-time dealer. I thought I would have sailboats and houses around the world–all the dreams that don't really come true.

I lived in a place where there was a variety of drugs to be had so I started to use different types. Within a very short while (by the time I was about 12 years old), I began taking pills. I was snorting heroin by the time I was 13 years old. Within three years, I had used all the drugs I knew about.

I found certain drugs that I liked more than others. I knew right from the beginning that narcotics were very addictive and I didn't want to get hooked. I wanted drugs that I could have fun with and I had fun alright. My addiction lasted for sixteen years and for the first ten years of it, I had great times. Of course, there were some bad experiences. But, all in all, it was good and I loved it. I thought of those years as a happy and successful part of my life.

It was a long time before my problems started but once they did, they lasted for years. I lost my wife. She left me over my insanity with drugs, crime and association with crazy people. I didn't think it was a big deal. When she left, it hurt but I accepted such things as just part of life.

I never thought of myself as a criminal even though everything I did was illegal. I wasn't wrong; the laws were. I wasn't out there robbing stores and doing things like that. But I was involved in drug deals and guns were a part of my life. I began to get arrested for stupid things and I accepted that. It was the way I chose to live.

It wasn't until I was about 20 years old that everything in my life seemed to fall apart. I had a lot of very close friends who loved and cared about me. They began to look down on me. Every time I was around them they would lecture me, saying, "You're ruining your life. You can't use those types of drugs. Why don't you just smoke pot do a little coke and drink? You've got to leave narcotics alone." But I had fallen in love with heroin—it was my drug of choice.

I left the West Coast and moved east. I didn't find the drugs as good on the East Coast. I didn't like the heroin but was introduced to a lovely pill called Dilaudid. I fell in love with it.

Since I didn't know all the right people or have the connections to get the money and the types of drugs I liked, I started committing bigger crimes. I carried out armed robberies and burglaries. Then I realized that the best way to get big money and lots of drugs was to rob dealers. So that's how I made my living. Ripping off dealers was easy because they didn't dare to call the cops. Some people got shot, but I didn't care. I was at the point where I didn't care if I lived or died so I didn't care if anyone else died either. I felt nothing. All I wanted to do was get loaded. I was depressed most of the time and I used to think, "I wish it would just all end."

By the next year, I was in the hospital. That wasn't the first time, but it was one of the times when things started to work. I was sent to detox and then to rehab where I learned about the Program of Alcoholics Anonymous. I went to lots of meetings. I liked them and I liked the people. When I'd hear them talking about looking into medicine cabinets for drugs at parties, I knew exactly what they meant. But I thought I was worse than they were. My self-esteem was so low. I was sure that if everyone knew what I was like and what I had done, they wouldn't want me there. So, I went back out and I used for three more years.

In those three years, I went places emotionally that I had never been before. The darkness and the depression were constantly with me. I was a blackout user. I would go for days without knowing what had happened. I was no longer just using recreationally. I was a daily maintenance user. I would wake up in the morning and shoot dope so I wouldn't go into withdrawal. Steadily throughout the day, that's all I would do. I worked off and on but nothing in my life mattered. Eventually, I went into three more hospitals and detox units.

There was a pattern to my relapse behavior. Each time, I was told that I would never make it because I was unable to be honest with myself. The terrible thing was that I knew they were right. Coming in and out of the Program for about five years, I began to learn some things. I started to pick up values and I began to feel worse about myself.

I was strung out badly, I was physically shaky and I was having persistent convulsions. I couldn't even get loaded. No matter how much I'd shoot, I would either pass out or still be in withdrawal. I hated it so I checked myself into another hospital. I thought, "This is it. I don't like this anymore. It's no fun." I went through detox. Halfway through, I started to feel again. I came to and began to realize what was going on. I was filled with fear. I thought I would have to live without drugs from then on and I was afraid I couldn't do it. Because I felt I was such a failure, I thought I might be the type of person who couldn't make it without them.

When I got out of the hospital, I went to a rehab. But I was soon thrown out of there because I wasn't cooperative. I could talk one-on-one with the counselor about my pain but when I was around other people my ego wouldn't let that happen. I couldn't let anyone else know how badly I hurt. So, I started using again and I used for four months.

It was the worst it had ever been. I didn't shoot dope for the first three-and-a-half months. All I did was drink and smoke pot every day. I became a blackout drinker. I would black out in the mornings and come to the next day. Then I'd drink and black out, again.

For the first time in my life, I began to think about killing myself. I was so miserable. I was not afraid to die. I was afraid to be alive. Somehow, I was able to start going back to meetings. I knew everything about the Program–I'd been going for so many years. But this time I went in with the attitude "If my life doesn't get better in a year, I'm going to kill myself because I *cannot live* like this any longer. "

That was eight years ago. I haven't picked up a drug or a drink since then. That's a miracle. What worked is that I tried to listen to what people told me. I knew all the Steps and I knew all the clichés. I knew everything about the Program *except* how to do it. I looked back over all the years of going in and out of the Program and knew I had to do something different or it wouldn't work this time either.

I started meeting some people and because I was at such a terrible point in my life, I decided, "What the hell. I'd better trust these people." Learning to trust *anybody* was very hard. I went to meetings every day. I got a sponsor and hung out with people after the meetings.

But, I didn't want to do those things, and I didn't like the people. Everyone was always so happy and positive. I thought if they knew how awful I felt, and how much I hurt, they wouldn't be in there laughing. Of course, I wasn't going to tell them that. I couldn't admit to them that I was in pain, because I didn't know them. It seems so stupid, but I believed that these people would recognize me as the failure I believed I was if I let them know where I was coming from.

I didn't talk at the meetings for the first four months that I was in the Program. I couldn't bring myself to open my mouth because I was afraid of what I might say and I didn't want to humiliate myself. But I would talk afterwards. My sponsor and Jack, another member, would talk to me for long periods of time after the meetings and they taught me how to have fun. Jack openly spoke about a higher power, and he made it easy for me to learn to start praying and begin working the Steps.

I got another sponsor after four months and I went to his house every day. We would talk for hours and hours. I got rid of some of the nonsense and a lot of the fears that I had bottled up. I learned to become comfortable with myself. I started living for today instead of in the past.

After I was in A.A. for about six months, Chemically Dependent Anonymous was started and I got involved in the Program. I started by making coffee and I felt responsible for that duty. As I saw that I was doing my job well, I came to realize that this was the first time I had ever done anything well. My sponsor and I continued to talk about working the Steps.

In the beginning, I was told that the Steps *are* the Program and that the only way I was going to get better was by following them. Everything I had to do was completely against the way I had always lived. I didn't like doing most of it but found out that when I did what CDA said to do, things were a little bit easier. I didn't get a job for the first year or so, partly because I was too burnt out to think, but mostly out of laziness. I had a lot of time on my hands. So if there were three meetings a day, I'd go to three meetings.

When I did start to work, it was with my sponsor. He taught me that it was o.k. to screw up in the job I was doing. He used to tell me, "That's why they make erasers on pencils." What he did for me and for my program was to give me permission to make mistakes. I had been so terrified of doing things wrong that I often wound up not doing anything. Now I could start accepting the fact that I am human. Therefore, I will, at times, be less than perfect.

When I came into the Program everything began to get better. The relationship I had been involved in took a long time to turn into a healthy one. I had been told in rehab that if the girl I lived with and I wanted to stay together we were both going to need luck. I now know why they said that. It is much harder for two addicts to try to recover together than it is for each of them to try to do it alone. But for some reason, it has worked out for us.

The turning points in my program came when I got backed up against the wall. I'd hurt so badly that I would be willing to work the next Step. I did my 4th and 5th Steps when I had about eight months in the Fellowship. The Steps allowed me to let go of my past and stop living in it. They gave me time in the present without the drugs, alcohol and crazy behavior to look back at the eight months and say, "Well, I haven't done all those things in eight months. I'm just not that same person."

They also let me go on. Instead of basing all my decisions on my sick past, I began to make decisions about myself and my life according to my life in the present. I started to build a pathway of program action and that opened up the world for me. My first couple of years was hard and painful, but the joy I got out of them was well worth it.

After a year or so, everything stopped being *new:* The first time I went to the dance without drugs, the first time I went to the job without using. All these "firsts" were old hat now. The excitement had worn off. I had to start looking at just living one day at a time. Going through the Steps though caused most of my fears to ease, and I did begin to live.

I no longer looked to other people for my standards for growth. I looked at myself and saw that I was O.K. I had come a long way! I had been taught not to judge my insides by other people's outsides. And the true miracle that happened in my life was that I had really tried to work the Program this time. Even though I had gone back out so many times before, I was now clean and sober.

Going forward and working the Steps opened up all the doors. I started to let go of my character defects, something that was very difficult for me. Each evening I began to look over my day to see if there were things that

I had done wrong. I tentatively made conscious contact with my God. When I first came into the Program, I believed in anything. After a long time, my definition or concept became more particular. I found more faith and that faith kept me going.

Slowly, I started to feel more a part of the world. When I first came into CDA, I was told that it had taken me 16 years to get there so I wasn't going to be able to change overnight. I accepted that from the first day. It also helped me not to have expectations of having this after one year or that after three years and something else after five years. I didn't go by such guidelines. If I had, I would probably have gone crazy and gotten loaded.

Instead, I went to the meetings, worked the Steps and lived one day at a time. Just give me one day, and I could succeed. I did the very best I could, but some days that meant just staying in bed–not getting out, but also not getting loaded. And some days that meant going out there in the world and doing everything I could to live normally.

I came into the Program unfeeling and uncaring. Today, I have all the feelings any other person has. I care about people. I have learned how to love people. I've even learned to like them. That is one of the greatest gifts I have received. My life has changed completely since I started working the Steps. People in the Fellowship told me that happiness comes from within and it is from within that I am happy now. I have a successful life, but my happiness is where my true success lies.

CDA has given me many other great gifts in my life. When I first heard the saying, "With responsibility comes freedom," I thought, "I don't want to be responsible. Freedom is in my backpack." However, I have found that freedom does come with the responsibility that I accept. I am employed now and I'm responsible for my job. I go to work even though I don't *like* to work. I like *going* to work because the things that I get from working *are working for me*. And the job gives me the opportunity to do other things that I like to do.

I've got a commitment in life not only to the Program, but also to my wife. We've been married for five years (and have been living together for seven). That's a real commitment, one that gives me freedom to love. I don't have any of the bad feelings I had with all my other past relationships because I know that this time I am being true.

My wife and I have bought a house. It's not a house at the beach or a mansion. It's just a little place but it is ours, and it's not going to be taken away because of the next drug deal I blow. I'm living a life I never thought possible and I owe all of that to the Program.

I believe that my Higher Power put the people of CDA in my life. I'm very grateful for them. They have helped make me into someone I never thought I could be. I owe God and them everything. I have to have people in my life, and that's great. I used to think that not needing anyone was the way to be. Today, I know better. The people I sponsor give me so much too. To be able to watch them change and grow is a truly wonderful gift. The miracle is that I haven't had to have a fix, a pill or a drink for six-and-a-half years. I couldn't have done that alone. I just did my part by doing a little bit of the footwork. The Program and the people of the Fellowship are responsible for the rest.

Anybody who wants this program can have it. It states: "If you want what we have, here it is—just take these simple Steps. And one day at a time, your life will change."

CDA saved my life. It can save yours, too.

29 Miserable Mike

    The story begins in the Midwest. My Mother was a Lutheran and my Father was a Catholic. The move to Dad's home down South was short-lived. Mom became unhappy and left my father. She then took custody of her son (me), returned to the Midwest and remarried.
    My entire family and most of our friends drank on a daily basis. Some of us drank more heavily than others and, as a result, had to pay the consequences. My stepfather died from an alcohol-induced seizure in the late Sixties when he was only 39 years old. A brother-in-law got so depressed while drinking that he blew his brains out onto the living room floor one evening, much to the horror of his wife and two young children. An aunt drank until she passed out in the bathroom one afternoon, never to regain consciousness. My stepbrother partied so hard that he overdosed and died when he was just 18 years old. Both my stepsisters still like to drink socially and are married to men who use chemicals in order to function on a regular basis. By the age of 36, I was suicidal, wondering why I had to endure the pain of this life twice as long as my little brother, and knowing that I could not survive as long as my stepfather had.
    I remember being melancholy as a child. I didn't like attending the Lutheran grammar school. The teachers said that I had the intellectual potential but that I just would not apply myself. Maybe that had something to do with my stepfather. He was a bartender who was absent from home much of the time. Or maybe it was due to the

fact that we had a well-stocked bar at home. As the oldest child, I was responsible for acting as the family bartender. I could make all the house-favorite cocktails by the time I was 8 years old. I had to attend summer school more than once because of my bad grades. As a cute little kid, I sometimes drank until I passed out. And sometimes I awoke in my own vomit.

Things began to change when, due to financial pressures, I had to attend a public high school. Now I had peers who liked to drink and smoke. I got my first pair of contact lenses, shed my thick glasses and discovered girls. I played football and loved the hard physical contact at the defensive position of middle linebacker. It seemed as though I had died and been reborn. I was enjoying life. I seemed to be so much more capable of doing things. I was even studying. In fact, I graduated as a member of the National Honor Society. But as my drinking increased, my blackouts were not all at home anymore and my driving record proved it.

After graduation, I got a job working for a large corporation as a computer operator/programmer and it was here that I met the young lady I was to marry within a few years. Her family lived on the other side of town but they loved to drink as much as I did. All our dating and social engagements revolved around alcohol.

Somehow it was decided that I should resume my education and, the following year, I enrolled in a Christian university. Of course, I pledged the fraternity that had a beer machine hidden in the basement. College football was intimidating because it seemed as if everybody but me had put on about a 100 pounds. But unfortunately, sports had now started to interfere with my partying. Disciplinary problems ensued and I was asked to leave school during my sophomore year.

When I joined the Army near the end of the Sixties, it seemed to be a big mistake. I didn't like the barracks life with the guys so I married right after basic training. Eventually, I secured a position as a computer programmer, and everything seemed fine until my wife (who must have gotten tired of living with my self-centeredness) began to have affairs. I believe now that she was merely seeking the love and attention that a practicing alcoholic cannot give. But at the time, I just consoled myself by drinking more heavily.

I received orders for Vietnam but was instead diverted, purely by chance, to duty in a state far to the north. My wife and I tried to make the relationship work again, but neither of us had changed and her affairs continued. Flying was now my big love and I received my private pilot's license. I began to experiment with marijuana socially at this time since it was legal in that state.

I was given an honorable discharge from the Army after two years and returned to college. But my finances dwindled until I was forced to seek employment. Now living out West, I had a real "Catch-22" experience. I found that I couldn't get a position in the computer field without a degree and that I couldn't get a degree without a decent job. The Air Force Bootstrap Program appealed to me, so I was off to the West Coast where I majored in psychology, visited the local wineries and cultivated my own herb.

After completing my bachelor's degree requirements, as a distinguished graduate from the School of Military Sciences, I was commissioned as an officer. Neither my wife nor I appreciated my assignment back East. Since she had continued to seek love outside of the marriage relationship, it was decided that she should stay behind and seek a legal separation.

My next relationship lasted approximately five years, during which time I drank daily and smoked grass on occasion. I carried the scars of my broken marriage and I found that, besides not being able to love, I was now unable even to trust. So I began cheating in order to keep from being hurt again. I enjoyed the status of being an officer and, during this time, I returned to college and took some undergraduate pre-med courses. At the age of 27, I was too old to be accepted by a medical school so I completed a master's degree in business management and supervision. It was really an extension of my psychology degree in counseling but I just couldn't see working with a clientele of emotionally disturbed people every day.

One dreary morning, I returned home to find my girlfriend in bed with my best friend (a fellow officer). Of course, I reacted immaturely and, as a direct result, both my best friend and I were subsequently released from active duty and honorably discharged. Somehow, the Air Force decided that our using marijuana constituted conduct unbecoming of officers and that our behavior was not that of gentlemen. My sick relationship with the woman was renewed however and continued until she again had an affair. This time, it was with my *new* best friend. She eventually married him.

On my own, with no woman to give me any heartache, was how I started my career as a federal employee. I was still in the computer field and I was determined to work hard and play hard. I was finished with formal education for a while, but I became an avid student in the field of parapsychology. I bought my first house. I had been addicted to running so I was in relatively good health. Now I added weight training in order to become more *macho.*

It was while working a part-time job with a company running weekend ski trips that I was introduced to cocaine. Initially, it was used as just a stimulant to allow me to party all Friday night, ski all day Saturday, party all Saturday night again, ski all day Sunday and then keep awake for the drive home Sunday evening. I enjoyed this drug so much that my next part-time job was that of a nightclub bouncer. The fringe benefits included free drinks, better coke and exposure to opiated hash, mushrooms, PCP, barbiturates and other drugs as well as lots of fun-loving women.

Although my absenteeism from my government job increased and my ability to function as a computer specialist was becoming more and more impaired, my capacity to fabricate stories grew to meet my needs. It was at this time that I was introduced to freebasing cocaine and I fell so much in love with this new high that I became a dysfunctional addict. It wasn't long before I experienced every symptom of mental illness that I had studied in abnormal psychology: schizophrenic paranoia with full-blown audio-visual hallucinations, the overdoses, the sweats, the shakes and, finally, the deep suicidal depression and complete inability to cope.

My roommates feared that they might be in danger so they volunteered me for treatment on an outpatient basis. I was able to quit freebasing, but I continued to drink and use coke and other chemicals daily for another year. My last weekend binge six years ago started at an office picnic. I knew I had a problem but I was still trying to find out how I could drink socially. I figured one hot dog or hamburger per beer would be a safe ratio. But after the first beer, I was unable to stop. And eventually I had to score some coke too. The usual blackout ensued and when I came to on Sunday, I did a line of coke and began to cry.

This was the first time that coke had let me down and I was embarrassed because there were people around. I dropped back to "old reliable" and drank a fifth of l00-proof vodka straight down, but that alone didn't help. Next, I grabbed a quart of rum, downed it and faded into oblivion. When I was revived, I found myself wrapped up in my own vomit and bleeding from both ends. I showered and went to work, came home and vowed not to drink again. The

D.T.'s were very bad Monday night and I found no rest amid all the horror of the hallucinations. I returned to work the next day only to have a mental breakdown. I finally sought medical help in a hospital with a detox ward and this is where God introduced me to Alcoholics Anonymous.

My only prayer up to this time had gone like this: "Look God, if you don't allow me to quit hurting so bad, I'm just going to kill myself and you're going to lose one of your little experiments down here." I guess this concept of God was left over from my parapsychology days. But now, in A.A., I was being told that I no longer had to drink or use drugs, that there was a program designed to show me how to live a better life and that I didn't have to die. I wept. It was too good to be true.

I went manic-depressive in detox and was sedated with antidepressants for two weeks. After release, I was too depressed to return to work but I started attending local A.A. meetings. There I was told about another fellowship for people who used drugs as well as alcohol and I started attending Chemically Dependent Anonymous. I went to one of their meetings at a local rehabilitation center and apparently was still in bad enough shape after 30 days clean and sober that they admitted me for 28 days of inpatient treatment. There, I received the tools necessary for success in my recovery.

I learned that I needed to get down on my knees every morning and ask God to remove the compulsion to drink and use drugs. I was told to return again on my knees at night to thank God for another day clean and sober. The medical aspects of what I had done to myself, the valuable lessons on the importance of fellowship, keeping honest, open-minded and willing to try, along with the Twelve Steps were slowly absorbed as I began to work the Program.

After returning to work, I found that I had changed one addiction for a much healthier one and I began to attend meetings as if my life depended on them. I was allowed to go to lunchtime meetings. With the one or two meetings I also went to each evening during my first 90 days, I managed to make it to about 200 meetings. The emotional high I was on is called a "pink-cloud" and I enjoyed it until an incapacitating depression brought me once again to my knees around six months into the Program. I just could not stop crying so I called work and explained my embarrassing condition. Then I sought medical assistance.

The empathic physician who patiently listened to my predicament said, "You're just lazy and what you need is a good swift kick in the ass." To this kindly statement I replied, "But I'm going to die." He referred me to a psychiatrist who also listened patiently (for $100 an hour) and explained to me that I was having a normal reaction. I had lost my best friend and lifelong companion, Alcohol, who had always been there to help me celebrate or consoled me when I was down.

I was just undergoing a mourning process and, once it was over, I would be a lot stronger psychologically. Once again, I stated, "I'm going to die." But he said he couldn't help me or give me anything to ease my pain because I was an addict.

Just about ready to give up and take my own life, I stopped in at a meeting place. One of the guys there came to my assistance and told me that this sort of depression sometimes occurred as part of a protracted withdrawal as was explained in *Under the Influence* by James R. Milam, Ph.D. and Katherine Ketcham. This volume showed pictures of healthy blood samples and compared them to the alcoholic's microscopic electron views with the organelles and mitochondria all blown apart and oozing their life-sustaining properties. In the sequel,

Eating Right to Live Sober by Katherine Ketcham and L. Ann Mueller, M.D., it was shown that a nutritional approach of eliminating caffeine, nicotine, sugar and red meats was indicated for recovery.

Being compulsive, I eliminated even the legal stimulants from my diet. I went so far as to fast regularly and eat nothing but organically grown fresh, raw fruits and vegetables for a period of one year. After dropping from 185 pounds to 125 (with my friends fearing I had contracted either cancer or AIDS), I added whole grains and occasionally some meats to my diet. I then regained a healthier 150 pound average weight for one who is my height.

During this time, I had what I choose to call my "spiritual awakening." While attending a seminar on the Book of Revelation in the Holy Bible, I accepted Jesus Christ as my personal higher power. My first year of sobriety was filled with some 600 meetings, three spiritual retreats and one baptism. The sponsor I've had ever since I first went into treatment was a real blessing through all of this. He listened to my crying and, although he had never personally gone through the deep depression I was experiencing, he encouraged me to stick with not picking up, to continue to attend the meetings and to keep on praying. Seeking his approval, I told him that I had answered an altar call and was going to be baptized. He confided in me that he had already done the same thing and said that it was o.k.

Having God in my life is not a universal panacea, but it does provide me with strength to carry on with the help of the Fellowship. God works through people. But even though life in recovery is a series of relationships with other men and women, sometimes there are heartaches that only God can heal. Some of your buddies or members of your family won't get the Program and they can end up in jails, institutions or even the grave. An intimate relationship breaks up and you can't use to relieve the pain, as you used to do.

There can be other heartaches too. After buying that new house and a new car and after years of being clean and sober, you lose the job you've had for 10 years and your confidence is shot. It's not always easy to remember that the Lord gives but that He also takes away, that all things work together for the good for those who love the Lord and are called according to His purpose. Thank God there is the Program and the words of encouragement that are found in the Holy Bible.

The opportunities I have for growth are always there as long as I continue to show up and reach out to help someone else. It might be through sponsorship, speaking on radio talk shows, doing TV commercials, leading Bible studies, sharing in meetings, listening to a troubled friend or sending cards and letters to loved ones. Faith without works is dead.

Working the Steps to the best of my ability is a major challenge. A crying man wrapped in his own vomit and blood knows that his life is unmanageable, but I had harbored such resentment against God that coming to believe that He had my best interests at heart was extremely difficult. Taking a personal inventory was something I had never done before and I was afraid that I would not like what I was going to find out, let alone be able to share it with another human being. I still struggle with character defects but, today, I ask God for help in eliminating the ones He points out.

Personally making amends to people wasn't easy either. But even though they didn't always accept me or my apologies, I felt better for having tried. I remember in particular making amends to my beloved grandfather. When I blurted out that I hadn't visited him for a few years because I was too embarrassed about my alcoholism and my drug addiction he said, "It's been more like five years and, even then, it wasn't any fun to have you around." But on my next visit when he saw that I was still sober, he was so impressed that he took me around to his friends and showed me off. Continuing to take a personal inventory and admitting my wrongs allows me the opportunity to grow spiritually.

In making decisions, I use the 3rd and 11th Steps, trying to seek God's way, praying that He will close the doors where He would not have me enter in and open those doors where He wants me to proceed. To me, prayer means talking to God. And meditation means that I have to listen (at meetings, in Bible studies or in church) and that I have to keep an open mind as to what God's will is for me each day.

A.A.'s *Dr. Bob and the Good Oldtimers* has shown me where the Twelve Steps came from and the importance of studying the Bible and applying what I learn to my daily life. The slogan "First Things First" refers to seeking first the kingdom of God and His righteousness, after which all other things shall be gathered unto you. And "One Day at a Time" means that we are not to worry about tomorrow for today has troubles enough of its own.

Today finds me between relationships, unemployed and melancholy from time to time. But I am strong in my faith that God can still use this beaten-up, tired shell of a man to help someone else in recovery, to be of service to someone in need, to encourage the less fortunate or to pray for a brother's salvation. I enjoy reading the Scriptures and sharing the light that I find, so much so that I've applied to a small Christian Bible college to study pastoral counseling. I'm not sure where tomorrow may find me, but I'm sure that God will be with me and with anyone in CDA who is looking for Him, always, even until the end.

30 A Sixties Idealist

During the Sixties, like many drug-experimenting members of my generation, I believed that taking psychedelics and smoking pot were positive, beneficial things to do. I thought that if the whole country would "turn on, tune in, and drop out," America and the whole world would be a better place in which to live. In my mind, my drug taking was connected with being for the civil rights movement, civil liberties and environmental protection and also being against war, racism and classism. Most of the people who were part of the counterculture in that era also smoked marijuana.

Therefore, it was very difficult later in the Eighties to admit that I had become an addict. To make the admission and acknowledge that marijuana was addicting seemed also to mean that I had sold out all my values and that I was renouncing my ideals and politics at the same time. Fortunately, attaining sobriety, which was the most difficult thing I have ever done in my life, did not require that I become a conservative.

I was born on a farm. I received a nurturing and stable upbringing from my liberal parents. They inculcated in me the idea that when the government or any authority wrongly interfered in my right to privacy, it was my duty as an American to oppose them provided that my opposition was peaceable and within the system.

In college in the late Fifties, I was introduced to marijuana which was very rarely used on campuses at the time. In my sophomore year, I was also given pure

Sandoz LSD once. The drug was still legal at the time and had not yet received attention from the press. The acid trip (and the state of consciousness which I experienced during the trip) was the most significant thing that had ever happened to me. After this experience, I found that I was able to understand certain mystical poetry and philosophical writings which had previously been incomprehensible to me. I was also able to appreciate modern art for the first time. This led me to believe that the path to greater intuitive insight as well as wisdom and spiritual enlightenment lay in experimenting further with psychedelics and in finding other psychedelic devotees.

So, two years later when I graduated from college, I headed for the West Coast city known as the world capital for such experimentation. My most hopeful expectations were fulfilled when I had a spiritual experience while under the influence of a psychedelic. During this epiphany, I felt a union with the One and completely understood the first chapter of the Gospel according to St. John.

After that revelation my life seemed changed as it is when a person has a religious conversion except that I wasn't converted to any specific belief system. I just felt at peace with the Universe as if my own individual wants and needs were not so important and everything was o.k. I thought, "God's in His Heaven and all's well with the world." I stopped doing psychedelics after about 10 or 12 trips because I ceased to have new experiences or breakthroughs and I thought that was what these chemicals were for. They did not seem to be the types of drugs one would want to get high on.

I went to law school and became a lawyer and did very well. Not only was I successful financially, but I was able to become involved in various types of "movement" cases that would allow me to attack and help change the system. I smoked marijuana and believed that it helped me to be creative. Often, I edited things I wrote when I was high on marijuana. Although I drank heavily off and on, I considered marijuana my drug of choice. I considered myself a "head" not a "juicer." Because I believed strongly that more widespread use of marijuana would help society, I actively and publicly worked to repeal laws prohibiting *Cannabis sativa.*

In the middle Seventies following the breakup of my marriage, I began to drink in the morning and this really alarmed me. I went to see a highly regarded psychiatrist and told him I was afraid I was becoming an alcoholic. He said, "No, you just have a lot of anxiety and you are self-medicating. If you come to therapy and get to the root of your problem, your anxieties will diminish and you will not need to drink so much."

While in therapy with this doctor, my drinking and marijuana use increased. I would get up at 6 a.m. feeling acutely suicidal and would often cry out, "I want to die." Then I would have two martinis, followed that by smoking a joint and, by 10 a.m. after a couple more martinis, I'd go to work. If I had to go to court, I would refrain from smoking the joint.

After two years of therapy, my psychiatrist started showing up late for my appointments and then began not showing up at all. I got very depressed and concluded that psychiatry was a sham and that my real problem was America and practicing law. So I closed down my practice and went to the Far East for 18 months. There, I stopped drinking in the morning, stopped smoking grass every day, and stopped feeling depressed and suicidal.

When I moved back to the United States, I decided the answer to my alcohol and drug problem was to get out of the fast lane, mellow out, live on less money and work fewer hours. I thought that with a smaller amount of stress, I would not abuse alcohol and drugs. But even though I wasn't working and was leading a very laid-back lifestyle, as soon as I came back to America I again began drinking compulsively beginning in the morning.

I went to a couple of Alcoholics Anonymous meetings and identified and bonded with my brother-and-sister alcoholics right off. But I didn't like the fact that the A.A. Program involved total abstinence. I walked out of my first meeting chuckling to myself, "Of course they can solve their alcohol problems if they don't drink anything at all." It seemed much too simplistic a solution. "A well-rounded individual must drink," I thought, "and I would be a failure at life if I admitted I couldn't handle booze and recreational drugs." There must be a therapist or therapeutic method which would help me get myself together so I could drink as I had in the good old days of my late twenties and early thirties.

While I was searching around for a solution which would not require abstinence, I met and fell in love with a beautiful young lover who thought everything I did was just great. This person was especially impressed with my debauchery. My lover regarded this as some sort of achievement. Being involved in this affair and traveling around the country reenacting Hunter S. Thompson's *Fear and Loathing in Las Vegas* kept me from feeling I had a problem for a year. But when the affair broke up, I found myself staying high on pot continuously. So, back I went to the therapists.

I even paid a nice sum of money to go to a six-week workshop which promised to teach people how to smoke marijuana moderately. Until that time, I hadn't known other people who felt they were addicted to marijuana. At the workshop, I met some people including other professionals who like me, were still "functioning" and practicing their vocations. I was particularly startled to meet a psychotherapist who was a pothead and who went to her sessions while she was high. The workshop used behaviorist methods to cut down, set goals and so on. I found I could cut back and control my marijuana use but when I did, my alcohol consumption shot up. Although a local newspaper article touted the workshop and the psychologists who ran it as being 90% successful, my research on the people in my group revealed that several months afterwards they were all smoking as much, if not more, than they had before the workshop.

I continued to drink more and more until finally, after a ten-day binge, I went to two A.A. meetings and stopped drinking for thirteen months. I didn't continue to go to A.A. during that time because I felt I didn't really need it and I found it too corny. What would my sophisticated friends think if they knew I was getting together with a group of losers at life, holding hands and saying the Lord's Prayer?

Although I used no alcohol, I continued to use marijuana. I attempted to control my use of grass in various ways. I would only buy nickel bags or joints and I'd have a friend hold my marijuana for several days so I could get clean temporarily. Rarely did I get really stoned on pot and seldom did I smoke more than one or two joints a day. I smoked just enough to get high and stay high with a mild buzz. Of course, as throughout my life, every so often I would take coke, MDA, opium or hashish when they were offered in social settings. But I seldom bought or used them by myself.

Being off the alcohol completely, I became very healthy physically and I looked great. I ate health food and did yoga. But I was increasingly panicky and anxiety-ridden. It was a big effort for me to do any work or to do anything except party and have sex. I did less and less legal work and made less and less money. Increasingly, I felt estranged from people and alienated from society. More and more, I became depressed and I realized I didn't really care about anyone or anything except, "What is wrong with me?" I was concerned only with whatever therapy, therapist, religion, lover, sex practice, career change or new political cause could provide the answer to that question.

I felt like a fraud as a human being. When I told people I loved them, I suspected I was lying. When they told me they loved me, I thought something was wrong with them. I thought that they must have some grave, sick dependency if they could care about me or that they must have some hustle going. To bolster my eroding self-esteem, I sought to encourage people to think that I was the answer to their problems, the fulfillment of their fantasies. But if my self-promotion efforts were successful, I would feel trapped by the very demands that I had worked to arouse.

Also, I no longer had any real interest in participating in political causes or professional associations. I felt society's institutions were hopelessly corrupt and decadent and there was no way I could relate to any of them. Secretly, I believed a nuclear war might not be so bad after all.

After thirteen months I started drinking again. I thought that drinking would be preferable to using marijuana all the time because I might be able to work better on booze. Using marijuana was inconsistent with trying to make a living at doing "left-brain" type mental work. Even if I didn't use every day, I knew that there was a fuzzy-brain aftermath for several days afterwards. Never did the idea that I could or should come off all mood-changing and mind-altering chemicals occur to me. Instead it was a question of which ones or what combination to discontinue.

I began to drink and use grass as well as coke and speed for four months in an increasingly compulsive manner. In complete despair, I decided I must stop everything. I realized that whatever joyful, enlightening function alcohol and marijuana might have played in my life earlier I was now using drugs and alcohol solely for escape and avoidance of reality. I no longer thought it to be mind-expanding or beneficial in any way.

So to start, I came off the alcohol. I knew I could stop the alcohol use because I had done it before. I could not imagine how I'd ever be able to stop using marijuana. I didn't know anyone who was in Narcotics Anonymous nor did I know anything about that program. But five days after I stopped drinking, out of desperation I called N.A. (Chemically Dependent Anonymous was not in the city where I started to get clean and sober.) I asked the person on the phone, "Do you take people who only have a problem with marijuana?"

I was embarrassed to ask this because I felt ashamed that I was addicted to such a mild drug. I thought that if I was going to have a drug habit, I ought to be using something like heroin or cocaine. But to be addicted to pot was ludicrous. The person on the telephone said, "Yes," and I went to my first meeting seven years ago. I have been clean and sober ever since.

Well, actually, I did have three or four Dalmanes after that meeting. I had persuaded a doctor to write a prescription for 100 of them for me before I stopped using. I couldn't imagine how I was going to sleep if I gave up both marijuana and alcohol. When I mentioned to my first temporary sponsor that I had some Dalmane in case I couldn't sleep, she informed me, "In 'the Program,' we don't do any drugs at all." I asked, "But how will I sleep?" and she said, "You may not sleep for a while, but eventually you will."

This advice at first seemed dogmatic and fanatical, since I had never had a problem with prescription drugs, even though I had taken them off and on to ease off of alcohol and street drugs. Furthermore, I had proved (so I thought) that I was not generally an addict since I could take or leave cocaine, barbiturates and even opiates. So some wimpy, boring drug like Dalmane certainly wasn't going to get its hooks into me. But I decided to do it the way "the Program" suggested and I got rid of all my sleeping pills and tranquilizers. I have not used any drugs since that time.

I announced myself as a "marijuana addict" in my first meeting. After the meeting, a young man told me that he had had the same problem. He said he had never seemed to get addicted to the stronger drugs even though he had used them off and on. He figured he couldn't have an "addict personality" or he would have become addicted to the so-called addictive drugs. He asked, "Who can be addicted to marijuana?" He too reported that he'd spent a lot of time and money on therapists because he seemed to lack the motivation and ability to get his life together and to use his creative potential. Finally, it dawned on him that his marijuana use might be "The Problem."

So, that night I had another spiritual experience, a blinding revolutionary insight: *My* "Problem" was caused by my use of drugs! Before that, I had thought that my compulsive drug use was a result of my screwed-up psychological state and that if I got cured psychologically; my drug, work and motivation problems would all be solved. But I had it backward. So long as I kept using, I would have work problems, anxiety and feelings of alienation from people and society.

The first priority was to stop using all drugs and alcohol. And I knew that there was a power in the room, a force tapped by a group of addicts with a common desire to stop using. While I had not been able to stop by myself, with the power that was accessible through the group I would never have to use again. I was free.

As the sedatives, marijuana and alcohol gradually left my system, I experienced a succession of anxiety attacks and rages. These emotions had been there all along, but my "self-medication" had prevented me from feeling them. While the cravings for drugs and alcohol were lifted from the very beginning, I felt I was on the verge of insanity most of the time for well over six months. But the people in "the Program," by now CDA, kept assuring me that my reactions and anxieties were not atypical and that I could survive it all, clean and sober, one day at a time.

The anxiety provided a great incentive to do the Steps and gain some insight into why I was so upset. I would then be able to change some of the maladaptive patterns which had resulted in putting myself in no-win, stress-producing situations. A lot of my anxiety centered around my fear that I was permanently brain-damaged because I found that I couldn't concentrate. I was afraid I would end up having to give up my profession and take a menial job for the rest of my life.

When the anxiety became so great I decided, "To Hell with it all! How do I know that it is not best in the total scheme of things to be poor and brain-damaged?" My anxiety did subside and my concentration improved. Eventually, after several years my full mental capacity returned. As long as I was so attached to my intellectual ability, I was prevented from using it. Before I could use it again, I had to "let go" and put it in its proper perspective.

CDA has allowed me to live the life I had always wanted to live and to relate to people the way I had aspired to do when I was a flower child and peacenik. I now have a set of guidelines to live by: the Steps. They are nothing more than a compendium of principles found in many religions, philosophies and psychologies from both East and West. They are not a mere gimmick that some self-help book writer has just discovered. I also have a group of people who are attempting to practice the same guidelines for life who I can talk to, be with, and turn to when I feel overwhelmed. By working with others, especially newcomers, I am relieved of the hell of self-preoccupation.

I feel that I initially turned to drugs because I wanted a fuller, richer, more deeply-conscious life. Perhaps, in the beginning, drugs do open the doors to perception. But as I increasingly used them for escape, my life became narrower, poorer and less conscious. When I became addicted, no amount of personal effort or self-discipline, no new religion, therapy, or lover was able to remove my craving and compulsion. Since coming to CDA (and the other Twelve-step programs) and working the Steps, my desire to use any mood-changing or mind-altering chemical has left me. I hope that someone may read this story and see that there is a way to freedom from slavery to chemicals in this Program.

31 Evening the Odds

My story is just like a lot of others. I never had any intention of growing up to be a drug addict and an alcoholic. It just seemed to happen that way.

When I was 15, I took my first drink. Not long after that, I got drunk for the first time when three friends and I got hold of two fifths of wine. We had drunk about half a bottle when one of the kids bet me that I couldn't finish the rest of that bottle and drink another one. That was a 75¢ bet, and I won it. As a result, my first experience with alcohol was that I had a total blackout. I got sick, vomited and woke up the next morning with a hangover. That should have told me something, but the next weekend I got drunk again. This time the effects weren't quite so bad. I actually enjoyed drinking. This was the way I started off my career of chemical dependency.

During high school, I was an athlete. I played varsity sports, track and football. I didn't abuse alcohol full time, but every weekend I would go out drinking and would always get drunk. Everyone I ran around with did the same thing. We were wild and crazy and had a lot of fun. From the very beginning, the only thing I associated with drinking was getting stoned. Alcohol allowed me to do all the things I couldn't do or didn't want to do when I was straight.

At the end of my senior year, I thought I was going to get a football scholarship to a small university in the South. The recruiter came to my house and talked to my parents but my academic record just didn't cut the mustard. The following Fall, I received my draft notice to report for a physical and I was classified I-A. Two months later, I received another notice to report to the Army.

The Army is where I found drugs. I was introduced to people who had been doing drugs since they were 13 years old. I was 19 when I entered the service and had never even seen any drugs before. I learned about marijuana, speed, rug cleaners and cough syrup and I immediately became an abuser. I decided that I wanted to live my life using drugs as often as I could. I heard Timothy Leary say, "Turn on and drop out," and I was very ready to do that. The only problem was that I was in the Army and I couldn't drop out.

I was discharged two years later after almost getting busted for possession. I decided that I was going to live my life exactly the way I wanted to. I was going to do whatever I wanted and whenever I wanted to do it. I was going to have fun and do everything in a different way than my parents had.

I had a girlfriend back home who I kept in touch with while I was in the service. We decided to move into an apartment together. I enrolled in college, with the GI Bill paying my tuition. She was a school teacher and had a steady job. I supplemented my GI Bill money and supported myself by dealing marijuana.

I grew my hair long and did everything hippies did back then. I got high, went to concerts, demonstrations and parties. I had a great time. I even went to Woodstock, which was a fantastic experience. I tripped the entire time I was there on acid, mescaline, Dolophine and any other drug I could get.

Basically, I was tripping all the time. After Woodstock, I went back to school. I got through college only because a good friend of mine supplied me with speed. I took it not only for exams, but just to be able to go to class. And, of course, I was smoking grass too. It's a miracle that I managed to graduate.

After college, I found a job in sales which turned out to be my lifelong profession. A friend my age owned a silk-screening t-shirt factory and he offered me a job selling the shirts. Everybody who worked at the factory was also young and we all got stoned.

My job was to call on head shops, surf shops, and department stores. The majority of our shirts were drug paraphernalia lines in a wide variety of designs. They appealed primarily to people who were users. This was when customized, silk-screened t-shirts were becoming popular for advertising and bar owners ordered them to promote their establishments. Most of the customers I called on were also getting loaded.

Shortly after I was hired, we had the first boutique show in New York. We had just set up an elaborate display when my sales manager pulled out a bag of pharmaceutical Black Beauties and gave them to everybody. I was even more certain that I had found the perfect job.

My alcoholism started to take shape too. I had become friends with some of the bar owners and managers I did business with. I would go in high on speed and they would give me free drinks. I wound up in the bar drinking the entire day and not making any sales calls. It progressed to where I was doing this on a daily basis. Sometimes I wouldn't leave until eleven o'clock at night. I would call my girlfriend and tell her I wouldn't be home for dinner. As a result, after almost nine years of living together, we broke up. I felt that this was the best thing that could have happened to me.

My addiction was really on a downhill course. I was getting DWIs. I started losing things (like my relationship with this girl). I wasn't feeling too good about myself either. I quit the job selling t-shirts and sold drugs for a few months while I was unemployed.

I finally got a really good job selling ladies' sportswear. A head shop owner I did business with introduced me to another drug addict who hired me. He couldn't cover his whole territory and was still making $100,000 a year. The potential was there for me to make a lot of money by helping him. All I had to do was take samples to stores and show them five times a year. But I couldn't do it.

By this time, I had been introduced to cocaine and when I was on the road, I was also doing barbiturates and Quaaludes. My routine was to take about an ounce of coke with me and some speed. I would get a motel room, go to a liquor store and buy a fifth of liquor, go back to the room and start making my calls. After a couple of trips, I no longer made the calls. I would just sit in the motel room and get strung out from all the drinking and drugs.

Needless to say, that job didn't last very long. I found myself unemployed, broke and addicted. I decided I would just deal drugs for a while until I found something else, but I wasn't a very good dealer either. It seemed that everybody was willing to front me the drugs. But I would use them myself and then have a very hard time trying to pay back the people who fronted me the dope. It got to the point where I owed thousands of dollars to my drug dealers and they refused to give me any more.

I was still in the bars everyday acting like a big shot and pretending I had money. I cashed checks at the bars for $10 and $15 wondering where I was going to get the money to cover the checks. I borrowed from everybody I could think of, from my friends to my mother, until nobody would lend me any more money. I was living with two practicing drug-and-alcohol addicts. We were renting a house together. I was even writing bad checks to one of them to pay my rent.

Then one of my roommates decided that he was going to leave the country and, since the lease was in his name, the rest of us had to find another place to live. I kept putting it off, but finally a guy who frequented one of the bars I hung out in said that I could move in with him. Although I felt the move would be good for me because I would be away from my former roommates, it proved to be the beginning of my bottom.

I had found another sales job but everything else was getting worse. I became more and more paranoid. I experienced more despair than I had ever known before. Yet at no time did I associate those feelings with drug and alcohol abuse. I was not ready to quit yet.

Then something happened. My former roommate and best friend, Ronnie, was someone I'd always compared myself to, but only to the extent that if I ever got as bad as he was, I might think about doing something about it myself. He was a *real* drug addict. He hadn't worked in about a year and he had become totally unemployable (except for selling and manufacturing PCP). He was doing every kind of drug imaginable. He was the person I got many of my drugs from and then, all of a sudden, he decided to quit using drugs and alcohol. He joined a Program called Alcoholics Anonymous.

And here he was staying straight! He would tell me about A.A. and how he hadn't done any chemicals for two weeks, a month, two months, three months. He started calling me all the time to tell me what was happening with his life and I saw a miraculous change take place in him. I truly believe that there are miracles in these Programs. But sometimes you have to experience them in order to start believing.

For me, it had to be the combination of hitting my own bottom and seeing this miracle happen to my friend Ronnie. In a three month period, I saw him completely change from a nonfunctional person barley able to talk to someone who began to look better and sound really good. He actually got a job and was working, something I had never thought he'd be able to do. Ronnie was the one who took me to my first meeting.

At that meeting, I was given a copy of the Big Book of Alcoholics Anonymous and I was told to keep coming back. I took the book home but I didn't even open it up. I just put it in a closet somewhere and forgot about it for a couple of months.

In those months, my life got worse and I started experiencing physical as well as emotional problems. For the first time in my life, all the drugs I was doing started affecting my body. I began having mini-convulsions but I didn't know what was causing them. My emotional state was really bad. I was experiencing more and more despair and paranoia. So I decided maybe I should do something about myself.

My friend Ronnie said "Well, o.k. You don't have to go to meetings or anything. But I'll bet you that you can't beat this on your own." That was just what I wanted to hear. I had been brought up to believe that if you put your mind to it, you could do anything you really wanted to. "And I've got plenty of willpower," I thought to myself. It was a perfect opportunity to show him and myself that if I wanted to do something about my problem, I could.

So I took the bet. It was for $50 (a lot of money at that time) and I was thinking, "If I don't win this bet, I don't know where I'm going to get the money to pay him." I locked myself in my room and just didn't go anywhere. Those 30 days were the hardest I've ever gone through in my entire life. But I won the bet! I went 30 days without taking a drink or any drugs.

I was very uncomfortable without those chemicals though—one mean, miserable person. So after I won the bet, I went out to a bar and drank six or seven vodka gimlets straight down. Then my roommate came in with a sheet of LSD and gave me a hit of that. I remember staying in that bar until it closed. I had a pretty good time– that night.

  That bet played a very significant part in my recovery, because it showed me the difference between drying out by simply not using and becoming sober through working the Program. However, that was something I would not recognize until later on when I had experienced true sobriety. I wasn't ready to quit for good yet, even though I'd been able to do it on my own and win the bet. I went right back to where I had started and continued to use on a daily basis, getting loaded to the max. I didn't hit any gigantic bottoms. I didn't get busted and go to jail or anything like that.

  Something did happen that brought me up short though. My best friend since childhood had spent quite some time traveling and I had not seen him for 6 or 7 years. He got back in town, called me up and suggested we get together. So, we went out to a bar and both got drunk. Then we got into an argument. I had been so glad to see him after such a long time and here we were arguing. I can't even recall what the disagreement was about. But he said something to me that really caused me to hit my emotional bottom that night. "You know something?" he told me. "You think you're better than everybody else."

  That proved to be my moment of truth. I had never thought I was better than anybody else. I didn't think I was as good. But I had always presented an image that I was o.k. I think the big lie of my addiction had finally caught up with me. I had been using the chemicals to change my mood and to make me believe that I felt great when I actually didn't. My friend's words now made me realize that I needed those drugs to get up, to talk, to do so many things. That hadn't changed since the first time I had used them. But they were not working anymore.

I felt that maybe there was a better way of living. I thought of Ronnie, of the changes that had taken place in him and I said to myself "Well maybe I'll give this Program thing a try. Maybe I can get my act together. Then we'll see what happens from there." I still hadn't made any real decision to quit my drug use, but I had at least made a decision to try.

I let Ronnie take me to some meetings where he introduced me to different people. I started listening to what they said. We had a mutual friend who had come into A.A. the year before and there was a miraculous change in him too. He and Ronnie reinforced what I was hearing about the need to get a home group so I picked a meeting not too far from where I was living and signed up to be on their home group list.

That was one of the most important things I did in my early recovery: I made a commitment. The people in the group gave me the job of cleaning up after the meetings–emptying ashtrays and coffee cups, things like that. I had to be there every week to do my job. That's how I began to get into the routine of attending meetings. In my home group, I started meeting people and was soon venturing out to other meetings in my area. I met young people, with lifestyles just like mine who had experienced many of the same things. I found myself relating to them. I didn't just listen however. I went home and found that A.A. Big Book I had thrown in the closet and started reading it. For the first time in my life, I began to understand the concept that alcoholism and drug addiction were diseases.

The Fellowship is what really put me on the road to recovery. The people who reached out and helped me, especially those in my home group, made me feel so comfortable. I began to realize so many things. First of all, I had to share what I felt with other human beings, something completely contrary to what I had been taught. I was one of those people who kept everything inside and never shared anything with anybody. But the Program said that I would have to let people know me in order to recover.

I first started letting people know me in my home group. I started to talk about feelings because that's what I heard other people talking about and that's what I related to. I can remember going home from those first meetings after having heard things that just turned a light bulb on in my brain and saying, "Boy, I feel the same way." And that was how recovery started for me. I found people who were happy and content with smiles on their faces. And I said, "I want that too."

But there were a lot of obstacles, both within me and in front of me, if I wanted to continue in A.A. I had so many reservations. I could not comprehend how I would ever be able to abstain from using drugs and alcohol for the rest of my life. How could I have fun without drugs? How could I go to work? How could I be in any kind of a relationship? I had been using drugs and alcohol since I was 15 years old, just so I could do all of these things. Now I was being told that I had to give up my crutch.

I discovered that you only have to do it one day at a time. That was the most important thing I ever learned because that made it all possible. Everything else (working, having fun) I could find out about later. But that "one day at a time" was the beginning of my recovery. It gave me the means intellectually to make it. I knew I could go one day at a time without using.

The next thing that really perplexed me was the concept of God in these twelve-step Programs. I had rejected God at the age of about 16 because of the influence of my alcoholic older brother. He explained to me one day that there wasn't any God. I immediately latched onto that point of view. It appealed to me because of the injustices I saw in the world and because of the strictness of my Catholic upbringing. Not believing allowed me to be free of guilt; if I didn't believe, then everything I did was o.k. My life and what I made of it depended on me. I was in control. It was up to me to decide for myself.

I really had a hard time coming into the Program when I found out that God was mentioned in the Steps and all throughout the literature. When the group said the Lord's Prayer at the end of the first meeting I attended, I couldn't even remember the words. I cringed when I thought about the very idea of God. Then I heard somebody say that you can believe in the God of your understanding. That means that He doesn't have to be the God that you were brought up with. He can be whatever you want Him to be.

Looking at it that way made it so much easier for me to find the God of my understanding. At first, I used the group because that was a power greater than me and I saw how God worked within it. Then I found the Serenity Prayer. Finding out how effective it could be was another great influence in my recovery.

My earlier physical problems caused by taking too many drugs had included over-amping: when I took too much speed and cocaine, I would often get so high that my heart would jump out of my chest. The only way I could bring myself down in a hurry was to drink or take a barbiturate.

When I was about three months into the Program, I had a similar reaction despite the fact that I was no longer drinking or drugging. I was driving on a major highway and I had to pull over to the side of the road. I later discovered that I had suffered an anxiety attack. This is what it is called when it happens to someone who is straight.

While I was hyperventilating, I said, "Well, I can't go to the liquor store and I don't have any drugs." Then I remembered the Serenity Prayer. I said it over and over. In about ten minutes, the attack went away and I felt normal again. That was the first time in my entire life that I had used a prayer and found that it actually changed my mood, just as the chemicals had done in the past. A very important part of finding my Higher Power was the realization that prayer worked. Through further investigation and reading A.A.'s *Came to Believe* and a few other similar books, I found a power, a God of my understanding, which I still use today.

Another of the stumbling blocks I had to overcome was that old question about how I was going to be able to function without drugs and alcohol. I had invested some time in the Program and was beginning to wonder about such things. After about six months, that question was answered when the compulsion to use finally left me. I realized that I could do what I needed to do. I could go to work, have relationships and even live with myself without the chemicals. It was a tremendous breakthrough, one I had never thought possible.

About 10 months into the Program, though, everything came crashing down on me. I had been working the first three Steps, and I now faced the Fourth, or inventory, Step. I had looked at it when I first came into A.A. and it really scared me. But I knew that I had to get honest with myself. I had to look at and find out more about who I really was. I had been avoiding that introspection for so long. I had been putting up walls my entire life, refusing to face the real me. One day, I woke up feeling as bad physically and emotionally as I ever had when I was using. It was then that I finally came to the conclusion that I desperately needed to do my Fourth Step.

I went to my sponsor and told him how I was feeling. He agreed that it was time for me to do my Fourth Step. I always did whatever my sponsors told me to do. At first, I didn't know how to go about it. I went to my sponsor's house for a couple of hours one night and he explained the various methods recommended in Program literature, for working this Step. He suggested I read the A.A. Big

Book, the A.A. *Twelve Steps and Twelve Traditions* or the Hazelden *Guide to the Fourth Step Inventory.* I decided that I was going to do it all three ways. I wanted to make sure I did a thorough inventory.

The first time I sat down to do my Fourth Step, I began to lie to myself on the paper especially when it came to fears and resentments. After a half-hour or so, I put the pen down and thought to myself, "This is really ridiculous. Here I am trying to do this Step and I'm lying, instead of trying to help myself." I tore up that sheet of paper and said, "I don't care how painful this is. I'm going to write and be honest and fearless."

I started writing the truth and even though I was uncomfortable, it was the most valuable thing I have ever done. For the first time in my life, I looked inside and put what I found on paper. It took me two months to complete my Fourth Step and I covered about 12 yellow, legal-sized pages. I did the entire Hazelden guide as well. I really reached down and did the best job I could.

I called my sponsor after I had completed my inventory and he asked me to come right over to do the Fifth Step. His house was on a military base. It was a spring evening. While I was driving there I saw kids playing tennis and softball, all sorts of people having a good time. I thought, 'I'm going to have to tell this person things I've never told anyone in my entire life." I was really scared about it. But people in A.A. had told me that this Step (admitting my faults to God, myself and another human being) would set me free and that is what I wanted.

When I reached my sponsor's house, we got into his car and drove out to a lake on the base to be alone together outdoors. All of a sudden, it got really cloudy and the wind started blowing. Then it started raining and the temperature dropped. So I had to do my Fifth Step in the car. It took about three hours from beginning to end. And when I was finished, it felt like a great weight had been lifted from my shoulders.

All the fear and anxiety I had anticipated were unfounded. I had trusted my sponsor. He had shared his experiences with me. A wonderful feeling of fellowship had developed between us. After I completed my Fifth Step, my sponsor told me to go home to a quiet place and meditate on what we had just done. By then, it was getting quite late, so I went home and did exactly what he had said to do, and then I fell asleep.

That was the most restful night I had ever had in my life. When I woke up the next morning, it was as if a whole new world had opened up to me. I had now become a part of this Program of recovery. I felt that I finally fit in and that I had really done something important towards changing my life. Since that day, my life has gotten nothing but better.

I continued working the rest of the Steps and got very involved in a newly-established fellowship, Chemically Dependent Anonymous. I became committed to service work, did twelve-step work, took meetings to hospitals and institutions, became part of Intergroup and took on all sorts of responsibilities. I was willing to be the secretary at meetings and do anything I could, because I realized that you do have to give it away in order to keep this Program.

Today, I still make it a habit to do whatever I have to do to grow in my Program. I sponsor many people. I go to retreats. I even do things that I don't want to do. And that seems to be what makes it work.

Since the time I came in the Program for help with nothing but misery, despair and fear, my life has turned 180 degrees. I have everything I need now and almost everything I want. I have peace of mind. I have love. I care about all of *you*. And it's all a result of working this twelve-step Program called Chemically Dependent Anonymous. When I came in, I was told, "This is not a

Program for people who need it. It's a Program for people who want it." That is so true. I really believe that anyone who wants it can get what I have received from CDA.

If I want to continue to grow, get closer to my Higher Power and maintain some semblance of the serenity that I have experienced so far, I have to keep wanting it too. Just because I've been clean and sober for awhile, I can't expect to live happily ever after by simply not doing what I did before I came into the Program. That is not enough. I know that the addict in me will always be too strong for that. If I stop going to meetings, stop praying, stop helping others and stop reaching out and sharing with others about myself, I'm going to revert back to that miserable, fearful person I was before I came into the Fellowship of CDA. I don't want to go back. I'm not taking chances with the life I have today.

32 Happiness Too Is Inevitable

As far back as I can remember, I always looked for a way to avoid the reality of living in the present moment. Life was scary and unpredictable and there was nothing solid to hang on to or believe in. I was a great dreamer as a child and I would fantasize for hours about being in a different family or a different city, looking prettier and being anyone other than the person I was. I thought that there was something wrong with me and that I was not a worthy person.

Our house was not a happy one. There was constant fighting and tension in our family. My mother would close the windows so the neighbors wouldn't hear what went on behind the normal-looking façade of our family. I often felt that I was the cause of my parents' unhappiness and that they therefore could not love me. I stayed awake many nights thinking of running away so the pain would stop.

Growing up continued to be difficult, particularly in school where I was picked on and frequently rejected. I thought that if I weren't so skinny or ugly, I would be accepted and I would feel normal. I turned the hurt and anger from these experiences onto myself. Believing that I wasn't "as good as" other people and that I was unlovable, I began to hate myself for what I saw as my fault. That feeling became ingrained in my mind and I carried it with me into adulthood.

For some reason, I was ashamed to communicate my sense of rejection to my parents. The few times I did talk about it didn't bring me the support and reassurance that I needed to overcome my burden. I began to hide my feelings and eventually to deny them. I'm not blaming my upbringing or my childhood for being the reasons for my addiction. However, those experiences do explain the insecurity, the low self-esteem and the desire to escape reality that led to my later problems with drugs.

Around the age of 11 when I began junior high school, I started to develop problems falling asleep at night and staying asleep. I was hanging around with a crowd of people who were, like me, a little bit different; people I thought would accept me. I became what they call in the Program a total people pleaser. To speak my true feelings or to confront anyone when I didn't like something they said or did was a struggle for me. I wondered if life was painful like this for other people, but was too ashamed to ask anyone else.

When I was around 14, my parents sent me to the first in a long line of psychiatrists to be treated for insomnia and depression. The only thing I remember of my relationship with this first doctor is that I was given sleeping pills. I loved the way they changed how I felt and I began to stay up and nod out instead of sleeping. I found that I could manipulate the doctor to get more and I quickly built up a tolerance. It became a pattern—going to doctors and getting pills.

My father was a pharmacist so if I needed additional pills (and I always did), I could call him and he would bring them home for me. Our relationship became centered on the drugs, but we pretended that everything was normal—the typical denial of the disease. Today, I believe that he enabled me by giving me pills out of fear that I would get drugs from someplace more dangerous. It was not because he didn't love me. My addiction had now become a "family disease."

When I was 16, I finally began to attract the opposite sex. However, I didn't' date then, (or for many years) for fear of getting close and letting someone get to know me. That developed into another pattern of not letting anyone get too near or of ending a relationship as soon as I felt exposed and vulnerable to pain.

Fearful and depressed, the only thing that got me through this time was knowing that I would soon graduate from high school. I was going to college where I could further my love of both writing and photography by majoring in journalism. I was always waiting for something to change my life and I thought that once I got away from home, everything would be all right. Never once did it enter my mind that I was addicted to pills in any *negative* way. They were medicine, something to help me sleep. The pills dulled the edges of reality so well that I started to feel that this was how life was supposed to be.

College wasn't what I had hoped it would be. I was very unhappy there. I felt I was an imposter amidst the human race. Drugs became even more important to me because I now had to hide from the shame of not being (or so it seemed) accepted again. At that time, drugs on campus were not as popular as alcohol. I lived in a dorm so I had to hide my drugs. I smoked a lot of pot and I took large quantities of sleeping pills. I also started taking Valium on a daily basis. I experienced hangovers in the morning and I lost my concentration. I walked stiffly and slowly. My reflexes were off.

I went home on vacation one semester and it became evident that I had a serious problem when I couldn't wake up one morning. I was in such bad shape that my sister and my mother became hysterical trying to get me up. They called the psychiatrist and he had them pour coffee into me and walk me around the bedroom until I was finally alert. It was a very bad experience for all of us. The family could no longer deny my drug abuse.

Unfortunately, this experience frightened them a lot more than it frightened me because I wasn't awake for their ordeal. At first, they thought that I had tried to commit suicide. I assured them I hadn't and that was the truth—then. I had just forgotten how many pills I had taken, another pattern that would become more dangerous as I began drinking along with the pills.

When I came home from college the next summer, my life and my addiction took a turn for the worse. A friend and I went to the beach to get summer jobs. I held my job for a couple of weeks but I was getting too high to keep it so I quit. I began to meet people who were using narcotics and, for the duration of the summer, I did nothing but fire or snort dope and nod out completely unaware of what was going on.

My parents attempted to intervene. They knew that I was using drugs from the way I talked on the phone. One weekend, my roommate and I had a surprise visit from our mothers. They pleaded with us to come back home, but I wouldn't go. Rebellious as ever, I stayed the summer to finish out my rampage of drugging.

When I returned home, I discovered a crowd of people who liked to get down. We all became addicted to cough syrup and Doriden sleeping pills and we would drive to a nearby city every day to cop cases of syrup. At the time, all you had to do was sign a book and you could get quite a few bottles. You could also go to some doctors there and get prescriptions for Dolophine very cheaply. Just "living for the high" became a way of life. Nothing else existed. But something was still wrong inside. The only time I felt o.k. was when I was high. And even then I wasn't happy. I just didn't feel pain.

Not long after I had a serious car accident caused by my drug use I went into my first mental institution. My psychiatrist, who believed my depression was too severe for him to treat, sent me there. He was not then completely aware of the severity of my drug problem. I was almost eager to go because I felt so suicidal.

However, the hospital, like my psychiatrist, never addressed the problem of addiction. They just gave me more drugs to fight my depression.

Eight months later, I left the hospital as depressed as the day I had walked in. I had no idea how I was going to live out the rest of my life. I came home and tried to do all the right things, but I had no fervor for life. The only thing I looked forward to was the temporary escape that drug use afforded me. What followed, until the time I finally came into the Program, was a series of jobs, attempts to finish college, different apartments, many psychiatrists, a hypnotist, two more mental institutions, many failed relationships, all adding up to a dreadfully lonely existence. I had become someone I hated so much that I didn't want to live.

When I was 26 years old, my father died after a long illness. That was a very significant event in my life as it was also the beginning of the end of my addiction. I had very mixed feelings about my father's death. I was grief-stricken but there was also a sense of relief, not only because he had been so ill but because I felt that the chain of my dependence on him had now been broken. As long as Dad was alive, he had picked up the pieces of my life even though he knew he couldn't put them back together. Scared and depressed, I needed the drugs more than ever.

Later that year, I got a job as a technician in a pharmacy the worst place I could have been. I stole drugs and was totally out of control. One of the employees started to suspect me and I knew it was only a matter of time before I was caught. I quit the job shortly thereafter with a sense of relief. The amount of drugs I was taking had begun to frighten even me.

After leaving that job, I went to work in the mental health field in a day-care center. Many of my so-called "normal" friends were also employed there. I was able to maintain this job for a few years even though I was still getting high. I rationalized that now was my chance to have a normal life.

Of course, it didn't work. I found it harder and harder to get to work in the morning. The hangovers were just incredible. It was as though I were sleepwalking. My supervisor, a very kind woman, found it difficult to confront me about these situations. Once again, I was able to get away with addictive behavior and keep my job.

When I eventually left this job, I took another one to see if that would fix me. I was even more miserable. I would go to a bar after work or sometimes I would take home a bottle and drink, take more pills and smoke some pot alone. Many nights, I would fall down in the apartment and wake up later with bruises.

Then the drugs and alcohol stopped working. The feelings of pain just wouldn't evaporate whether I was high or not. I had reached my bottom. I finally realized that nothing was going to change or improve until I *stopped*. I just wanted that whole cycle of addiction to end.

After years of steady addiction, I knew that I would need to be hospitalized in order to get clean. I had never been detoxified before, and I was terrified by the prospect. But the fear of continuing to live the way I had been was greater than my fear of withdrawal. And so for the first time in my life, I reached out for help.

I called a local drug agency, but there wasn't much aid available locally. Thirty-day Programs did not yet exist in my area so the only alternative was a long-term, out-of-state Program somewhere else. I knew that the farther from home I went, the better my chance of recovery. I called the contact given to me and went to detox just a few weeks later.

As soon as I saw the detox unit, I wanted to leave. It was such a depressing place. But there was nowhere else to go. The first 10 days went smoothly. It seemed all too easy. I wondered why I had put this off so long. And then in the second week of detox, I started to feel the withdrawal. It seemed as if every part of my body burned and itched. I was unable to sleep and experienced auditory and visual hallucinations. I reached a point where I felt I couldn't handle any more and would surely go insane. But the other addicts told me it would pass and that I would get high if I left.

I remained in detox for almost a month. A deep depression overwhelmed me. I remember thinking that I'd waited so long to finally give up the drugs and alcohol, but now withdrawal was causing me unbearable physical discomfort. I wanted immediate relief.

After I was released from the detox, I went into a treatment center for approximately the next six months. Around my second week at the center, I experienced one of the worst depressions of my life. I felt I was a complete failure. This time there was nothing to blot out those feelings. I also feared that I wasn't making any progress and withdrawal would never end. Each day I told myself that I would leave "tomorrow," but I never did.

That therapeutic community was the beginning of my physical recovery, but I credit the twelve-step fellowships for my entry into emotional recovery. During treatment, we didn't go to any meetings. But I had been to one Alcoholics Anonymous meeting many years before, although I didn't remember much about it. I did however somehow keep in mind the name and location of the church where the meeting had been held. Remembering this meeting would soon become very important to me.

I left the treatment center prematurely because I knew intuitively that there had to be another way. After seven months, the only change I saw in myself was that I wasn't using. There had to be more to being clean than just existing and enduring life as I had done before. I was determined to start a new life and it had to begin right back where I had fallen. When I called my family however I was given an ultimatum. I was to go back to treatment or I couldn't return home.

With my little resources, I managed to get to the home of a woman who had been in treatment with me but had left after only a month. I needed some time to think and plan my next steps. That was a *very* slippery place. My friend's mother had a pill problem and she offered me Valium when she saw how anxious I was. I did want those pills–very badly. But I didn't take them. A lot of pot smoking went on in that house and I am sure that I inhaled enough to affect my mood when I was not even aware of it. There was also one occasion when I took a hit off the pipe, although I can't recollect that time very clearly now. I was in a state of shock at the time.

I left after two days. I experienced an enormous anxiety attack on the bus ride home and began to suffer recurring withdrawal symptoms. When we pulled into the station, I began to walk. About five o'clock in the evening, I arrived at the very church where I had attended an A.A. meeting, years before. There was to be a meeting there that night and attending it marked the true beginning of my recovery Program.

The people there were wonderful to me. A woman I had been watching during the meeting came to me afterwards and told me she was going to be my sponsor. Someone else said they would find me a place to stay if I didn't have one. But I wanted to go to my mother's house to try and mend our relationship.

When I arrived there, my mother was very angry and would not let me in. She had lost all trust in me. But she finally opened the door when she saw the spark in my eyes and realized that I was sober. I guess she began to have a glimmer of hope too. I told her I would be going to A.A. meetings, and she said I would have to attend the meetings regularly if I wanted to stay.

Almost immediately, I found that I had to cut off all ties with any people who were using. Remarkably, this was very easy for me to do because I was so desperate. It would be nice to say that from this point on everything went smoothly, but it didn't. I was still experiencing compulsions to use.

But they told me in the A.A. meetings that I could work it "one day at a time." I had never heard that concept before. The A.A. people told me to break it down into any block of time I had to. I would tell myself for instance that just for the period of time I was sitting in the meeting that night, I was not going to get high. And I would find I had made it through another day free of drugs and alcohol.

The first three months that I was in the Program, I primarily went to A.A. meetings and then I found Narcotics Anonymous. I attended meetings of both groups, but I wasn't working the Program the way it was suggested I still had reservations and the old mentality of the quitter. And I was terribly lonely. There weren't many people my age in those meetings. I soon got into a relationship with someone I met in the Fellowship. Although it turned out to be a very painful experience for me, today I am grateful because I think that the pain is what boosted my participation in the Program. While I was still in the relationship, I had a relapse because I was holding on to a resentment towards this man. For the first time, I realized that I had picked up a drink simply because of my inability to be honest about my emotional state. This became a clue to me about my whole life and its basic dishonesty.

Ashamed of my slip, I changed my sobriety date but found it difficult to talk about it in the meetings. Instead, I threw myself into the Program's service work. I felt so *needed* by the Fellowship. It gave me a reason to keep on going and to stay straight.

I kept very busy at this work but there was still something wrong inside. I continued to harbor many of the old feelings, ideas and attitudes. I knew that the Big Book of A.A. said that we had to let go of our old ideas but they were all I had ever known. I didn't trust people. There was self-pity, jealousy and resentment in my life. I began to understand that I wouldn't be able to stay straight for long if I didn't change.

At this time, God chose to put someone in my path who has been one of the most significant influences in my recovery. She showed me how to work the Steps. She was very patient and loving, yet firm and honest with me at the same time. She encouraged me to work on my relationship with God through prayer. I am so grateful to her for being in my life as my sponsor and for showing me the way to live an honest life.

As I began to work the Steps with her guidance, she told me that "surrender" in the Third Step meant not only surrendering our drugs and alcohol but the rest of our lives as well. The Third Step was the most difficult part of the Program for me. In order to begin the process of turning my life over to God, I had to change my concept of God.

I could not love or pray to the punishing God of my childhood. The longer I stayed in the Program however the more I realized that I needed a higher power. Dependence on my fellows was not sufficient. I did see however that the love and caring I had found in the Fellowship were manifestations of that Power. Now I know that God works through people, and that is how I came to believe that there is a good and loving God.

For many years, I still attached some blame to my father for what I believed was his part in my addiction. I was never able to forgive him completely. But as a result of working the Steps, I recently had a wonderful healing experience. I was able to make my peace with him. I was filled with a genuine love and compassion for my father and a true understanding of the situation he had been placed in during my addiction. Today, I know that I can't hold on to anger and resentment because they will destroy me and any relationship that I might have with God.

The painful process of looking within was taught to me by my sponsor. I have gone over several written inventories with her and I have gained tremendous insight into myself and what needs to be done in the Seventh Step. I'm not working alone and the Steps tell us that God can and will remove defects of character if He is asked.

Many wonderful things have happened to me in sobriety. I have a career today in the field of addictions. I have also worked in other organizations related to this field and have been placed in positions where I believe that I've been of service. I care about what I'm doing for the first time. I'm interested in what happens with my life and other people's lives. That's a tremendous change for a self-centered person like me.

When I was clean for about six months, I attended my first Chemically Dependent Anonymous meeting. I was attracted to the people in the Fellowship and found I could relate with many of them. I also liked the very comfortable atmosphere in the group.

It was at that meeting that I met a gentleman who would later become my husband. Our relationship was the opposite of any I had experienced before. Neither of us was good at sharing our feelings and there were many times when I didn't want to get to know another person or work on a relationship. But I learned in the Program that anything worth having has to be nurtured. The bond deepened between us and we married four years later.

Six months before we became engaged, I moved away from home to be with my fiancé. That meant that I had to change the meetings I had been attending, and I became resentful. Many nights I wanted to hide and not go out to meetings. I was asked to take my "dis-ease" to the meeting when I was in that state. And that made sense to me.

After about a year of attending different Programs, I still felt most accepted at the CDA meetings. I thought I was being almost disloyal to my former fellowship, but I had to work through that and come to realize that it really didn't matter where I found my recovery as long as it helped me treat my disease. The CDA meetings were smaller in size so I was able to get to know many of the members on a very deep level, and I have grown to love them. Because CDA wasn't as well established as N.A. or A.A., there was also a greater need for people to do service work. I always feel my Program is incomplete when I am not involved so I immersed myself in service to CDA and developed a loyalty to its fellowship.

Things are going well for me today. The gift of a second chance that I have received was never promised to me and I certainly didn't earn it. There are still those days when I feel that I don't deserve it and I try to do something to ruin it. That's when I have to exercise faith in this Program, remember how devastated my life was before and realize that it is God's will that I remain free of drugs and alcohol.

I know that the only way I can repay God is by passing on what I have received to someone else. And my message is that there is hope and a life without drugs and alcohol. The compulsion to use leaves and the willingness to live does return. When I was new on one of those bleak days when I was certain that I was going to leave the Program, I read something in a book by Albert Camus: "Happiness, too, is inevitable." Somehow I knew that it applied to me. And I decided that I would wait just *one* more day because it is true: If you work at this Program, happiness, too, *is* inevitable.

33 I Couldn't Knock the Love

My name is Sterling S. and I'm chemically dependent. I'm going to try to tell some of my story, what it was like for me in terms of addiction to booze and other drugs (the chemicals) what happened to get me into recovery Programs and what it's like for me today. I guess the standard operating procedure is to start from the beginning right?

My childhood was fine—I imagine what you could call "normal." I liked toys, television, girls, my family, sports and music. I was a pesky little sucker, very energetic. But when I hit that puberty period, I became directionless. Before then, I'd been involved with horses and I liked the feelings that I got from showing horses and achieving little goals, riding and winning ribbons. But after a couple of years of that, at around the age of 12, I got bored with it and needed a challenge again and a new pursuit.

Many of the guys in the neighborhood (those my age or a little older) were into other sports and I soon got into the game of football. I also discovered the guitar and found that I had a knack for it and for singing. I picked it up pretty quickly and soon my life became sports and music. It made me feel good to do well and to get all the accolades and trophies for sports and the applause for the music. My ego needed feeding. Looking back, I see that I needed to do good, good, good and to have people tell me I was good. And I had to feel that I was good.

With music there seemed to come some attention (maybe this just comes with age and everybody goes through it) especially from girls, and I liked that. I liked to mix with them but I was extremely shy. The girls liked the older guys and I noticed that these fellows got a little loose if they had a beer. So I had a beer. But it really didn't do a whole lot for me. I guess I was a latent alcoholic but I still got much more thrill out of the natural pursuits.

I was only 16 when I got into one particular band whose members were really "older people" who were already out of school. Football was going o.k. for me and I was making C-average grades in school. Let's face it, I liked to play, not work, but I didn't mind practicing for football or practicing music. This group of older musicians got lots of attention from our peers. So to be like them, I got drunk a few times (not just drinking a beer or two). I was with this band for almost a year and I remember a few nights when I got out-and-out drunk. I was just a silly child, and I thought it would help me get girls. Drinking made it easier to talk to them, but they were not really interested in such a wild little kid.

I got out of that group when I was a high school senior. I was still doing o.k. in football, but I got into another band. I also got drunk a few more times, but getting loaded wasn't the light of my life at this time.

Then I went away to college but I got homesick and came home to go to school. I got in with some of my musician friends who were also in school around my local area. I attended a community college, and we put a nice little band together. We did really well locally and then when I was still only 18 years old, we moved the band to a nearby big city. We had good chemistry, a lot of energy and we were superb. We were all on natural highs just from the exhilaration of it all.

Within the next year though, my father died. I suffered terribly. I loved my whole family but my dad's death just rocked me. I felt I had lost my best friend. I had experimented with a little pot before in addition to the booze. So I got stoned on the way to the airport to pick up my dad's mother for the funeral. I got stoned the next day and I got stoned again for the funeral. My little chemical-dependent-and-addiction career really got started then, I believe, because I wanted to escape those feelings of pain.

After that, I started using something every day. I did speed, went back to college and played music. I did so well that I was earning the equivalent of $700 to $800 a week in today's terms (this was during the Vietnam War era). It was a lot for a 19 year old kid. I dropped out of school.

A year later, I was still getting loaded every day. Looking back now, I can see that I began to let myself go around that time. My clothes started going from nice, elaborate outfits to just blue jeans, sandals and an old vest. But I got into another head change and decided that even though I had been playing in the best clubs and making good money for quite a while, I needed something new. So I went back into athletics again. I was now 20 years old.

This time, I returned to a small-town, out-of-state college. I did very well there by taking plenty of Dexedrine, amphetamine sulfate, marijuana, wine and beer. I still trained, though and ran and stayed up late studying hard. I wasn't in a band now and I was just exercising my body for sports to be ready for the next year. I was at this little school for three years during which time I became a walk-on in football the first year and did all right at it during the next two years.

But of course, I ended up finding all the other addicts too. We wound up hanging together. The long-hairs and I wound up hanging together even though I was a jock with *my* long hair hanging out of the back of my football helmet. I was a *little different* from all the locals and the up-North boys. I was the weird one from the big city. I even looked different in all these wild clothes I had brought to school. I was still doing o.k. in school, in spite of the fact that I was getting loaded all the time. After a year at this college, I got married and my wife moved to be there with me. By now I was doing a lot of marijuana, speed and booze.

Two years later, I had another head change and decided to leave that school and come back to my home town so I could play music again while I finished school closer to home. In my senior year, I quit college altogether only 20 credits short of graduation. But I figured, "What the heck did I need college for?" I had inherited a business from my dad and I was obviously going to be a rich and famous rock-and-roll star right? Since I wanted to be one, everyone else who mattered in that kind of enterprise would naturally want me to be one too.

I thought I'd go back home, play in bars and get plenty of fringe benefits (perks like booze, money and attention). So, I did that and I got that. But I had another head change and my wife and I split up. We were only 21 when we married which is too young. She wanted me to get straightened and just do a regular gig. And she was probably right, but I couldn't. My head wasn't there. I wanted to rock-and-roll and do the night scene. So we parted company.

I went back to the nightclubs and got into plenty more booze, drugs and women—the old wine, women and song. I had about four years of wild times from the time I was 23 until I was 27. There was pretty good money and plenty of those fringe benefits. I felt good about myself and I actually saw a bright future about to happen right about the time I probably crossed over into real alcoholism. I also felt rocky and I was starting to drink and drug most of the day, but lightly, of course.

My typical day went like this: I'd wake up, grab the glass on the nightstand left over from the night before, flick out whatever was floating in it, and drink what was left. That was to get rid of the shakes from the previous night and so I could get to the icebox to drink a couple of beers. Then I'd switch to something else, maybe a soda pop, and lay off the booze until later in the afternoon.

Of course I didn't even get up until 2 p.m. But late in the afternoon and into the evening, I'd stop the beers and make the calls to get some speed or psychedelics (LSD or mescaline) because they'd act like speed and they got me wound up. I'd get to the club just flying but not guzzling any booze. I'd drink ginger ales and cola drinks for the first three sets from 9 p.m. to Midnight and then it was my time. Now, I deserved it—my reward—and I'd switch to the hard stuff and just inhale it for a nice, mellow last set.

Then I'd look for a party. And I always found one. I'd drink the hard stuff there, smoke some PCP, snort some more stuff and just get in somewhere (hopefully my apartment) before the sun came up. I used to hate the sounds of the birds, crickets, and the garbage men banging around! It was my duty now to get some good, solid sleep. So I'd pass out and come to around 2:00 in the afternoon the next day and just start in at the nightstand, again.

My whole band was all messed up too. Everybody was on something, and we'd switch around trying to cut this out and cut that down. We knew we had problems but we didn't know what to do about them. Deep inside we knew we should stop all of it, but that was kind of ridiculous. Come on now, everybody has to be able to do a little something! Each of us was stuck in a vicious cycle–switching from one drug to another, only to stay with it for a couple of days before returning to our original drug of choice, and ending up hooked all over again. In the mid-Seventies no one around my circle of friends knew what was really going on as far as their drug use was concerned.

I changed bands and got out of that group of people for a while. I was going to play with a decent group of some renown in a major city. It just didn't work out though, probably because they could spot me as an alcoholic. I came back home with the money I'd borrowed from my older brother still in my pocket. Since I had the money and the time off, I drank way too much. I ran into about three girls in a row who were the same kind of drinkers and we binged out every night. I don't know if I latched onto them or they latched onto me, but I ended up broke.

There was nothing to stay straight for anymore. I didn't have any shows to do. So I wound up in a stupor for several months. Then I got into a fight with my brother and got busted up pretty badly because I didn't really want to fight him. I just wanted to run my mouth but he'd heard enough. I had to leave my apartment because he was living right down the hall. Since I had nowhere else to go, I went to live with my mother.

The fact that my mother had a gigantic liquor cabinet for entertaining her friends was probably what influenced me to move in with her for a while when my she suggested it. Within a couple of months, I'd wiped out the entire contents of that liquor cabinet. She didn't realize it at first because she didn't even look. My mother didn't drink much except to be sociable or when she went out once in a while. But after a couple of months, she did begin to notice my drinking and smoking.

She also saw that I wasn't doing anything with my life. I was now 29 years old, and I was getting nowhere. I was just sitting around consuming everything, and getting fatter. She began to think I had a drug problem. I was always crying and I seemed to be feeling sorry for myself all the time. She called Alcoholics Anonymous. I heard her call someone, but I wasn't sure whether she was calling the mental hospital or A.A. Thank God it was A.A.!

On the phone my mother explained what she had been seeing. By this time, I was up to about two quarts of booze (one of my mother's and one of mine) or a case of beer and a quart of booze per day. If you start early in the morning and go until you pass out at night, you can get rid of that much booze.

When my mother laid it all out for me, I had to listen to her because I really respected her. She wasn't like the rest of the people I hung around with who were all messed up. She added up the facts and said that maybe, if there was such a drug problem and I had it, someone could give us some guidance on how to correct it or turn it around. It was hard to deny the facts so I admitted that I might need help because I wasn't doing such a good job on my own.

So, Sandra F. from A.A. came over and got to the core of it which was that I probably wanted to live more than I wanted to die. She assured me that people could die from continuing to live the way that I was. I believed that she had been in some of the same places I had been, with all the discouragement and despair and so I told her I could use some help. She said, "Let's go to an A.A. meeting" and I agreed, but I was afraid. She told me, "Don't drink for the rest of today and I'll come back to get you tonight."

That night, she brought me to a medical Intergroup headquarters of Alcoholics Anonymous where they also held A.A. meetings. I was so scared and I was withdrawing from alcohol because I hadn't had a drink all day. I was sweating and it was hot. It seemed hot as Hell, smoky and I got this flash that somebody had handed out reports about my activities and that these people knew all about me. It was kind of a conspiracy and now they were laughing. But I wasn't.

I didn't understand what was going on there, but they didn't look the way I felt. I understand now that they were recovering–they weren't using anymore. The stuff wasn't contaminating their bodies and spirits. But it had mine and it had *me* and I withdrew (all over the floor.) I got sick right on the steps I was sitting on.

A guy, Rick R., walked me out of there and helped me. He was a contemporary, an artist. He took me outside and then helped clean up that mess–*my* mess. Oh my God, he didn't even know me and he did something like that instead of letting me wallow around forever with it or in it! He watched me continue to get sick for a couple more hours and then he talked me into giving recovery a bigger shot. He said, "Hey, do yourself a favor and go to the hospital. Just go ahead and relax, get a shot and warm yourself up inside. Go to sleep and in a few days you will come out of there feeling pretty chipper. We'll see what happens then."

He was a con man, he was.

He, Sandra, Stella D., my mother and some other people got me into that hospital. They called my illness gastritis because the hospital refused to admit patients for alcoholism in those days. I got my shot and some sleep. After a couple of days, I even got my appetite back (which was a miracle).

I was then told, "Do yourself a really big favor now and invest in your life. Take the big step. Take two weeks out of your busy life and go to a rehab." My attitude was that I couldn't see how the world out there could possibly get along without me in circulation for that long, and I really believed that. But I was told, "You can die from this disease or condition of yours. Why go through that? Take a couple of weeks and get some education, some meals and get back on your feet." So I said I would reluctantly–very reluctantly.

When I went to that rehab I was afraid to go in. Then after I started to feel good, I was afraid to leave because they were taking care of everything. The world looked pretty scary when I got off the stuff. But I got off it all. And I came out believing that I had taken the first step by admitting that there was alcohol in my life, and that the reason I probably drank so much was because of all the drugs that I took. I got out of there convinced that I didn't want to do *any* of it anymore and I went to some more A.A. meetings.

But somehow I just didn't get the picture. I still had a lot of denial about letting other people help me–too much false pride. I thought I could deal with my problem on my own. I went to the meetings and when people talked about alcohol, I wondered why. If we were trying to stay away from drinking it, why did we go there and talk about it so much? I asked my mother that question too. Since she was my best friend and she thought that I made some sense, she didn't push me. So I didn't go to any more meetings.

I went for a "geographical" cure by moving from one side of town to another with some guys who worked at a boat yard. I thought a change of career would help so I started working there with them. It was nice, decent exercise and some cash, and I could lay low. It turned out that these guys drugged though. One Friday after I had gone a couple of weeks without drinking, I had a beer. I wasn't going to meetings so when the next Friday came, and I had another beer. The Friday after that, I had two beers, then three beers and I was off and running.

I'd binge out somewhere then straighten up and wouldn't do anything (no alcohol or drugs) for a week or two. Then I'd have a little pot, then a little more pot, then a beer and then a few more beers. Or maybe I'd use PCP or Crystal Meth. I'd do one of everything I had ever done before and it would eventually turn into two. Then I'd get thirsty so I'd end up binge drinking again. I was in that vicious cycle. I would use, straighten out, and then I'd do the same thing again.

Ten years ago, I had my last beer. It was 11 months from the rehab to my last drink. During that time, I still didn't understand what was wrong: that I was an addict and an alcoholic, together making me a chemically dependent person. Then one day I looked at my hand. It had a can in it. I was trying to get a job in a band again and wound up at one rehearsal where I couldn't play three notes in a row, no matter how much I wanted to. "Do, re mi." Anybody can do that right?

But I couldn't. With all my years of playing the guitar, I couldn't play now because of this stuff in my hand. Right there, I finally realized and admitted that I was powerless over the stuff. That's when I picked up the phone and asked for help. But not before finishing the six-pack of beer I had. Actually, I drove around a little while thinking about it too before I phoned. But I knew that was it, and I had a kind of sadness in me because I knew I was actually going to let it go. I knew what I had to do. I was going back to that outfit, A.A.

Then I went to see a guy I didn't really know. When I'd stopped at the body shop where he worked to get my car fixed during that year of my own "Program," I had noticed an "Easy Does It" sticker on his desk. And I remembered that now. It had haunted me. I didn't even like to drive by that place after that because he might see me. I suspected he was in a fellowship. But now I went there, drunk, and asked him what the sticker meant.

He talked to me for about an hour–just shut his door and refused to take any business during that time. And he listened to me and gave me hope. He said, "Go ahead and call your buddy Rick. He'll come help you." So I went home and did that and finished that last beer while I talked to Elin R., who said Rick would be over as soon as he came home from work. When he arrived, he laughed because he told me a long time ago what would happen. Then he said that it was all over if I wanted it to be. I could do anything I wanted to do with my life. Anything was possible now if I'd let go and just follow along, follow these Steps that we're all taking today. I would have a spiritual life now, a spiritual Program.

That made me feel good and kind of relieved because I always knew there was a God. Even in the barrooms, somehow or another I felt a spiritual bond with all the people there. We were not communicating and just kind of bouncing off each other. And we were all in there, lonely, looking for love in whichever kind of way we could get it or had gotten used to having it. But we had this wall between us and our Creator which kept us from knowing how to communicate love to each other in a healthy sense.

Through the love demonstrated to me by the A A people, and by the fact that these total strangers did things for me and did not ask for anything in return on the few occasions when I'd met them. I'd seen that they understood real love. That was what attracted me. They wanted nothing but they offered me a way out of the hell I was in. I couldn't knock that love. And so I started going to meetings, started to live and began to do my own thing, to get music jobs, again. I worked in bars but now I did it cold sober.

I've been in the music business off and on since then and played at bars. I've found out (and this is important) that you *can* do whatever you want to do. I want to play and even though there's booze and all those other elements in the bars, if I want to go do my work I can. If you've got business being in one of those places, it's o.k. as long as you make sure you're talking to your sponsors and other people in meetings about the chemicals. I go in and play and enjoy it because I'm always plugged in to my universe with my music. It's super (like I am a kid in my teens). I'm feeling good about doing things, sounding good, performing well and having fun playing again. And it's all right. But at the same time, I have to go to meetings, pray, and use the tools we all hear about in this Program.

And I can do other things too besides play music. I had a lot of false pride about not wanting to take day jobs. That attitude kept me on a cheap-beer budget for quite a while, but I found out that there were other things I could do to earn a living. And I have done them.

About a year after my reentry into A.A., a few of us who were members and who had used more than one substance created a sort of catch-all Program for ourselves and others like us. We knew what our problem was–we were addicted to chemicals. We called ourselves Chemically Dependent Anonymous and, in the 10 years since the Fellowship's founding, our growth has been phenomenal. My recovery was strengthened as CDA's Program brought me to realize how my use of chemicals had blocked my own growth.

Today I feel at peace with myself in my recovery with my recovery tools. I know what to do to stay clean and sober. In my ongoing adventures, I have many peaks and valleys. But I know that anything is possible. There are many things I still want in life; there are also things I have to keep working on. I want to grow in my music career. I've peaked and valleyed with that and with finances too but right now I'm fine. I have to work through so I've started a little courier company. Last year, I got married and I also bought a house.

I've done some recordings and I'm still trying to make contacts to help that area of my music grow into something more fulfilling. I really feel that I've outgrown working in bars on a nightly basis to generate income and express myself. I can't see playing for five hours a night, five days a week forever. That's behind me. I'd also like to get into concert work, something else I'm constantly working on. I've got to get going and keep growing.

There are plenty of tools and people here to help me: my beautiful wife, my wonderful friends, all the co-founders of CDA, all the new people and Phil C., my sponsor in A.A., who keeps it simple for me. I've learned to let out my emotions and they get more intense as time goes by. I guess I'm peeling the onion and getting down to more raw nerves. I'm taking more chances so I'm feeling more rejections, but more triumphs as well. And that makes for a good life.

Each of us has to keep doing the same things, using the tools. We have so many *other* "things" to do in our lives sometimes that living the Program seems more difficult than it used to. But we have to keep increasing our efforts. All of us who have grown up together in these Programs are living more now; experiencing more and have much less free time. Often, it seems we tend to take too much for granted. It seems to be more of an effort to say the prayers, go to the meetings, or listen to the newcomer on the phone. But we do it; we follow through, because the root of it all *is* the Program. We have to be willing to work and not let it get stale for us.

I hope anyone who is exposed to my story will be helped by it, whether you're a drug addict, an alcoholic, or a chemically dependent. I'm sure you will because it comes from the heart. I thank all of those who have come before me to pave the way and I consider them the wisest people I know. All the newcomers are the luckiest people I know to have reached a point to be reading this material. I wish us all, in CDA and in all of the world good luck and Godspeed.

34 A Medical Miracle

I was raised in an alcoholic family. My father was an alcoholic, but I didn't actually know that until I came into the Program. I knew that he drank a lot and that he slept much of the time. My sister and I were very afraid of him because when he was drinking he had such severe mood swings. When he'd first start drinking, he'd be really nice. Then he'd pass out for a little while and as soon as he woke up, we learned to try to stay as far away from him as we could.

When I was 11, my mother died. I think that's the most devastating thing that has ever happened to me in my entire life. The day of her funeral was the day I took my first drink. I heard somebody tell my father, "Here, have another drink. That will make you feel better." I needed to feel better too. I hurt a lot. So I sneaked into the kitchen, poured myself a small glass of whiskey and drank it straight down.

I remember that it tasted terrible and I thought it wasn't going to stay down. But after it did, I got a warm sensation inside. It made things seem different. I wasn't any happier or any better, but it made me almost numb about the situation. So right from the very beginning, I always drank to make things feel better, to make *me* feel better.

When I was 12, I was hospitalized with stomach pains. Doctors couldn't find any reason for these pains so I started seeing a psychiatrist. The doctors eventually gave me some kind of drug (belladonna) to slow my stomach muscles down, but I continued seeing the psychiatrist too. He in turn started me on mild tranquilizers.

I couldn't seem to cope with anything once my mother died. I couldn't handle school. I'd get through one or two classes and then I'd tell the teachers that I was sick. I had this panic that came over me, a fear that I was going to die, and I had to get out of there. Sometimes, the teachers would not let me go home and all I would do for the rest of the day was put my head on my desk and cry. I just wanted to be in my bedroom at home and to be left alone. And that's the way I always wanted to go through life. I could only be around people for a short period of time. Then after a while, I just wanted to be by myself and have everybody go away.

Early in high school, I started sneaking alcohol from my father. I would take some out of his bottle and fill it back up with water so he wouldn't notice I had taken any. I would go up to my room or go outside and drink. The more I did it, the more the alcohol made me feel better. It made me happy.

It also helped me get along with people. I was so afraid of the way I acted around my family. Since I'd started going to see the psychiatrist, I thought that if I didn't behave perfectly around them, they were going to put me back in the hospital. I always had to pretend I felt fine and the alcohol helped me do that. When I got home from school, before my father got home from work, I would drink, almost on a daily basis.

I started hanging around with older kids, mostly guys who had dropped out of school and didn't have very good reputations. They always had booze and I just wanted to drink. I started getting into some trouble. I used to "hook" from school quite a lot. I would walk to school where the guys would pick me up and we'd go off to the beach or just hang out at somebody's house where we could drink all day long.

It seemed that I always got caught, but I would use the excuse that my father was a drunk, my mother had died and I was so confused. I turned on the tears and everybody would look at me and say, "Poor Cathy." That is how I used to get out of trouble. When I was called in to the police station a few times, I gave them the same story and they felt sorry for me too.

By the time I was a senior in high school, I had to get out of my father's house; his drinking was much worse. He had hit me when I was younger but I soon found that with a little more alcohol inside me, I could hit back. So we had some pretty serious fights. I used to run away from home. He'd call the State Police, and they'd come looking for me. It was just a God-awful, ugly scene all the time. I started hanging around with one particular guy and I really fell in love with him. Before graduation, I was married.

I married another alcoholic, someone who drank and treated me exactly the way my father had. But I let him do it. I didn't want to be alone and I didn't want to have to go back to my father. I figured marriage was the lesser of two evils.

I did graduate from high school that year but I don't know how. I spent more time out of school than in it. My marriage only lasted three months. After too many drunken fights and my husband's extramarital affairs, someone where I worked started paying attention to me. He was much older than I was but I didn't mind. I just felt that finally somebody cared. After work on Fridays, we used to hop in the car and drive to out-of-state bars where we would drink all night. Once again, I was mixed up with an alcoholic.

A few months later I met my second husband. Our relationship was a turning point in my life. I had never tried drugs before; I had only drunk alcohol. But this guy introduced me to all sorts of drugs: marijuana, cocaine, LSD. They were wonderful. I didn't have hangovers in the morning when I used them. I didn't get into fights. At first, I didn't get into a lot of trouble. This man not only had drugs, he was very wealthy. I knew I didn't really love him. I didn't have the feelings that you should have to marry someone, but he had what I wanted most in the world. He had something that let me escape.

I don't think there had been too many days since I was a young child when I hadn't taken a drink. But now I had something more wonderful I thought than I had ever experienced in my whole life. I can't explain it but drugs of any kind made me feel, for the first time, that I had control and that I knew what I was going to do. I was going to do such marvelous, magnificent things. I was just sitting on top of the world.

My husband's family owned a glass factory. We first met when they opened up a new factory in my hometown and I went to work there. After my husband and I married, we went out West to open up a new plant. He trained the men, and I took care of the women. I thought that was a perfect arrangement. I had a management job and I felt like somebody. But after work and on all our weekends, we were getting high. There wasn't much else to do in that town.

After we were there about five or six months, I got pregnant. When my husband's family heard about it, they said no daughter-in-law of theirs was going to work. I was sent back East to set up housekeeping for my new family. I really hated it right from the start. I didn't like the idea of living next door to my in-laws. I felt I could never live up to the expectations of such a very wealthy family. They immediately tried to teach me everything I needed to know. It was almost like *My Fair Lady*. They wanted to turn me into something that I wasn't. They taught me the proper way to set a table. I was even given Amy Vanderbilt's book on etiquette.

While I was pregnant with my son, I was really afraid that something was going to be wrong with him so I stopped using cocaine. I just drank a little bit and smoked pot. After he was born, it was a relief to find that he was alright. And I was finally free to go back to using my preferred drug cocaine.

I used to justify my use of this drug by telling myself that it made me a better mother. When I wasn't getting high on coke, I felt tired all the time and I would often doze off when I knew I needed to be awake to take care of my son. So I'd snort a couple of lines of cocaine and then I felt like Supermom. I not only could care for my son and have time to read to him and play with him, but I could also keep my house clean.

That was very important to my husband. He insisted on a clean house. Some days when I was tired and had had a bad day with my son, my husband would come home and say, "What have you done all day?" I always felt under pressure to be perfect. I had to look great, my son had to be bathed and the house had to be immaculate. Dinner had to be on the table. With the help of cocaine, I could do it all

When my son was under a year old, our marriage began to go sour. I thought another child would make it better so I got pregnant. We had our second child, a little girl, before my son was not quite 2 years old. Our daughter came six weeks early. To this day, I think it's because I used drugs a lot more heavily when I was pregnant with her. Since my son had been alright, I felt that this child would be too. Still, I did cut down on my use of drugs although I drank a little more than in my first pregnancy. I smoked much more pot and I did cocaine off and on the whole time. My daughter was born not only premature but also underweight (five pounds) and she was very jaundiced at birth.

That really scared me. I prayed to God that everything was going to be alright with her and I promised that if He answered my prayer, I wouldn't use drugs anymore. But of course once she came home from the hospital, started putting on weight and wasn't as yellow as she had been, I felt that I could celebrate. I pulled out my stash and got high.

Now that I had two children, I had to do more cocaine. There was so much more work to be done each day. So I just started snorting cocaine all day long. I began to have some physical problems which led to my needing a partial hysterectomy. I found that I enjoyed being in the hospital, having somebody else take care of my children, my husband and my house. I didn't have to do anything except rest and get pain medication every four hours. I was in the hospital for about a week. When I got home, my husband had hired somebody to take care of the children until I could recuperate. I could now stay in bed all day, take my pain medication, snort some coke, watch television and not have any responsibilities at all. That was wonderful.

About six months after my operation, I had some problems with my back. I had had back pain off and on when I was growing up but this seemed a lot worse. I went to my general physician and he said that I had a disc problem and put me on Valium. After I had taken the first few of them, I was in heaven. I had no pain. I felt as calm and as cool as a cucumber. When I did my coke, it was completely different than when I did it without the Valium. Using the two together gave me a new kind of high. I stayed on the Valium for five years. By the end of that time, I was getting it from three different doctors.

About six months after my back problems, I became very depressed. I called my gynecologist because someone told me it probably had something to do with my hysterectomy. The doctor put me on antidepressants. Between these pills, Valium, coke, pot, and the booze, I never seemed to touch down. I went into the hospital two more times for my back and for migraine headaches. I was falling apart physically. But I enjoyed going into the hospital because, again, I didn't have to handle any responsibilities when I was sick.

I then found a really good drug connection—my hairdresser. When I went to get my hair done, he'd have something waiting for me and I'd go into the bathroom and snort a couple of lines, or try this pill or that drug. I'd sit in his chair while he was doing my hair and just be flying! When I told him I was really having some trouble coming down off the coke, he said he knew an out-of-town doctor who would give me a prescription for Quaaludes as long as they got filled at his brother-in-law's pharmacy across the street. So, twice a week we'd take a trip to get our "ludes."

I was still very unhappy in my marriage so I thought that my problems were largely due to my marital difficulties. If I ended the marriage, everything else would be fine. One day I called a lawyer, made an appointment, and told him I wanted to get a divorce without ever discussing anything with my husband. Only two weeks later, I left with the children to go back to my hometown. During the five years of my marriage, I had pictured all my friends still back home partying, getting high, and doing all the same old things. I had wanted to be a part of that and now was my chance.

I was so sick by the time I got home that I didn't want to be alone and I had no connections there. So I hooked up with my first husband again, forgetting all about the problems we had before. By that time, he had been in a fellowship but he hadn't been able to stay sober. It just seemed that the two of us were meant to be together; we were two really sick people. He connected me with a drug dealer and I still had plenty of money from my divorce settlement so I was able to get my drugs again. To this day, I still can't believe I subjected my children to all that. I had taken them away from their father and immediately moved in with someone who was a complete stranger to them, another addict.

About two weeks later, I woke up one morning and knew that I had to get away. I called my second husband and asked him to please come and pick up the children. I was going to be away for a while. Within two hours, I was on my way to the opposite coast to a place I had never been to before. I do not know what prompted me to do that. I bought a first-class ticket to get there because I knew you were allowed to drink all you wanted to in first class without paying.

I can't really tell you very much about the trip, because I was in a fog the whole time. I know I got back with my first husband out there and we ended up in another great big fight. He knocked me out–right into the bathtub. At that point, a light came on and I realized that something wasn't right. I was back into the same physical abuse, again. I had sent my children away and I was in a part of the world that I didn't even know.

I returned to my hometown and made an appointment to see a drug-and-alcohol counselor I had seen as a teenager, when I got my first DWI. He told me he had known then that I had a problem. He offered to get help for me and sent me to a state hospital. I really believed I was crazy by now and that the reasons for my insanity were people, places and things. I never once thought the drugs or alcohol might be responsible. I stayed in the institution for 10 days locked in a cell. I was later told that I had about 9 seizures in the hospital, but I don't remember any of it. I had almost been arrested, too, because I was holding speed when I went into the institution. I was one pretty sick cookie when I went in there.

When my head started clearing a little, I realized that what I had been doing wasn't good for my children or for me. I talked to my counselor and we discussed my going into a rehabilitation center. I agreed and he entered me into a twenty-eight day Program. I was scared to death. I knew that I wanted to feel better but I hadn't thought about quitting drugs, yet. That was the farthest thing from my mind. I think what I probably wanted was to feel better only so I could go back out and use again.

But I learned a lot in rehab. I began to feel better physically. I started to eat, something I had been doing very little of lately. I had probably weighed about 90 pounds when I entered the rehab. I was advised not to go back to my hometown when I got out. And I finally found the courage to break off with my first husband.

The rehab people had recommended that I try to go to 90 meetings in 90 days, but I thought I could recover on my own. I had never tried to do it alone before and I really wanted to try. My first week out of rehab, I applied for three jobs and I was chosen for all three. I accepted one of the positions and started to work. When I got my first paycheck at the end of the week, without even thinking I stopped at a liquor store and bought myself a six-pack of beer to celebrate. I had forgotten all about the rehab; I had forgotten all that I had been through.

A week later, my second husband brought the children back to me. I was now living with a man I had met at rehab. Not too long after, we began getting high together. Then he decided that he really wanted to get straight, so he left me and moved in with his parents. I was just devastated.

A few nights after he moved out, I made up my mind that I was going to see what this Alcoholics Anonymous was all about. Chemically Dependent Anonymous hadn't been formed yet so A.A. was the only organization I had heard about when I started going to meetings. I heard the people say, "It gets better." I heard, "Day at a time. Don't drink, a day at a time." I heard so many things that stuck in my mind. The people there planted a seed. They also reminded me of a lot of things I had been taught in rehab.

I went to some more meetings. I stopped drinking but still continued to smoke pot. I figured that was o.k. I hadn't heard much about other drugs around the rooms only that I shouldn't drink. My boyfriend moved back in with me and we began going to meetings together. I also met some other people, including a couple who were trying to start a new fellowship called Chemically Dependent Anonymous, and I was asked to help. About five or six of us would go out to the founders' house once or twice a week, sit around their living room and talk about why we were forming this new group. We tried to write some literature about it.

You know, when I look back on it today, God was really acting in my life when He helped me find these people. Who would ever have believed that anyone as sick as I was at that time would become part of something so beautiful, an organization that has helped so many people? Since I have been straight, I have seen people come into the rooms feeling so hopeless and so sick, just as I once did. But the happiness and the caring that they experience is truly a miracle. Every one of us is a miracle.

We started holding CDA meetings at Rick and Elin R.'s house. Then the big night came when we finally got a church, and had our first official CDA meeting. There were about six or seven people there, and the man I was living with chaired the first meeting. He had been clean about six months by now. It was a really special night in that small room which we called "The Dungeon." That was how it all started.

After the CDA meetings began, I heard, from this new group that anything that affects me from the neck up also affects my stability and cuts off communication between my God and me. I realized that I couldn't even use pot. It was rough trying to come off everything. I had never realized how addictive pot was until I tried to quit. But I managed to do it. I stayed clean for about three months and then my boyfriend moved out again. I didn't want to feel the pain so I went back out from the Fellowships.

Before getting high, one night I gave my children $2 each. I was feeling guilty because I knew what I was about to do. My children had been really proud of me, watching me get a one-month chip, a two-month chip and then my three-month chip. They knew why I got those awards and that they meant mommy had not taken a drug for three months. But this night, I went out to see a girl I was working with and she gave me some pot and some Quaaludes. I came home again, sat the children in front of the TV, went into the bathroom and commenced to get high.

A friend of mine from A.A. came over that evening and saw that I was on pot. She told me that as long as I didn't take a drink, I could still go back to A.A. and keep my sobriety date. Thanks to CDA I knew she was wrong. I was high and I knew it didn't matter what I used, whether in liquid form, pill form or whatever form. I was being affected; I was using a mood-changing and mind-altering chemical. They were all the same.

But I had no idea how that night would change my life and that nothing would ever be the same again. When my 6 year old son saw the condition I was in, he was heartbroken. He packed up his suitcase and put his coat on. Then he ripped up the $2 I had given and threw them at me, saying "Mommy, I hate you! You're a drunk!" He was looking at me the same way I had looked at my father when I was younger. I was ashamed and deeply embarrassed.

A girlfriend took the children to spend the night with her. Then, when I was alone, I talked to God for the first time since my mother had died. From the time I was 11 years old, I had hated God. He had taken my mother away from me and left me with a father who was a drunk. I said all these things to Him now. I let out all the anger and told Him about all the unfairness that I thought was His fault. I talked to Him for most of the night.

Finally, I believe He answered me. It became clear to me what I had to do. I had to get better. I didn't hate God; I just hated my life. I hated what I was putting my children through. It had to change. At that point, I realized that drugs were my problem. All the denial was gone, all the blaming of people, places and things. I turned my life over to God and to the members of CDA. I was going to listen, I was going to take suggestions and I was going to try to stop hurting.

I went back into the rooms the next day and told everybody what had happened. I said that I now had an honest desire to be a part of the Fellowship. I wanted to get better. That was seven years ago. My first year in the Program was very hard. I had to learn everything all over again. Just functioning on a day-to-day basis without any chemicals seemed almost impossible. But it slowly started getting easier.

My third year was the real test. I had to have major back surgery and needed to take pain medication. I was very frightened. I didn't know what it would be like to be back on drugs. And I really didn't know if once I got on them, I would be able to stop. But thank God for the Fellowship. I don't think I would have been able to come off the drugs as I did if it hadn't been for the people in the Program. Every day, somebody came to offer support.

They even brought meetings to my house so I could attend.

I had to have another back operation 13 weeks after the first one. I was sure I would not be able to stop taking the drugs if I had to start taking them again. I had been on them for a while the first time. But I never abused the medications and I managed to use them just as the doctor prescribed. Again, thanks to the people of CDA and to the Program, I made it!

I hope that my experience will give hope to others in the Fellowship that might have to undergo surgery someday. I think there will come a time in most people's lives when they will legitimately need some kind of medication for one reason or another. But if they have a firm foundation in the Program, I know they can get through it. You can get through anything just as I did. And you'll never have to do any of it alone.

When I came off the medication the second time, I experienced another miracle. For the first time in the three years that I had been in the Program, I found that I would rather be straight than loaded. I had gained unbelievable control over my feelings and emotions so that I hadn't become addicted again when I was on the drugs. Now I preferred the way my head felt straight to the effects of the medicine.

It's really hard for me to list all of the other miracles that have taken place in my life since then. My children are still with their father and I know that this is probably God's will. I have been able to accept that. Today, I have a wonderful relationship (better than I could have ever imagined) with a remarkable man who is also in the Program. We've been married for five years. He has given me so much help and support. And I have faith in a higher power now that is incredible. God has always been there for me. It just took this fellowship for me to find Him. I don't need to look for happiness now through a bottle, pills, or snorting something up my nose. It comes from working the Steps of CDA. The miracle has happened in my life, and it continues happening a day at a time. I hope those who read my story will let miracles happen to them too.

35 No More Excuses

A lot of my excuses and the things I used for excuses to keep me out there drinking and drugging for as long as I did began right at birth. One of the big ones was that my natural mother left me in the hospital and never came back for me. As a result, for years in all my relationships, I always thought I was going to be abandoned.

Soon after my birth the medical staff in the hospital discovered that I wasn't normal. I didn't respond to light or to sound like other kids. I didn't even cry right. They thought I was going to have all kinds of problems. I wouldn't be able to see, hear or talk. Doctors started performing operations. So, one of my main excuses for feeling sorry for myself was that I had a right to get on the "pity pot" about my handicap. After all, I was different from other kids.

My behavior patterns began to form at a very early age. The operations started when I was less than four months old. Between that time and my 15th birthday, I had 49 operations: on my eyes, my ears, my throat, my feet everywhere. One thing I learned from being in the hospital (and I was a long-term hospital patient) was that I could push a button and a nurse would come in and give me a shot for the pain. I loved that. A nurse would come and shoot me with a needle and I could feel the drugs going up through my body and making me feel good. Using drugs to relieve pain was the behavior I learned as a child.

Before I start making everything sound as if my whole life was total misery though, let me back up one second and mention something really positive that happened to me at a very young age. The man who is now my father adopted me. When he decided to adopt, he had every opportunity to choose a perfectly normal child but he took me the one with the disabilities, the one he knew would have a physical handicap, the one he knew would have to have many operations. I was the one he chose to bring into his life and to love.

I understand now how difficult that must have been for him. And I also realize what my father did for me and what he did for my life. He played a big part in my development, in enabling me to be the person I have become. Even though I could not have recognized it for what it was at the time, I know now that his adopting me was one of the circumstances that led to my being in Chemically Dependent Anonymous today. My father has been one of the major influences in my life especially as an example for my recovery.

I had some problems fitting in with my new family. I felt so out of place. My father and a neighbor used to sit out at a picnic table and drink beer and I liked to sit there with them. I was just a little kid, they were the big men and I looked up to them. Often, when I sat with them, they would let me have some of their beer. That made me feel like I belonged. It was such a big deal to me to be allowed to be with them there. And so, another behavioral trait that I acquired very early was equating alcohol with companionship.

My belief that I was always being abandoned by women also made me feel I was not normal. It was not just that my mother had left me in the hospital. I became close to a grandmother and she died. A sister I cared about left to get married. My adoptive mother also left and she created another family without me. These abandonments made me think that I was fated always to be a loser in relationships. So I approached most of them with the attitude that they wouldn't last.

I also had problems with the educational system from the very beginning. When I went to kindergarten, I didn't fit in. I was kind of an obnoxious kid. The teacher used to write things on the board and ask me what they were. Since I couldn't see what she wrote, I made things up.

After a year of that, the County said that I wasn't able to function in public school with normal children so they sent me to a school for the retarded for two years. I'm not sure how I ever got out of there. I told the school counselors all sorts of fantastic stories about my life. None of my tales were true but they were my way of surviving in that environment.

I didn't feel that I fit in anywhere–not at that school and not with the kids in my neighborhood. I didn't attend the same school as everyone else did and I was ashamed to admit where I had to go. That made for a very uncomfortable life. I went around with a chip on my shoulder. I thought people picked on me because I couldn't see. After a while, I felt that I had fought every single kid in elementary school.

When I got to an age where it seemed very important to have friends, go to parties and be able to associate with and talk to girls, I didn't know what to do. But then I discovered that drinking and pot were the "in" things. If I had pot, the other kids would befriend me and the girls would talk to me. So I always had pot. And all through junior high and high school, I was a popular kid. Still, I never really got into marijuana or the other street drugs myself.

I turned 13 when I was in the fifth grade. At that point, I was sent to a private school where I was given an aptitude test. As a result, I was moved up a grade. I had to struggle for a while, but I started having some enthusiasm about getting an education now because of the encouragement I received. I began to study much more on my own. I also got involved with the wrestling team at school and the track team and I began to be enthusiastic about these activities too.

When I started using drugs, all of that went out the window. Suddenly, the only thing that was important seemed to be the partying. High school for me became one big party. It was a wild time. I did everything under the sun. I was so reckless that I should have been killed.

On my 18th birthday some friends and I got drunk as hell and took a ride on a rough country road on top of a station wagon acting as if it was a surfboard. Later that night as I was leaving a party, I walked out onto a porch landing that was 12 feet above the ground. I figured that I would walk to the edge of the porch and follow the railing to the stairs. When I came to the edge, I found there was no railing so I thought I was at the steps. Then I took my first step and I realized that it was much steeper than I had expected. I did a complete flip and ended up on the ground on my back. I just bounced up on my feet and staggered around laughing about it. Everyone who saw this little episode found it quite amusing. Something must have been watching out for me that night or I would surely not have survived it.

But I thought I had my drinking and drugging under control. In high school I was able to party in the morning and then stop. In college, I cut all of that out. My first two years, I only partied on weekends. I stayed straight during the school week, took a lot of courses and really studied.

I always had a plan for the weekends though. I had a good drinking buddy and I would get in touch with him about the middle of the week and set it up so he came over to my house at the end of the day on Friday with a case of my favorite brew. My part was to provide the pot. And that's how we began our weekends. I would live it up until Monday when I would return to my rigid routine.

All week, I would get up early in the morning, start studying, have a heavy schedule of classes, come home and eat dinner, go to bed and then get up early to study again. I was very obsessive about this routine and I got through junior college doing very well. I even received high honors.

But something happened at that point. I'm not sure exactly why, but I started acting the way I had in high school all over again. I was partying every day. After a couple of weeks of this, I was ready to go back home. I enrolled in a guide-dog school near my home and met lots of people there who really liked to party too.

Once, we decided to go on a camping trip. A bunch of us were going to get back to nature–live in the woods for a while and act like men. We practically died. When we were preparing to go, we made sure we had plenty of bottles of beer, found the pot and had everything we needed. Somehow we forgot to bring the food. I forgot my sleeping bag too, but it was August. It should be warm in August right? I almost froze my butt off.

I tried to get back into college, but I couldn't get it together and I couldn't face a single day without starting it with a drink. I couldn't remember things anymore so college just didn't work out. Finally, I went to a rehab to learn vocational training because I'd decided that college was not for me. I would just acquire some skills and get a job. They trained me very well there.

When I got out, I figured that the best way to get a job was to go somewhere and prove to an employer that I could do the work. I found a place that would take me and I worked for them for nine weeks without pay. I thought that would be the best investment I could make to get a permanent position. But at the end of the nine weeks, they told me they didn't have anything for me.

It got to the point where I decided I would have to go back to college. I'd take one class. I should be able to handle that. Anybody could take one class a week. I borrowed money from my father to pay for the class. I went once. I couldn't handle it.

By the time I was ready to come into the Program, I was someone I didn't like very much. I was depressed about myself because I was a blind bum. I was living off my father and collecting welfare checks or their equivalent. I wasn't working. I wasn't going to school. And I wasn't nice to people most of the time.

That's where I was when all of a sudden the drugs stopped working for me. A typical example of what I was doing at the time was drinking shots and chasing them with beer as well as doing bongs. I remember this particular night because I'd had about seven shots and was just starting to get a buzz from the pot when it was exactly like a switch being turned off–that quick. Nothing! The next day there I was at home with a hangover feeling miserable. But I'd had none of the enjoyment from the drinking or drugging. It was all gone. I had just blacked out and that was it.

And on top of that, I was very depressed. While I was in this state, depressed, broke, and therefore unable to get my drug of choice (which was pot used on an almost-daily basis), an old friend of mine dropped over. He was a couple of years older, an old drinking buddy. He had been out of town for a while and I thought he might have brought back some good drugs.

But he said, "No, I don't have any drugs." And he started talking about how great his life was and how well things had been going for him. He ran down to the new truck he had just bought and brought back a book. Then he began to read out of it and he started telling me about these meetings that he'd been attending.

So I asked him a couple of dumb questions. First, I asked, "How often do you go to these meetings?" and he said that he went every night. Then I asked him an even more stupid question; "Are you going to one tonight?" He replied, "Yeah. Do you want to go?" And I said that I did. To this day, I don't know why. I kind of surprised myself.

My buddy was on his way to his father's house. He told me, "You get a shower because you need one and I'll be back to get you." He was a little late and when he didn't return at the time he told me to expect him, I thought "Good. Maybe he won't show up. What do I want to go along to this meeting for anyhow?" But he did show up.

Another important influence on my decision to go with my buddy just at this point was my father's example. He had been in the Program for quite a while and that had also started me thinking. He went out to a meeting every night. He would tell me before he left, "Hey, I'm going to such-and-such place to a meeting," and I would think to myself, "Now, isn't this weird? Here I am in my early twenties sitting alone in this house. And there he is in his early sixties going out every night with his friends. There's something wrong here." So I was proud when I could tell him that I was going to a meeting too, with *my* friends.

I don't remember much at all about that meeting. But I told my old drinking buddy I would follow up and go again the next night. The only thing I do recall is getting home, calling my girlfriend and telling her where I had gone.

The following night before someone came to take me to the meeting, another friend dropped by with some drugs. He asked me if I wanted to get high. I said, "Yes. But first, I'm supposed to go to this meeting with someone." So I talked my druggie friend into attending the meeting with me. After we sat through it, the guy with the drugs walked up to me and asked, "Do you want to go out and get high with me or do you want to stay here with these people?" And I told him I wanted to stay. That was a major step for me because I had seldom, if ever, turned down drugs before that night. I hadn't had a drink or a drug for two days at the time. I haven't had a drink or a drug since then.

Many other changes have taken place in my life since that night. At first, it was a struggle to get up every day and start doing something positive and not just doing without the alcohol and drugs. For the first few months, I smoked a lot of pipe tobacco and cigarettes. Then I started becoming more active which was hard after sitting at home for so long. I had to work myself up just to do some simple things like wash the dishes, fold some laundry or help my father is some way around the house (anything to get motivated and moving) Most days my greatest accomplishment was to take a shower and get dressed so I would be ready for someone to take me to a meeting.

Because I wasn't able to drive, people from the Program literally carried me to my first meetings. They made sure I got there every day and I needed that. Still, my biggest problem was wondering if I really wanted to do all of this. I said, "Yeah, I feel miserable. But give it up for life? That's outrageous!" So the people told me, "Don't worry about that. Just think that you want to give it up today. You want to stay clean and sober today."

That's how I had to start living. For a while I had to think, "One hour at a time." After about a month, I realized that smoking cigarettes and pipe tobacco was just an extension of my compulsive, addictive behavior. In kind of an angry mood, I threw away my pipe and said, "I'm going to have to stop." I knew I was doing the same type of thing, sitting back and smoking, that I used to do with pot.

Then I went through a stage of depression for a while where I felt very sorry for "poor me." I thought that I wanted to die. If I weren't blind, I knew I could find a job anywhere–at a gas station, waiting on tables, or what have you. I wouldn't need a job that I was specifically trained for either. If there hadn't been someone in the

Program to tell me that it was probably God's will that I didn't have a job right then and that I had to be patient, I don't know what would have happened to me. They told me to pray about it.

Eventually, I got the good job which I still have today. That is a miracle because when I was still using, I thought I would never be able to handle getting up in the morning and going to work every day. I didn't want that kind of responsibility in my life.

One night, a friend who had promised to take me to a meeting didn't show up. That was a turning point in my sobriety because it proved to me how much I really did want to go. I called people I knew were going to be there and I even called a hotline, but I just couldn't find a ride. Finally, I got an old friend of mine (a guy I had once drank with) to take me to the meeting place. I was really determined to get there that night. I arrived at the location for the meeting and realized I couldn't figure out how to get in. There was snow on the ground and my dog and I were wandering around in the snow wondering how we would ever find the door and the meeting room. Somebody finally saw me out there and yelled out the door with directions for me. That incident convinced me that I really did want the Program. I wanted to stay clean and sober.

After that night, I got a sponsor. I also started to consider working the Steps. Up to that point when I had heard people talk about the Fourth Step, I would think to myself, "Writing a personal inventory? No way. Not for me!" But I learned that I must do these kinds of things. I began to get more involved in the Program too. It was around this time that I started going to CDA meetings as well as to Alcoholics Anonymous.

There are all kinds of very exciting things that have happened since then. What has really changed for me today is my whole outlook on sobriety, especially where spirituality is concerned. Before coming into the Program, my attitude was that I sort of admitted I was an alcoholic and a drug addict, but it didn't really matter. Today I care very much that I stay sober. I did not have any faith that a higher power, God, was needed in my life and I totally resented that type of thinking and that type of principle. But I was miserable because I thought that I had all the answers. If everyone would just leave me alone, I would be o.k. Today I know that I need to get on my knees and pray. I also read a little spiritual literature every day. Now that I am able to work the Program by using the Steps and by trying to keep an open mind (I'm kind of a hardheaded, stubborn type) life is immensely better.

Since relationships have always been tough for me to handle, the really good relationship that I have with my father today is very important. I'm able to appreciate so many things about him now. When I was as young as 14, he had tried to get me to go to meetings because he thought I had a problem. I didn't agree then so there was a lot of conflict between us. That was when he was trying to get sober and I was just beginning to use. Now we don't have any need to fight. In fact, I don't think we've had any serious arguments since I've been in the Fellowship. That's miraculous. Also, today I have a relationship with a lady which has lasted–a big change in my life.

One of the most important improvements is that I'm able to feel much better about myself, these days. I not only have some self-esteem, but I'm even able to get up and talk in front of people and feel comfortable about that. Speaking at meetings has gone a long way towards making me realize that I belong in a world where I once thought I'd never fit in. I can deal with my problems. I don't need excuses anymore.

What I pray for is that something in my message will be an inspiration to you just as the things I heard when I first came in were an inspiration to me: to stay in the Program, to keep coming back and to associate associating with the winners here. When these people set examples for me to follow and gave me advice, they helped me become clean and sober as I am today. Most of what I've heard in these meetings I've been able to apply in my everyday life and that has made it so much easier. A very important part of CDA is the fellowship, the caring among the people.

    Thank you for this opportunity to share with you the things that have given me my strength, my faith and my hope.

36 Keep An Open Mind: Something May Fall In

I love the memories of my childhood. It was a healthy one. My parents loved me and as the first son after two daughters, I may have been a bit spoiled. But I was a basically a good kid who learned right from wrong and didn't make trouble. Other kids, I assume, thought I was intelligent; girls thought I was handsome. I had respect from my peers. At least that's the way I think people saw me then. I was small for my age and not really physically fit, but I tried hard in the inner-city Catholic school I attended and I received good grades.

When I was 8 years old, I started smoking cigarettes. The association between smoking tobacco and cancer was just beginning to be made by the medical profession. But fear of cancer couldn't stop me. I wanted to be cool. So I secretly smoked with a friend who was 9 and also wanted to be cool.

Being small for my age was no fun. Throughout grammar school and into high school, most kids I knew always seemed to be a head taller. I put up with this because I had no choice. But I always wondered, "What if I hadn't started smoking so young?" I attended an all-boys' high school where I refused leadership opportunities and became introverted and shy. Yet life still seemed nice and secure throughout those years.

But all was not well in our family. I had three sisters, each quite different from the other. My oldest sister married an alcoholic who is now in recovery. My second sister has been married twice and is chemically dependent. Only my youngest sister seems to have escaped unscathed. She earned master's degree in sociology and works in the field of addiction. And then there was me.

My parents, who have never had problems with substance abuse, are extraordinary. No matter how much I messed up or how much they were disappointed by my arrests, my need for the help of institutions, my failure at jobs and my lack of love relationships and friendships with others, they always eventually adjusted, forgave me and went on with their lives. I truly believe that my parents did the best they could. God knows that by the time I got through with me, I didn't leave myself or anyone else too much to work with.

My college years were when I really began to get out of control. After attending a community college for two years, I went away to a university for a lot of good reasons. It was time to be on my own. I would be able to make more friends where I didn't have my family to depend on. I could escape the service and the risk of being killed since the U.S. was involved in Vietnam at the time. Finally, my first relationship had turned out badly and I wanted some kind of escape from that rejection. I turned to drugs and booze with reckless abandon. My mother's father had been an alcoholic for over 50 years. It now seemed that I was going to follow in his footsteps.

Classes had not even started yet when I decided to get drunk on my second night away from home. I had never been drunk before. But I decided to loosen up, to try it, to really live. I was with some more experienced guys who were seniors. I thought they would show me which end was up and how to drink. But that's not exactly how it went. I started drinking beer at six o'clock in the evening and didn't stop until close to three the following morning. It was difficult, but I was still standing. I had kept up with the best drinker in the house. He finally admitted that he couldn't out drink me and we both set out for our rooms. That's the last thing I can remember clearly. I was in and out of a blackout the rest of that night.

The next day, I felt that I had competed with the best senior and had not been beaten. I had done well, had won his respect and had been able to articulate my views and opinions. I felt that I belonged and that I was important. I had found courage, knowledge and euphoria. I knew that I had found the answer. Alcohol worked for me.

The truth was that I was in trouble the first time I got drunk—blacking out, vomiting and having diarrhea for three days. But the blackouts were a price I was willing to pay. I was having fun it seemed for the very first time. I knew I would be getting drunk a lot from now on as a way to relax. I relaxed my way right out of school, out of friendships, out of jobs and out of my mind.

Drugs were given the same priority. I liked getting high. It was cool. Being high was my act of rebellion against authority. I had the same reason for drugging as I did for drinking. And if I could do both, I was a double winner.

The result of this attitude was an overdose. I ate four grams of hash while I was drunk and became mentally ill, paranoid and psychotic. I had to be hospitalized for over three months and I never really recovered from being in the hospital. Ten years elapsed and the same behaviors, using and abusing drugs and alcohol, were still present. I did want to be well. I just didn't want to consider the obvious fact that drugs and alcohol were the problem and not the solution. I had a disease whose major symptom was that I thought it was okay to use the problem *as* the solution.

Let me tell you about being hospitalized. There are many words to describe psychiatric units and they are not usually kind or flattering terms. The one I like best is "nuthouse." It implies the lack of therapeutic values to be found there. People with mental problems are simply put into the nuthouse. You might be a sociopath or merely a maladjusted neurotic. No matter what your degree of trauma, you can be almost certain that you won't be attended to or categorized according to your real problem. A molester might well be placed in with the molested or catatonics might be housed with the extremely anxious. There will be no cure in the nuthouse. Survival is the name of the game.

Inhabitants of the nuthouse learn to adapt. They put their time in, warehoused, hoping to survive long enough to be discharged. Patients become conditioned to this lifestyle and then simply revert to the type of behavior that got them placed in the nuthouse in the first place when they are finally released. They repeat this process over and over–sometimes, unfortunately, for the rest of their lives.

My first hospitalization took a lot out of me. When I was discharged, I was not really ready to leave. Just before my release, one of the aides I respected and had become friends with said to me, "You'll be all right. Just don't drink or use drugs." And I didn't, but I let that fact fool me and I began to rationalize that my ability to abstain proved that I wasn't an alcoholic. I could stop when I wanted to; of course, I also started up again when I wanted to.) After discharge, college seemed out of the question. Employment was something I was becoming fearful of. What was I going to do now?

Not knowing what else to do, I signed up for group therapy. There were two whiz kids leading the group. One was a semi-attractive social worker in her middle twenties and the reason I had signed up for therapy. I might best describe her as a liberated woman, a hippie with a job. The psychiatrist, the other half of the team, was not yet 30 years old. He had shoulder-length hair. He also had indefatigable energy. His drive came not from within himself, however, but from the pharmacy downstairs.

It was pop psychology time and I didn't have the foggiest notion of what was going on. I was dazed and confused, a walking contradiction–"partly truth and partly fiction" as I think a songwriter once wrote. My skilled team and the group couldn't crack me. I was already cracked. I refused to open up and talk about my feelings. During the two-and-a-half years that the group existed, various members came and went. There were four of us clients however who stuck with our therapy religiously for most of that time.

One was a woman of about 25, not especially good-looking, who had been in medical school. I felt closest to her and we dated a few times. I opened up to her more than to anyone else which was not very much. But I could make her laugh. To some slight degree, I felt at ease with her and her with me. Knowing her brought me out of myself a little bit.

While we were still in group, she had to be put back into the psycho ward (the same one we had both been in only 18 months before). We had both talked about suicide but even though I was always worried and was in deep despair, I somehow knew that she was sicker than I was. It was when her roommate attempted to take her own life that my friend had to be hospitalized again. I started visiting her and was able to make her laugh, even in the hospital. I would make fun of the older generation and of our own age group. Being cynical and sarcastic seemed to come naturally to me. It was easier to tear things down than to build them up. She liked that attitude too. It was our escape.

I even made fun of myself. My friend thought it was hysterical when I gave her my theory about why I had gone crazy and had to attend group therapy. I told her that

I couldn't deal with the phase I was going through in my life, the crisis state I was in. Coping with the fact that at age 20, I was going through menopause was too much for me to bear. No wonder I had lost my mind–anyone would. She laughed long and hard at my absurdity which was difficult for her to do, especially since she was on so much medication that repressed her emotions. My only good times were when I was visiting her.

Another faithful member of our therapy group was a young black woman whose estranged husband was in jail for most of the time that she was in therapy. I found her most attractive and she liked me. When I had a car, I would sometimes give her rides to group meetings. But at this point in my life in my early twenties, the female members of the group didn't have to worry about my acting out sexually. I had been badly burned in my first try at love and was scared to death to have any kind of relationship. I avoided letting anyone get close enough to talk about intimate feelings. I tried not to feel.

These members of the group and its leaders were very special in my life. I still think of them fondly. But therapeutically, I don't think any of us were very great or got any revelations from our group experience. We were merely trying to tread water in the sea of our emotions. I know I had very few insights. I did develop some good self-pity skills though. About two years after therapy. I was still contemplating suicide constantly. But the group did keep me out of the psycho ward for 30 months.

When the group disbanded, the freaky young psychiatrist made an interesting suggestion to me. Throughout the entire therapy, never had there been any mention of anyone in group having drug or alcohol problems. All that time, all of us except the black woman were getting high and it was never considered an issue. I thought my problem concerning drugs and alcohol was that I was not getting enough. But my group leader told me that I needed additional therapy and further help.

He was right. Within a year after the group dispersed, I found myself spending the night in the city jail because of my disruptive behavior. I had been living alone in the big city for about three months drinking bourbon, smoking reefer every day, and working at a clerical job at a downtown freight-forwarding office. I had worked my way up from messenger to making lots of important decisions on a daily basis concerning thousands of dollars. I took all my responsibilities very seriously. I worked there nine months altogether. For the last month, another employee and I ran the office while the boss went on vacation.

During that month, I started acting out more in every way. I became more dedicated to work but also more dedicated to drugs and alcohol. And I was more sexually active in the red-light district and with a woman I had met in connection with my work. The candle was definitely burning at both ends. I was 23 now, ego gone amuck and I thought I was invincible.

When the boss returned from his vacation, he gave me a big raise. I certainly deserved the monetary reward. The work had been done, there had been no complaints from the main office and the customers were satisfied. But the angry young clerk who greeted him on his return had turned into a hungry, broken, vicious psycho case. I was a wild man full of paranoia. I had been starving myself so I could spend all my money on sex, drugs and rock-and-roll. I quit my job.

Realizing that I was once again in trouble emotionally, I put myself back into the hospital. But there was nothing the hospital could do for me. I didn't go to the emergency room. I went directly to my old psycho ward. Breaking procedure like that is forbidden and I was arrested. It took half-a-dozen men to restrain me. The police directed me to another psychiatric hospital across town. I was so completely paranoid that I had to be put in a straitjacket. Off and on, the hospital staff tried talking me down for many hours. I refused sedation.

Then a kind male nurse approached me and I physically resisted him when he tried to coax me into taking some liquid Thorazine. I finally picked him up and threw him across the room. As a result, I spent the night in jail and was then transferred to a locked ward in the same quarters as the criminally insane. I was charged with assault. I spent three months in Hell in cramped quarters with a bunch of crazies.

I celebrated my 24th birthday in that locked ward for the criminally maladjusted. Everyone in there was up on some kind of charge. Everyone was probably as guilty as sin, but we were all feeling persecuted (mistreated, unwanted, unloved). However, because of the medications we were being given we were unable to feel anything more. And I was grateful for that. I was tired of suffering and I didn't want to have to face what was happening to me.

The first time I had been in a locked ward I had been unfeeling due to the tranquilizer, Thorazine, which I had been given. This nuthouse however prescribed Stelazine. They juiced me up pretty well. There were times when I was so medicated that I was completely at anyone's mercy. There was a guy there who liked my shoulder-length shag haircut a little too much and in the wrong way. He was 50 pounds heavier than I was. On many nights after being medicated, I had to fight off his advances. I acted out a lot yelling and hitting him, because I was afraid of being raped.

As a result, I spent a good deal of time in seclusion. This solitary confinement could last for hours or days. It all depended on your attitude. I was in there quite a bit. But that wasn't as bad I thought as having a boyfriend. Even though living in reality was not my strong point, being victimized was a real fear. My big accomplishment in that locked ward was not being attacked by Dr. Strangelove.

When the male nurse I had assaulted dropped the charges a few months later, I was put on a nicer, less-restricted ward that was not so crowded. Some of the patients there were even voluntary ones. After a month on that unit, I was given ground privileges. I got a girlfriend—someone from another building.

But this institution left me emotionally scarred. After I took leave of it, I went into a severe depression that seemed never-ending, although it actually lasted two years. I retired from society for the most part and went into isolation at my parents' home. I really wanted to die. And it was many years before I wanted to live again.

Even though I had learned how to survive in the nuthouse, I had never learned how to survive outside. I reverted to my old ways when I was discharged and repeated the process of going in and out of hospitals ten times in ten years. It was all pretty disgusting. I was hopeless, helpless and unable to realize that I could change, that I if I just surrender to the fact that I could not use safely. If I had only been willing to change my lifestyle, I could have had a life worth living so much sooner.

Denial was my biggest obstacle. Something had to happen and when "it" did, recovery also started to take place. Now, every day that I don't put chemicals into my body to alter my mood since "it" happened, I've been recovering. And it keeps on happening with every day of continuous abstinence.

So what did happen? It's very simple. My last drunk lasted for five days and occurred after a two-year binge. I had taken only four drinks of alcohol. I wasn't even using pot. But on this occasion, I found myself a naked vagrant in a police station 200 miles from home babbling incoherently. My disease had progressed to the point where I had to suffer D.T.'s and hospitalization again.

This time however I was willing to want something different. I was given a second chance by something greater than myself, something greater than any nuthouse. I like to think that God intervened in my life at this point to help me become aware that I was going nowhere but that I could matter in this world. All I had to do was to want change and ask for help. If I did this, love, in the person of mankind, could also intervene.

Thus I was given hope. When I'm doing the footwork and doing whatever it takes to abstain today, I realize that I am still receiving the miracle that I did back then. It was a miracle for someone as sick as I was to become so willing to abstain. But such willingness begets change and change begets learning. Learning begets growth, and growth, in turn, begets recovery. And there is no end to recovery. Yet it all starts with the simple task of not using on a daily, continuous basis.

My recovery was not easy at the start. Being in jail and withdrawing from alcohol there was a horrendous experience. I suffered extreme delusionary thinking, running the gamut from believing that I was the savior of the world to knowing that I was the antichrist. I saw imaginary rats coming out of the ceiling, and I shot them dead with a just-as-imaginary gun in my hand. After explaining to my jailers all night long that I was crazy and an alcoholic (I had admitted my craziness before, but never the alcoholism), they began to believe me about the insanity but didn't seem to care very much about my other problem.

They transferred me to a state hospital, my tenth institution in ten years. I was used to the routine by now. You wake up or rather get up (I was never getting much sleep when I was in this kind of altered state), roam around the day room and mix with the other patients until breakfast. Meals are the big event each day. I thought to myself, "Nothing has changed. I'm in another institution where the only things to look forward to (eating and medication) involve waiting in lines." It was the same old procedure that had always occurred before of being warehoused until I was stabilized and could then be released.

Although the routine never changed, the situation and the environment had gotten progressively worse. I was severely beaten one day two weeks into my stay. I had conned my way into the day room. A drunken aide was there harassing a patient who was a former professional middleweight boxer. The aide was very big, about 225 pounds, and very drunk. The patient wanted no trouble and just took the verbal and physical abuse without fighting back. I was very hyperactive which was normal for me whenever I quit drinking. I was jumpy and anxiety-ridden and my mind was going a thousand miles per hour. I was in a bad way.

But my insanity told me to protect this poor patient and I asked the aide, "Why don't you pick on someone your own size?" (By this, I did not mean me.) The aide and I started to fight. He hit me very hard all over my body, but mostly in the ribs and stomach. And I fought back with all the psychotic viciousness I could muster. Somehow, I caught him flush on the jaw and he went down like a dead tree.

Other aides were watching us the entire time and didn't expect a patient to get the upper hand. But at this point, I was not about to observe the Marquis of Queensbury rules of boxing. I wanted blood. So I started racing toward the aide as if I were a kicker in a football game. I had decided to tee off his head. I was not a nice person. I was very mean and very sick.

A couple of aides intervened, fortunately. I don't doubt that I would have tried to kill that drunken aide if they hadn't stopped me. They threw me to the ground. Many other aides then came to help, and I was held down and struck repeatedly for what seemed to be an eternity. I was shaken up pretty badly and afraid that I was bleeding internally.

This experience was the beginning of my spiritual awakening. I finally became ready to start admitting that I had a problem with alcohol and drugs. I made a vow to God that if I got out of that hospital, I would seek help through Alcoholics Anonymous. I called my father and told him what had happened. He raised a lot of Cain with the hospital and I was released two weeks later.

About eight months after I joined A.A., Chemically Dependent Anonymous was founded. I became aware of it because I knew its founders. I respected them and so I went to their meetings, but only occasionally since I was very active in A.A. by then. But the members of this new fellowship impressed me as being sincere in their efforts to make CDA grow.

My problem was that I didn't have the same goal for myself. I went to CDA mostly as a speaker to share my experience, strength and hope. I went, usually, only when invited to chair a meeting and I liked the Fellowship only to the extent that it gave me a platform from which to talk about my sobriety. I wasn't a member; I was a guest lecturer! I was totally ignorant of CDA's ability to enhance the credibility of the group.

I lived in this unenlightened state for some time. Finally, the hard work of the members paid off. I realized that Chemically Dependent Anonymous was not merely an extension of Alcoholics Anonymous. In my mind, CDA began to achieve the status of a support group which could really increase my quality of living. People were staying clean in this fellowship because they were involved, not in spite of their involvement. Up until now, my devotion to A.A. and my ignorance had blinded me to these facts. After four years of recovery, I started using the three Fellowships of Alcoholics Anonymous, Narcotics Anonymous and Chemically Dependent Anonymous, much more in unison.

I was now working in a treatment center for alcoholics and addicts and I played a part in getting CDA and the center to hold a CDA meeting there. Both sides agreed on an open-group format. It has since become a useful meeting not only for patients but for other substance abusers as well.

By the time I was five years into recovery, I was utilizing all three support groups as a way to stay clean. A.A. and N.A. gave me the exposure to quality and quantity experience. But in CDA, I found both quality and camaraderie. The love and enthusiasm of its members broke through my denial and ignorance of the Program's God-given effectiveness and I started involving myself more and more. I got a home group, a sponsor and I became active.

As the saying goes, "CDA is not my life but it [certainly] *gives* me life." It has shown me a dimension of recovery that I had been lacking: love and forgiveness of myself. I have healed greatly because of the love I have found in CDA's rooms. I am very grateful to be a member in good standing today. The Fellowship helps keep that sick, nuthouse patient (the person I used to be) away.

I still work in a drug-and-alcohol treatment center, but in another state, now. We have CDA here too and a Step group has been started. The Fellowship is so small that it meets in my apartment. But I feel it enhances the quality of my own recovery and so I'm committed to being a part of CDA wherever I am. I know it helps others also. I understand only too well about those feelings of denial and ignorance. Higher Power willing, CDA will survive and flourish in this new state. I feel confident that the

Fellowship will grow. Its members are too positive for it not to succeed.

    A state trooper gave me a speeding ticket today. Then, I arrived late at my job. But I did a good day's work and had dinner with a wonderful woman who cooked a delicious meal for us. As we took a walk, on this cold winter night we talked and part of our conversation was about dreams coming true. During active addiction, my dreams never included trying to recover, establishing friendships or caring about people. And they certainly never included being anything but hopeless and helpless.

    Today I got a ticket. If it had been the old days and I was still using, such an occurrence might have set me off like a stick of TNT. Instead, I talked out my frustration and anger with some friends. I was able to laugh about what had happened. I thanked God for another day of not using chemicals to control myself. Talk about dreams coming true! I've come to love life and to face it daily, however difficult, non-chemically. Isn't that great?

37 A Love Story

What I want to share with you is my experience, my story and my own particular opinions. Mine is a love story, not a tale of horror, because what I have experienced through Alcoholics Anonymous, Chemically Dependent Anonymous and all the twelve-step Programs, is a new love of life and the discovery of the meaning of love. Once, I knew nothing about love. Even now, I'm certainly not speaking as an expert. I'm more an explorer of love. I'm new at it but I think this is the most exciting adventure I've ever been on.

As far as I am concerned, there isn't just a spiritual *part* of the Program of CDA. The Program *is* a spiritual one. And the major discovery I have made since coming into the Fellowship is learning how to get close to and become comfortable with the God of my understanding.

Here is a story relating to that God which took place a couple of thousand years ago when He sent down what I believe to be the most positive example to have ever walked on this earth. This man was performing many miracles. And one day, He came upon a blind man standing at a gate who really wanted to be healed so he could see again. The blind man called out, "Lord, help me!" And all His disciples said, "Leave Him alone. He's busy." But the blind man called out one more time, "Please Lord!" And He walked over to the blind man and asked him, "What can I do for you?" The blind man replied, "I'd like to be able to see." So He leaned down and spat in the dirt. He picked up the mud He had just made from the dirt and put it on the blind man's eyes. And he was able to see.

This story explains exactly how I was when I first came into these rooms. I was completely blind to life and had no idea what it was all about. I had no principles and no values. But those in the Fellowship loved me until I was able to establish some principles and values to use in everyday living.

What kept me sober for my first six months in the Program, besides your love, was the fact that I couldn't wait to get up there and tell you what a bad-ass I was—how much alcohol and how many drugs I had used. I was really going to impress everybody with my story. But when the time finally came and I got the opportunity and to throw some of my worst horror stories at you, nobody blinked an eye. So I thought, "If I can't impress these people with how bad I am, maybe if I take all that energy, to try to use it in a positive way, try to do well and work this Program the right way, which will impress them. Maybe I'll get them to love me that way." What happened instead was that after a few months of doing what I was supposed to do, and following directions, I was able to love you. And I was able to love myself.

Today, I am no longer so proud of all my drug stories. But as the Program asks us to do, I want to share some of the way it was with you. The first thing I must say is that I honestly don't remember the pain now. My life is not about pain anymore. It's about challenges, not problems. Hearing that statement is one of the reasons I got into the Program. I went up to a guy at a step meeting one night and said "I've got a lot of other problems besides drinking and drugs." And he told me, "Ronnie, so did I. But when I came into these Programs, my problems turned into challenges." And that was an attractive concept.

I grew up in an alcoholic family and I swore I would never drink because I didn't want to be like my father. I drank for the first time because of peer influence and had a blackout. It was a Christmas Eve many years ago. I vomited in my family's living room, passed out and knocked over the Christmas tree. Then it was off to the races from that very first drink. At that time, I had a promising athletic career, but I flushed that right down the toilet. As soon as I found that magic in alcohol, it became the number one item in my life.

The reason alcohol was so magical for me was not in the taste. I never liked that from the first time I drank until the day when (I hope) I took my last drink. Alcohol's magic was that it enabled me to tell people I was angry at them. For the first time in my life, I was able to express what I wanted to say. It made everything so much easier.

At first, I just drank on weekends and then daily through my high school years. In college, I got into the love-peace-hippie movement and grew long hair. I also went to work as a bouncer at a nightclub. But in order to get to work, I'd have to drink half-pints of vodka straight. Then I'd go into the club and drink beer all night. I started hanging around with the band. I'd always had this terrible need to be in with the "in" crowd.

One night, a whole bunch of girls and a few guys came into the club. One of the guys came up to me and said, "Look, if you want to be able to stay up all night and party, and the odds look good that you will be doing that, you don't want to be falling asleep." I told him I felt fine, but he insisted "Here. Try one of these," and opened up his suitcase. In it, he had literally thousands of Dexedrine pills. I told him I didn't want to become a dope user. I liked my beer. But he persuaded me to try "just a couple." I tried them and they made me feel like Superman. I couldn't quit talking. Eight days later, I still hadn't slept and I was taking 16 pills a day.

That says a lot about this disease. The first time, I wasn't willing to take two. But eight days later, I was up to sixteen. Nothing compulsive about that! By the eighth day, I not only hadn't slept but I was hallucinating too, seeing fights in the bar that weren't really happening. I was told not to come back to work.

I was frightened enough to swear off the drugs and leave town. I met a teenage girl (I was only 21 at the time) and we got together. I was soon on drugs again and I upset her life, as I did everyone's while I was using. Eventually, she became pregnant and my drug use progressed even more after that.

We agreed that she would give the baby up for adoption. But once she started to feel life, she got all excited and wanted me to feel the baby kicking. I refused to do it. I didn't want to get attached to that baby. Deep down I suspected that she was never going to be able to give it up and after the seventh month, she admitted it. So I left her. I couldn't handle the responsibility.

I took LSD, for the first time. But I don't want to de-emphasize the importance of my alcoholism because I was blitzed all day, every day too. I considered that just a normal part of everyday living. One day while on a hit of LSD, I decided that I should do the right thing and go back, get a job and raise my child. But it wasn't until three months later after the baby was born that I finally got around to doing that. In the meantime, I partied until I got a call from the hospital. I hurried there and sat in a waiting room for three days, awaiting the arrival of my son.

For the next three-and-a-half years, I tried to live with my girlfriend and be the best at what I thought a father should be. The only problem was that I didn't want to get married. I never wanted to hold my son. I never changed diapers. I could never tell him I loved him. Other people who came to see him told me how great he was, and I would agree. But he was more like a big bother to me, an accident in my life. That's not easy to admit, but I am trying to be honest about it.

I used to watch television and I'd see all these family shows and wonder, "Why isn't my family like that: all happy and everything?" I know why now. There was some part of me that didn't want to be there–a disease inside me that made me unable to handle the responsibility and just wanted to chase that buzz all the time. The mother of my son finally left me. And, at the time, I was glad. For the next eight years, I set about doing exactly what I wanted to do which was making money off other people's weaknesses, dealing drugs, and just running, ripping and drinking.

Eventually, I got busted for possession of a couple of hundred pounds of pot and all kinds of pills and I had to go court. But I had a good lawyer and he got me off. That episode taught me nothing. I stayed high up until the day of my court appearance because I was afraid. When the day came and I wasn't convicted, I just thought, "Well, I'll always get off."

Shortly thereafter, I got into another relationship. This time it was with a girl who had a six-month-old baby and I completely upset *her* life for five years. Usually, we sent her little girl to daycare every day even though neither of us had jobs. But eventually my girlfriend got a job. (By this time, her little girl was in kindergarten.) One day, my girlfriend asked me to babysit with daughter. It was the only time she had ever done that. She went off to work and I rolled a couple of joints of PCP and smoked them. When my girlfriend arrived home from work, she found me hiding behind the refrigerator naked in a fetal position. Her daughter was just standing there. She just stared at me, horrified.

I spent eight years under the influence of PCP on a daily basis, convulsing every time. I took sets (uppers and downers together) on a regular basis for 15 years, often forgetting how many of each I had taken. Then I would O.D. on them.

After the babysitting incident, I moved out of state, and tried to start a new way of life. I also needed to get away from the mess I had gotten into. I had been busted again for manufacturing PCP, possession and dealing. But the move didn't work out, either. My brother owned a bar and I stayed stone drunk for a year. I drank every day and night, passing out on the bar in his restaurant.

So I went back home and stayed there for the next two years. At one time, I even had a nice house, two cars, a good stereo—all a result of dealing dope. But I eventually ended up on welfare and food stamps because I had to feed my habit too.

One day I looked in the mirror. By now I was 30 years old, and I wondered, "What is the matter with me? How come everybody else is getting it together and I am such a loser? Am I retarded? Is this the result of all the drugs and alcohol I've put in my body? Where did I get these circles under my eyes? How did I get up to 205 pounds? What the hell has gone wrong?" I was afraid, but I had no one to share my fear with. I didn't know anyone who really cared. I had never dared to confess to the people I was running around with that I was weak, that I was hurting or that I had any feelings at all.

Finally, I started shooting drugs intravenously. There is such a feeling of desperation and disgust when you wake up and your arms look like hamburger. You don't care whether you live or not. I felt that way a lot of the time by now then.

Then I got a phone call. Someone said that I'd better get to the hospital because my father had been brought in and he wasn't going to make it through the night. I took a handful of Percodan and went to see him. I was horrified. I saw a man dying of the same disease that I had. I realized that there was very little difference between us—I was dead inside already. It just cut right through the denial.

Something else strange occurred that night. One of my brothers was there (one I'd not been particularly close to over the years). But as my father was dying, he put his hand out, and we all said the Lord's Prayer together. I was deeply moved by that experience. I couldn't remember the words very well, but it didn't matter. We came together at that moment. Afterwards, my brother and I started to talk and I found out that he was in a Program and hadn't taken a drink in six months. I thought, "Man, that's pretty good. How do you *do* that?"

Not too long after my father's death, I found myself in a church. I was going to light a candle and say some prayers for him. But I found myself lighting two candles–one for him and one for me. I'd finally reached my bottom. I was being subpoenaed by the grand jury for manufacturing drugs. I had been thrown off welfare which I have to admit is the best thing that ever happened to me. I just didn't know what to do. So I asked, "God, please give me some direction. What can I do?" I wish I could tell you that from that moment on I was saved, and I never found it necessary to take a drink or drug again. But that was not the case. I went right back out and used again for quite a while.

Then all of a sudden, the drugs just quit working. The alcohol didn't give me the buzz anymore. And I found myself alone in a room with a hypodermic needle, the alcohol, the drugs, and I couldn't get high. The hardest thing I've ever done was to pick up that telephone and call my brother. But I did. I told him that I needed some help. And he put me in touch with people from A.A.

At the time I called my brother I was living in the downtown area of a major city. I had a car, but I was incapable of following directions. It was all just too overwhelming, even when people tried to tell me how to get to the meetings. But the subway wasn't too far from the house and I managed to get there. People from the

Fellowship would meet me at the other end every night and take me to the meetings. They welcomed me, but I couldn't look them in the eye when I first got there because of my lack of self-esteem. I *knew* there was nothing honest about me. I had been out there for 17 years beating myself, lying and cheating.

When I got into the Program, it was not what I didn't know that hurt. It was what I "knew" that just wasn't so. I was completely confused. There was one thing I did know however. When people were at the meetings, they were laughing from their hearts. I liked that. They gave me their phone numbers and told me to keep coming back. They were talking about positive things so I kept showing up.

The first year, I went to four house meetings. But I had a few little slips in the first year because I had something called "a habit." That's something I don't hear much talk about in the rooms. I had a habit of drinking and drugging when I came into A.A. I wanted to stay straight, but I wanted even more, to stay straight and still be allowed to use once in a while.

In the beginning I came to meetings every day, but I had a slip after seven days, then after 19 days and again after 31 days. I'll never forget the last time I used. I had met a girl at my sister's wedding. I called her up and said, "I don't know what I'm going to do. I'm getting tired of coming into these meetings and telling the people that I have been slipping." She replied, "I think you've got to make up your mind. Do you want to get loaded or do you really want to get straight?" Her question was the big crossroads for me.

I moved out of my house in town and knocked on the door of an elderly aunt. I told her I was a drug addict, but she couldn't accept that. I said, "Believe what I tell you. I have a lot of credentials, a lot of history. I just happen to be *sharing* it with you." She said, "Why don't you go upstairs and take a nap and then you'll be alright."

When I came back down two days later, I think my aunt began to believe me. Anybody who can sleep for two days must have some sort of problem. But she was good to me. She helped me. She let me stay there and she did my laundry. So I tried to get a job.

For the first year in A.A., all I did was come to meetings and not use drugs. I left the rooms when people began talking about their particular God. I didn't want to hear anything about the spiritual Program. All I wanted was to stay straight. That was good enough for me. And I made it!

I had some time to fill when I had been straight for about six months. I had heard that you should try to do things, in sobriety that you always wanted to do when you were using but had never had time for. So when I was 34 years old, I wrote my first letter to a guy in prison. He was someone I had dealt drugs with. I was all excited about being straight and I enclosed that "Acceptance" pamphlet—the one with the dove on it. I wrote, "Man, I haven't used drugs for one hundred and eighty days. I've got a new way of life, and I want to share that with you." I'm sure he was thrilled to hear my news, while he was sitting in the penitentiary while he was serving five years.

But four years later, I got a phone call from that guy. He was once the biggest PCP manufacturer in the United States. But this year he'll be celebrating two years in the Fellowship. As a matter of fact, he now goes back to the penitentiary to give the Program away to others. That's the way it works.

I was looking for more things to do in sobriety so on Mother's Day that same year I called the mother of my son. By this time, my son was 13 years old and he had been legally adopted by his mother's husband. Up until then the only times I had been allowed to see my boy were on Christmas and his birthday. And I had always been loaded when I arrived to visit him and give him his presents. I had to be loaded to get up the courage to show up at all.

I told my son's mother that I was straight and she said that he had been asking questions about me. She had recently separated from her husband and wondered if I would like to take our boy for the weekend. She had heard I was in a recovery Program. I couldn't believe my ears. That was one part of my past that I had never thought I'd be able to make up for. I'd never dreamed that I might be able to have a real relationship with my son.

He and I spent the weekend together. It was tough because I still didn't know how to be a father. I had no idea how to give him love; I didn't know what to do with him. So I just prayed and went with my heart. When I first sat down with my son I said "Look I haven't been here in a long time. I've been sick but I'm getting better now. I hope that I'll be able to put back into your life some of the things that I wasn't able to give you before." Eventually, the walls between us came tumbling down. We went sailing–he was a controller and so was I. We had problems deciding which way we were going to go. But I'm here to tell that you we didn't sink.

I thought maybe my son would like to go to camp since I had enjoyed that when I was young. I took him to the same one I had gone to. He was all excited and also a little bit scared when it came time for me to leave. But I came back on Parent's Day. There's this big kid inside me who still likes to have fun. So when we were at the pool, I had to go off the diving board. One of my son's friends asked him, "Hey, who's the guy?" My boy looked at him and said, "That's my dad!" That may not sound like much to you but they were three of the most important words I'd ever heard. I still couldn't tell him that I loved him; I wasn't able to express myself with him in that way yet. But he had acknowledged me.

Through my efforts and with the grace of God, my relationship with my son has kept growing stronger and better. This past year, I went up to his high school and watched him play football. Since I was an athlete when I was young, I had always dreamed of having a son on the team. I watched him play tight end, hit a block and do well. And I was finally able to say, "That's my son!" We have something real together now. That is one more lesson in my on-going education, in learning about love.

Another lesson had to do with my love life. I was still dating my sister's friend in the first year of my recovery. And here is where the real love story begins. While I was dating her, I was also starting to look around at other girls. I was feeling a little better now and I was sprucing up a bit. When I had come into the Fellowship, I still weighed over 200 pounds and had those dark circles under my eyes. I also had quite a few teeth missing. In addition to my physical defects, I had many personality ones. I had started trying to correct my faults and had also begun to work out. After a while, I felt good enough about myself to wonder if I had had enough experience with women. Maybe I should be free to date around.

When I asked my sponsor what he thought, he asked me, "Is this so important to you that you need to tell your girl about it? Do you have to make that decision today?" I said that I didn't so he suggested, "Why don't you just hang in there? You're going through a lot of changes and she's been going to Al-Anon. Maybe things will get better." I thought that was good advice so I kept going to meetings, and my girl accepted the fact that she would only get to see me after the meeting on Saturday nights. She kept going to Al-Anon, I hung in there and our relationship grew.

I did my Fourth Step right after my first anniversary in A.A. That was a tremendous awakening. I came to realize how self-centered I was and saw a lot of other defects that

I hadn't noticed before. I tried to work on them for the next year.

Today I believe that if something is bothering you, and you're afraid of it in sobriety, you should run at it and not away from it. That's the challenge and that's where I find my achievement. It's all too easy to do what I want to do. I did that for 17 years and it got me in trouble. I had always believed that anything that looked good and felt good was something I should do. And I would do it constantly until I had exhausted every bit of pleasure from it. But doing what I sometimes don't want to do has been a big change in my attitude since I have entered the Program.

A good example is what happened at my second Sessions by the Sea early in my recovery. I could not believe the incredible feelings I had there. I was sky-high. I had gotten up early in the morning to see the sunrise, and I was walking along in the sand. I suddenly saw a church. I had told myself that I didn't want to fear anything in sobriety. I had been brought up a Catholic and I looked at that church and thought, "I'd like to go in there. Why don't I?" I realized that I was still full of guilt. And I didn't go in.

But also, as I was walking down that beach, I thought about the fact that there were 3,500 recovering alcoholics and addicts at the convention. The recovery rate for people like me was only one out of every ten. I asked myself why I was one of them. What had I done to deserve this gift of sobriety? I knew that I hadn't done anything to deserve it. My only conclusion was that somebody's prayers had been answered and I had been given a gift from God. I was a child of God. It wasn't too long after that day when I finally did walk into a church.

The feelings I'd had that day by the sea were ones I wanted to investigate further. What I learned was that we don't have any exclusive rights to spirituality here in the Program. There are many other people outside who have it too. As time went by, it got easier and easier for me to be comfortable with the idea of spirituality and I found the God of my own understanding. That completely changed my life. It changed my attitudes. Now I believe that as long as we keep trying to get closer and open our hearts, whatever God we believe in will see to it that we never have the desire to drink or drug when we have the opportunity. God will protect us from temptation.

About my third year in A.A., my employment situation improved. I became a very successful salesperson. I also started becoming inquisitive about something that had never interested me before. I went to a meeting and was asked to lead it. I began by asking questions about love. I told the people there I had been in a relationship for two or three years, but that there was something I didn't understand about it. I shared, "Where are all the fireworks?" When I had relationships before, there were always fireworks and even sirens at times."

And they asked me, "What makes you think you know anything about love? 17 years, all you've been doing is grasping and taking everything you can get out of your relationships because you are a self-centered alcoholic." Those may not be their exact words but that's what I heard. And they were right. That meeting really opened my eyes and those people helped me learn much more about love.

Just about that time I had finally learned my lesson, however, something happened that really jolted me. My girl had come back from an out-of-town Christmas visit with her family to be with me on New Year's Eve. She surprised me by saying that she thought I was becoming too serious about our relationship. She also felt that after four years, we might be getting a little complacent about being together. She said that we ought to give each other some space for a while.

I was overwhelmed and angry. I couldn't believe it. I said, "Do you realize that this is the only relationship I've ever had where I've been faithful? I've never cheated on you once, and now you tell me you want some time off?" The only thing I felt I had to offer her was my fidelity even though I had thought about fooling around during our relationship. I had always heard it's not what you think, but what you do, that counts.

I didn't know what to do about my problem. So I went to meetings every day, talked about it there and I prayed. I wanted to call my girl, every day, and sell myself to her all over again. Then I'd change my mind and want to call her and say, "Forget it! I don't want anything more to do with you." Those were my old tapes, the old pride speaking. After ten days, it all worked out, and we did get back together. With time to think it over, she decided that she knew what she really wanted. And I had learned another valuable lesson. By giving her the space she needed, I had won her back.

My fifth anniversary was a high point in my recovery. When I had first come into the Fellowship, there was only one person at the meetings that I knew from our old drug-using days. I had always wondered what I was going to do about all my old friends once I got straightened out. At my 5th anniversary celebration, 22 people attended who were friends from the days when we used to drink and get high together. That's amazing growth in just five years' time. I hope that encourages all of you who are new to sobriety. God has made it really easy for me. This is a piece of cake compared to the pain and frustration I went through when I was using drugs.

Right after my fifth anniversary, I went on a CDA camp-out with my girl. I had decided that this might be the right time to pop the question. Two years before, I had not even considered marrying. But one night as we were walking on the beach, I just looked over at her and said,

"I'm making this walk towards God. And I was wondering if you would like to come along with me?" She knew exactly what I meant and she answered, "I would."

Six months ago, I had the privilege of walking her down the aisle. That was an extremely important step in my life because I think I finally understand what love is. I know I deeply care about someone other than myself. I've learned more about life and love from this lady than I would ever have believed possible. I may be a little new at marriage but my wife and I have known each other for almost seven years. We've grown together. And we're still growing because we both have Programs and because ours is a triangular relationship. It isn't just the two of us alone against the world. We have God with us too.

So that's my love story. If I have one wish for you, it's that you keep coming back to CDA. Then maybe one day you'll have your own love story to share with us.

Appendices

A. The Twelve Steps of Alcoholics Anonymous*

B. The Twelve Traditions of Alcoholics Anonymous*

*Reprinted with permission of Alcoholics Anonymous World Services, Inc.

Appendix A

THE TWELVE STEPS OF ALCOHOLICS ANONYMOUS*

1. We admitted we were powerless over alcohol—-that our lives had become unmanageable.
2. Came to believe that a Power greater than ourselves could restore us to sanity.
3. Made a decision to turn our will and our lives over to the care of God as we understood Him.
4. Made a searching and fearless moral inventory of ourselves.
5. Admitted to God, to ourselves, and to another human being the exact nature of our wrongs.
6. Were entirely ready to have God remove all these defects of character.
7. Humbly asked Him to remove our shortcomings.
8. Made a list of all persons we had harmed, and became willing to make amends to them all.
9. Made direct amends to such people wherever possible, except when to do so would injure them or others.
10. Continued to take personal inventory and when we were wrong promptly admitted it.
11. Sought through prayer and meditation to improve our conscious contact with God *as we understood Him*, praying only for knowledge of His will for us and the power to carry that out.
12. Having had a spiritual awakening as the result of these steps, we tried to carry this message to alcoholics, and to practice these principles in all our affairs.

*Reprinted with permission of Alcoholics Anonymous World Services, Inc.

Appendix B

THE TWELVE TRADITIONS OF ALCOHOLICS ANONYMOUS*

1. Our common welfare should come first; personal recovery depends upon A.A. unity.
2. For our group purpose there is but one ultimate authority-a loving God as He may express Himself in our group conscience. Our leaders are but trusted servants; they do not govern.
3. The only requirement for A.A. membership is a desire to stop drinking.
4. Each group should be autonomous except in matters affecting other groups or A.A. as a whole.
5. Each group has but one primary purpose-to carry its message to the alcoholic who still suffers.
6. An A.A. group ought never endorse, finance or lend the A.A. name to any related facility or outside enterprise, lest problems of money, property and prestige divert us from our primary purpose.
7. Every A.A. group ought to be fully self-supporting, declining outside contributions.
8. Alcoholics Anonymous should remain forever nonprofessional, but our service centers may employ special workers.
9. A.A., as such, ought never be organized; but we may create service boards or committees directly responsible to those they serve.
10. Alcoholics Anonymous has no opinion on outside issues; hence the A.A. name ought never be drawn into public controversy.
11. Our public relations policy is based on attraction rather than promotion; we need always maintain personal anonymity at the level of press, radio and films.
12. Anonymity is the spiritual foundation of all our Traditions, ever reminding us to place principles before personalities.

* Reprinted with permission of Alcoholics Anonymous World Services, Inc.

Notes

Notes

Notes

+HB137 .A525 1987

HB137 .A525 1987 C.1 STACKS 1987

HB
137
A525
1987

Andersen, Erling B.
Statistics for
economics, business
administration, and
the social sciences

Erling B. Andersen · Niels-Erik Jensen
Nils Kousgaard

Statistics for Economics, Business Administration, and the Social Sciences

With 122 Figures

Springer-Verlag
Berlin Heidelberg New York
London Paris Tokyo

Professor Erling B. Andersen
Professor Niels-Erik Jensen
Professor Nils Kousgaard

Institute of Statistics
University of Copenhagen
Studiestræde 6
DK-1455 Copenhagen K., Denmark

ISBN 3-540-17720-5 Springer-Verlag Berlin Heidelberg New York Tokyo
ISBN 0-387-17720-5 Springer-Verlag New York Heidelberg Berlin Tokyo

This work is subject to copyright. All rights are reserved, whether the whole or part of the material is concerned, specifically the rights of translation, reprinting, reuse of illustrations, recitation, broadcasting, reproduction on microfilms or in other ways, and storage in data banks. Duplication of this publication or parts thereof is only permitted under the provisions of the German Copyright Law of September 9, 1965, in its version of June 24, 1985, and a copyright fee must always be paid. Violations fall under the prosecution act of the German Copyright Law.

© by Springer-Verlag Berlin · Heidelberg 1987
Printed in Germany

The use of registered names, trademarks, etc. in this publication does not imply, even in the absence of a specific statement, that such names are exempt from the relevant protective laws and regulations and therefore free for general use.

Printing: Kiliandruck Grünstadt
Bookbinding: G. Schäffer GmbH u. Co. KG., Grünstadt
2142/7130-543210

Preface

This book is a revised version in English of a text originally written in Danish for a first course in applied statistics for students of economics, public administration and business administration.

A limited knowledge of mathematics is required for understanding the text, except for a single chapter where some knowledge of elementary matrix algebra is necessary. Complicated mathematical proofs are avoided and the explanations are based on intuition and numerical examples.

The aim of the book is to enable the student to understand the reasoning underlying a statistical analysis and to apply statistical methods to problems likely to be met within the fields of economy, public administration and business administration.

The content of the book can be divided into four parts:

methods for exploratory data analysis are presented in chapter 2;
probability theory and standard statistical distributions are discussed in chapter 3-9;
statistical inference theory is presented in chapter 10-12;
and the application of statistical methods is discussed in chapter 13-19.

Chapter 13 deals with simple models related to the normal distribution. The subject of chapter 14 is simple linear regression and that of chapter 15, multiple linear regression. In chapter 16, problems related to heteroscedasticity and autocorrelation in regression models are treated. The presentation of the regression models is based on the application of the least squares method, stressing the importance of methods for evaluating the influence of the individual cases. Chapter 17 contains an introduction to survey sampling, and, finally, chapters 18 and 19 deal with the application of the multinomial distribution and the Poisson distribution for the analysis of categorical data, in particular the analysis of contingency tables.

The applications are illustrated by numerical examples, most of which originate from the fields in which the respective authors are engaged. Most of these examples have never been presented before in English text books. However, due to space restrictions and the complexity of the original problems, these examples are usually not presented in full.

We are indebted to our colleague at the Institute of Statistics, University of Copenhagen, Anders Milhøj, who read and commented on the draft of the manuscript, and to George W. Leeson who has made a heroic attempt to correct the existing text. In particular, we are indebted to Mirtha Cereceda and Joan N. Rasmussen, who typed the manuscript.

Erling B. Andersen
Niels-Erik Jensen
Nils Kousgaard

Contents

1. **Introduction** 1
   1.1. Statistical methods 1
   1.2. Examples 2

2. **Descriptive Statistics** 7
   2.1. Data and variables 7
   2.2. Description of the observed distribution of a categorical variable 8
   2.3. Description of the observed distribution of a quantitative variable 11
   2.4. Description of a grouped distribution of a quantitative variable 16
   2.5. Linear relationship between two quantitative variables.. 20
   2.6. Multiplicative and additive structures in two-way tables 22

3. **Probability Theory** 26
   3.1. Observations and events 26
   3.2. Combinations of events 28
   3.3. Relative frequencies and probabilities 31
   3.4. The axioms of probability theory 34
   3.5. Conditional probabilities 38
   3.6. Stochastic independence 42

4. **Probability Distributions on the Real Line and Random Variables** 47
   4.1. Probability distributions on the real line 47
   4.2. Random variables 49
   4.3. Discrete random variables 52
   4.4. Continuous random variables 56
   4.5. Transformations 62
   4.6. Empirical frequencies and density functions 64

5. **Mean Values and Variances** 66

5.1.	The mean value	66
5.2.	The variance	71
5.3.	Theorems about mean values and variances	74
5.4.	Other moments and distributional measures	76
5.5.	Applications of location and dispersion measures	80

6. Special Discrete Distributions... 89

6.1.	The binomial distribution	89
6.2.	The Poisson distribution	95
6.3.	The Pascal distribution	102
6.4.	The multinomial distribution	107
6.5.	The hypergeometric distribution	108

7. Special Continuous Distributions... 112

7.1.	The normal distribution	112
7.2.	The log-normal distribution	122
7.3.	The exponential distribution	125
7.4.	The Pareto distribution	129
7.5.	The gamma distribution	132
7.6.	A comparison of six distributions	135

8. Multivariate Distributions... 137

8.1.	Multi-dimensional random variables	137
8.2.	Discrete m-dimensional random variables	137
8.3.	Continuous m-dimensional random variables	140
8.4.	Marginal distributions	143
8.5.	Conditional distributions	145
8.6.	Independent random variables	147
8.7.	Mean values and variances for sums of random variables	148
8.8.	The covariance and the correlation coefficient	151
8.9.	The multinomial distribution	159
8.10.	The distribution of sums of random variables	161
8.11.	The multivariate normal distribution	165

9. The Distribution of Sample Functions and Limit Theorems... 169

9.1.	Introduction	169
9.2.	The distribution of $\overline{X}$ and S^2 for normally distributed random variables	169
9.3.	The t-distribution and the F-distribution	174
9.4.	The law of large numbers	176
9.5.	Limit theorems	179

10. Estimation 184

    10.1. The statistical model 184
    10.2. Estimation 185
    10.3. Maximum likelihood estimation 187
    10.4. Unbiased estimators 192
    10.5. Consistency 197
    10.6. The properties of ML-estimators 199

11. Confidence Intervals 202

    11.1. Point estimates and confidence intervals 202
    11.2. Confidence intervals 202
    11.3. Confidence intervals for the mean value and the variance in the normal distribution 204
    11.4. Confidence intervals for the parameters in the binomial distribution and the hypergeometric distribution 209
    11.5. Approximate confidence intervals 211
    11.6. Concluding remarks 213

12. Testing Statistical Hypotheses 214

    12.1. The statistical hypothesis 214
    12.2. Significance tests 215
    12.3. Construction of tests 217
    12.4. Tests in discrete distributions 220
    12.5. Conditional tests 222
    12.6. Approximate tests 228
    12.7. The power of a test 231
    12.8. Hypothesis testing and interval estimation 233

13. Models and Tests Related to the Normal Distribution 235

    13.1. The u-test 235
    13.2. The t-test 240
    13.3. The Q-test 241
    13.4. The comparison of two independent normally distributed samples 246
    13.5. A model for pairwise observations 253
    13.6. The model for pairwise observations and the model for two independent samples 256
    13.7. The analysis of variance 258
    13.8. Distribution free tests 267

14. Simple Linear Regression 275

14.1.	Regression analysis...	275
14.2.	Simple linear regression..	276
14.3.	Estimation of the parameters....................................	278
14.4.	Properties of the LS-estimator..................................	281
14.5.	Analysis of variance..	286
14.6.	Interpretation of the estimated regression parameters and R^2..	289
14.7.	Examination of the residuals....................................	292
14.8.	Predictions...	295
14.9.	Experimental and non-experimental data..........................	302
14.10.	Transformations..	303
14.11.	Comparison of two regression lines.............................	310

15. Multiple Linear Regression................................. 316

15.1.	The multiple linear regression model................	316
15.2.	Estimation of the parameters........................	319
15.3.	Properties of the LS-estimator......................	321
15.4.	Residual analysis...................................	323
15.5.	Hypothesis testing..................................	325
15.6.	Case analysis.......................................	334
15.7.	Collinearity..	338
15.8.	Predictions...	343

16. Heteroscedasticity and Autocorrelation................ 347

16.1.	Heteroscedasticity...............................	347
16.2.	Autocorrelation..................................	354

17. Survey Sampling... 362

17.1.	Introduction...	362
17.2.	Simple random sampling.................................	363
17.3.	Simple random sampling in the binary case..............	365
17.4.	Simple random sampling in the general case.............	368
17.5.	Stratified sampling....................................	373

18. Applications of the Multinomial Distribution........ 386

18.1.	Hypothesis testing in the multinomial distribution.......	386
18.2.	Goodness-of-fit tests of discrete distributions..........	392
18.3.	Goodness-of-fit tests of continuous distributions........	396
18.4.	Comparison of k Poisson distributions....................	399

19. Analysis of Contingency Tables........................... 403

19.1.	The test of independence.....................	403

- 19.2. The test of homogeneity................................. 409
- 19.3. Comparison of binomial distributions.................... 411
- 19.4. The multiplicative Poisson model........................ 412
- 19.5. The effect of the sampling procedure................... 417
- 19.6. Analysis of the marginals of a two-way table........... 418
- 19.7. Three-way contingency tables............................ 423

Appendix Table... 431

Index... 432

Index of Examples with Real Data................................. 438

1. Introduction

1.1. Statistical methods

The discussion of many problems in the social sciences is based on the collection and analysis of data. For example, to investigate how the value of a house depends on such things as the size of the house or the location, the values of these quantities must be measured for a sample of houses. If the problem is to describe the production of electricity at a power plant as a function of the fuel consumption, monthly or weekly joint observations of production and consumption must be collected. For the study of the employment pattern of married women, information about variables like present employment status, education, age and area of residence must be obtained, for example from a survey of a selected group of married women. To evaluate the information in such data, a statistical analysis can be performed.

A statistical analysis is based on a scientific theory called theoretical statistics, which provides the rules for describing, summarizing and evaluating information in data. The fundamental concept in theoretical statistics is the statistical model, by which a formal separation of the observed variability in data into a structural and a random component can be obtained. The description of the random component is based on probability theory, which is a mathematical discipline.

In the initial phase of a statistical analysis, descriptive or explorative methods are used to investigate important structural features of the data in easily interpretable ways. A characteristic property of such simple methods is that they are based on very broad assumptions concerning the nature of the data. This part of the analysis plays an important role for the choice of a statistical model which is required for a more detailed evaluation of the information available from the data.

Since the conclusions of a statistical analysis depend on the chosen statistical model, it is essential that the model gives an appropriate description of the variability in the data. Therefore, prior knowledge of the problem under consideration and the methods for collecting the data should be taken into account when a statistical model is formulated. But it is equally important to check empirically that the variability prescribed by the model is matched by the actual variability in the data. Such a model check is obviously an important part of any statistical analysis.

After a brief introduction to exploratory data analysis, the elements of probability theory that are necessary for understanding and performing a statistical analysis are presented. This is followed by the general theory of inference which is applied to a number of statistical models and methods, frequently used for the analysis of problems within the social sciences.

1.2. Examples

This book emphasises examples as a mean of illustrating the applicability of the theory. Many of the examples originate from actual applications of statistical methods, but in most cases neither the original data set nor the original analysis of the data can be presented in detail, so simplifications of the problems are discussed on the basis of selected parts of the original data set. The data sets presented all relate with few exceptions to problems in the social sciences, primarily economics, business administration, public administration and sociology.

Example 1.1. Contingency tables

Many investigations in the social sciences are based on interviews or written questionnaires concerning socio-demographic or socio-economic issues. Each of the questions gives rise to a classification of the interviewed persons into one of several possible categories. Based on several of the questions, the persons can, therefore, be cross-classified according to the given categories. The resulting table is called a **contingency table**. Table 1.1 shows a two-dimensional contingency table, in which 2610 married women are classified according to degree of urbanization and type of employment. The categories for each criterion follow from the headings of the table. The data in table 1.1 are collected in order to investigate the extent to which the employment pattern of married women depends on the degree of urbanization. Initially it could be assumed (quite unrealistically) that the employment pattern is the same for all five urbanization levels. If this assumption holds, the same percentage distribution should be found in all five rows of table 1.1. These distributions are shown in table 1.2 where the numbers are obtained by dividing the numbers in table 1.1 by their row totals.

Table 1.1. Married women in Denmark classified according to degree of urbanization and type of employment, 1964.

| Degree of urbanization | Employment ||||
	Work at home	Part-time work	Full-time work	Assist in husband's business
Copenhagen,City	188	66	139	16
Copenhagen,Suburbs	145	32	98	14
Towns	401	114	239	65
Villages	81	24	53	25
Country	364	118	164	264

Source: Women in family and employment. Danish National Institute of Social Research. Publication No. 37, 1969.

Table 1.2. Percentage distribution of married women according to type of employment, given the degree of urbanization.

| Degree of urbanization | Employment ||||
	Work at home	Part-time work	Full-time work	Assist in husband's business
Copenhagen,City	46.0	16.1	34.0	3.9
Copenhagen,Suburbs	50.2	11.1	33.9	4.8
Towns	49.0	13.9	29.2	7.9
Villages	44.2	13.1	29.0	13.7
Country	40.0	13.0	18.0	29.0

The calculations in table 1.2 represent an example of the application of a descriptive statistical method, on the basis of which one obtains an overview of the structure in the data. Table 1.2 thus reveals that there are differences in the employment patterns, but also that some differences seem to be more significant than others. Some differences may even be so small that they do not represent structural differences in the population from which the persons have been selected. To settle this question, more sophisticated statistical methods are needed. An analysis of the data based on a statistical model is given in section 19.1.△.

Example 1.2. Survey sampling

An estimate of the percentage of the Danish population aged 20 to 69 years participating in sports-activities at least once a week can be obtained from a survey sample. In 1977, the Danish National Institute of Social Research conducted a survey, in which 5166 persons aged 20 to 69 years were asked a whole variety of questions. Among these, 25% said they participate in a sports-activity at least once a week. How close is the observed percentage to the true percentage in the population? In order to answer this question, the method of sampling must be known. The frequency of persons participating in some form of sport probably varies considerably between population groups. The frequency may thus turn out to be different for men and for women and for persons from different social groups or age groups. The precision of the estimate accordingly depends on the representation of these various population groups in the sample and on the variation of the frequency from group to group.

In the following it is assumed as a simplification that the sample is drawn at random from the population consisting of Danes, aged 20 to 69 years. This means that the sample is drawn so that each person in the population has the same probability of being included in the sample. The population in question consisted in 1976 of 3 111 892 persons. From this population numerous different samples consisting of 5166 persons can be drawn, and the percentage of these actively participating in some form of sport may vary considerably between the potential samples. Therefore, the percentage observed in the sample is not necessarily identical with the percentage in the population as a whole. The percentage in the population can in principle be almost any number between 0 and 100. Based on theoretical statistical arguments, it can be claimed, however, that the percentage in the population with "a certainty of 95%" will be in the interval from 23.8 to 26.2. In the computation of these limits, knowledge of the sample size and of the percentage in the sample claiming to participate in sports at least once a week is utilized.

In selecting the actual sample considered above, it was attempted to account for the fact that different groups in the population behave differently. This was done by applying a two-stage stratified sampling scheme. According to this scheme, the 275 Danish municipalities were grouped in strata in such a way that the municipalities within a stratum were similar with respect to degree of urbanization and demographic structure. At the first stage a number of municipalities were then selected in such a way that the strata were represented in the total sample with predetermined frequencies and at the second stage a number of individuals were selected from these municipalities in such a way that each stratum was represented in the final sample with predetermined frequencies. The aim of this procedure was, among other things, to increase the precision of the estimate of the percentage of the sports-active in the population. Thus it would seem reasonable to claim that the sampling uncertainty is in fact less than that expressed by the interval (23.8%, 26.2%). △.

Example 1.3. Regression analysis

A problem often met in economics is that of describing the value of an economic variable as a function of one or more so-called explanatory variables. Table 1.3 shows the joint observations of production of electricity and fuel consumption (oil or coal) for a Danish power plant in 24 consecutive months.

In order to investigate the relationship between the variables, the electricity production can be plotted against the fuel consumption as in fig. 1.1.

Table 1.3. Monthly fuel consumption measured in Giga Joule and electricity production measured in MegaWatt-hours. Asnæs Power Plant, block 3.

	1982 Electricity production	Fuel consumption	1983 Electricity production	Fuel consumption
January	150 638	1 422 044	124 743	1 178 430
February	139 907	1 338 445	115 333	1 078 701
March	127 849	1 225 643	112 994	1 086 166
April	117 390	1 144 123	123 239	1 176 552
May	96 450	967 955	58 400	561 176
June	113 148	1 150 605	17 677	192 242
July	141 873	1 342 686	3 394	39 189
August	177 661	1 736 447	136 598	1 310 817
September	20 296	216 282	69 840	692 139
October	92 359	865 543	69 941	689 855
November	92 735	879 298	122 615	1 166 354
December	131 728	1 267 052	116 869	1 129 953

Source: El-Kraft Production Company.

It follows from the figure that there is an almost perfect linear relationship between fuel consumption and electricity production. In order to determine the straight line that fits the data best and in order to evaluate the goodness of the fit, a statistical model has to be formulated. The appropriate model is called a linear regression model. In such a model, the structural variation represented by the line can be distinguished from the random variation represented by the deviations from the line. △ .

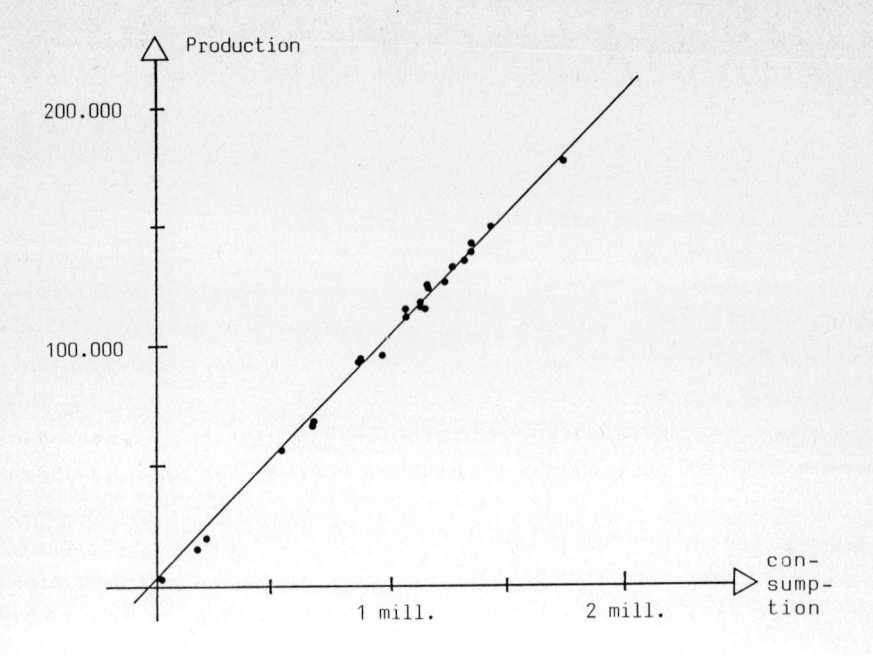

Fig. 1.1. Monthly values of the fuel consumption and electricity production for two years at the Asnæs Plant, Block 3.

2. Descriptive Statistics

2.1. Data and variables

A **data set** is a collection of observed values of one or more variables. In the simplest case, data consist of repeated measurements of one variable. In table 2.1 the differences between the exchange rate for American Dollars (US$) on the first day of each month from January 1983 to December 1984 are shown. The exchange rate is defined as the value in DKK (Danish Kroner) of 100 US$.

Table 2.1. Differences between the exchange rate for US$ on the first day of the month, January 1983 to December 1984.

```
+31.10, + 0.65, - 9.40, +18.70, +33.45, + 0.50, +49.25,
+ 6.40, -20.10, + 8.20, +19.15, +14.60, +28.30,
-61.55, - 4.55, +49.15, - 3.35, +29.00, +40.25,
- 9.25, +56.10, -20.55, +30.70.
```

The exchange rate is a **quantitative** variable, i.e. a variable measurable on the real line, so the monthly difference is also a quantitative variable.

Table 2.2 is a summary of a data set consisting of pairs of observations, recording personal income and type of holiday for 3111 Danes. The type of holiday is a categorical variable with five categories: Holidays at home, at week-end cottage, in Denmark, abroad and no holidays. A measurement of a **categorical variable** with a finite number of categories is simply a statement of one of the categories. Personal income is a quantitative variable. For the purpose of presentation, however, the variable has been **grouped**, i.e. the range of the variable has been divided into a finite number of intervals and the recorded personal incomes replaced by indications of the intervals, to which they belong.

Table 2.2. 3111 Danes distributed according to type of holiday and personal income.

Income, DKK	At home	Type of holiday Week-end cottage	In Denmark	Abroad	No holiday	Total
- 19999	33	15	81	51	120	300
20000- 39999	100	20	125	90	165	500
40000- 59999	155	28	166	100	105	554
60000- 79999	157	43	152	119	71	542
80000- 99999	132	52	146	108	33	471
100000-149999	141	79	164	141	39	564
150000-	31	31	34	66	18	180
Total	749	268	868	675	551	3111

Source: Living Conditions in Denmark. Compendium of Statistics 1976. Danmarks Statistik and the Danish National Institute of Social Research.

The grouped variable personal income is a categorical variable but in contrast to a categorical variable such as type of holiday, its categories can be ordered with respect to income, whereas no natural ordering exists for the categories of the type of holiday.

In this chapter, a number of simple data analytic methods for exploring and displaying important features of these data are discussed. These methods involve the computation of elementary summary measures and the construction of graphs. In contrast to those discussed in the later chapters, however, they are not based on detailed assumptions concerning the distribution of the observations.

2.2. Description of the observed distribution of a categorical variable

For n observations $x_1, \ldots, x_n$ of a categorical variable with m categories, let

a_j = number of observations belonging to category j, j=1,...,m,

and

$f_j = a_j/n$ = the relative frequency of observations belonging to category j, j=1,...,m.

The set $(a_1, \ldots, a_m)$ constitutes the **observed** or **empirical distribution** of the variable, and $(f_1, \ldots, f_m)$ the corresponding **frequency distribution**.

The observed distribution of the type of holiday, for example, is obtained from the column sums of table 2.2 as

$(a_1, a_2, a_3, a_4, a_5) = (749, 268, 868, 675, 551)$

and the corresponding frequency distribution as

$(f_1, f_2, f_3, f_4, f_5) = (0.24, 0.08, 0.28, 0.22, 0.18)$.

The frequency distribution can be displayed graphically by means of a **pie chart**, where the proportion f_j is depicted as a slice of a circle, the area of which is the fraction f_j of the total area of the circle. Fig. 2.1 shows the pie chart for the frequency distribution of type of holiday.

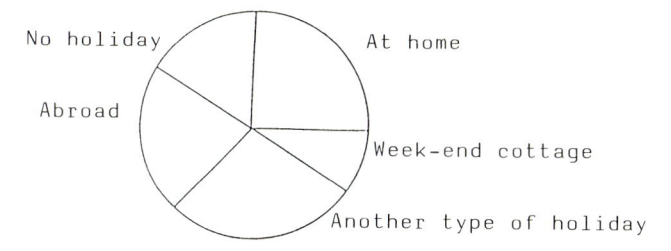

Fig. 2.1. Pie chart for the frequency distribution of type of holiday.

Alternatively, the frequency distribution can be depicted by means of a **block diagram** where the blocks represent categories and the areas of the blocks are proportional to the frequencies of the respective categories. The block diagram for the frequency distribution of type of holiday is shown in fig. 2.2.

A third way of illustrating the frequency distribution is by means of a **histogram**, in which the relative frequencies are represented by vertical bars on a horizontal axis. Again the areas of the bars are proportional to the corresponding relative frequencies. The histogram for type of holiday is shown in fig. 2.3. It should be noted that the order of the bars in fig. 2.3 is arbitrary.

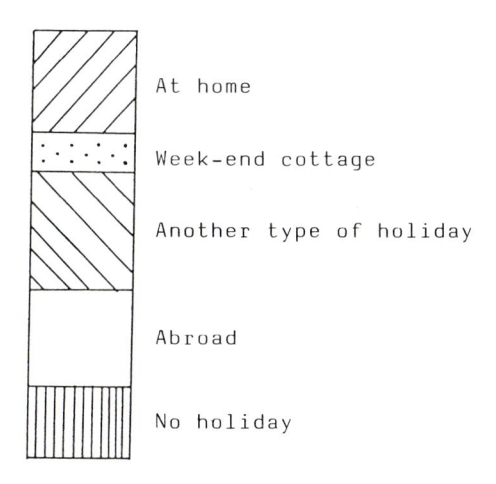

Fig. 2.2. Block diagram for type of holiday.

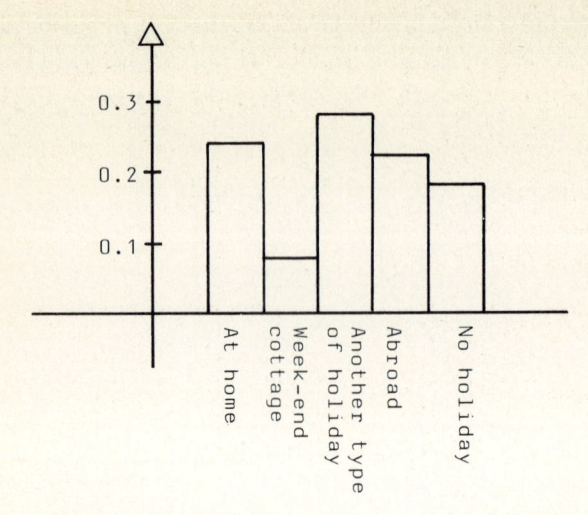

Fig. 2.3. Histogram for type of holiday.

Graphical displays are particularly useful for the comparison of two or more distributions. Fig. 2.4 shows the pie charts for the distribution of type of holiday for persons with incomes below 20000 DKK and for persons with incomes above 150000 DKK, respectively. These pie charts clearly reveal the differences between the frequencies of the categories "no holidays" and "holidays abroad" for persons with low incomes and persons with high incomes. The corresponding block diagrams are shown in fig. 2.5.

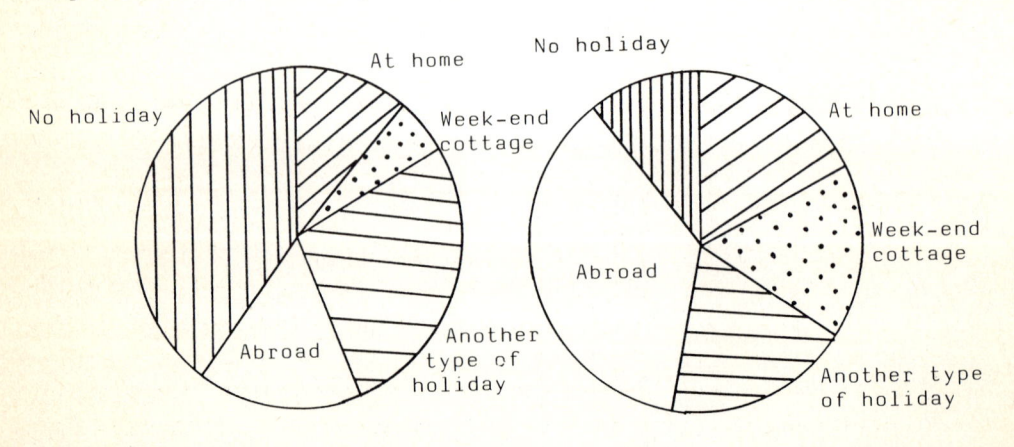

Fig. 2.4. Pie charts for type of holiday for a low-income group and a high-income group.

Fig. 2.5. Block diagrams for a low-income group and a high-income group.

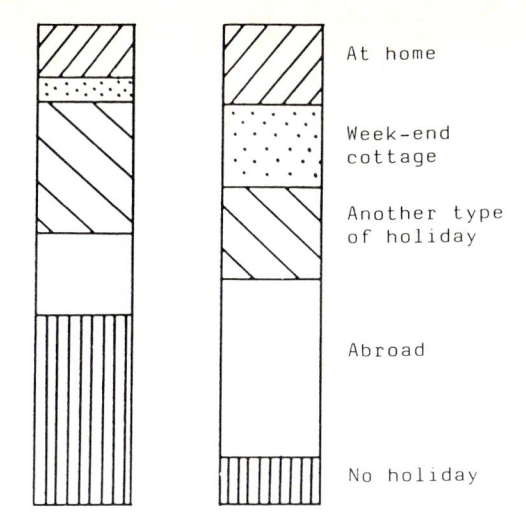

2.3. Description of the observed distribution of a quantitative variable

Let $x_1,\ldots,x_n$ be n observations of a quantitative variable. The first step in an explorative analysis of such data is to organize and display them so that emphasis is placed on important features of the data, such as properties of location and symmetry, the spread of the observations and the existence of extreme or outlying observations.

A useful form of display is offered by the **stem and leaf diagram**. In order to construct this diagram, each observation is split into two parts, the stem and the leaf. The stem consists of the leading digits of the observation, while the remaining part of the observation is represented by the leaf. The values in the stem are written in a column and for each observation the leaf is placed on a line to the right of the stem. To separate the stem from the leaves, a vertical line is drawn between them.

To facilitate the construction and interpretation of the diagram, the observations are often rounded beforehand. Consider, for example, the stem and leaf diagram for the data in table 2.1. In order to construct this diagram, each of the monthly changes of the exchange rate is rounded to an integer value. As the stem, the 10 digit is chosen and as the leaf, the 1 digit. For example, the first observation, 31.10, is rounded to 31 and split as

                    31 = 3(stem) + 1(leaf)

The stem values, running from -6 to +5, are written in ascending order as a column (note that all integer values between -6 and +5 are written) and for each observation, the leaf is written to the right of its stem value. Finally, for each value of the stem, the leaves are written in ascending order.

In the stem and leaf diagram in fig. 2.6, the first observation can be found as the second leaf corresponding to the stem value 3. Fig. 2.6 shows that the monthly differences of the exchange rate are located around a value between 10 and 20 and that the distribution seems to be asymmetric. Furthermore, x=61.55 is clearly distinct from the bulk of the observations and may therefore be denoted as an outlier.

Stem	Leaves
-6	2
-5	
-4	
-3	
-2	1 0
-1	
-0	9 9 5 3
0	1 1 6 8
1	5 9 9
2	8 9
3	1 1 3
4	0 9 9
5	6

Fig. 2.6. Stem and leaf diagram for the monthly differences of the exchange rate.

Consider now figures 2.7(a) and 2.7(b). The data used to construct these figures were obtained from an experiment in which four mono loudspeakers were compared with respect to timbre by a panel of judges. The judges were instructed to score the loudspeakers on a scale ranging from 0 to 9. The observations consist of the scores given by two judges in different settings.

In these diagrams, the stem values have been chosen so that the leaves are neither too numerous nor too sparse. In fig. 2.7(a), this has been achieved by letting two stem values represent each value of the integer part of the observation. The first stem value, marked with an asterisk, corresponds to observations with a fractional part between 0 and 4 while the second value, marked with a dot, corresponds to observations with a fractional part between 5 and 9. Similarly, in fig. 2.7(b), each value of the integer part of the observations is represented by five different stem values. The first, marked with an asterisk, corresponds to observations with a fractional part which is either 0 or 1; the second, marked with a T, refers to fractional parts 2 and 3; the third, marked with an F, refers to fractional parts 4 and 5; the fourth, marked with an S, refers to fractional parts 6 and 7; and the fifth, marked with a dot, refers to fractional parts 8 and 9.

a)
```
3*  | 04
3.  | 56899
4*  | 000011133334444
4.  | 555555567777889999
5*  | 00001222333334
5.  | 55677789999
6*  | 000111233344
6.  | 556677889
7*  | 0111123
```

b)
```
6F  | 55555
6S  |
6.  | 8
7*  | 000000000000000000000
7T  |
7F  | 55555555555555555555555555
7S  | 7
7.  | 888
8*  | 0000000000000000000000000
8T  | 23
8F  | 55555555
```

Fig. 2.7. Stem and leaf diagrams for scores of loudspeakers given by two judges.

The stem and leaf diagrams reveal that the judges apply the scales in widely different manners, both as regards the level, the range and the actual scores used. While the scores of judge 1 range from 3 to 7 with a level around 5, the scores of judge 2 range from 6.5 to 8.5 with a level around 7.5. In addition, judge 2 seems to prefer the values

6.5, 7.0, 7.5, 8.0 and 8.5, whereas judge 1 uses a broader range of scores. Thus, the scores of the two judges as measurements of a quantitative variable are not directly comparable.

The stem and leaf diagram for the monthly differences of the exchange rate can also be constructed without rounding the observations as shown in fig 2.8. In this way the original observations are sorted in ascending order.

Stem	Leaves
-6	1.55
-5	
-4	
-3	
-2	0.55 0.10
-1	
-0	9.40 9.25 4.55 3.55
0	0.50 0.65 6.40 8.20
1	4.60 8.70 9.15
2	8.30 9.00
3	0.70 1.10 3.45
4	0.25 9.15 9.25
5	6.10

Fig. 2.8. Stem and leaf diagram for the monthly changes of the exchange rate.

The ordered set of the observations $x_1, \ldots, x_n$ is denoted $x_{(1)}, x_{(2)}, \ldots, x_{(n)}$ where

$$x_{(1)} \leq x_{(2)} \leq \cdots \leq x_{(n)},$$

and the values $x_{(1)}, \ldots, x_{(n)}$ are called the **order statistics**. For the monthly differences of the exchange rate in table 2.1, $x_{(1)} = -61.55$, $x_{(2)} = -20.55$ and $x_{(23)} = 56.10$. If two or more observations are equal their mutual order is of course arbitrary.

From the order statistics the **percentiles** can be computed. Let $0 < p < 1$ and let

$$p(n+1) = i + f$$

where $i = [p(n+1)]$ is the integer part of $p(n+1)$ (i.e. the largest integer less than or equal to $p(n+1)$) and f is the fractional part of $p(n+1)$. The p percentile x_p is then obtained by interpolating between $x_{(i)}$ and $x_{(i+1)}$ as

(2.1) $\quad x_p = (1-f)x_{(i)} + fx_{(i+1)}.$

The 0.5 percentile, called the **median**, divides the sample into two equally large portions and is a measure of the **location** of the sample, i.e. a value centrally located in the distribution of the sample. If $n=2m+1$, then $[0.5(2m+1+1)]=m+1$ and $f=0$ such that according to (2.1)

$$x_{0.5} = 1 \cdot x_{(m+1)} + 0 \cdot x_{(m+2)} = x_{(m+1)}.$$

If $n=2m$, then $[0.5(2m+1)]=m$ and $f=0.5$ such that

$$x_{0.5} = (1-0.5)x_{(m)} + 0.5x_{(m+1)} = (x_{(m)} + x_{(m+1)})/2.$$

The **lower** and **upper quartiles** are defined as the 0.25 and the 0.75 percentiles, respectively. The **interquartile** distance is defined as

$$d_q = x_{0.75} - x_{0.25}$$

and is a measure of the spread or the variation of the observations around the median. Finally, the smallest and the largest observation, $x_{(1)}$ and $x_{(n)}$, are called the **extremes**.

From fig. 2.8, the percentiles of the data in table 2.1 are easily computed. Since $n=23=2 \cdot 11+1$, the median becomes $x_{(12)}=14.60$. The 0.25 percentile becomes $x_{(6)}=-4.55$ since $0.25(23+1)=6+0$ and finally $x_{0.75}=x_{(18)}=31.10$ since $0.75(23+1)=18+0$. If the sample had consisted of $n=24$ observations, the median would have been $(x_{(12)}+x_{(13)})/2$ and the quartiles $0.75x_{(6)}+0.25x_{(7)}$ and $0.25x_{(18)}+0.75x_{(19)}$, respectively.

Important features of the distribution of quantitative observations can be displayed graphically by means of a **box plot**. The box plot consists of a rectangular box, the length of which is equal to the interquartile distance d_q. A vertical line through the box indicates the position of the median. The extremes $x_{(1)}$ and $x_{(n)}$ are connected to the edges of the box by horizontal lines. On more sophisticated box plots, outliers, defined as observations smaller than $x_{0.25}-1.5d_q$ or larger than $x_{0.75}+1.5d_q$, are marked by crosses on the line connecting the extremes to the box.

From the box plot, the symmetry of the distribution of the observations can be evaluated. Symmetry means that the distribution to the right and to the left of the median have similar shapes. This implies that the distances $x_{0.50}-x_{0.25}$ and $x_{0.75}-x_{0.50}$ are approximately equal and that the incidence of outlying observations is the same in each side of the distribution.

Fig. 2.9 shows the box plot for the monthly differences of the exchange rate in table 2.1. Again the lower extreme, $x_{(1)}=-61.55$, is clearly distinct from the remaining observations. Furthermore, the distance between the median and the lower quartile is somewhat smaller than the distance between the upper quartile and the median, indicating lack of symmetry.

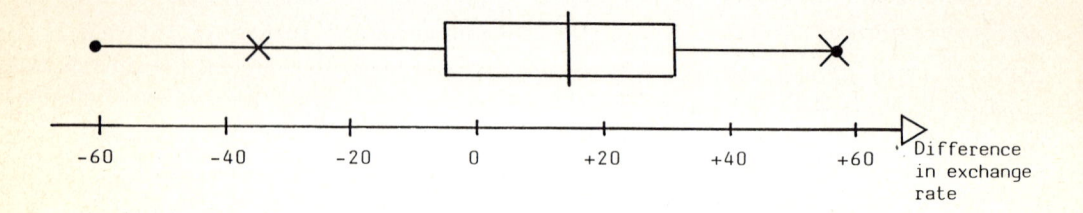

Fig. 2.9. Box plot for the monthly differences of the exchange rate.

2.4. Description of a grouped distribution of a quantitative variable

Let $x_1,\ldots,x_n$ be a set of n observations of a quantitative variable and assume that the range of the observations is divided into m intervals by the points $t_0, t_1,\ldots,t_m$. If a_j is the number of observations contained in the j'th interval $(t_{j-1}, t_j]$, $a_1,\ldots,a_m$ represents a **grouped distribution**. In many cases, data are presented in the form of a grouped distribution and the values of the original observations are unknown.

The histogram provides a graphical representation of a grouped distribution. In a **histogram**, the frequencies $f_j = a_j/n$ corresponding to each interval are graphed as vertical columns or bars above the intervals, so that the areas of the columns are proportional to the relative frequencies. The height of the column for the j'th interval is therefore proportional to

$$f_j^* = f_j/(t_j - t_{j-1}).$$

If all intervals are of equal length, it is not necessary to adjust the heights for interval length.

In many cases, one or both of the end intervals are open, i.e. $t_0=-\infty$ and/or $t_m=+\infty$. In such situations, the part of the histogram corresponding to the extreme intervals cannot be constructed directly. However, the histogram can be completed by taking values believed to be close to the unknown values of t_0 and t_m, but it should be borne in mind that unless the relative frequencies of the end intervals are very low the appearance of the histogram can be seriously influenced by the choice of endpoints.

The cumulative frequency corresponding to the interval $(t_0, t_j]$ is defined as

$$F_j = \sum_{i=1}^{j} f_i.$$

A connected graph of the points (t_j, F_j), $j=1,\ldots,m$ (if $t_m=+\infty$, $j=1,\ldots,m-1$) is called a **cumulative frequency function**.

In some cases, the percentiles of a grouped distribution are required. If $p=F_j$ for some j, then the p percentile t_p is simply defined as t_j. For values of p between F_j and F_{j+1}, the percentile is computed by linear interpolation. Suppose that $F_j < p < F_{j+1}$, then t_p is defined by

$$t_p = (1-f)t_j + ft_{j+1},$$

where $f=(p-F_j)/(F_{j+1}-F_j)$. Note that t_m must be different from $+\infty$ if $p > F_{m-1}$ and t_0 must be different from $-\infty$ if $p < F_1$.

Since t_p is obtained by linear interpolation, it can be derived directly from the plot of the cumulative frequency function. A line **parallel** to the abscissa through the point $(0,p)$ is drawn, and from the intersection between this line and the cumulative frequency function a line perpendicular to the abscissa is drawn. This line intersects the abscissa in t_p.

Table 2.3 shows the distribution of Danish farms according to size in 1980 together with the quantities f_j^* and F_j. Since no upper limit is given for the last interval, it is arbitrarily set to 150 ha. The frequency of this interval is so low that the choice of endpoint has little effect on the appearance of the histogram, shown in fig. 2.10.

Fig. 2.11 shows the cumulative frequency function for the distribution of the farm size and illustrates the computation of the median of the distribution by interpolation.

Table 2.3. A grouped distribution of Danish farms according to size in 1980, with frequencies and cumulative frequencies.

Size (in ha)	Length of interval	f_j	f_j^*	F_j
0.0 - 4.9	5	0.1317	0.0263	0.1317
5.0 - 9.9	5	0.1721	0.0344	0.3038
10.0 - 19.9	10	0.2589	0.0259	0.5627
20.0 - 29.9	10	0.1750	0.0175	0.7377
30.0 - 49.9	20	0.1637	0.0082	0.9014
50.0 - 99.9	50	0.0807	0.0016	0.9821
100.0 - 150.0	50	0.0180	0.0004	1.0001

Source: Danmarks Statistik.

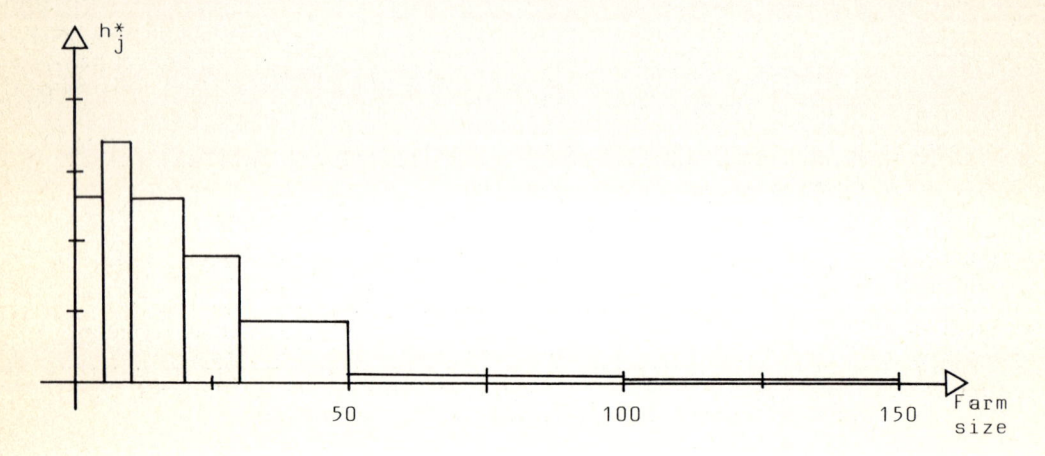

Fig. 2.10. Histogram for the distribution of Danish farms according to size.

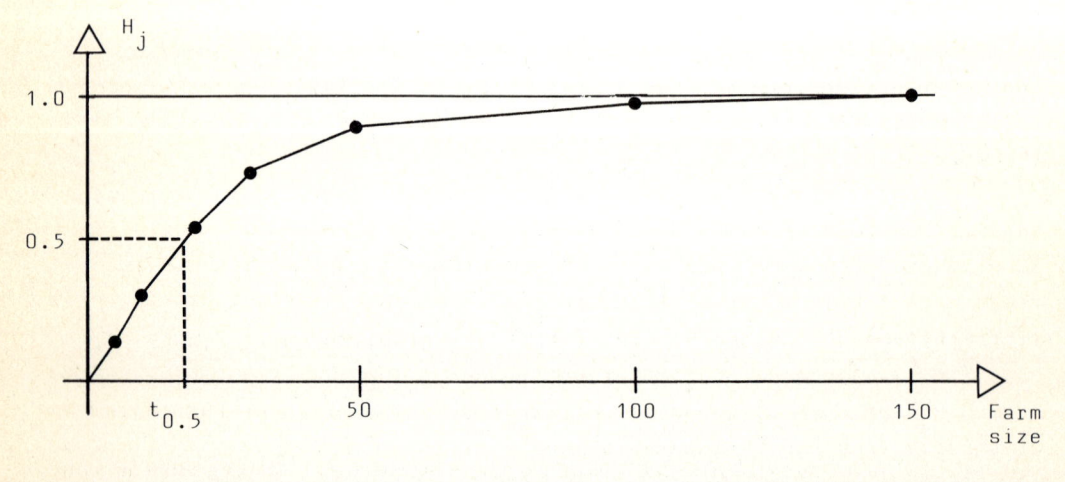

Fig. 2.11. Cumulative frequency function for the distribution of Danish farms according to size.

To illustrate the use of box plots for grouped distributions, consider the income distributions in table 2.4. By means of box plots, the differences in income distributions between single persons and couples can be studied, as well as variations in income distribution for families according to the number of children. The medians and quartiles necessary for drawing the box plots in fig. 2.12 are obtained by interpolation as described above.

Table 2.4. Percentage distributions of gross income for a random sample of 6930 Danes in 1974, shown for single persons and couples (in the taxation sense) and according to the number of children living at home .

	Single persons			Couples				
	Number of children			Number of children			
Gross income	0	1	2 or more	0	1	2	3	4 or more
- 19999	43	17	19	2	1	0	1	1
20000- 39999	24	30	32	24	4	2	4	5
40000- 59999	19	29	28	18	13	12	12	19
60000- 79999	9	17	13	19	20	24	26	24
80000- 99999	2	4	3	14	24	24	19	22
100000-119999	1	1	2	10	16	18	13	17
120000-139999	1	1	1	5	10	9	8	6
140000-	1	1	2	8	12	11	17	6

Source: Living Conditions in Denmark. Compendium of Statistics 1976. Danmarks Statistik and The Danish National Institute of Social Research.

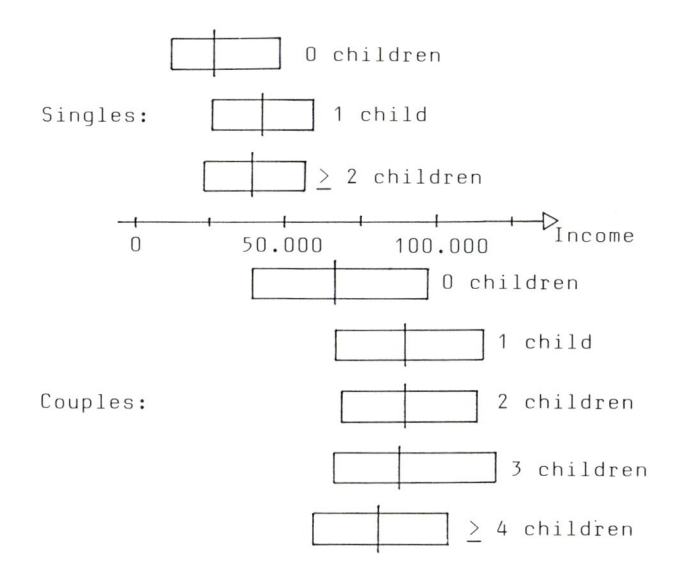

Fig. 2.12. Box plots for gross income for single persons and couples according to number of children.

From fig. 2.12 it can be concluded that:

1) The income is lower for single persons than for couples, given the humber of children, and the variation of the incomes, measured by the interquartile distance, is greater for couples.

2) For both single persons and couples, the income levels are lowest for the group without children, highest for the group with one child and thereafter decreasing with the number of children.

This, of course, could also be seen directly from table 2.4 but it would have required more experience in reading tables.

2.5. Linear relationship between two quantitative variables

Let (x_i, y_i), $i=1,\ldots,n$, be n pairs of observations of two quantitative variables x and y. To explore the relationship between the observed values of the variables, it is often useful to plot their observed values against each other. If one is interested in studying the variation of y as a function of x, the observed values of x should be plotted along the abscissa. If the plot indicates that the relationship is linear, i.e. if the points are scattered randomly around a straight line, a straight line can be fitted to the points. If, however, the relationship is considered non-linear, the data can perhaps be transformed to obtain an approximate linear relationship between the transformed observations. A logarithmic transformation of one or both variables is often suitable.

A description of the relationship between the variables by a straight line is preferred because it is easier to understand and interpret, and because deviations from linearity are often more evident than deviations from a curved non-linear function.

Table 2.5 shows the observed values of the Danish Consumer Price Index and the Land Value per square meter for each of the years 1964 to 1982. These variables are plotted against each other in fig. 2.13. Even though the relationship between the variables for the whole period is not approximated particularly well by a straight line, no simple transformations of the variables can improve the situation.

Table 2.5. The Danish Consumer Price Index and Land Value in Danish Kroner per square meter, 1964-1982.

Year	Consumer Price Index	Land Value per square meter
1964	44.2	15.54
1965	46.9	12.88
1966	50.4	16.07
1967	54.0	17.19
1968	58.4	18.80
1969	60.2	22.35
1970	64.2	23.17
1971	68.1	28.38
1972	72.4	34.21
1973	79.2	45.86
1974	91.2	55.35
1975	100.0	67.86
1976	109.0	76.29
1977	121.1	86.28
1978	133.3	97.28
1979	146.1	112.99
1980	164.1	117.89
1981	183.3	109.23
1982	201.9	97.15

Source: Danmarks Statistik.

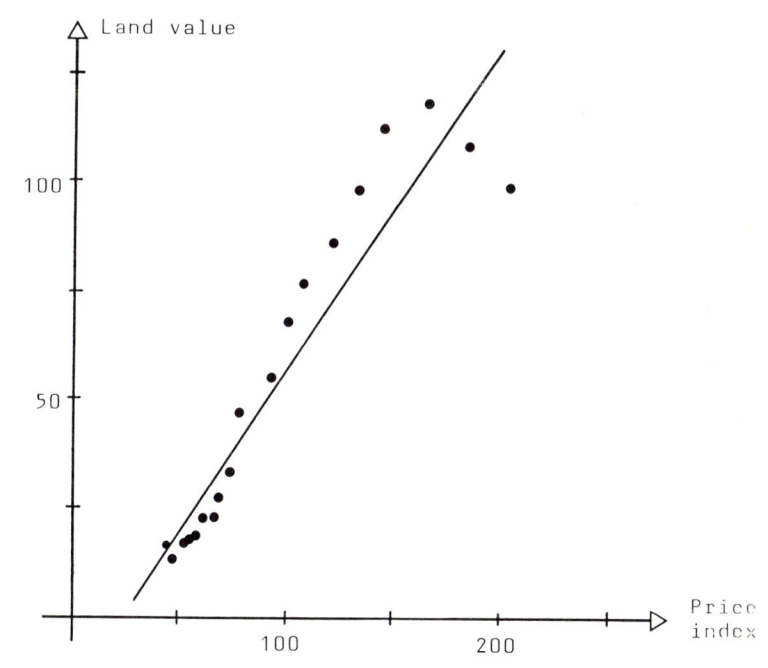

Fig. 2.13. Plot of the Consumer Price Index against Land Value, 1964 to 1982.

2.6. Multiplicative and additive structures in two-way tables

A data set for which the observations can be arranged in an IxJ matrix as

$$\begin{bmatrix} x_{11} \cdots x_{1j} \cdots x_{1J} \\ \vdots \\ x_{i1} \cdots x_{ij} \cdots x_{iJ} \\ \vdots \\ x_{I1} \cdots x_{Ij} \cdots x_{IJ} \end{bmatrix}$$

is said to constitute a **two-way table**. For example, table 2.2 shows 3111 persons grouped according to two qualitative variables with 7 and 5 categories respectively, and x_{ij} is the number of persons belonging to category i of variable 1 and to category j of variable 2.

The structure of a two-way table is said to be **additive** if

$$x_{ij} \simeq a_i + b_j \quad \text{for } i=1,\ldots,I, \text{ and } j=1,\ldots,J,$$

which means that x_{ij} for all combinations of i and j can be written approximately as the sum of two unknown constants representing the row number and the column number, respectively.

Under an assumed additive structure, the row and the column averages $\bar{x}_{i.}$ and $\bar{x}_{.j}$ satisfy

$$\bar{x}_{i.} = \frac{1}{J} x_{i.} = \frac{1}{J} \sum_{j=1}^{J} x_{ij} \simeq a_i + \bar{b}$$

and

$$\bar{x}_{.j} = \frac{1}{I} x_{.j} = \frac{1}{I} \sum_{i=1}^{I} x_{ij} \simeq \bar{a} + b_j$$

where $\bar{b} = \frac{1}{J} \sum_{j=1}^{J} b_j$ and $\bar{a} = \frac{1}{I} \sum_{i=1}^{I} a_i$.

Furthermore, $\bar{x}_{..} = \frac{1}{IJ} \sum_{i=1}^{I} \sum_{j=1}^{J} x_{ij} \simeq \bar{a} + \bar{b}$ so that

(2.2) $$x_{ij} \simeq \bar{x}_{i.} + \bar{x}_{.j} - \bar{x}_{..} .$$

The assumption of additivity can then be checked by plotting, for each value of j, the points $(\bar{x}_{i.}, x_{ij})$, $i=1,\ldots,I$. From (2.2) it follows that these points should cluster around a straight line with slope 1.

The structure of a two-way table is said to be **multiplicative** if

(2.3) $x_{ij} \simeq a_i b_j$ for $i=1,\ldots,I$, and $j=1,\ldots,J$,

i.e. if x_{ij} for all values of i and j can be approximated by the product of two numbers, representing the row and the column of the table, respectively.

The existence of a multiplicative structure can be checked as above by checking for additivity since (2.3) for $x_{ij} > 0$ implies that

(2.4) $\ln(x_{ij}) \simeq \ln(a_i) + \ln(b_j)$

so that the presence of a multiplicative structure in the x_{ij}'s is equivalent to the presence of an additive structure in the logarithms of the x_{ij}'s.

However, since

(2.5) $x_{ij} \simeq \dfrac{x_{i.} x_{.j}}{x_{..}}$

under the assumption of multiplicativity, this structure can also be checked by plotting, for each value of j, the points $(x_{i.}, x_{ij})$, $i=1,\ldots,I$. These points should cluster around a straight line through (0,0).

The graphical checks for additivity and multiplicativity are illustrated using the data in table 2.6 for the number of traffic accidents with serious personal injuries in Sweden on 15 Sundays in the summer of 1962, distributed according to the type of road.

Table 2.6. Traffic accidents in Sweden on 15 Sundays, distributed according to type of road, 1962.

Day No.	Trunk road	Major road	Minor road	Total
1	2	7	4	13
2	8	8	4	20
3	7	9	9	25
4	7	4	8	19
5	3	5	7	15
6	5	4	4	13
7	4	5	7	16
8	4	4	12	20
9	7	3	8	18
10	3	8	12	23
11	4	12	15	31
12	4	5	14	23
13	9	12	10	31
14	10	9	17	36
15	10	9	14	33
Total	87	104	145	336

It has been suggested that the number of accidents on a given type of road is proportional to the total number of accidents on the day considered. This suggestion implies that the table must have a multiplicative structure. Therefore, the points $(x_{i.}, x_{ij})$, $i=1,\ldots,I$, are plotted for each value of j as shown in fig. 2.14, where the slopes of the lines are $x_{.1}/x_{..}$, $x_{.2}/x_{..}$ and $x_{.3}/x_{..}$, respectively. Since the points are scattered randomly around the lines, it can be concluded that the data in fact have an additive structure.

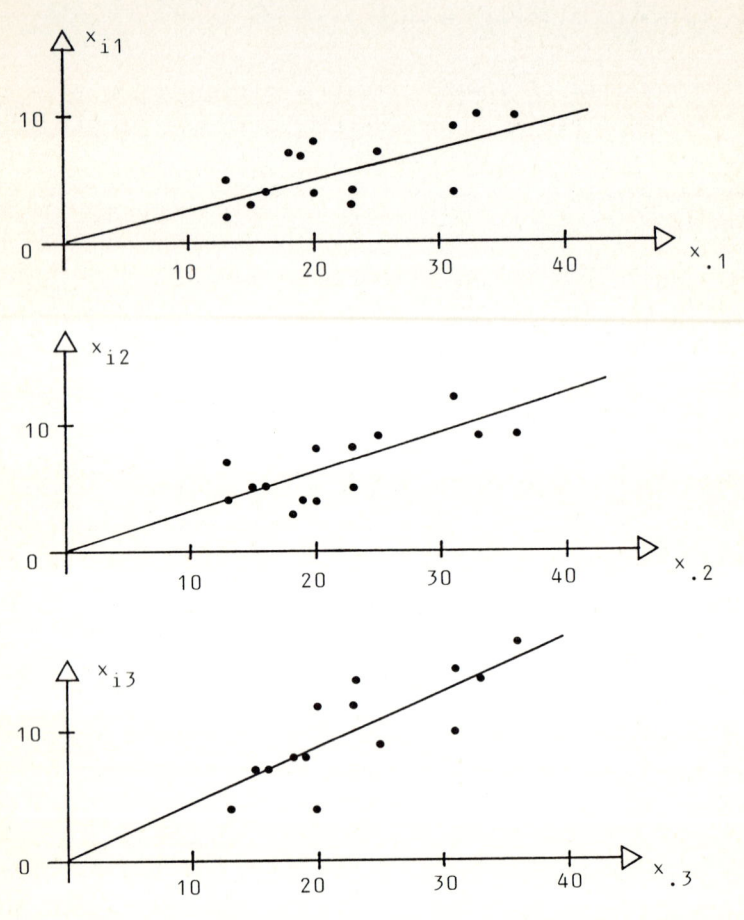

Fig. 2.14. Graphical check of multiplicativity in the data of table 2.6.

The existence of a multiplicative structure in table 2.6 implies that the structure of the table of logarithms is additive. Fig. 2.1 shows the check for additivity performed on the basis of the logarithms of the numbers of traffic accidents. As was to be expected, the points are scattered randomly around straight lines with slope 1, confirming the assumption of additivity.

Fig. 2.15. Graphical check of multiplicativity of the data in table 2.6 after a logarithmic transformation.

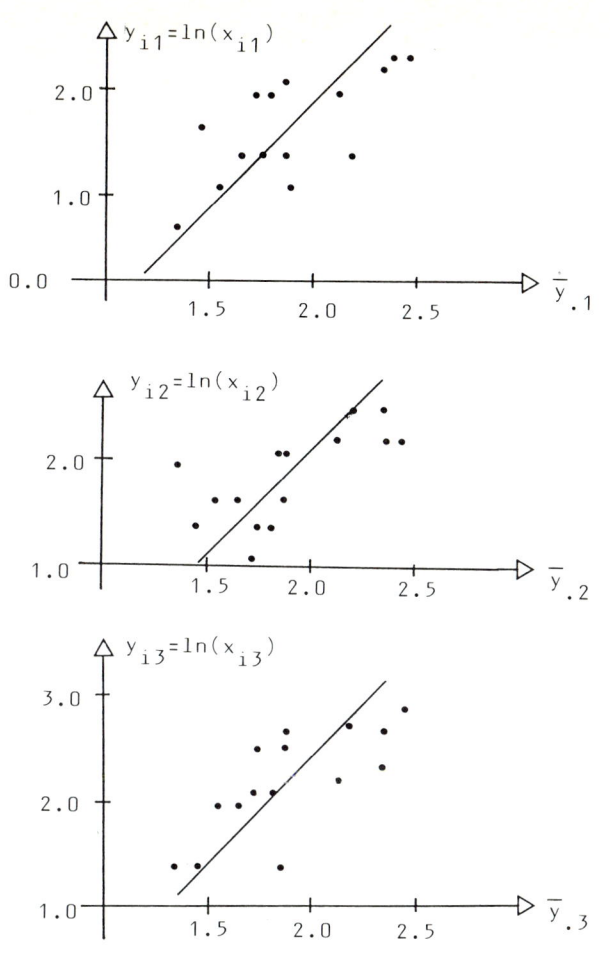

3. Probability Theory

3.1. Observations and events

Probability theory plays an important role in statistics because the concept of probability allows us to describe observable phenomena, the occurrence of which seems to be governed partly by chance. Faced with real data, the analyst needs to be able to differentiate between that which may be caused by an underlying structure and that which may be considered as random variation. Probability theory is the mathematical discipline that connects law and chance. In other words, with the help of probability theory, randomness can be described by mathematical law.

A fundamental concept underlying the following considerations is that of an **observation**. An observation may be **quantitative** such as "the output measured in giga joule of a power plant in May 1982 is 150000", or is may be **qualitative** such as " a randomly selected person intends to vote for the Conservative Party at the coming election". Probability theory can be used to describe and analyse both quantitative and qualitative observations.

An observation can be regarded as the result or the **outcome** of a random experiment. By random we mean that the outcome cannot be predicted with certainty prior to the experiment being carried out. For example, a random experiment would be casting a die since it is not possible to state with certainty the outcome of the cast. However, the concept of an experiment has to be understood in a very broad sense. Many of the observations we consider arise from a "natural" experiment rather than a planned experiment, for example observations from some process which takes place in the course of time.

The collection of all possible outcomes of a random experiment is called the **sample space**, and a subset of the sample space is called an **event**. An event consisting of a single outcome is called an **elementary event**. The sample space is denoted by E and events by capital letters (A, B, C,... for example).

To illustrate the concepts of a sample space, an event and an elementary event consider the situation where a die is cast. The outcome of this experiment is of course the number of eyes shown on the face of the die that turns up. Hence, the sample space E comprises six elementary events a_1, a_2, a_3, a_4, a_5 and a_6, i.e.

$$E = \{a_1, a_2, a_3, a_4, a_5, a_6\}.$$

The subset A of E consisting of the elementary events a_2, a_4 and a_6 is in itself an event corresponding to "the result of a cast is an even number".

The **complementary event** to the event A consists of all outcomes not contained in A and is denoted by $\bar{A}$. The complementary event to the sample space E is denoted by Ø and is called the **empty event** as it contains no outcomes at all.

Example 3.1

Table 3.1 shows the population in Denmark on 1.January 1985 distributed according to sex and geographical region (residence).

<u>Table 3.1.</u> The population in 3 regions of Denmark on 1.January 1985 distributed according to sex. Numbers are in thousands.

	The Copenhagen metropolitan area	The Islands, excl. Copenhagen	Jutland	All Denmark
Females	890	523	1181	2594
Males	833	514	1170	2517
Total	1723	1037	2351	5111

Source: Statistical Yearbook 1985. Danmarks Statistik.

Assume that a person is chosen at random from the population and that the sex and place of residence of the person is observed. The selection of a person can be regarded as a random experiment with elementary events $a_1, \ldots, a_6$ corresponding to the six combinations of sex and place of residence:

a_1 = {Female, Copenhagen}

a_2 = {Male, Copenhagen}

a_3 = {Female, The Islands}

a_4 = {Male, The Islands}

a_5 = {Female, Jutland}

a_6 = {Male, Jutland}.

The event A corresponding to "the person is male" can be written as

$$A = \{a_2, a_4, a_6\}$$

The event B corresponding to "the person lives in Copenhagen" can be written as

$$B = \{a_1, a_2\},$$

and the complementary event $\overline{B}$ to B is

$$\overline{B} = \{a_3, a_4, a_5, a_6\}.$$

In fig. 3.1, the sample space E, the events A and B and the elementary events $a_1, \ldots, a_6$ are illustrated. △.

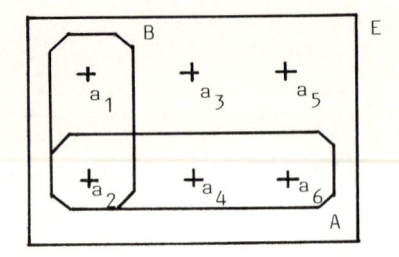

Fig. 3.1. The sample space and two events A and B.

3.2. Combinations of events

Let A and B be any two events in the sample space E. If we consider the set of all outcomes that are in A or B or both, a new event C is defined. This event C is called the **union** of A and B and is written as

$$C = A \cup B.$$

Note that C also contains outcomes that are in A as well as in B. The concept of a union can be illustrated graphically as shown in fig. 3.2 where the sample space is symbolized by a rectangle and the events A and B by subsets of this rectangle.

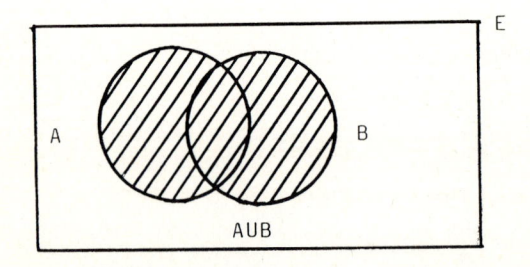

Fig. 3.2. The union of A and B.

The set of all outcomes that belong to A as well as to B is called the **intersection** of A and B. The intersection D of A and B is written as

$$D = A \cap B.$$

The concept of an intersection is illustrated in fig. 3.3.

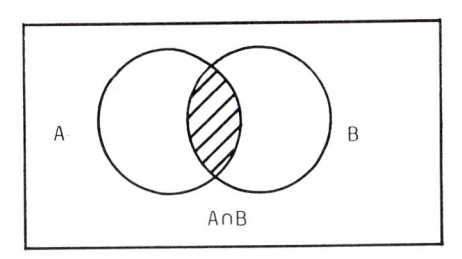

Fig. 3.3. The intersection of A and B.

Two events, the intersection of which is the empty event, are said to be **disjoint**.

The definition of a union and an intersection can be extended to more than two events. Let $A_1, \ldots, A_m$ be a sequence of m events. The union C of $A_1, \ldots, A_m$ is the set of all outcomes that belong to at least one of the m events and is written as

$$C = A_1 \cup A_2 \cup \ldots \cup A_m = \bigcup_{i=1}^{m} A_i$$

The intersection D of $A_1, \ldots, A_m$ is similarly defined as the set of all outcomes that belong to each of the A_i's and is written as

$$D = A_1 \cap A_2 \cap \ldots \cap A_m = \bigcap_{i=1}^{m} A_i.$$

Further extensions of the concepts of intersection and union to infinite sequences of events are straightforward. If $A_1, A_2, \ldots, A_i, \ldots$ is an infinite sequence of events, the union C of these events is written as

$$C = A_1 \cup A_2 \cup \ldots \cup A_i \cup \ldots = \bigcup_{i=1}^{\infty} A_i$$

and consists of all outcomes contained in at least one of the events of the sequence. The intersection of the events of the sequence is written as

$$D = A_1 \cap A_2 \cap \ldots \cap A_i \cap \ldots = \bigcap_{i=1}^{\infty} A_i$$

and consists of all outcomes that are in each of the events of the sequence.

The union and the intersection of the three events A, B and C are illustrated in fig. 3.4.

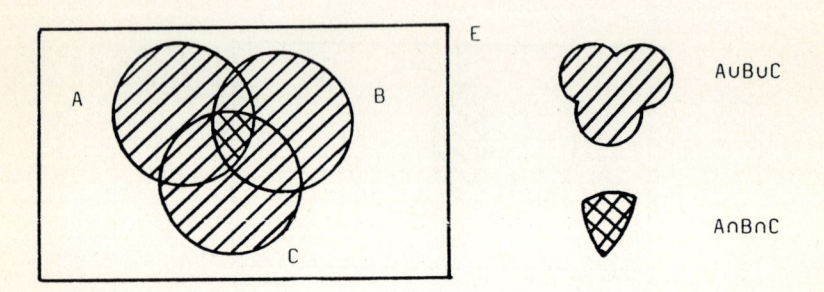

Fig. 3.4. The union and the intersection of the events A, B and C.

A sequence of events $A_1,\ldots,A_m$ is said to be disjoint if no elementary event is contained in more than one of the events of the sequence.

Example 3.2

Table 3.2 shows a sample of 3620 Danes, distributed according to social group and employment status. The selection of a person from the population can be regarded as a random experiment with 12 outcomes corresponding to the 12 combinations of social group and employment status.

Table 3.2. A sample of 3620 persons aged 20-69 years in Denmark 1976, by employment status and social group.

Social group	Self-employed	Salaried employees	Workers	Total
I + II	84	372	-	456
III	460	430	-	890
IV	127	785	352	1264
V	-	-	1010	1010
Total	671	1587	1362	3620

Source: Living Conditions in Denmark. Compendium of Statistics 1980. Danmarks Statistik and Danish National Institute for Social Research.

The elementary events are denoted a_{ij}, $i=1,2,3,4$ and $j=1,2,3$, where i represents social group and j employment status.

Let A be the event "the person is self-employed" and let B be the event "the person belongs to social group I+II". The union C of A and B, i.e. $C = A \cup B$, is then the event "the person is either self-employed or belongs to social group I+II". Likewise, the intersection D of A and B, i.e. $D = A \cap B$, is the event "the person is self-employed and belongs to social group I+II". The events A, B, C and D are illustrated in fig. 3.5.△.

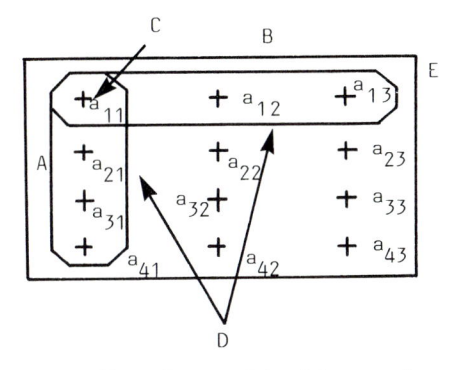

Fig. 3.5. Events corresponding to combinations of social group and employment status.

3.3. Relative frequencies and probabilities

As early as the 17'th century, mathematicians discovered that certain random phenomena exhibited the same sort of systematic behaviour. In a single cast of a die, the number of eyes shown is governed by chance. But if the die is cast many times, the frequency with which a six is observed approaches 1/6. This may be taken as evidence that the chance or the probability of observing a six is 1/6. The empirical fact that relative frequencies tend to stabilize in long series of random experiments is fundamental for the application of probability theory.

It is an empirical fact that if a random experiment is repeated many times under essentially the same conditions, then the relative frequency $h(A)$ for a given event A, defined as

(3.1) $\qquad h(A) = \dfrac{\text{number of times A occurs}}{\text{number of repetitions}}$,

approaches a number that only depends on the event A and the experiment, but not on the actual series. It is tempting to call this limiting number the probability of the event A. From a mathematical point of view, however, it is inconvenient to operate with quantities for which the definitions depend on long sequences of experiments. Thus, in establishing the mathematical framework for the computation of probabilities, an axiomatic approach is chosen. Probabilities between 0 and 1 are assigned to the events of an experiment in such a way that a certain consistency exists between the probabilities of the individual events. Moreover, before implementing those probabilities in practice, it is important to check the consistency of the probabilities with the real world. This may be done by comparing the postulated probabilities of certain events with the corresponding relative frequencies obtained by repeating the experiment a large number of times.

We can illustrate these considerations by returning to the experiment with a die. If the die is fair, i.e. if all six faces have the same chance of coming up, it may be reasonable to assign the probability 1/6 to each of the six elementary events. If A denotes the event that a six is thrown we may say that the probability of A, P(A), is 1/6. If the die is thrown many times and the relative frequencies

$$0.183, 0.163 \text{ and } 0.173$$

for a six after 500, 1000 and 1500 throws respectively are observed, it seems reasonable to accept 1/6 as the probability of A. If, however, the relative frequencies

$$0.205, 0.210 \text{ and } 0.225$$

are observed, one is likely to reject the model, i.e. the assignment of the probabilities 1/6 to each of the elementary events, as the difference between the relative frequency after 1500 throws and the postulated probability seems rather large.

In 1812, the French mathematician **Laplace** introduced a particularly simple method for the assignment of probabilities to events. Laplace considered the important case where the sample space E has a finite number of outcomes, all of which are **equally likely**. This framework covers examples such as throwing a die, tossing a coin and playing roulette. Assume that E consists of m equally likely outcomes and that g of these are in the event A. These g outcomes are called the **favourable** ones and Laplace suggested that the probability of A, P(A), should be defined as

(3.2) $P(A) = \frac{g}{m}$.

This simple formula permits us to establish a set of rules for calculations with probabilities. All rules for the calculation of probabilities derived from **Laplace's** formula (3.2) in the simple case of equally likely outcomes should also hold for the calculation of probabilities in more complicated situations.

Example 3.3

In example 3.2, a selection of a sample of 3620 Danes aged 20-69 years was considered, and in table 3.2 this sample was shown distributed according to social group and employment status. The contents of this table can be considered as a summary of the outcomes of 3620 random experiments in each of which a person is selected and his/her social group and employment status observed.

If each person in the population has an equal chance of being selected in each of the experiments, it follows from Laplace's formula that the probability of selecting a self-employed person belonging to social group I+II (event A) is identical to the proportion of self-employed persons belonging to social group I+II in the population. Hence the relative frequency in the sample

$$h(A) = \frac{84}{3620} = 0.023$$

is an approximation to the probability P(A) of A. $\triangle$.

In order to check that h(A) actually tends to stabilize around P(A) given by Laplace's formula (3.2), long series of random experiments have been carried out. The British statistician Karl Pearson tossed a coin 12000 times and 24000 times respectively and observed 6019 heads in the first series and 12012 heads in the second series. He thus found h(A)=0.5016 and h(A)=0.5005 for the event A={head}, strongly suggesting that $P(A)=\frac{1}{2}$, i.e. the coin is fair. The South African statistician Kerrich constructed a false coin by glueing a wooden disc to a lead disc of the same size. He found after 10, 50 and 100 tosses that the wooden side came up with frequencies 0.90, 0.78 and 0.73. After 1000 throws this frequency had stabilized at 0.68. Thus, it is not reasonable to assume that the two possible outcomes in Kerrich's experiment are equally likely.

From time to time empirical evidence rejects seemingly reasonable models. One could assume that for a given birth the events A={a boy} and B={a girl} are equally likely, such that $P(A)=P(B)=\frac{1}{2}$ according to Laplace's formula. However, from records of a large number of births, it is found that

$$h(A) \simeq 0.52.$$

Why slightly more boys than girls are born is not known.

3.4. The axioms of probability theory

For a sample space with a finite number of equally likely outcomes, the probability of any event is already defined by Laplace's formula (3.2). For this particular case

(3.3) $\qquad 0 \leq P(A) \leq 1,$

because $0 \leq g \leq m$, and

(3.4) $\qquad P(E) = 1,$

since m is the number of favourable outcomes for E.

For two disjoint events A, with g_1 favourable outcomes, and B, with g_2 favourable outcomes, the number of favourable outcomes in A∪B is g_1+g_2, since no outcome can be in both events. Hence

(3.5) $\qquad P(A \cup B) = P(A) + P(B).$

The general rules for probabilities must apply in particular to the case of a finite number of equally likely outcomes, so the rules (3.3), (3.4) and (3.5) must hold for probabilities in general.

The surprising thing is that the rules (3.3), (3.4) and (3.5) ensure a satisfactory definition of a probability for any finite sample space.

If E is a finite sample space and P a real-valued function defined on the events in E, P is said to be a **probability** if the following three axioms are satisfied:

Axiom 1: For any event A

$\qquad 0 \leq P(A) \leq 1.$

Axiom 2: For the sample space E

$\qquad P(E) = 1.$

Axiom 3: For any pair of disjoint events A and B

$\qquad P(A) + P(B) = P(A \cup B).$

If the three axioms are satisfied, then all reasonable requirements of probabilities on finite sample spaces are satisfied. To illustrate this, a number of useful consequences of the axioms are derived.

Theorem 3.1

If $A \subseteq B$, i.e. if every outcome in A is also in B, then $P(A) \leq P(B)$.

Proof

Let C be the event depicted by the shaded area in fig 3.6. Since A and C are disjoint and $B = A \cup C$, it follows from axiom 3 that

$$P(B) = P(A) + P(C),$$

and the theorem then follows from the fact that $P(C) \geq 0$. $\square$.

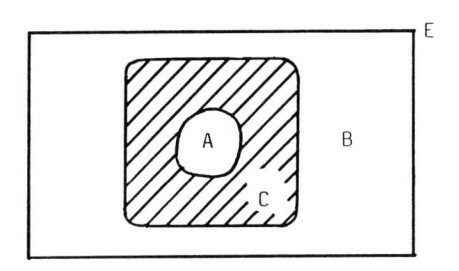

Fig. 3.6. Representation of the events A, B and C.

Theorem 3.2

For the empty event ∅

$$P(\emptyset) = 0.$$

Proof

Since $\emptyset \cup E = E$ and ∅ and E are disjoint, $P(\emptyset) + P(E) = P(E)$. The theorem then follows, since $P(E) = 1$ according to axiom 2. $\square$.

Theorem 3.3

For any event A

$$P(\overline{A}) = 1 - P(A).$$

Proof

Since A and $\overline{A}$ are disjoint and $\overline{A} \cup A = E$, axiom 3 gives

$$P(\overline{A}) + P(A) = P(E)$$

and the theorem then follows from axiom 2. $\square$.

The axioms are formulated so that they are in agreement with Laplace's definition of a probability. But since it is natural to require that relative frequencies approach probabilities in long series of repetitions of random experiments, it is equally important to check that the axioms are in accordance with the rules for computing relative frequencies. Denoting the numerator in (3.1) by $n(A)$

$$(3.6) \qquad h(A) = \frac{n(A)}{n} \ .$$

From (3.6) it follows that axioms 1 and 2 are satisfied if probabilities are replaced by frequencies. Also axiom 3 is valid since

$$n(A \cup B) = n(A) + n(B)$$

when A and B are disjoint, and accordingly

$$h(A \cup B) = h(A) + h(B).$$

These results imply that a probability P, defined as a limiting value for a sequence of relative frequencies, is consistent with a definition of P based on axioms 1 to 3.

Theorem 3.4

If $A_1, \ldots, A_m$ are disjoint events, then

$$(3.7) \qquad P(A_1 \cup A_2 \cup \ldots \cup A_m) = P(A_1) + P(A_2) + \ldots + P(A_m).$$

Proof

According to axiom 3, the theorem holds for $m=2$. Suppose that it holds for $A_1, \ldots, A_k$ with $k < m$. If

$$B = A_1 \cup \ldots \cup A_k,$$

it follows that B and A_{k+1} are disjoint and that

$$P(B \cup A_{k+1}) = P(A_1 \cup \ldots \cup A_{k+1}) = P(B) + P(A_{k+1})$$
$$= P(A_1) + \ldots + P(A_k) + P(A_{k+1}).$$

But since the theorem holds for $m=2$, it also holds for any fixed m larger than 2. □.

Theorem 3.5

For arbitrary events A and B

(3.8)   P(A∪B) = P(A) + P(B) - P(A∩B).

Proof
Let C be the event depicted by the shaded area in fig. 3.7.

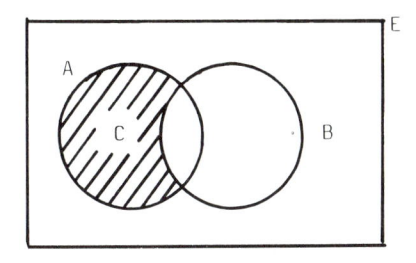

Fig. 3.7. The event C=A∩B̄.

From axiom 3,

P(A∪B) = P(C) + P(B)

and

P(A) = P(C) + P(A∩B).

By subtraction

P(A∪B) - P(A) = P(B) - P(A∩B),

and the theorem follows. □.

Theorems 3.4 and 3.5 are called **additivity theorems**.
For sample spaces with infinitely many outcomes, axioms 1 to 3 do not ensure a satisfactory definition of a probability. Therefore axiom 3 is replaced by

Axiom 3': If $A_1, \ldots, A_m, \ldots$ is an infinite sequence of disjoint events then

(3.9) $$P(\bigcup_{i=1}^{\infty} A_i) = \sum_{i=1}^{\infty} P(A_i).$$

Axiom 3' cannot be deduced from axioms 1, 2 and 3 but axiom 3 is a special case of axiom 3'.

Example 3.4

In example 3.1, we considered the random selection of a person from the Danish population, and described the experiment by a sample space with 5 111 000 equally likely outcomes.

Let A be the event that a male is selected. Laplace's formula gives

$$P(A) = \frac{833+514+1170}{5111} = 0.49.$$

Similarly, the probability P(B) that a person living in the Copenhagen area is selected is

$$P(B) = \frac{833+890}{5111} = 0.34$$

and the probability that a male living in the Copenhagen area is selected is

$$P(A \cap B) = \frac{833}{5111} = 0.16.$$

The probability of the union of A and B is obtained using the additivity theorem 3.5 as

$$P(A \cup B) = P(A) + P(B) - P(A \cap B) = 0.49+0.34-0.16 = 0.67.$$

The event corresponding to selecting a person living outside the Copenhagen area is the complement $\bar{B}$ of B and from theorem 3.3 follows that

$$P(\bar{B}) = 1-P(B) = 1-0.34 = 0.66. \triangle.$$

3.5. Conditional probabilities

Assume that the event B has occurred, i.e. the outcome observed is one of the outcomes in B. Based on this information, we want to compute the probability of the event A. First, consider the case with finitely many, equally likely outcomes. If B has occurred, the only possible outcomes are those contained in B, and the favourable outcomes are those contained in A∩B. If n(A∩B) and n(B) denote the number of outcomes in A∩B and in B respectively, application of Laplace's formula gives

$$P(A|B) = \frac{n(A \cap B)}{n(B)}.$$

Dividing the numerator and denominator by the number of outcomes in E, say n, gives

(3.10) $$P(A|B) = \frac{P(A \cap B)}{P(B)}.$$

We call P(A|B) the **conditional probability** of A given B. As seen from (3.10), P(A|B) is only defined when P(B)>0.

In the case of a general sample space, (3.10) under the assumption P(B)>0 is taken as the definition of a conditional probability. It can be shown that a conditional probability defined by (3.10) satisfies the axioms 1, 2 and 3' for a fixed B and hence is a probability in the ordinary sense.

Multiplying both sides of (3.10) by P(B) gives

(3.11) $$P(A \cap B) = P(A|B)P(B).$$

Formula (3.11) is known as the **multiplication rule**. Note that A and B can change place on the right hand side of (3.11), provided P(A)>0.

Example 3.5

Referring again to table 3.1 in example 3.1, define the events A and B as

A = {Male}
B = {Copenhagen} .

The event A|B occurs when a male is selected among the persons living in the Copenhagen area. There are 1 723 000 persons living in the Copenhagen area, of which 833 000 are males. Hence

$$P(A|B) = \frac{833}{1723} = 0.4835.$$

From formula (3.10), with P(A∩B)=0.16 and P(B)=0.34, follows that

$$P(A|B) = \frac{0.16}{0.34} = 0.4835 \quad . \triangle .$$

From the definition of conditional probabilities, two important results can be derived. If the events $A_1,\ldots,A_m$ in the sample space E are disjoint and

$$E = A_1 \cup \ldots \cup A_m,$$

then $A_1,\ldots,A_m$ constitute a **classification** of E. If $A_1,\ldots,A_m$ is a classification, then

$$P(A_1)+\ldots+P(A_m) = 1,$$

since $P(E)=1$.

Theorem 3.6

If $A_1,\ldots,A_m$ is a classification and B an arbitrary event, then

(3.12) $\quad P(B) = P(B|A_1)P(A_1)+\ldots+P(B|A_m)P(A_m).$

Proof

As $A_1,\ldots,A_m$ is a classification, both the events and their intersections with B are disjoint. Hence B can be rewritten as

$$B = (B \cap A_1) \cup (B \cap A_2) \cup \ldots \cup (B \cap A_m),$$

so that theorem 3.4 yields

$$P(B) = P(B \cap A_1) + P(B \cap A_2)+\ldots+P(B \cap A_m).$$

Using the definition (3.11), (3.12) follows immediately. □.

Formula (3.12) is called the **law of total probability**. For m=2, (3.12) becomes

$$P(B) = P(B|A)P(A) + P(B|\overline{A})P(\overline{A}).$$

Theorem 3.7

If $A_1,\ldots,A_m$ is a classification and B an arbitrary event with $P(B)>0$, then

(3.13) $\quad P(A_i|B) = \dfrac{P(B|A_i)P(A_i)}{\sum\limits_{j=1}^{m} P(B|A_j)P(A_j)}.$

Proof

From (3.10) follows that

$$P(A_i|B) = \frac{P(A_i \cap B)}{P(B)}.$$

Applying (3.11) to the numerator and the law of total probability to the denominator, (3.13) follows. □.

Theorem 3.7 is called **Bayes' theorem**.

Since A and $\overline{A}$ constitute a classification it follows from theorem 3.7 with m=2 that

(3.14) $\qquad P(A|B) = \dfrac{P(B|A)P(A)}{P(B|A)P(A)+P(B|\overline{A})P(\overline{A})}.$

Example 3.6

For a potential oil field consider the following three events:

A_1 = {the field contains enough oil and gas for a profitable production}

A_2 = {the field contains gas, which can be profitably produced, but oil production is not profitable}

A_3 = {the amount of oil and gas does not permit a profitable production}.

Based on previous experience in the area, the chances that a drilling will result in A_1, A_2 and A_3 can be set to

$P(A_1) = 0.6$
$P(A_2) = 0.3$
$P(A_3) = 0.1$.

These three probabilities represent our prior knowledge about the field.

A geological/seismic test is now performed. This test can result in two outcomes:

B = {the field is promising}

$\overline{B}$ = {the field is not promising}.

Knowing the effectiveness of the geological and seismic methods used, we are in a position to evaluate the chance of each of the outcomes B and $\overline{B}$ given A_1, A_2 and A_3 respectively. These conditional probabilities are given as

	$P(B\|A_i)$	$P(\bar{B}\|A_i)$
A_1	0.8	0.2
A_2	0.6	0.4
A_3	0.3	0.7

Using Bayes' formula (3.13) with m=3, the probabilities $P(A_i|B)$ and $P(A_i|\bar{B})$ for A_1, A_2 and A_3 can be calculated. For A_1 we obtain for example

$$P(A_1|B) = \frac{(0.8)(0.6)}{(0.8)(0.6)+(0.6)(0.3)+(0.3)(0.1)} = 0.7.$$

The probabilities shown below are computed in the same way.

	$P(A_i\|B)$	$P(A_i\|\bar{B})$
A_1	0.70	0.39
A_2	0.26	0.39
A_3	0.04	0.23

These probabilities represent the posterior knowledge, i.e. information about the potential oil field after data in the form of a geological/seismic test has been obtained.

The chance of finding enough oil and gas for a profitable production increases from 0.6 without a posteriori information to 0.7 if B is the outcome of the geological/seismic test. And if $\bar{B}$ is observed it drops from 0.6 to 0.39. △.

3.6. Stochastic independence

As mentioned earlier, the concepts of a probability and a relative frequency are closely related. Hence, the discussion of the properties of probabilities should reflect what is known about relative frequencies. With this in mind, the concept of stochastic independence is introduced by studying the properties of relative frequencies in a 2x2 table.

Example 3.7

Using data collected in the autumn of 1983 by Gallup, Denmark, we shall evaluate the extent to which two Danish political parties, Conservatives and Socialists, attract self-employed persons and employees respectively.

Table 3.3 shows the distribution according to employment status for those persons in the sample, who claimed to have voted for either the conservative party or the socialist party in the last election.

If the two parties attract self-employed persons and employees to the same extent, the two parties would be expected to have approximately the same proportion of employees among their voters.

Table 3.3. The distribution of 2143 persons according to political affiliation and type of employment.

Party	Employees	Self-employed	Total
Conservative	1020	347	1367
Socialist	754	22	776
Total	1774	369	2143

Source: Gallup Marketing Index 1983.

From table 3.3, it follows that the proportion of employees among the socialist voters is 754/776=0.972, while the proportion of employees among the conservative voters is 1020/1367=0.746. These figures are admittedly different, but this does not mean that the proportion of employees in the population voting for the Socialists is different from the proportion in the population voting for the Conservatives. It must be remembered that the 2143 persons in the survey do not include all persons voting for the two parties.

Next, consider the probabilities corresponding to the two proportions. Let the events A and B be defined as

A = {a randomly chosen voter voted for the Socialists}

B = {a randomly chosen voter is an employee}.

The two proportions computed above correspond to the conditional frequencies

$$h(B|A) = 0.972$$

and

$$h(B|\bar{A}) = 0.746.$$

If the proportions of employees among voters from the two parties were identical in the last election, then

$$P(B|A) = P(B|\bar{A}),$$

since the chance of choosing an employee among the socialist voters would be the same as that of choosing an employee among the conservative voters. In this situation, the events A and B are said to be stochastically independent. This means that the chance of B occurring is the same regardless of whether it is known that A has occurred or that $\bar{A}$ has occurred. △.

Example 3.7 justifies the definition of A and B being **stochastically independent** if

(3.15) $P(B|A) = P(B|\bar{A})$,

provided $P(A)>0$ and $P(\bar{A})>0$.

However, the commonly used definition of stochastic independence is that A and B are independent if

(3.16) $P(A \cap B) = P(A) \cdot P(B)$.

There are several reasons for preferring (3.16) to (3.15). Firstly, (3.16) does not operate with conditional probabilities, and secondly it is not assumed in (3.16) that $P(A)>0$ or $P(\bar{A})>0$.

A third definition, which can be intuitively justified, is that A and B are independent if

(3.17) $P(B|A) = P(B)$, where $P(A)>0$.

If (3.17) holds, then the chance of B occurring does not depend on A.

Theorem 3.8

The definitions (3.15), (3.16) and (3.17) of stochastic independence are equivalent if $P(A)>0$ and $P(\bar{A})>0$.

Proof

In order to prove that

$$(3.15) \Leftrightarrow (3.16) \Leftrightarrow (3.17)$$

it is sufficient to show that $(3.15) \Rightarrow (3.16)$, $(3.16) \Rightarrow (3.17)$ and $(3.17) \Rightarrow (3.15)$.

If (3.15) holds, it follows from the law of total probability that

$$P(B) = P(B|A)P(A) + P(B|\overline{A})P(\overline{A})$$

$$= P(B|A)(P(A) + 1-P(A)) = P(B\cap A)/P(A),$$

from which (3.16) follows.

If (3.16) holds and $P(A)>0$, then

$$P(B\cap A)/P(A) = P(B),$$

from which (3.17) follows, using (3.10).

If (3.17) holds, it follows from the law of total probability that

$$P(B) = P(B|A)P(A) + P(B|\overline{A})P(\overline{A}) = P(B)P(A) + P(B|\overline{A})P(\overline{A})$$

or

$$P(B)(1-P(A)) = P(B|\overline{A})P(\overline{A}),$$

from which (3.15) follows, using theorem 3.3, since it is assumed that $P(\overline{A})>0$. □.

The m events $A_1, A_2, \ldots A_m$ are said to be independent if

(3.18) $\quad P(A_{i_1} \cap \ldots \cap A_{i_k}) = P(A_{i_1}) \cdot \ldots \cdot P(A_{i_k})$

$$1 \leq i_1 < \ldots < i_k \leq m.$$

In general, i.e. when the events are not necessarily independent, we have

(3.19) $\quad P(A_1 \cap \ldots \cap A_m) = P(A_m | A_{m-1} \cap \ldots \cap A_1) \cdot$

$$P(A_{m-1}|A_{m-2} \cap \ldots \cap A_1) \cdot \ldots \cdot P(A_2|A_1) P(A_1).$$

According to (3.19), the chance of A_m occurring, for example, may be influenced by knowledge of the occurrence of the remaining events. Formula (3.19) can be derived from (3.11) by induction and is called the **multiplication rule**.

Example 3.8

Sampling theory deals with methods for the selection of samples from finite populations. Suppose that a population consists of N persons, M of which have a certain attribute. Consider for example the population of all Danes above 18 years of age and let the attribute be "opposed to Danish membership of the EEC". From this population a sample of size two is selected in two steps. In the first step, every person in the population has the same chance of being selected. Let A be the event that the first person selected is an EEC-opponent. It follows then from Laplace's formula that

$$P(A) = M/N.$$

The second member of the sample can be selected in two ways. If the selection is at random from among those not yet selected, the method is called simple random sampling **without replacement**. If, however, the selection in the second step is again at random from among all members of the population, the method is called simple random sampling **with replacement**.

Let B be the event that the second person selected is an opponent of Danish membership of the EEC. For sampling with replacement, Laplace's formula gives

$$P(B|A) = P(B|\overline{A}) = M/N,$$

since the number of possible outcomes is N and the number of favourable outcomes is M, whatever the outcome of the first selection. Hence the events A and B are independent.

For sampling without replacement, Laplace's formula yields

$$P(B|A) = \frac{M-1}{N-1}$$

since the number of possible outcomes is now N-1 and the number of favourable outcomes is M-1. Similarly,

$$P(B|\overline{A}) = \frac{M}{N-1}.$$

Thus, the events A and B are not independent, when the sampling is without replacement.

It is interesting to note, however, that for both methods

$$P(B) = M/N.$$

For sampling with replacement,

$$P(B) = \frac{M}{N},$$

and for sampling without replacement theorem 3.6 yields

$$P(B) = P(B|A)P(A) + P(B|\overline{A})P(\overline{A})$$

$$= \frac{M-1}{N-1} \cdot \frac{M}{N} + \frac{M}{N-1} \cdot \frac{N-M}{N} = \frac{M^2 - M + MN - M^2}{(N-1)N} = \frac{M}{N} \cdot \triangle.$$

4. Probability Distributions on the Real Line and Random Variables

4.1. Probability distributions on the real line

Many data sets from the social sciences are composed of real numbers. Alternatively, they are transformed into real numbers, in the course of the statistical analysis. Probabilities or probability distributions on the real line R are therefore of particular importance.

Probabilities for a sample space that is the entire real axis or a subset thereof can be defined by a real function. Consider events that are intervals of the type $(-\infty, x]$. The probability of such events then depends only on x and defines a function given as

(4.1) $\quad F(x) = P((-\infty, x])$, $x \in R$.

The function F is called a **distribution function** and it can be shown that F uniquely determines the probability for any subset of the real line of practical importance, i.e. F defines a **probability distribution** on the real line.

From (4.1) and axiom 1 follows that

(4.2) $\quad 0 \leq F(x) \leq 1$.

If $x_1 < x_2$ are real numbers, axiom 3 yields

(4.3) $\quad P((-\infty, x_2]) = P((-\infty, x_1]) + P((x_1, x_2])$,

since $(-\infty, x_1]$ and $(x_1, x_2]$ are disjoint. Applying (4.1) and axiom 1, we then obtain

(4.4) $\quad F(x_2) - F(x_1) \geq 0$,

i.e. a distribution function is non-decreasing. If we define

$$F(+\infty) = \lim_{x \to +\infty} F(x)$$

as the probability of the complete sample space, it follows from axiom 2 and axiom 3', that

(4.5) $F(+\infty) = 1.$

Defining

$$F(-\infty) = \lim_{x \to -\infty} F(x)$$

as the probability of the empty event, theorem 3.2 and axiom 3' gives

(4.6) $F(-\infty) = 0.$

The results (4.2), (4.4), (4.5) and (4.6) can be summarized by the following theorem:

Theorem 4.1

A distribution function F is a real-valued, non-decreasing and right continuous function, for which $\lim_{x \to +\infty} F(x) = 1$ and $\lim_{x \to -\infty} F(x) = 0$.

The distribution function is continuous from the right because the upper end point has been included in the interval for which F(x) is the probability.

Theorem 4.2

Let F be a distribution function. Then

(4.7) $P((x, +\infty)) = 1 - F(x)$

and

(4.8) $P((x_1, x_2]) = F(x_2) - F(x_1)$ for $x_1 < x_2$.

Proof

Since $R = (-\infty, x] \cup (x, +\infty)$, and the intervals $(-\infty, x]$ and (x, ∞) are disjoint, axioms 2 and 3 give

$$1 = F(x) + P((x, +\infty)),$$

from which (4.7) follows. Formula (4.8) follows from (4.3) and (4.1). □

4.2. Random variables

Most data analysed by statistical methods are real numbers or vectors of real numbers. If the experiment under consideration refers to a sample space E, which is not a subset of the real line, it is necessary therefore to establish a connection between E and the real line. The mappings used for this purpose are called random variables.

Example 4.1

Suppose a respondent tries to solve a problem, and assume for the sake of simplicity that the solution is either correct or wrong. Let A be the event that the solution is correct and $\bar{A}$ the event that the solution is wrong. Thus the sample space consists of two elementary events A and $\bar{A}$. If we assign the value 1 to A and the value 0 to $\bar{A}$, the sample space $E = \{A, \bar{A}\}$ is replaced by $S = \{0, 1\}$, so that each elementary event in E corresponds to exactly one elementary event in S. We can express the correspondance between E and S through the set function X, given by

$$X(A) = 1 \text{ and } X(\bar{A}) = 0.$$

The real-valued function X, which is defined on the elementary events of E, is called a random variable. This name refers to the fact that the value of X depends on the outcome of the random experiment in which the respondent tries to solve the problem. $\triangle$.

Example 4.2

We can extend the experiment considered in example 4.1 by letting the respondent solve k problems in turn. For each problem, 1 denotes a correct solution and 0 denotes a wrong solution. The sample space E consists of all sequences of k 0's or 1's, such that a particular elementary event in E can be written as $(x_1, \ldots, x_k)$, where x_i takes the value 1, if the solution to problem number i is correct, and 0, if it is wrong.

In the analysis of an aptitude test of the form just described, the score, i.e. the number of correct solutions, is an important quantity. The score is given by $x = x_1 + \ldots + x_k$, and can be considered as the outcome of an experiment with sample space $S = \{0, 1, \ldots, k\}$. The correspondence between E and S is expressed by the random variable X, where

$$X(x_1, \ldots, x_k) = x_1 + \ldots + x_k. \triangle.$$

Examples 4.1 and 4.2 can be generalized as follows. In a random experiment with sample space E, we want to assign real numbers to the elementary events of E. The set S⊆R of these numbers defines a new sample space, and the correspondence between E and S is expressed by the **random variable** X, which assigns a value X(a)∈S to each elementary event a∈E. The sample space S of X can be written

$$S = \{x \in R | x = X(a), a \in E\}.$$

The concept of a random variable is illustrated in fig. 4.1 which shows the sample space E, the sample space S and the function X. Note that for each a∈E, there is only one value x∈S. But for a value x∈S, there may be several values a∈E for which x=X(a). Since the value of X depends on the outcome of a random experiment, X is called a random variable.

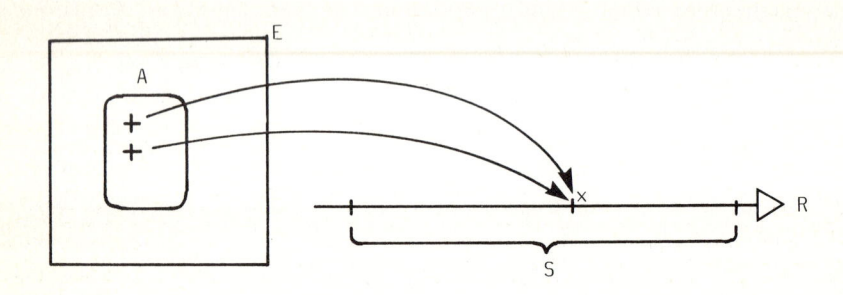

Fig. 4.1. Illustration of the concept of a random variable.

A probability P defined on the sample space E and a random variable X defined on E with sample space S specifies a probability distribution with distribution function F given by

(4.9) $F(x) = P(X \leq x) = P(\{a \in E | X(a) \leq x\}).$

The expression $(X \leq x)$ is read as "the random variable X takes a value less than or equal to x" and F is called the **distribution function** of X. A random variable represents the possible outcomes of a random experiment with sample space E. To each of these outcomes is assigned a real number and the proabilities of various events are defined by the distribution function F. When the experiment has been carried out, the value of X will be known and this value, denoted by x, is called the **observed value** of X.

Random variables are usually denoted by capital latin letters, while observed values are denoted by small latin letters. If x is the observed value of X, the probability of the outcome x is written as $P(X=x)$.

Example 4.3

Suppose an aptitude test consists of three problems, each of which can be solved either correctly or incorrectly. As in the previous examples, the number 1 indicates a correct solution and 0 indicates an incorrect solution. The sample space is given by

$$E = \{111, 110, 101, 011, 100, 010, 001, 000\}.$$

The number of correct solutions, X, has sample space $S=\{0,1,2,3\}$.

From axiom 3, the probability of exactly two correct solutions is

$$P(X=2) = P(110) + P(011) + P(101),$$

where the probabilities on the right hand side of the equation are defined on E. In the same way, the probability of at most 1 correct solution is computed as

$$F(1) = P(x \leq 1) = P(000) + P(100) + P(010) + P(001). \triangle.$$

A random variable has been defined as a mapping of the outcomes of a random experiment on a subset of the real line. The concept of a random variable is often used when no mapping seems to be involved, as is the case if the outcomes of the random experiment are themselves real numbers. In example 2.1, incomes for a random sample of Danes were observed. Let X denote the income for a randomly selected person, and let x be the income actually reported by the selected person. In principle, we can compute the distribution function F as

$$F(x) = \frac{\text{number of Danes with income less than or equal to x}}{\text{number of Danes}}$$

provided the incomes of all Danes are known.

A distinction is usually made between continuous and discrete random variables. A random variable X is **discrete** if the sample space S of X is finite or countable. An example of a countable sample space is the set of all non-negative integers. A random variable is **continuous** if the sample space is the real line or an interval on the real line, and if $P(X=x)=0$ for all $x \in S$. A continuous random variable is characterized by the fact that intervals, but not single points, are assigned positive probabilities.

4.3. Discrete random variables

Let X be a discrete random variable, i.e. the sample space S of X is a countable subset of R. In order to define the probability distribution of X, only knowledge of the probabilities $P(X=x)$ for each $x \in S$ is needed. The probability of an arbitrary event A is then computed as

$$P(A) = \sum_{x \in A} P(X=x),$$

where the summation is over all outcomes $x \in A$. The real-valued function f defined as

$$f(x) = P(X=x), \quad x \in S,$$

denotes the **point probability** of X. The values $f(x)$ of f are usually referred to as point probabilities.

In most applications, a discrete random variable represents the outcome of a count. This means that its sample space is a subset of the non-negative integers. If the sample space is finite and defined as $S=\{0,1,\ldots,k\}$, the point probability satisfies the following two conditions

$$f(x) \geq 0, \quad x=0,1,\ldots,k,$$

and

$$\sum_{x=0}^{k} f(x) = 1.$$

The first condition follows from axiom 1 and the second condition from axioms 2 and 3.

In the countable case, where $S=\{0,1,2,\ldots,\}$, the point probability satisfies

$$f(x) \geq 0, \quad x=0,1,\ldots, \text{ and } \sum_{x=0}^{\infty} f(x) = 1,$$

where the second condition now follows from axioms 2 and 3'.

In general, the point probability for a discrete random variable satisfies the conditions

(4.10) $$f(x) \geq 0, \quad x \in S$$

and

(4.11) $$\sum_{x \in S} f(x) = 1.$$

In (4.11), the summation is over all outcomes in the sample space, and for notational simplicity (4.11) is often written as

$$\sum_{x} f(x) = 1 \quad \text{or} \quad \sum f(x) = 1.$$

Example 4.4

Consider an aptitude test consisting of four equally difficult problems. For each problem, there are two possible solutions, one of which is correct. If a correct solution is denoted by 1 and an incorrect solution by 0, the sample space consists of 16 sequences:

$$E = \{1111, 1110, 1101, 1011, 0111, 1100, 1010$$
$$0110, 1001, 0101, 0011, 0001, 0010, 0100,$$
$$1000, 0000\}.$$

Assume that all of the problems are extremely difficult so that the respondents have to guess a solution for each problem. The probability of a correct solution is then 0.5 for each of the four problems. Assume further that the respondents solve - or try to solve - each problem independently of the other problems. Under these assumptions, all elementary events in E will have the same probability, which according to (3.18) becomes

$$p = (\frac{1}{2})^4 = 0.0625.$$

The random variable X is defined as the number of correctly solved problems. The sample space of X is then given by S={0,1,2,3,4} and the point probability f(x) is obtained by counting the number of sequences in E belonging to the event (X=x). Thus

$$f(0) = 1/16 = 0.0625$$
$$f(1) = 4/16 = 0.25$$
$$f(2) = 6/16 = 0.375$$
$$f(3) = 4/16 = 0.25$$
$$f(4) = 1/16 = 0.0625.$$

Note that $\Sigma f(x)=1$, as required. Fig. 4.2 shows the point probabilities.
The distribution derived in this example is a special case of the **binomial distribution**, discussed in more detail in chapter 6. △.

Some tables of discrete distributions show the distribution function F rather than the point probability f. For values of x in the sample space S={0,1,2,...}, F(x) is defined as

(4.12) $$F(x) = \sum_{z=0}^{x} f(z).$$

For other values of x, F(x) is defined as

(4.13) $$F(x) = \sum_{z=0}^{[x]} f(z)$$

where [x] is the largest number in S less than or equal to x. Note that the function defined by (4.13) is a step function with steps at each x∈S.

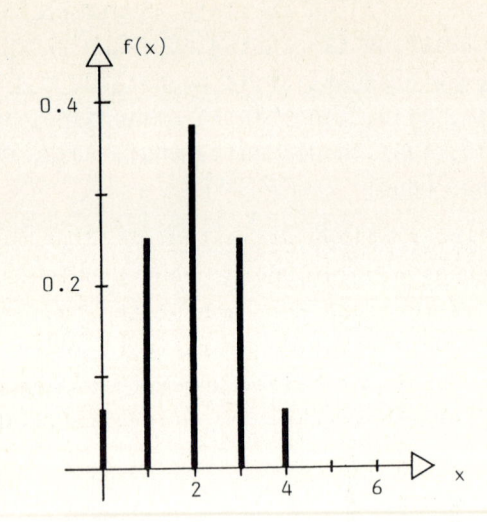

Fig. 4.2. The point probabilities for the number of correct solutions to four problems.

From the distribution function, the point probabilities are calculated as

$$f(x) = F(x) - F(x-1)$$

for integer x.

Example 4.5
Table 4.1 shows the distribution of the number of inhabitants per apartment in Denmark in 1965. If the random variable X represents the number of inhabitants in a randomly selected apartment, Laplace's formula (3.2) gives the point probabilities for X.

Table 4.1. Number of inhabitants per apartment in 1965.

Number of inhabitants	Number of apartments	Relative distribution	Distribution function
1	287170	0.182	0.182
2	438860	0.278	0.460
3	324700	0.206	0.666
4	292510	0.185	0.851
5	145620	0.092	0.943
6	57510	0.036	0.979
7	20610	0.013	0.992
8	11420	0.007	1.000
Total	1578400	0.999	

Source: The Danish Census 1965.

For x=3, f(3)=324 700/1 578 400=0.206, since there are 324 700 apartments out of a total of 1 578 400 apartments with three inhabitants. The values of the distribution function in column 4 of table 4.1 are computed using formula (4.12). Fig. 4.3 shows the point probabilities and fig. 4.4 the distribution function for the number of inhabitants per apartment.△.

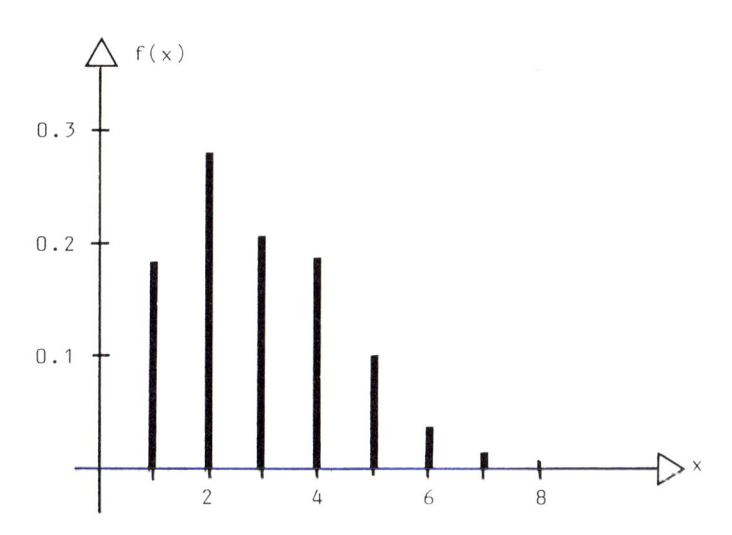

Fig. 4.3. The point probabilities for the number of inhabitants per apartment in Denmark in 1965.

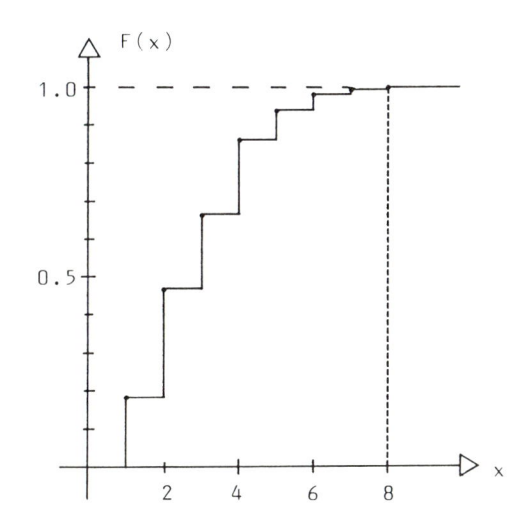

Fig. 4.4. The distribution function for the number of inhabitants per apartment in Denmark in 1965.

4.4. Continuous random variables

A continuous random variable X has the real line or an interval S on the real line R as sample space, and a probability distribution for which $P(X=x)=0$ for any $x \in S$. The latter characteristic corresponds to the distribution function of F being continuous. As $P(X=x)=0$, the probability distribution of a continuous random variable cannot be represented by its point probabilities as in the discrete case. Assuming that F is differentiable, a function analogous to the point probability can, however, be defined as

$$(4.14) \qquad f(x) = F'(x).$$

The real-valued function f is called the **density function** of X. Alternatively, f can be defined by

$$(4.15) \qquad F(x) = \int_{-\infty}^{x} f(y)dy.$$

For $x_1 < x_2$, (4.15) gives

$$(4.16) \qquad P(x_1 < X \leq x_2) = F(x_2) - F(x_1) = \int_{x_1}^{x_2} f(x)dx.$$

Hence, interval probabilities can be calculated by integrating the density function over a suitable subset of R. This is illustrated in fig. 4.5.

If $S=(a,b)$, $f(x)$ must be 0 for $x \leq a$ and $x \geq b$. In this case (4.15) becomes

$$F(x) = \begin{cases} 0 & \text{for } x \leq a \\ \int_a^x f(x)dx & \text{for } a < x < b \\ 1 & \text{for } x \geq b. \end{cases}$$

Since for a continuous random variable X, $P(X=x)=0$ for all $x \in R$, it is of no significance whether or not end points of the interval are included in the calculation of (4.16). Thus

$$P(x_1 < X < x_2) = P(x_1 \leq X \leq x_2) = F(x_2) - F(x_1)$$

and

$$P(X < x) = P(X \leq x) = F(x).$$

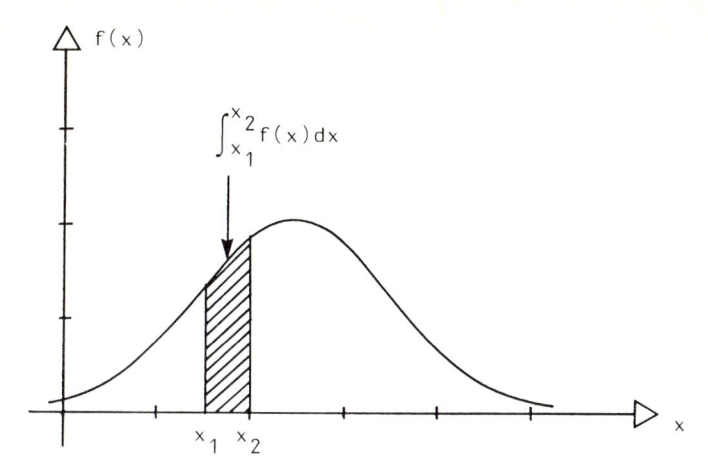

Fig. 4.5. The density function for a continuous random variable.

Theorem 4.3

For a density function f,

(4.17) $f(x) \geq 0$ for all x,

and

(4.18) $\int_{-\infty}^{\infty} f(x)dx = 1.$

Proof

If $f(x) < 0$ for $c_1 < x \leq c_2$, and f is a density function, it follows from (4.16) that

$$P(c_1 < X \leq c_2) = \int_{c_1}^{c_2} f(x)dx < 0,$$

which contradicts axiom 1. As

$$F(+\infty) = \int_{-\infty}^{\infty} f(x)dx,$$

(4.18) is an immediate consequence of (4.5). □

An intuitive interpretation of the density function can be obtained from the approximation of the probability of a short interval

$$(x - \frac{\Delta x}{2}, x + \frac{\Delta x}{2})$$

of length Δx by

$$(4.19) \quad P(x - \tfrac{\Delta x}{2} < X \leq x + \tfrac{\Delta x}{2}) = \int_{x-\frac{\Delta x}{2}}^{x+\frac{\Delta x}{2}} f(y)dy \simeq f(x)\Delta x.$$

The approximation (4.19) is illustrated in fig. 4.6. The area of the rectangle is equal to the right hand side of (4.19), while the area under the curve between $x - \tfrac{\Delta x}{2}$ and $x + \tfrac{\Delta x}{2}$ is equal to the left hand side of (4.19). It is clear that the probability of observing a value of X close to x increases with the value of f(x). Hence, f(x) describes how densely one can expect to find observed values of X in the neighbourhood of X. This motivates the name density function.

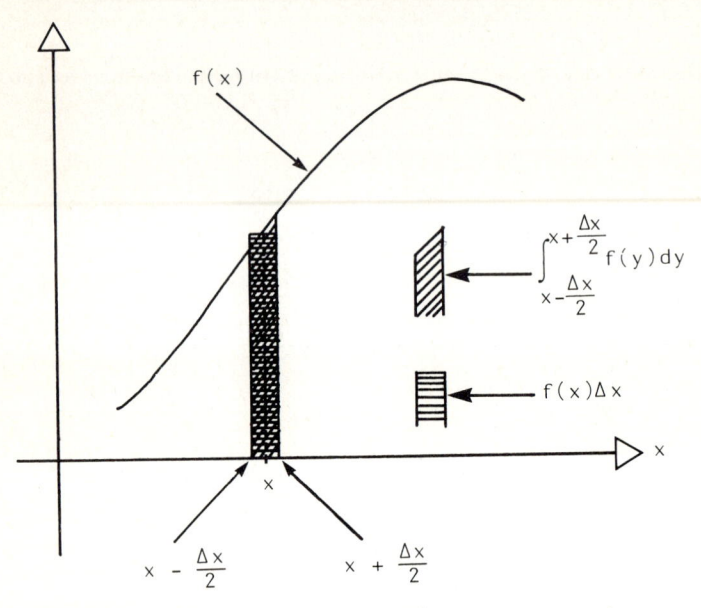

Fig. 4.6. Comparison of $f(x)\Delta x$ and $P(x - \tfrac{\Delta x}{2} < X \leq x + \tfrac{\Delta x}{2})$.

Example 4.6

Let (a,b) be an interval on the real line and let S=(a,b) be the sample space of a random variable X. If all values between a and b are equally likely in the sense that the probability of any interval is proportional to the length of its intersection with (a,b), the distribution function F of X becomes

$$F(x) = P(X \leq x) = \begin{cases} 0 & \text{for } x \leq a \\ \frac{x-a}{b-a} & \text{for } a < x < b \\ 1 & \text{for } x \geq b \end{cases}$$

From F(x), the density function f(x) is obtained by differentiation with respect to x, i.e.

(4.20) $$f(x) = \begin{cases} \dfrac{1}{b-a} & \text{for all } a<x<b \\ 0 & \text{otherwise.} \end{cases}$$

The assumption of all values between a and b being equally likely thus implies that f(x) is constant in the interval. A distribution with density (4.20) is called a **uniform distribution**. The graphs of f(x) og F(x) for a uniform distribution are shown in figures 4.7 and 4.8.

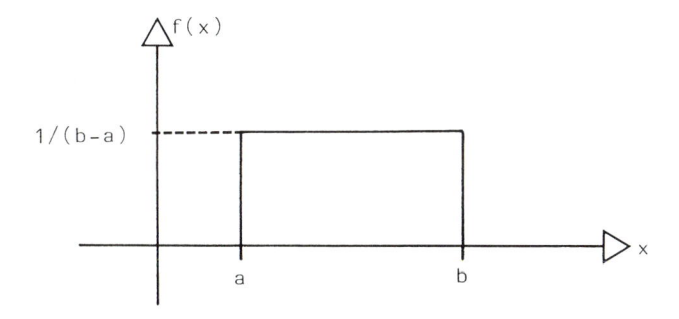

Fig. 4.7. The density function for a uniform distribution.

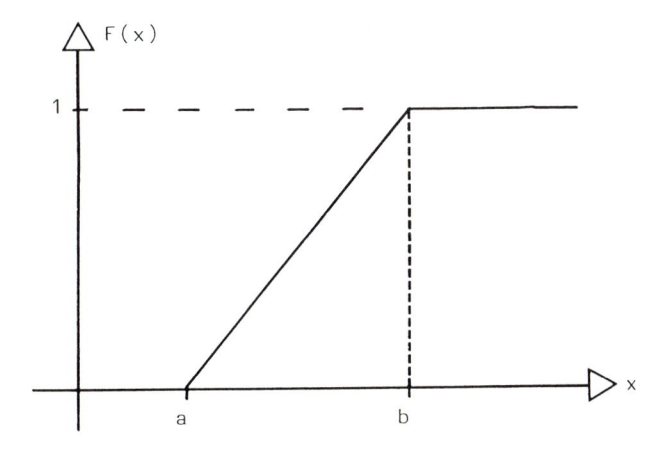

Fig. 4.8. The distribution function for a uniform distribution.

If $f(x)=0$ for $x \notin (a,b)$, the density given by (4.20) satisfies (4.17). Condition (4.18) is satisfied since

$$\int_a^b f(x)dx = \int_a^b \frac{1}{b-a} dx = 1. \triangle$$

Example 4.7

In order to describe the amount of time a shop assistant spends with a customer, let the random variable T denote the time it takes to serve a customer. Assume that T has the density function

(4.21) $$f(t) = \begin{cases} 0 & \text{for } t<0 \\ \lambda e^{-\lambda t} & \text{for } t \geq 0, \end{cases}$$

where λ is a given positive constant, called the intensity. A distribution with density (4.21) is called an **exponential distribution**.

Since $f(t) \geq 0$ for all t and

$$\int_{-\infty}^{\infty} f(t)dt = \lambda \int_0^{\infty} e^{-\lambda t} dt = \lambda [e^{-\lambda t}/(-\lambda)]_0^{\infty} = 1,$$

the conditions (4.17) and (4.18) for f to be a density are satisfied.

From (4.15) it follows that the distribution function F for T is

$$F(t) = \int_0^t f(z)dz = \lambda \int_0^t e^{-\lambda z} dz = 1-e^{-\lambda t}.$$

Hence

(4.22) $$P(T > t) = 1-P(T \leq t) = e^{-\lambda t}.$$

Suppose now that the shop assistant is still serving the same customer after t_0 more time units. What then is the probability that the customer is still being served after another t_1 time units? From (3.10) and (4.22)

$$P(T > t_1+t_0 | T > t_0) = e^{-\lambda(t_1+t_0)}/e^{-\lambda t_0} = e^{-\lambda t_1}.$$

If the distribution of the service time follows an exponential distribution, the probability distribution of the remaining service time is thus independent of its present duration. Among all distributions on the positive part of the real axis, the exponential distribution is the only one with this property. It is often expressed by saying that the exponential distribution is without memory.

In fig. 4.9, the density function for the exponential distribution is shown for three values of λ. The density function is seen to be monotonically decreasing and has the value λ when x=0. This implies that for a given value of λ, an interval of length Δt will have a larger probability of containing an observation the closer the interval is to 0. Therefore, if we are dealing with exponentially distributed service times, the majority of the observations will be rather small, while longer service times are observed less frequently. Fig. 4.9 also reveals that the larger the value of λ, the larger the probability of very small service times. Further discussion of the exponential distribution is given in chapter 7.3.△.

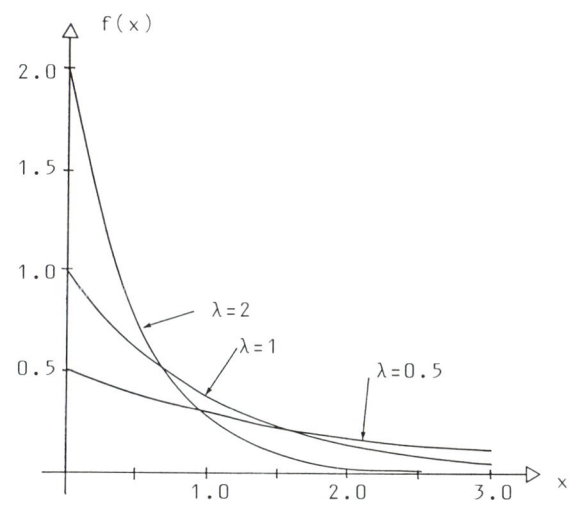

Fig. 4.9. Density functions for exponential distributions with λ=0.5, 1 and 2.

Until now, it has been assumed that the distribution function of a continuous random variable is differentiable. However, examples 4.6 and 4.7 show that this condition need not hold for all values of x in the sample space. In example 4.6, F is not differentiable for x=a and x=b, and in example 4.7, F is not differentiable for t=0. It is usually at the end points of the sample space that F fails to be differentiable. Fortunately such points do not cause problems, as long as they are finite in number. In general it is sufficient to require that F is differentiable, except at a finite number of points. At these points, the value of the density is of no importance.

In the preceding examples, we have considered distributions which depend on quantities determining the exact form of the density. Such quantities are called **parameters**. The exponential distribution considered in example 4.7 thus depended on the parameter λ, and a random variable with density

$$f(t) = \lambda e^{-\lambda t}$$

is said to be exponentially distributed with parameter λ.

4.5. Transformations

Assume there are n observations $x_1, x_2, \ldots, x_n$ of a random variable X. Instead of these observations, one may be interested in analysing the transformed observations $y_1 = \varphi(x_1)$, $y_2 = \varphi(x_2), \ldots, y_n = \varphi(x_n)$, where φ is a real-valued function. This involves studying the distribution of the random variable $Y = \varphi(X)$, where Y is said to be a **transformation** of X.

Two important examples of transformations are the **linear transformation**

$$Y = aX + b,$$

where a and b are given constants, and the **logarithmic transformation**

$$Y = \ln(X).$$

The linear transformation is often used in order to change the scale of the original observations. If, for example, X is a random variable which describes the time in minutes spent serving a customer it might be convenient to change the scale and measure time in hours instead. In this case, the linear transformation

$$Y = \frac{1}{60} X$$

gives the random variable Y measuring time in hours.

In the following examples, it is shown how the distribution function and the density function of a transformed random variable are derived from the distribution function of the original random variable.

Example 4.8

Let X be uniformly distributed with distribution function

$$F(x) = \begin{cases} 0 & \text{for } x \leq -2 \\ \frac{x+2}{4} & \text{for } -2 < x < 2 \\ 1 & \text{for } x \geq 2 \end{cases}$$

and consider the transformation
$$Y = \frac{1}{4} X + \frac{1}{2}.$$

In order to determine the density function g(y) of Y, compute
$$G(y) = P(Y \leq y) = P(\frac{1}{4} X + \frac{1}{2} \leq y)$$
$$= P(X \leq (y - \frac{1}{2})4)$$
$$= \begin{cases} 0 & \text{for } y \leq 0 \\ y & \text{for } 0 < y < 1 \\ 1 & \text{for } y \geq 1. \end{cases}$$

Then
$$g(y) = G'(y) = \begin{cases} 1 & \text{for } 0 < y < 1 \\ 0 & \text{otherwise} \end{cases}$$

so that Y is uniformly distributed over the interval (0,1). △.

Example 4.9

Let T be an exponentially distributed random variable with distribution function
$$F(t) = \begin{cases} 1 - e^{-\lambda t} & \text{for } t \geq 0 \\ 0 & \text{otherwise} \end{cases}$$

and let $Y = \alpha T$ where $\alpha > 0$. Then
$$G(y) = P(Y \leq y) = P(\alpha T \leq y) = P(T \leq y/\alpha) = 1 - e^{-\lambda y/\alpha}$$

for $y \geq 0$. Hence the density function for Y becomes
$$g(y) = \frac{\lambda}{\alpha} e^{-\lambda y/\alpha} = \rho e^{-\rho y}, \quad y \geq 0,$$

where $\rho = \lambda/\alpha$. It follows that Y is exponentially distributed with parameter λ/α. △.

Example 4.10

Let T be exponentially distributed, and consider the transformation
$$Y = e^t.$$
As the distribution function of Y is given by
$$G(y) = P(Y \leq y) = P(e^T \leq y) = P(T \leq \ln y) = 1 - e^{-\lambda \ln y} = 1 - y^{-\lambda},$$

the density function of Y becomes

$$(4.23) \qquad g(y) = \lambda y^{-\lambda} \frac{1}{y} = \frac{\lambda}{y^{\lambda+1}}, \quad y \geq 1,$$

since $t \geq 0$ corresponds to $y \geq 1$. A random variable with density function (4.23) is said to follow a **Pareto distribution**. This distribution is frequently used to describe income distributions. △.

4.6. Empirical frequencies and density functions

The histogram introduced in chapter 2 can be interpreted as an approximation to the density function of a continuous random variable X. Assume that n observations of X have been grouped and let a_j denote the number of observations in the interval $(t_{j-1}, t_j]$, $j=1,\ldots,m$. The area of the block in the histogram corresponding to the interval $(t_{j-1}, t_j]$ is

$$h_j^*(t_j - t_{j-1}) = h_j = a_j/n,$$

i.e. the relative frequency of the event

$$A_j = \{t_{j-1} < X \leq t_j\}.$$

If f is the density function of X and t_j^* the midpoint of the j'th interval, then

$$P(A_j) = \int_{t_{j-1}}^{t_j} f(x)dx \simeq f(t_j^*)(t_j - t_{j-1}).$$

Hence, the histogram is seen to be an approximation to the density function, because the relative frequency h_j of A_j is an approximation to the probability $P(A_j)$.

Example 4.11

Table 4.2 shows the time intervals between 100 successive arrivals at a check-out in a supermarket. We shall examine how well an exponential distribution with $\lambda = 0.035$ fits the data in table 4.2. The determination of λ is described in chapter 10. The fit is evaluated by comparing the histogram and the density function

$$f(t) = 0.035\, e^{-0.035t},$$

shown in fig. 4.10.

Table 4.2. Time intervals between 100 successive arrivals at a check-out in a supermarket.

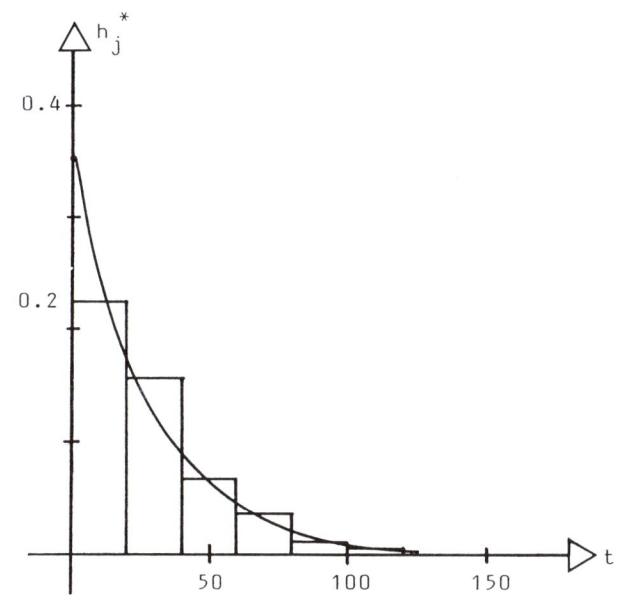

Time interval in sec.	Number of arrivals	h_j	h_j^*
0- 20	45	0.45	0.225
21- 40	31	0.31	0.155
41- 60	14	0.14	0.070
61- 80	7	0.07	0.035
81-100	2	0.02	0.010
101-120	1	0.01	0.005
Total	100	1.00	

Fig. 4.10. Histogram and an exponential density function for arrivals at a check-out.

Since there is a reasonable agreement between the histogram and the density function, it may be concluded that the fit of the exponential distribution is satisfactory.△.

5. Mean Values and Variances

5.1. The mean value

Let X be a discrete random variable with a finite or countable sample space S and with point probabilities $f(x)$. The **mean value** or the **mathematical expectation** $E[X]$ of X is defined as

$$(5.1) \qquad E[X] = \sum_{x \in S} x f(x),$$

i.e. as a weighted sum of the elements of the sample space with the corresponding probabilities as weights. The mean value of X can be interpreted as a long run average of the outcomes of an experiment with sample space S and probability $f(x)$ of the outcome x. This is illustrated in the following example.

Example 5.1

Consider a simple game with 8 equally likely outcomes, e.g. a game of roulette with 8 squares. The stake is 2 DKK and the pay-off is 0 DKK for four of the squares, 2 DKK for two of the squares and 5 DKK for the remaining two squares. Assume that the game is played n times and that the observed pay-offs are 0 DKK in n_0 games, 2 DKK in n_2 games and 5 DKK in n_5 games. The average pay-off per game is therefore

$$a_n = 0 \cdot \frac{n_0}{n} + 2 \cdot \frac{n_2}{n} + 5 \cdot \frac{n_5}{n}.$$

Let now X be a random variable representing the pay-off of a game. The sample space of X is $S = \{0, 2, 5\}$, and according to Laplace's formula the point probabilities are given by $f(0) = 0.5$, $f(2) = 0.25$ and $f(5) = 0.25$. As the number of games played increases, the relative frequencies n_0/n, n_2/n and n_5/n approach the corresponding probabilities $f(0)$, $f(2)$ and $f(5)$ and the average pay-off a_n accordingly approaches the value

$$E[X] = 0 \cdot f(0) + 2 \cdot f(2) + 5 \cdot f(5),$$

called the expected pay-off of the game or the expectation of the random variable X.△.

If the sample space is countable and the series (5.1) is divergent, the mean value of X does not exist. If the sample space only consists on non-negative numbers, the mean value of X exists if large values of X have very small probabilities. Formally the mean value exists if

(5.2) $\sum_{x \in S} |x| f(x) < \infty.$

Condition (5.2) ensures both that the series in (5.1) converges and that the mean value is uniquely defined.

Example 5.2

Consider a game in which a person tosses a coin until "heads" comes up for the first time. If this happens in the n'th toss the person is paid 2^n DKK. Let X be the amount paid to the person. The sample space of X is S={2,4,8,16,...} and the point probabilities are

$$P(X=2^n) = 1/2^n \quad \text{for } n=1,2,...$$

For this game, the mean value does not exist since the series (5.2)

$$\sum_{n=1}^{\infty} 2^n (1/2^n) = 1+1+...$$

is divergent. This result is known as the Petersburg paradox.△.

Example 4.5 (continued)

In example 4.5, we studied the distribution of apartments in Denmark in 1965 according to the number of residents. Let X be a random variable with point probability f that represents the number of residents in a randomly selected apartment. Assume for convenience that $f(x)=0$ for $x \geq 9$, so the mean value of X becomes

$$E[X] = 1 \cdot 0.182 + 2 \cdot 0.278 + ... + 8 \cdot 0.007 = 2.919.$$

Thus, on average there were just under 3 persons per apartment in Denmark in 1965. Fig. 5.1 shows the position of the mean value in the distribution.△.

The mean value is an important summary measure for the location of the distribution, but it does not necessarily give any information about the shape of the distribution. Suppose for example that $P(X=-1)=1/3$ and $P(X=1)=2/3$. The mean value is then

$$E[X] = -1 \cdot \frac{1}{3} + 1 \cdot \frac{2}{3} = \frac{1}{3}.$$

But the fact that $E[X]=1/3$ does not reveal that this is a two point distribution. Other distributions with a substantially different shape, for example a distribution with $P(X=3)=P(X=2)=P(X=-4)=1/3$, also has mean value 1/3. Note that the mean value does not have to be a value in the sample space.

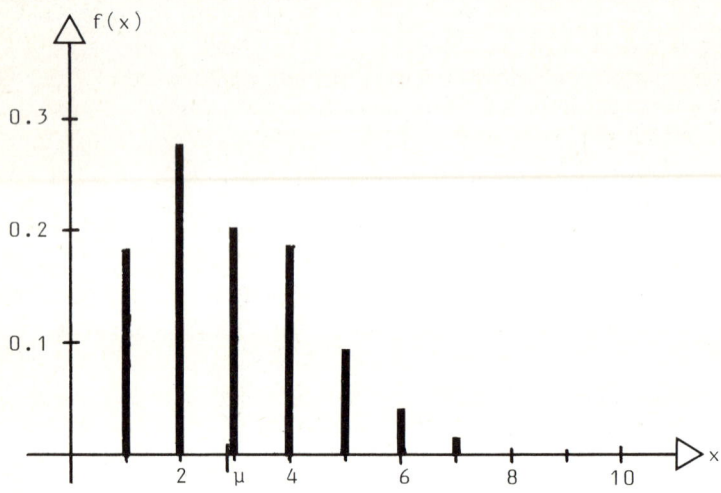

Fig. 5.1. The distribution of apartments according to the number of residents and the location of the mean value.

For a continuous random variable with density function f the mean value is defined as

(5.3) $$E[X] = \int x f(x) dx,$$

provided that

$$\int |x| f(x) dx < \infty.$$

If this condition does not hold, the mean value of the distribution does not exist. In the remainder of this chapter it will be assumed that all mean values exist.

The definition (5.3) can be justified by approximating the continuous distribution by a suitable discrete distribution. Let

$$E[X] = \int_{-\infty}^{\infty} xf(x)dx \simeq \int_{a}^{b} xf(x)dx,$$

where a and b are chosen such that

$$\int_{-\infty}^{a} xf(x)dx$$

and

$$\int_{b}^{\infty} xf(x)dx$$

are negligible. Divide the interval from a to b in sub-intervals by the points $t_0 = a < t_1 < \ldots < t_{n-1} < t_n = b$. Then $E[X]$ can be approximated as follows

(5.4) $$E[X] = \int_{-\infty}^{\infty} xf(x)dx \simeq \sum_{i=1}^{n} t_i^* f(t_i^*)(t_i - t_{i-1})$$

where $t_i^* = (t_i + t_{i-1})/2$, if the differences $\Delta t_i = t_i - t_{i-1}$ are suitably small. In section 4.4, it was mentioned that

$$f(t_i^*)\Delta t_i \simeq P(t_{i-1} < X \leq t_i).$$

If follows accordingly from (5.4) that $E[X]$ is approximated by the mean value of a discrete random variable Y with sample space $S = \{t_1^*, \ldots, t_n^*\}$ and point probabilities

$$P(Y = t_i^*) = P(t_{i-1} < X \leq t_i).$$

A parallel to the definition (5.3) of a mean value is found in classical mechanics. If $f(x)$ describes the distribution of a given mass along the x-axis, then $E[X]$ is the centre of gravity.

Example 5.3

Let X be uniformly distributed over the interval (a,b). Then

$$E[X] = \int_a^b x \cdot \frac{1}{b-a} dx = \frac{1}{b-a}\left[\frac{x^2}{2}\right]_a^b = \frac{1}{2}\frac{b^2 - a^2}{b-a} = \frac{b+a}{2}.$$

The mean value is thus the center of the interval as illustrated in fig. 5.2. △

Example 5.4

Let X be exponentially distributed with density function

$$f(x) = \lambda e^{-\lambda x}, \quad x \geq 0.$$

The mean value can be computed by partial integration as

$$E[X] = \lambda \int_0^\infty x e^{-\lambda x} dx = \lambda [x e^{-\lambda x}/(-\lambda)]_0^\infty - \lambda \int_0^\infty e^{-\lambda x}/(-\lambda) dx$$

$$= 0 + [e^{-\lambda x}/(-\lambda)]_0^\infty = \frac{1}{\lambda} . \triangle .$$

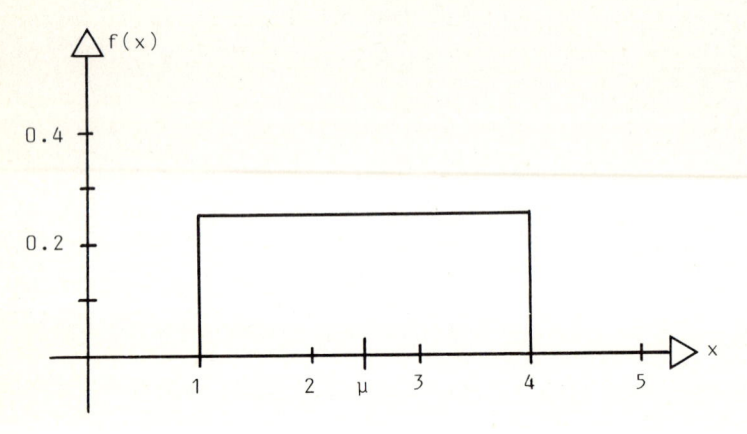

Fig. 5.2. The location of the mean value for a uniform distribution.

Example 5.5

A random variable X with density function

$$f(x) = \lambda/x^{\lambda+1}, \quad x \geq 1,$$

where $\lambda > 0$, is said to be Pareto distributed (cf. example 4.10). The mean value of X is

$$E[X] = \lambda \int_1^\infty (x/x^{\lambda+1}) dx = \lambda \int_1^\infty x^{-\lambda} dx = \lambda \left[\frac{x^{-\lambda+1}}{-\lambda+1} \right]_1^\infty = \lambda/(\lambda-1),$$

if $\lambda > 1$. For $0 < \lambda \leq 1$, the mean value does not exist. $\triangle$.

In chapter 4, it was shown that the distributional properties of a random variable can be expressed through the form of the distribution function, the density function or the point probability. Moreover, one is often interested in summarizing the properties of the distribution by means of a few key measures. The mean value is a so-called **measure of location** or **location parameter.** These names derive from the fact that the mean value is located centrally among the possible values of X and hence is a measure of the location of the distribution on the real axis.

5.2. The variance

The variance of a discrete random variable X with point probability f is defined as

$$(5.5) \qquad \text{var}[X] = \sum_x (x-\mu)^2 f(x)$$

where $\mu = E[X]$. The variance of a continuous random variable X with density function f is defined as

$$(5.6) \qquad \text{var}[X] = \int (x-\mu)^2 f(x) dx.$$

The variance of a random variable or a probability distribution is usually denoted by σ^2. For some distributions the series (5.5) or the integral (5.6) are divergent. For such distributions, the variance does not exist.

Theorem 5.1

For a discrete random variable X with point probability f and mean value μ

$$(5.7) \qquad \text{var}[X] = \sum_x x^2 f(x) - \mu^2,$$

and for a continuous random variable X with density function f and mean value μ

$$(5.8) \qquad \text{var}[X] = \int x^2 f(x) dx - \mu^2.$$

Proof

In the discrete case

$$\text{var}[X] = \sum (x^2 - 2\mu x + \mu^2) f(x) = \sum x^2 f(x) - 2\mu \sum x f(x) + \mu^2 \sum f(x)$$

$$= \sum x^2 f(x) - \mu^2,$$

since $\sum x f(x) = \mu$ and $\sum f(x) = 1$.

Formula (5.8) is obtained simply by substituting the summation signs with integration signs.□.

Example 5.6

If X is uniformly distributed over the interval (a,b), then

$$\text{var}[X] = \int_a^b x^2 \frac{1}{b-a} dx - \left(\frac{b+a}{2}\right)^2 = \frac{1}{b-a}\left(\frac{b^3}{3} - \frac{a^3}{3}\right) - \frac{(b+a)^2}{4}.$$

But since $b^3 - a^3 = (b-a)(b^2+ab+a^2)$ this gives

$$\text{var}[X] = \frac{4(b^2+ab+a^2) - 3(b^2+2ab+a^2)}{12} = \frac{b^2-2ab+a^2}{12} = \frac{(b-a)^2}{12}.$$

It follows that the larger the length of the interval, the larger the variance. △.

The variance is a measure of the dispersion of the distribution around its mean value. The larger the variance of the distribution, the more the density or the point probabilities spread out over the real line.

The square root σ of the variance $σ^2$ is called the **standard deviation**, and this is often preferred to the variance as a **measure of dispersion** because the standard deviation, in contrast to the variance, is measured in the same units as X.

To illustrate the role of the variance or the standard deviation as a measure of dispersion, consider the following example with three simple discrete distributions.

Example 5.7

Consider three discrete random variables X_1, X_2 and X_3 with point probabilities $f_1(x)$, $f_2(x)$ and $f_3(x)$ given by

x	0	1	2	3	4	5
$f_1(x)$	1/6	1/6	1/6	1/6	1/6	1/6
$f_2(x)$	1/12	2/12	3/12	3/12	2/12	1/12
$f_3(x)$	1/18	3/18	5/18	5/18	3/18	1/18

For all three distributions, the mean value is 2.5, but according to (5.7), the variances are

$$\text{var}[X_1] = 9.17 - (2.5)^2 = 2.92$$

$$\text{var}[X_2] = 8.17 - (2.5)^2 = 1.92$$

$$\text{var}[X_3] = 7.83 - (2.5)^2 = 1.58.$$

The three distributions are shown in fig. 5.3. The figure illustrates that the variance is an indicator of how much the distribution is "spread out" around the mean value.△.

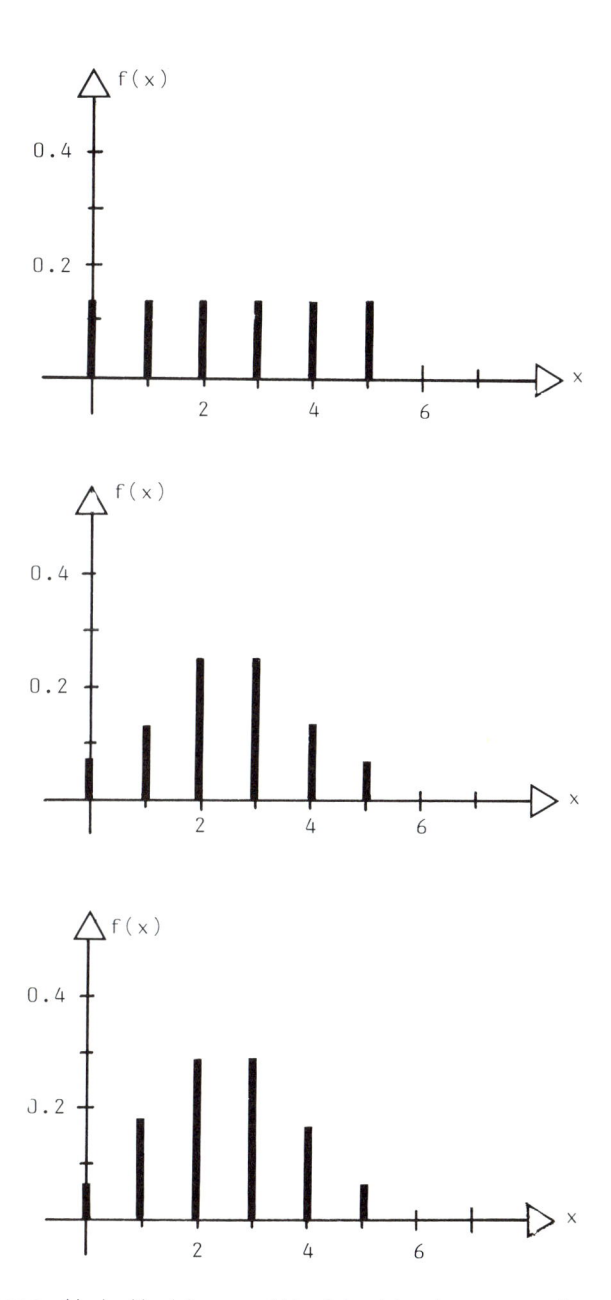

Fig. 5.3. Three distributions with identical mean values, but different variances.

5.3. Theorems about mean values and variances

There exists a number of results that can facilitate the computation of mean values and variances of transformations of random variables. Assume that Y is defined by

(5.9) $\quad Y = \varphi(X),$

i.e. Y is a random variable derived from X by the transformation φ.

Theorem 5.2

If Y is given by (5.9) and X is a discrete random variable with point probability f, then

$$E[Y] = \Sigma \varphi(x) f(x).$$

If X is a continuous random variable with density function f,

$$E[Y] = \int \varphi(x) f(x) dx.$$

Proof

In the discrete case it follows from the definition (5.1) of a mean value that with $S_y = \{x | y = \varphi(x)\}$

$$E[Y] = \Sigma_y y P(Y=y) = \Sigma_y y P(\varphi(X)=y) = \Sigma_y \{\Sigma_{x \in S_y} \varphi(x) P(X=x)\} = \Sigma_x \varphi(x) f(x),$$

which proves the discrete part of the theorem. $\square$.

If Y is a transformation of X, it is according to theorem 5.2 not necessary to compute the point probability or the density function of Y in order to compute the mean value of Y.

From theorem 5.2, it follows that

$$\sigma^2 = \Sigma(x-\mu)^2 f(x) = E[(X-\mu)^2]$$

in the discrete case and that

$$\sigma^2 = \int (x-\mu)^2 f(x) dx = E[(X-\mu)^2]$$

in the continuous case which shows that the variance is the expected value of the squared distance from X to the mean value. From theorem 5.2 and formulas (5.7) and (5.8), it follows that the variance can be written as

(5.10) $\quad \text{var}[X] = E[X^2] - (E[X])^2$

both in the discrete and in the continuous case.

Theorem 5.3

If $Y=aX+b$, then

$$E[Y] = aE[X] + b$$

and

$$\text{var}[Y] = a^2 \text{var}[X].$$

Proof

In the discrete case, theorem 5.2 yields that

$$E[Y] = \sum_x (ax+b)f(x) = a\sum_x xf(x) + b\sum_x f(x) = aE[X]+b.$$

and, with $E[X]=\mu$, that

$$\text{var}[X] = \sum_x (ax+b-a\mu-b)^2 f(x) = \sum_x a^2(x-\mu)^2 f(x) = a^2 \text{var}[X].$$

The proof is analogous for the continuous case. $\square$.

The **factorial moment** of the second order, defined as

(5.11) $\quad \tau^2 = E[X(X-1)],$

is useful for the computation of variances in discrete distributions.

Theorem 5.4

The factorial moment of the second order, τ^2, and the variance, σ^2, are related via

(5.12) $\quad \sigma^2 = \tau^2 - \mu(\mu-1).$

Proof

In the discrete case,

$$\sigma^2 = \sum_x x^2 f(x) - \mu^2 = \sum_x (x^2-x)f(x) + \sum_x xf(x) - \mu^2$$

$$= \sum_x x(x-1)f(x) + \mu - \mu^2 = \tau^2 - \mu(\mu-1). \square.$$

Let X be a random variable with mean value μ and variance σ^2. The random variable Z, defined as

$$Z = (X-\mu)/\sigma,$$

is called a **standardized random variable**.

Theorem 5.5

A standardized random variable has mean value 0 and variance 1.

Proof

Since $Z=X/\sigma-\mu/\sigma$, theorem 5.3 yields that

$$E[Z] = \frac{\mu}{\sigma} - \frac{\mu}{\sigma} = 0,$$

and that

$$\text{var}[Z] = \frac{1}{\sigma^2}\sigma^2 = 1 \;.\;\Box.$$

5.4. Other moments and distributional measures

The mean value and the variance are examples of what are termed **moments** in statistical theory. The **k'th central moment** of a random variable X is defined as

(5.13) $$\mu_k = E[(X-\mu)^k]$$

provided that $E[|X|^k] < \infty$.

According to this definition, $\mu_1=0$ and $\mu_2=\sigma^2$. If the non-central k'th moment is defined as $E[X^k]$, the mean value is the non-central moment of the first order. Among other things, moments can be used to characterize the shape of a distribution.

A distribution is said to be **symmetric** with c as the point of symmetry if $c-x \in S$ whenever $c+x \in S$ and

$$f(c-x) = f(c+x) \quad \text{for all } (c+x) \in S \;.$$

The distributions in example 5.7 are all symmetric with c=2.5 as the point of symmetry as can be seen from the fact that

$$f(0) = f(5), \; f(1) = f(4) \text{ and } f(2) = f(3).$$

Theorem 5.6

If a distribution is symmetric around c and μ and μ_3 exist, then $\mu=c$ and $\mu_3=0$.

If the right hand tail of a distribution is longer than the left hand tail, the distribution is said to be **skew to the right** and if the left hand tail is longer than the right hand tail, the distribution is said to be **skew to the left**. Fig. 5.4 shows the densities for distributions, which are skew to the left and right respectively. If a distribution is skew to the right, large positive values of $(x-\mu)^3$ have relatively larger probabilities than for a symmetric distribution and therefore μ_3 becomes positive. If a distribution is skew to the left, large negative values of $(x-\mu)^3$ have relatively larger probabilities than for a symmetric distribution and μ_3 becomes negative. The third central moment μ_3 is thus a measure of lack of symmetry or skewness with $\mu_3>0$ when the distribution is skew to the right and $\mu_3<0$ if the distribution is skew to the left.

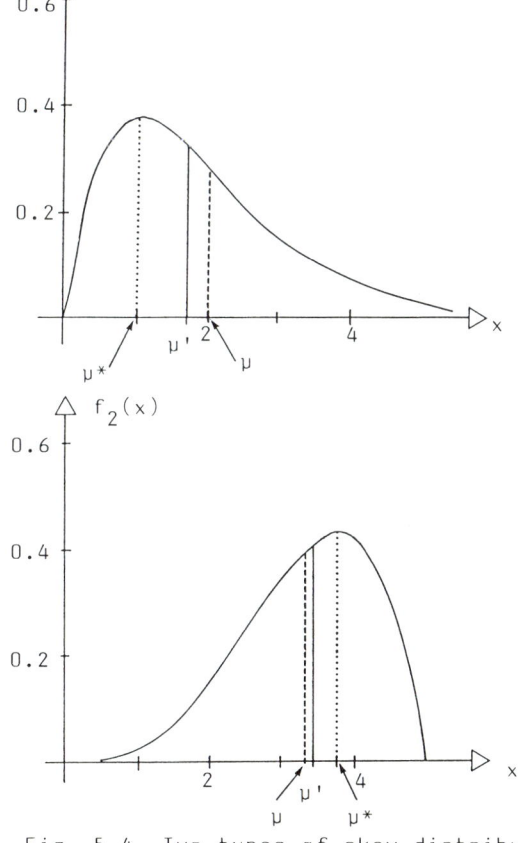

Fig. 5.4. Two types of skew distributions.

The degree of skewness is usually measured by the standardized central third moment

$$\mu_3^* = \mu_3/\sigma^3.$$

The factor $1/\sigma^3$ makes the measure of skewness invariant to changes of the scale. The random variable X and the standardized random variable $Z=(X-\mu)/\sigma$ thus have the same degree of skewness.

Example 5.8

For an exponentially distributed random variable X partial integration gives

$$\sigma^2 = \int_0^\infty (x-1/\lambda)^2 \lambda e^{-\lambda x} dx = [-(x-1/\lambda)^2 e^{-\lambda x}]_0^\infty$$

$$+ 2\int_0^\infty (x-1/\lambda)e^{-\lambda x} dx = 1/\lambda^2 + (2/\lambda)\int_0^\infty (x-\mu)f(x)dx = 1/\lambda^2,$$

since $\mu = E[X] = 1/\lambda$, as derived in example 5.4.

The third central moment becomes

$$\mu_3 = \int_0^\infty (x-1/\lambda)^3 \lambda e^{-\lambda x} dx = [-(x-1/\lambda)^3 e^{-\lambda x}]_0^\infty$$

$$+ 3\int_0^\infty (x-1/\lambda)^2 e^{-\lambda x} dx = -1/\lambda^3 + (3/\lambda)\sigma^2 = 2/\lambda^3.$$

Since $\mu_3 > 0$ the exponential distribution is skew to the right, and the degree of skewness is

$$\mu_3^* = \mu_3/\sigma^3 = \frac{2/\lambda^3}{1/\lambda^3} = 2.$$

All exponential distributions thus have the same degree of skewness. △

The **median** μ' of a continuous random variable with distribution function F is defined by the equation

(5.14) $F(\mu') = 0.5.$

Since (5.14) implies that

(5.15) $P(X \leq \mu') = P(X \geq \mu') = 0.5,$

the median divides the sample space into two equally likely parts and is, therefore, in a certain sense, located in the centre of the distribution. In contrast to the mean, the median exists for all distributions and is to a much lesser extent influenced by the skewness of the distribution. For these reasons, the median rather than the mean is often used as a measure of the location of a distribution.

The median is an important example of a theoretical percentile. The theoretical **α percentile** for $0<\alpha<1$ is defined as the value μ_α that satisfies the condition

$$F(\mu_\alpha) = P(X \leq \mu_\alpha) = \alpha.$$

From (5.14) follows that the median is the 0.5 percentile, i.e. $\mu'=\mu_{0.5}$.

Other useful percentiles are the **quartiles** $\mu_{0.25}$ and $\mu_{0.75}$. The **quartile distance** $d_q = \mu_{0.75} - \mu_{0.25}$ is often used as a measure of dispersion for a distribution, as an alternative to the standard deviation.

The **mode** μ^* for a random variable with density function or point probabilities $f(x)$ is the value of x for which $f(x)$ attains its maximum, i.e. μ^* satisfies

(5.16) $f(\mu^*) \geq f(x)$ for all x.

Theorem 5.7

For unimodal, continuous and symmetric distributions, the mode, the median and the mean are equal.

Example 5.9

For the exponential distribution with density function

$$f(x) = \lambda e^{-\lambda x}, x>0,$$

the mean value is $\mu=1/\lambda$ as shown in example 5.4. Since

$$F(x) = 1-e^{-\lambda x},$$

it follows from (5.14) that the median is given by $\mu'=(\ln 2)/\lambda=0.69/\lambda$. It finally follows from fig. 4.9, that $\mu^*=0$. Thus

$$\mu^* < \mu' < \mu.$$

This relationship is typical for a distribution which is skew to the right as illustrated in fig. 5.4. △.

5.5. Applications of location and dispersion measures

Suppose we want to describe the distribution of a data set consisting of n quantitative measurements $x_1,\ldots,x_n$, assumed to be observations of a continuous random variable X with density function f. In chapter 4, a histogram was used to approximate the shape of the density function. Frequently, however, it is better to summarize the data with a few numerical measures, e.g. by measures of the location and the dispersion of the observations. Such measures are derived as analogues to the quantities used to describe a theoretical distribution, e.g. percentiles, mean values or variances.

The median is a measure of location, and as a measure of the dispersion the empirical quartile distance, i.e. the difference between the empirical 0.75 percentile and the empirical 0.25 percentile can be used.

Since empirical percentiles in large data sets differ only slightly from the theoretical percentiles, the empirical median and the empirical quartile distance may give a good impression of the location of the true distribution of the observations and of the variation around this location.

An alternative set of summary measures for the location and the dispersion of a random variable is the mean value and the variance. The corresponding empirical measures are the average

$$(5.17) \quad \bar{x} = \frac{1}{n} \sum_{i=1}^{n} x_i$$

and the sample variance

$$(5.18) \quad s^2 = \frac{1}{n-1} \sum_{i=1}^{n} (x_i - \bar{x})^2.$$

Computation of the average and the variance is facilitated by the formulae

$$(5.19) \quad \begin{cases} S = \sum_{i=1}^{n} x_i, \quad SS = \sum_{i=1}^{n} x_i^2 \\ \bar{x} = S/n, \quad s^2 = \frac{1}{n-1}(SS - S^2/n). \end{cases}$$

The use of $\bar{x}$ and s^2 is justified by letting the data define a discrete distribution with point probabilities

$$f(x) = 1/n \quad \text{for} \quad x = x_1, \ldots, x_n$$

and sample space $S = \{x_1, \ldots, x_n\}$. Then $\bar{x}$ is the mean value and s^2, with n-1 replaced by n, the variance in this distribution. Another justification is that $\bar{x}$ approximates $E[X]$ and s^2 approximates $\text{var}[X]$ for large data sets.

The application of empirical measures to summarize data can thus be seen as an attempt to approximate a number of quantities describing a theoretical distribution. However, an empirical measure may also be chosen because it describes important characteristics of the data. These two points of view are in no way contradictory. The next example emphasizes the latter point of view.

Example 5.10

Consider the observed incomes for 19 families that built a house with 4 rooms in the municipality of Elsinore in 1962. The incomes in DKK were, in order of magnitude,

16371, 22331, 25928, 27593, 32088, 33458,
34554, 39017, 39759, 42129, 43376, 45734,
49027, 52898, 58116, 62893, 73450, 82455,
116779.

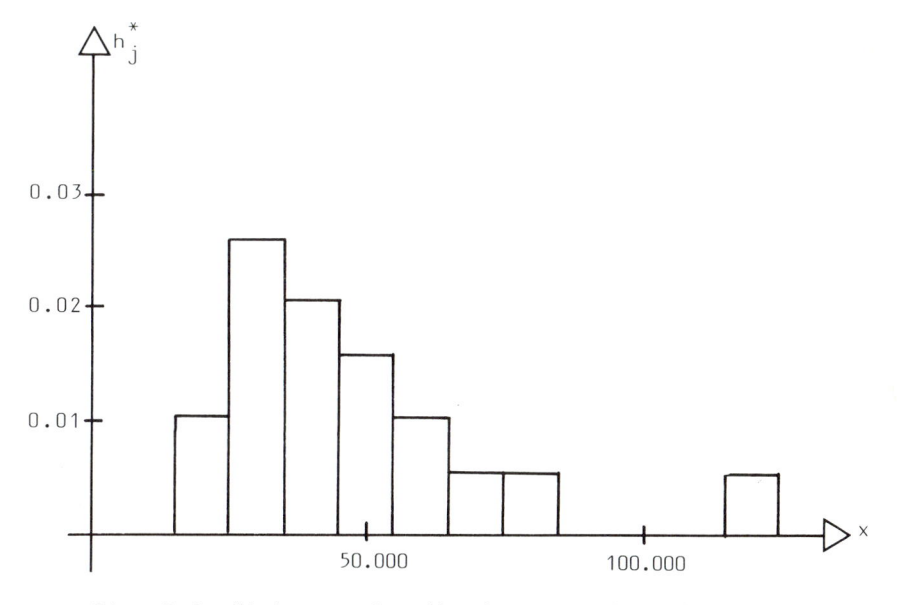

Fig. 5.5. Histogram for the incomes of 19 families.

The histogram in fig. 5.5 shows that the distribution of the incomes is skew to the right. This skewness is also evident in the box plot in fig. 5.6 as a shorter distance between the lower quartile and the median than between the upper quartile and the median. Furthermore, the distance from the smallest observation to the lower quartile is much shorter than the distance from the upper quartile to the largest observation.

In the first column of table 5.1, the median, the two quartiles, the quartile distance, the average and the empirical standard deviation are shown. Note that the median is smaller than the average, a feature typical of distributions which are skew to the right. In fact, the average is strongly influenced by the large incomes in the right hand tail of the distribution. The median is in general not influenced by the magnitude of extreme observations. Since the average is more sensitive to the actual magnitude of large observations than the median, the latter is often used to describe the location of a skew distribution.

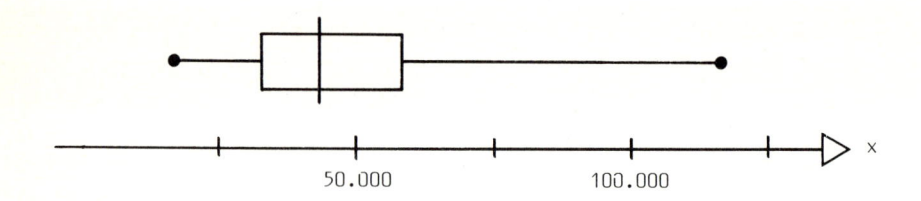

Fig. 5.6. Box plot for the incomes of 19 families.

Table 5.1. Comparison of empirical location and dispersion measures for the incomes of 19 families.

	All observations	18 observations
Median	42129	40944
Average	47261	43399
Upper quartile	58116	54202
Lower quartile	32088	30964
Quartile distance	26028	23238
Standard deviation	23947	17525

In order to measure the influence of an extreme observation on the quantities computed above, the largest observation is removed and all the quantities are recalculated. The results are shown in the second column of table 5.1.

It is obvious from table 5.1 that the value of the median is less influenced by the presence of a large observation than is the average. Similarly, the quartile distance is less influenced by the large observation than the standard deviation is. These conclusions are general ones, and are often used to justify the description of empirical distributions by percentiles rather than by the average and the sample variance. It is not unusual that data contain observations which, due to registration or measurement errors, deviate from the majority of the observations. If such outliers are not detected, the use of percentiles may serve as a safeguard against erroneous conclusions.

For various reasons, we often prefer to describe data using a symmetric rather than a skew distribution. As the income distribution is skew to the right, the distribution of the logarithms of the incomes may appear to be more symmetric than the distribution of the incomes. The logarithms of the incomes are

9.703, 10.014, 10.163, 10.225, 10.376,
10.418, 10.450, 10.572, 10.591, 10.649,
10.678, 10.731, 10.800, 10.876, 10.970,
11.049, 11.204, 11.320, 11.668.

The histogram and the box plot for the transformed observations are shown in fig. 5.7 and 5.8. Both figures indicate that the logarithmic transformation has attained its goal. The median, the quartiles, the average and the standard deviation for all 19 observations as well as for the 18 smallest observations are shown in table 5.2. The difference between the median and the average is now negligible. This confirms the symmetry of the distribution, since according to theorem 5.7, the theoretical median and the mean value are equal for a symmetric distribution.

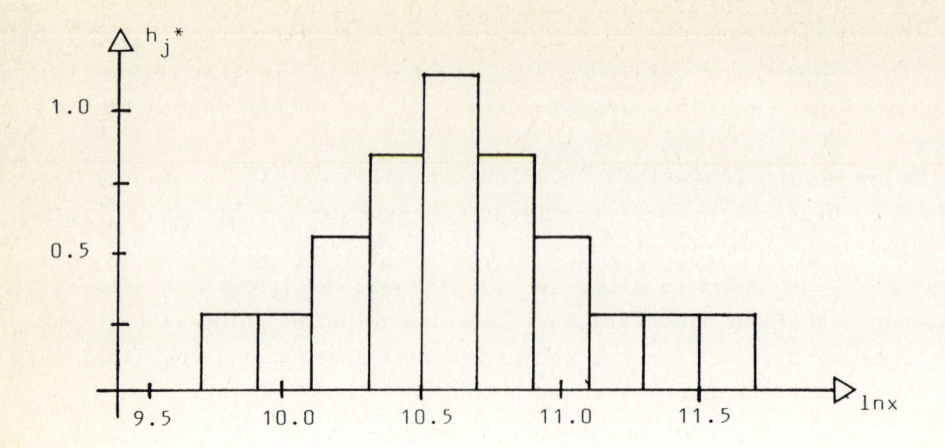

Fig. 5.7. Histogram for the logarithms of the incomes of 19 families.

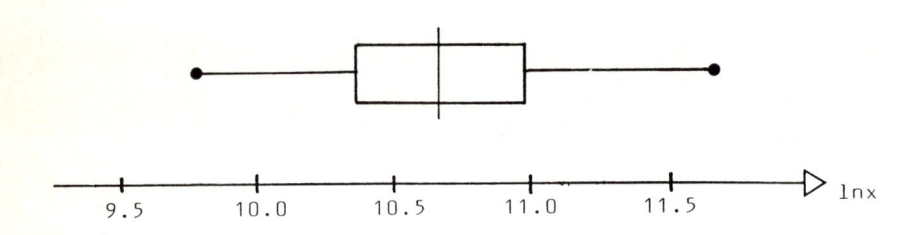

Fig. 5.8. Box plot for the logarithms of the incomes of 19 families.

Table 5.2. Comparisons of location and dispersion measures for the logarithms of the incomes of 19 families.

	All observations	18 observations
Median	10.648	10.620
Average	10.656	10.599
Upper quartile	10.970	10.900
Lower quartile	10.376	10.339
Quartile distance	0.594	0.561
Standard deviation	0.473	0.417

Finally, it can be seen from table 5.2 that the relative change in the standard deviation is larger than the relative change in the quartile distance when the largest observation is omitted.△.

If the data available are in the form of a set of observations grouped in disjoint intervals, percentiles, averages and variances based on the original observations cannot be computed. In chapter 2, it was shown how to calculate the percentiles when the data are on grouped form. Similar approximations can be derived for the average $\bar{x}$ and the sample variance s^2.

Assume that data consists of n observations, grouped in the intervals $(t_{i-1}, t_i]$, $i=1,2,\ldots,m$, and let further the interval $(t_{i-1}, t_i]$ contain a_i observations. The midpoint of the i'th interval is denoted by $t_i^* = (t_i + t_{i-1})/2$. An approximation to the average of the n original observations is then given by

$$(5.20) \qquad \bar{t} = \frac{1}{n} \sum_{i=1}^{m} a_i t_i^*,$$

and an approximation to the sample variance by

$$(5.21) \qquad s_t^2 = \frac{1}{n-1} \sum_{i=1}^{m} a_i (t_i^* - \bar{t})^2 = \frac{1}{n-1} (\Sigma a_i (t_i^*)^2 - n\bar{t}^2).$$

If the number of observations is reasonably large and the number of intervals not too small, (5.20) and (5.21) are usually satisfactory approximations to $\bar{x}$ and s^2 computed from the original observations.

However, there may be problems if the end points of the extreme intervals t_0 and t_m are unknown. This case also caused problems in connection with the construction of a histogram. Values for t_0 and t_m can of course be selected arbitrarily, but the choice of t_0 and t_m may have serious consequences for the calculated values of $\bar{t}$ and s_t^2. This is particularly the case if the extreme intervals contain relatively many observations.

Example 5.11

Suppose we want to describe the income distributions in table 2.2 by means of the average and the standard deviations, calculated using (5.20) and (5.21). From (5.20), with $t_0=0$ and $t_7=300$ and with units of 1000 DKK, follows

$$\sum_{i=1}^{7} a_i t_i^* = 237030 \text{ and } \bar{t} = 76.191,$$

and from (5.21) follows

$$\Sigma a_i (t_i^*)^2 = 26260900,$$

and

$$s_t^2 = \frac{1}{3110}(26260900-(237030)^2/3111) = 2637.1.$$

If $t_7=400$, then

$$\Sigma a_i t_i^* = 246030, \quad \bar{t} = 79.084$$

$$\Sigma a_i (t_i^*)^2 = 30760900$$

and

$$s_t^2 = \frac{1}{3110}(30760900-(246030)^2/3111) = 3624.7. \triangle.$$

Example 5.11 shows that a grouped distribution in some cases is unsuitable for determining approximations to $\bar{x}$ and s^2 because of the influence from arbitrarily chosen interval end points. However, when calculating percentiles, only the interval ordering between the observations is used. If a percentile is not in one of the two extreme intervals, the choice of t_0 and t_m are, therefore, of no consequence for the values of the percentiles.

Let now $x_1,\ldots,x_n$ be observations of a discrete random variable with point probabilities $f(x)$. Such observations often represent counts and the sample space is accordingly the set of non-negative integers. If the observed values are large and show a considerable degree of variation, the observations can often be treated as continuous and the same methods be used for describing the data as for continuous observations. If, on the other hand, the observations only attain a limited number of values, e.g. the integers between 0 and m, many observations will have identical values. The appropriate procedure is then for each integer j between 0 and m to count the number a_j of observations taking the value j. Data can then be presented as shown in table 5.3.

The relative frequencies $h_0,\ldots,h_m$ are approximations to the point probabilities $f(0),\ldots,f(m)$. As summary measures the average and the sample variance are normally used. For grouped discrete data these are computed as

(5.22)
$$\begin{cases} S = \sum_{i=1}^{n} x_i = \sum_{j=0}^{m} j \cdot a_j \\ \bar{x} = S/n, \end{cases}$$

and

(5.23) $\begin{cases} SS = \sum_{i=1}^{n} x_i^2 = \sum_{j=0}^{m} j^2 a_j \\ s^2 = \frac{1}{n-1} (SS - S^2/n). \end{cases}$

Table 5.3. Presentation of a discrete data set.

j	a_j	$h_j = a_j/n$	$j \cdot a_j$	$j^2 \cdot a_j$
0	a_0	h_0	$0 \cdot a_0$	$0^2 \cdot a_0$
1	a_1	h_1	$1 \cdot a_1$	$1^2 \cdot a_1$
2	a_2	h_2	$2 \cdot a_2$	$2^2 \cdot a_2$
.	.	.	.	.
.	.	.	.	.
.	.	.	.	.
m	a_m	h_m	$m \cdot a_m$	$m^2 \cdot a_m$
Sum	n	1	$\sum_{i=1}^{n} x_i$	$\sum_{i=1}^{n} x_i^2$

Example 5.12

Consider a data set consisting of the observed number of arrivals at the check-out counter at a supermarket in 45 consecutive 2 minute intervals. There were at most five arrivals in any interval. Hence the observations $x_1, \ldots, x_{45}$ only take the values 0, 1, 2, 3, 4 and 5. The data are summarized in table 5.4.

Table 5.4. The distribution of number of arrivals at a supermarket check-out.

Number of arrivals j	Observed number of j arrivals a_j	Frequency h_j	$j \cdot a_j$	$j^2 \cdot a_j$
0	6	0.13	0	0
1	18	0.40	18	18
2	9	0.20	18	36
3	7	0.16	21	63
4	4	0.09	16	64
5	1	0.02	5	25
Sum	45	1.00	78	206

Formulae (5.22) and (5.23) yield

$$\bar{x} = S/n = 78/45 = 1.73$$

and

$$s^2 = \frac{1}{n-1}(SS-S^2/n) = \frac{1}{44}(206-78^2/45) = 1.61. \triangle$$

6. Special Discrete Distributions

6.1. The binomial distribution

The binomial distribution typically applies to finite sequences of experiments or trials, in each of which it is observed whether or not an event A occurs.

Consider n trials and assume that

(i) the probability p=P(A) of the outcome A is the same in all trials

(ii) the outcomes of the trials are independent.

Let X be a random variable representing the number of times A occurs in n trials. In order to determine the point probabilities f(x) for X, consider a certain sequence of outcomes in which A occurs x times and $\bar{A}$ occurs n-x times, for example

$$\underbrace{A\bar{A}A A \bar{A} \ldots \bar{A} A}_{n}.$$

The probability of observing this sequence is

(6.1) $\qquad p^{x}(1-p)^{n-x},$

since the trials are independent. The event {X=x} is the union of all sequences with exactly x A's and n-x $\bar{A}$'s. All of these sequences have the probability (6.1) and hence

$$P(X=x) = C(n,x)p^{x}(1-p)^{n-x},$$

where C(n,x) is the number of possible sequences of length n with exactly x A's, i.e. the number of different ways in which x elements can be selected from n elements. Using combinatorial arguments, it can be proved that C(n,x) is given by

(6.2) $\qquad C(n,x) = \binom{n}{x} = \dfrac{n!}{x!(n-x)!} = \dfrac{n(n-1)\ldots(n-x+1)}{x!},$

where $n! = n(n-1) \cdot \ldots \cdot 2 \cdot 1$. $C(n,x)$ is called a **binomial coefficient**. The point probabilities of X are, therefore, given by

$$(6.3) \qquad f(x) = \binom{n}{x} p^x (1-p)^{n-x}, \quad x = 0, 1, \ldots, n.$$

A random variable X with point probabilities (6.3) is said to follow a **binomial distribution** with parameters (n,p) and we write $X \sim b(n,p)$. The parameter p is called the **probability parameter**.

Since f is a point probability

$$(6.4) \qquad \sum_{x=0}^{n} \binom{n}{x} p^x (1-p)^{n-x} = 1.$$

This result can be derived from the binomial formula

$$(6.5) \qquad (a+b)^n = \sum_{x=0}^{n} \binom{n}{x} a^x b^{n-x}.$$

The name of the distribution is derived from this formula, of which (6.4) is a special case with $a=p$ and $b=1-p$.

From the definition (6.2) of the binomial coefficient, it follows immediately that

$$(6.6) \qquad \binom{n}{x} = \binom{n}{n-x},$$

so that if $X \sim b(n,p)$, $Y = n-X \sim b(n, 1-p)$.

To get an impression of the shape of the distribution, consider the inequality

$$\frac{f(x+1)}{f(x)} \geq 1.$$

As long as $f(x+1) > f(x)$, the point probabilities increase as x increases. From (6.2) and (6.3),

$$\frac{f(x+1)}{f(x)} = \frac{n-x}{x+1} \cdot \frac{p}{1-p} \geq 1,$$

for

$$x \leq (n+1)p - 1 = x_0.$$

Hence, the point probabilities increase to a certain point and then decrease unless $x_0 < 0$ or $x_0 > n-1$. These extreme cases correspond respectively to

and
$$p < \frac{1}{n+1}$$
$$p > \frac{n}{n+1}$$

In the former case, the point probabilities are strictly decreasing and in the latter case they are strictly increasing. One of the extreme cases is shown in fig. 6.1 for n=8 and p=0.1.

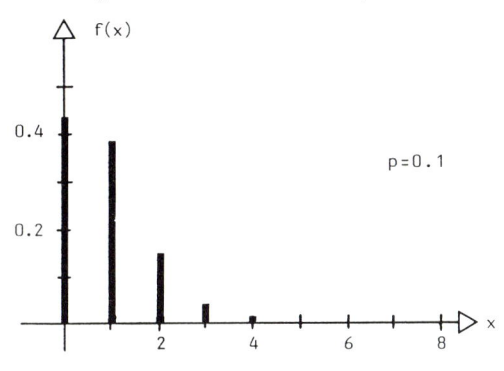

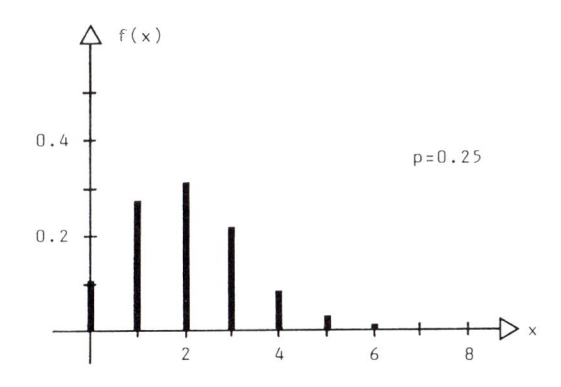

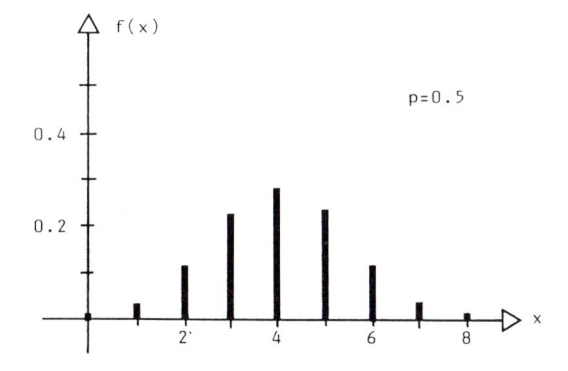

Fig. 6.1. Three binomial distributions, n=8.

The other two distributions in fig. 6.1 show the characteristic shape of the binomial distribution. Fig. 6.1 also illustrates that the binomial distribution is symmetric around n/2 for p=0.5.

The point probabilities of the binomial distribution are usually computed by means of tables showing the cumulative distribution function F(x). From such tables, the point probabilities are computed as

(6.7) $f(x) = F(x) - F(x-1)$, $x=1,\ldots,n$.

Example 4.4 (continued)

Consider an aptitude test with 4 equally difficult problems. A respondent tries to solve each problem independently of the other problems. If a problem is solved correctly, the event A is said to occur. Hence, assumption (i) and (ii) are satisfied for n=4. If it is further assumed that the probability of solving a given problem correctly is p=0.5, the point probabilities f(0), f(1), f(2), f(3) and f(4) can be computed as follows:

$$f(0) = \binom{4}{0}(0.5)^0(0.5)^4 = (0.5)^4 = 0.0625$$
$$f(1) = \binom{4}{1}(0.5)^1(0.5)^3 = 4(0.5)^4 = 0.25$$
$$f(2) = \binom{4}{2}(0.5)^2(0.5)^2 = 6(0.5)^4 = 0.375.$$

Since the distribution is symmetric, f(3)=f(1) and f(4)=f(0). Note that $\binom{n}{0}=1$ since $0!=1$. △.

The event A in the binomial distribution is often referred to as a success, such that p becomes the probability of a success. With this terminology, the binomial distribution is the distribution of the number of successes in n independent trials, where the probability of a success is constant over the trials.

Example 6.1

Table 6.1 shows the distribution of the number x of correct solutions to 20 problems in an American aptitude test, SAT (Scholastic Aptitude Test), for 1000 respondents.

If each of the respondents tries to solve any problem independently of the other problems, and if all respondents solve any of the problems correctly with the same probability p, table 6.1 is a summary of 1000 observations from a binomial distribution with parameters (20,p).

To check these assumptions, the point probability f in a binomial distribution with n=20 and p=0.473 are calculated, where 0.473 is the relative frequency of correctly solved problems for all the respondents. In chapter 10, this particular choice of the probability parameter is motivated. Table 6.1 displays the relative frequencies h(x) and the point probabilities f(x).

Table 6.1. The distribution of the number of correct answers in the SAT for 1000 respondents and the point probabilities of a binomial distribution with n=20 and p=0.473.

Number of correct solutions x	Number of persons with x correct solutions	h(x)	f(x)
0	18	0.018	0.000
1	25	0.025	0.000
2	25	0.025	0.001
3	41	0.041	0.002
4	46	0.046	0.009
5	57	0.057	0.026
6	56	0.056	0.058
7	53	0.053	0.102
8	55	0.055	0.147
9	69	0.069	0.174
10	95	0.095	0.170
11	93	0.093	0.137
12	95	0.095	0.091
13	81	0.081	0.050
14	82	0.082	0.022
15	58	0.058	0.008
16	33	0.033	0.002
17	11	0.011	0.001
18	4	0.004	0.000
19	3	0.003	0.000
20	0	0.000	0.000
Total	1000	1.000	1.000

It is obvious from table 6.1 that the point probabilities do not correspond at all well to the relative frequencies. There are three possible explanations for this:

(1) The problems are not equally difficult so that p is not constant over all 20 "trials". This violates assumption (i).

(2) The "trials" are not independent. For example, there may be a learning effect so that the chance of solving a given problem correctly depends on whether the previous problems have been solved correctly or incorrectly. Assumption (ii) is then violated.

(3) Finally, the respondents may have different abilities. Since the observations are collected from 1000 individuals, the probability parameter p is likely to change from respondent to respondent. In this case, the binomial distribution cannot describe the complete set of data, even though it may describe the number of correct answers for each respondent.△.

Theorem 6.1

If X is binomially distributed with parameters n and p, then

(6.8) $\quad E[X] = np$

and

(6.9) $\quad \mathrm{var}[X] = np(1-p)$.

Proof

From definition (5.1),

$$E[X] = \sum_{x=0}^{n} x \binom{n}{x} p^x (1-p)^{n-x}.$$

Using (6.2) this can be rewritten as

$$E[X] = np \sum_{x=1}^{n} \binom{n-1}{x-1} p^{x-1} (1-p)^{n-x}.$$

Since n-x=n-1-(x-1) and x-1 runs from 0 to n-1 as x runs from 1 to n, the sum in this expression for E[X] is identical to the sum in (6.4) with n replaced by n-1. Hence,

$$E[X] = np.$$

According to (5.12)

$$\mathrm{var}[X] = E[X(X-1)] - E[X](E[X]-1),$$

where

$$E[X(X-1)] = \sum_{x=0}^{n} x(x-1) \binom{n}{x} p^x (1-p)^{n-x} =$$

$$n(n-1)p^2 \sum_{x=2}^{n} \binom{n-2}{x-2} p^{x-2} (1-p)^{n-x}.$$

The sum in the last expression is a sum of binomial probabilities with n replaced by n-2 so that

$$\mathrm{var}[X] = n(n-1)p^2 - n^2 p^2 + np = np(1-p). \square$$

6.2. The Poisson distribution

In 1837, the French mathematician Poisson discovered that the binomial distribution could be approximated by a simple distribution when n is large and p small. This distribution is called the Poisson distribution.

Theorem 6.2

If $p \to 0$ and $n \to \infty$ in such a way that $np = \lambda$ remains constant, or np converges to λ, then

(6.10) $$f(x) = \binom{n}{x} p^x (1-p)^{n-x} \to \frac{\lambda^x}{x!} e^{-\lambda}.$$

Proof

Write $f(x)$ as

$$f(x) = \frac{n(n-1)\ldots(n-x+1)}{x! n^x} (np)^x \left(1 - \frac{np}{n}\right)^{n-x}.$$

For fixed x,

$$\frac{n(n-1)\ldots(n-x+1)}{n^x} = \left(1 - \frac{1}{n}\right)\ldots\left(1 - \frac{x-1}{n}\right) \to 1 \quad \text{for } n \to \infty.$$

Furthermore,

$$\left(1 - \frac{np}{n}\right)^{n-x} = \left(1 - \frac{\lambda}{n}\right)^n / \left(1 - \frac{\lambda}{n}\right)^x.$$

As $n \to \infty$, $(1-\lambda/n)^x$ converges to 1, while it can be shown that

$$\left(1 - \frac{\lambda}{n}\right)^n \to e^{-\lambda} \quad \text{for } n \to \infty.$$

Inserting these results in the expression for $f(x)$ yields

$$f(x) \to \frac{\lambda^x}{x!} e^{-\lambda}. \quad \Box$$

Consider now the sample space $S = \{0, 1, \ldots\}$ and the function

(6.11) $$f(x) = \frac{\lambda^x}{x!} e^{-\lambda}, \quad x \in S.$$

If $\lambda > 0$, then $f(x) > 0$ for all $x \in S$ and

(6.12) $$\sum_{x=0}^{\infty} f(x) = \sum_{x=0}^{\infty} \frac{\lambda^x}{x!} e^{-\lambda} = e^{-\lambda} e^{\lambda} = 1,$$

since $\sum \lambda^x / x!$ is the Taylor expansion of e^λ. Therefore, f can be interpreted as a point probability for a discrete random variable, the values of which depend on the parameter λ. A random variable X with point probabilities (6.11) is said to be **Poisson distributed** with parameter λ and this is written as X~Ps(λ). For selected values of λ, the form of f(x) is shown in fig. 6.2.

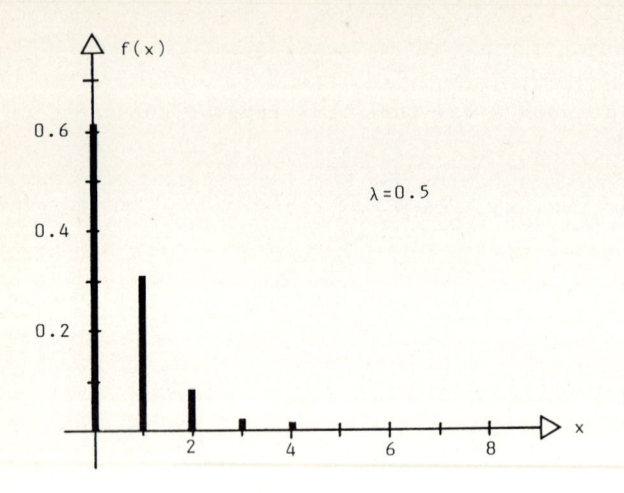

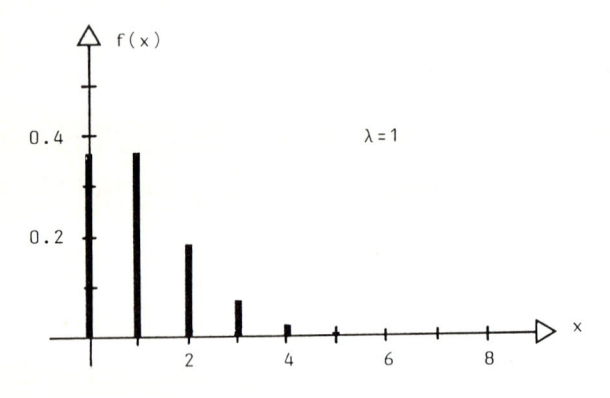

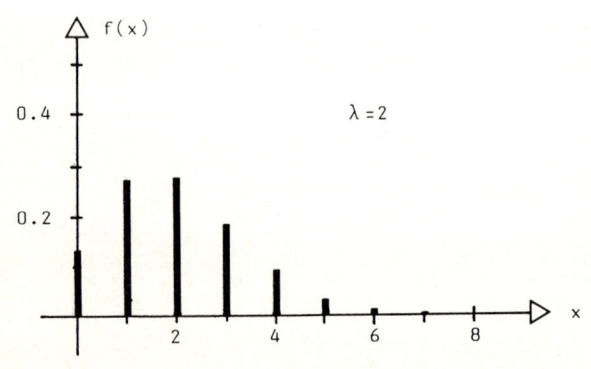

Fig. 6.2. Three Poisson distributions.

The result in theorem 6.2 can be used to approximate binomial probabilities. For n sufficiently large and p sufficiently small, it follows from the theorem that the difference between $\binom{n}{x}p^x(1-p)^{n-x}$ and $(np)^x e^{-np}/x!$ is so small that it does not matter in practice whether the one or the other of the expressions is used for f(x). For many practical purposes, the difference is considered negligible if p<0.1 and n>30.

Example 6.2

A wild cat oil discovery is a minor discovery which is not part of a large systematic search. Table 6.2 shows the number of wild cat oil discoveries per month in Alberta, Canada from 1953 to 1971.

The observation period consists of 228 months. Assume that 1) two wild cat discoveries are not made on the same day, 2) the discoveries are made independently of each other and 3) the probability p of making a discovery on a given day is constant within each month. Under these assumptions, the number of discoveries in a given month will follow a binomial distribution with parameters (n,p), where n is the number of days in the month. Since n is reasonably large and p is presumably small, a Poisson distribution may be used to describe the number of wild cat discoveries per month.

In table 6.2, the point probabilities f(x) of a Poisson distribution with $\lambda=0.68$ are shown together with the relative frequencies h(x) of the number of discoveries per month. As can be seen, the Poisson distribution fits the observed distribution reasonably well.

Table 6.2. Number of wild cat oil discoveries per month together with a fitted Poisson distribution.

Number of discoveries x	Number of months	h(x)	f(x)
0	123	0.539	0.507
1	67	0.294	0.344
2	27	0.118	0.117
3	10	0.044	0.027
4	0	0.000	0.004
5	1	0.004	0.001
Total	228	0.999	1.000

The number of days per month changes slightly from month to month, so the monthly numbers of discoveries are not identically distributed, even under the given assumptions. However, this complication has been disregarded for the sake of simplicity. △ .

Theorem 6.3

If X follows a Poisson distribution with parameter λ, then

(6.13) $\qquad E[X] = \lambda$

and

(6.14) $\qquad var[X] = \lambda.$

Proof

From (5.1),

$$E[X] = \sum_{x=0}^{\infty} x \frac{\lambda^x e^{-\lambda}}{x!} = \lambda \sum_{x=1}^{\infty} \frac{\lambda^{x-1}}{(x-1)!} e^{-\lambda}$$

$$= \lambda \sum_{y=0}^{\infty} \frac{\lambda^y}{y!} e^{-\lambda} = \lambda.$$

Furthermore,

$$E[X(X-1)] = \sum_{x=0}^{\infty} x(x-1) \frac{\lambda^x}{x!} e^{-\lambda} = \lambda^2 \sum_{x=2}^{\infty} \frac{\lambda^{x-2}}{(x-2)!} e^{-\lambda}$$

$$= \lambda^2 \sum_{y=0}^{\infty} \frac{\lambda^y}{y!} e^{-\lambda} = \lambda^2.$$

Then according to (5.12)

$$var[X] = E[X(X-1)] - E[X](E[X]-1) = \lambda^2 - \lambda(\lambda-1) = \lambda,$$

which proves the theorem. $\square$.

The Poisson distribution can alternatively be introduced by considering a process such as the one shown in fig. 6.3 where an event A occurs at time points t_1, t_2, t_3, t_4 and t_5. The process may refer to a customer entering a supermarket, a patient arriving at the casualty department of a hospital or a telephone call coming in to a switchboard.

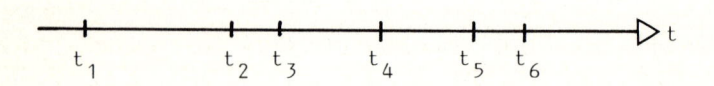

Fig. 6.3. A time process.

The number of times the event occurs in a given time interval (0,t] is a random variable X(t), the distribution of which depends on the value of t. Considered as a function of t, X(t) is called a **stochastic process**.

The following three assumptions about the occurrence of the events are made:

(i) The probability that the event occurs in a short time interval of length Δt is

$\lambda \Delta t + o(\Delta t)$,

where λ is a positive constant, and $o(\Delta t)$ approaches zero faster than Δt, i.e.

$o(\Delta t)/\Delta t \to 0$ for $\Delta t \to 0$.

(ii) The probability of the event occurring two or more times in a short time interval of length Δt is $o(\Delta t)$.

(iii) The number of occurrences of the event in two non-overlapping time intervals are independent.

A process satisfying these three assumptions is called a **Poisson process**. It is implicit in (i) that the value of λ does not depend on the position of the interval on the time axis.

Assumption (i) means that the probability of the event occurring in a sufficiently small time interval is proportional to the length of the interval. Assumption (ii) means that the probability of the event occurring twice in a short time interval is negligible, which in turn means that in practice it should be possible to separate any two occurrences of the event in time. Assumption (iii) means that the process has no memory, i.e. what happens in any one time interval does not influence what happens in subsequent intervals.

Theorem 6.4

Under assumption (i) to (iii) the random variable X(t), which denotes the number of times a given event occurs in the time interval (0,t], is Poisson distributed with parameter λt, i.e.

(6.15) $\qquad P(X(t)=x) = \dfrac{(\lambda t)^x}{x!} e^{-\lambda t}, \quad x=0,1,\ldots$.

The proof is complicated and omitted in favour of the following intuitive argument. Suppose the interval from 0 to t is subdivided in n intervals of length t/n. If n is large, t/n becomes small and the probability of two or more occurrences of the event in an interval of length t/n will be of the order of magnitude $o(\Delta t)$ in accordance with assumption (ii). Hence we need only pay attention to the possibilities that the event A or its complement $\bar{A}$ occurs. From (i), the probability p_n that A occurs in an interval of length t/n can be written as

$$p_n = \lambda \frac{t}{n} + o(\frac{t}{n}).$$

Since there are n intervals of length t/n in (0,t] and occurrences in these intervals are independent (assumption (iii)), X(t) must be approximately binomially distributed, i.e.

$$P(X(t)=x) \simeq \binom{n}{x} p_n^x (1-p_n)^{n-x}.$$

As np_n converges to λt as $n \to \infty$, (6.15) follows from theorem 6.2.

From theorem 6.3, it follows that the mean value of a Poisson process is λt, i.e. λ is the expected number of occurrences per time unit. This motivates calling λ the **intensity** of the process.

Assumptions (i), (ii) and (iii) can be used to justify the description of a given set of observations by a Poisson distribution. In practice, we can thus check whether or not the circumstances under which the data have been collected are in accordance with the assumptions of the Poisson process. An indirect way of checking the assumptions is to check whether the Poisson distribution fits the data by comparing relative frequencies and point probabilities, as illustrated in example 6.3.

Example 6.3

In a supermarket, the number of customers arriving at the check-out counter in two-minute intervals over a period of 1½ hour are observed. Table 6.3 shows the distribution of the numbers of customers in the 45 intervals.

The use of a Poisson distribution as a model for the number of arrivals to the check-out counter can be justified by checking each of the assumptions (i) - (iii).

    (i)   It is not unrealistic to assume that the probability of an arrival in a small time interval Δt is proportional to Δt. The proportionality factor λ is interpreted as the intensity of arrivals since arrivals occur more frequently the larger the value of λ.

(ii) This assumption requires that the customers arrive separately at the check-out counter so that any two arrivals can be separated in time. This assumption is therefore not satisfied if two persons (a married couple, for example) arrive at the same time and are recorded as two arrivals.

(iii) If the customers arrive independently of each other to the check-out counter, (iii) is satisfied. It is not satisfied if a long queue discourages other customers from using a particular counter.

Table 6.3. The distribution of the number of arrivals at a check-out counter for 45 time intervals of length 2 minutes.

Number of arrivals	Observed number of intervals	Frequency $h(x)$	Poisson probability $f(x)$
x = 0	6	0.13	0.17
1	18	0.40	0.30
2	9	0.20	0.27
3	7	0.16	0.16
4	4	0.09	0.07
5	1	0.02	0.03
Total	45	1.00	1.00

The observations in table 6.3 represent 45 repetitions of an experiment. For each repetition, it is argued that the Poisson distribution may describe the number of arrivals. In order to describe the data in table 6.3 by a Poisson distribution, the parameter λ must be assumed constant over the 45 repetitions. This means that the intensity of arrivals must stay constant over the entire period of 90 minutes in which arrivals are observed.

In order to evaluate the fit of the Poisson distribution empirically, the point probabilities of a Poisson distribution with intensity 1.73 are shown in the last column of table 6.3. The determination of this value is discussed in chapter 10. It may be noted that 1.73 is the average number of arrivals per 2 minutes over the period of observation. It can be seen that there is a reasonably good correspondance between the Poisson probabilities and the relative frequencies. $\triangle$.

Example 6.4

Table 6.4 shows the number of cars passing a counting station in each of 120 intervals of length 30 seconds. The last column shows the point probabilities of a Poisson distribution with $\lambda = 2.2$.

Table 6.4. Number of cars passing a counting station in 120 time intervals of length 30 seconds.

Number of cars x	Observed number of intervals	Frequency h(x)	Poisson probability f(x)
0	19	0.16	0.11
1	29	0.24	0.24
2	23	0.19	0.27
3	23	0.19	0.20
4	15	0.12	0.11
5	7	0.06	0.05
6	2	0.02	0.02
≥ 7	2	0.02	0.01
Total	120	1.00	1.00

As it can be seen, the Poisson distribution fits the data reasonably well. This result is rather surprising because assumption (iii) would appear to be questionable in this instance. A car which intends to overtake another car needs an opening in the opposite traffic flow, so road traffic is to some extend characterized by queue formations. Hence, cars will not pass a counting station independently of each other.

The chance of a car passing the station immediately after another car depends on whether the first car is at the head of a queue. The existence of queues will in effect mean that large values and the value zero ought to be observed more frequently than would be expected according to the Poisson distribution. In table 6.4, there is a weak tendency in this direction. For example, the frequencies for $x \geq 4$ are all slightly larger than the corresponding Poisson probabilities. $\triangle$.

6.3. The Pascal distribution

In section 6.1, the distribution of the number of successes or events occurring in n independent trials was discussed. The probability p of a success was assumed constant in all trials. Consider now the same basic set up, but without a limit on the number of trials performed. Observation ceases once the event occurs the k'th time. The random variable Y is the number of the trial in which the k'th success occurs so that the event $\{Y=y\}$ occurs if the k'th success is observed in the y'th trial.

In order to derive the point probability for Y, consider the events

B_1 = {k-1 successes in the y-1 first trials}

and

$$B_2 = \{\text{success in trial number } y\}.$$

Note that $\{Y=y\} = B_1 \cap B_2$ and that B_1 and B_2 are independent, since the trials are independent. Obviously, $P(B_1)$ is the point probability of observing k-1 successes in a binomial distribution with parameters y-1 and p, such that

$$P(B_1) = \binom{y-1}{k-1} p^{k-1} (1-p)^{y-1-(k-1)},$$

and since $P(B_2) = p$, it follows that

(6.16) $\qquad P(Y=y) = P(B_1) P(B_2) = \binom{y-1}{k-1} p^{k-1} (1-p)^{y-k} p.$

Substituting x for y-k, the point probabilities become

(6.17) $\qquad f(x) = \binom{x+k-1}{k-1} p^k (1-p)^x, \quad x = 0, 1, 2, \ldots.$

A random variable X with sample space $S = \{0, 1, 2, \ldots\}$ and point probabilities (6.17) is said to follow a **Pascal distribution**. The domain of variation for p is the interval (0,1).

Since Y is the number of trials until the k'th succes is observed, X is the number of fiascoes preceeding the k'th success. The Pascal distribution (6.17) is also called the **negative binomial distribution**. Fig. 6.4 shows a number of Pascal distributions.

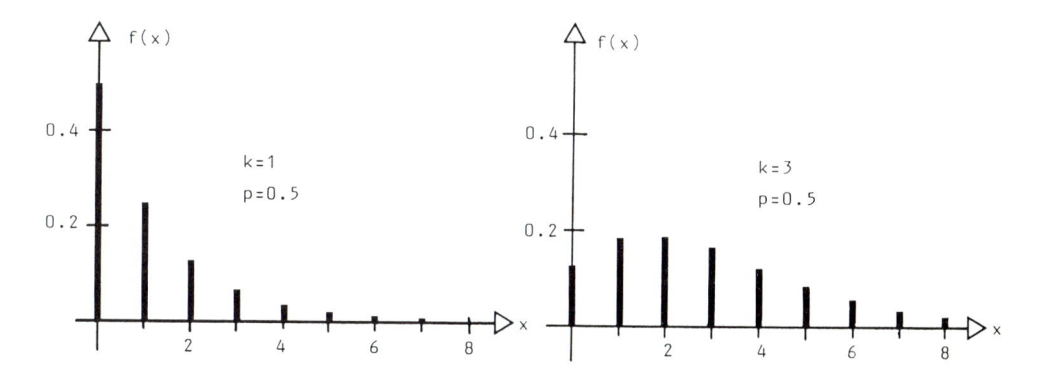

Fig. 6.4. Pascal distributions for k=1 and 3 and p=0.5.

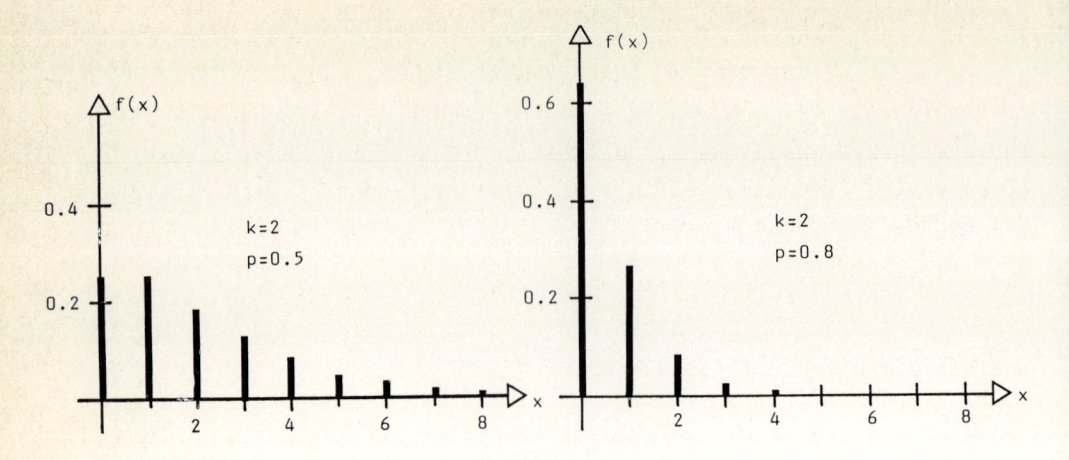

Fig. 6.4. Pascal distributions for k=2 and p=0.5 and 0.8.

Theorem 6.5

For a random variable X with point probabilities (6.17)

(6.18) $E[X] = k(1-p)/p$,

and

(6.19) $\text{var}[X] = k(1-p)/p^2$.

Since $1/p > 1$, when $p < 1$,

$$E[X] < \text{var}[X]$$

for a Pascal distributed random variable X.
For a Poisson distributed random variable X,

$$E[X] = \text{var}[X]$$

and since $(1-p) < 1$ for $p > 0$, it follows from theorem 6.1, that

$$E[X] > \text{var}[X]$$

for a binomially distributed random variable X.
The relationship between the mean and the variance thus distin-

guishes the three distributions in a characteristic way.

The Pascal distribution is often used to describe observed distributions with "long tails", i.e. distributions for which large values occur more frequently than would be expected in a Poisson distribution. One such example is the queue length in stable queues.

Suppose we have a queueing system with one server, for example a supermarket with one open check-out counter. Assume that customers arrive and depart independently of each other at and from the check-out counter according to Poisson processes. The arrival intensity, i.e. the expected number of arrivals per time unit, is called λ, and the departure intensity is called μ. Under certain supplementary assumptions it can then be shown that the length X of the queue, including the person being served, at any given time has point probabilities

(6.20) $f(x) = \rho^x(1-\rho)$, $x = 0, 1, \ldots$,

where $\rho = \lambda/\mu$. The point probability (6.20) can be recognized as a Pascal distribution with $p = 1-\rho$ and $k = 1$. In order for (6.20) to give the point probability in a discrete distribution, ρ must be less than 1. However, ρ depends on both the intensity of arrivals λ and the intensity of departures μ. Thus $\rho \geq 1$ means that customers arrive faster than they can be served, so the queue continues to grow and no stable queue with a probability distribution exists. The distribution (6.20) is called the **geometric distribution.**

Applications of the Pascal distribution can be motivated by an alternative argument. Assume that the number of entries per time unit in a queue is Poisson distributed with parameter λ, but that λ varies randomly over the observation period. If λ varies according to a gamma distribution, cf. section 7.5, it can be shown that the number of arrivals in a given time interval is Pascal distributed. This means that the Pascal distribution can be applied in situations where the parameter λ for the Poisson process fails to be constant during the observation period.

Example 6.5

In example 6.4 it was mentioned that the distribution of the number of cars passing a counting station is influenced by the formation of queues. It was also noted that the existence of queues should entail a distribution with a somewhat longer right tail than would be expected for a Poisson distribution. Since the Pascal distribution is related to the description of queues, it is reasonable to suggest a Pascal distribution as an alternative to the Poisson distribution when trying to describe traffic data such as those presented in table 6.4.

In order to compare the description by a Pascal and by a Poisson distribution, consider data from an observation period of three hours. The data thus consist of the number of cars passing in 360 time intervals of length 30 seconds each. The observed distribution is shown in table 6.5 together with a fitted Poisson distribution with $\lambda=2.269$ and a a fitted Pascal distribution with $k=7$ and $p=0.755$.

Table 6.5. Number of cars observed in 360 time intervals of length 30 seconds and fitted Poisson and Pascal distributions.

Number of cars x	Number of intervals	Frequencies h(x)	Poisson probabilities	Pascal probabilities
0	56	0.156	0.103	0.140
1	79	0.219	0.235	0.240
2	79	0.219	0.266	0.235
3	65	0.181	0.201	0.173
4	44	0.122	0.114	0.106
5	19	0.053	0.052	0.057
6	12	0.033	0.020	0.028
≥ 7	6	0.017	0.009	0.022
Total	360	1.000	1.000	1.001

As can be seen, the Pascal distribution describes the observed frequencies better than the Poisson distribution. This is true in particular for $x=0$ and $x \geq 6$. This was to be expected since the variance is larger in the Pascal than in the Poisson distribution (should the mean values be equal). $\triangle$.

The Pascal distribution and the binomial distribution are both connected with a sequence of independent trials where a certain event A occurs or does not occur in each trial. The assumption of independent trials and constant probability of success are the same for the two distributions. The difference between the distributions lies in what is being observed. In the binomial distribution, the number of successes in a given number of trials is observed. In the Pascal distribution, the "waiting time" until a given number of successes have occurred is observed.

6.4. The multinomial distribution

Consider a sequence of n independent trials, each of which can result in one of m possible events $A_1,\ldots,A_m$, such that $A_1,\ldots,A_m$ form a classification of the sample space of the individual trials. Let

$$P(A_j) = p_j, \quad j=1,\ldots,m,$$

with

$$\sum_{j=1}^{m} p_j = 1.$$

The number of occurrences of each of the events $A_1,\ldots,A_m$ can be observed, and the random variables $X_1,\ldots,X_m$ defined as

$$X_j = \text{number of times } A_j \text{ occurs}, \quad j=1,\ldots,m.$$

This gives an m-dimensional vector $(X_1, X_2,\ldots,X_m)$, where each component is a random variable. Such a vector is called an **m-dimensional random variable**. The sample space consists of all vectors $(x_1,\ldots,x_m)$ of non-negative integers satisfying the condition $\Sigma x_i = n$ since only one of the A_j's can occur in each trial.

Let

$$B = \{X_1 = x_1\} \cap \ldots \cap \{X_m = x_m\}.$$

In order to determine the probability of B, the probability of a sequence, where A_1 occur x_1 times, A_2 occur x_2 times etc. must be derived. Such a sequence could be

$$\underbrace{A_1 \ldots A_1}_{x_1} \underbrace{A_2 \ldots A_2}_{x_2} \ldots \underbrace{A_m \ldots A_m}_{x_m}.$$

Since the trials are independent, the probability of this particular sequence is

$$p_1^{x_1} p_2^{x_2} \ldots p_m^{x_m}.$$

All sequences with x_1 A_1's, x_2 A_2's and so on have, however, the same probability, but since B is the event that one of these sequences occur and the sequences represent disjoint events, the probability of B is according to theorem 3.4 the sum of the probabilities for all the particular sequences. Hence,

$$P(\{X_1=x_1\} \cap \ldots \cap \{X_m=x_m\}) = K p_1^{x_1} p_2^{x_2} \ldots p_m^{x_m} ,$$

where the **multinomial coefficient** K is the number of possible sequences with exactly x_1 A_1's, x_2 A_2's and so on.

By combinatorial arguments, it can be shown that

$$(6.21) \qquad K = \frac{n!}{x_1! \ldots x_m!} = \binom{n}{x_1 \ldots x_m} .$$

Hence, the point probabilities of $(X_1, \ldots, X_m)$ can be written as

$$(6.22) \qquad f(x_1, \ldots, x_m) = \binom{n}{x_1 \ldots x_m} p_1^{x_1} \ldots p_m^{x_m} .$$

The random variable $(X_1, \ldots, X_m)$ with point probability (6.22) is said to follow a **multinomial distribution** and we write $(X_1, \ldots, X_m) \sim M(n, p_1, \ldots, p_m)$.

6.5. The hypergeometric distribution

The hypergeometric distribution is used in connection with sampling without replacement from a finite population, the units of which can be divided into two distinct categories. Assume that the population consists of N units and that a sample of size n is to be drawn, i.e. n units are to be selected from the population. If the units are selected one by one so that those units not already drawn have an equal chance of being selected, the sample is said to have been drawn randomly and without replacement.

Let the units of the first category be denoted as marked units and let the random variable X be defined as the number of marked units in a sample of size n drawn randomly and without replacement from the population. It can then be shown that all samples, i.e. all sets of n different units, have the same probability of being drawn, and the point probabilities of X can, therefore, be derived by an application of Laplace's law.

The number of possible outcomes is the number of different samples

$$m = \binom{N}{n} .$$

If there are M marked units in the population, the number of favourable outcomes, i.e. the number of samples with exactly x marked units, is

$$g = \binom{M}{x} \binom{N-M}{n-x}$$

since the marked units can be selected in $\binom{M}{x}$ different ways and for each of these, the remaining n-x units can be selected in $\binom{N-M}{n-x}$ different ways. The point probabilities f(x) of X are, therefore, given by

(6.23) $$f(x) = g/m = \binom{M}{x}\binom{N-M}{n-x}/\binom{N}{n}, \quad x = 0, 1, \ldots, \min(n, M),$$

as x cannot exceed the sample size or the number of marked units in the population.

A random variable with point probabilities (6.23) is said to follow a **hypergeometric distribution**. The parameters of this distribution are n, M and N.

Theorem 6.6

If X follows a hypergeometric distribution,

(6.24) $$E[X] = n\frac{M}{N},$$

and

(6.25) $$\text{var}[X] = n\frac{M}{N}\left(1 - \frac{M}{N}\right)\frac{N-n}{N-1}.$$

Proof

For convenience, assume that n<M. Formula (6.2) then gives

$$E[X] = \sum_{x=0}^{n} x\binom{M}{x}\binom{N-M}{n-x}/\binom{N}{n} = \frac{Mn}{N}\sum_{x=1}^{n}\binom{M-1}{x-1}\binom{N-M}{n-x}/\binom{N-1}{n-1}.$$

Since the last sum in this expression is the sum of all the point probabilities for a hypergeometric distribution with n, M and N replaced by n-1, M-1 and N-1, (6.24) follows. Similarly,

$$E[X(X-1)] = \sum_{x=0}^{n} x(x-1)\binom{M}{x}\binom{N-M}{n-x}/\binom{N}{n}$$

$$= \frac{M(M-1)n(n-1)}{N(N-1)}\sum_{x=2}^{n}\binom{M-2}{x-2}\binom{N-M}{n-x}/\binom{N-2}{n-2}$$

$$= \frac{M(M-1)n(n-1)}{N(N-1)},$$

noting that the last sum is a sum of hypergeometric probabilities. Hence, using (5.12),

$$\text{var}[X] = \frac{M(M-1)n(n-1)}{N(N-1)} - \frac{Mn}{N}\left(\frac{Mn}{N} - 1\right) = \frac{Mn(N-n)(N-M)}{N^2(N-1)},$$

from which (6.25) follows.☐.

If $N\to\infty$ and $M\to\infty$ in such a way that the ratio $p=M/N$ of marked units in the population remains constant, the situation will become more and more similar to a binomial situation. In the limiting situation, the outcome of the selection of one unit will hardly influence the result of the next selection since both M and N are large. The probability of selecting a marked unit is, therefore, approximately constant during the n trials necessary to create the sample. It also follows that the selections are approximately independent, and therefore the distribution of the x marked units in the sample ought to be approximately binomially distributed.

Theorem 6.7

If $N\to\infty$ and $M\to\infty$ in such a way that $p=M/N$ is constant, or such that M/N converges to p, then

$$\binom{M}{x}\binom{N-M}{n-x}/\binom{N}{n} \to \binom{n}{x}p^x(1-p)^{n-x}$$

for each value of $x \geq 0$ and $n \geq 0$.

If, after each selection, the selected unit is put back in the population before the next unit is selected, the sampling is said to be **with replacement**. In this situation, the conditions for the binomial distribution are satisfied. The result of one selection does not influence the result of the next selection, and the fraction of marked units remains constant during the entire sampling process. It follows that the number of marked units in the sample is binomially distributed when sampling with replacement.

There are several "rules of thumb" for when it is safe to use the binomial distribution as an approximation to the hypergeometric distribution. For most practical purposes, if $n<N/10$ and $0.1<p<0.9$, the approximation can be used. It is interesting to compare the mean value and variance of the hypergeometric distribution with those of the binomial distribution for a given sample size n. The mean values are obviously equal when $p=M/N$. For this value of p, the variance of the hypergeometric distribution is smaller than the variance of the binomial distribution for $n>1$, as can be seen from (6.9) and (6.25). The factor

$$\frac{N-n}{N-1} = \frac{N}{N-1} - \frac{n}{N-1} = \frac{1-n/N}{1-1/N}$$

depends primarily on the ratio between n and N. The smaller n is in relation to N, the less does the factor influence the variance in the hypergeometric distribution.

Expressed in terms of the parameter p rather than M, the hypergeometric distribution takes the form

$$f(x) = \binom{Np}{x}\binom{N(1-p)}{n-x} / \binom{N}{n}.$$

7. Special Continuous Distributions

7.1. The normal distribution

A continuous random variable X with density function

(7.1) $$f(x) = \frac{1}{\sigma\sqrt{2\pi}} \exp\left\{-\frac{(x-\mu)^2}{2\sigma^2}\right\}, \quad -\infty < x < \infty,$$

where $-\infty < \mu < +\infty$ and $\sigma > 0$, is said to be **normally distributed** with parameters μ and σ^2, and we write $X \sim N(\mu, \sigma^2)$.

Theorem 7.1
If X is normally distributed with density function (7.1), then

(7.2) $$E[X] = \mu$$

and

(7.3) $$\text{var}[X] = \sigma^2.$$

Proof
The density function (7.1) is symmetric around μ, i.e.

$$f(\mu-x) = f(\mu+x)$$

for all x. Hence (7.2) follows from the fact that the mean value is equal to the point of symmetry (theorem 5.6). The more complicated proof of (7.3) is omitted. □

It follows from (7.1), (7.2) and (7.3) that the normal distribution can be characterized by its mean value and variance. Fig. 7.1 shows three normal distributions. Note that the shape of the density function is unaffected by the value of μ. Changes in μ merely change the location of the density. If the variance σ^2 is changed, however, the shape of the density changes: Small values of σ^2 give a high and steep density, whereas large values of σ^2 give a low and flat density.

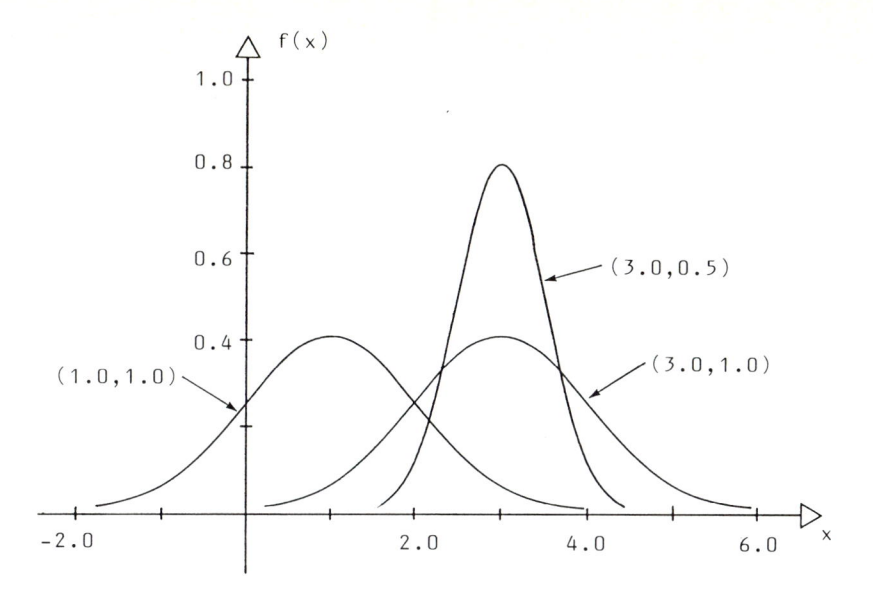

Fig. 7.1. Normal densities with different mean values and variances.

Theorem 7.2
If X is normally distributed with mean value μ and variance σ^2, then

$$Y = aX + b$$

is normally distributed with mean value

$$E[Y] = a\mu + b$$

and variance

$$\text{var}[Y] = a^2\sigma^2.$$

Proof
For a>0, the distribution function of Y is given by

$$P(Y \leq y) = P(aX + b \leq y) = P(X \leq \frac{y-b}{a})$$

$$= \int_{-\infty}^{\frac{y-b}{a}} f(x)dx = \int_{-\infty}^{y} f(\frac{v-b}{a})\frac{dv}{a},$$

where v=ax+b is substituted for x in the last integral. From this expression and from (4.17), it follows that the density function of Y is given by

$$f(y) = \frac{1}{\sigma\sqrt{2\pi}} \frac{1}{a} \exp\{-\tfrac{1}{2}(\tfrac{y-b}{a} - \mu)^2/\sigma^2\}$$

$$= \frac{1}{a\sigma\sqrt{2\pi}} \exp\{-\tfrac{1}{2}(y-(a\mu+b))^2/(a\sigma)^2\},$$

from which the theorem follows by comparison with (7.1). □.

Theorem 7.2 shows that the class of normal distributions is invariant to linear transformations, i.e. if a normally distributed random variable is transformed linearly, then the transformed variable is also normally distributed.

It follows from theorem 7.2, that if $X \sim N(\mu, \sigma^2)$, then

(7.4) $\quad U = (X-\mu)/\sigma$

is normally distributed with mean value 0 and variance 1. U is said to follow a **standardized normal distribution** or a **standard normal distribution**. The density function of U is given by

(7.5) $\quad \varphi(u) = \dfrac{1}{\sqrt{2\pi}} e^{-u^2/2}.$

The symbol φ is always used to denote the density function (7.5). The distribution function of the standardized normal distribution,

(7.6) $\quad \Phi(x) = \int_{-\infty}^{x} \varphi(u) du,$

is tabulated in most statistical tables.

We now show, step by step, how the probabilities

(7.7) $\quad P(a < X \leq b)$

are calculated from knowledge of Φ when $X \sim N(\mu, \sigma^2)$ and μ and σ^2 are known. From theorem 4.2 follows that

(7.8) $\quad P(a < X \leq b) = P(\tfrac{a-\mu}{\sigma} < \tfrac{X-\mu}{\sigma} \leq \tfrac{b-\mu}{\sigma}) = \Phi(\tfrac{b-\mu}{\sigma}) - \Phi(\tfrac{a-\mu}{\sigma}),$

since $U = (X-\mu)/\sigma \sim N(0,1)$.

In order to determine the value of (7.7), three operations have to be performed:

1) The end points a and b are standardized by subtraction of μ and division by σ.

2) The standardized end points are used as entries in a table of Φ.

3) The one resulting value of Φ is substracted from the other.

Suppose, for example, that X is normally distributed with μ=1.5 and σ²=2 and that P(0<X≤2) is wanted.

Steps 1), 2) and 3) then become:

1) Since σ=√2=1.414, the standardized end points are -1.061 and 0.354.

2) From a table of Φ, the values 0.144 and 0.638 are obtained.

3) The probability is finally calculated as

$$P(0 < X \leq 2) = 0.638 - 0.144 = 0.494.$$

It follows from (7.8) that

(7.9) $\qquad P(\mu - c\sigma < X \leq \mu + c\sigma) = \Phi(c) - \Phi(-c)$

only depends on c.

Typical examples of formula (7.9) are

$$P(\mu - \sigma < X < \mu+\sigma) = \Phi(1)-\Phi(-1) = 0.682$$

and

$$P(\mu - 2\sigma < X < \mu+2\sigma) = \Phi(2)-\Phi(-2) = 0.955.$$

Suppose that we want to check whether a given empirical distribution or a set of observations can be described by a normal distribution. If the observations are grouped, or it is reasonable to perform a grouping, the check can be based on a comparison of the histogram and the normal density function. As mentioned in chapter 4.6, the area of the bars in the histogram and the corresponding areas under the density must be approximately equal if it is to be accepted that the normal distribution describes the data. For a given interval $(t_{j-1}, t_j]$ the area of the bar in the histogram is

(7.10) $\qquad h_j^*(t_j - t_{j-1}) = h_j$,

where h_j is the relative frequency of the event that an observation is contained in the interval. The corresponding probability is

$$(7.11) \qquad p_j = P(t_{j-1} < X \leq t_j) = \int_{t_{j-1}}^{t_j} f(x)dx.$$

Since h_j approximates p_j with a large number of observations, a comparison of the histogram and the density function for suitable choices of μ and σ^2 can serve as a basis for evaluating the fit of the normal distribution to the observations.

Example 7.1

The observations in table 7.1 are from a health investigation carried out in the USA between 1971 and 1974. The table shows the distribution of heights (inches) for 772 American men between the ages of 18 and 24 years. The table shows the relative frequency h_j, the cumulative frequency H_j and h_j^* given by (7.10) for 9 intervals.

The extent to which a normal distribution can describe the data is to be evaluated. This is done by comparing the empirical distribution with a normal distribution with mean value $\bar{x}$ and variance s^2, since as we saw in section 5.6, $\bar{x}$ and s^2 can be used as estimates for μ and σ^2 in the distribution from which the 772 observations originate. From table 7.1, $\bar{x}=69.2$ and $s^2=8.43$. With μ and σ in (7.8) as 69.2 and $\sqrt{8.43}$ respectively, the probabilities p_j for the intervals of table 7.1 can be calculated.

Table 7.1. Observed numbers, relative and cumulative frequencies for the heights in inches of 772 American men aged 18 to 24 years.

Interval	a_j	h_j^*	h_j	H_j
$(-\infty, 61.5]$	3	0.002	0.004	0.004
$(61.5, 63.5]$	17	0.011	0.022	0.026
$(63.5, 65.5]$	50	0.033	0.065	0.091
$(65.5, 67.5]$	133	0.086	0.173	0.264
$(67.5, 69.5]$	207	0.134	0.269	0.533
$(69.5, 71.5]$	208	0.134	0.268	0.801
$(71.5, 73.5]$	107	0.069	0.138	0.939
$(73.5, 75.5]$	29	0.019	0.038	0.977
$(75.5, +\infty)$	18	0.012	0.023	1.000
Sum	772		1.000	

Source: Weight and Height of Adults 18-24 years of age: United States, 1971-74. U.S. Department of Health, Education and Welfare. Hyattsville 1979.

For the interval (67.5,69.5], the standardized interval end points are -0.586 and 0.103. The corresponding values of Φ are 0.279 and 0.541, and by substraction p_j=0.262.

In table 7.2, the results of the corresponding computations are shown for the remaining intervals. As can be seen, there is a high degree of similarity between the values of p_j and the values of h_j so that the distribution of the heights of American men can be described by a normal distribution.

Table 7.2. A normal distribution fitted to the empirical distribution of the heights of 772 American men.

Interval	h_j	$\dfrac{t_j - \bar{x}}{s}$	$\Phi\left(\dfrac{t_j - \bar{x}}{s}\right)$	p_j
(- ∞ , 61.5]	0.004	-2.652	0.004	0.004
(61.5,63.5]	0.022	-1.963	0.025	0.021
(63.5,65.5]	0.065	-1.274	0.101	0.076
(65.5,67.5]	0.173	-0.586	0.279	0.178
(67.5,69.5]	0.269	0.103	0.541	0.262
(69.5,71.5]	0.268	0.792	0.786	0.245
(71.5,73.5]	0.138	1.481	0.931	0.145
(73.5,75.5]	0.038	2.170	0.985	0.054
(75.5, + ∞	0.023	-	1.000	0.015

Fig. 7.2 shows the histogram h_j^* and a normal density function with μ=69.2 and σ^2=8.43. $\triangle$.

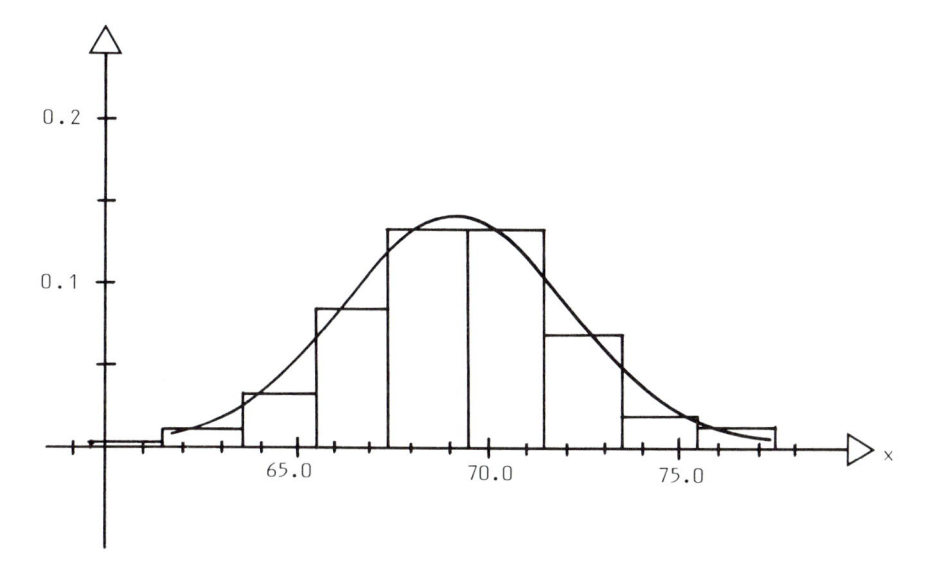

Fig. 7.2. Histogram and fitted normal distribution for the heights of 772 American men.

A widely used graphical technique to evaluate the fit of a normal distribution to a set of observations is the probability plot. This method is based on a comparison of the cumulative frequencies H_j and $\Phi((t_j-\mu)/\sigma)$. Since H_j is the relative frequency for the event $\{X \leq t_j\}$, H_j approximates the probability of this event, which according to (7.8) is given by

$$(7.12) \qquad P_j = P(X \leq t_j) = \Phi\left(\frac{t_j-\mu}{\sigma}\right) .$$

The P_j's can be calculated from (7.12) if the estimates $\bar{x}$ and s^2 for μ and σ^2 are used and H_j can be plotted against P_j. It is possible, however, to avoid the use of $\bar{x}$ and s^2 if both H_j and P_j are transformed using Φ^{-1}. Thus

$$(7.13) \qquad \Phi^{-1}(H_j) \simeq \frac{t_j-\mu}{\sigma} = u_j,$$

where the sign "$\simeq$" means that the two sides of the equation are approximately equal. Since the right hand side is a linear function of t_j, a plot of $\Phi^{-1}(H_j)$ against t_j should, if the normal distribution fits the data, give points clustered around a straight line. The function Φ^{-1} corresponds to a "backward" reading of a table of Φ, which is slightly odd. For this reason, special **probability paper** has been constructed, where the y-axis is marked with Φ^{-1} as scale. Using probability paper H_j can therefore be plotted directly against t_j. The H_j-scale and the $\Phi^{-1}(H_j)$-scale are shown simultaneously in fig. 7.3. A graph of $\Phi^{-1}(H_j)$ against t_j is called a **normal probability plot**. Since the probability in (7.12) refers to the event $\{X \leq t_j\}$, t_j is used as abscissa.

In addition to checking the fit of the normal distribution, the probability plot can be used to determine graphical estimates $\tilde{\mu}$ and $\tilde{\sigma}^2$ of μ and σ^2. Formula (7.13) shows that $t_j = \mu$ corresponds approximately to $H_j = 0.5$ on the probability plot, since $\Phi(0) = 0.5$. Furthermore, $t_j = \mu+\sigma$ and $t_j = \mu-\sigma$ correspond to $H_j = 0.841$ and 0.159, respectively, since $\Phi(1) = 0.841$ and $\Phi(-1) = 0.159$. After fitting a straight line to the points in the probability plot, the t-values corresponding to the ordinates 0.159, 0.5 and 0.841 can be read from the plot. These are approximate values of $\mu-\sigma$, μ and $\mu+\sigma$, and graphical estimates $\tilde{\mu}$ and $\tilde{\sigma}$ of μ and σ can be calculated respectively as the middle one of these and as half of the difference between the last and first value.

Example 7.1 (continued)

For the heights of 772 American men, H_j is given in the last column of table 7.1. The probability plot is constructed according to (7.13) by plotting 0.004 against 61.5, 0.026 against 63.5 etc. on probability paper. Since the last interval is open the point (t_j, H_j) for j=9 cannot be plotted. The resulting probability plot is shown in fig. 7.3. The plot shows both of the possible y-axes, $\Phi^{-1}(H_j)$ on the left hand side and H_j on the right hand side. As the points cluster around a straight line, the normal distribution would appear to fit the data in a satisfactory way. Graphical estimation of μ and σ^2 is illustrated in fig. 7.3, and it can be seen that $\tilde{\mu}$=69.2 and $\tilde{\sigma}$=2.8. These estimates differ very little from $\bar{x}$=69.2 and $s=\sqrt{8.43}$=2.90. $\triangle$.

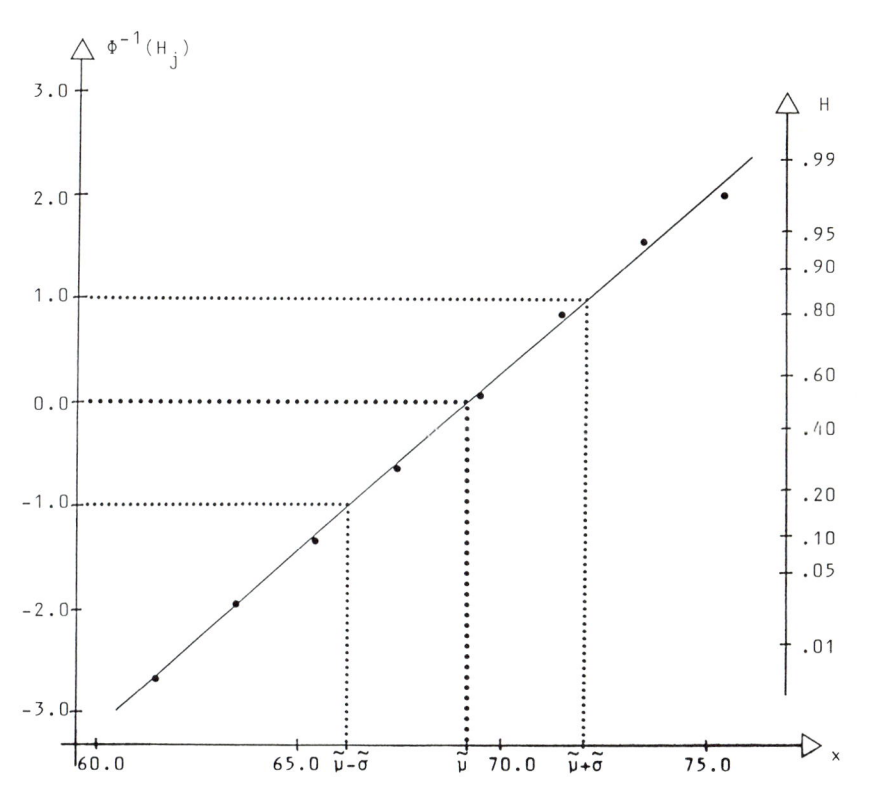

Fig. 7.3. Probability plot of the distribution of height of 772 American men.

In cases with few observations a grouping does not make sense and instead the probability plot is based on the ordered observations $x_{(1)}, \ldots, x_{(n)}$. Since i/n is the cumulative frequency for all x-values in the interval $[x_{(i)}, x_{(i+1)})$ and (i-1)/n the cumulative frequency for all x-values in $[x_{(i-1)}, x_{(i)})$, the average

$$0.5(i/n + (i-1)/n) = (i-0.5)/n$$

can be regarded as an estimate of the distribution function $F(x_{(i)})$ at $x_{(i)}$. Hence the probability plot is constructed by plotting $(i-0.5)/n$ against $x_{(i)}$ on probability paper.

Many computer programmes produce probability plots by plotting a so-called normal score z_i against the value of the i'th ordered observation. The i'th normal score is the expected value of $x_{(i)}$ if the n observations are from a standardized normal distribution. A satisfactory approximation to z_i for most practical purposes is

$$z_i \simeq \Phi^{-1}\left(\frac{i-\frac{1}{2}}{n}\right),$$

and in this case a computer-made probability plot and the one described above are almost identical.

When evaluating the fit of a model to the data using a probability plot, there are several problems to take into consideration. Firstly, the points in the plot will tend to wind around a straight line even though the model fits the data. This is due to the fact that being cumulated frequencies a random positive deviation from the line in one interval tends to generate a positive deviation also in the next interval. Secondly, the points in the probability plot tend to cluster more closely around the line in the middle than at the extremes of the range of the x's. This is due to the fact that H_j is expected to be closer to P_j in the middle of a distribution than in its tails. Thirdly, the sample size must be taken into consideration. When the number of observations is small, it is more likely that the points exhibit an apparent systematic pattern even though the deviations from the line are in fact random.

Example 7.2

Consider fluctuations in the exchange rate between American dollars and Danish Kroner (DKK) in 1983 and 1984. The 23 observations listed below are the differences between the exchange rates (the value in DKK of 100 dollars) on the first day of each month from January 1983 to December 1984:

+31.10, + 0.65, - 9.40, +18.70, +33.45, + 0.50, +49.25,
+ 6.40, -20.10, + 8.20, +19.15, +14.60, +28.30,
-61.55, - 4.55, +49.15, - 3.35, +29.00, +40.25,
- 9.25, +56.10, -20.55, +30.70.

Table 7.3. Ordered values, $x_{(i)}$, of the differences in monthly exchange rates and cumulative frequencies.

i	$x_{(i)}$	$(i-\frac{1}{2})/n$
1	-61.55	0.022
2	-20.55	0.065
3	-20.10	0.109
4	- 9.40	0.152
5	- 9.25	0.196
6	- 4.55	0.239
7	- 3.35	0.283
8	+ 0.50	0.326
9	+ 0.65	0.370
10	+ 6.40	0.413
11	+ 8.20	0.457
12	+14.60	0.500
13	+18.70	0.543
14	+19.15	0.587
15	+28.30	0.630
16	+29.00	0.674
17	+30.70	0.717
18	+31.10	0.761
19	+33.45	0.804
20	+40.25	0.848
21	+49.15	0.891
22	+49.25	0.935
23	+56.10	0.978

Table 7.3 shows $x_{(i)}$ and $(i-\frac{1}{2})/n$. The probability plot based on table 7.3 is shown in fig. 7.4. Apart from the smallest observation, -61.55, which seems to be very untypical, the points cluster more or less around a straight line. The tendency to a "wave" in the middle of the plot is not sufficiently pronounced to justify a rejection of the normal distribution as a description of the data, if we exclude the smallest observation. △.

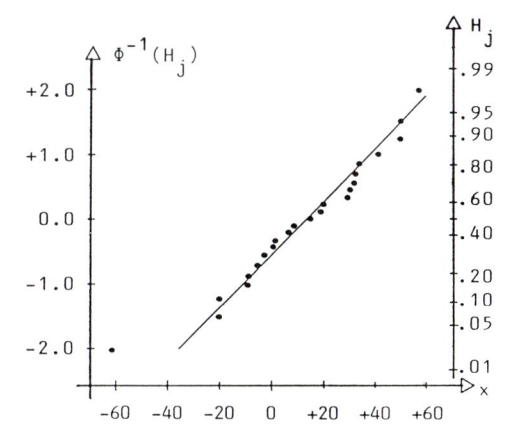

Fig. 7.4. Probability plot for the monthly changes in the exchange rate.

7.2. The log-normal distribution

Assume that the random variable Y is normally distributed with mean μ and variance σ^2 and define X by the transformation

$$X = e^Y.$$

Then X is said to be **log-normally distributed** because $\ln X = Y \sim N(\mu, \sigma^2)$. This distribution is useful when a normal distribution does not fit the original observations and the points on the probability plot cluster around a convex curve as shown in fig. 7.6(a). In such situations, a logarithmic transformation may generate points which cluster around a straight line as shown in fig. 7.6(b).

Theorem 7.3

Let Y be a normally distributed random variable with mean μ and variance σ^2. The density function for $X = e^Y$ is then

(7.14) $\qquad f(x) = (\sigma x \sqrt{2\pi})^{-1} \exp\{-\tfrac{1}{2}(\ln x - \mu)^2 / \sigma^2\}.$

Proof

Since

$$F(x) = P(e^Y \leq x) = P(Y \leq \ln x) = \frac{1}{\sigma\sqrt{2\pi}} \int_{-\infty}^{\ln x} \exp\{-\tfrac{1}{2}(y-\mu)^2/\sigma^2\} dy,$$

it follows that

$$f(x) = F'(x) = \frac{1}{\sigma\sqrt{2\pi}} \exp\{-\tfrac{1}{2}(\ln x - \mu)^2/\sigma^2\} \frac{1}{x} \quad \square.$$

The log-normal distribution is skewed to the right as shown in fig. 7.5. If the observations $x_1, \ldots, x_n$ are all positive and the histogram for these observations is skewed to the right, then a log-normal distribution could perhaps describe the observations. If $x_1, \ldots, x_n$ follow a log-normal distribution, the transformed observations $y_1 = \ln x_1, \ldots, y_n = \ln x_n$ follow a normal distribution so the fit of the log-normal distribution can in fact be checked using a probability plot for $y_1, \ldots, y_n$.

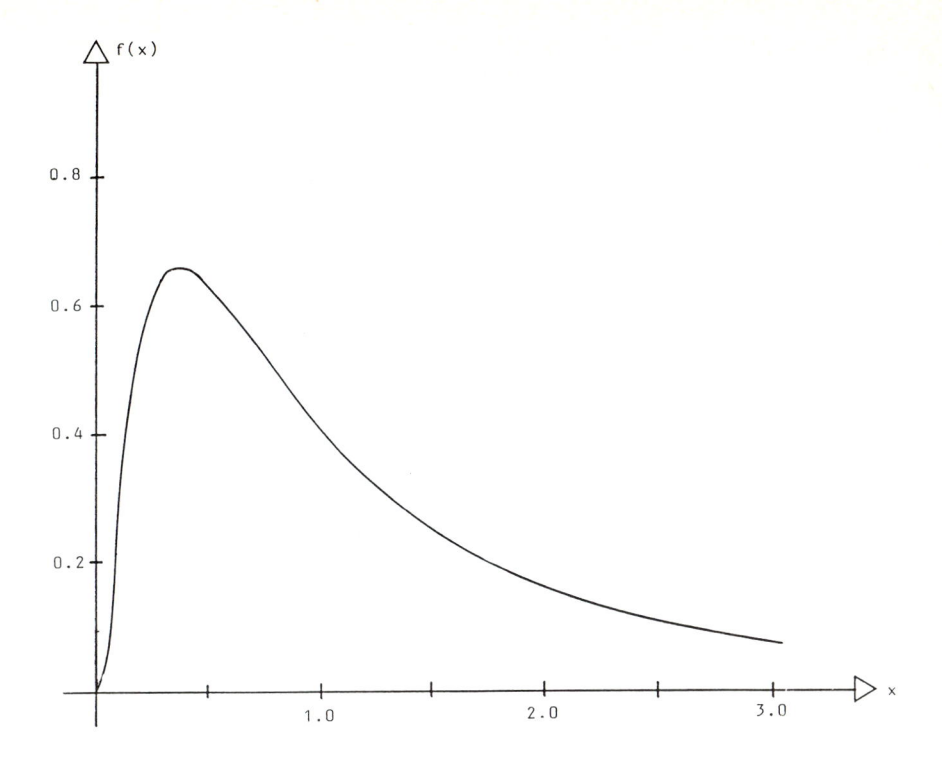

Fig. 7.5. The density function for the log-normal distribution for µ=0 and $\sigma^2=1$.

Example 7.3

The content of cholesterol in blood is an important health indicator in human populations. Cholesterol measurements are thus important elements in many large scale health investigations. The figures in table 7.4 are taken from an investigation of 6768 American children between 12 and 17 years of age carried out from 1966 to 1970. The table shows the distribution of measured content of cholesterol in the blood (measured in mg. pr. 100 ml. blood) of 14-year old boys.

Fig. 7.6(a) shows the probability plot based on the figures of table 7.4. The points do not cluster around a straight line and their curvature suggests that the distribution is skewed to the right. Therefore, it seems reasonable to apply a logarithmic transformation and check the fit of a normal distribution to the transformed data. This would also correspond well with general experience within the biological field, where many data sets follow log-normal distributions.

In fig. 7.6(b), $\Phi^{-1}(H_j)$ is plottet against $\ln t_j$. In contrast to the plot in fig. 7.6(a), the points now cluster around a straight line.

Hence a log-normal distribution seems to describe satisfactory the distribution of the content of cholesterol in the blood of 14-year American boys.△.

Table 7.4. Content of cholesterol in the blood of 618 14-year old American boys, 1966-1970, in mg. per 100 ml.

$(t_{j-1}, t_j]$	Number of boys	h_j	H_j	$\ln t_j$
- 99.5	2	0.3	0.3	4.60
99.5 - 109.5	6	1.0	1.3	4.70
109.5 - 119.5	15	2.4	3.7	4.78
119.5 - 129.5	18	3.0	6.7	4.86
129.5 - 139.5	45	7.3	14.0	4.94
139.5 - 149.5	72	11.7	25.7	5.01
149.5 - 159.5	77	12.4	38.1	5.07
159.5 - 169.5	91	14.8	52.9	5.13
169.5 - 179.5	72	11.6	64.5	5.19
179.5 - 189.5	72	11.6	76.1	5.24
189.5 - 199.5	57	9.2	85.3	5.30
199.5 - 209.5	32	5.2	90.5	5.34
209.5 - 219.5	25	4.0	94.5	5.39
219.5 - 229.5	13	2.2	96.7	5.44
229.5 - 239.5	9	1.4	98.1	5.48
239.5 - 249.5	5	0.8	98.9	5.52
249.5 - 259.5	4	0.6	99.5	5.56
259.5 - 269.5	1	0.2	99.7	5.60
269.5 -	2	0.3	100.0	
Total	618	100.0		

Source: Total Serum Cholesterol Values for Youths 12-17 years. United States. Vital and Health Statistics. Series 11. Number 156. U.S. Department of Health, Education and Welfare. 1976.

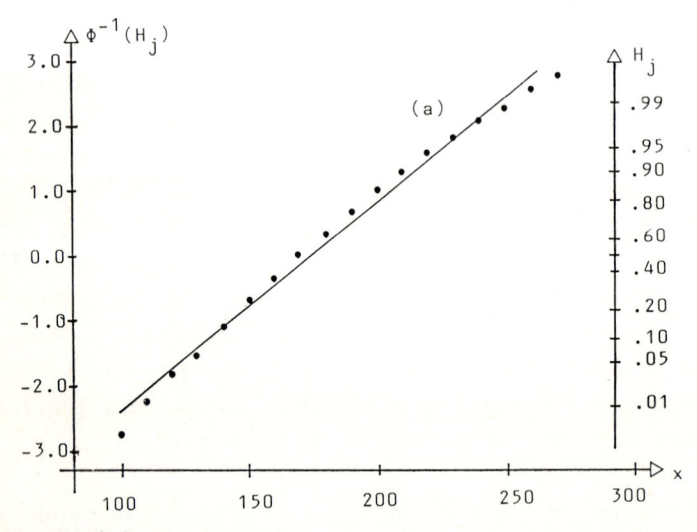

Fig. 7.6(a). Probability plot for the cholesterol data.

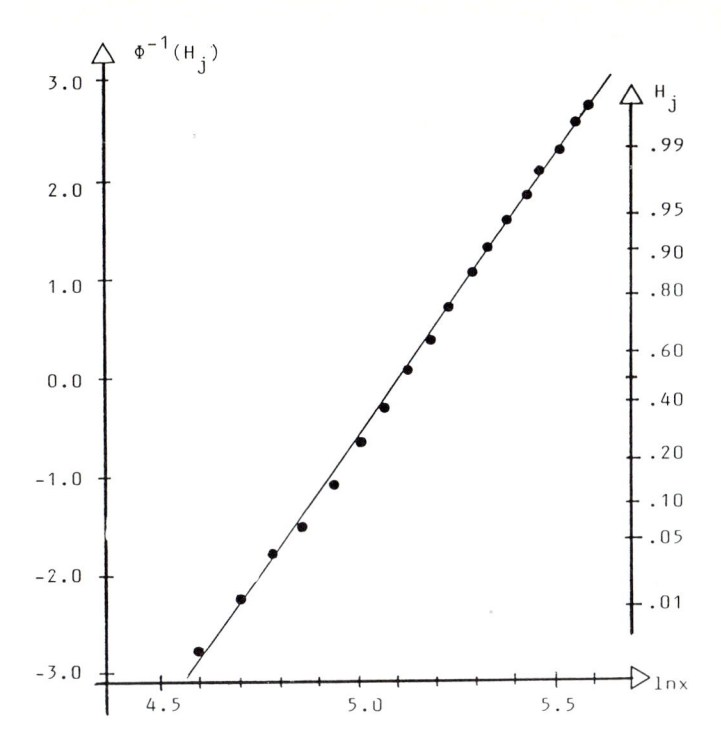

Fig. 7.6 (b). Probability plot for the logarithms of the cholesterol data.

7.3. The exponential distribution

In section 6.2, the conditions under which the number of occurrences of an event in a fixed time interval is Poisson distributed were discussed. Now the Poisson process is approached from another angle. Let T be a random variable representing the time elapsing from observation of the process starts until the event occurs for the first time. Suppose further that the assumptions for theorem 6.4 are satisfied so that the number of occurrences in a time interval of length t is Poisson distributed with mean λt. The probability of no event occurring in the time interval is accordingly equal to the probability of 0 in a Poisson distribution with parameter λt. Hence

$$P(T > t) = e^{-\lambda t}.$$

But since $P(T>t)=1-F(t)$, where $F(t)$ is the distribution function of T, it follows that

$$F(t) = 1-e^{-\lambda t}.$$

Differentiation of F(t) with respect to t yields the density function

(7.15) $\qquad f(t) = \lambda e^{-\lambda t}, \quad t \geq 0,$

where $\lambda > 0$. A random variable T with density function (7.15) is said to follow an **exponential distribution** with parameter λ.

It can be shown that the time interval between two consecutive occurrences of the event is also exponentially distributed with parameter λ. The fact that the exponential distribution can be interpreted as a **waiting-time distribution** makes it useful in connection with planning and control problems.

Theorem 7.4

If T follows an exponential distribution with parameter λ and a>0, then Y=aT is also exponentially distributed with parameter $\rho = \lambda/a$.

Proof
Let F be the distribution function of Y. Then

$$F(y) = P(aT \leq y) = P(T \leq y/a) = 1-e^{-y\lambda/a},$$

so the density f of Y becomes

$$f(y) = \frac{\lambda}{a} e^{-y\lambda/a} \quad \square.$$

According to theorem 7.4 the exponential distribution is invariant under scale changes. This is an important property if the distribution is used for the description of waiting times, since a waiting time distribution necessarily has to be independent of the time unit chosen. If, for example, the waiting time is measured in minutes instead of in hours, all waiting times are multiplied by 60, and in accordance with theorem 7.4, the distribution is then still exponential but with a parameter equal to the original parameter divided by 60.

Theorem 7.5

If T follows an exponential distribution with density function (7.15), then

(7.16) $E[T] = 1/\lambda$

and

(7.17) $\text{var}[T] = 1/\lambda^2$.

It follows that the mean value in an exponential distribution is inversely proportional to λ.

When the exponential distribution is used to describe waiting times in queues, $1/\lambda$ is the expected waiting time between arriving customers. The more frequently the customers arrive, the smaller the value of $1/\lambda$ and the larger the value of λ.

The degree to which an exponential distribution fits a given data set can be checked graphically. The method is related to the probability plot for a normal distribution, and is based on a comparison of the cumulative frequency H_j and the value of the distribution function at t_j. It follows that H_j is compared with

(7.18) $P_j = P(T \leq t_j)$.

In case of an exponential distribution, however,

$$P_j = 1-e^{-\lambda t_j},$$

so the approximate relation $H_j \approx P_j$ can be written

(7.19) $\ln(1-H_j) \approx -\lambda t_j$.

Thus, if the points $(t_j, \ln(1-H_j))$ are plotted in a coordinate system, the points should cluster randomly around a straight line through $(0,0)$ with slope $-\lambda$.

Example 7.4

Table 7.5 shows the time intervals measured in seconds between 150 consecutive arrivals to a queue including the waiting time to the first arrival.

Table 7.5 also shows the relative frequencies for the grouped distribution of waiting times and the corresponding probabilities for an exponential distribution with parameter $\lambda=0.037$. This estimate of λ is chosen to give the best possible fit between h_j and p_j.

As can be seen, there is reasonably good correspondance between the observed frequency distribution and the areas under the density function of the exponential distribution, computed with $\lambda=0.037$ as

$$p_j = \lambda \int_{t_{j-1}}^{t_j} e^{-\lambda x} dx = e^{-\lambda t_{j-1}} - e^{-\lambda t_j}.$$

The model check is carried out by plotting $\ln(1-H_j)$ against t_j as shown in fig. 7.7. As the points cluster around a straight line, the hand-drawn line can be used to derive a graphical estimate of λ by simply taking the negative value of the slope. For the data of table 7.5, the graphical estimate of λ is 0.035. $\triangle$.

Table 7.5. The distribution of time intervals between 150 arrivals to a queue.

Time interval (sec.)	Number of arrivals	h_j	p_j	H_j	$\ln(1-H_j)$
(0.0, 9.5]	45	0.300	0.299	0.300	-0.357
(9.5,19.5]	28	0.187	0.226	0.487	-0.667
(19.5,29.5]	29	0.193	0.143	0.680	-1.139
(29.5,39.5]	15	0.100	0.104	0.780	-1.514
(39.5,49.5]	9	0.060	0.071	0.840	-1.832
(49.5,59.5]	6	0.040	0.049	0.880	-2.120
(59.5,69.5]	5	0.033	0.034	0.913	-2.412
(69.5,79.5]	5	0.033	0.023	0.946	-2.919
(79.5,89.5]	1	0.007	0.016	0.953	-3.058
(89.5,99.5]	3	0.020	0.011	0.973	-3.612
(99.5,+∞)	4	0.027	0.024	1.000	
Total	150	1.000	1.000		

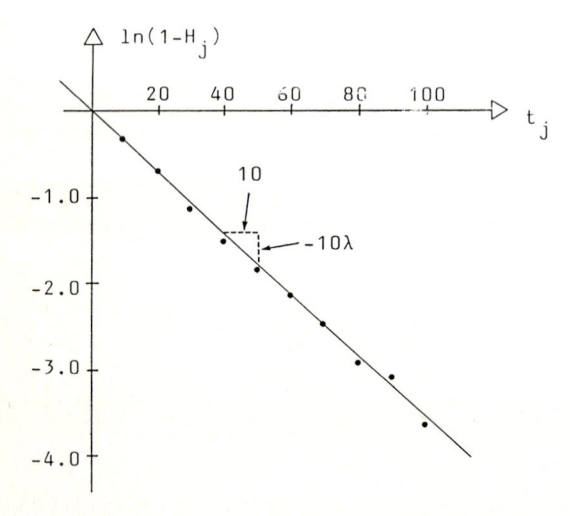

Fig. 7.7. Probability plot for an exponential distribution.

7.4. The Pareto distribution

A random variable X is said to follow a **Pareto distribution** with parameters α and x_0 if it has density function

(7.20) $\qquad f(x|\alpha,x_0) = \begin{cases} \alpha x_0^{\alpha}/x^{\alpha+1} & \text{for } x \geq x_0 \\ 0 & \text{otherwise.} \end{cases}$

Both parameters α and x_0 must be positive. The distribution function is

(7.21) $\qquad F(x) = \int_{x_0}^{x} \alpha x_0^{\alpha}/y^{\alpha+1} dy = 1-(x_0/x)^{\alpha}$.

Fig. 7.8 shows the density functions for (α,x_0) equal to (1,1) and (2,1).

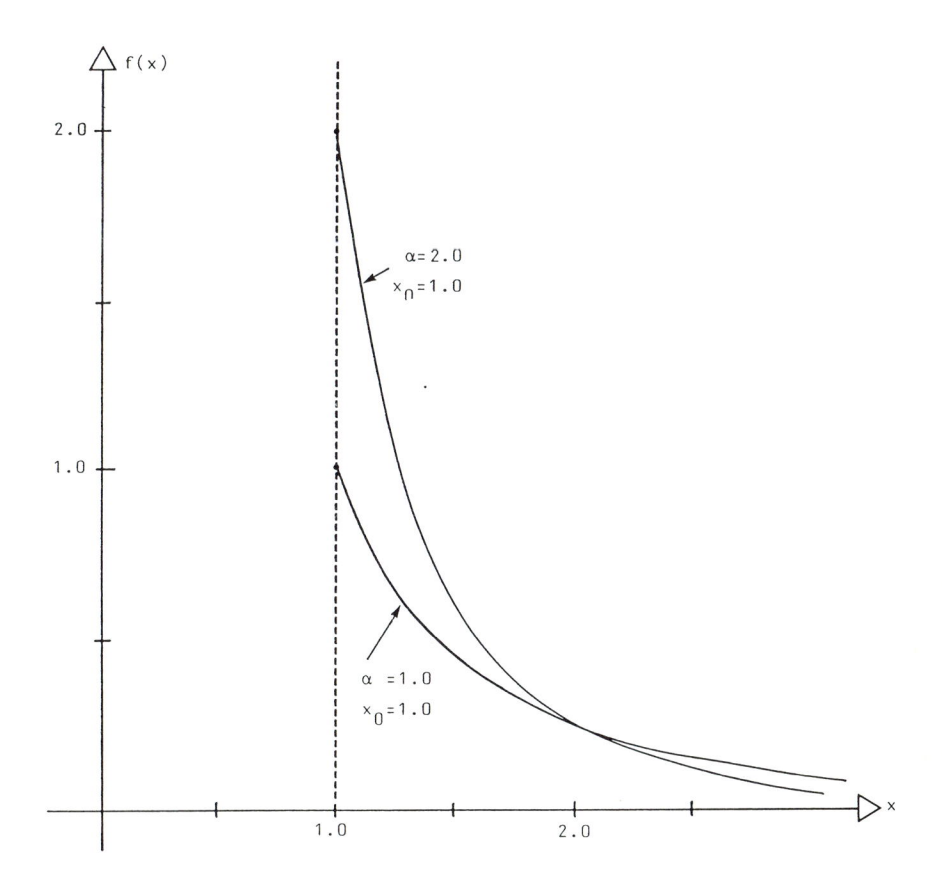

Fig. 7.8. Density functions for two Pareto distributions.

Theorem 7.6

If X follows a Pareto distribution with parameters α and x_0, then the distribution of X given that $X \geq x_1$, where $x_1 > x_0$, is again a Pareto distribution with parameters α and x_1.

Proof

From (7.21),

$$P(X \geq x | X \geq x_1) = \left(\frac{x_0}{x}\right)^\alpha / \left(\frac{x_0}{x_1}\right)^\alpha = \left(\frac{x_1}{x}\right)^\alpha.$$

or

$$F(x | X \geq x_1) = 1 - (x_1/x)^\alpha.$$

Hence

$$f(x | X \geq x_1) = \alpha x_1^\alpha / x^{\alpha+1},$$

and the theorem is proved. □.

It follows from theorem 7.6 that the Pareto distribution is **invariant under truncation** if a truncation at x_1 means that only values larger than x_1 are considered. Under truncation α is unchanged, while x_0 is changed to the point of truncation.

Theorem 7.7

If X follows a Pareto distribution with parameters α and x_0, then

$$E[X] = \frac{\alpha}{\alpha-1} x_0 \qquad \text{for } \alpha > 1$$

and

$$\text{var}[X] = \alpha x_0^2 / [(\alpha-2)(\alpha-1)^2] \qquad \text{for } \alpha > 2.$$

The mean does not exist for $\alpha \leq 1$ and the variance does not exist for $\alpha \leq 2$. The mean decreases towards the limiting value x_0 as α increases. As α tends to infinity, the distribution will accordingly tend to be more and more concentrated in the neighbourhood of x_0.

The fit of a Pareto distribution of a set of grouped observations can also be checked graphically by a probability plot. The cumulative frequency H_j for the j'th interval and $P_j = P(X \leq t_j)$, where t_j is the upper end point for the j'th interval, are compared. According to (7.21) the relationship $H_j \approx P_j$ can be written

(7.22) $\qquad \ln(1 - H_j) \approx \alpha(\ln x_0 - \ln t_j) = -\alpha \ln t_j + \alpha \ln x_0.$

Hence, if $\ln(1-H_j)$ is plotted against $\ln t_j$, the points should cluster around a straight line with slope $-\alpha$.

The Pareto distribution is often used for the description of income distributions and other distributions skewed to the right.

Example 7.5

We shall try to determine whether or not the distribution of the gross incomes for employee's in Denmark in 1981 follow a Pareto distribution. Since a Pareto distribution is only defined for $x \geq x_0 > 0$, the complete distribution of incomes, including negative incomes and zero incomes cannot be covered. Only the distribution of gross incomes above a certain limit x_0 is considered. This limit can be chosen arbitrarily since it follows from theorem 7.6 that if the Pareto distribution describes the income distribution for $x \geq x_0$, then it will also describe the distribution of incomes larger than any $x_1 > x_0$.

Table 7.6 shows the gross incomes in Denmark in 1981 with the income grouping used by Danmarks Statistik.

Table 7.6. Gross incomes for employee's in Denmark in 1981.

Income - DKK -	Number - 1000 persons -	H_j $(x \geq 100\ 000)$	$\ln(1-H_j)$	$\ln(t_j)$
- 39 999	117.8			10.597
40 000 - 69 999	374.7			11.156
70 000 - 99 999	533.9			11.513
100 000 - 149 999	805.4	0.677	-1.130	11.918
150 000 - 199 999	247.2	0.885	-2.165	12.206
200 000 - 249 999	78.6	0.951	-3.024	12.429
250 000 - 299 999	28.7	0.975	-3.710	12.612
300 000 - 399 999	18.7	0.991	-4.739	12.899
400 000	10.4	1.000		
Total	2215.4			

Source: Income and Wealth. Danmarks Statistik. 1981.

The Pareto distribution does not fit the data satisfactory if x_0 is chosen as 40 000 or 70 000 DKK. Fig. 7.9 shows the probability plot for the Pareto distribution with $x_0 = 100\ 000$ DKK. The necessary computations are shown in the last three columns of table 7.6. Note that the frequencies are calculated from the 1 189 000 employee's with incomes larger than 100 000 DKK. In fig. 7.9, $\ln(1-H_j)$ is plotted against $\ln(t_j)$. The points cluster rather close around a straight line, indicating a satisfactory fit by a Pareto distribution. $\triangle$.

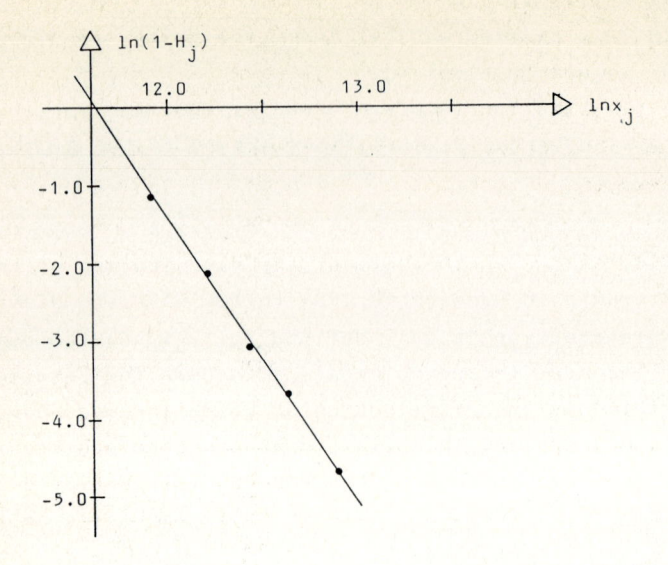

Fig. 7.9. Probability plot for the gross incomes for employees in Denmark.

7.5. The gamma distribution

The exponential distribution is a special case of the **gamma distribution** which has density function

$$(7.23) \qquad f(x) = \begin{cases} C(\beta,\lambda)x^{\beta-1}e^{-\lambda x} & , x \geq 0 \\ 0 & , x < 0. \end{cases}$$

The parameters β and λ both have to be positive. Since $f(x)$ is a density function

$$\int_0^\infty C(\beta,\lambda) x^{\beta-1} e^{-\lambda x} dx = 1,$$

or

$$\int_0^\infty x^{\beta-1} e^{-\lambda x} dx = 1/C(\beta,\lambda).$$

With $y = \lambda x$,

$$(7.24) \qquad \frac{1}{\lambda^\beta} \int_0^\infty y^{\beta-1} e^{-y} dy = 1/C(\beta,\lambda).$$

The integral

$$(7.25) \qquad \Gamma(\beta) = \int_0^\infty y^{\beta-1} e^{-y} dy$$

cannot be expressed explicitly. As a function of β, it is called the **gamma function**. For integer values of β, integration by parts gives

$$\Gamma(k) = (k-1)!$$

with $\Gamma(1)=1$.

From (7.24) and (7.25), the gamma distribution has the density function

$$(7.26) \qquad f(x) = \frac{\lambda^\beta}{\Gamma(\beta)} x^{\beta-1} e^{-\lambda x} , \quad x>0,$$

which reduces to the exponential distribution for β=1.

Theorem 7.8

If X follows a gamma distribution with parameters β and λ and if a>0, then Y=aX is gamma distributed with parameters β and λ/a.

From theorem 7.8 follows that the gamma distribution is scale invariant.

Theorem 7.9

If X follows a gamma distribution with parameters β and λ, then

$$(7.27) \qquad E[X] = \beta/\lambda$$

and

$$(7.28) \qquad var[X] = \beta/\lambda^2 .$$

Since a change in β changes the shape of the density function, β is called the **shape parameter** and since λ is only changed under a change of scale (theorem 7.8), λ is called the **scale parameter**. When β is integer-valued, a random variable with density function (7.26) is said to follow an **Erlang distribution**. The density function of the Erlang distribution is

$$(7.29) \qquad f(x) = \frac{\lambda^k}{(k-1)!} x^{k-1} e^{-\lambda x} , \quad x>0,$$

where k has replaced β to emphasize that the shape parameter is integer-valued. Fig. 7.10 shows the density function for three Erlang distributions.

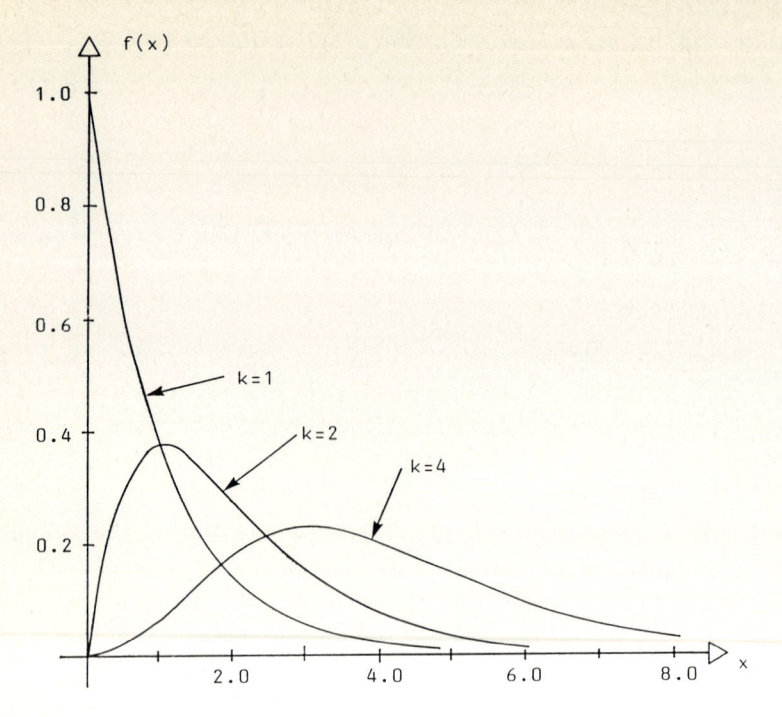

Fig. 7.10. Three Erlang distributions with $\lambda=1$.

Theorem 7.10

If conditions (i) to (iii) of theorem 6.4 are satisfied, the waiting time until the event occurs for the x'th time has the density function

$$f(t|x,\lambda) = \frac{\lambda^x}{(x-1)!} t^{x-1} e^{-\lambda t}, \quad t>0.$$

Proof

Let T_x be the waiting time until the event occurs for the x'th time, and let X_t be the number of occurrences of the event in an interval of length t. Then

$$P(T_x > t) = P(X_t < x).$$

Since X_t is Poisson distributed, it follows that

$$1 - F(t|x,\lambda) = \sum_{z=0}^{x-1} \frac{(\lambda t)^z}{z!} e^{-\lambda t}.$$

Differentiating both sides of this expression with respect to t yields

$$-f(t|x,\lambda) = \sum_{z=0}^{x-1} \frac{z(\lambda t)^{z-1}}{z!} e^{-\lambda t}(\lambda) + \sum_{z=0}^{x-1} \frac{(\lambda t)^z}{z!} e^{-\lambda t}(-\lambda)$$

$$= \lambda \sum_{z=0}^{x-2} \frac{(\lambda t)^z}{z!} e^{-\lambda t} - \lambda \sum_{z=0}^{x-1} \frac{(\lambda t)^z}{z!} e^{-\lambda t} = -\lambda \frac{(\lambda t)^{x-1}}{(x-1)!} e^{-\lambda t},$$

which proves the theorem. □.

The waiting time from an arbitrary starting time until the event has occurred exactly x times thus follows an Erlang distribution with parameters λ and x. The Erlang distribution is, in other words, the waiting time distribution for the Poisson process with the exponential distribution as a special case for x=1.

7.6. A comparison of six distributions

A random variable X(t) defined for each time point, $\{X(t), t \geq 0\}$, is called a **stochastic process in continuous time**. If the process is only defined at certain given times, it is called a **stochastic process in discrete time**. If these time points are n=0,1,..., we write $\{X(n), n=0,1,...\}$, where n is used to indicate that the time is discrete.

The Poisson process is an example of a stochastic process in continuous time, if X(t) denotes the number of times the given event occurs in the time interval (0,t]. As an example of a stochastic process in discrete time, consider the following situation: Perform n independent trials, where the observed outcome is A or $\bar{A}$, and let X(n) be the number of times A occurs in the n trials. If p=P(A) is constant, then X(n) is binomially distributed and $\{X(n), n=0,1,...\}$ is a stochastic process in discrete time. This process is called the **binomial process**.

For the binomial process, it is easy to see that the Pascal distribution and the geometric distribution are waiting time distributions corresponding to the waiting time until A occurs for the k'th time and the first time, respectively. Thus, they are the analogues of the Erlang distribution and the exponential distribution in the continuous case. Table 7.7 summarizes the relationships between these distributions.

Table 7.7. Comparison of six distributions.

Random variable	Discrete time.	Continuous time.
Number of times an event occurs in a time interval	The binomial distribution. Section 6.1	The Poisson distribution. Section 6.2
The waiting time until an event occurs for the first time	The geometric distribution. Section 6.3.	The exponential distribution. Section 7.3.
The waiting time until an event occurs for the k'th time.	The Pascal distribution. Section 6.3	The Erlang distribution. Section 7.5.

8. Multivariate Distributions

8.1. Multi-dimensional random variables

When analysing statistical data, it is often necessary to work with models, which involve several random variables. This is obviously the case if the purpose of the analysis is to draw inference about the relationship between two or more variables in a population from their observed values in a sample drawn from the population. Also when discussing the structure of statistical models, the simultaneous distribution of several random variables is an important concept. Assume that the data consist of the n observations $x_1,\ldots,x_n$. For theoretical reasons, $x_1,\ldots,x_n$ are regarded as the observed or realized values of n random variables $X_1,\ldots,X_n$. The statistical model for such data is a specification of the joint or simultaneous distribution of $X_1,\ldots,X_n$. For example, suppose that $x_1,\ldots,x_n$ form a random sample from a population or from a distribution, the mean of which is to be estimated using the sample mean $\bar{x}=(x_1+\ldots+x_n)/n$. From knowledge of the simultaneous distribution of $X_1,\ldots,X_n$, it is possible to derive the distribution of the random variable $\bar{X}=(X_1+\ldots+X_n)/n$. Using this distribution, it is then possible to formulate statements concerning the precision of the estimate.

A vector $(X_1,\ldots,X_m)$, the components of which are random variables as defined in chapter 4, is called an **m-dimensional random variable**. It is said to be discrete if its components are discrete random variables and continuous if its components are continuous random variables.

8.2. Discrete m-dimensional random variables

The sample space S for an m-dimensional **discrete** random variable $(X_1,\ldots,X_m)$ is a countable subset of R^m. The joint distribution of $(X_1,\ldots,X_m)$ is defined by the **joint point probabilities**

(8.1) $\quad f(x_1,\ldots,x_m) = P\{(X_1=x_1)\cap\ldots\cap(X_m=x_m)\} \quad , \quad (x_1,\ldots,x_m)\in S.$

The probabilities for any event A in the sample space can be calculated as

$$P\{(X_1,\ldots,X_m)\in A\} = \sum_{(x_1,\ldots,x_m)\in A}\ldots\sum f(x_1,\ldots,x_m),$$

where the summation is over all outcomes in A. Hence, the distributional properties of $(X_1,\ldots,X_m)$ are completely characterized by f.

Example 8.1

Assume that two dice are cast. Let X_1 be the number of eyes shown on the first and X_2 the number shown on the second die. The sample space then becomes

$$S = \{x_1,x_2 | x_1=1,\ldots,6 \text{ and } x_2=1,\ldots,6\}.$$

If the dice are regular and are cast independently of one another, then the 36 outcomes of S are equally likely, and from Laplace's formula it follows that

$$f(x_1,x_2) = 1/36 \text{ for all } (x_1,x_2)\in S. \triangle$$

Example 8.2

Based on a test for psychic vulnerability a number of persons have, at two different points in time, been assigned a vulnerability index, defined as the number of yes-answers to 12 questions of the type "Do you often suffer from headaches?" and "Do you often suffer from stomach troubles?". Let X_1 denote the vulnerability index for a randomly selected person at time t_1 and X_2 the index for the same person at time t_2. Table 8.1 shows the distribution of the observed values of the two-dimensional discrete random variable (X_1,X_2) for 3237 persons. For example, 1341 persons with index 0 at time t_1 and index 0 at time t_2 have been observed.

Table 8.1. Vulnerability indices for 3237 persons.

		Vulnerability index at t_2					Total
		0	1	2	3	≥ 4	
Vulnerability index at t_1	0	1341	315	58	8	1	1723
	1	386	417	120	23	2	948
	2	81	144	137	40	10	412
	3	17	22	38	40	6	123
	≥ 4	1	4	8	11	7	31
Total		1826	902	361	122	26	3237

Based on the data in table 8.1 and a psychological theory of the development of psychic vulnerability over time, a model has been formulated for the joint distribution of (X_1, X_2). The point probabilities of this model are shown in table 8.2.

Table 8.2. Point probabilities for a model for psychic vulnerability.

		Vulnerability index at t_2					Total
		0	1	2	3	≥ 4	
Vulnerability index at t_1	0	0.312	0.096	0.029	0.009	0.003	0.449
	1	0.096	0.069	0.037	0.016	0.008	0.226
	2	0.029	0.037	0.029	0.016	0.013	0.124
	3	0.009	0.016	0.016	0.012	0.018	0.071
	≥ 4	0.003	0.008	0.013	0.018	0.088	0.130
Total		0.449	0.226	0.124	0.071	0.130	1.000

In fig. 8.1 these point probabilities are presented graphically. △.

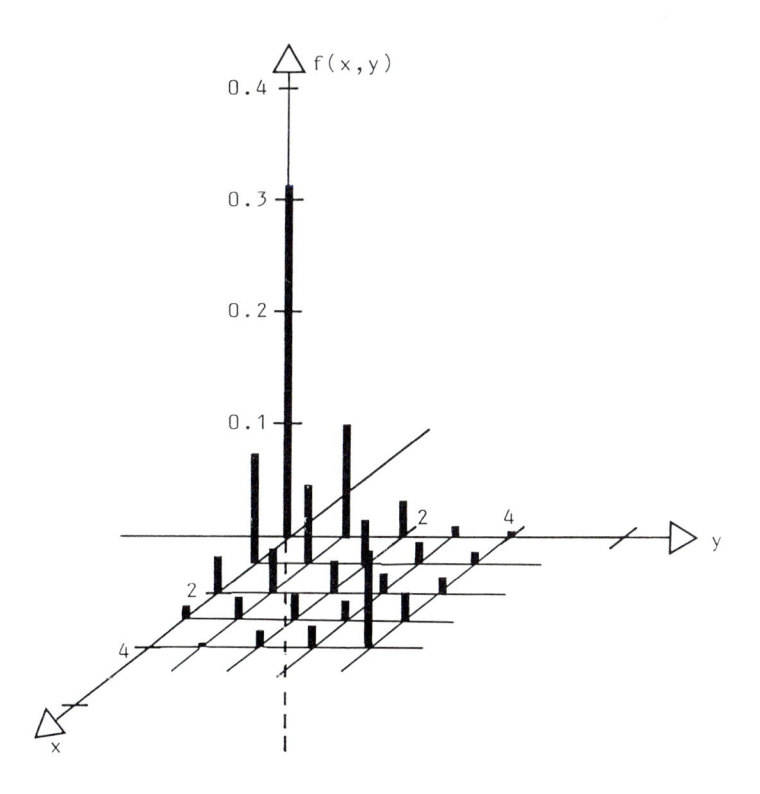

Fig. 8.1. Point probabilities of the model for the vulnerability index.

8.3. Continuous m-dimensional random variables

The sample space S for an n-dimensional continuous random variable is a subset of R^m. The **joint distribution function** of $(X_1,\ldots,X_m)$ is defined as

$$F(x_1,\ldots,x_m) = P(X_1 \leq x_1,\ldots,X_m \leq x_m).$$

The **joint density function** $f(x_1,\ldots,x_m)$ is a non-negative function which satisfies the condition

(8.2) $\qquad F(x_1,\ldots,x_m) = \int_{-\infty}^{x_m}\ldots\int_{-\infty}^{x_m} f(z_1,\ldots,z_m)dz_1\ldots dz_m$

for all $(x_1,\ldots,x_m) \in R^m$. It can be shown that $f(x_1,\ldots,x_m) = 0$ if $(x_1,\ldots,x_m) \notin S$. The meaning of the density function is illustrated by considering the probability of the event

$$B = \{x_1 - \tfrac{\Delta}{2} \leq X_1 \leq x_1 + \tfrac{\Delta}{2},\ldots,x_m - \tfrac{\Delta}{2} \leq X_m \leq x_m + \tfrac{\Delta}{2}\}.$$

If Δ is so small that f is practically constant on B then P(B) can be approximated as

(8.3) $\qquad P(B) \simeq f(x_1,\ldots,x_m)\Delta^m.$

The expression (8.3) shows that the larger the value of $f(x_1,\ldots,x_m)$, the larger the probability of observing vectors close to $(x_1,\ldots,x_m)$. This means that the observation $(x_1,\ldots,x_m)$ is more likely than another observation $(x'_1,\ldots,x'_m)$ for which $f(x'_1,\ldots,x'_m)$ is smaller than $f(x_1,\ldots,x_m)$.

If the partial derivatives of F exist, it can be shown that

$$f(x_1,\ldots,x_m) = \frac{\partial^m F(x_1,\ldots,x_m)}{\partial x_1 \ldots \partial x_m}.$$

The joint density function and the joint point probability are fundamental concepts in the theory of statistics. As mentioned at the beginning of this chapter, a **statistical model** for a set of data $x_1,\ldots,x_n$ can be specified through the joint distribution of a set of random variables with observed values $x_1,\ldots,x_n$. This specification is usually given in the form of a joint density function in the continuous case and a joint point probability in the discrete case.

Many of the concepts discussed above are more easily understood if we limit ourselves to the two-dimensional case. For a continuous random variable (X_1, X_2), the probability of the event $\{(a_1 \leq X_1 \leq b_1) \cap (a_2 \leq X_2 \leq b_2)\}$ is calculated from the joint density function $f(x_1, x_2)$, using (8.2), as

$$(8.4) \quad P(a_1 \leq X_1 \leq b_1, a_2 \leq X_2 \leq b_2) = \int_{a_1}^{b_1} \int_{a_2}^{b_2} f(x_1, x_2) dx_2 dx_1 ,$$

and the approximation (8.3) takes the form

$$P(x_1 - \frac{\Delta}{2} \leq X_1 \leq x_1 + \frac{\Delta}{2}, x_2 - \frac{\Delta}{2} \leq X_2 \leq x_2 + \frac{\Delta}{2}) \simeq f(x_1, x_2) \Delta^2.$$

This is illustrated in fig. 8.2 which also shows an example of a two-dimensional density function.

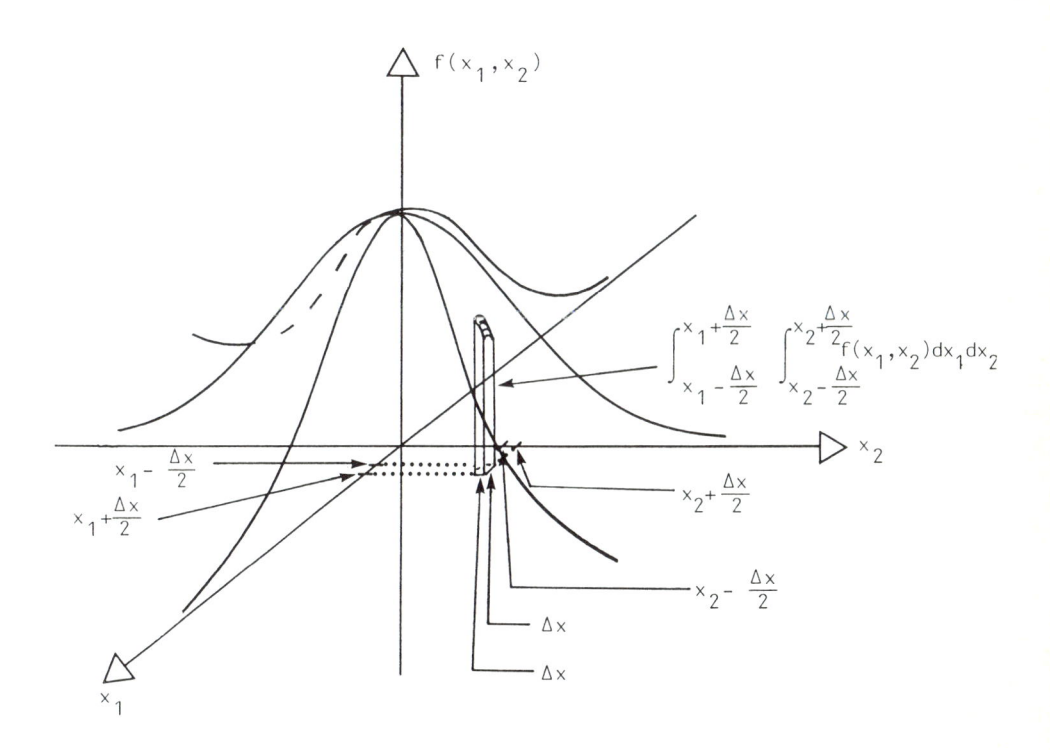

Fig. 8.2. A two-dimensional density function.

Example 8.3

The two-dimensional uniform distribution has density function

$$f(x_1, x_2) = \begin{cases} c & \text{for } a_1 < x_1 < b_1 \text{ and } a_2 < x_2 < b_2 \\ 0 & \text{otherwise.} \end{cases}$$

Since $P(-\infty < X_1 < +\infty, -\infty < X_2 < +\infty) = 1$, (8.4) gives

$$\int_{-\infty}^{-\infty} \int_{-\infty}^{-\infty} f(x_1, x_2) dx_1 dx_2 = \int_{a_1}^{b_1} \int_{a_2}^{b_2} c \, dx_1 dx_2 = c(b_2 - a_2) \cdot (b_1 - a_1) = 1,$$

such that

$$f(x_1, x_2) = \begin{cases} \dfrac{1}{(b_2 - a_2)(b_1 - a_1)} & \text{for } a_1 < x_1 < b_1, \; a_2 < x_2 < b_2 \\ 0 & \text{otherwise.} \end{cases}$$

Fig. 8.3 shows the density function. △.

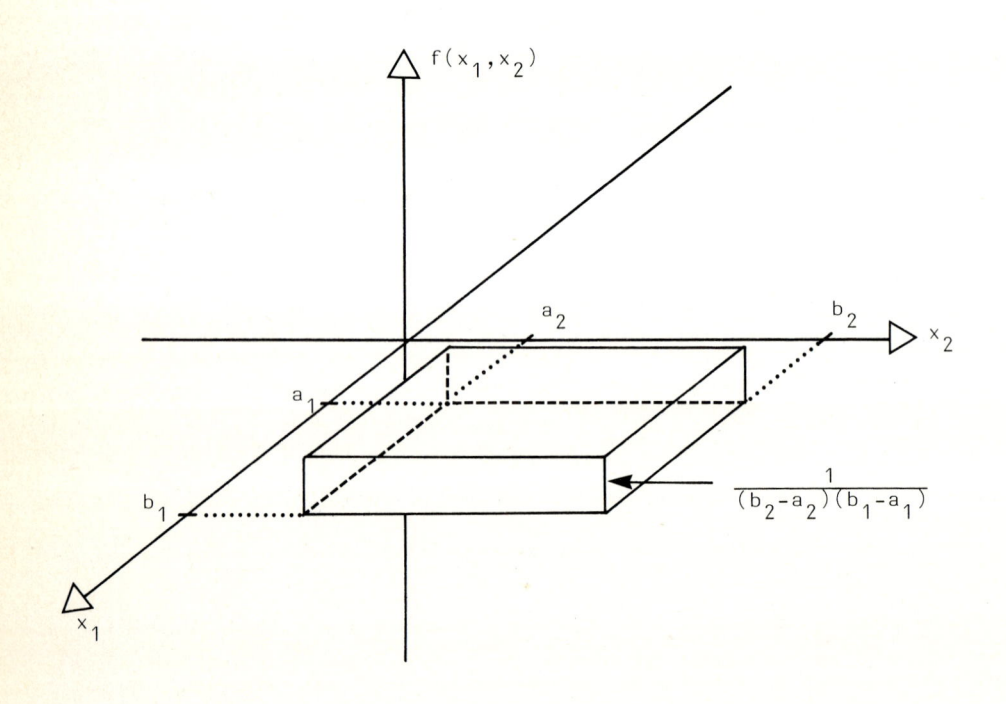

<u>Fig. 8.3.</u> The density function for the two-dimensional uniform distribution.

8.4. Marginal distributions

From the joint distribution of the variables X_1 and X_2, the **marginal distributions** of X_1 and X_2 can be derived. The marginal distribution of X_1 is the distribution of X_1, determined independently of the value of X_2. In the discrete case, the **marginal point probabilities** of X_1 are thus given by

$$f_1(x_1) = P(X_1 = x_1).$$

Theorem 8.1

If (X_1, X_2) is a discrete two-dimensional random variable, the marginal point probability of X_1 is

(8.5) $$f_1(x_1) = \sum_{x_2} f(x_1, x_2),$$

and the marginal point probability of X_2 is

(8.6) $$f_2(x_2) = \sum_{x_1} f(x_1, x_2).$$

Proof

The event $\{X_1 = x_1\}$ can be written

$$\{X_1 = x_1\} = \bigcup_{S(x_1)} \{(X_1 = x_1) \cap (X_2 = x_2)\},$$

where $S(x_1) = \{x_2 \mid (x_1, x_2) \in S\}$ is the set of possible values of X_2, when $X_1 = x_1$. Since the events in the union are all disjoint

$$f_1(x_1) = P(X_1 = x_1) = \sum_{S(x_1)} P\{(X_1 = x_1) \cap (X_2 = x_2)\} = \sum_{x_2} f(x_1, x_2)$$

and (8.5) follows. $\square$.

Example 8.1 (continued)

If $f_1(x_1)$ and $f_2(x_2)$ are computed from (8.5) and (8.6), it follows that

$$f_1(x_1) = f_2(x_2) = 1/6. \triangle.$$

Example 8.2 (continued)

In table 8.2 the marginal point probabilities are derived by adding the point probabilities vertically and horizontally, respectively. The marginal distributions for X_1 and X_2 are thus shown in the last column and the last row of the table. The marginal distributions of X_1 and X_2 are identical in this particular case. △.

Theorem 8.2

If (X_1, X_2) is a continuous two-dimensional random variable, the marginal density functions of X_1 and X_2 are

$$(8.7) \quad f_1(x_1) = \int_{-\infty}^{+\infty} f(x_1, x_2) dx_2$$

and

$$(8.8) \quad f_2(x_2) = \int_{-\infty}^{+\infty} f(x_1, x_2) dx_1.$$

Proof

The event $A = \{X_1 \leq x_1\}$ can also be written

$$A = \{-\infty < X_1 \leq x_1, \; -\infty < X_2 < +\infty\}.$$

Hence, from (8.4)

$$F_1(x_1) = P(X_1 \leq x_1) = \int_{-\infty}^{x_1} \left[\int_{-\infty}^{+\infty} f(z_1, x_2) dx_2 \right] dz_1.$$

Since the density function f_1 for X_1 is defined by

$$F_1(x_1) = \int_{-\infty}^{x_1} f_1(z_1) dz_1$$

for all values of x_1, (8.7) follows directly. Formula (8.8) is proved in the same way. □.

Example 8.3 (continued)

Consider again the two-dimensional uniform distribution. Using (8.7),

$$f_1(x_1) = \begin{cases} \int_{a_2}^{b_2} \dfrac{dx_2}{(b_1 - a_1)(b_2 - a_2)} = \dfrac{1}{b_1 - a_1} & \text{for } a_1 < x_1 < b_1 \\ 0 & \text{otherwise,} \end{cases}$$

i.e. X_1 is uniformly distributed. It is easy to show that X_2 is also uniformly distributed. △.

Given the joint distribution of m random variables, in the discrete case the marginal distribution of X_1 is given by

$$f_1(x_1) = \sum_{x_2 \cdots x_m} \cdots \sum f(x_1, \ldots, x_m),$$

where the summations are over all vectors $(x_2, \ldots, x_m)$ for which $(x_1, \ldots, x_m) \in S$. In the continuous case, the marginal distribution of X_1 is given by

$$f_1(x_1) = \int \cdots \int f(x_1, \ldots, x_m) dx_2 \cdots dx_m.$$

8.5. Conditional distributions

Assume that the joint distribution of two random variables X_1 and X_2 is known. In some cases, the distribution of X_2, given that the value x_1 of X_1, has been observed, is of interest. This is called the **conditional distribution** of X_2 given X_1. Consider in the discrete case the probability of the event $(X_2 = x_2)$, given the event $(X_1 = x_1)$. According to definition (3.10) of a conditional probability,

$$P(X_2 = x_2 | X_1 = x_1) = \frac{P\{(X_2 = x_2) \cap (X_1 = x_1)\}}{P(X_1 = x_1)}.$$

If $f(x_1, x_2)$ is the joint point probability of (X_1, X_2) and $f_1(x_1)$ the marginal probability of X_1, the **conditional point probability** of X_2, given $X_1 = x_1$, is

(8.9) $\qquad f_2(x_2 | x_1) = f(x_1, x_2) / f_1(x_1),$

assuming that $f_1(x_1) \neq 0$. For each fixed value x_1, (8.9) defines the point probabilities of a discrete distribution since

$$f_2(x_2 | x_1) > 0 \quad \text{for} \quad (x_1, x_2) \in S$$

and

$$\sum_{x_2} f_2(x_2 | x_1) = 1.$$

For continuous random variables (X_1, X_2), the **conditional density function** of X_2 given $X_1 = x_1$ is defined as

(8.10) $\qquad f_2(x_2 | x_1) = f(x_1, x_2) / f_1(x_1),$

where $f(x_1,x_2)$ is the joint density function of X_1 and X_2 and $f_1(x_1)$ the marginal density function of X_1, again assuming that $f_1(x_1)>0$.

Since

$$f_2(x_2|x_1) \geq 0 \quad \text{for } (x_1,x_2) \in S$$

and

$$\int_{-\infty}^{+\infty} f_2(x_2|x_1)dx_2 = 1,$$

it follows that $f_2(x_2|x_1)$ is a density function.

The conditional distribution of X_2 given X_1 in the discrete case is thus expressed through the conditional point probabilities (8.9) and in the continuous case through the conditional density (8.10). In the discrete case the mean value of a conditional distribution is defined as

$$(8.11) \qquad E[X_2|X_1=x_1] = \sum_{x_2} x_2 f_2(x_2|x_1) = \mu_{x_2|x_1}$$

and in the continuous case as

$$(8.12) \qquad E[X_2|X_1=x_1] = \int x_2 f_2(x_2|x_1)dx_2 = \mu_{x_2|x_1}.$$

The expressions (8.11) and (8.12) are called **conditional mean values** of X_2 given $X_1=x_1$. The **conditional variance** of X_2 given $X_1=x_1$ is defined as

$$(8.13) \qquad \text{var}[X_2|X_1=x_1] = \sum_{x_2} (x_2-\mu_{x_2|x_1})^2 f_2(x_2|x_1)$$

in the discrete case, and in the continuous case as

$$(8.14) \qquad \text{var}[X_2|X_1=x_1] = \int (x_2-\mu_{x_2|x_1})^2 f_2(x_2|x_1)dx_2.$$

Example 8.2 (continued)

In order to illustrate the calculation of conditional probabilities, consider again table 8.2. According to formula (8.9), the probability $f_2(x_2|x_1)$ of observing vulnerability index x_2 at time t_2, given that the index at time t_1 was x_1, is obtained by dividing each of the probabilities in table 8.2 with the corresponding row sum as shown in table 8.3. △.

Table 8.3. Conditional distributions of the vulnerability index at time t_2 given the value of the index at time t_1.

x_1 \ x_2	0	1	2	3	4	Total
0	0.694	0.214	0.065	0.020	0.007	1.000
1	0.425	0.305	0.164	0.071	0.035	1.000
2	0.234	0.298	0.234	0.129	0.105	1.000
3	0.127	0.225	0.225	0.169	0.254	1.000
4	0.023	0.062	0.099	0.137	0.679	1.000

8.6. Independent random variables

In the discrete case, two random variables X_1 and X_2 are said to be **independent** if the events $\{X_1=x_1\}$ and $\{X_2=x_2\}$ are independent for each pair (x_1,x_2) in the sample space S of (X_1,X_2). Thus, according to formula (3.16), X_1 and X_2 are independent if $P(\{X_1 = x_1\} \cap \{X_2 = x_2\}) = P(X_1=x_1)P(X_2=x_2)$ for all $(x_1,x_2) \in S$. From the definitions (8.1), (8.5) and (8.6) it then follows that X_1 and X_2 are independent if

(8.15) $f(x_1,x_2) = f_1(x_1)f_2(x_2)$ for every pair $(x_1,x_2) \in S$.

Two continuous random variables X_1 and X_2 with joint density function $f(x_1,x_2)$ and marginal density functions $f_1(x_1)$ and $f_2(x_2)$ are said to be independent if

(8.16) $f(x_1,x_2) = f_1(x_1)f_2(x_2)$ for all $(x_1,x_2) \in S$.

Since, in the discrete case, X_1 and X_2 are independent if the events $\{X_1=x_1\}$ and $\{X_2=x_2\}$ are independent, independence can also by theorem 3.8 be expressed as

(8.17) $P(X_2=x_2 | X_1=x_1) = P(X_2=x_2)$.

Hence, definitions (8.15)-(8.16) are equivalent to saying that the two random variables are independent if knowledge of the observed value of one of the variables does not influence the probability distribution of the other.

Example 8.2 (continued)

Table 8.3 shows the conditional probabilities for the vulnerability index x_2 at time t_2 given that the index at time t_1 was x_1. The table reveals a strong dependence of $f_2(x_2|x_1)$ on x_1. In view of (8.17), this means that X_1 and X_2 are not independent random variables.

This dependency has a clear direction. A low value of x_1 tends to entail a low value of x_2, and a high value of x_1 is more likely to lead to a high value of x_2. This effect can be illustrated by calculating the conditional expectation of X_2 given that $X_1=x_1$. From (8.11) and table 8.3,

$$E[X_2|X_1=0] = 0\cdot 0.694 + 1\cdot 0.214 + 2\cdot 0.065 + 3\cdot 0.020 + 4\cdot 0.007 = 0.432,$$

and correspondingly

$$E[X_2|X_1=1] = 0.986$$
$$E[X_2|X_1=2] = 1.573$$
$$E[X_2|X_1=3] = 2.198$$
$$E[X_2|X_1=4] = 3.387.$$

The expected vulnerability index at time t_2 thus increases from 0.43 to 3.39 as x_1 increases from 0 to 4. $\triangle$.

The random variables $(X_1,\ldots,X_m)$ with joint point probability or joint density function f and sample space S are said to be **independent**, if

(8.18) $\qquad f(x_1,\ldots,x_m) = f_1(x_1)\ldots f_m(x_m), \quad (x_1,\ldots,x_m) \in S,$

where $f_j(x_j)$ is the marginal density function or the marginal point probability of X_j, $j=1,\ldots,m$.

From (8.18) the joint point probabilities or the joint density function for m independent random variables can be calculated if the marginal point probabilities or the marginal density functions are known for each of the m variables.

8.7. Mean values and variances for sums of random variables

Sums of random variables play an important role in many statistical analyses. In this section, the calculation of the mean and variance of a sum of random variables $X_1,\ldots,X_n$ with known joint density function or joint point probability $f(x_1,\ldots,x_n)$ will be presented.

Theorem 8.3

If $Y = \varphi(X_1,\ldots,X_m)$, the mean value of Y is calculated as

(8.19) $E[Y] = E[\varphi(X_1,\ldots,X_m)] = \sum_{(x_1,\ldots,x_m) \in S} \varphi(x_1,\ldots,x_m) f(x_1,\ldots,x_m)$

in the discrete case and as

(8.20) $E[Y] = E[\varphi(X_1,\ldots,X_m)] = \int\cdots\int_{(x_1,\ldots,x_m) \in S} \varphi(x_1,\ldots,x_m) f(x_1,\ldots,x_m) dx_1\ldots dx_m$

in the continuous case.

It follows from this theorem that it is not necessary to derive the distribution of Y in order to determine the mean value of Y.

Theorem 8.4

If $X_1,\ldots,X_m$ are random variables with mean values $\mu_1,\ldots,\mu_m$ and $Y = X_1 + \ldots + X_m$, then

(8.21) $E[Y] = \mu_1 + \ldots + \mu_m.$

Proof

In the discrete case, it follows from theorem 8.3 that

$$E[X_1 + \ldots + X_m] = \sum_{x_1}\cdots\sum_{x_m}(x_1+\ldots+x_m) f(x_1,\ldots,x_m)$$

$$= \sum_{x_1} x_1 \sum_{x_2}\cdots\sum_{x_m} f(x_1,\ldots,x_m) + \ldots + \sum_{x_m} x_m \sum_{x_1}\cdots\sum_{x_{m-1}} f(x_1,\ldots,x_m)$$

$$= \sum_{x_1} x_1 f_1(x_1) + \ldots + \sum_{x_m} x_m f_m(x_m) = \mu_1 + \ldots + \mu_m.$$

The proof is analogous in the continuous case. □

Theorem 8.5

If $X_1,\ldots,X_m$ are independent random variables with variances $\sigma_1^2,\ldots,\sigma_m^2$ and $Y = X_1 + \ldots + X_m$, then

(8.22) $\text{var}[Y] = \sigma_1^2 + \ldots + \sigma_m^2.$

Proof

Since, according to theorem 8.4, $E[Y] = \mu_1 + \ldots + \mu_m$,

$$\text{var}[Y] = E[(X_1 + \ldots + X_m - \mu_1 - \ldots - \mu_m)^2],$$

and hence, again using theorem 8.4,

$$\text{var}[Y] = E[(X_1-\mu_1)^2]+\ldots+E[(X_m-\mu_m)^2]$$
$$+ 2\underset{i<j}{\Sigma\Sigma} E[(X_i-\mu_i)(X_j-\mu_j)].$$

If X_i and X_j for $i \neq j$ are independent, then

$$E[(X_i-\mu_i)(X_j-\mu_j)] = \underset{x_i x_j}{\Sigma \Sigma}(x_i-\mu_i)(x_j-\mu_j)f_i(x_i)f_j(x_j)$$

$$= \underset{x_i}{\Sigma}(x_i-\mu_i)f_i(x_i)\underset{x_j}{\Sigma}(x_j-\mu_j)f_j(x_j) = 0,$$

which proves the theorem in the discrete case. The proof in the continuous case is analogous. □.

It is important to take note of the different assumptions in theorems 8.4 and 8.5. Theorem 8.4 is generally valid, while theorem 8.5 only applies if $E[(X_i-\mu_i)(X_j-\mu_j)]=0$ for $i \neq j$. In this case the random variables X_i and X_j are said to be **uncorrelated**.

Theorem 8.6

If $X_1,\ldots,X_n$ are independent, identically distributed random variables with mean μ and variance σ^2, then

(8.23) $E[\bar{X}] = \mu$

and

(8.24) $\text{var}[\bar{X}] = \sigma^2/n,$

where $\bar{X}=(X_1+\ldots+X_n)/n$.

Proof
The theorem follows immediately from theorems 5.3, 8.4 and 8.5. □.

8.8. The covariance and the correlation coefficient

For two random variables X_1 and X_2 with $\mu_1=E[X_1]$, $\mu_2=E[X_2]$, $\sigma_1^2=\text{var}[X_1]$ and $\sigma_2^2=\text{var}[X_2]$, it follows from the proof theorem 8.5 with m=2 that

$$(8.25) \quad \text{var}[X_1+X_2] = E[(X_1+X_2-\mu_1-\mu_2)^2]$$

$$= E[(X_1-\mu_1)^2+(X_2-\mu_2)^2+2(X_1-\mu_1)(X_2-\mu_2)]$$

$$= \sigma_1^2+\sigma_2^2+2E[(X_1-\mu_1)(X_2-\mu_2)].$$

Hence, the variance of a sum of random variables is the sum of the variances alone if and only if the last term in (8.25) is 0. The quantity

$$\text{cov}(X_1,X_2) = E[(X_1-\mu_1)(X_2-\mu_2)]$$

is called the **covariance** between X_1 and X_2. The covariance between X_1 and X_2 is often denoted by σ_{12}.

According to (8.19), the covariance between two discrete random variables X_1 and X_2 is calculated from the point probabilities $f(x_1,x_2)$ of (X_1,X_2) as

$$(8.26) \quad \text{cov}(X_1,X_2) = \sum_{x_1}\sum_{x_2}(x_1-\mu_1)(x_2-\mu_2)f(x_1,x_2).$$

According to (8.20), the covariance for continuous random variables is calculated as

$$(8.27) \quad \text{cov}(X_1,X_2) = \int_{-\infty}^{+\infty}\int_{-\infty}^{+\infty}(x_1-\mu_1)(x_2-\mu_2)f(x_1,x_2)dx_1dx_2,$$

where $f(x_1,x_2)$ is the joint density function for X_1 and X_2.

From (8.26) and (8.27), it is easy to show that the covariance can be written in the alternative form

$$(8.28) \quad \text{cov}(X_1,X_2) = E[X_1X_2]-\mu_1\mu_2.$$

The covariance is used as a measure of the degree of linear covariation between two random variables. Broadly speaking, a positive value of $\text{cov}(X_1,X_2)$ means that a positive value of $X_1-\mu_1$ is more likely to be observed together with a positive value of $X_2-\mu_2$, and a negative value of $X_1-\mu_1$ is more likely to be observed together with a negative value of $X_2-\mu_2$. In the same way, a negative value of $cov(X_1,X_2)$ means that values of $X_1-\mu_1$ and $X_2-\mu_2$ with opposite signs are more likely to be observed together than values of $X_1-\mu_1$ and $X_2-\mu_2$ with identical signs.

Example 8.2 (continued)

In the two-dimensional distribution of the vulnerability indices, the random variables were not independent. From table 8.2, it follows that it is most likely that small values of X_1 are observed together with small values of X_2, and that large values of X_1 are observed together with large values of X_2. Therefore, the covariance between X_1 and X_2 can be expected to be positive.

Table 8.4 shows all 25 values of the product $(x_1-\mu_1)(x_2-\mu_2)$. Comparing this table with table 8.2, it can be seen that values of (x_1,x_2) for which the product is positive have large probabilities, while values of (x_1,x_2) for which the product is negative have small probabilities.

Table 8.4. Values of the product $(x_1-\mu_1)(x_2-\mu_2)$ for all pairs of observed vulnerability indices.

x_1 \ x_2	0	1	2	3	4
0	1.464	0.254	-0.956	-2.166	-3.376
1	0.254	0.044	-0.166	-0.376	-0.586
2	-0.956	-0.166	0.624	1.414	2.204
3	-2.166	-0.376	1.414	3.204	4.994
4	-3.376	-0.586	2.204	4.994	7.784

If the values in table 8.4 are multiplied with the probabilities of table 8.2, we find $cov(X_1,X_2)=1.374$, i.e. the covariance between X_1 and X_2 is positive, as expected. △.

In general, it is impossible without further information to say whether a given covariance between two variables indicates a strong or a weak dependency between the variables. The main reason is that the value of the covariance depends on the scales of measurement for the variables. If all the values of one of the variables are multiplied by 1000, then obviously the covariance is also multiplied by 1000.

In order to compensate for this scale dependency, the covariance can be standardized. Dividing $cov(X_1,X_2)$ by the product of the standard deviations σ_1 and σ_2 yields

(8.29) $\quad \rho = \text{cov}(X_1, X_2)/(\sigma_1 \sigma_2)$,

which is called the **correlation coefficient** between X_1 and X_2.
If a_1, a_2, b_1 and b_2 are arbitrary constants then

(8.30) $\quad \text{cov}(a_1 X_1 + b_1, a_2 X_2 + b_2) = a_1 a_2 \text{cov}(X_1, X_2)$.

From (8.29), (8.30) and theorem 5.3, it then follows that

$$\rho(a_1 X_1, a_2 X_2) = \rho(X_1, X_2),$$

i.e. the correlation coefficient is independent of the scales of measurement for X_1 and X_2.

Theorem 8.7

If ρ is the correlation coefficient between the random variables X_1 and X_2,

(8.31) $\quad -1 \leq \rho \leq 1$.

If ρ is equal to +1 or -1, then

$$P(X_2 = aX_1 + b) = 1,$$

where
$$a = \rho \frac{\sigma_2}{\sigma_1}$$
and
$$b = \mu_2 - \rho \frac{\sigma_2}{\sigma_1} \mu_1.$$

Proof

Let
$$U_1 = (X_1 - \mu_1)/\sigma_1$$
and
$$U_2 = (X_2 - \mu_2)/\sigma_2.$$

Then, according to (8.25) and theorem 5.5,

(8.32) $\quad \text{var}[U_1 + U_2] = \text{var}[U_1] + \text{var}[U_2] + 2\text{cov}(U_1, U_2) = 2 + 2\text{cov}(U_1, U_2)$.

From (8.30) it follows that

$$\text{cov}(U_1, U_2) = \text{cov}(X_1, X_2)/\sigma_1\sigma_2 = \rho,$$

and since $\text{var}[U_1+U_2] \geq 0$, (8.32) gives

$$\rho \geq -1.$$

From the relationship $\text{var}[U_1-U_2] = \text{var}[U_1] + \text{var}[U_2] - 2\text{cov}(U_1, U_2) \geq 0$, the same argument gives

$$\rho \leq 1,$$

thus proving (8.31).

It should be noted that $\rho=+1$ and $\rho=-1$ means that $\text{var}[U_1-U_2]=0$ and $\text{var}[U_1+U_2]=0$. This implies however that the events $A=\{U_1=U_2\}$ and $B=\{U_1=-U_2\}$ have probability 1, which proves the second part of the theorem. $\square$.

Theorem 8.8

If X_1 and X_2 are independent, then

$$E[X_1 \cdot X_2] = E[X_1] \cdot E[X_2]$$

and

$$\text{cov}(X_1, X_2) = \rho = 0.$$

Proof

Applying theorem 8.3 in the discrete case gives

$$E[X_1 \cdot X_2] = \sum_{x_1} \sum_{x_2} x_1 x_2 f_1(x_1) f_2(x_2)$$

$$= \sum_{x_1} x_1 f_1(x_1) \sum_{x_2} x_2 f_2(x_2) = E[X_1]E[X_2].$$

It then follows from (8.28) that $\text{cov}(X_1, X_2) = 0$. $\square$.

If the covariance or the correlation coefficient between two random variables X_1 and X_2 is 0, they are said to be **uncorrelated**. If X_1 and X_2 are independent, it follows from theorem 8.8 that they are also uncorrelated. However, the fact that the variables are uncorrelated does not necessarily imply independence.

The correlation coefficient is used as a measure of the degree of **linear dependence** between two random variables. The closer the numerical value of the correlation coefficient between the random variables X_1 and X_2 comes to 1, the closer observed values of X_1 and X_2 can be expected to cluster around a straight line. It is essential to emphazise, however, that the correlation coefficient is a measure of linear relationship only. If for example

$$X_1^2 + X_2^2 = c^2,$$

such that the observed values of X_1 and X_2 with probability 1 fall on a circle, then ρ may well be 0 in spite of the exact functional relationship between X_1 and X_2.

For n independent observations $(x_{11}, x_{12}), \ldots, (x_{n1}, x_{n2})$ of (X_1, X_2), the **empirical covariance** is defined as

(8.33) $$s_{12} = \frac{1}{n-1} \sum_{i=1}^{n} (x_{i1} - \bar{x}_1)(x_{i2} - \bar{x}_2)$$

where $\bar{x}_j = \frac{1}{n} \sum_{i=1}^{n} x_{ij}$, $j = 1, 2$, and the **empirical correlation coefficient** as

(8.34) $$r_{12} = s_{12}/(s_1 s_2),$$

where s_1^2 and s_2^2 are the empirical variances for the x_1's and x_2's respectively.

The empirical correlation coefficient (8.34) is an estimate of the correlation coefficient (8.29) between X_1 and X_2, just as $\bar{x}$ and s^2 are estimates of the mean and the variance. Thus, the degree of linear relationship between X_1 and X_2 is reflected in the empirical correlation coefficient r_{12}. By arguments similar to those used in the proof of theorem 8.7, it can be shown that

$$|r_{12}| \leq 1.$$

If $r_{12} = 1$, the observations all lie on a straight line with a positive slope and if $r_{12} = -1$ the observations all lie on a straight line with a negative slope.

The empirical correlation coefficient is an important quantity in descriptive statistics. A value of r_{12} close to +1 or -1 can thus be interpreted as an indication of a strong linear dependency between the variables. On the other hand a value of r_{12} close to 0 implies a weak dependency between the variables. If r_{12} is used as a descriptive statistic, the observations do not have to be connected with random variables.

Suppose that the data are grouped with respect to x_1 and x_2, i.e. the x_1-axis and the x_2-axis are divided into intervals by the points $t_0,\ldots,t_m$ and $v_0,\ldots,v_k$ respectively. The empirical covariance s_{12} is then approximated by

$$(8.35) \qquad s^*_{12} = \frac{1}{n-1} \sum_{j=1}^{m} \sum_{\ell=1}^{k} (t^*_j - \bar{x}_1)(v^*_\ell - \bar{x}_2) a_{j\ell},$$

where $a_{j\ell}$ is the number of observed pairs (x_{i1}, x_{i2}), for which

$$t_{j-1} < x_{i1} \leq t_j \quad \text{and} \quad v_{\ell-1} < x_{i2} \leq v_\ell,$$

and where

$$t^*_j = (t_j + t_{j-1})/2 \quad \text{and} \quad v^*_\ell = (v_\ell + v_{\ell-1})/2.$$

If X_1 and X_2 are discrete random variables, formula (8.33) can be simplified. Let $a(x_1, x_2)$ be the number of times the pair (x_1, x_2) has been observed. Then (8.33) can be written as

$$(8.36) \qquad s_{12} = \frac{1}{n-1} \sum_{x_1} \sum_{x_2} (x_1 - \bar{x}_1)(x_2 - \bar{x}_2) a(x_1, x_2).$$

For practical purposes, there exist a simple formula for the computation of the empirical covariance. Define SP_{12} (Sum of Products) as

$$SP_{12} = \sum_{i=1}^{n} x_{i1} x_{i2}$$

when the observations are ungrouped and as

$$SP_{12} = \sum_{j\ell} t^*_j v^*_\ell a_{j\ell},$$

when the observations are grouped.

If $S_1 = \Sigma x_{i1}$ and $S_2 = \Sigma x_{i2}$, (8.33) can be written as

$$s_{12} = (SP_{12} - S_1 S_2/n)/(n-1).$$

If SPD_{12} (Sum of Products of Deviations) is defined as

$$SPD_{12} = SP_{12} - S_1 S_2/n,$$

then

$$s_{12} = SPD_{12}/(n-1).$$

Example 8.2 (continued)

It was claimed earlier that the point probabilities in table 8.2 constitute an appropriate model for the data in table 8.1. This model can be partially checked by comparing the empirical and the theoretical correlation coefficients. The correlation coefficient between the two indices of vulnerability, computed from table 8.2, is $\rho=0.690$. The empirical correlation coefficient (8.36) can be written as

$$s_{12} = \frac{1}{n-1}(\sum_{x_1 x_2} \sum x_1 x_2 a(x_1,x_2) - n\bar{x}_1 \bar{x}_2)$$

From table 8.1, the values $s_1=0.899$, $\bar{x}_1=0.700$, $s_2=0.880$, $\bar{x}_2=0.647$ and $s_{12}=0.456$ can be computed, such that $r_{12}=0.576$.

The fact that the empirical correlation coefficient has a substantially lower value than the theoretical correlation coefficient indicates that the fit of the model is not good. $\triangle$.

Example 8.4

Table 8.5 shows the age of the wife, x_1, and the husband, x_2, at the time of divorce for married couples in Denmark in 1982. In order to calculate the covariance s_{12} between x_1 and x_2, (8.35) can be used with $(t_1^*,\ldots,t_m^*)=(17,22,\ldots,72)$ and $v_1^*=(18.5,22,\ldots,67,72)$. This gives

$$SP_{12} = 18396039,$$
$$S_1 S_2/n = 17203910.8,$$
$$s_{12} = 1192128.2/13325 = 89.47$$

and
$$r_{12} = 89.47/[9.92 \cdot 10.49] = 0.860. \triangle.$$

Table 8.5. Divorces in Denmark in 1982 distributed according to the age of the wife and husband.

Age of wife in years	18-19	20-24	25-29	30-34	35-39	40-44	45-49	50-54	55-59	60-64	65-69	70-
15 - 19	4	42	19	3	3	2	-	-	-	-	-	-
20 - 24	4	433	796	238	52	12	3	1	-	2	-	-
25 - 29	-	95	1423	1301	229	65	18	8	4	2	-	-
30 - 34	-	25	290	1526	993	231	84	27	14	6	2	1
35 - 39	-	2	39	212	802	625	192	70	31	15	4	-
40 - 44	-	1	9	39	129	495	385	137	50	17	10	1
45 - 49	-	1	12	11	29	101	328	277	91	31	11	-
50 - 54	-	-	3	-	4	13	98	218	153	60	24	10
55 - 59	-	-	-	1	1	5	19	43	124	89	33	8
60 - 64	-	-	-	-	1	4	2	12	37	58	42	11
65 - 69	-	-	-	-	-	-	1	2	3	25	33	28
70 -	-	-	-	-	1	1	-	-	1	3	7	32

Source: Statistical Yearbook 1979. Danmarks Statistik.

8.9. The multinomial distribution

In chapter 6, the **multinomial distribution** was presented by considering n independent trials, where one of m possible events $A_1,\ldots,A_m$ is observed in each trial. With $X_1,\ldots,X_m$ as random variables representing the number of times each of the m events occurs in the n trials, the point pro bility is then given by

$$(8.37) \qquad f(x_1,\ldots,x_m) = \binom{n}{x_1 \cdots x_m} p_1^{x_1} \cdots p_m^{x_m},$$

where

$$p_j = P(A_j).$$

Example 8.5

As part of a large scale investigation of living conditions in Denmark carried out in 1976 by the Danish National Institute for Social Research, a sample of 6000 persons between 20 and 69 years of age was selected without replacement. Interviews were obtained from 5166 persons. Table 8.6 shows the sample distributed according to marital status.

Table 8.6. A sample of Danes between 20 and 69 years of age in 1976, distributed according to marital status.

Marital status	Single	Married	Separated	Divorced	Widowed	Total
Number in the sample	954	3696	28	277	211	5166
Percentage distribution	18.5	71.5	0.5	5.4	4.1	100

Source: The distribution of living conditions. The Danish National Institute for Social Research. Publication No.82. 1978.

It is assumed that the 5166 persons constitute a random sample from the population of Danes between 20 and 69 years of age. This population consisted in 1976 of 3 111 892 persons. Since the sample size is small compared with the size of the population, it is assumed that the outcomes of the 5166 selections are independent. It is further assumed that the probability of selecting a person in a given category, for example a widowed, is the same in all 5166 selections. Under these assumptions, a multinomial distribution with m=5 and n=5166 describes the data in table 8.6. The parameters $p_1,\ldots,p_5$ are the probabilities of observing a person in one of the five categories in any given selection. The parameter p_1 is thus the actual proportion of single persons in Denmark in 1976 aged between 20 and 69 years. △.

If $(X_1,\ldots,X_m)$ is multinomially distributed, the marginal distribution of X_j is a binomial distribution for $j=1,\ldots,m$. This follows for X_1 from

$$f_1(x_1) = \sum_{x_2}\ldots\sum_{x_m} \binom{n}{x_1\ldots x_m} p_1^{x_1}\ldots p_m^{x_m}$$

$$= p_1^{x_1} \sum_{x_2}\ldots\sum_{x_m} \binom{n}{x_1\ldots x_m} p_2^{x_2}\ldots p_m^{x_m} = p_1^{x_1}\binom{n}{x_1}(1-p_1)^{n-x_1},$$

so that

$$f_1(x_1) = \binom{n}{x_1} p_1^{x_1}(1-p_1)^{n-x_1},$$

showing that X_1 follows a binomial distribution with parameters (n_1, p_1). This result can also be established intuitively since X_1 is the number of times A_1 occurs in n independent trials with $P(A_1)=p_1$ in each trial.

Since

(8.38) $X_j \sim b(n,p_j)$, $j=1,\ldots,m$,

it follows that

(8.39) $E[X_j] = np_j$

and

(8.40) $\text{var}[X_j] = np_j(1-p_j)$.

The random variables $X_1,\ldots,X_m$ are not independent since

$$X_1+\ldots+X_m = n.$$

This means for example that if X_1 is close to n, then $X_2,\ldots,X_m$ must all be close to 0. The covariance between any two X's should then be negative. In fact,

(8.41) $\text{cov}(X_i, X_j) = -np_i p_j$, $i \neq j$.

From (8.41) and (8.40), the correlation coefficient between X_i and X_j is

$$\rho_{ij} = -\sqrt{\frac{p_i p_j}{(1-p_i)(1-p_j)}},$$

which is independent of the parameter n.

8.10. The distribution of sums of random variables

Many widely used statistical methods involve the computation of sums of the observations. As the observations are assumed to be observed values of random variables, it is therefore important to be able to derive the distribution of such sums from knowledge of the joint distribution of the random variables, i.e. from knowledge of the probability model used for the description of the observations.

Theorem 8.9

If $f(x_1, x_2)$ is the joint point probability of the discrete random variables X_1 and X_2 with sample space S, the point probability g of $Y = X_1 + X_2$ is given by

(8.42) $g(y) = \sum_{x_1} f(x_1, y-x_1)$,

where the summation is over all values of x_1 for which $(x_1, y-x_1) \in S$.

Proof

As illustrated in fig. 8.4

$$(Y=y) = \bigcup_{x_1+x_2=y} (\{X_1=x_1\} \cap \{X_2=x_2\}) = \bigcup_{x_1} (\{X_1=x_1\} \cap \{X_2=y-x_1\}).$$

It follows that

$$P(Y=y) = P(X_1+X_2=y) = \sum_{x_1+x_2=y} \sum f(x_1, x_2) = \sum_{x_1} f(x_1, y-x_1). \quad \square$$

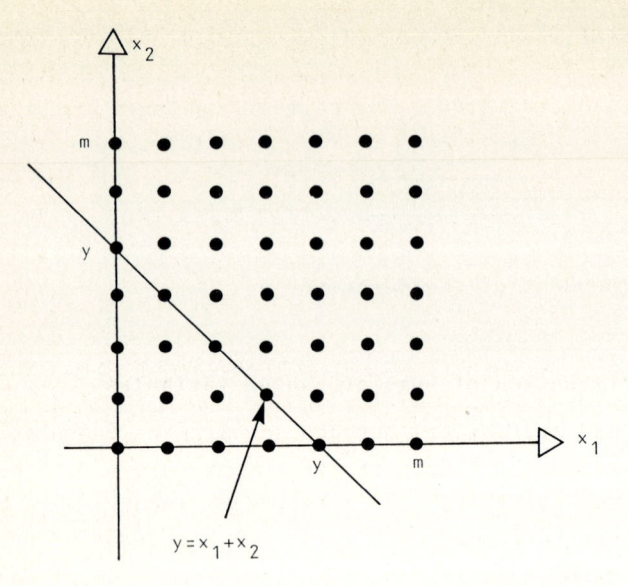

Fig. 8.4. Values of x_1 and x_2 for which $x_1+x_2=y$.

Theorem 8.10

If $f(x_1,x_2)$ is the joint density function of the continuous random variables X_1 and X_2, the density function g of $Y=X_1+X_2$ is given by

$$g(y) = \int f(x_1, y-x_1)dx_1.$$

Theorems 8.9 and 8.10 show how the density function or the point probability for a sum of two random variables can be derived. Theorems 8.11 to 8.14 below are all applications of these two theorems.

Theorem 8.11

If $X_1,\ldots,X_m$ are independent Poisson distributed random variables with parameters $\lambda_1,\ldots,\lambda_m$, then $Y=X_1+\ldots+X_m$ is Poisson distributed with parameter $\lambda=\lambda_1+\ldots+\lambda_m$.

Proof

Since $f(x_1,y-x_1)=f_1(x_1)f_2(y-x_1)$ when X_1 and X_2 are independent, (8.42) and (6.11) give

$$g(y) = \sum_{x_1} \lambda_1^{x_1} \lambda_2^{y-x_1} e^{-\lambda_1-\lambda_2}/(x_1!(y-x_1)!)$$

$$= (\lambda_1+\lambda_2)^y e^{-(\lambda_1+\lambda_2)} \frac{1}{y!} \sum_{x_1} \binom{y}{x_1} \left(\frac{\lambda_1}{\lambda_1+\lambda_2}\right)^{x_1} \left(\frac{\lambda_2}{\lambda_1+\lambda_2}\right)^{y-x_1}.$$

The last sum in this expression is the sum of the point probabilities of a binomial distribution with parameters (y,p) where $p=\lambda_1/(\lambda_1+\lambda_2)$. Hence,

$$g(y) = \frac{(\lambda_1+\lambda_2)^y}{y!} e^{-(\lambda_1+\lambda_2)}$$

which proves the theorem for $m=2$. For arbitrary m, the theorem follows by induction. ☐.

Theorem 8.12

If $X_1,\ldots,X_m$ are independent, binomially distributed random variables with parameters $(n_1,p),\ldots,(n_m,p)$, then $Y=X_1+\ldots+X_m$ is binomially distributed with parameters (n,p), where $n=n_1+\ldots+n_m$.

Proof

The result can be established intuitively. For $m=2$, the value of X_1 can be interpreted as the number of successes in n_1 independent trials with probability p of a success, while X_2 can be interpreted as the number of successes in n_2 independent trials with the same probability p of a success. The sum Y of X_1 and X_2 can then be interpreted as the number of successes in n_1+n_2 trials with success probability p. It follows from this interpretation that Y is binomially distributed with parameters n_1+n_2 and p, assuming the n_1 first and the n_2 last trials are independent. The assumption of independence between X_1 and X_2 implies, however, that the result of the n_1 first trials is independent of the result of the last n_2 trials. This proves the theorem for $m=2$. For arbitrary m, the result follows by induction. ☐.

Theorem 8.13

If $X_1,\ldots,X_m$ are independent, exponentially distributed random variables with parameter λ, then $Y=X_1+\ldots+X_m$ follows an Erlang-distribution with shape parameter m and scale parameter λ.

Proof

As X_1 and X_2 are independent

$$f(x_1, y-x_1) = f_1(x_1)f_2(y-x_1).$$

From (7.15) and theorem 8.10 then follows

$$g(y) = \int_0^y \lambda^2 e^{-\lambda x_1 - \lambda(y-x_1)} dx_1 = \lambda^2 e^{-\lambda y} \int_0^y dx_1 = y\lambda^2 e^{-\lambda y},$$

which is the density function for an Erlang-distribution with shape parameter 2 and scale parameter λ. The proof for higher values of m follows by induction. □.

Theorem 8.14

If $X_1,\ldots,X_m$ are independent, normally distributed random variables with mean values $\mu_1,\ldots,\mu_m$ and variances $\sigma_1^2,\ldots,\sigma_m^2$, then $Y=X_1+\ldots+X_m$ is normally distributed with mean value $\mu=\mu_1+\ldots+\mu_m$ and variance $\sigma^2=\sigma_1^2+\ldots+\sigma_m^2$.

In section 8.7 two important results concerning the mean and the variance of sums of random variables were discussed. Theorem 8.4 was generally valid, while theorem 8.5 was only valid for independent random variables. If the m random variables are dependent, covariances must be included in the expression for the variance of their sum.

For m=2, (8.25) and the definition of $cov(X_1,X_2)$ gives

$$(8.43) \quad var[X_1+X_2] = var[X_1] + var[X_2] + 2cov(X_1,X_2).$$

For the difference between X_1 and X_2, (8.25) gives

$$(8.44) \quad var[X_1-X_2] = var[X_1] + var[X_2] - 2cov(X_1,X_2).$$

Theorem 8.5 can be generalized in the following way:

Theorem 8.15

For m random variables $X_1,\ldots,X_m$ and arbitrary constants $a_1,\ldots,a_m$,

$$(8.45) \quad var[Y] = \sum_{i=1}^{m} a_i^2 var[X_i] + 2\sum\sum_{i>j} a_i a_j cov(X_i,X_j)$$

for

$$Y = \sum_{j=1}^{m} a_j X_j.$$

Proof

The proof follows easily from the proof of theorem 8.5, formula (8.30) and theorem 5.3. □.

8.11. The multivariate normal distribution

The density function for a two-dimensional normal distribution is given by

(8.46) $$\begin{cases} f(x_1,x_2) = (2\pi\sigma_1\sigma_2\sqrt{1-\rho^2})^{-1} \exp\{-\tfrac{1}{2}q\} \\ q = (u_1^2 - 2\rho u_1 u_2 + u_2^2)/(1-\rho^2), \end{cases}$$

where
$$u_1 = (x_1-\mu_1)/\sigma_1$$
and
$$u_2 = (x_2-\mu_2)/\sigma_2.$$

It can be shown that μ_1 and μ_2 in (8.46) are the mean values and σ_1^2 and σ_2^2 the variances of X_1 and X_2 respectively while ρ is the correlation coefficient between X_1 and X_2.

Fig. 8.5 shows a two-dimensional normal density function.

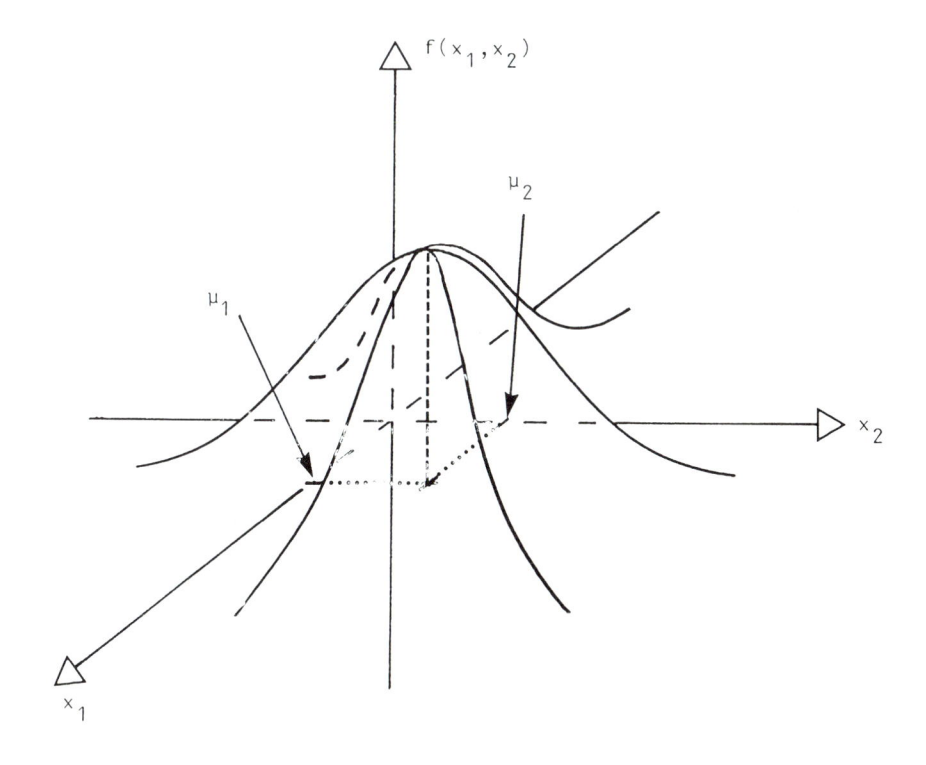

Fig. 8.5. Graph of the two-dimensional normal density function.

The marginal distributions of X_1 and X_2 are one-dimensional normal distributions. For $\rho=0$, the density (8.46) factorizes into the marginal densities of X_1 and X_2. Hence, two uncorrelated normally distributed random variables are also independent. Comparing this result with theorem 8.8 shows that two normally distributed random variables are independent if and only if they are uncorrelated.

What is more, the conditional distribution of X_2, given that $X_1=x_1$, is normal. The conditional mean value of X_2, given that $X_1=x_1$, is

$$(8.47) \qquad E[X_2|X_1=x_1] = \mu_2 + \rho\frac{\sigma_2}{\sigma_1}(x_1-\mu_1),$$

and the conditional variance

$$(8.48) \qquad \text{var}[X_2|X_1=x_1] = \sigma_2^2(1-\rho^2).$$

Similar results are obtained for the distribution of X_1, given $X_2=x_2$.

Formula (8.47) shows that for the two-dimensional normal distribution, the conditional mean value of X_2 given that $X_1=x_1$ is a linear function of x_1. The variance formula (8.48) shows that the variance of X_2, given that $X_1=x_1$, is less than the unconditional variance of σ_2^2 if $\rho \neq 0$, i.e. if X_1 and X_2 are dependent. If ρ approaches 1, then $\text{var}[X_2|X_1=x_1]$ approaches 0, as should be expected.

The joint density function of a two-dimensional normally distributed random variable (X_1,X_2) is completely characterized by the mean values and the variances in the marginal distributions and the correlation coefficient ρ. These parameters can be summarized in

$$\mu = \begin{bmatrix} \mu_1 \\ \mu_2 \end{bmatrix} \qquad \text{and} \qquad C = \begin{bmatrix} \sigma_1^2 & \sigma_{21} \\ \sigma_{12} & \sigma_2^2 \end{bmatrix}$$

where $\sigma_{12}=\sigma_{21}=\rho\sigma_1\sigma_2$. The vector μ is called the mean value vector and the matrix C is called the covariance matrix.

Similarly, the distributional properties of an m-dimensional normal random variable $(X_1,\ldots,X_m)$ can be characterized completely by the **mean value vector**

$$\mu = \begin{bmatrix} E[X_1] \\ \vdots \\ E[X_m] \end{bmatrix} = \begin{bmatrix} \mu_1 \\ \vdots \\ \mu_m \end{bmatrix}$$

and the **covariance matrix**

$$C = \begin{bmatrix} \sigma_1^2 & \sigma_{12} & \cdots & \sigma_{1m} \\ \sigma_{12} & \sigma_2^2 & \cdots & \sigma_{2m} \\ \vdots & \vdots & & \vdots \\ \sigma_{1m} & \sigma_{2m} & \cdots & \sigma_m^2 \end{bmatrix},$$

where $\sigma_{ij} = \text{cov}(X_i, X_j)$, $i \neq j$. As $\text{cov}(X_i, X_j) = \text{cov}(X_j, X_i)$, the covariance matrix is symmetric. Furthermore it can be shown that the covariance matrix is non-negative definite, i.e. $\mathbf{x'Cx} \geq 0$ for any $\mathbf{x'} = (x_1, \ldots, x_m) \in R^m$. If C is non-singular, the joint density function of an m-dimensional normally distributed random variable can be written as

(8.49) $f(\mathbf{x}) = (2\pi)^{-m/2} |C|^{-\frac{1}{2}} \exp\{-q/2\},$

where
$$q = (\mathbf{x} - \boldsymbol{\mu})' C^{-1} (\mathbf{x} - \boldsymbol{\mu}).$$

The normal distribution is invariant under linear transformations. In the one-dimensional case, this follows from theorem 7.2. In the m-dimensional case, a linear transformation of $(X_1, \ldots, X_m)$ can be written as

(8.50) $\mathbf{Y} = \mathbf{AX} + \mathbf{b},$

where

$$\mathbf{Y} = \begin{bmatrix} Y_1 \\ \vdots \\ Y_k \end{bmatrix},$$

$$\mathbf{A} = \begin{bmatrix} a_{11} & \cdots & a_{1m} \\ \vdots & & \vdots \\ a_{k1} & \cdots & a_{km} \end{bmatrix},$$

$$\mathbf{X} = \begin{bmatrix} X_1 \\ \vdots \\ X_m \end{bmatrix}$$

and
$$\mathbf{b} = \begin{bmatrix} b_1 \\ \vdots \\ b_k \end{bmatrix}.$$

Theorem 8.16

If **Y** is given by (8.50) and **X** is an m-dimensional normally distributed random variable with covariance matrix **C** and mean value vector μ, then **Y** follows a k-dimensional normal distribution with

$$E[Y] = A\mu + b$$

and covariance matrix

$$\text{var}[Y] = ACA'.$$

It should be noted, however, that the density function of **Y** can only be written in the form (8.49) if var[**Y**] is non-singular.

One of the consequences of theorem 8.16 is that a sum of normally distributed random variables is again normally distributed, even when the random variables are correlated. This can be seen by writing $Y = X_1 + \ldots + X_m$ as

$$Y = (1 \ldots 1) \begin{bmatrix} X_1 \\ \vdots \\ X_m \end{bmatrix}.$$

Then Y follows a normal distribution with

$$E[Y] = (1 \ldots 1) \begin{bmatrix} \mu_1 \\ \vdots \\ \mu_m \end{bmatrix} = \mu_1 + \ldots + \mu_m$$

and

$$\text{var}[Y] = (1 \ldots 1) \begin{bmatrix} \sigma_1^2 & \cdots & \sigma_{1m} \\ \vdots & & \vdots \\ \sigma_{1m} & \cdots & \sigma_m^2 \end{bmatrix} \begin{bmatrix} 1 \\ \vdots \\ 1 \end{bmatrix}$$

$$= \sum_i \sigma_i^2 + 2 \sum_{i<j} \sigma_{ij}.$$

9. The Distribution of Sample Functions and Limit Theorems

9.1. Introduction

A **statistic** or a **sample function** is a real-valued function of the observations. By means of statistics, extensive data can be reduced to a limited number of descriptive quantities. Statistics can be used as summary measures of data, e.g. as estimates of unknown parameters in a probability model, or they can form the basis for testing statistical hypotheses. Statistics are thus key elements in the theory for drawing conclusions from data based on a probability model, so-called **theory of inference**.

For a statistic to be useful, its distribution must be known at least approximately under the given statistical model. In this chapter, the distributional properties of sums and sums of squares of normally distributed random variables are considered. These results are essential for a variety of standard statistical methods. Situations in which it is difficult or even impossible to derive the exact distribution of a statistic from the statistical model are then considered. In such situations, however, it is often possible to approximate the distribution of the statistic if there is a sufficiently large number of observations. Such approximations are justified by the so-called **limit theorems**. For example, it can be shown that the distribution of statistics obtained as the sum of random variables are approximately normal under slightly restrictive conditions.

9.2. The distribution of $\bar{X}$ and S^2 for normally distributed random variables

Let $x_1, \ldots, x_n$ be observations of independent, identically distributed random variables $X_1, \ldots, X_n$. In chapter 5, the statistics $\bar{x}$ and s^2, i.e. the sample mean and the sample variance respectively, were proposed as estimates of the mean μ and the variance σ^2. These estimates can be regarded as the observed values of the random variables

$$\bar{X} = (\sum_{i=1}^{n} X_i)/n$$

and

$$S^2 = \sum_{i=1}^{n} (X_i - \overline{X})^2 / (n-1),$$

respectively.

To evaluate the precision of $\overline{x}$ and s^2 as estimates of μ and σ^2 and to test statistical hypotheses concerning the values of μ and σ^2, the distributions of $\overline{X}$ and S^2 need to be derived.

Theorem 9.1

Let $X_1, \ldots, X_n$ be independent random variables, where $X_i \sim N(\mu, \sigma^2)$, $i = 1, \ldots, n$, and let

$$\overline{X} = (X_1 + \ldots + X_n)/n.$$

Then

(9.1) $\overline{X} \sim N(\mu, \sigma^2/n)$.

Proof

The result follows from theorem 8.14 with $\mu_1 = \ldots = \mu_n = \mu$ and $\sigma_1^2 = \ldots = \sigma_n^2 = \sigma^2$, and from theorem 7.2 for $a = 1/n$ and $b = 0$. □

In order to derive the distribution of S^2, a number of results concerning the distribution of sums of squares of independent, normally distributed random variables with mean 0 and variance 1 are needed. The distribution function F of U^2, when $U \sim N(0,1)$, is

$$F(q) = P\{U^2 \leq q\} = P\{-\sqrt{q} \leq U \leq \sqrt{q}\} = \Phi(\sqrt{q}) - \Phi(-\sqrt{q}).$$

The density function f of U^2 then follows by taking the derivative of F with respect to q, i.e.

(9.2) $$f(q) = \frac{1}{2\sqrt{q}} \frac{1}{\sqrt{2\pi}} e^{-q/2} + \frac{1}{2\sqrt{q}} \frac{1}{\sqrt{2\pi}} e^{-q/2} = \frac{1}{\sqrt{2\pi}} q^{-\frac{1}{2}} e^{-q/2}.$$

U^2 is said to follow a chi-square (χ^2) distribution with one degree of freedom.

Definition 9.1

If $U_1, \ldots, U_n$ are independent, normally distributed random variables with mean 0 and variance 1, then

$$Q = U_1^2 + \ldots + U_n^2$$

follows a χ^2-distribution with n degrees of freedom, written as $Q \sim \chi^2(n)$.

It can be shown that the density function of Q is

(9.3) $$f(q) = \frac{1}{2^{n/2}\Gamma(n/2)} q^{\frac{n}{2}-1} e^{-q/2},$$

where the gamma function Γ is defined by (7.25). For n=1, (9.3) reduces to (9.2) since it can be shown that $\Gamma(\frac{1}{2})=\sqrt{\pi}$.

The χ^2-distribution depends on the integer-valued parameter n, called the **number of degrees of freedom**. For n=2, the χ^2-distribution is an exponential distribution with $\lambda=1/2$, cf. section 7.3. If n is integer-valued and even, the χ^2-distribution is an Erlang-distribution with shape parameter n/2 and scale parameter 1/2, cf. section 7.5.

The mean value and the variance for the χ^2-distribution are given by

(9.4) $$\begin{cases} E[Q] = n \\ var[Q] = 2n. \end{cases}$$

In fig. 9.1, the density function of the χ^2 distribution is shown with 1, 2, 3 and 4 degrees of freedom.

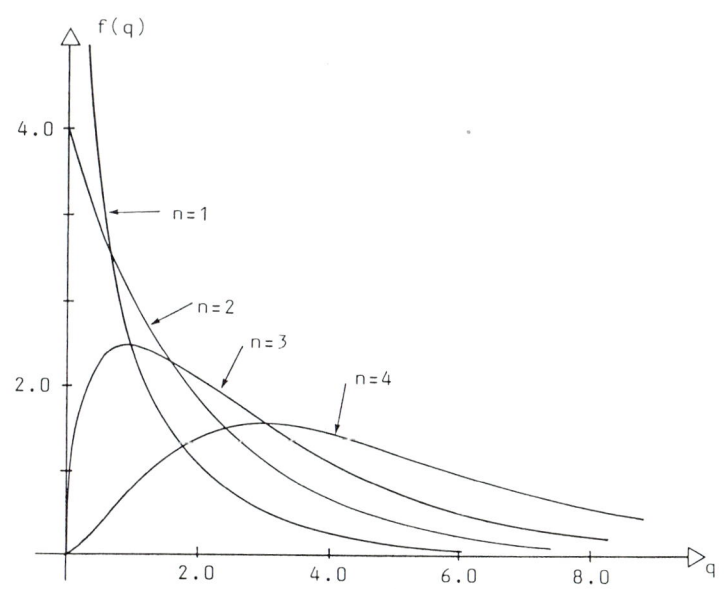

Fig. 9.1. The density function of the χ^2-distribution with 1, 2, 3 and 4 degrees of freedom.

Theorem 9.2

Let $Q_1,\ldots,Q_k$ be independent random variables with $Q_i \sim \chi^2(n_i)$, $i=1,\ldots,k$. Then

$$Q = Q_1 + \ldots + Q_k \sim \chi^2(n),$$

where $n = n_1 + \ldots + n_k$.

Theorem 9.2 is called the **additivity theorem** of the χ^2-distribution. If, in accordance with definition 9.1, Q_i is assumed to be the sum of n_i squared, standardized and normally distributed random variables, then theorem 9.2 follows directly from definition 9.1. For $n_1 = n_2 = \ldots = n_k = 2$, theorem 8.13 is obtained.

Let $X_1, \ldots, X_n$ be independent, normally distributed random variables with mean 0 and variance 1, and let a_{ij} $i,j=1,\ldots,n$, be constants with $a_{ij} = a_{ji}$. Then

$$Q = \sum_{i=1}^{n} \sum_{j=1}^{n} a_{ij} X_i X_j$$

is said to be a **quadratic form** in $X_1, \ldots, X_n$. If the a_{ij}'s are chosen in such a way that Q is non-negative regardless of the values of $X_1, \ldots, X_n$, then Q is said to be a **non-negative definite quadratic form**. Let **A** be the matrix with elements a_{ij} and **X** the column vector with elements $X_1, \ldots, X_n$. Then Q can be written

$$Q = \mathbf{X'AX}.$$

The rank of the n×n matrix **A** is said to be the rank of the quadratic form Q.

From definition 9.1, it follows that $Q_0 = X_1^2 + \ldots + X_n^2$ is χ^2-distributed with n degrees of freedom. We also note that Q_0 is the non-negative quadratic form $\mathbf{X'I_n X}$, where $\mathbf{I_n}$ is the (n×n) identity matrix. Suppose now that Q_0 can be written as

$$Q_0 = Q_1 + \ldots + Q_k,$$

where $Q_1, \ldots, Q_k$ are quadratic forms in $X_1, \ldots, X_n$. Then $Q_1, \ldots, Q_k$ is said to represent a decomposition of the quadratic form Q_0.

Theorem 9.3

Let $X_1, \ldots, X_n$ be independent random variables with $X_i \sim N(0,1)$, $i=1,\ldots,n$, and assume that

(9.5) $$\sum_{i=1}^{n} X_i^2 = Q_1 + \ldots + Q_k,$$

where $Q_1, \ldots, Q_k$ are non-negative definite quadratic forms in $X_1, \ldots, X_n$ with ranks $n_1, \ldots, n_k$. A necessary and sufficient condition for $Q_1, \ldots, Q_k$ to be independent is that $n = n_1 + \ldots + n_k$. If this is the case, then $Q_i \sim \chi^2(n_i)$.

Theorem 9.3 is called the **Cochran-Fisher theorem** or the **decomposition theorem** for the χ^2-distribution. While the additivity theorem specifies the distribution of a sum of independent, χ^2-distributed random variables, the decomposition theorem specifies the conditions under which quadratic forms, adding up to a χ^2-distributed random variable, are independent and χ^2-distributed.

Theorem 9.4

Let Q, Q_1 and Q_2 be non-negative definite quadratic forms in $X_1, \ldots, X_n$, where $X_i \sim N(0,1)$, $i = 1, \ldots, n$.

If $Q = Q_1 + Q_2$, where $Q \sim \chi^2(n)$ and $Q_1 \sim \chi^2(n_1)$ with $n_1 < n$, then

$$Q_2 \sim \chi^2(n - n_1).$$

Let A_1 and A_2 be the matrices connected with the quadratic forms Q_1 and Q_2. If $A_1'A_2 = 0$ then Q_1 and Q_2 are independent.

Theorem 9.5

Let $X_1, \ldots, X_n$ be independent, identically distributed random variables with $X_i \sim N(\mu, \sigma^2)$, $i = 1, \ldots, n$. Then

1) $\quad \overline{X} \sim N(\mu, \sigma^2/n),$

2) $\quad \dfrac{(n-1)S^2}{\sigma^2} = \sum\limits_{i=1}^{n} \dfrac{(X_i - \overline{X})^2}{\sigma^2} \sim \chi^2(n-1),$

and

3) $\quad \overline{X}$ and S^2 are independent.

Proof

The result 1) is proved in theorem 9.1. In order to prove 2), consider the decomposition

$$\sum_{i=1}^{n} (X_i - \mu)^2 = \sum_{i=1}^{n} (X_i - \overline{X})^2 + n(\overline{X} - \mu)^2.$$

Divided by σ^2 the left hand side becomes χ^2-distributed with n degrees of freedom. The second term on the right hand side becomes the square of a standardized normally distributed random variable, i.e. becomes

χ^2-distributed with 1 degree of freedom. From theorem 9.4, it then follows that $(n-1)S^2/\sigma^2 \sim \chi^2(n-1)$. Checking the last condition of theorem 9.4, it can be proved that the two χ^2-distributed quantities $\Sigma(X_i-\bar{X})^2/\sigma^2$ and $n(\bar{X}-\mu)^2/\sigma^2$ are independent. Hence, 3) also follows. □

9.3. The t-distribution and the F-distribution

Definition 9.2

Let U and Q be independent random variables with $U \sim N(0,1)$ and $Q \sim \chi^2(n)$. The random variable

$$T = U/\sqrt{Q/n}$$

is then said to follow a t-distribution with n degrees of freedom, written as $T \sim t(n)$.

Fig. 9.2 shows the density function for the t-distribution with 1, 2 and 10 degrees of freedom respectively. Also shown in fig. 9.2 is the density function for the standard normal distribution. As illustrated in the figure, the t-distribution has heavier tails than the standard normal distribution and as the degrees of freedom increase, the density function of the t-distribution approaches the standard normal density function.

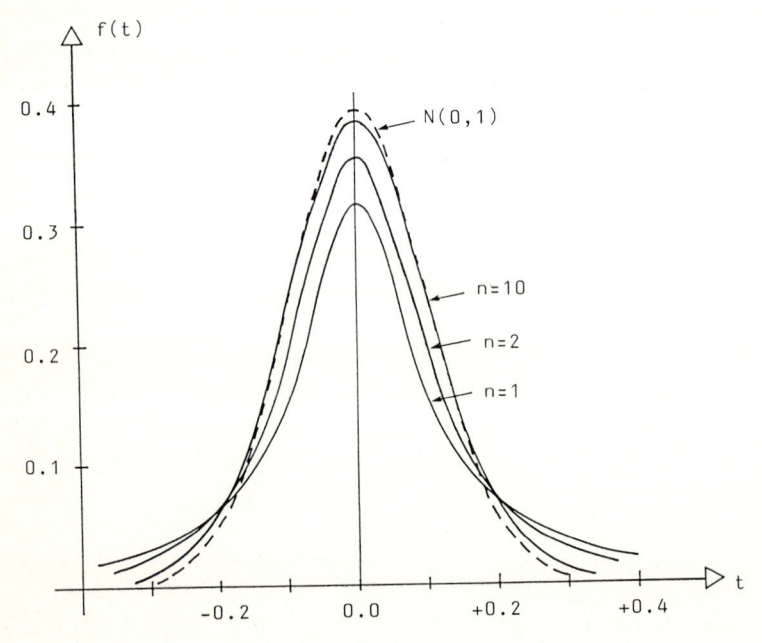

Fig. 9.2. Density functions for three t-distributions and the standard normal distribution.

It can be shown that when $T \sim t(n)$,

$$E[T] = 0 \quad \text{for } n \geq 2$$

and

$$\text{var}[T] = \frac{n}{n-2} \quad \text{for } n \geq 3.$$

For $n=1$, the mean value in the t-distribution does not exist and for $n \leq 2$ the variance does not exist. The t-distribution with one degree of freedom is called the **Cauchy-distribution**.

Theorem 9.6

If $X_1, \ldots, X_n$ are independent random variables with $X_i \sim N(\mu, \sigma^2)$, then

$$T = \sqrt{n}(\bar{X} - \mu)/S \sim t(n-1).$$

Proof
The result follows from theorem 9.5 and definition 9.2. □.

Definition 9.3

If Q_1 and Q_2 are independent random variables with $Q_1 \sim \chi^2(n_1)$ and $Q \sim \chi^2(n_2)$, then

$$V = \frac{Q_1/n_1}{Q_2/n_2}$$

follows an F-distribution with (n_1, n_2) degrees of freedom, written as $V \sim F(n_1, n_2)$.

An F-distribution is also called a **Fisher-distribution** after R.A. Fisher. Fig. 9.3 shows the F-distribution for three different combinations of degrees of freedom. Note that an F-distribution is skewed to the right.

From the definition of the F-distribution, it follows immediately that if $V \sim F(n_1, n_2)$ then

(9.6) $\qquad V^* = 1/V \sim F(n_2, n_1).$

Let

(9.7) $\qquad T = U/\sqrt{Q/f},$

where $U \sim N(0,1)$, $Q \sim \chi^2(f)$ and U and Q are independent. Squaring (9.7) gives

$$T^2 = fU^2/Q.$$

Since $U^2 \sim \chi^2(1)$, it thus follows that T^2 is F-distributed with $(1,f)$ degrees of freedom.

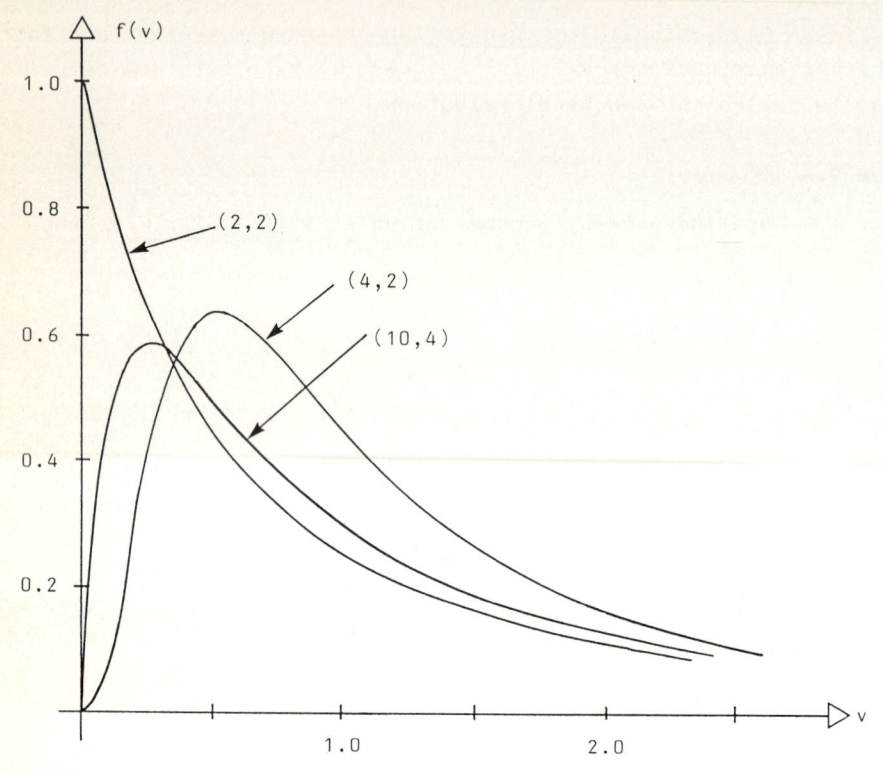

Fig. 9.3. Density functions of F-distributions with different numbers of degrees of freedom.

9.4. The law of large numbers

In chapter 3, the existence of a connection between the relative frequency $h(A)$ of an event in n independent repetitions of a random experiment and the probability $P(A)$ of the same event was mentioned. Empirically, this corresponds to $h(A)$ in some sense converging to $P(A)$ as the number of repetitions increases.

Definition 9.4

Let $X_1, X_2, \ldots$ be a sequence of random variables and c a constant such that for each $\varepsilon > 0$

(9.8) $P(|X_n - c| \le \epsilon) \to 1$ for $n \to \infty$.

The sequence is then said to converge in probability to c, which is written as $X_n \overset{P}{\to} c$.

The kind of convergence observed empirically when the relative frequency of an event stabilizes around some limiting value is convergence in probability, and the limiting value is the probability of the event.

Theorem 9.7

If $h_n(A)$ is the relative frequency of the event A in n independent repetitions of a random experiment and P(A) is the probability of A, then

$$P(|h_n(A) - P(A)| \le \epsilon) \to 1 \quad \text{as } n \to \infty$$

for every $\epsilon > 0$.

The theorem may be interpreted as follows. Assume that P(A) is surrounded by an interval. No matter how small this interval is, the probability of $h_n(A)$ being in the interval can be brought arbitrarily close to 1 by choosing n sufficiently large.

Theorem 9.8

Let X be a random variable with mean μ and variance σ^2. Then for every $\epsilon > 0$

(9.9) $P(|X - \mu| > \epsilon) \le \sigma^2 / \epsilon^2$.

Proof

Only the proof of the theorem in the continuous case will be given. Let f be the density function of X. Then

$$\sigma^2 = \int (x-\mu)^2 f(x) dx =$$

$$\int_{|x-\mu|>\epsilon} (x-\mu)^2 f(x) dx + \int_{|x-\mu|\le\epsilon} (x-\mu)^2 f(x) dx \ge \int_{|x-\mu|>\epsilon} (x-\mu)^2 f(x) dx \ge$$

$$\epsilon^2 \int_{|x-\mu|>\epsilon} f(x) dx = \epsilon^2 P(|X-\mu|>\epsilon).$$

It follows from this inequality that $P(|X-\mu|>\epsilon) \le \sigma^2/\epsilon^2$. $\square$.

Formula (9.9) is called **Tchebychev's inequality**.

Theorem 9.9

Let $X_1, X_2, \ldots$, be a sequence of independent, identically distributed random variables for which the mean μ exists. Let $\overline{X}_n = (X_1 + \ldots + X_n)/n$. Then for every $\varepsilon > 0$

$$P(|\overline{X}_n - \mu| \leq \varepsilon) \to 1 \quad \text{as } n \to \infty,$$

i.e. $\overline{X}_n$ converges in probability to μ.

Proof

The theorem is proved assuming that $\sigma^2 = \text{var}[X_i]$ exists. This condition is not necessary for the theorem to be valid, however. From Tchebychev's inequality, it follows that

$$P(|\overline{X}_n - \mu| > \varepsilon) \leq \sigma^2/(n\varepsilon^2) \to 0 \quad \text{for } n \to \infty$$

and hence

$$P(|\overline{X}_n - \mu| \leq \varepsilon) \to 1 \quad \text{for } n \to \infty. \square$$

Theorem 9.9 is called the **law of large numbers**.

Consider n repetitions of a random experiment and let X_i be a random variable for which

$$X_i = \begin{cases} 1 & \text{if the event } A \text{ occurs in the i'th repetition} \\ 0 & \text{if the event } \overline{A} \text{ occurs in the i'th repetition.} \end{cases}$$

Then

$$\overline{X}_n = h_n(A)$$

and

$$E[X_i] = 1 \cdot P(A) + 0 \cdot (1 - P(A)) = P(A).$$

Theorem 9.7 is therefore a special case of theorem 9.9.

Estimation theory is based on the study of sample functions which can be used as approximations to the values of unknown parameters. For example, if $X_1, \ldots, X_n$ are independent random variables with mean μ and variance σ^2, then (8.23) and (8.24) with $\overline{X} = \overline{X}_n$ give

$$E[\overline{X}] = \mu$$

and

$$\text{var}[\overline{X}] = \sigma^2/n.$$

According to theorem 9.9, $\overline{X}$ converges in probability to μ, so that with a sufficiently large n, the probability that $\overline{X}$ deviates more than ε from μ becomes arbitrarily small. Thus, with a probability approaching one, it can be ensured that the observed value of $\overline{X}$ is close to μ. This justifies the use of the average $\bar{x}$ as an estimate of the mean μ.

9.5. Limit theorems

Many sample functions used in the course of statistical analyses have distributions, which are difficult to derive and for which it is difficult to compute exact probabilities. However, in many cases, it is possible to compute approximate probabilities. Such approximations are usually based on so-called **limit theorems** which describe the behavior of the distribution of certain sample functions when the number of observations is large. The limiting distributions obtained by such theorems are called **asymptotic distributions**.

First a limit theorem for the binomial distribution is considered. Let $F(x)$ be the distribution function for a binomial distribution with parameters (n,p). If n is large, $F(x)$ can be approximated by a normal distribution function. This result is known as the **de Moivre-Laplace theorem** and is the oldest known limit theorem.

Theorem 9.10

Let $X_n \sim b(n,p)$ and let Φ be the distribution function for the standard normal distribution. If $U_n = (X_n - np)/\sqrt{np(1-p)}$, then for every u

(9.10) $P(U_n \leq u) \to \Phi(u)$ for $n \to \infty$.

For large values of n, it follows from theorem 9.10 that

(9.11) $P(X \leq x) = P\{(X-np)/\sqrt{np(1-p)} \leq (x-np)/\sqrt{np(1-p)}\} \simeq \Phi\left(\dfrac{x-np}{\sqrt{np(1-p)}}\right)$

for $X \sim b(n,p)$. Using (9.11), binomial probabilities can be calculated approximately as normal probabilities. This is an important and convenient result since it is impossible to tabulate the binomial probabilities for all combinations of n and p. The approximation

(9.12) $P(X \leq x) \simeq \Phi\left(\dfrac{x+0.5-np}{\sqrt{np(1-p)}}\right) = \Phi(u^*)$

is often preferred to (9.11) since it is more precise. Since

$P(a \leq X \leq b) = P(X \leq b) - P(X \leq a-1)$,

it follows from (9.12) that

(9.13) $$P(a < x \leq b) \simeq \Phi\left(\frac{b+0.5-np}{\sqrt{np(1-p)}}\right) - \Phi\left(\frac{a-0.5-np}{\sqrt{np(1-p)}}\right).$$

For the majority of situations, the approximations (9.12) and (9.13) are satisfactory if $np(1-p)>9$. The closer p is to 0 or 1, the larger the value of n needs to be in order to ensure a good approximation.

Table 9.1 shows a comparison of binomial probabilities and the corresponding normal approximations for $n=8$ and for $p=0.5$ and 0.2. These figures reveal that the approximation for a given value of n is much better for p close to 0.5 than for values of p close to 0 or 1. It can also be seen that the approximation is very good for $n=8$ and $p=\frac{1}{2}$, even though $np(1-p)$ in this case is less than 9.

<u>Table 9.1</u>. Numerical illustration of the approximation (9.12) for $n=8$ and $p=0.5$ and 0.2.

	p = 0.5			p = 0.2		
x	F(x)	$\Phi(u^*)$	$F(x)-\Phi(u^*)$	F(x)	$\Phi(u^*)$	$F(x)-\Phi(u^*)$
0	0.004	0.007	-0.003	0.168	0.166	0.002
1	0.035	0.038	-0.003	0.503	0.464	0.039
2	0.145	0.145	0.000	0.797	0.788	0.009
3	0.363	0.363	0.000	0.944	0.953	-0.009
4	0.637	0.637	0.000	0.990	0.995	-0.005
5	0.855	0.855	0.000	0.999	0.999	0.000
6	0.965	0.962	+0.003	1.000	1.000	0.000
7	0.996	0.993	+0.003	1.000	1.000	0.000
8	1.000	1.000	0.000	1.000	1.000	0.000

The de Moivre-Laplace theorem can also be used to approximate the α percentile x_α in a binomial distribution. Assume that $X \sim b(n,p)$. Then

$$\alpha = P(X \leq x_\alpha) \simeq \Phi\left(\frac{x_\alpha + 0.5 - np}{\sqrt{np(1-p)}}\right) = \Phi(u_\alpha),$$

such that

(9.14) $$x_\alpha \simeq np - 0.5 + u_\alpha \sqrt{np(1-p)}.$$

Example 9.1

Suppose we want to approximate the .90 percentile in a binomial distribution with $n=50$ and $p=0.5$. From a standard normal distribution table, we find $u_{.90}=1.28$ and hence, according to (9.14),

$$x_{.90} \simeq 50 \cdot 0.5 - 0.5 + 1.28\sqrt{50/4} = 29.03.$$

From a binomial distribution table, it is seen that x=29 corresponds to the 0.899 percentile. △.

The de Moivre-Laplace theorem is a special case of a more general result known as the **central limit theorem**. This theorem establishes the limiting distribution of the average $\bar{X}$ of n random variables under very general conditions. In the form stated here it applies to independent, identically distributed random variables.

Theorem 9.11

Let $X_1,\ldots,X_n$ be independent, identically distributed random variables for which $\mu=E[X_i]$ and $\sigma^2=\text{var}[X_i]$ exists. Then

(9.15) $$P\left(\frac{\bar{X}-\mu}{\sigma/\sqrt{n}} \leq u\right) \to \Phi(u) \quad \text{for } n\to\infty,$$

where $\bar{X}=(X_1+\ldots+X_n)/n$.

Since $E[\bar{X}]=\mu$ and $\text{var}[\bar{X}]=\sigma^2/n$, it follows from the theorem that the distribution of $\bar{X}$ can be approximated by a normal distribution with the same mean and variance as the distribution of $\bar{X}$, i.e.

(9.16) $$P(\bar{X} \leq x) \simeq \Phi\left(\frac{x-\mu}{\sigma/\sqrt{n}}\right).$$

Theorem 9.11 is remarkable because the form of the limiting distribution does not depend on the distribution of the random variables involved. The required size of n for the approximation to be satisfactory depends strongly on the form of the common distribution of the X's.

Example 9.2

The χ^2-distribution with one degree of freedom has mean 1 and variance 2. Let
$$Q = Q_1+\ldots+Q_n,$$
where $Q_1,\ldots,Q_n$ are independent, identically χ^2-distributed random variables with one degree of freedom. It then follows from definition 9.1 that $Q\sim\chi^2(n)$. The central limit theorem gives that Q is approximately normally distributed with mean n and variance 2n for n sufficiently large. △.

Theorem 9.12

Let X be Poisson distributed with parameter λ. Then

$$P\left(\frac{X-\lambda}{\sqrt{\lambda}} \leq u\right) \to \Phi(u) \quad \text{for } \lambda \to \infty.$$

From this theorem, it follows that the probabilities from a Poisson distribution with sufficiently large λ can be approximated by probabilities computed from a normal distribution with the same mean and variance as X. If X is Poisson distributed with parameter λ and λ is sufficiently large, then

(9.17) $\qquad P(X \leq x) \simeq \Phi\left(\frac{x+0.5-\lambda}{\sqrt{\lambda}}\right),$

where the term 0.5 improves the approximation as in (9.12). The approximation is satisfactory if the size of λ ensures that the Poisson distribution is almost symmetric. For most purposes the approximation is considered satisfactory for $\lambda > 9$.

For the hypergeometric distribution, limit theorems can be established in several ways. To avoid unnecessary complications, the approximation corresponding to (9.12) and (9.17) will be presented. Let X be hypergeometrically distributed with point probabilities

$$P(X = x) = \frac{\binom{N\theta}{x}\binom{N(1-\theta)}{n-x}}{\binom{N}{n}}.$$

Then

(9.18) $\qquad P(X \leq x) \simeq \Phi\left(\frac{x+0.5-n\theta}{\sqrt{n\theta(1-\theta)\frac{N-n}{N-1}}}\right)$

if N is large, θ is not too close to 0 or 1 and n is small compared with N.

If $X \sim b(n,p)$, X can be written as

$$X = X_1 + \ldots + X_n,$$

where $X_i \sim b(1,p)$ and $X_1, \ldots, X_n$ are independent. Hence, $E[X_i] = p$, $\text{var}[X_i] = p(1-p)$ and theorem 9.10 follows by substituting these values in theorem 9.11. Theorem 9.12 can also be established as a special case of theorem 9.11. If $X \sim Ps(\lambda)$, the random variable X might have been generated as a sum of independent variables $X_1, \ldots, X_n$ where $X_i \sim Ps(\lambda/n)$. Theorem 9.12 then follows by inserting $\mu = E[X_i] = \lambda/n$ and $\sigma^2 = \text{var}[X_i] = \lambda/n$ in (9.15).

The result (9.18) is on the other hand not a special case of theorem 9.11, since a random variable following a hypergeomtric distribution cannot be written as a sum of independent, identically distributed random variables.

10. Estimation

10.1. The statistical model

A statistical analysis enables one to draw conclusions based on a description of a given data set by means of a **statistical model**. The model should describe both the systematic and the random variation in the data so that all likely questions can be formulated within the framework of the model.

Most statistical models are based on the assumption that the data comprise observations $x_1, \ldots, x_n$ of n random variables $X_1, \ldots, X_n$. The statistical model is then a set of assumptions concerning the joint distribution of $X_1, \ldots, X_n$, usually expressed in the form of their density or point probability, f.

In most of the models considered in this book, it is assumed that f is known except for the values of a finite number of real-valued parameters. The statistical model thus takes the form

$$(10.1) \quad f(x_1, \ldots, x_n | \theta), \quad \theta \in \Theta,$$

where $\theta = (\theta_1, \ldots, \theta_k)$ represents unknown parameters. In this way, a model is a set of probability distributions or a family of probability distributions indexed by a finite number of real parameters. The **parameter space** Θ gives the range of the parameters and is an essential part of the model. In many cases, Θ is defined in an obvious manner, and a specification of Θ is omitted in such cases.

The **statistical inference theory** is a collection of rules or principles used for the interpretation of a set of data described by a model. The main question dealt with in statistical inference theory are how to assess the consistency between the data and the model, and how to draw inference about the parameters of the model, i.e. how to estimate the parameters and make conclusions about their values.

Example 10.1

As an example of a situation where data can be regarded as generated by a statistical model, consider a random sample from a finite population. Assume that the population consists of N units of which $M=N\theta$ are of type A, while the remaining N-M are of type B, and assume that a random sample of size n is drawn without replacement. As seen in section 6.5, the number x of units of type A in the sample is the observed value of a random variable X which follows a hypergeometric distribution with point probabilities

$$(10.2) \qquad P(X=x) = f(x|\theta) = \frac{\binom{N\theta}{x}\binom{N(1-\theta)}{n-x}}{\binom{N}{n}}$$

and parameter space $\Theta = \{0, \frac{1}{N}, \frac{2}{N}, \ldots, 1\}$. △.

Example 10.2

Suppose that the observations $x_1, \ldots, x_n$ are collected under identical conditions such that they can be regarded as observed values of n independent, identically distributed random variables $X_1, \ldots, X_n$. If the variation of the observations can be described by a normal distribution, it is possible to formulate a statistical model for the data in terms of the simultaneous density function for $X_1, \ldots, X_n$ as

$$f(x_1, \ldots, x_n | \mu, \sigma^2) = \prod_{i=1}^{n} \frac{1}{\sigma\sqrt{2\pi}} \exp\{-\tfrac{1}{2}(x_i - \mu)^2/\sigma^2\}.$$

The model depends on the unknown parameters (μ, σ^2) with parameter space $\Theta = \{-\infty < \mu < +\infty, \ 0 < \sigma^2 < +\infty\}$. △.

10.2. Estimation

Suppose that the data $x_1, \ldots, x_n$ are described by the model $f(x_1, \ldots, x_n | \theta)$. Furthermore, assume that f is known except for the value of the real parameter θ.

In this section we shall discuss the calculation of the "best" value of the parameter from the existing data. This value is called a **point estimate** of θ. A point estimate of θ is denoted by $\hat{\theta}$ and can be written as

$$\hat{\theta} = \hat{\theta}(x_1, \ldots, x_n),$$

thus emphasizing that the estimate is a function of a given set of observations.

Since $x_1, \ldots, x_n$ are observations of random variables, repeated calculations of $\hat{\theta}$ from different sets of data cannot be expected to result in identical estimates, so that uncertainty is an inevitable part of the estimation problem.

To describe the uncertainty, consider the random variable

$$\hat{\theta} = \hat{\theta}(X_1,\ldots,X_n) ,$$

called an **estimator** of θ. Since $x_1,\ldots,x_n$ are observations of $X_1,\ldots,X_n$, the estimate $\hat{\theta}$ is an observation of the estimator $\hat{\theta}$ (note that identical symbols are used for the estimate and the corresponding estimator). The uncertainty connected with the estimation can, therefore, be described in terms of the distribution of the estimator, which in principle can be determined from knowledge of the joint distribution of $X_1,\ldots,X_n$.

The estimation problem can also be formulated as follows. The given data are assumed to be generated by the model for a fixed but unknown value of the parameter, the so-called **true value**, and the estimate represents an approximation to this true value. However, random variation makes it impossible to guarantee that the estimate is identical with the true value or even that it is close to the true value. On the other hand if the distribution of $\hat{\theta}$ is concentrated around the true value of the parameter, whatever this may be, the estimator can be regarded as satisfactory.

Example 10.3

Suppose we want to estimate the probability θ of heads in the toss of a coin, and let x be the number of heads observed in 10 tosses. As an estimate for θ, one may choose $\hat{\theta}=x/10$, since the relative frequency of an event is expected to be close to the probability of the event in a large number of independent random experiments. The number of heads x and the estimate $\hat{\theta}(x)=x/10$ obtained in 10 repetitions each consisting of 10 tosses with the coin are shown in the tabel below.

x	4	6	7	4	4	4	3	3	5	4
$\hat{\theta}(x)$	0.4	0.6	0.7	0.4	0.4	0.4	0.3	0.3	0.5	0.4

Each value of $\hat{\theta}(x)$ is an estimate of the same unknown parameter θ, but since the estimates are based on different samples, their values are different, and it is impossible to determine which one, if any, is the true value of θ. In the present case, it should be noted that the estimates vary around 0.5, which could be the true value of θ if the coin were symmetrically balanced. This is illustrated in fig. 10.1, where the distribution of the estimator $\hat{\theta}=X/10$ is shown under the assumption that $X \sim b(10, 0.5)$. $\triangle$

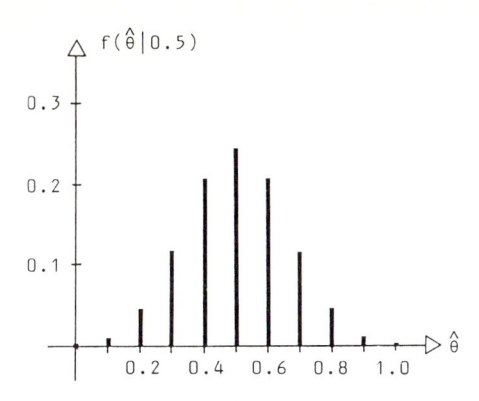

Fig. 10.1. Point probabilities $f(\hat{\theta}|0.5)$ for the estimator $\hat{\theta}=X/10$ when $\theta=0.5$.

10.3. Maximum likelihood estimation

The most widely used method for deriving an estimator for a parameter in a statistical model is the so-called **maximum likelihood** (ML) **method**.

Consider first the case where θ is real-valued and $\mathbf{x}=(x_1,\ldots,x_n)$ are assumed to be observations of discrete random variables $\mathbf{X}=(X_1,\ldots,X_n)$ with point probability $f(\mathbf{x}|\theta)$. It is assumed that f is known except for the value of the parameter θ with sample space Θ.

If $f(\mathbf{x}|\theta)$ is regarded as a function of θ given the data $\mathbf{x}$, the **likelihood function** $L(\theta|\mathbf{x})$ is defined as

(10.3) $\qquad L(\theta|\mathbf{x}) = f(\mathbf{x}|\theta)$.

The difference between L and f is simply that f is a function of $\mathbf{x}$ for a given value of θ, while L is a function of θ for given $\mathbf{x}$.

The value of the likelihood function for a fixed value θ_0 of θ can be regarded as an expression of the degree of agreement between the data and θ_0. The larger the value of $L(\theta_0|\mathbf{x})$, the larger the probability that a model with parameter θ_0 has generated the data. The function L thus describes the degree of agreement between the values of $\theta \in \Theta$ and the data.

If this interpretation of L is adopted, it is natural to estimate the unknown parameter θ by the value $\hat{\theta}$ which maximizes the likelihood function, i.e. to choose $\hat{\theta}$ as the estimate of θ if

$$L(\hat{\theta}|\mathbf{x}) = \max_{\theta} L(\theta|\mathbf{x}) \; .$$

The value $\hat{\theta}$ determined in this way is called the **ML-estimate** of θ. Since

$\hat{\theta}$ is a function of **x** it is written $\hat{\theta}(\mathbf{x})$, so $\hat{\theta}$ can be regarded as an observation of the random variable $\hat{\theta}(\mathbf{X})$, the **ML-estimator** of θ.

In practice the ML-estimate is often computed as the solution of the **likelihood equation**

(10.4) $$\frac{dl(\theta|\mathbf{x})}{d\theta} = 0 ,$$

where

$$l(\theta|\mathbf{x}) = \ln L(\theta|\mathbf{x}) ,$$

i.e. by maximizing the **log-likelihood function** $l(\theta|\mathbf{x})$. Since the logarithm is an increasing function, l and L both attain their maximum at the same parameter value. However, it should be noted that a solution to the likelihood equation does not necessarily correspond to a maximum of $l(\theta|\mathbf{x})$, local or global. If (10.4) has only one solution, $\hat{\theta}$, this corresponds in regular cases to an absolute maximum if $d^2 l(\theta|\mathbf{x})/d\theta^2|_{\theta=\hat{\theta}} < 0$. If, on the other hand, $d^2 l(\theta|\mathbf{x})/d\theta^2|_{\theta=\hat{\theta}} > 0$ the maximum of the likelihood function must usually be searched for on the boundary of the parameter space. If there is more than one solution to (10.4), the local maxima must be compared in order to determine the absolute maximum.

Example 10.4

Let $x_1,\ldots,x_n$ be observations of independent, identically distributed random variables $X_1,\ldots,X_n$ with point probabilities

$$f(x|\theta) = \theta^x (1-\theta)^{1-x}, \quad x=0,1 \text{ and } \theta \in (0,1).$$

The point probabilities of $X_1,\ldots,X_n$ are

$$f(x_1,\ldots,x_n|\theta) = \prod_{i=1}^{n} f(x_i|\theta) = \theta^{\Sigma x_i}(1-\theta)^{n-\Sigma x_i}.$$

Hence the likelihood function is

$$L(\theta|x_1,\ldots,x_n) = \theta^{\Sigma x_i}(1-\theta)^{n-\Sigma x_i},$$

while the log-likelihood function becomes

$$l(\theta|x_1,\ldots,x_n) = \Sigma x_i \ln\theta + (n-\Sigma x_i)\ln(1-\theta).$$

The ML-estimate of θ is computed as a solution to

$$\frac{\Sigma x_i}{\theta} - \frac{n-\Sigma x_i}{1-\theta} = 0 ,$$

so that

$$\hat{\theta} = \frac{\Sigma x_i}{n}.$$

Note that the likelihood function, and hence the ML-estimate, only depends on the observations through Σx_i. Which of the x_i's are 0 and which are 1 is of no consequence for the value of $\hat{\theta}$. The log-likelihood function for $n=20$ and $\Sigma x_i=7$ is illustrated graphically in fig. 10.2.△.

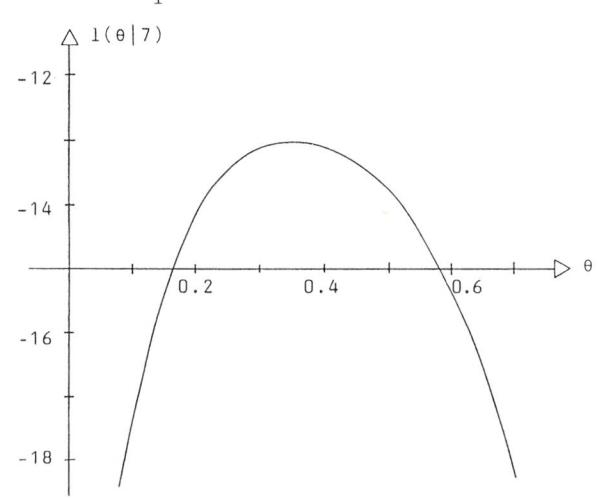

Fig. 10.2. The log-likelihood function for $n=20$ and $\Sigma x_1=7$.

Example 10.5

Let $x_1,\ldots,x_n$ be observed values of independent, identically Poisson distributed random variables $X_1,\ldots,X_n$ with parameter λ. The point probability of $X_1,\ldots,X_n$ is then given by

$$f(x_1,\ldots,x_n|\lambda) = \prod_{i=1}^{n} e^{-\lambda} \frac{\lambda^{x_i}}{x_i!} = e^{-n\lambda} \frac{\lambda^{\Sigma x_i}}{\prod x_i!}.$$

The log-likelihood function takes the form

$$l(\lambda|x_1,\ldots,x_n) = -n\lambda + (\Sigma x_i)\ln\lambda - \sum_{i=1}^{n} \ln(x_i!),$$

and accordingly the likelihood equation becomes

$$\frac{\partial l(\lambda|x_1,\ldots,x_n)}{\partial \lambda} = -n + \frac{1}{\lambda}\sum_{i=1}^{n} x_i = 0.$$

Solving this equation with respect to λ yields the ML-estimate

$$\hat{\lambda} = \sum_{i=1}^{n} x_i/n . \triangle.$$

Example 10.6

Suppose x is the observed value of a binomially distributed random variable with parameters (n,θ). The likelihood function is

$$L(\theta|x) = \binom{n}{x}\theta^x(1-\theta)^{n-x} , \quad \theta \in (0,1) .$$

This function is proportional to the likelihood function considered in example 10.4 with $x=\Sigma x_i$. Since the proportionality factor $\binom{n}{x}$ does not depend on θ, it follows that the ML-estimate of θ in this example and the ML-estimate of θ in example 10.4 are identical, i.e.

$$\hat{\theta} = x/n .$$

This is a consequence of the fact that all information about θ contained in $x_1,\ldots,x_n$ in example 10.4 is summarized by the sum Σx_i. In such a case, Σx_i is said to be a sufficient statistic for the parameter θ. $\triangle$.

Let $\mathbf{x}=(x_1,\ldots,x_n)$ be observations of continuous random variables $\mathbf{X}=(X_1,\ldots,X_n)$ with simultaneous density function $f(\mathbf{x}|\theta)$. The likelihood function $L(\theta|\mathbf{x})$ is then defined as

(10.5) $\qquad L(\theta|\mathbf{x}) = f(\mathbf{x}|\theta) .$

In the continuous case, $L(\theta|\mathbf{x})$ cannot be interpreted as the probability of observing the given data set $x_1,\ldots,x_n$. It follows, on the other hand, from the definition of a density function, that $f(\mathbf{x}|\theta)$ is proportional to the probability of observing a set of observations in a small neighbourhood of $\mathbf{x}$ with a proportionality factor which is independent of θ. Accordingly, the value of the likelihood function at θ_0 can still be interpreted as a measurement of the degree of agreement between θ_0 and $\mathbf{x}$.

Analogous to the discrete case, the ML-estimate $\hat{\theta}$ is defined as that value of θ which maximizes $L(\theta|\mathbf{x})$. It is usually convenient to determine $\hat{\theta}$ as a solution to the likelihood equation (10.4), where, as in the discrete case, $l(\theta|\mathbf{x})$ is defined as

$$l(\theta|\mathbf{x}) = \ln L(\theta|\mathbf{x}) .$$

If θ is vector-valued, i.e. $\boldsymbol{\theta}=(\theta_1,\ldots,\theta_k)$, the ML-estimate

$\hat{\theta} = (\hat{\theta}_1, \ldots, \hat{\theta}_k)$ is still defined as the value $\hat{\theta}$ for which

$$L(\hat{\theta}|x) = \max_{\theta} L(\theta|x) .$$

The ML-estimate is then as a rule obtained as the solution to the likelihood equations

(10.6) $\qquad \dfrac{\partial l(\theta_1, \ldots, \theta_k | x)}{\partial \theta_j} = 0 , \quad j=1,\ldots,k .$

As in the one-dimensional case, it must be ensured that a set of solutions to (10.6) is also a global maximum of the likelihood function.

Example 10.7

Let $x_1, \ldots, x_n$ be observed values of independent, identically distributed random variables $X_1, \ldots, X_n$ with $X_i \sim N(\mu, \sigma^2)$. The likelihood function is

$$L(\mu, \sigma^2 | x_1, \ldots, x_n) = \prod_{i=1}^{n} \dfrac{1}{\sigma\sqrt{2\pi}} \cdot \exp\{-\tfrac{1}{2}(x_i - \mu)^2 / \sigma^2\}$$

$$= \sigma^{-n} (2\pi)^{-n/2} \exp\{-\tfrac{1}{2} \Sigma (x_i - \mu)^2 / \sigma^2\} ,$$

and the log-likelihood function is

$$l(\mu, \sigma^2 | x_1, \ldots, x_n) = -\tfrac{1}{2}(n \ln \sigma^2 + n \ln(2\pi) + \Sigma (x_i - \mu)^2 / \sigma^2) .$$

The ML-estimate of μ can be determined as the solution, $\hat{\mu}$, to the likelihood equation

$$\dfrac{\partial l(\mu, \sigma^2 | x_1, \ldots, x_n)}{\partial \mu} = \sum_{i=1}^{n} (x_i - \mu)/\sigma^2 = 0 ,$$

so that

$$\hat{\mu} = \sum_{i=1}^{n} x_i / n ,$$

which is seen to be independent of the value of σ^2.

If both μ and σ^2 are to be estimated, the joint solution, $(\hat{\mu}, \hat{\sigma}^2)$, to the equations

$$\dfrac{\partial l(\mu, \sigma^2 | x_1, \ldots, x_n)}{\partial \mu} = \Sigma (x_i - \mu)/\sigma^2 = 0$$

and

$$\dfrac{\partial l(\mu, \sigma^2 | x_1, \ldots, x_n)}{\partial \sigma^2} = -\dfrac{n}{2} \dfrac{1}{\sigma^2} + \dfrac{1}{2} \dfrac{\Sigma (x_i - \mu)^2}{(\sigma^2)^2} = 0$$

must be obtained. Then

$$\hat{\mu} = \sum_{i=1}^{n} x_i/n = \bar{x}$$

and

$$\hat{\sigma}^2 = \frac{\sum_{i=1}^{n}(x_i-\bar{x})^2}{n} \quad .\triangle.$$

10.4. Unbiased estimators

Let $x_1,\ldots,x_n$ be the observed values of random variables $X_1,\ldots,X_n$ with density or point probability $f(x_1,\ldots,x_n|\theta)$, where θ is a fixed but unknown value, called the true value. In section 10.2, it was mentioned that it is impossible to guarantee that the estimate is in all cases close to the true parameter value. It is, therefore, necessary to summarize the properties of an estimation method by distributional properties of the estimator. In general, an estimator is considered more attractive, the more its distribution is concentrated around the true parameter value, no matter what this value may be.

Definition 10.1

If

$$E[\hat{\theta}(X_1,\ldots,X_n)|\theta] = \theta$$

for any $\theta \in \Theta$, then $\hat{\theta}$ is said to be an unbiased estimator of θ.

In definition 10.1, the notation $E[\hat{\theta}|\theta]$ is used to emphasize that the mean value of $\hat{\theta}$ is calculated in a distribution with parameter value θ. That an estimator is **unbiased** thus means that even if one cannot be sure that an individual estimate is close to the true value, then in repeated applications of the method the average value of the estimates will be close to the true parameter value.

Example 10.8

A population consists of N individuals of which θN ($0<\theta<1$) are of type A, while the remaining $(1-\theta)N$ are of type B. From the population a sample of size n is drawn at random and without replacement. Let x be the number of individuals of type A sampled and consider

$$\hat{\theta} = x/n$$

as an estimate of θ. Since x is the observed value of a hypergeometrically distributed random variable X with point probabilities given by (10.2), then

$$E[\hat{\theta}|\theta] = E[X/n|\theta] = \frac{n\theta}{n} = \theta,$$

and $\hat{\theta}$ is thus seen to be an unbiased estimator of θ. This means that if a large number of samples are drawn independently from the population, the average value of the estimates must be close to θ, the true proportion of individuals of type A. △

If $\hat{\theta}$ is an unbiased estimator, var[$\hat{\theta}$] can be used as a measure of the precision of the estimate, since the more concentrated the distribution of $\hat{\theta}$ is around its mean θ, the smaller var[$\hat{\theta}$] is. If two unbiased estimators $\hat{\theta}_1(X_1,\ldots,X_n)$ and $\hat{\theta}_2(X_1,\ldots,X_n)$ of θ are available, the estimator with the smallest variance should be preferred.

In certain situations, it is possible to find an unbiased estimator whose variance is smaller than the variance of any other unbiased estimator. Such an estimator is said to be a **minimum variance unbiased estimator**.

Definition 10.2

The bias, b, of an estimator $\hat{\theta}$ is given by

$$b = E[\hat{\theta}(X_1,\ldots,X_n)|\theta] - \theta.$$

Theorem 10.1

Let $\hat{\theta}$ be an estimator of θ with bias b. Then

$$E[(\hat{\theta}-\theta)^2] = \text{var}[\hat{\theta}] + b^2.$$

Proof

$$\begin{aligned}E[(\hat{\theta}-\theta)^2] &= E[(\hat{\theta}-E[\hat{\theta}]+E[\hat{\theta}]-\theta)^2]\\ &= E[(\hat{\theta}-E[\hat{\theta}])^2] + E[(E[\hat{\theta}]-\theta)^2] + 2E[(\hat{\theta}-E[\hat{\theta}])(E[\hat{\theta}]-\theta)]\\ &= \text{var}[\hat{\theta}] + b^2 + 2(E[\hat{\theta}]-\theta)E[(\hat{\theta}-E[\hat{\theta}])]\\ &= \text{var}[\hat{\theta}] + b^2. \quad \square\end{aligned}$$

The quantity $E[(\hat{\theta}-\theta)^2]$ is called the **mean square error** or the **estimation error**. For an unbiased estimator, the estimation error is equal to the variance of the estimator. If an estimator is biased, the estimation error is a better measure of precision than the variance.

An unbiased estimator should not unconditionally be prefered to a biased estimator. Let $\hat{\theta}_1$ and $\hat{\theta}_2$ be two estimators for θ, where $\hat{\theta}_1$ is unbiased with variance σ_1^2 and $\hat{\theta}_2$ is biased with bias b and variance σ_2^2. According to theorem 10.1,

$$E[(\hat{\theta}_1-\theta)^2] = \sigma_1^2$$

and

$$E[(\hat{\theta}_2-\theta)^2] = \sigma_2^2+b^2 .$$

If σ_2^2 is so much smaller than σ_1^2 that $\sigma_2^2+b^2<\sigma_1^2$, then $\hat{\theta}_2$ should be preferred to $\hat{\theta}_1$, as $\hat{\theta}_2$ has the smallest estimation error. In this case the bias of $\hat{\theta}_2$ is more than counterbalanced by its smaller variance, as illustrated in fig. 10.3.

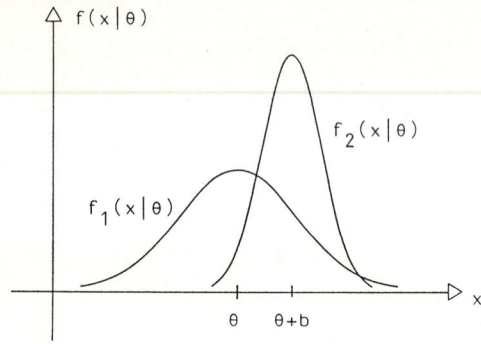

Fig.10.3. Comparison of the density function f_1 for an unbiased estimator $\hat{\theta}_1$ and the density function f_2 for a biased estimator $\hat{\theta}_2$.

The type of comparisons exemplified in fig. 10.3 are often complicated by the fact that the bias usually depends on the unknown value of the parameter θ. Hence, the difference between $\sigma_2^2+b^2$ and σ_1^2 also depends on θ.

A less attractive property of unbiased estimators is their lack of invariance under transformations. If $\hat{\theta}$ is unbiased for θ, it is natural to estimate $g(\theta)$ by $g(\hat{\theta})$, where g is a real-valued function. But $g(\hat{\theta})$ is only an unbiased estimator of $g(\theta)$ if $g(\theta)$ is a linear function of θ.

Example 10.9

Let $X_1,\ldots,X_n$ be independent, identically distributed random variables, with $X_i \sim N(\mu,\sigma^2)$. As an estimator of σ^2, when μ is unknown, consider

$$S^2 = \frac{1}{n-1}\Sigma(X_i-\overline{X})^2 \ .$$

From theorem 9.5, it follows that $(n-1)S^2/\sigma^2$ is χ^2-distributed with $n-1$ degrees of freedom. The mean value of a χ^2-distribution is according to (9.4) equal to the number of degrees of freedom. Hence,

$$E[(n-1)S^2/\sigma^2] = n-1 \ ,$$

such that

$$E[S^2] = \sigma^2 \ ,$$

and S^2 is an unbiased estimator of σ^2. As an estimator of the standard deviation σ, $S=\sqrt{S^2}$ can be used. However, S is not an unbiased estimator of σ. The ML-estimator of σ^2 is, according to example 10.7,

$$\hat{\sigma}^2 = \frac{n-1}{n}S^2 \ .$$

This estimator is biased since

$$E[\hat{\sigma}^2] = \frac{n-1}{n}E[S^2] = \frac{n-1}{n}\sigma^2 \ .$$

The precision of $\hat{\sigma}^2$ and S^2 can be compared through their estimation errors. Since $(n-1)S^2/\sigma^2 \sim \chi^2(n-1)$, it follows from formula (9.4) that

$$\text{var}[(n-1)S^2/\sigma^2] = 2(n-1) \ ,$$

and hence that

$$\text{var}[S^2] = \frac{2\sigma^4}{n-1} \ .$$

On the other hand, it follows from theorem 10.1 that

$$E[(\hat{\sigma}^2-\sigma^2)^2] = \text{var}[\hat{\sigma}^2]+\left(\frac{n-1}{n}\sigma^2-\sigma^2\right)^2 = \left(\frac{n-1}{n}\right)^2\frac{2\sigma^4}{n-1}+\frac{\sigma^4}{n^2}=\frac{2n-1}{n^2}\sigma^4 \ ,$$

and since $2/(n-1)>(2n-1)/n^2$ for all $n\geq 2$, the ML-estimator is more precise than S^2. If unbiasedness were sacrificed, it would be acceptable to use $\hat{\sigma}^2$.

S^2 is usually preferred to $\hat{\sigma}^2$, not because it is unbiased, but because of other convenient distributional properties. $\triangle$.

Example 10.10

If X is binomially distributed with parameters (n,θ), then the ML-estimator of θ is

$$\hat{\theta} = X/n,$$

as seen in example 10.6. Since

$$E[\hat{\theta}|\theta] = E[X/n|\theta] = \frac{1}{n}E[X|\theta] = \frac{1}{n}\cdot n\theta = \theta,$$

$\hat{\theta}$ is an unbiased estimator of θ with variance

$$\text{var}[\hat{\theta}|\theta] = \text{var}[X/n|\theta] = \frac{\text{var}[X|\theta]}{n^2} = \frac{\theta(1-\theta)}{n}. \triangle.$$

Example 10.11

Let $X_1, \ldots, X_n$ be independent, identically Poisson distributed variables with parameter λ. In example 10.5, it was shown that

$$\hat{\lambda} = \frac{1}{n}\sum_{i=1}^{n} X_i = \overline{X}$$

is the ML-estimator of λ. From (8.21), it follows that

$$E[\hat{\lambda}] = \Sigma E[X_i]/n = \frac{n\lambda}{n} = \lambda,$$

so that $\hat{\lambda}$ is unbiased. The variance of $\hat{\lambda}$ is

$$\text{var}[\hat{\lambda}] = \frac{1}{n^2}\Sigma\text{var}[X_i] = \frac{n\lambda}{n^2} = \lambda/n.$$

Note that in this example and in example 10.10, the variance of the ML-estimator is proportional to 1/n and thus decreases as n increases. $\triangle$.

Example 10.12

From the data in table 10.1, we want to estimate the probability that a live birth child in Greater Copenhagen is a boy.

Table 10.1. Live births in Greater Copenhagen distributed according to municipality and sex, 1960.

Municipality \ Sex	Girls	Boys	Total
City of Copenhagen	4857	5019	9876
Frederiksberg	556	635	1191
Gentofte	491	574	1065
Other municipalities	4119	4343	8462

Source: Vital statistics 1960. Danmarks Statistik.

Let n_1, n_2, n_3 and n_4 be the total number of live births in each of the four regions and let X_1, X_2, X_3 and X_4 be random variables representing the number of boys in each region. Assume that $X_1,\ldots,X_4$ are independent with $X_i \sim b(n_i,\theta)$. Let us compare the following estimators of θ:

$$\hat{\theta}_1 = \frac{X_1+X_2+X_3+X_4}{n_1+n_2+n_3+n_4}$$

and

$$\hat{\theta}_2 = \frac{1}{4}\left(\frac{X_1}{n_1} + \frac{X_2}{n_2} + \frac{X_3}{n_3} + \frac{X_4}{n_4}\right).$$

Both estimators are unbiased, since

$$E[\hat{\theta}_1] = \frac{1}{n_1+n_2+n_3+n_4}E[X_1+X_2+X_3+X_4]$$

$$= \frac{1}{n_1+n_2+n_3+n_4}(n_1\theta+n_2\theta+n_3\theta+n_4\theta) = \theta$$

and

$$E[\hat{\theta}_2] = \frac{1}{4}\left(\frac{1}{n_1}E[X_1]+\frac{1}{n_2}E[X_2]+\frac{1}{n_3}E[X_3]+\frac{1}{n_4}E[X_4]\right) = \theta.$$

Furthermore,

$$\mathrm{var}[\hat{\theta}_1] = \frac{1}{(n_1+n_2+n_3+n_4)^2}\mathrm{var}[X_1+X_2+X_3+X_4] = \frac{\theta(1-\theta)}{n_1+n_2+n_3+n_4}$$

and

$$\mathrm{var}[\hat{\theta}_2] = \frac{1}{16}(n_1^{-2}\mathrm{var}[X_1]+n_2^{-2}\mathrm{var}[X_2]+n_3^{-2}\mathrm{var}[X_3]+n_4^{-2}\mathrm{var}[X_4])$$

$$= \frac{\theta(1-\theta)}{16}\left(\frac{1}{n_1}+\frac{1}{n_2}+\frac{1}{n_3}+\frac{1}{n_4}\right).$$

Thus, since

$$\frac{1}{n_1+n_2+n_3+n_4} = \frac{1}{9876+1191+1065+8462} = \frac{1}{20594} = 0.49 \cdot 10^{-4}$$

and

$$\frac{1}{16}\left(\frac{1}{9876}+\frac{1}{1191}+\frac{1}{1065}+\frac{1}{8462}\right) = 1.25 \cdot 10^{-4},$$

it follows that the ML-estimate $\hat{\theta}_1$ has the smaller variance and therefore should be preferred to $\hat{\theta}_2$. It can be shown that $\mathrm{var}[\hat{\theta}_1]$ is less than or equal to $\mathrm{var}[\hat{\theta}_2]$, regardless of the values of n_1, n_2, n_3 and n_4. △

10.5. Consistency

As the sample size increases, it is reasonable to expect that the precision of an estimator increases. It is therefore quite natural to require that the estimate be very close to the true parameter value if the sample size is large enough. In order to study the properties of an estimation method as the sample size increases, the dependency of the estimator on the sample size must be determined. Consider thus the sequence of estimators

$$\hat{\theta}_n = \hat{\theta}(X_1,\ldots,X_n) \quad, \quad n=n_0, \; n_0+1, \ldots$$

Definition 10.3
Let $\hat{\theta}_1, \hat{\theta}_2, \ldots$ be a sequence of estimators of the parameter θ. The sequence is then said to be consistent for θ if, for any $\varepsilon > 0$,

(10.7) $\qquad P(|\hat{\theta}_n - \theta| \leq \varepsilon | \theta) \to 1 \text{ for } n \to \infty$.

Hence, $\hat{\theta}_n$ is consistent if the probability of observing an estimate deviating more than ε from θ can be made arbitrarily small if n is made large enough, however small ε may be. This means that the distribution of $\hat{\theta}_n$ becomes more and more concentrated around θ as n increases so that $\hat{\theta}_n$ can be expected to be very close to θ for large values of n.

Definition 9.4 and (10.7) gives that $\hat{\theta}_n \xrightarrow{P} \theta$, i.e. $\hat{\theta}_n$ is consistent if the estimator converges in probability to the true value. The concept of consistency is illustrated in fig. 10.4.

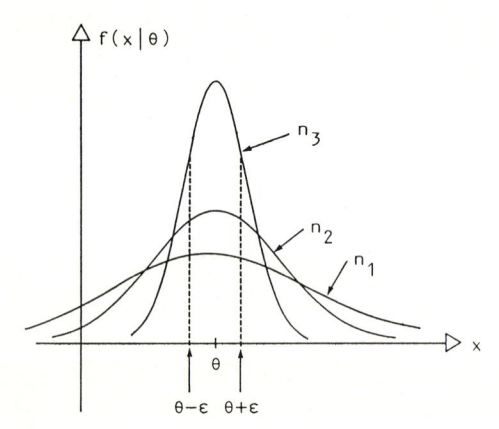

Fig.10.4. The density function of a consistent estimator $\hat{\theta}_n$ for $n_1 < n_2 < n_3$.

Consistency is an asymptotic property. The fact that an estimator is consistent does not, therefore, give any information about its small sample properties. Consequently, consistency in itself cannot justify the use of an estimator.

From Tchebychev's inequality, theorem 9.8, it follows that $\hat{\theta}_n$ is a consistent estimator of θ if

1) $E[\hat{\theta}_n] = \theta$

and

2) $\text{var}[\hat{\theta}_n] \to 0$ for $n \to \infty$.

In fact, if 1) and 2) hold, then

$$P(|\hat{\theta}_n - \theta| > \varepsilon) \le \frac{\text{var}[\hat{\theta}_n]}{\varepsilon^2} \to 0 \quad \text{for } n \to \infty .$$

Example 10.13

In example 10.5, it was shown that if $X_1, \ldots, X_n$ are independent, identically Poisson distributed variables with parameter λ, then $\hat{\lambda} = \overline{X}$ is the ML-estimator of λ. In example 10.11, it was further shown that $E[\hat{\lambda}] = \lambda$ and $\text{var}[\hat{\lambda}] = \lambda/n$. Thus, conditions 1) and 2) are satisfied and $\hat{\lambda}$ is a consistent estimator of λ.

What is more, the central limit theorem, theorem 9.12, gives that $\hat{\lambda}$ is asymptotically normally distributed with mean λ and variance λ/n. △.

Example 10.14

In example 10.7, the ML-estimators $\hat{\mu}$ and $\hat{\sigma}^2$ of the mean and the variance based on n independent random variables $X_1, \ldots, X_n$ with $X_1 \sim N(\mu, \sigma^2)$ were derived as

$$\hat{\mu} = \frac{1}{n} \Sigma X_i$$

and

$$\hat{\sigma}^2 = \frac{1}{n} \Sigma (X_i - \overline{X})^2 .$$

From (8.23) and (8.24), it follows that $E[\hat{\mu}] = \mu$ and $\text{var}[\hat{\mu}] = \sigma^2/n$. Hence, conditions 1) and 2) are satisfied so that $\hat{\mu}$ is unbiased and consistent. In example 10.9 the mean of $\hat{\sigma}^2$ was shown to be

$$E[\hat{\sigma}^2] = E\left[\frac{n-1}{n} S^2\right] = \frac{n-1}{n} \sigma^2 .$$

For $n \to \infty$, however, $E[\hat{\sigma}^2] \to \sigma^2$, and $\hat{\sigma}^2$ is said to be asymptotically unbiased. △.

10.6. The properties of ML-estimators

The use of the ML-method is based on the assumption that all information in the data about the parameters is concentrated in the likelihood function given the distributional assumptions of the model. Hence, as estimates of the parameters of the model, it is natural to choose those parameter values that maximize the likelihood function.

In small samples, it is not possible to formulate general results concerning the properties of ML-estimators. It should be mentioned, however, that the ML-method is invariant under monotone transformations of the parameter space. Assume that g is a monotone function and $\hat{\theta}$ is the ML-estimate of the parameter θ in some given model. Then the ML-estimate of the parameter $g(\theta)$ is $g(\hat{\theta})$. For example, if $\hat{\sigma}^2$ is the ML-estimate of the variance σ^2, then the ML-estimate of the standard deviation σ is $\hat{\sigma} = \sqrt{\hat{\sigma}^2}$.

In large samples, general results concerning the approximate distribution of ML-estimators can be formulated under certain assumptions about the properties of the likelihood function.

In the general case the assumptions are rather complicated, but if attention is restricted to a class of models known as the exponential family, only a few assumptions are necessary. It is beyond the scope of this book to formulate the exact assumptions in either case, but the main result is stated below in theorem 10.2, where the necessary assumptions are refered to as "regularity conditions".

Theorem 10.2

Let $X_1, \ldots, X_n$ be independent, identically distributed with common density function or point probabilities $f(x|\theta)$. Under regularity conditions the ML-estimator $\hat{\theta}$ is consistent and the asymptotic distribution of $\sqrt{n}(\hat{\theta}-\theta)$ is a normal distribution with mean 0 and variance $1/J(\theta)$, where

$$J(\theta) = E[-d^2 \ln f(X|\theta)/d\theta^2],$$

i.e.

$$P(\sqrt{n}(\hat{\theta}-\theta)\sqrt{J(\theta)} \leq u) \to \Phi(u)$$

as $n \to \infty$.

It follows from theorem 10.2 that the distribution of the ML-estimator θ for large values of n can be approximated by a normal distribution with mean value θ and variance $(nJ(\theta))^{-1}$.

Example 10.15

Let $x_1, \ldots, x_n$ be observations of independent Poisson distributed random variables with common point probability

$$f(x|\lambda) = \frac{\lambda^x}{x!}e^{-\lambda} = \exp\{-\lambda+x\ln\lambda-\ln(x!)\}.$$

From theorem 10.2, it follows that $\hat{\lambda}$ is asymptotically normally distributed with mean value λ and variance $J(\lambda)^{-1}/n$, where

$$J(\lambda) = E[-\partial^2 \ln f(X|\lambda)/\partial\lambda^2] = E[X/\lambda^2] = 1/\lambda.$$

Thus

$$\text{var}[\hat{\lambda}] \simeq \lambda/n. \triangle.$$

11. Confidence Intervals

11.1. Point estimates and confidence intervals

A point estimate may be regarded as an approximation to a fixed but unknown value of a parameter in a statistical model. Due to the variability in data, however, estimates from different samples are not the same, and one can never know with certainty how close an estimate is to the true value of the parameter. This uncertainty can be expressed by means of the distribution of the estimator, but can also be summed up quite simply in terms of an interval around the point estimate that is believed to contain the true parameter value with a certain degree of confidence. Such an interval is called a **confidence interval**.

A point estimate can also be regarded as that value of the parameter for which there is optimal agreement between the model and the data. Instead of only stating a single value of the parameter, one could, however, choose to state the values of all parameters for which the agreement between the model and the data is acceptable in a certain sense. This usually results in an interval surrounding the point estimate, and this interval is called an **interval estimate** of the parameter.

Example 11.1

Suppose $x=0$ is an observation from a binomial distribution with parameters $(10,\theta)$, and that an interval $[0,c]$, consisting of all values of θ consistent with the observation $x=0$ is to be constructed. Such an interval can be composed of those values of θ for which $P(X=0|\theta) = (1-\theta)^{10} \geq 0.05$, since values of θ satisfying this inequality could be regarded as reasonably consistent with the observation. Since $(1-c)^{10} = 0.05$ has the unique solution $c=0.259$, and since $(1-\theta)^{10}$ is a decreasing function of θ, it follows that the interval $[0, 0.259]$ contains all values of θ for which $P(X=0|\theta) \geq 0.05$. The interval $[0, 0.259]$ is said to constitute an interval estimate for θ, based on the observation $x=0$. $\triangle$

11.2. Confidence intervals

Let $x_1,\ldots,x_n$ be observed values of continuous random variables $X_1,\ldots,X_n$ with density function $f(x_1,\ldots,x_n|\theta)$, $\theta \in \Theta \subseteq \mathbb{R}$, and let

$$\overline{C} = \bar{c}(X_1,\ldots,X_n)$$

be a sample function for which

(11.1) $P(\overline{C} > \theta | \theta) = 1-\alpha$ for any θ.

Thus if the probability is computed in a distribution with parameter value θ, then the inequality $\overline{C} > \theta$ is satisfied with probability $1-\alpha$, whatever the value of θ.

If $\bar{c}$ is the observed value of $\overline{C}$, the interval $(-\infty, \bar{c}]$ is called a **confidence interval** for θ with **confidence level** $1-\alpha$, or a level $1-\alpha$ confidence interval and $\bar{c}$ is called an **upper confidence limit** for θ.

Confidence intervals may be interpreted in the following way. Assume that level $1-\alpha$ confidence intervals are computed from a large number of independent samples, all generated by a probability model with a fixed parameter value. It then follows from the law of large numbers that the frequency with which the computed intervals include this parameter value is approximately $1-\alpha$.

It should be noted, that a confidence statement is not a probability statement as the expression "$\bar{c} > \theta$" does not involve a random variable. In fact, $\bar{c}$ is an observation and θ is an unknown, but fixed parameter value, so the statement "$\bar{c} > \theta$" is simply either true or false. To indicate that $(-\infty, \bar{c}]$ is a level $1-\alpha$ confidence interval for θ we may write

$$Cf\{\theta < \bar{c}\} = 1-\alpha.$$

Let now $\underline{C} = \underline{c}(X_1,\ldots,X_n)$ be a sample function for which

$$P(\underline{C} < \theta | \theta) = 1-\alpha \text{ for any } \theta.$$

With the notation introduced above, we then have the confidence statement

$$Cf\{\underline{c} < \theta\} = 1-\alpha,$$

where $\underline{c}$ is the observed value of $\underline{C}$. The interval $[\underline{c}, \infty)$ is thus a level $1-\alpha$ confidence interval for θ and $\underline{c}$ is called a **lower confidence limit** for θ.

Suppose finally that the sample functions $\underline{C}$ and $\overline{C}$ have been determined such that

$$P(\underline{C}<\theta<\overline{C}|\theta) = 1-\alpha \text{ for any } \theta.$$

The corresponding confidence statement is

$$Cf\{\underline{c}<\theta<\overline{c}\} = 1-\alpha,$$

where $\underline{c}$ and $\overline{c}$ are the observed values of $\underline{C}$ and $\overline{C}$ respectively. The interval $[\underline{c},\overline{c}]$ is said to be a **two-sided confidence interval** for θ with level $1-\alpha$. In the following, upper and lower confidence limits for a parameter θ are denoted by $\overline{\theta}$ and $\underline{\theta}$ respectively.

11.3. Confidence intervals for the mean value and the variance in the normal distribution

Let $x_1,\ldots,x_n$ be observations of independent, identically distributed random variables $X_1,\ldots,X_n$ with mean value μ and variance σ^2.

Suppose σ^2 is known and that an upper confidence limit for μ with confidence level $1-\alpha$ is to be constructed. According to theorem 9.5,

$$\overline{X} = \frac{1}{n}\sum_{i=1}^{n} X_i \sim N(\mu,\sigma^2/n)$$

so

$$P\left(\frac{\overline{X}-\mu}{\sigma/\sqrt{n}} \leq u_\alpha \bigg| \mu\right) = \alpha$$

and

(11.2) $$P\left(\frac{\overline{X}-\mu}{\sigma/\sqrt{n}} \geq u_\alpha \bigg| \mu\right) = 1-\alpha,$$

where u_α is the α percentile in the standard normal distribution. It then follows that

(11.3) $$P(\mu \leq \overline{X}-u_\alpha \sigma/\sqrt{n}|\mu) = 1-\alpha,$$

which is a probability statement for $\overline{X}$. According to (11.1), the interval $(-\infty, \overline{x}-u_\alpha \sigma/\sqrt{n}]$ is then a confidence interval for μ with confidence level $1-\alpha$ and

(11.4) $$\overline{\mu} = \overline{x}-u_\alpha \sigma/\sqrt{n}$$

is an upper confidence limit for μ.

A lower confidence limit can be derived in a similar way as

$$\text{(11.5)} \qquad \underline{\mu} = \bar{x} - u_{1-\alpha}\sigma/\sqrt{n} ,$$

with $[\bar{x}-u_{1-\alpha}\sigma/\sqrt{n}, \infty)$ as a level 1-α confidence interval for μ.

A two-sided confidence interval for μ with confidence level 1-α has limits

$$\text{(11.6)} \qquad \begin{cases} \overline{\mu} = \bar{x} + u_{1-\alpha/2}\sigma/\sqrt{n} \\ \underline{\mu} = \bar{x} - u_{1-\alpha/2}\sigma/\sqrt{n} \end{cases}$$

since $u_{\alpha/2} = -u_{1-\alpha/2}$.

Example 11.2

Suppose that the data consist of 10 observations of independent, identically distributed random variables, all following a normal distribution with variance 9. A two-sided confidence interval for μ with confidence level 0.95 is to be calculated. The observations are 12.7, 1.4, 5.6, 9.8, 8.2, 8.0, 10.0, 5.2, 7.1 and 2.7 so that $\bar{x}=7.07$. From (11.6), the confidence limits are calculated as

$$\overline{\mu} = 7.07 + 1.96 \cdot 3/\sqrt{10} = 8.93$$

and

$$\underline{\mu} = 7.07 - 1.96 \cdot 3/\sqrt{10} = 5.21 .$$

Changing the level of confidence to 0.90, the limits become

$$\overline{\mu} = 7.07 + 1.645 \cdot 3/\sqrt{10} = 8.63$$

and

$$\underline{\mu} = 7.07 - 1.645 \cdot 3/\sqrt{10} = 5.51 .$$

Comparing the two intervals, it can be seen that the interval with confidence level 0.90 is shorter than the interval with confidence level 0.95. Thus increasing the confidence level increases the length of the confidence interval.

Suppose now that the data consist of 20 observations, and that $\bar{x}$ is still 7.07. A confidence interval with confidence level 0.95 then has the limits

$$\overline{\mu} = 7.07 + 1.96 \cdot 3/\sqrt{20} = 8.38$$

and

$$\underline{\mu} = 7.07 - 1.96 \cdot 3/\sqrt{20} = 5.76 .$$

Thus, increasing the sample size shortens the confidence interval for a fixed confidence level. △

The results in example 11.2 are quite general: the larger the sample size, the shorter the confidence interval for a fixed confidence level, and the larger the confidence level for a fixed sample size, the longer the confidence interval.

For a fixed confidence level, the smallest number of observations that ensures that the confidence interval has a maximum length 2L can be determined. From (11.6), it follows that the length of a two-sided confidence interval with confidence level $1-\alpha$ based on the sample size n is

$$2u_{1-\alpha/2} \cdot \sigma/\sqrt{n} \ .$$

To ensure that the length of the interval does not exceed 2L, n must thus satisfy

$$u_{1-\alpha/2} \sigma/\sqrt{n} \leq L \ ,$$

so that

(11.7) $$n \geq \left(\frac{u_{1-\alpha/2} \sigma}{L}\right)^2 \ .$$

Example 11.3

Suppose we have to construct a two-sided confidence interval of length 2L=4 with confidence level 0.95 for the mean value in a normal distribution with variance $\sigma^2 = 9$. Inserting these values in formula (11.7) yields

$$n \geq \frac{(1.96)^2 \cdot 9}{4} = 8.6 \ .$$

Hence, at least 9 observations are needed for a confidence interval of length at most 4. △

Suppose now that σ^2 as well as μ are unknown and let

$$\overline{X} = \frac{1}{n} \sum_{i=1}^{n} X_i$$

and

$$S^2 = \frac{1}{n-1} \sum_{i=1}^{n} (X_i - \overline{X})^2 \ .$$

According to theorem 9.5 and definition 9.2,

$$T = \frac{\bar{X}-\mu}{S}\sqrt{n}$$

follows a t-distribution with n-1 degrees of freedom. Let $t_\alpha(n-1)$ be the α percentile in this distribution. Then

$$P\{t_{\alpha/2}(n-1) \leq T \leq t_{1-\alpha/2}(n-1)|\mu\} = 1-\alpha$$

or, by inserting $T=(\bar{X}-\mu)\sqrt{n}/S$ and rearranging,

$$P\{\bar{X}-t_{1-\alpha/2}(n-1)S/\sqrt{n} \leq \mu \leq \bar{X}-t_{\alpha/2}(n-1)S/\sqrt{n}\} = 1-\alpha.$$

Substituting the observed values $\bar{x}$ and s^2 for $\bar{X}$ and S^2 and using the fact that $t_{\alpha/2}(n-1) = -t_{1-\alpha/2}(n-1)$, the limits for a confidence interval with confidence level $1-\alpha$ become

(11.8)
$$\begin{cases} \bar{\mu} = \bar{x}+t_{1-\alpha/2}(n-1)s/\sqrt{n} \\ \underline{\mu} = \bar{x}-t_{1-\alpha/2}(n-1)s/\sqrt{n} . \end{cases}$$

The limits (11.8) for a symmetric two-sided confidence interval such as (11.8) are usually written as $\bar{x} \pm t_{\alpha/2}(n-1)s/\sqrt{n}$.

Note that (11.8) corresponds to (11.6) with σ^2 replaced by s^2 and the percentiles in the u-distribution replaced by the corresponding percentiles in a t-distribution with n-1 degrees of freedom. One-sided confidence intervals for μ with σ^2 unknown can be constructed by substituting s^2 for σ^2 and $t_{1-\alpha/2}(n-1)$ for $u_{1-\alpha/2}$ in (11.4) and (11.5).

Example 11.4

Consider again the observations in example 11.2 for which $\bar{x}=7.07$ and $s^2=11.86$. Suppose now that we want to determine a two-sided confidence interval for μ with confidence level 0.95, for an unknown value of σ^2. From (11.8), it follows that the limits of this interval are

$$\bar{\mu} = 7.07+2.262\sqrt{11.86}/\sqrt{10} = 9.53$$

and

$$\underline{\mu} = 7.07-2.262\sqrt{11.86}/\sqrt{10} = 4.61 .$$

It is interesting to compare the length of the interval (11.6) with the length of the interval (11.8), given confidence level and sample size. If (by coincidence) $s^2=\sigma^2$, then (11.6) is shorter than (11.8), since $t_{1-\alpha/2}(n-1) > u_{1-\alpha/2}$. Obviously the lack of uncertainty as regards the value of σ^2 means that the same level of confidence is obtained with a shorter interval. If n is large, the difference is, however, negligible. In general, if we compare a confidence interval given by (11.6) with an interval given by (11.8), based on the same observations, it is not possible to say which interval is the shorter one. This is due to the fact that s^2 varies around σ^2. On average, however, (11.6) is shorter than (11.8). △.

Consider again $x_1,\ldots,x_n$, observations of independent, normally distributed random variables with common mean value μ and variance σ^2, both of which are unknown. From theorem 9.5,

$$\frac{(n-1)S^2}{\sigma^2} \sim \chi^2(n-1) .$$

Let $\chi_\alpha^2(f)$ denote the α percentile in a χ^2-distribution with f degrees of freedom. Then

$$P\left(\chi_{\alpha/2}^2(n-1) \le \frac{(n-1)S^2}{\sigma^2} \le \chi_{1-\alpha/2}^2(n-1) \mid \sigma^2\right)$$

$$= P\left(\frac{1}{\chi_{1-\alpha/2}^2(n-1)} \le \frac{\sigma^2}{(n-1)S^2} \le \frac{1}{\chi_{\alpha/2}^2(n-1)} \mid \sigma^2\right)$$

$$= P\left(\frac{(n-1)S^2}{\chi_{1-\alpha/2}^2(n-1)} \le \sigma^2 \le \frac{(n-1)S^2}{\chi_{\alpha/2}^2(n-1)} \mid \sigma^2\right) = 1-\alpha .$$

Inserting the observed value of s^2 for S^2 yields the limits

(11.9)
$$\begin{cases} \overline{\sigma}^2 = (n-1)s^2/\chi_{\alpha/2}^2(n-1) \\ \underline{\sigma}^2 = (n-1)s^2/\chi_{1-\alpha/2}^2(n-1) \end{cases}$$

for a two-sided confidence interval for σ^2 with confidence level 1-α.

In spite of the fact that a slightly shorter interval can be obtained by cutting off less than $\alpha/2$ in the left hand tail of the χ^2-distribution and cutting off correspondingly more in the right hand tail of the distribution,(11.9) is normally used. The limits of a two-sided confidence interval for the standard deviation are obtained by taking the square roots of the limits (11.9).

Example 11.5

Suppose a confidence interval for the variance in a normal distribution with confidence level 0.95 is to be determined. With 20 observations and an estimated variance $s^2 = 8.9$, (11.9) gives

$$\begin{cases} \bar{\sigma}^2 = \dfrac{19 \cdot 8.9}{8.91} = 18.98 \\ \underline{\sigma}^2 = \dfrac{19 \cdot 8.9}{32.85} = 5.15 \end{cases}$$

since $\chi^2_{0.975}(19) = 32.85$ and $\chi^2_{0.025}(19) = 8.91$.

The interval [2.27, 4.36] is then a confidence interval for σ with level 0.95. △.

11.4. Confidence intervals for the parameters in the binomial distribution and the hypergeometric distribution

Suppose that X follows a binomial distribution with parameters (n, θ). The methods presented above cannot be used to derive exact confidence intervals for θ. For small values of n, confidence intervals can, however, be constructed from tables of the binomial distribution, as illustrated in example 11.1. For large values of n, approximate confidence intervals can be constructed using the de Moivre-Laplace theorem, according to which

$$P\left\{ u_{\alpha/2} < \frac{X - n\theta}{\sqrt{n\theta(1-\theta)}} < u_{1-\alpha/2} \mid \theta \right\} \simeq 1 - \alpha.$$

Solving the two inequalities with respect to θ then yields an approximate confidence interval.

The computations are simplified if $\sqrt{n\theta(1-\theta)}$ is replaced by $\sqrt{nh(1-h)}$, where $h = x/n$. This approximation is justified by the fact that $\sqrt{\theta(1-\theta)}$ is only slightly sensitive to changes in θ as long as θ is not close to 0 and 1. Since

$$\frac{X/n - \theta}{\sqrt{h(1-h)/n}}$$

approximately follows a standard normal distribution,

$$P\left\{ u_{\alpha/2} \leq \frac{X/n - \theta}{\sqrt{h(1-h)/n}} < u_{1-\alpha/2} \right\} \simeq 1 - \alpha.$$

The approximate confidence limits become

(11.10) $\begin{cases} \overline{\theta} = h+u_{1-\alpha/2}\sqrt{h(1-h)/n} \\ \underline{\theta} = h-u_{1-\alpha/2}\sqrt{h(1-h)/n}. \end{cases}$

Assume now that X follows a hypergeometric distribution with point probabilities

$$f(x|\theta) = \binom{N\theta}{x}\binom{N(1-\theta)}{n-x}/\binom{N}{n}$$

where $0 \leq \theta \leq 1$. According to (9.18),

$$U = \frac{X/n - \theta}{\sqrt{\frac{\theta(1-\theta)}{n} \cdot \frac{N-n}{N-1}}}$$

is approximately normally distributed with mean 0 and variance 1. As above also

$$U' = \frac{X/n - \theta}{\hat{\sigma}_n},$$

where $\hat{\sigma}_n^2 = \frac{1}{n} h(1-h)(N-n)/(N-1)$, approximately follows a standard normal distribution. Hence, the approximate probability statement

$$P\left(u_{\alpha/2} < \frac{X/n - \theta}{\hat{\sigma}_n} \leq u_{1-\alpha/2}\right) \approx 1-\alpha$$

gives the approximate limits

(11.11) $\begin{cases} \overline{\theta} = h+u_{1-\alpha/2}\hat{\sigma}_n \\ \underline{\theta} = h-u_{1-\alpha/2}\hat{\sigma}_n \end{cases}$

for a two-sided confidence interval with level $1-\alpha$.

Example 11.6

From among the 22000 inhabitants above the age of 18 in the city of Horsholm in Denmark, a simple random sample of 150 persons was drawn. When asked whether they were for or against the preservations by law of an old mansion, x=69 said they were for a preservation. On the basis of this information, a confidence interval for the proportion, θ, of inhabitants in Horsholm for a preservation is to be determined. Assuming that x is an observation from a hypergeometric distribution with parameters n=150, M=22000·θ and N=22000 and with

$$h = x/n = 0.46,$$

and
$$\hat{\sigma}_n^2 = 0.001656,$$

the confidence interval with level 0.95 is

$$0.46 \pm 1.96 \cdot 0.0407 = \begin{cases} 0.38 \\ 0.54 \end{cases}. \triangle.$$

11.5. Approximate confidence intervals

Approximate confidence intervals are used either when it is impossible or when it is considered too complicated to determine exact intervals. The determination of approximate intervals is usually based on a statistic which is approximately normally distributed.

Let $x_1, \ldots, x_n$ be observed values of independent, identically distributed random variables $X_1, \ldots, X_n$ with common mean μ and variance σ^2. From theorem 9.11, $\sqrt{n}(\bar{X}-\mu)/\sqrt{\sigma}$ follows approximately a standard normal distribution for large values of n. An approximate confidence interval for μ with level $1-\alpha$ is accordingly determined by the limits given in (11.6), i.e. as

$$\bar{x} \pm u_{1-\alpha/2} \sigma/\sqrt{n}.$$

If σ^2 is unknown, (11.8) gives the approximate interval

$$\bar{x} \pm u_{1-\alpha/2} s/\sqrt{n},$$

since the distribution of $\sqrt{n}(\bar{X}-\mu)/S$ can also be approximated by a standard normal distribution for large values of n.

Assume that the estimator $\hat{\theta}$ of a parameter θ has been obtained from a sample of size n, and that $\hat{\theta}$ is approximately normally distributed with mean θ and an estimated variance $\hat{c}^2$. An approximate confidence interval with level $1-\alpha$ is then given by

(11.12) $$\hat{\theta} \pm u_{1-\alpha/2} \hat{\sigma}.$$

The usefulness of this result lies in the fact that many estimators, including most ML-estimators, are asymptotically normally distributed. The variance $\hat{\sigma}^2$ of the estimator often depends on θ, but the approximation to the normal distribution is as a rule almost equally good when the true value of the parameter is replaced by the estimate $\hat{\theta}$ in the expression for $\hat{\sigma}^2$.

Let $x_1,\ldots,x_n$ be observed values of independent, identically distributed random variables $X_1,\ldots,X_n$, where X_i follows an exponential distribution with parameter $\lambda>0$, i.e. the density function of X_i is

$$f(x|\lambda) = \lambda e^{-\lambda x}, \quad x>0.$$

The likelihood function is

$$L(\lambda|x_1,\ldots,x_n) = \lambda^n e^{-\lambda \Sigma x_i},$$

and the ML-estimate of λ is given by

$$\hat{\lambda} = \frac{n}{\Sigma x_i} = \frac{1}{\bar{x}}.$$

Since the ML-estimator is invariant under monotone transformations, the ML-estimate of $\theta=1/\lambda$ becomes

$$\hat{\theta} = 1/\hat{\lambda} = \frac{\Sigma x_i}{n} = \bar{x}.$$

According to (7.16) and (7.17), $E[X_i]=\lambda^{-1}$ and $\text{var}[X_i]=\lambda^{-2}$. The central limit theorem gives that $\hat{\theta}$ is asymptotically normally distributed with mean value $\lambda^{-1}=\theta$ and variance $(\lambda^2 n)^{-1}=\theta^2/n$. Applying (11.12), an approximate confidence interval for θ with confidence level 0.95 is

$$(\underline{\theta},\overline{\theta}) = (\bar{x}-1.96\bar{x}/\sqrt{n},\ \bar{x}+1.96\bar{x}/\sqrt{n}),$$

where the ML-estimate $\bar{x}$ is inserted for θ in the expression for the variance. The confidence interval for the parameter λ is obtained by inverting the limits of the interval for θ, i.e.

$$(\underline{\lambda},\overline{\lambda}) = (\overline{\theta}^{-1},\underline{\theta}^{-1}).$$

Example 11.7

In example 7.4, 150 time intervals between consecutive arrivals to a queueing system were considered. The analysis showed that the observations could be described adequately by an exponential distribution. Since $\bar{x}=26.73$, $\hat{\lambda}=0.0374$. The lower and upper limits of a confidence interval for θ with level 0.95 are respectively

$$\underline{\theta} = 26.73-1.96\cdot 26.73/\sqrt{150} = 22.45$$

and
$$\overline{\theta} = 26.73+1.96 \cdot 26.73/\sqrt{150} = 31.01,$$

The corresponding interval for λ is

$$\begin{cases} \underline{\lambda} = 1/\overline{\theta} = 0.0322 \\ \overline{\lambda} = 1/\underline{\theta} = 0.0445 \end{cases} . \triangle.$$

11.6. Concluding remarks

Confidence intervals are used as a summary description of the uncertainty concerning the value of a parameter estimated from a sample. This uncertainty is represented in detail by the probability distribution of the estimator. A confidence interval has the advantage that its intuitive meaning is easier to grasp than the meaning of a probability distribution. The formal interpretation of a confidence interval is, however, somewhat more complicated. The basic interpretation of a confidence interval is in terms of frequencies, i.e. the confidence level of an interval is interpreted as the long-run frequency with which the calculated intervals include the true value of the unknown parameter.

The interval may alternatively be interpreted as an interval estimate. This means that the interval contains all values of the parameter, for which the model is considered reasonably consistent with the observations. This interpretation is discussed in more detail in the next chapter.

The probability statements leading to the two-sided confidence intervals in sections 11.3-11.5 are all of the form

$$(11.13) \quad P(y_{\alpha_1} < Y(X_1,\ldots,X_n;\theta) < y_{1-\alpha_2}) = 1-\alpha_1-\alpha_2 = 1-\alpha,$$

where $Y(X_1,\ldots,X_n;\theta)$ is a random variable, the (exact or approximate) distribution of which does not depend on the parameter θ, and where y_α is the α percentile in the distribution of Y. The confidence interval was then determined by isolating the parameter θ in an interval $\underline{c} < \theta < \overline{c}$. This method is fairly general, in particular for the construction of approximate confidence intervals, where Y may be chosen as the ML-estimator of θ.

12. Testing Statistical Hypotheses

12.1. The statistical hypothesis

A **statistical hypothesis** is an assumption concerning the distribution of random variables. For example, let $X_1,\ldots,X_n$ be independent and identically distributed random variables. A typical statistical hypothesis could then be that these variables are Poisson distributed with mean 2. Such a hypothesis is called a **simple hypothesis** because it completely specifies the distribution of the random variables. A different hypothesis would be that the random variables are normally distributed with mean 0 and unknown variance σ^2. Such a hypothesis is said to be **composite**, since a class of distributions is specified.

A **statistical test** is a method for evaluating the consistency of data with a statistical hypothesis. The hypothesis to be tested is called the **null hypothesis** and is denoted H_0. In order to carry out a meaningful test of H_0 it is necessary to specify departures from the null hypothesis which are of special interest. Such departures are described by an **alternative hypothesis** H_1. The statistical test then evaluates the consistency of the data with H_0 in relation to the possibility of better consistency with H_1.

Example 12.1

In a supermarket it is known that on the average two customers can be served at the check-out counter per minute. If, therefore, the average number of arrivals per minute exceeds two, the manager has to face a queue of increasing length in front of the check-out counter, as discussed in section 6.3.

Within one minute the manager observed 4 arrivals at the counter. This number is certainly larger than 2, but if the customers arrive at random to the counter, one may ask how likely it is to observe as many as 4 arrivals, given that the expected number is 2. To answer this question it is assumed that the number of arrivals in a one-minute period is Poisson distributed with parameter λ. This means that $x=4$ is an observation of a Poisson distributed random variable X with mean value $\lambda=2$. Under this model

$$p = P(X \geq 4 | \lambda = 2) = 0.1429,$$

so the probability of observing four or more arrivals within one minute is 0.1429 if the expected number of arrivals per minute is 2. If $\lambda < 2$ it is easy to see that this probability is even less than 0.1429. It can be argued that p is a measure of the extent to which the value x=4 supports the hypothesis $\lambda \leq 2$ against the alternative $\lambda > 2$. The larger the value of p, the stronger the support of H_0 against H_1. △.

12.2. Significance tests

Let $x_1, \ldots, x_n$ be observations of random variables $X_1, \ldots, X_n$ with density or point probability $f(x_1, \ldots, x_n | \theta)$, where θ is a real-valued parameter, θ∈Θ, and suppose that the observations can be adequately described by a particular distribution within this model, characterized by the parameter value θ_0. This assumption is equivalent to the null hypothesis

$$H_0: \theta = \theta_0.$$

If the detection of departures in the direction $\theta > \theta_0$ are important, then the alternative hypothesis is

$$H_1: \theta > \theta_0.$$

This form of alternative hypothesis is said to be **one-sided** since only departures from H_0 in one direction are considered.

Let T be a sample function,

$$T = t(X_1, \ldots, X_n),$$

such that large values of T support H_1 against H_0 and such that the larger the value of T, the stronger the support of H_1 against H_0. Such a sample function is called a **test statistic**. This means that all points in the sample space of $X_1, \ldots, X_n$ through T are ordered with respect to how much they support H_1 against H_0. The quantity

(12.1) $\quad p = P(T \geq t | H_0) = P(T \geq t | \theta_0),$

where t is the observed value of T, can, therefore, be used as a measure of how strongly the observed value t supports H_1 against H_0. This interpretation follows if it is assumed that the observed value t is accepted as adequate support for H_1 against H_0. Then all values t'>t must support H_1 even more against H_0, and p is the probability of observing one of these extreme values, should H_0 be true. Thus the smaller the value of p, the more t supports H_1 against H_0.

The probability defined by (12.1) is called the **level of signifi-**

cance. If the level of significance is sufficiently small, H_0 is rejected.

One may choose to reject H_0 in favour of H_1 if the level of significance is less than some chosen value α, i.e. H_0 is rejected if $t \geq t_{1-\alpha}$, where $t_{1-\alpha}$ is the $(1-\alpha)$ percentile in the distribution of T, or

(12.2) $\alpha = P(T \geq t_{1-\alpha} | H_0)$.

This procedure for deciding whether or not to reject H_0 is called a **significance test** of H_0 with **test level** α. A significance test divides the sample space into two regions: the **critical region**, R, consisting of all samples $(x_1,\ldots,x_n)$ for which H_0 is rejected, i.e. for which $t(x_1,\ldots,x_n) \geq t_{1-\alpha}$, and the **acceptance region**, $\overline{R}$, consisting of all samples for which H_0 is accepted, i.e. for which $t(x_1,\ldots,x_n) < t_{1-\alpha}$.

A significance test is defined by its critical region, and the test level is the probability of rejecting H_0 when it is in fact true. The test level is often chosen as 0.05 or 0.01. This choice reflects the fact that the null hypothesis is usually only rejected if the evidence against it is very strong. It should be noted that acceptance of the null hypothesis does not necessarily imply that it is true but only that the evidence against it is not sufficiently strong.

Example 12.1 (continued)

In example 12.1 the null hypothesis

$$H_0 : \lambda \leq \lambda_0 = 2$$

was tested against the alternative

$$H_1 : \lambda > 2$$

on the basis of a single observation from a Poisson distribution. The level of significance for this test is

$$p = P(X \geq 4 | \lambda = 2) = 0.1429 .$$

For discrete distributions critical regions can only be determined for selected test levels. With test level α, the critical region for a test of H_0 against H_1 is given by $R=\{c, c+1,\ldots\}$ where c, according to (12.2), satisfies

$$P(X \geq c | \lambda = 2) = \alpha.$$

For $c=5$, α is obtained from a table of a Poisson distribution with $\lambda=2$ as 0.0527 and likewise for $c=6$, $\alpha=0.0166$. For test levels between

0.0166 and 0.0527 (for example α=0.05), there is no unique critical region. Therefore, when testing hypotheses in discrete distributions, it is advisable to compute levels of significance. △.

In example 12.1 a null hypothesis of the form $H_0: \theta \leq \theta_0$ was tested against the alternative $H_1: \theta > \theta_0$. In the subsequent sections the null hypothesis always takes the form $\theta = \theta_0$. However, the results obtained in this case can be used when the null hypothesis is $\theta \leq \theta_0$ since the level of significance for values of θ less than θ_0 is usually less than or equal to the level of significance for θ_0, i.e.

$$P(T \geq t | \theta) \leq P(T \geq t | \theta_0) \quad \text{for } \theta < \theta_0 .$$

The level of significance for $\theta = \theta_0$ is therefore the maximum value of the level of significance for all values of θ under the null hypothesis.

12.3. Construction of tests

Intuitively, it would be preferable to base the test of a statistical hypothesis concerning a parameter θ on a suitable estimator of θ or on a sample function whose mean is a monotone function of θ.

Assume that $\hat{\theta} = L(x_1, \ldots, x_n)$ is an estimator of θ and that the hypothesis $\theta = \theta_0$ is to be tested against the alternative $\theta \neq \theta_0$. It would be quite natural to use $|\hat{\theta} - \theta_0|$ as a test statistic since the larger the value of $|\hat{\theta} - \theta_0|$, the stronger the evidence of the sample against the null hypothesis. In some cases $\hat{\theta}/\theta_0$ is used as a test statistic and H_0 is then rejected if $|\hat{\theta}/\theta_0 - 1|$ is large or close to 1.

To illustrate how this intuitive method works, the problem of testing a hypothesis concerning the mean in a normal distribution is considered. Let $x_1, \ldots, x_n$ be the observed values of independent, normally distributed random variables $X_1, \ldots, X_n$ with mean μ and known variance σ_0^2. As a test statistic for the null hypothesis $\mu = \mu_0$ against the alternative $\mu \neq \mu_0$, $|\bar{x} - \mu_0|$ can be used, since $\bar{x}$ is the ML-estimate of μ. It is obvious that the larger the value of $|\bar{x} - \mu_0|$, the more the data suggests rejection of H_0.

Under H_0, $\bar{X} \sim N(\mu_0, \sigma_0^2/n)$. Hence, the level of significance is

(12.3) $\quad p = P(|\bar{X} - \mu_0| \geq |\bar{x} - \mu_0|) = P(\sqrt{n}|\bar{X} - \mu_0|/\sigma_0 \geq \sqrt{n}|\bar{x} - \mu_0|/\sigma_0)$.

Since, however, $\sqrt{n}|\bar{X} - \mu_0|/\sigma_0 = U \sim N(0,1)$, and the distribution of U is symmetric around 0 it follows that

(12.4) $\quad p = 2P(U > \sqrt{n}|\bar{x}-\mu_0|/\sigma_0) = 2(1-\Phi(\sqrt{n}|\bar{x}-\mu_0|/\sigma_0))$.

Let $u_{1-\alpha/2}$ be the $(1-\alpha/2)$ percentile of the standardized normal distribution. Then, under H_0,

$$P(\sqrt{n}|\bar{x}-\mu_0|/\sigma_0 \geq u_{1-\alpha/2}) = \alpha.$$

and the critical region with level α consists of data sets for which

$$|\bar{x}-\mu_0| > u_{1-\alpha/2}\sigma_0/\sqrt{n},$$

or values of $\bar{x}$ which satisfy one of the two inequalities

(12.5) $\quad \begin{cases} \bar{x} > \mu_0 + u_{1-\alpha/2}\sigma_0/\sqrt{n} \\ \bar{x} < \mu_0 - u_{1-\alpha/2}\sigma_0/\sqrt{n} \end{cases}$

A test with critical region (12.5) is called a **u-test**.

A formal method for the construction of a test is based on the so-called **likelihood ratio**, presented in the following.

Let $\mathbf{x}=(x_1,\ldots,x_n)$ be observed values of the random variables $\mathbf{X}=(X_1,\ldots,X_n)$ with density function or point probability $f(\mathbf{x}|\theta)$ where the parameter space Θ is a subset of the real line, and assume that the hypothesis $H_0: \theta=\theta_0$ is to be tested against the two-sided alternative $H_1: \theta \neq \theta_0$. The likelihood ratio is defined as

(12.6) $\quad r(\mathbf{x}) = \dfrac{L(\theta_0|\mathbf{x})}{\max_{\theta \in \Theta} L(\theta|\mathbf{x})} = \dfrac{L(\theta_0|\mathbf{x})}{L(\hat{\theta}|\mathbf{x})}$,

where $L(\theta|\mathbf{x})$ is the likelihood function. The likelihood ratio $r(\mathbf{x})$ is seen to be the ratio between the value of the likelihood function under H_0 and the maximum value of the likelihood function for $\theta \in \Theta$.

The closer the value of the likelihood function at $\theta=\theta_0$ is to its maximum value, the closer the likelihood ratio is to its maximum $r(\mathbf{x})=1$, and the stronger the evidence is in favour of H_0. Thus all potential samples $\mathbf{x}$ are ordered by the value of $r(\mathbf{x})$.

The level of significance for a test based on the test statistic $r(\mathbf{X})$ is given by

$$p = P(r(\mathbf{X}) < r(\mathbf{x})|H_0),$$

and a significance test at level α based on the test statistic $r(\mathbf{x})$ has critical region

$$R = \{\mathbf{x} | r(\mathbf{x}) < r_\alpha\},$$

where r_α is the α percentile in the distribution of $r(\mathbf{X})$ under H_0, i.e.

$$\alpha = P(r(\mathbf{X}) < r_\alpha | H_0).$$

A test based on the likelihood ratio is called a **likelihood ratio test**. In order to apply a likelihood ratio test, the distribution of $r(\mathbf{X})$ under H_0 must be known. In some cases, a simple transformation of r has a known distribution, but in most cases asymptotic results, related to the second part of theorem 10.2, must be invoked. Under reasonably general conditions it can be shown that the distribution of $Q=-2\ln r(\mathbf{X})$ for large values of n can be approximated by a χ^2-distribution with one degree of freedom.

The likelihood ratio test is popular for two main reasons: $r(\mathbf{x})$ is relatively easy to derive, even in complicated models; and the asymptotic result concerning the distribution of the likelihood ratio facilitates approximation of the level of significance.

The likelihood ratio test can be extended to hypotheses involving vector-valued parameters. If the quantities in the numerator and denominator of (12.6) are vectors $\boldsymbol{\theta}_0 = (\theta_{01}, \ldots, \theta_{0k})$ and $\hat{\boldsymbol{\theta}} = (\hat{\theta}_1, \ldots, \hat{\theta}_k)$ the limiting χ^2-distribution of $-2\ln r(\mathbf{X})$ has k degrees of freedom, provided the estimates $\hat{\theta}_1, \ldots, \hat{\theta}_k$ are not functionally related.

Example 12.2

The u-test with level of significance (12.4) is also a likelihood ratio test. This can be seen by letting $x_1, \ldots, x_n$ be observed values of n independent, identically distributed random variables $X_1, \ldots, X_n$ with $X_i \sim N(\mu, \sigma_0^2)$. Consider a test of the hypothesis

$$H_0: \mu = \mu_0$$

against the alternative

$$H_1: \mu \neq \mu_0.$$

Since $\bar{x}$ is the ML-estimate of μ, the likelihood ratio is given by

$$r(x) = \frac{(2\pi\sigma_0^2)^{-n/2}\exp\left\{-\frac{1}{2\sigma_0^2}\Sigma(x_i-\mu_0)^2\right\}}{(2\pi\sigma_0^2)^{-n/2}\exp\left\{-\frac{1}{2\sigma_0^2}\Sigma(x_i-\bar{x})^2\right\}}$$

$$= \exp\left\{-\frac{1}{2\sigma_0^2}[\Sigma(x_i-\mu_0)^2-\Sigma(x_i-\bar{x})^2]\right\} = \exp\left\{-\frac{n}{2\sigma_0^2}(\bar{x}-\mu_0)^2\right\}.$$

Solving with respect to $u=\sqrt{n}(\bar{x}-\mu_0)/\sigma_0$ yields

$$u = \sqrt{n}\frac{\bar{x}-\mu_0}{\sigma_0} = \pm\sqrt{-2\ln(r(x))} \ .$$

The level of significance is, therefore,

$$p = P(r(X_1,\ldots,X_n)<r) = P((U<-\sqrt{-2\ln(r)})+P(U>\sqrt{-2\ln(r)}) \ .$$

Since $|u|=\sqrt{-2\ln(r)}$, it follows from (12.4) that the u-test and the likelihood ratio test are identical. Notice that $u^2=-2\ln(r)$ so the transformed likelihood ratio test statistic in this case has an exact χ^2-distribution with one degree of freedom. As mentioned above, this result in general holds only approximately. $\triangle$.

12.4. Tests in discrete distributions

Example 12.1 illustrates the basic ideas of testing statistical hypotheses. The method used in that example applies in fact to all discrete distributions. For convenience, only distributions with sample space $S=\{0,1,\ldots,m\}$ or $\{0,1,2,\ldots\}$ are considered.

Let X be a discrete random variable with sample space S and point probability $f(x|\theta)$, where θ is a real valued parameter, and consider a test of the hypothesis

$$H_0: \theta=\theta_0$$

against the alternative

$$H_1: \theta>\theta_0 \ .$$

Assume that a large value, x, of X suggests a large value of θ. This could be because the mean of X is an increasing function of θ. Under the alternative $\theta>\theta_0$, H_0 is, therefore, rejected when x is suitably large. The level of significance is calculated as

(12.7) $$p = P(X \geq x|H_0) = \sum_{z \geq x} f(z|\theta_0) \ ,$$

and H_0 is rejected if p is smaller than a fixed level α. Under the alternative $\theta < \theta_0$, the level of significance is given by

(12.8) $\qquad p = P(X \leq x | H_0) = \sum_{z \leq x} f(z | \theta_0)$.

For a two-sided alternative both large and small values of x support the alternative. If x is larger than the median of the distribution under H_0, the level of significance can be calculated as

$$p = 2 \sum_{z \geq x} f(z | \theta_0) .$$

It is thus assumed that there also exists a set of small x-values, all of which support the alternative. Furthermore, this set is assumed to have the same probability as the set $\{X \geq x\}$. If, on the other hand, x is smaller than the median, p is calculated as

$$p = 2 \sum_{z \leq x} f(x | \theta_0) .$$

With a two-sided alternative the level of significance is, therefore, computed as

(12.9) $\qquad p = 2 \min \left\{ \sum_{z \leq x} f(z | \theta_0), \sum_{z \geq x} f(z | \theta_0) \right\}.$

Example 12.3

The migraine clinic at the Copenhagen University Hospital is interested in investigating the effect of ferrum quartz as a treatment for migraine. A patient has over a long period of time kept a record of his migraine attacks. This shows that a strong attack occurs on average every 9th day. Over a period of three months, he was treated with ferrum quartz. During this period strong attacks only occurred on 7 out of the 90 days. Since 7 is clearly below the expected number of attacks, which is 10, it is tempting to conclude that the treatment with ferrum quartz has in fact had an effect. In order to check this conclusion statistically it is assumed that the number of migraine attacks X during a 90 day period is Poisson distributed. The parameter λ is the expected number of attacks over the period considered. An attack is expected every 9th day if ferrum quartz has no effect, so the hypothesis $\lambda = 10$ is tested against the alternative $\lambda < 10$. This alternative is chosen because there should be fewer attacks if the treatment has any effect.

The level of significance is

$$p = \sum_{x=0}^{7} \frac{10^x}{x!} e^{-10} = 0.2202.$$

Even though the observed number of days with migraine attacks points in the direction of the alternative, the evidence against H_0 is accordingly not sufficient to conclude that ferrum quartz has an effect on migraine. △.

The methods developed above for a single observation from a discrete distribution can often be used in situations with n observations from the same discrete distribution.

Assume for example that $x_1, \ldots, x_n$ are observations of independent, Poisson distributed random variables $X_1, \ldots, X_n$ with mean λ. Then $T = X_1 + \ldots + X_n$ is Poisson distributed with mean $n\lambda$, according to theorem 8.11. A test of the hypothesis $\lambda = \lambda_0$ can, therefore, be carried out exactly like a test based on a single observation from a Poisson distribution. The level of significance can be computed from (12.7), (12.8) or (12.9), depending on the alternative, where f is the point probability of a Poisson distribution with parameter $n\lambda_0$.

As another example, let $x_1, \ldots, x_n$ be the observed values of independent random variables $X_1, \ldots, X_n$ where $X_i \sim b(n_i, \theta)$. Since $T = X_1 + \ldots + X_n \sim b(\Sigma n_i, \theta)$, according to theorem 8.12, a test of the hypothesis $\theta = \theta_0$ can be carried out using the same procedure as for a test based on a single observation from a binomial distribution. The level of significance is again computed from (12.7), (12.8) or (12.9) where f is the point probability of the binomial distribution with parameters $(\Sigma n_i, \theta_0)$. Note that the binomially distributed random variables need not be identically distributed. It is sufficient that they are independent with the same probability parameter θ.

12.5. Conditional tests

Assume that the model $f(x_1, \ldots, x_n | \theta, \tau)$ for the observations $x_1, \ldots, x_n$ depends on two real-valued parameters θ and τ and consider the null hypothesis

$$H_0: \theta = \theta_0 .$$

Since H_0 only involves the parameter θ, one often eliminates τ from the model by conditioning with respect to a suitable sample function, so that the test of H_0 can be based on this conditional distribution. Such a test is called a **conditional test**.

A number of conditional tests are related to discrete distributions. Let $X_1,\ldots,X_n$ be discrete random variables with point probabilities

(12.10) $\quad P(X_1=x_1,\ldots,X_n=x_n) = f(x_1,\ldots,x_n|\theta,\tau)$

and assume that there exists a sample function $Y=y(X_1,\ldots,X_n)$ for which the conditional distribution

(12.11) $\quad P(X_1=x_1,\ldots,X_n=x_n|Y=y) = g(x_1,\ldots,x_n|\theta,y)$

does not depend on τ. Let $T=t(X_1,\ldots,X_n)$ be a test statistic for the hypothesis $\theta=\theta_0$ against the alternative $\theta>\theta_0$. The level of significance is then given by

(12.12) $\quad p = P(T \geq t|\theta_0,y) = \sum_{R(t,y)} g(x_1,\ldots,x_n|\theta_0,y)$

where $R(t,y)=\{x_1,\ldots,x_n|y=y(x_1,\ldots,x_n) \text{ and } t(x_1,\ldots,x_n) \geq t\}$. An essential feature of a conditional test is thus the fact that the observed data set $(x_1,\ldots,x_n)$ is only compared to other data sets $(x_1',\ldots,x_n')$ for which $y=y(x_1',\ldots,x_n')$, and the probability of observing more extreme values than $t=t(x_1,\ldots,x_n)$ is therefore evaluated only among those data sets for which y has the same value as that observed.

Theorem 12.1

If X_1 and X_2 are independent, Poisson distributed random variables with parameters λ_1 and λ_2, then

(12.13) $\quad P(X_1=x_1|X_1+X_2=y) = \binom{y}{x_1} \left(\frac{\lambda_1}{\lambda_1+\lambda_2}\right)^{x_1} \left(1-\frac{\lambda_1}{\lambda_1+\lambda_2}\right)^{y-x_1}$,

i.e. X_1 given $X_1+X_2=y$ is binomially distributed with parameters $(y,\lambda_1/(\lambda_1+\lambda_2))$.

Proof

From theorem 8.11 it follows that $Y=X_1+X_2$ is Poisson distributed with parameter $\lambda_1+\lambda_2$. The conditional point probability of X_1, given that

$X_1+X_2=y$, is therefore

$$P(X_1=x_1|X_1+X_2=y) = P(X_1=x_1)P(X_2=y-x_1)/P(X_1+X_2=y)$$

$$= \frac{\lambda_1^{x_1}}{x_1!}e^{-\lambda_1} \frac{\lambda_2^{y-x_1}}{(y-x_1)!}e^{-\lambda_2} / \left[\frac{(\lambda_1+\lambda_2)^y}{y!}e^{-(\lambda_1+\lambda_2)}\right]$$

$$= \frac{y!}{x_1!(y-x_1)!}\left(\frac{\lambda_1}{\lambda_1+\lambda_2}\right)^{x_1}\left(\frac{\lambda_2}{\lambda_1+\lambda_2}\right)^{y-x_1},$$

which coincides with (12.13), since

$$\frac{\lambda_2}{\lambda_1+\lambda_2} = 1 - \frac{\lambda_1}{\lambda_1+\lambda_2}. \ \square$$

Consider now two independent, Poisson distributed random variables, X_1 and X_2, with parameters λ_1 and λ_2, and let the null hypothesis be

(12.14) $\quad H_0: \lambda_1 = k\lambda_2$,

where k is a known constant. This is seen to be a two-parameter test problem, as discussed above, with $\tau=\lambda_2$ and $\theta=\lambda_1/\lambda_2$. The hypothesis (12.14) is equivalent to

$$H_0: \theta = k,$$

which does not involve the parameter τ. The conditional distribution (12.11) is obtained from theorem 12.1 for $y=X_1+X_2$ as

(12.15) $\quad g(x_1,x_2|\theta,y) = \binom{y}{x_1}\left(\frac{\theta}{\theta+1}\right)^{x_1}\left(\frac{1}{\theta+1}\right)^{y-x_1},$

since

$$\frac{\lambda_1}{\lambda_1+\lambda_2} = \frac{\lambda_1/\lambda_2}{\lambda_1/\lambda_2+1} = \frac{\theta}{\theta+1}.$$

Since the probability parameter of (12.15) is $k/(k+1)$ if $\theta=k$, the level of significance is calculated in a binomial distribution with parameters (y, $k/(k+1)$). Under the alternative $\lambda_1 \neq k\lambda_2$, H_0 is rejected if x is close to 0 or to y.

Example 12.4

In Denmark general speed limits were introduced in 1974, resulting in a marked decline in the number of persons killed in road accidents. The actual number of persons killed was 1132 in 1973 and 766 in 1974. In Elsinore Police District the number of persons killed in road accidents was 22 in 1973 and 11 in 1974. Do these data support a hypothesis to the effect that the risk of being killed in a road accident decreased by the same factor in Elsinore as in the rest of Denmark? In order to test this hypothesis, it is assumed that the number of persons killed in Elsinore in road accidents in 1973 and 1974, respectively, are observations of independent, Poisson distributed random variables X_1 and X_2 with parameters λ_1 and λ_2. Since the parameter in a Poisson distribution is equal to the mean value, λ_1 and λ_2 can be interpreted as the risks of being killed in a road accident in Elsinore in 1973 and 1974 respectively. With this interpretation, the hypothesis under consideration is

$$\frac{\lambda_1}{\lambda_2} = \frac{1132-22}{766-11} = 1.470$$

The ratio for the rest of Denmark, 1.470, is here assumed to be known. In section 19.3 a method is discussed, in which it is taken into consideration that this ratio is actually subject to random variation.

The hypothesis in question can also be expressed as

$$H_0: \lambda_1 = 1.470\lambda_2$$

and the alternative as $\lambda_1 \neq 1.470\lambda_2$. This means that H_0 has the form (12.14) and can be tested by means of a conditional test in the binomial distribution $X_1|y \sim b(33, \lambda_1/(\lambda_1+\lambda_2))$.

Under H_0, $\lambda_1/(\lambda_1+\lambda_2) = 0.595$ such that the level of significance is given by

$$p = 2\min\left\{\sum_{x=22}^{33} f(x|33,0.595), \sum_{x=0}^{22} f(x|33,0.595)\right\}$$

$$= 2\min\{0.276, 0.831\} = 0.552,$$

where $f(x|33,0.595)$ is the point probability for a binomial distribution with parameters $(33, 0.595)$.

With this level of significance, the data do not contradict the hypothesis that the decline in the risk of being killed in a road accident in Elsinore from 1973 to 1974 is of the same magnitude as in the rest of Denmark. △.

Theorem 12.2

Let X_1 and X_2 be independent, binomially distributed random variables with parameters (n_1,θ) and (n_2,θ). Then

(12.16) $$P(X_1=x_1|X_1+X_2=y) = \binom{n_1}{x_1}\binom{n_2}{y-x_1}/\binom{n_1+n_2}{y},$$

i.e. the distribution of X_1 given $X_1+X_2=y$ is hypergeometric with parameters (y, n_1, n_1+n_2).

Proof

From theorem 8.12 it follows that $Y=X_1+X_2 \sim b(n_1+n_2,\theta)$. An application of the definition of a conditional probability then yields (12.16) directly. $\square$.

Assume that X_1 and X_2 are independent with $X_1 \sim b(n_1,\theta_1)$ and $X_2 \sim b(n_2,\theta_2)$ and consider a test of the hypothesis

$$H_0: \theta_1=\theta_2$$

against the alternative

$$H_1: \theta_1>\theta_2.$$

Consider the reparametrization

$$\tau = \theta_2/(1-\theta_2)$$

and

$$\lambda = \frac{\theta_1}{1-\theta_1} \frac{1-\theta_2}{\theta_2}.$$

Then H_0 is equivalent to $\lambda=1$ and H_1 to $\lambda>1$, since $(1-\theta_1)/(1-\theta_2)<1$ and $\theta_1/\theta_2>1$, whenever $\theta_1>\theta_2$. With this parametrization the conditional distribution of (X_1,X_2), given that $X_1+X_2=y$, is independent of τ. From theorem 12.2 it follows for $\lambda=1$ that

$$g(x_1,x_2|y) = \binom{n_1}{x_1}\binom{n_2}{x_2}/\binom{n_1+n_2}{y}.$$

The alternative $\theta_1>\theta_2$ is supported by values of x_1 close to $\min(y,n_1)$ and the level of significance is accordingly

(12.17) $$p = \sum_{z \geq x_1} \binom{n_1}{z}\binom{n_2}{y-z}/\binom{n_1+n_2}{y}.$$

Example 12.5

As part of an investigation in 1981 of the indoor climate at the Faculty of Arts at the University of Copenhagen, the aim of which was to relate a number of health complaints from the staff to environmental factors associated with the building, members of the staff were asked to complete a questionnaire. Table 12.1 shows the answers given by a group of 46 persons to the question "Do you often suffer from smarting eyes", cross tabulated with type of floor material in their office. The floor material could either be traditional linoleum or needle felt.

Table 12.1. Distribution of 46 staff members according to the sufferance from smarting eyes and flooring material.

Suffering from smarting eyes	Flooring material		Total
	Linoleum	Needle felt	
Yes	1	18	19
No	5	22	27
Total	6	40	46

Let X_1 and X_2 be the number of persons suffering from smarting eyes with linoleum or with needle felt flooring respectively. It is assumed that X_1 and X_2 are independent with $X_1 \sim b(6, \theta_1)$ and $X_2 \sim b(40, \theta_2)$ where θ_1 and θ_2 can be interpreted as the relative risk of suffering from smarting eyes with linoleum and with needle felt, respectively.

Needle felt is suspected of causing smarting eyes, so the null hypothesis $\theta_1 = \theta_2$, i.e. the type of flooring does not affect the occurrence of smarting eyes, should be tested against the alternative $\theta_1 < \theta_2$, i.e. that there is a significantly higher number of persons suffering from smarting eyes among those working on needle felt.

The null hypothesis is tested by means of the conditional test derived from theorem 12.2. The observed value x_1 of X_1 is related to the conditional distribution with point probability

$$f(x_1 | X_1 + X_2 = 19) = \binom{6}{x_1}\binom{40}{19-x_1} / \binom{46}{19},$$

which is the true distribution under H_0. Since $E[X_1 | X_1 + X_2 = 19] = 19 \cdot 6/46 = 2.48$, small values of X_1 suggest rejection of H_0. According to (12.8), the level of significance is

$$p = \sum_{x=0}^{1} \binom{6}{x}\binom{40}{19-x} / \binom{46}{19} = 0.1954.$$

Even though there is some evidence in favour of the alternative hypothesis, the difference between the frequencies of the occurrence of smarting eyes on the two types of flooring can be interpreted as random variation. △.

12.6. Approximate tests

It is difficult in many cases to derive the exact distribution of the test statistic under the null hypothesis. For example, suppose that the random variable X is binomially distributed with parameters (n,θ), and that the hypothesis $H_0: \theta = \theta_0$ is to be tested. With X as test statistic and the alternative $\theta > \theta_0$, the level of significance $p = P(X \geq x)$ cannot be found in a table of the binomial distribution if n is sufficiently large. However, according to theorem 9.10, X is approximately normally distributed with mean $n\theta_0$ and variance $n\theta_0(1-\theta_0)$ under H_0 for large n. Therefore the test statistic

$$(12.18) \qquad U = \frac{X - n\theta_0}{\sqrt{n\theta_0(1-\theta_0)}}$$

is approximately standardized normally distributed and the level of significance can be approximated by

$$p \simeq P\left(U \geq \frac{x - n\theta_0}{\sqrt{n\theta_0(1-\theta_0)}}\right) = 1 - \Phi\left(\frac{x - n\theta_0}{\sqrt{n\theta_0(1-\theta_0)}}\right).$$

If the level of significance is computed from an approximation to the distribution of the test statistic, the test is called an **approximate test**.

Example 12.6

A motor magazine claims that 30% of the private cars in Denmark are Japanese. In order to obtain a quick check of this claim the number of Japanese cars passing a check point on a road near Copenhagen is observed one morning over a period of two hours. Out of a total of 633 observed cars, 211 were Japanese. Assume that the observed value, x=211, follows a binomial distribution with parameters $(633,\theta)$. If the claim is correct, then θ should be equal to 0.3, corresponding to the hypothesis $H_0: \theta = 0.3$. The observed value of the test statistic (12.18) is

$$u = \frac{211 - 633 \cdot 0.3}{\sqrt{633(0.3)(0.7)}} = 1.83,$$

and the level of significance against the alternative $\theta \neq 0.3$ is approximately

$$p \simeq 2P(U>1.83) = 0.067 \ .$$

Hence the observed number of Japanese cars supports the alternative hypothesis but not strongly enough to reject the hypothesis at test level 0.05. △.

In the case of a Poisson distribution, theorem 9.12 can be used to calculate approximate levels of significance. According to this theorem, when $X \sim Ps(\lambda)$

(12.19) $\quad U = \dfrac{X-\lambda}{\sqrt{\lambda}}$

is approximately normally distributed with mean 0 and variance 1 for $\lambda > 9$. For a test of the hypothesis $\lambda = \lambda_0$ against the alternative $\lambda > \lambda_0$, the level of significance is approximately

$$P\left(\dfrac{X-\lambda_0}{\sqrt{\lambda_0}} \geq u\right) = 1-\Phi(u), \text{ where } u = \dfrac{x-\lambda_0}{\sqrt{\lambda_0}} \ .$$

When the random variable X is hypergeometrically distributed with point probabilities

$$f(x) = \binom{N\theta}{x}\binom{N(1-\theta)}{n-x} / \binom{N}{n}$$

the hypothesis $H_0: \theta = \theta_0$ can be tested by an approximate test. According to (9.18), X is approximately normally distributed with mean $n\theta_0$ and variance

(12.20) $\quad \sigma_0^2 = n\theta_0(1-\theta_0)\dfrac{N-n}{N-1}.$

For an observed value x, the level of significance for a test of H_0 against the alternative $\theta > \theta_0$ is thus approximately

(12.21) $\quad p \simeq P(U \geq u),$

where $u = (x-n\theta_0)/\sigma_0$ and U is approximately normally distributed with mean 0 and variance 1.

Example 12.7

In the spring of 1975, 204 students sat for their final examinations in business economics at the Copenhagen School of Business Administration. Of these, 172 passed the examinations. In the spring of 1976, 272 took the examinations and 207 passed. The question is, whether these observations support a claim to the effect that the chance of passing the examinations has decreased from 1975 to 1976. This means that we must check whether there were relatively more students who passed in 1976 than in 1975.

Let X_1 and X_2 be random variables representing the numbers of students who passed in 1975 and 1976, respectively, and consider the null hypothesis, that there is an equal chance of passing in the two years under consideration. Under this hypothesis X_1 can be considered as the number of students who passed in 1975 in a random sample of size 379, drawn from the total population of 476 students. Hence the conditional distribution of X_1, given that $X_1+X_2=379$, is under the null hypothesis hypergeometric with parameters (379, 204, 476).

The expected number of students who would have passed in 1975 under the null hypothesis is

$$379 \cdot \frac{204}{476} = 162.4 .$$

The alternative, that there has been a decrease in the chance of passing from 1975 to 1976, is supported by large values of X_1. For the observed value $x_1=172$, the significance probability is

$$p = P(X_1 \geq 172 | X_1+X_2=379) .$$

According to (12.20) and (12.21), the hypergeometric distribution can be approximated by a normal distribution with mean 162.4 and variance

$$\sigma^2 = 379 \cdot \frac{204}{476} \cdot \frac{272}{476} \cdot \frac{476-379}{476-1} = 18.95 .$$

Hence

$$p \simeq 1-\Phi\left(\frac{172-162.4}{\sqrt{18.95}}\right) = 0.014$$

This level of significance is so low that the hypothesis of equal chances must be rejected. A possible explanation for this could be that the examinations in 1976 were more difficult than the corresponding examinations in 1975. △.

In section 12.5 it was shown how to compare the probability parameters of two binomial distributions by means of a conditional test. As an alternative to this method, a direct comparison of two frequencies is possible. Let x_1 and x_2 be observations of two independent, binomially distributed random variables X_1 and X_2, where $X_1 \sim b(n_1,\theta_1)$ and $X_2 \sim b(n_2,\theta_2)$. An intuitive test statistic for the hypothesis $H_0: \theta_1 = \theta_2$ is given by

$$\hat{\theta}_1 - \hat{\theta}_2 = x_1/n_1 - x_2/n_2 ,$$

i.e. the difference between the ML-estimates for θ_1 and θ_2. Hence, a large value of $|\theta_1-\theta_2|$ suggests rejection of H_0 in favour of the alternative $\theta_1 \neq \theta_2$. If n_1 and n_2 are sufficiently large, $\hat{\theta}_1 - \hat{\theta}_2$ is approximately normally distributed with mean 0 and variance $\theta(1-\theta)(1/n_1+1/n_2)$ under H_0, where θ is the common value of θ_1 and θ_2. Under H_0 the ML-estimator of θ is

$$\hat{\theta} = (X_1+X_2)/(n_1+n_2)$$

and it can be shown that approximately

(12.22) $$U = \frac{\hat{\theta}_1 - \hat{\theta}_2}{\sqrt{\hat{\theta}(1-\hat{\theta})(1/n_1+1/n_2)}}$$

follows a standardized normal distribution. The level of significance for a test of H_0 against the alternative $\theta_1 \neq \theta_2$ can therefore be approximated by

$$p = 2P(U \geq |u|) = 2(1-\Phi(|u|))$$

where u is the observed value of U. For small values of n_1 and n_2, the conditional test should be preferred to (12.22). For large values of n_1 and n_2 the conditional test and the test based on (12.22) are nearly equivalent.

12.7. The power of a test

By fixing the test level α, the probability of incorrectly rejecting the null hypothesis by chance is controlled. The error arising from an incorrect rejection of the null hypothesis is called a **type I error**. Since the purpose of performing a test is to detect a possible departure from the null hypothesis, the probability of detecting such departures is also of interest.

Consider a test with critical region R and test level α, based on the test statistic T. If the null hypothesis is $\theta = \theta_0$ (or $\theta \leq \theta_0$) and the alternative $\theta > \theta_0$, then

(12.23) $\quad \eta(\theta_1) = P(T \in R | \theta_1)$

is the probability that an observed value of T falls in the critical region when the parameter has the value θ_1. For $\theta_1 > \theta_0$, $\eta(\theta_1)$ is the probability of detecting a departure from the null hypothesis. This probability is called **the power of the test** at θ_1. The quantity $1 - \eta(\theta_1)$ is then the probability of erroneously accepting the null hypothesis if the parameter has the value $\theta_1 \neq \theta_0$. This kind of error is called a **type II error**. If the power of the test is considered as a function of θ_1, $\eta(\theta_1)$ is called the **power function** of the test. The power function expresses the probability of obtaining a value of the test statistic in the critical region as a function of θ. Notice that $\eta(\theta_0) = \alpha$, i.e. that the power of the test when θ has the value expressed by the null hypothesis is equal to the test level. Furthermore, for any reasonable test of $\theta \leq \theta_0$ against $\theta > \theta_0$, $\eta(\theta) \leq \alpha$ for $\theta < \theta_0$ and $\eta(\theta) \geq \alpha$ for $\theta > \theta_0$. Fig. 12.1 shows an example of a power function.

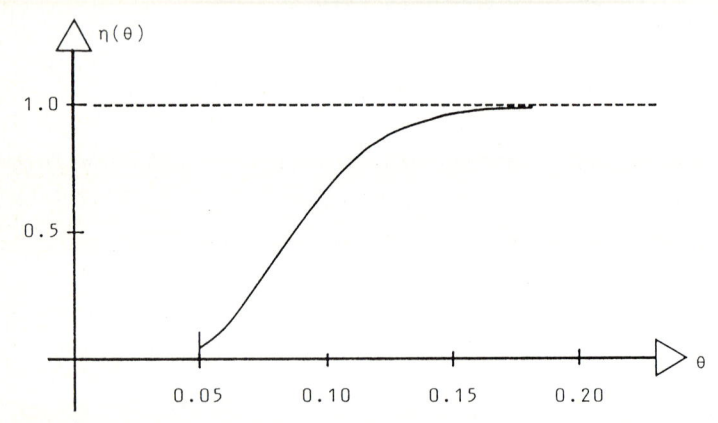

Fig. 12.1. The power of a test with critical region $\{x | x \geq 5\}$ for the hypothesis $\lambda \leq 2$ against the alternative $\lambda > 2$.

Example 12.1 (continued)

Suppose that a particularly critical situation occurs if the expected number of arrivals λ exceeds 3. It can thus be shown that if $\lambda > 3$ then there can after 5 minutes be expected to be more than 5 customers in the queue, after 10 minutes more than 10 customers and so on. The ability of the test procedure to detect that λ is in fact larger than or equal to 3 can be measured by the power of the test at $\lambda = 3$. For test level $\alpha = 0.0527$, the critical region is $R = \{x | x \geq 5\}$. The power of this test at $\lambda = 3$ is accordingly

$$\hat{\eta}(3) = P(X \geq 5 | \lambda = 3) = 0.1847 \ .$$

The proposed test is thus very weak. Even when the queue is clearly out of balance, there is a probability of more than 80% for accepting the null hypothesis. The reason for this lack of power is the very sparse information on which the test is based on. Clearly the queue need to be observed for a longer period. The power function of the considered test is shown in fig. 12.1.△.

As it has been shown, when testing statistical hypotheses, two kinds of errors can be committed. The null hypothesis may be rejected when it is in fact true, and it may be accepted when it is in fact false. Ideally the probabilities of both kinds of errors should be minimized.

If a choice has to be made between two tests, that test which minimizes the probability of falsely accepting the null hypothesis is usually preferred. For a test based on a fixed sample size, a reduction in size of the type I error or the test level will almost always entail an increase in the size of the type II error. Since it is not possible to minimize both types of errors simultaneously, it is common practice to fix the test level such that the probability of a type I error is controlled. This procedure reflects the different roles of the null hypothesis and the alternative hypothesis. The null hypothesis is accepted unless it is quite clearly contradicted by the data. An acceptance of the null hypothesis, however, does not necessarily mean that the hypothesis is true. The null hypothesis often represents a model for the data, which is more simple and easy to interpret than the alternatives. Hence it is desirable to reject H_0 only if there is clear evidence against it.

The table below illustrates the different types of errors and the probabilities with which they occur:

	H_0 is true	H_1 is true
$x \in R$	α Type I	$\eta(\theta)$
$x \notin R$	$1-\alpha$	$1-\eta(\theta)$ Type II

The power of a test reflects the efficiency of the test with regard to detecting specific alternatives from H_0 and is useful, therefore when different tests are to be compared.

12.8. Hypothesis testing and interval estimation

The methods of constructing confidence intervals and critical regions show that they are related - at least from a computational point of view. Let $x_1,\ldots,x_n$ be observations of independent, identically distributed random variables with unknown mean, μ, and known variance, σ_0^2. According to (11.6) a two-sided confidence interval for μ with level of confidence $1-\alpha$ is given by

(12.24) $\quad [\bar{x}-u_{1-\alpha/2}\sigma_0/\sqrt{n},\ \bar{x}+u_{1-\alpha/2}\sigma_0/\sqrt{n}]$,

and the acceptance region for a test of the hypothesis $\mu=\mu_0$ against the two-sided alternative $\mu \neq \mu_0$ is according to (12.5)

(12.25) $\quad [\mu_0-u_{1-\alpha/2}\sigma_0/\sqrt{n},\ \mu_0+u_{1-\alpha/2}\sigma_0/\sqrt{n}]$.

If μ_0 is a value in the interval (12.24), then

$$|\bar{x}-\mu_0| \leq u_{1-\alpha/2}\sigma_0/\sqrt{n} ,$$

and it follows that $\bar{x}$ is contained in (12.25). Hence, the confidence interval with level of confidence $1-\alpha$ consists of all parameter values, which would not be rejected as a null hypothesis at test level α on the basis of the observed value $\bar{x}$. A level α confidence interval can thus be constructed from a test with level α.

13. Models and Tests Related to the Normal Distribution

13.1. The u-test

Let $x_1,\ldots,x_n$ be observations of independent, identically normally distributed random variables $X_1,\ldots,X_n$ with mean μ and variance σ^2, and consider the hypothesis

$$H_0: \mu=\mu_0 .$$

Assume further that the value of σ^2 is known. Then (see section 12.3)

$$(13.1) \qquad U = \frac{\bar{X}-\mu_0}{\sigma}\sqrt{n}$$

can be used as a test statistic for H_0 against the alternative

$$H_1: \mu>\mu_0,$$

with large observed values of U suggesting a rejection of H_0 in favour of H_1. Under H_0, U follows a standardized normal distribution, so the level of significance is given by

$$p = P(U \geq u) = 1-\Phi(u)$$

where u is the observed value of U. The critical region of a significance test at level α consists of samples for which $u \geq u_{1-\alpha}$ or, equivalently, for which

$$\bar{x} \geq \mu_0 + u_{1-\alpha}\sigma/\sqrt{n} .$$

Also if the alternative hypothesis is $H_1: \mu<\mu_0$, U given by (13.1) can be used as test statistic. But the level of significance is then given by

$$P(U \leq u) = \Phi(u),$$

since small values of U support H_1.

In this case the critical region for a test at level α consists of samples for which

$$\bar{x} \leq \mu_0 + u_\alpha \sigma/\sqrt{n} .$$

The appropriate test statistic for testing H_0 against the two-sided alternative $H_1: \mu \neq \mu_0$ is $|U|$. This implies that values of $\bar{x}$ which are equidistant from μ_0 are regarded as supporting H_0 to the same degree. The level of significance is

$$p = P(|U| \geq |u|) = P(U \leq -|u|) + P(U \geq |u|) = 2(1-\Phi(|u|)),$$

and the critical region for a test at level α consists of samples for which

$$\bar{x} \leq \mu_0 + u_{\alpha/2} \sigma/\sqrt{n}$$

or

$$\bar{x} \geq \mu_0 + u_{1-\alpha/2} \sigma/\sqrt{n} .$$

Table 13.1 summarizes the calculations of significance levels and critical regions for testing H_0 against each of the alternatives $\mu < \mu_0$, $\mu > \mu_0$ and $\mu \neq \mu_0$.

Table 13.1. Levels of significance and critical regions for the u-test.

Alternative	Level of significance	Critical region
$\mu < \mu_0$	$\Phi(u)$	$u \leq u_\alpha$
$\mu > \mu_0$	$1 - \Phi(u)$	$u \geq u_{1-\alpha}$
$\mu \neq \mu_0$	$2(1-\Phi(|u|))$	$|u| \geq u_{1-\alpha/2}$

Tests based on test statistics of the form given by (13.1), following a standard normal distribution, are called **u-tests**.

Example 13.1

An instrument used for measuring the alcohol content in human blood is routinely checked every morning to determine whether or not it needs adjusting. The check is based on repeated measurements of the alcohol content in a blood solution and these measurements are compared with the known alcohol content.

It can be assumed that such measurements are independent and normally distributed with a variance of 0.0354^2. For 11 measurements of a solution with a known alcohol content of 1.514 0/00, the average was 1.477. The instrument is to be adjusted if the hypothesis

$$H_0: \mu = 1.514$$

is rejected against the alternative $\mu \neq 1.514$ at test level 0.05. In this case, a u-test can be employed, and the value of the test statistic (13.1) with $n=11$ and $\sigma=0.0354$ is

$$u = \sqrt{11}\frac{1.477-1.514}{0.0354} = -3.47 \quad,$$

corresponding to a level of significance

$$p = 2(1-\Phi(3.47)) \simeq 0.00052 \quad.$$

Even if the test level was $\alpha = 0.001$, the null hypothesis would be rejected and it is therefore concluded that the instrument needs adjusting. △.

Consider a test of $H_0: \mu = \mu_0$ against the one-sided alternative $H_1: \mu > \mu_0$ with test level α. Using the test statistic (13.1), table 13.1 shows that the critical region consists of samples for which

$$u = \frac{\overline{x}-\mu_0}{\sigma}\sqrt{n} \geq u_{1-\alpha},$$

i.e. for which

$$\overline{x} \geq \mu_0 + u_{1-\alpha}\sigma/\sqrt{n} \quad.$$

The power η of the test is the probability of observing $\overline{x}$ in the critical region, given that the mean is μ, i.e.

(13.2) $\quad \eta(\mu) = P(\overline{X} > \mu_0 + u_{1-\alpha}\sigma/\sqrt{n} | \mu)$

$$= P\left(\frac{\overline{X}-\mu}{\sigma}\sqrt{n} > \frac{\mu_0-\mu}{\sigma}\sqrt{n} + u_{1-\alpha} | \mu\right) = 1-\Phi\left(\frac{\mu_0-\mu}{\sigma}\sqrt{n} + u_{1-\alpha}\right).$$

Fig. 13.1 illustrates the calculation of the power for $\mu = \mu_1$. The complete power function is shown in fig. 13.2. Note that the power is equal to the test level α for $\mu = \mu_0$ and increases as μ departs from μ_0 in the direction given by the alternative. This means that larger values of μ corresponds to higher probabilities of correctly rejecting H_0.

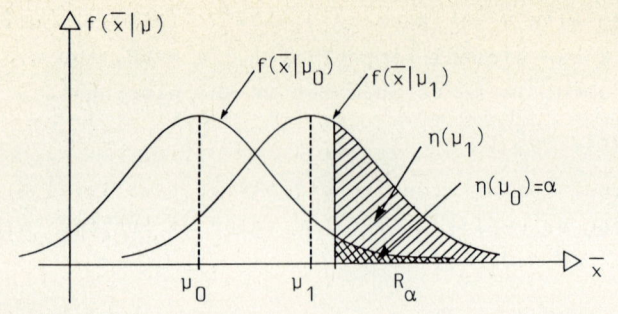

Fig. 13.1. Computation of the power for $\mu=\mu_1$.

Example 13.2

The dependence of the power of the u-test on the test level α and the sample size n can be illustrated numerically. Consider a test of $H_0:\mu=\mu_0$ against the alternative $H_1:\mu>\mu_0$ at level $\alpha=0.05$ based on sample size n=10 from a normal distribution. If the variance is 9, the critical region consists of all samples for which $\bar{x}$ is larger than $\mu_0+1.645\cdot 3/\sqrt{10}$.

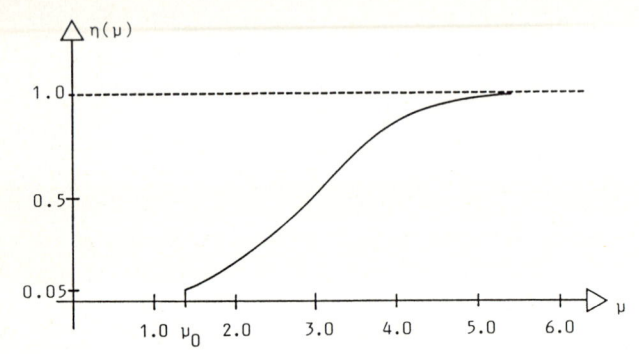

Fig. 13.2. The power function for a u-test of $H_0:\mu=\mu_0$ against the alternative $H_1:\mu>\mu_0$ at level $\alpha=0.05$.

For $\mu=\mu_0+1$, (13.2) yields

$$\eta(\mu_0+1) = 1-\Phi(-\frac{1}{3}\sqrt{10}+1.645) \simeq 0.28 .$$

Decreasing the level from 0.05 to 0.01 gives

$$\eta(\mu_0+1) = 1-\Phi(-\frac{1}{3}\sqrt{10}+2.326) \simeq 0.10 .$$

Thus if the level of significance is decreased, the power decreases, so a reduction in the risk of rejecting a correct hypothesis reduces the probability of detecting a departure in the direction given by the alternative.

Suppose now that the sample size is increased from 10 to 25. With test level 0.05,

$$\eta(\mu_0+1) = 1-\Phi(-\frac{1}{3}\sqrt{25}+1.645) = 1-\Phi(-0.02) = 0.508 ,$$

so that for a fixed test level, the power increases as the sample size is increased. In other words, the probability of detecting a given departure from the null hypothesis increases with increasing sample size.

△.

From (13.2) follows that $\eta(\mu) \to 1$ for every $\mu > \mu_0$, as $n \to \infty$. Hence, a deviation from μ_0, however small, is detected with arbitrary high probability by increasing the sample size. This property raises a problem concerning the choice of the level of significance for a given test. It is natural to distinguish between a result which is significant from a practical point of view, and a result which is significant in a statistical sense. From a practical point of view the detection of small deviations from the null hypothesis may be of little importance. If the size of the sample is large, however, H_0 would be rejected with a probability close to one, even when μ is very close to μ_0. If small deviations are of no practical importance, the test level may be decreased without risking that alternatives of practical importance pass unnoticed.

Traditionally, a test level of $\alpha=0.05$ is used in many applications. This may well be a reasonable choice if no supplementary information is available and if the sample size is moderate. However, if possible, the choice of test level should be based on a close examination of the problem at hand, and on the size and the quality of the sample.

It is possible to determine the smallest sample size for which a u-test at level α with probability η_0 rejects the null hypothesis when the true parameter value is $\mu > \mu_0$, i.e. to determine a sample size such that the power of the test attains the value η_0 at μ. The power is η_0 if

$$\eta_0 = 1-\Phi\left(\frac{\mu_0-\mu}{\sigma}\sqrt{n} + u_{1-\alpha}\right).$$

Since this function is monotonically increasing in n, the smallest sample size possible to attain the power η_0 is accordingly the smallest integer greater than or equal to

$$n_0 = (u_{1-\eta_0} - u_{1-\alpha})^2 \sigma^2 / (\mu_0-\mu)^2.$$

13.2. The t-test

Consider again n observations $x_1,\ldots,x_n$ of independent, identically distributed random variables $X_1,\ldots,X_n$, where $X_i \sim N(\mu,\sigma^2)$. As in section 13.1, the null hypothesis is

$$H_0: \mu=\mu_0 .$$

In contrast to the problem discussed above consider the situation with unknown variance. H_0 is called a **composite hypothesis**, since the statistical model depends on two parameters, only one of which is specified by the null hypothesis. Since there is no reference to the value of σ^2 in H_0, it would be convenient if the distribution of the test statistic does not depend on σ^2.

Substituting the estimator S for σ in (13.1) yields

$$(13.3) \qquad T = \frac{\overline{X}-\mu_0}{S}\sqrt{n} ,$$

where $S^2 = \Sigma(X_i-\overline{X})^2/(n-1)$. Under the alternative

$$H_1: \mu>\mu_0,$$

large observed values of $\overline{X}$ support the alternative hypothesis. Hence large observed values of T are evidence against H_0. According to theorem 9.6, (13.3) is under H_0 t-distributed with n-1 degrees of freedom. The level of significance is

$$(13.4) \qquad p = P(T \geq t | H_0) = 1-P(T \leq t | H_0) .$$

The critical region for a test with level α consists of samples for which T is larger than the $(1-\alpha)$ percentile in a t-distribution with n-1 degrees of freedom, i.e. for which $\overline{x} \geq \mu_0 + t_{1-\alpha}(n-1)s/\sqrt{n}$.

For a test of H_0 against the one-sided alternative $H_1: \mu<\mu_0$, the level of significance becomes

$$(13.5) \qquad p = P(T \leq t | H_0) ,$$

while the critical region with test level α consists of samples for which T is less than the α percentile in the t-distribution with n-1 degrees of freedom.

For a test of H_0 against the two-sided alternative, $H_1: \mu \neq \mu_0$, the test statistic is

$$|T| = \frac{|\overline{X}-\mu_0|}{S}\sqrt{n} .$$

The evidence against H_0 grows as the value of $|T|$ increases. If the values t and $-t$ are additionally assumed to support H_0 to the same degree, the level of significance becomes

$$(13.6) \quad p = P(|T| \geq |t|) = P(T \geq |t|) + P(T \leq -|t|) = 2P(T \geq |t|),$$

in view of the symmetry of the t-distribution. A test of H_0 at level α against a two-sided alternative thus has a critical region consisting of samples for which T is less than the $\alpha/2$ percentile or larger than the $(1-\alpha/2)$ percentile in a t-distribution with $n-1$ degrees of freedom.

A test based on the test statistic (13.3) is called a **t-test**. Table 13.2 summarizes levels of significance and critical regions for t-tests of $H_0: \mu = \mu_0$ against the alternatives $\mu > \mu_0$, $\mu < \mu_0$ and $\mu \neq \mu_0$.

Table 13.2. Levels of significance and critical regions for the t-test.

Alternative	Levels of significance	Critical region
$\mu > \mu_0$	$P(T \geq t)$	$t \geq t_{1-\alpha}(n-1)$
$\mu < \mu_0$	$P(T \leq t)$	$t \leq t_{\alpha}(n-1)$
$\mu \neq \mu_0$	$2P(T \geq |t|)$	$|t| > t_{1-\alpha/2}(n-1)$

13.3. The Q-test

As in the previous sections of this chapter, assume that $x_1, \ldots, x_n$ are the observed values of independent, identically distributed random variables $X_1, \ldots, X_n$, where $X_1 \sim N(\mu, \sigma^2)$, and consider this time the null hypothesis for the variance

$$H_0: \sigma^2 = \sigma_0^2$$

and the alternative

$$H_1: \sigma^2 > \sigma_0^2,$$

assuming that μ is unknown. The estimate of σ^2 is

$$s^2 = \frac{1}{n-1} \sum_{i=1}^{n} (x_i - \bar{x})^2,$$

and the evidence against H_0 grows as the value of s^2/σ_0^2 increases.

The test statistic

$$(13.7) \quad Q = (n-1)\frac{s^2}{\sigma_0^2},$$

where $S^2 = \sum_i (X_i - \bar{X})^2/(n-1)$, can, therefore, be used to test H_0.

From theorem 9.5, it follows that

$$Q \sim \chi^2(n-1),$$

so the level of significance becomes

$$p = P(Q \geq q),$$

where

$$q = (n-1)s^2/\sigma_0^2.$$

The critical region for a test with level α consists of samples for which the value of Q is larger than the $(1-\alpha)$ percentile in the χ^2-distribution with n-1 degrees of freedom, i.e. H_0 is rejected at level α, if

$$q > \chi^2_{1-\alpha}(n-1).$$

Against the alternative

$$H_1: \sigma^2 < \sigma_0^2,$$

the level of significance is

$$p = P(Q \leq q),$$

and the critical region for a test with level α consists of values of Q smaller than $\chi^2_\alpha(n-1)$.

If the alternative hypothesis is

$$H_1: \sigma^2 \neq \sigma_0^2,$$

H_0 is rejected both when the observed value of Q is large and when it is close to 0. In order to determine the level of significance under a two-sided alternative, two cases must accordingly be considered. If q is larger than the median of Q under H_0, then values of the test statistic larger than q support H_0 to a lesser degree than q. To the probability of observing such values must be added, however, values of Q in the lower tail of its distribution under H_0. If small values of the test statistic are included with the same weight as large values, the level of significance is given by

(13.8) $2P(Q \geq q)$ for $q > n-5/3$,

since the median for $Q \sim \chi^2(f)$ is approximately $f-2/3$. If the observed value q of the test statistic is less than the median under H_0, the same line of reasoning leads to the level of significance

(13.9) $2P(Q \leq q)$ for $q < n-5/3$.

A critical region based on the test statistic Q with level α comprises equally large areas in each of the tails of the density function of the χ^2-distribution with n-1 degrees of freedom, and thereby consists of values of Q, that are either larger than $\chi^2_{1-\alpha/2}(n-1)$ or smaller than $\chi^2_{\alpha/2}(n-1)$.

Example 13.3

Consider a sample $x_1, \ldots, x_{20}$ of observed values of normally distributed random variables $X_1, \ldots, X_{20}$ with common mean value μ and variance σ^2. Neither of the parameters are known. The hypothesis $H_0: \sigma^2 = 2.5$ is to be tested based on the observed values $\bar{x} = 22.1$ and $s^2 = 1.084$. Since $q = 19 \cdot 1.084/2.5 = 8.24 < 18.33$, the level of significance is, according to (13.9), given by

$$p = 2P(Q \leq 8.24) = 0.034,$$

where $Q \sim \chi^2(19)$.

The critical region for a test with level $\alpha = 0.05$ consists of values of Q, less than $\chi^2_{0.025}(19) = 8.91$ and greater than $\chi^2_{0.975}(19) = 32.9$. $\triangle$.

If μ is known, the variance σ^2 is estimated by

$$\hat{\sigma}^2 = \frac{1}{n} \sum_{i=1}^{n} (x_i - \mu)^2 .$$

From definition 9.1 it follows that $Q_0 = n\hat{\sigma}^2/\sigma_0^2$ is χ^2-distributed with n degrees of freedom. Hence, Q_0 can be used as test statistic for H_0. The level of significance is derived by replacing Q by Q_0 and n-1 by n in formulae (13.8) and (13.9). In the same way, the limits for a critical region with level α are given by $\chi^2_{\alpha/2}(n)$ and $\chi^2_{1-\alpha/2}(n)$.

Example 13.4

When bottling beer, it is important that the distance from the level of the beer to the rim of the bottle is neither too small nor too large. If this distance is too small, the bottle may explode during the subsequent process of pasteurization, and if it is too large, the keeping qualities and the taste of the beer are affected.

A brewery specifies that the expected distance between the beer and the rim of the bottle should be 50 mm, and that the probability of a distance less than 35 mm or more than 65 mm should be very small. These specifications are met if a normally distributed random variable X, describing the distance in question measured in mm, has mean $\mu=50$ and standard deviation at most $\sigma=5$, since then

(13.10) $P((X \leq 35) \cup (X \geq 65)) = \Phi(-3) + 1 - \Phi(3) = 0.0027$.

For a tapping machine, satisfying these specifications, a two year guarantee was issued. Towards the end of the guarantee period, the brewery wants to check if the machine still satisfies the specifications. Thus a random sample of 20 bottles is selected and the following filling distances are measured (in mm):

$$\begin{array}{cccccccccc} 49 & 53 & 41 & 60 & 58 & 38 & 33 & 44 & 52 & 52 \\ 46 & 64 & 45 & 49 & 60 & 52 & 45 & 48 & 55 & 51 \end{array}$$.

First of all, it is necessary to control that the data can be described by a normal distribution. The probability plot, shown in fig. 13.3, supports the assumption of normality. In passing, it should be noted that computations of tail probabilities like (13.10) can not be justified by a probability plot with only 20 observations.

The next step is to check whether the standard deviation of the distance is at most 5 mm. This is done by testing

$$H_0: \sigma^2 = 25$$

against the alternative

$$H_1: \sigma^2 > 25$$.

A one-sided alternative is chosen since only departures in the direction of larger standard deviations are of any interest.

The test statistic Q, given by (13.7), has the observed value

$$q = 19 \frac{59.36}{25} = 45.11$$.

Under H_0, $Q \sim \chi^2(19)$, so the level of significance is $p = P(Q \geq q) = 0.0007$.

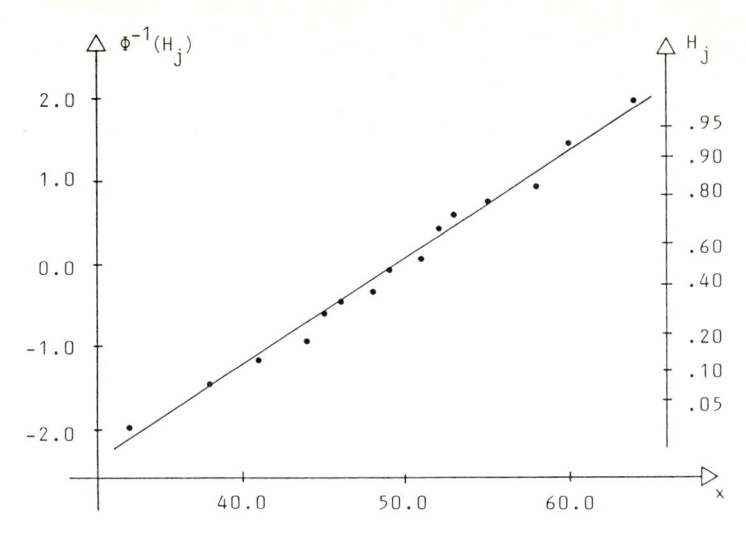

Fig. 13.3. Probability plot for the beer tapping data.

This means that H_0 is clearly rejected, even at level 0.001, and it can be concluded that the standard deviation is greater than 5. Thus the required standard is no longer met by the machine.

Finally it is checked whether the expected distance is still 50 mm. This is done by testing the null hypothesis

$$H_0: \mu=50$$

against the alternative

$$H_1: \mu \neq 50 \ .$$

Since σ^2 is unknown, it is necessary to use the test statistic T, given by (13.3). The observed value of T is

$$t = \frac{\bar{x}-50}{s}\sqrt{20} = -0.15 \ .$$

Since, under H_0, $T \sim t(19)$, the level of significance is

$$p = 2P(T>0.15) = 0.924 \ ,$$

implying that there is insufficient evidence to reject the hypothesis of an expected mean distance of 50 mm.

The over-all conclusion of the analysis is that although the expected distance between beer and rim still seems to be 50 mm, the standard deviation is now greater than the original 5 mm. △.

13.4. The comparison of two independent, normally distributed samples

Let each of two samples of sizes n_1 and n_2, respectively, be collected under essentially identical conditions with $x_{i1},\ldots,x_{in_i}$ denoting the observations of the i'th sample, $i=1,2$. If the samples are normally distributed, they can be compared with the help of the following model:

$\{x_{ij}, j=1,\ldots,n_i, i=1,2\}$ are observations of independent random variables $\{X_{ij}, j=1,\ldots,n_i, i=1,2\}$, where $X_{ij} \sim N(\mu_i, \sigma_i^2)$.

This model is called the **model for the comparison of two independent samples**, and can also be stated as

$$X_{ij} = \mu_i + e_{ij}, \quad i=1,2 \text{ and } j=1,\ldots,n_i,$$

where the e_{ij}'s are independent with $e_{ij} \sim N(0, \sigma_i^2)$.

In this form, the stochastic variation of the data is decomposed into a random error component, e_{ij}, and a structural component, μ_i, which represents the expected level of X_{ij}.

A comparison of the two samples can take the form of testing the equality of the means μ_1 and μ_2 or the equality of the variances σ_1^2 and σ_2^2.

Consider the hypothesis of equal means given that the variances σ_1^2 and σ_2^2 are known. This hypothesis can be formulated as

$$H_0: \delta = \mu_1 - \mu_2 = 0.$$

Since the ML-estimates for μ_1 and μ_2 are respectively

$$\bar{x}_1 = \frac{1}{n_1} \sum_{j=1}^{n_1} x_{1j} \quad \text{and} \quad \bar{x}_2 = \frac{1}{n_2} \sum_{j=1}^{n_2} x_{2j},$$

a test statistic should be based on the difference $d = \bar{x}_1 - \bar{x}_2$. From theorem 9.5, it follows that

1) $\bar{X}_1 \sim N(\mu_1, \sigma_1^2/n_1)$, $\bar{X}_2 \sim N(\mu_2, \sigma_2^2/n_2)$

and from independence of all the X_{ij}'s that

2) $\bar{X}_1$ and $\bar{X}_2$ are independent,

where $\bar{X}_1$ and $\bar{X}_2$ are the random variables corresponding to $\bar{x}_1$ and $\bar{x}_2$. Furthermore it follows from theorems 8.14 and 7.2 that

(13.11) $$\hat{\delta} = \bar{X}_1 - \bar{X}_2 \sim N\left(\mu_1 - \mu_2, \frac{\sigma_1^2}{n_1} + \frac{\sigma_2^2}{n_2}\right).$$

Hence, a test can be based on

(13.12) $U = (\bar{X}_1 - \bar{X}_2)/\sqrt{\sigma_1^2/n_1 + \sigma_2^2/n_2}$,

where $U \sim N(0,1)$ under H_0. The levels of significance of an observed value u and the critical regions for a fixed test level are those given in table 13.1.

In accordance with (11.6), confidence limits with level 1-α are given by

$$\underline{\delta} = \bar{x}_1 - \bar{x}_2 + u_{\alpha/2}\sqrt{\sigma_1^2/n_1 + \sigma_2^2/n_2}$$

and

$$\overline{\delta} = \bar{x}_1 - \bar{x}_2 + u_{1-\alpha/2}\sqrt{\sigma_1^2/n_1 + \sigma_2^2/n_2} .$$

If σ_1^2 and σ_2^2 are not known, they are estimated by the observed values of

$$S_1^2 = \frac{1}{n_1 - 1} \sum_{j=1}^{n_1} (X_{1j} - \bar{X}_1)^2$$

and

$$S_2^2 = \frac{1}{n_2 - 1} \sum_{j=1}^{n_2} (X_{2j} - \bar{X}_2)^2 ,$$

respectively. From theorem 9.5, it follows that $\bar{X}_1$, $\bar{X}_2$, S_1^2 and S_2^2 are all independent and that

$$\bar{X}_1 \sim N(\mu_1, \sigma_1^2/n_1), \quad \bar{X}_2 \sim N(\mu_2, \sigma_2^2/n_2),$$

$$\frac{(n_1-1)S_1^2}{\sigma_1^2} \sim \chi^2(n_1-1), \quad \frac{(n_2-1)S_2^2}{\sigma_2^2} \sim \chi^2(n_2-1) .$$

No simple test for the hypothesis $\mu_1 = \mu_2$ exists unless $\sigma_1^2 = \sigma_2^2$. Prior to testing a hypothesis of equal means, it is therefore necessary to test the hypothesis

$$H_0': \sigma_1^2 = \sigma_2^2 = \sigma^2$$

against the alternative

$$H_1': \sigma_1^2 \neq \sigma_2^2 .$$

As test statistic,

(13.13) $V = S_1^2 / S_2^2$,

is chosen. If the variances are equal, the ratio $v=s_1^2/s_2^2$ between the observed values of S_1^2 and S_2^2 can be expected to be close to 1. A value of V close to 0 supports the alternative $\sigma_1^2 < \sigma_2^2$, while a large value of V supports the alternative $\sigma_1^2 > \sigma_2^2$. The critical region for a test based on V should thus under the two-sided alternative H_1' consist of values of V near 0 or much greater than 1.

Under H_0',
$$\frac{(n_1-1)S_1^2}{\sigma^2} \sim \chi^2(n_1-1)$$
and
$$\frac{(n_2-1)S_2^2}{\sigma^2} \sim \chi^2(n_2-1) .$$

What is more, S_1^2 and S_2^2 are independent so definition 9.3 yields that
$$V \sim F(n_1-1, n_2-1) .$$

For a test of H_0' at level α, the critical region consists of values of V larger than $F_{1-\alpha/2}(f_1, f_2)$ or smaller than $F_{\alpha/2}(f_1, f_2)$, where $f_1 = n_1 - 1$ and $f_2 = n_2 - 1$.

In most statistical tables only percentiles above 0.50 are given for the F-distribution. However, since
$$P(V \leq v) = P\left(\frac{1}{V} \geq \frac{1}{v}\right)$$
it follows from definition 9.3 that

(13.14) $\quad F_{\alpha/2}(f_1, f_2) = 1/F_{1-\alpha/2}(f_2, f_1),$

so the percentiles for $\alpha/2 < 0.5$ can also be found. In fact, equation (13.14) can be used to define a new test statistic for testing H_0'. According to (13.14), the inequality
$$v \leq F_{\alpha/2}(f_1, f_2)$$
is satisfied if and only if
$$1/v \geq F_{1-\alpha/2}(f_2, f_1),$$
so the critical region for testing H_0' at level α consists of values v for which either $v \geq F_{1-\alpha/2}(f_1, f_2)$ or $1/v \geq F_{1-\alpha/2}(f_2, f_1)$. It can be easily

verified that this critical region comprises those values of the test statistic

(13.15) $\quad V^* = \max(S_1^2, S_2^2)/\min(S_1^2, S_2^2)$

for which

$$v^* \geq F_{1-\alpha/2}(f_1^*, f_2^*),$$

where

f_1^* = number of degrees of freedom for the numerator of V^*

and

f_2^* = number of degrees of freedom for the denominator of V^*.

It should be emphasized here that V^* does not follow an F-distribution. Since for any α between 0 and 1,

$$P(V^* \geq F_{1-\alpha/2}(f_1^*, f_2^*)) = \alpha,$$

the level of significance p for testing H_0' against the two-sided alternative $\sigma_1^2 \neq \sigma_2^2$ is given by the relation

$$v^* = F_{1-p/2}(f_1^*, f_2^*),$$

whereby $p = P(V^* \geq v^*)$ can be found using a table of the F-distribution.

If H_0' is accepted, the ML-estimator for the common value σ^2 of σ_1^2 and σ_2^2 becomes

$$S^2 = \frac{(n_1-1)S_1^2 + (n_2-1)S_2^2}{n_1+n_2-2}.$$

Under H_0',

$$\bar{X}_1 \sim N(\mu_1, \sigma^2/n_1)$$

and

$$\bar{X}_2 \sim N(\mu_2, \sigma^2/n_2).$$

From theorem 9.5, it then follows that $\bar{X}_1$, $\bar{X}_2$ and S^2 are independent and that

that if both n_1 and n_2 are large (e.g. both larger than 30), then

$$(13.18) \quad U^* = \frac{\bar{X}_1 - \bar{X}_2}{\sqrt{S_1^2/n_1 + S_2^2/n_2}}$$

follows a standard normal distribution approximately, and H_0 can then be tested with approximate levels of significance shown in table 13.1.

Example 13.5

The alcohol content in blood is estimated as the average of two measurements from different instruments. At regular intervals the instruments have to be controlled both with respect to the level of measurement and with respect to the precision. Such a control is based on two samples, each consisting of nine measurements of the alcohol content of a given blood sample. It is assumed that the repeated measurements made by the same instrument can be regarded as independent and identically distributed. The two samples can, therefore, be compared within the framework of a model for comparison of two independent, normally distributed samples.

Table 13.3. Alcohol contents in a blood sample measured by two different instruments.

Instrument 1	Instrument 2
1.075	0.982
1.068	1.029
1.030	0.984
1.031	1.002
1.029	1.028
1.016	1.001
1.024	1.018
1.020	0.980
1.000	0.965

The two sets of observations are shown in table 13.3, and the probability plots are shown in fig. 13.4. On the basis of these plots, it can only be said that there are no signs of systematic deviations from normality. Thus, it is assumed that the measurements made by instruments 1 and 2 are independent and normally distributed with parameters (μ_1, σ_1^2) and (μ_2, σ_2^2) respectively. The estimates of the parameters are $\bar{x}_1 = 1.0325$, $\bar{x}_2 = 0.9988$, $s_1^2 = 0.000580$ and $s_2^2 = 0.000518$.

The value of the test statistic (13.15) for the hypothesis $\sigma_1^2 = \sigma_2^2$ against the alternative $\sigma_1^2 \neq \sigma_2^2$ is 1.12. Since $F_{0.70}(8,8) = 1.1$, the level of significance is

$$\frac{(n_1+n_2-2)s^2}{\sigma^2} \sim \chi^2(n_1+n_2-2) \ .$$

A graphical check of the hypothesis $\sigma_1^2 = \sigma_2^2$ can be obtained by comparing the probability plots for the two samples. The slopes of the "fitted" lines are estimates of $1/\sigma_1$ and $1/\sigma_2$, so if $\sigma_1^2 = \sigma_2^2$, these lines should be parallel.

As in the case with known variances, the hypothesis of equal means is formulated as

$$H_0: \delta = 0 \ ,$$

where $\delta = \mu_1 - \mu_2$. Under H_0 and assuming that $\sigma_1^2 = \sigma_2^2$, the estimator $\hat{\delta} = \bar{X}_1 - \bar{X}_2$ is normally distributed with mean 0 and variance

$$\text{var}[\bar{X}_1 - \bar{X}_2] = \left(\frac{1}{n_1} + \frac{1}{n_2}\right)\sigma^2$$

as follows from theorems 8.14 and 7.2. According to definition 9.2, the test statistic

$$(13.16) \qquad T = (\bar{X}_1 - \bar{X}_2)/\sqrt{s^2\left(\frac{1}{n_1} + \frac{1}{n_2}\right)}$$

is then t-distributed with n_1+n_2-2 degrees of freedom. Levels of significance and critical regions for the alternatives $\delta > 0$, $\delta < 0$ and $\delta \neq 0$ are shown in table 13.2.

For a test of

$$H_0^*: \mu_1 - \mu_2 = \delta_0 \ ,$$

the test statistic

$$(13.17) \qquad T^* = (\bar{X}_1 - \bar{X}_2 - \delta_0)/\sqrt{s^2\left(\frac{1}{n_1} + \frac{1}{n_2}\right)}$$

is used. Since $E[\bar{X}_1 - \bar{X}_2] = \delta_0$ under H_0^*, T^* is t-distributed with n_1+n_2-2 degrees of freedom. Levels of significance and critical regions are again shown in table 13.2.

Confidence limits for δ with level $1-\alpha$ are given by

$$\underline{\delta} = \bar{x}_1 - \bar{x}_2 - t_{1-\alpha/2}(n_1+n_2-2)s\sqrt{\frac{1}{n_1} + \frac{1}{n_2}}$$

and

$$\overline{\delta} = \bar{x}_1 - \bar{x}_2 + t_{1-\alpha/2}(n_1+n_2-2)s\sqrt{\frac{1}{n_1} + \frac{1}{n_2}} \ .$$

The test statistic (13.16) does not follow a t-distribution if the assumption of equal variances does not hold. It can be shown, however,

$$p = P(V^* \geq 1.12) \simeq 0.60 ,$$

and the hypothesis of equal variances is not rejected. The estimate of the common variance is

$$s^2 = \frac{8 \cdot 0.000580 + 8 \cdot 0.000518}{16} = 0.000549 .$$

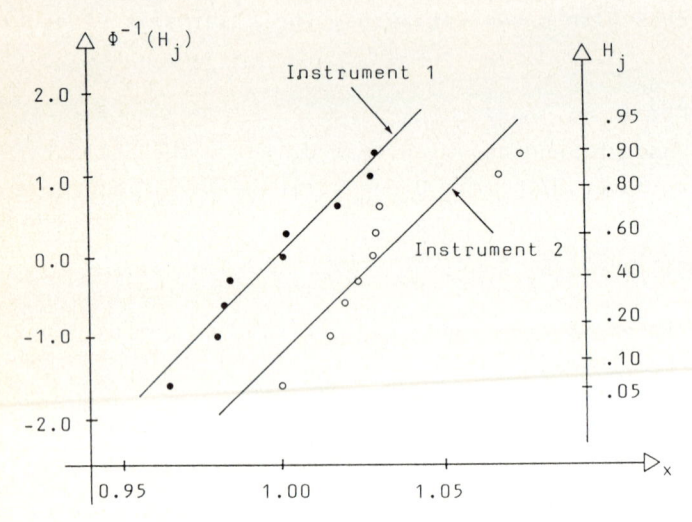

Fig. 13.4. Probability plots for content of alcohol in the blood.

To test the hypothesis $\mu_1 = \mu_2$ against the alternative $\mu_1 \neq \mu_2$, the test statistic (13.16) is used and the observed value is

$$t = \frac{1.0325 - 0.9988}{\sqrt{0.000549(1/9 + 1/9)}} = 3.057 .$$

Even at level $\alpha = 0.01$, the hypothesis is rejected, and it can be concluded that the two instruments do not operate with the same measurement level, even though the precision of the two instruments seems to be the same. The analysis does not indicate, of course, which instrument needs to be adjusted. Confidence limits for the difference δ with level 0.95 are given by

$$\underline{\delta} = 0.0337 - 2.120\sqrt{0.000549 \cdot 2/9} = 0.0103$$
$$\overline{\delta} = 0.0337 + 2.120\sqrt{0.000549 \cdot 2/9} = 0.0571 . \triangle$$

13.5. A model for pairwise observations

Example 13.6

Table 13.4 shows the annual profits of two Danish bonds over a period of 10 years. It can be assumed that the profit of a bond is primarily affected by two factors:

    1) the general level of interest, which changes from year to year,

and

    2) the bond specific interest, which depends on the nominal interest rate of the bond, the time elapsed since the bond was issued and the term of the bond.

The effects of these two factors on the profit may be called the year effect and the bond effect respectively. In a comparison of the two bonds, only the bond effect is of interest. Hence, it is necessary to formulate a model in which the year effect and the bond effect can be separated.

<u>Table 13.4</u>. The annual profit in % for two Danish bonds, 1955-1964.

Year	Bond 1	Bond 2	Difference
1955	5.67	5.83	-0.16
1956	5.96	5.92	0.04
1957	6.03	6.13	-0.10
1958	6.15	6.17	-0.02
1959	6.25	6.48	-0.23
1960	6.53	6.50	0.03
1961	6.74	6.70	0.04
1962	7.01	7.05	-0.04
1963	6.99	7.04	-0.05
1964	7.51	7.65	-0.14

Let the random variable X_{ij} represent the profit of the i'th bond ($i=1,2$) in year j ($j=1,\ldots,10$) and assume that the expected profit is the sum of a year effect α_j, $j=1,\ldots,10$, and a bond effect β_i, $i=1,2$, i.e.

(13.19) $E[X_{ij}] = \alpha_j + \beta_i$.

If (13.19) is true, a similar additive structure must be evident in the observed profits x_{ij}. This can be checked by the graphical method described in section 2.6. In fig. 13.5, x_{ij} is plotted against $\bar{x}_{\cdot j} = (x_{1j} + x_{2j})/2$ for fixed i and varying j. As the points cluster randomly around straight lines with slopes 1, the additive mean value structure (13.19) can be accepted.

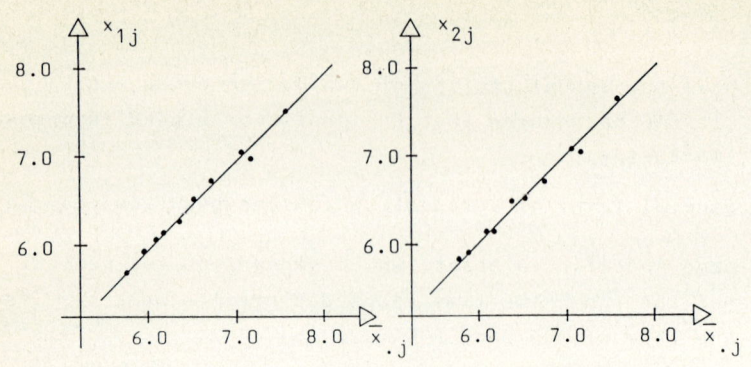

Fig. 13.5. The profits from bonds 1 and 2 plotted against the annual average $\bar{x}_{.j}$.

In this model, the α's can be eliminated by forming the differences

$$D_j = X_{1j} - X_{2j} .$$

Since

(13.20) $\quad E[D_j] = E[X_{1j}] - E[X_{2j}] = \beta_1 - \beta_2 ,$

the D_j's express the difference in profit between the bonds, irrespectively of the year in question. Assuming that the X_{ij}'s are independent and normally distributed with common variance σ^2, theorem 8.5 yields

$$\text{var}[D_j] = \text{var}[X_{1j}] + \text{var}[X_{2j}] = 2\sigma^2 ,$$

and hence

$$D_j \sim N(\beta_1 - \beta_2, \sigma_d^2)$$

where $\sigma_d^2 = 2\sigma^2$ and $D_1, \ldots, D_n$ are independent. Consider a test of the hypothesis of equal bond effects

$$H_0 : \beta_1 = \beta_2$$

against the alternative

$$H_1 : \beta_1 \neq \beta_2 .$$

Under H_0, $D_j \sim N(0, \sigma_d^2)$, so

$$\bar{D} = \frac{1}{10}\sum_j D_j \sim N(0, \sigma_d^2/10) .$$

Hence, H_0 can be tested using the test statistic

$$T = \frac{\bar{D}}{S_d}\sqrt{10} ,$$

where $S_d^2 = \frac{1}{9}\sum_j(D_j - \bar{D})^2$. Under H_0, T follows a t-distribution with 9 degrees of freedom, and the level of significance is given by

$$p = 2P(T \geq |t|) .$$

For the data in table 13.4, T has the observed value

$$t = \frac{-0.063}{\sqrt{0.00856}}\sqrt{10} = -2.15 ,$$

and the level of significance is

$$p = 2P(T \geq 2.15) = 0.06 .$$

Thus, the hypothesis of equal bond effects can not be rejected at level 0.05. △.

The important feature of the model applied in example 13.6 is the additive structure (13.19), which makes it possible to separate the effects of the two factors influencing the interest in order to study the difference in levels independently of the annual fluctuations in the general interest level. This type of model, called a **model for pairwise observations**, can, in a general form, be stated as follows:

$\{(x_{1j}, x_{2j}), j=1,\ldots,n\}$ are observed values of pairs of independent random variables $\{(X_{1j}, X_{2j}), j=1,\ldots,n\}$, where $X_{ij} \sim N(\alpha_j + \beta_i, \sigma^2)$.

The first step in the analysis of paired observations is to check the assumption of an additive mean value structure by plotting x_{ij} against $\bar{x}_{.j}$ for fixed i. The points should then cluster around straight lines with slope 1 if this structure is present. If the assumption of additivity is confirmed, the remaining part of the analysis is based on the differences $d_1,\ldots,d_n$ with $d_j = x_{1j} - x_{2j}$. The corresponding random variables $D_1,\ldots,D_n$ are independent, identically distributed random variables with common distribution $D_j \sim N(\beta_1-\beta_2, \sigma_d^2)$. The parameter of main interest, $\beta_1-\beta_2$, is estimated by

$$\overline{D} = \frac{1}{n}\sum_{j=1}^{n} D_j$$

which has the distribution

$$\overline{D} \sim N(\beta_1-\beta_2, \sigma_d^2/n)$$

where the variance σ_d^2 is estimated by

$$S_d^2 = \frac{1}{n-1}\sum_{j=1}^{n}(D_j-\overline{D})^2.$$

Tests concerning the value of $\beta_1-\beta_2$ are based on the test statistic

(13.21) $$T = \frac{\overline{D}-(\beta_1-\beta_2)}{S_d}\sqrt{n},$$

which is t-distributed with n-1 degrees of freedom. Levels of significance and critical regions are shown in table 13.2, and confidence limits for $\beta_1-\beta_2$ with level $1-\alpha$ are

$$\overline{d} \pm t_{1-\alpha/2}(n-1)s_d/\sqrt{n}.$$

13.6. The model for pairwise observations and the model for two independent samples

To illustrate the similarities and the differences between the model for paired observations and the model for two independent samples, consider the following hypothetical situation.

A company plans to test a new method of production by means of two different test-procedures. The company is assumed to have a number of machines producing the same unit. The suggested test-procedures are:

A. From the total of machines, a sample of size 2n is selected at random. From among these, n are randomly selected to produce units according to the old method, while the rest apply the new method. The data thus consist of two sets of observations: $x_{11}, \ldots, x_{1n}$, which are the units produced by the n machines applying the old method and $x_{21}, \ldots, x_{2n}$, which are observations for the machines applying the new method.

B. Each of n randomly selected machines applies the old method of production as well as the new method. For each machine a coin is tossed to determine which method is used first. The data then take the form (x_{11}, x_{21}), $(x_{12}, x_{22}), \ldots, (x_{1n}, x_{2n})$, where x_{1j} is the observed production for machine number j by the old method, and x_{2j} is the observed production for machine number j by the new method.

The structural variability of production is due to the method and to the machine used. In addition, the variability contains a purely random component due to the fact that even when the same machine repeatedly uses the same production method, the production will not be exactly the same.

For data collected by method A, the purely random variation cannot be separated from the variation between machines since only one measurement is available for each selected machine. The relevant statistical model for these data is that for two independent samples. The measure of the random variation, s^2, includes both the variation between machines and the purely random variation. Hence, dividing $\bar{x}_1 - \bar{x}_2$ by s^2, the estimated difference in the level of production between the old and new methods is compared with a measure of variability including both the pure random variation and the variation between machines.

For data collected by method B, $\bar{x}_1 - \bar{x}_2$ also estimates the difference in the level of production between the two methods. However, if there is an additive structure in the data and the data are analysed by means of the model for paired observations, the difference $\bar{x}_1 - \bar{x}_2$ is compared with a measure of variability which only depends on the purely random variation. In fact, the denominator in (13.21) depends only on the differences $x_{1j} - x_{2j}$, from which the levels of production for the machines are eliminated.

In summary, the difference in production is estimated in the same way under the two models, but the estimates are compared with different measures of variability.

If it is possible to eliminate the individual levels of production for the machines, and if there is a noticeable variation between these levels, the model for paired observations should be preferred because it gives a more precise estimate of the difference in production between the two methods. The model for two independent samples should be used only if the machines are very homogeneous. In this case a test based on (13.17) has a larger power than a test based on (13.21), since the t-test statistic in the former case is based on a larger number of degrees of freedom and the power of the t-test increases with the number of degrees of freedom.

13.7. The analysis of variance

The model presented above for two independent samples can be extended to situations, where more than two samples are to be compared. Let $x_{i1}, \ldots, x_{in_i}$ denote the observations in the i'th of k samples. The data consist of k samples of sizes $n_1, \ldots, n_k$ respectively as shown in the following table.

Sample	Observations
1	$x_{11}\ x_{12} \cdots x_{1j} \cdots x_{1n_1}$
2	$x_{21}\ x_{22} \cdots x_{2j} \cdots x_{2n_2}$
...	...
i	$x_{i1}\ x_{i2} \cdots x_{ij} \cdots x_{in_i}$
...	
k	$x_{k1}\ x_{k2} \cdots x_{kj} \cdots x_{kn_k}$

A comparison of the distributions of the samples can be based on the model:

$x_{i1}, \ldots, x_{in_i}$, $i=1, \ldots, k$, are observations of independent random variables $X_{i1}, \ldots, X_{in_i}$, $i=1, \ldots, k$, with distributions $X_{ij} \sim N(\mu_i, \sigma_i^2)$, $i=1, \ldots, k$, $j=1, \ldots, n_i$.

A model satisfying these assumptions is called an **analysis of variance model**. The model can alternatively be written as

$$(13.22) \quad X_{ij} = \mu_i + e_{ij}, \quad j=1, \ldots, n_i \text{ and } i=1, \ldots, k,$$

where the e_{ij}'s are independent random variables with $e_{ij} \sim N(0, \sigma_i^2)$.

According to (13.22), X_{ij} is the sum of a systematic component, μ_i, and a random error component, e_{ij}.

The ML-estimator for μ_i is

$$\overline{X}_i = \frac{1}{n_i} \sum_{j=1}^{n_i} X_{ij}$$

and σ_i^2 is estimated by

$$S_i^2 = \frac{1}{n_i - 1} \sum_{j=1}^{n_i} (X_{ij} - \overline{X}_i)^2 .$$

Usually interest is centered on comparing the means $\mu_1,\ldots,\mu_k$. Such a comparison is, however, rather complicated if the samples do not have the same variance. Therefore, the hypothesis

$$H_0': \sigma_1^2 = \ldots = \sigma_k^2 = \sigma^2$$

must be tested before proceeding with a comparison of the means.

If the variances are equal, their common value σ^2 is estimated by the weighted average

(13.23) $\qquad S^2 = \dfrac{1}{n-k} \sum_{i=1}^{k} (n_i - 1) S_i^2 \,, \quad n = \sum_{i=1}^{k} n_i \,,$

of the estimators S_i^2 for σ^2 from the individual samples. It follows from theorem 9.5 that

$$(n_i - 1) S_i^2 / \sigma^2 \sim \chi^2(n_i - 1) \,,$$

and hence from theorem 9.2 that

(13.24) $\qquad (n-k) S^2 / \sigma^2 = \sum_{i=1}^{k} (n_i - 1) S_i^2 / \sigma^2 \sim \chi^2(n-k) \,,$

because the S_i^2's are independent and

$$\sum_{i=1}^{k} (n_i - 1) = n - k \,.$$

Since the mean of a χ^2-distribution is equal to the number of degrees of freedom, $E[(n-k)S^2/\sigma^2] = n-k$. Thus $E[S^2] = \sigma^2$ and S^2 is an unbiased estimator for σ^2.

As a test statistic for H_0',

$$R' = (n-k)\ln(S^2) - \sum_{i=1}^{k} (n_i - 1)\ln(S_i^2) = \ln\left[\prod_{i=1}^{k} \left(\dfrac{S^2}{S_i^2}\right)^{n_i - 1}\right]$$

can be used. It is approximately χ^2-distributed with $k-1$ degrees of freedom if none of the factors $(n_i - 1)$, $i = 1, \ldots, k$, are too small. A better approximation to the χ^2-distribution is obtained by the test statistic

(13.25) $\qquad R = R'/c \,,$

where

$$c = 1 + \dfrac{1}{3(k-1)} \left(\sum_i \dfrac{1}{n_i - 1} - \dfrac{1}{n-k} \right) \,.$$

Obviously, c is close to unity if all the n_i's are moderately large.

The approximation is usually regarded as satisfactory if $n_i \geq 4$ for $i=1,\ldots,k$. The test based on R is called **Bartlett's test**.

Neither R, nor R', can be negative, and they only attain the value 0, if the S_i^2's are equal. Therefore, H_0' is rejected for large values of R, and the level of significance is $p = P(R \geq r)$, where r is the observed value of R. Since R is approximately χ^2-distributed with k-1 degrees of freedom

(13.26) $\qquad \tilde{p} \simeq P(Q_{k-1} \geq r)$,

where $Q_{k-1} \sim \chi^2(k-1)$. The critical region with level α consists of observed values of R larger than $\chi^2_{1-\alpha}(k-1)$. Bartlett's test has often been criticized because it is sensitive to departures from the assumption of normality: If the distributions of the X_{ij}'s differ substantially from normal distributions, R is no longer approximately χ^2-distributed.

If the hypothesis H_0' is accepted,

$$H_0: \mu_1 = \ldots = \mu_k$$

can be tested against the alternative that at least two μ's are different.

The test statistic for H_0 is obtained by decomposing the total sum of squares of deviations of the observations, q_T, as

$$q_T = \sum_{i=1}^{k} \sum_{j=1}^{n_i} (x_{ij} - \bar{x})^2 = \sum_{i=1}^{k} n_i(\bar{x}_i - \bar{x})^2 + \sum_{i=1}^{k} \sum_{j=1}^{n_i} (x_{ij} - \bar{x}_i)^2$$

$$= \sum_{i=1}^{k} n_i(\bar{x}_i - \bar{x})^2 + \sum_{i=1}^{k} (n_i - 1) s_i^2 = q_B + q_W$$

where

$$\bar{x} = \frac{1}{n} \sum_{i=1}^{k} \sum_{j=1}^{n_i} x_{ij} .$$

The components q_B and q_W are called the **variation between samples** and the **variation within samples**, respectively. The variation between samples is a measure of the extent to which the sample averages differ from the over-all average $\bar{x}$, while the variation within samples is a weighted average of the empirical variances in the k samples and thus measures the variability within samples. The random variables Q_T, Q_B and Q_W corresponding to q_T, q_B and q_W, respectively, satisfy the relationship

$$Q_T/\sigma^2 = Q_B/\sigma^2 + Q_W/\sigma^2 \ .$$

Under H_0, it follows from theorem 9.5 that $Q_T/\sigma^2 \sim \chi^2(n-1)$, and since $Q_W=(n-k)S^2$, it follows further from (13.24) that $Q_W/\sigma^2 \sim \chi^2(n-k)$. What is more, Q_B, Q_T and Q_W are all quadratic forms in the X_{ij}'s, so theorem 9.4 yields that $Q_B/\sigma^2 \sim \chi^2(k-1)$. Under H_0,

$$E[Q_B/(k-1)] = E[Q_W/(n-k)] = \sigma^2 \ ,$$

so the test statistic

(13.27) $\quad V = \dfrac{Q_B/(k-1)}{Q_W/(n-k)}$

should be close to 1 under H_0. If the sample means are not equal, it can be shown that

$$E[Q_B/(k-1)] = \sigma^2 + \frac{1}{k-1}\sum_{i=1}^{k} n_i(\mu_i - \bar{\mu})^2 \ ,$$

where $\bar{\mu} = \Sigma n_i \mu_i / n$. Hence V will tend to attain large values if there are substantial differences between the μ_i's and V can, therefore, be used as a test statistic for testing H_0.

Since Q_B and Q_W can be shown to be independent, $V \sim F(k-1, n-k)$ according to definition 9.3, and the level of significance is

(13.28) $\quad p = P(V>v) \ ,$

with $V \sim F(k-1, n-k)$. The critical region for a test with level α consists of values of V larger than $F_{1-\alpha}(k-1, n-k)$.

For k=2, the test statistics (13.27) and (13.16) are equivalent since then $T^2=V$.

A value of (13.27) close to zero can not be regarded as evidence against H_0, but such a value may raise doubts about the way in which the data have been collected. For example, for k=2, a small value of V may be due to the fact that the data consists of paired observations, which violates the assumption of independence between samples.

If neither H_0, nor H_0', is rejected, the observations can be assumed to be independent and identically, normally distributed with mean μ and variance σ^2, estimated by

$$\bar{x} = \frac{1}{n}\sum_{i=1}^{k}\sum_{j=1}^{n_i} x_{ij} = \frac{1}{n}\sum_{i=1}^{k} n_i \bar{x}_i$$

and

$$s_0^2 = \frac{1}{n-1} \sum_{i=1}^{k} \sum_{j=1}^{n_i} (x_{ij}-\bar{x})^2 = \frac{1}{n-1}(q_B+q_W) ,$$

respectively. Since

(13.29) $\quad T = \frac{\bar{X}-\mu}{S_0}\sqrt{n}$

is t-distributed with n-1 degrees of freedom, hypotheses about μ can be tested by a t-test according to table 13.2, while confidence intervals are given by (11.8).

The hypothesis H_0 is rejected both if only a single mean value differs from the others, and if all mean values are different. Hence, it is often of interest to inspect the data in order to detect likely alternatives. This can be done for example by computing confidence intervals for the various μ_i's. Since $\bar{X}_i$ and S_i^2 are independent, each $\bar{X}_i$ is independent of S^2, so that according to definition 9.2

(13.30) $\quad t_i = \frac{\bar{x}_i - \mu_i}{\sqrt{s^2/n_i}}$

is the observed value of a t-distributed random variable with n-k degrees of freedom. Note that under H_0', the estimate for σ^2 is based on information from all samples. By plotting confidence intervals for the μ_i's based on (13.30) and (11.8) in the same figure, those μ_i's with substantially different values can be detected. A test of the hypothesis $H_0'': \mu_i = \mu_h$ can be based on

(13.31) $\quad t_{ih} = \frac{\bar{x}_i - \bar{x}_h}{s\sqrt{\frac{1}{n_i}+\frac{1}{n_h}}} ,$

which under H_0'' is the observed value of a t-distributed random variable with n-k degrees of freedom. Test statistics of the form (13.30) and (13.31) must be applied with care. For example, if (13.31) is computed for all pairs of samples, there may be problems with the interpretation of the results. The various t-test statistics are not necessarily independent and the maximum value of the test statistics does not follow a t-distribution. To derive proper tests for such simultaneous hypotheses, more refined techniques known as **multiple comparisons** or **multiple decision procedures** must be used.

The conclusions to be drawn from an analysis of variance depend on the cicumstances under which the data are collected. Consider first the case, where the distribution of a variable x in k populations are to be compared. Assume that n_i units are selected randomly from the i'th population and the value of x for each of the sampled units is noted. According to the analysis of variance model the observations are normally distributed within each of the populations. If the hypotheses of equal variances and equal means are accepted, then the populations do not differ with regard to the distribution of x. This conclusion is dependent on random selection of the units from the populations.

Consider now observations from k groups of units which have been subjected to different treatments, e.g. in a medical experiment. If the hypotheses of equal means and equal variances in an analysis of variance model are accepted, the conclusion of the analysis depends on how the units have been assigned to the groups. If the units are selected at random from a given population and then assigned to the groups at random, the conclusion is that there are no noticeable differences between the effects of the k treatments. However, such a conclusion is only valid for the population from which the units are drawn. Whether or not it can be extended to another population depends on the degree of similarity between the two populations, and the data at hand will not necessarily reveal any such similarities.

Example 13.7

Table 13.5 shows the incomes for 43 families who built a new house in Elsinore in 1965, distributed according to the number of rooms in the house. Based on these data, the effect of income on the size of a new house is to be investigated.

If the incomes within each of the groups are regarded as a sample from a normal distribution, the income levels in the three groups can be compared by means of an analysis of variance.

The assumption of normality within each of the samples is checked by probability plots. The three plots shown as fig. 13.6 all exhibit the same convexity, indicating that the distributions are skewed to the right. In this situation a logarithmic transformation of the incomes may produce a better fit to a normal distribution. Table 13.6 shows the logarithms to the incomes. The corresponding probability plots in fig. 13.7 show that the assumption of normally distributed logarithmic incomes cannot be rejected.

Let x_{ij} denote the logarithm of the j'th income in the i'th sample. Estimates for the mean and variance in each sample together with the sums, sums of squares and sums of squares of deviations used to compute these estimates, are all shown in table 13.7.

Table 13.5. Incomes for 43 families distributed according to the number of rooms in their house.

	4 rooms i=1	5 rooms i=2	More than 6 rooms i=3
j= 1	16371	23529	33366
2	22331	32845	39377
3	25928	39758	40244
4	27593	43461	44501
5	32088	44249	52840
6	33458	47343	66235
7	34554	51804	75235
8	39017	54482	122007
9	39759	57779	
10	42129	59623	
11	43376	61950	
12	45734	67680	
13	49027	74289	
14	52898	86702	
15	58116	91073	
16	62893	128673	
17	73450		
18	82455		
19	116779		

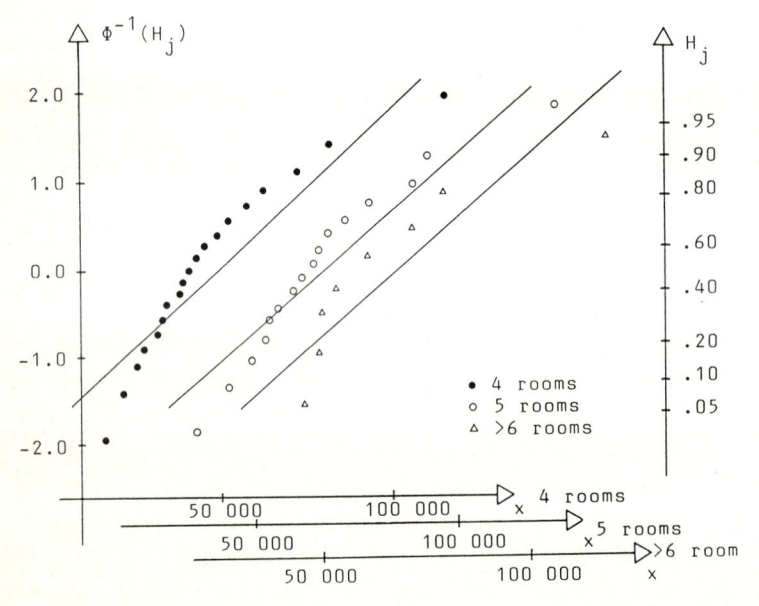

Fig. 13.6. Probability plots of incomes for 43 families.

Table 13.6. Logarithms of incomes for 43 families.

	4 rooms i=1	5 rooms i=2	More than 6 rooms i=3
j= 1	9.703	10.066	10.415
2	10.014	10.400	10.581
3	10.163	10.591	10.603
4	10.225	10.680	10.703
5	10.376	10.698	10.875
6	10.418	10.765	11.101
7	10.450	10.855	11.228
8	10.572	10.906	11.712
9	10.591	10.964	
10	10.648	10.996	
11	10.678	11.034	
12	10.731	11.122	
13	10.800	11.216	
14	10.876	11.370	
15	10.970	11.419	
16	11.049	11.765	
17	11.204		
18	11.320		
19	11.668		

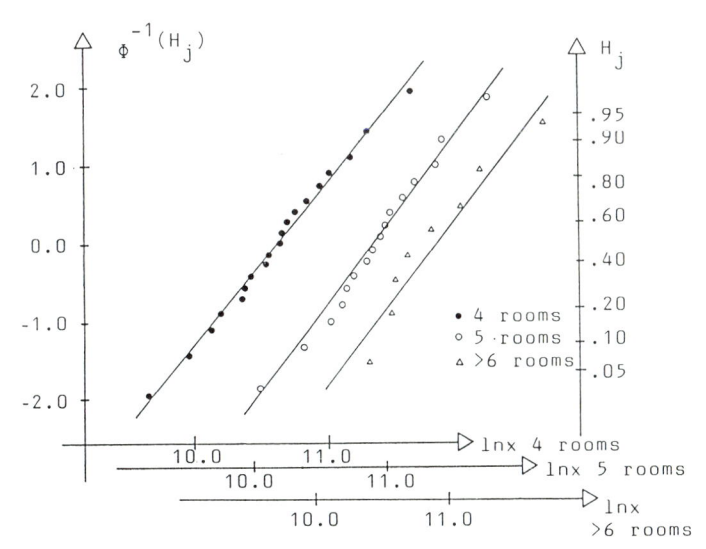

Fig. 13.7. Probability plots of logarithmic incomes for 43 families.

The hypothesis $\sigma_1^2 = \sigma_2^2 = \sigma_3^2$ is tested by means of Bartlett's test (13.25). It is found that

$$c = 1 + \frac{1}{3 \cdot 2}\left(\frac{1}{18} + \frac{1}{15} + \frac{1}{7} - \frac{1}{40}\right) = 1.0400$$

and

$$r' = -65.073 + 26.931 + 26.528 + 11.939 = 0.325 ,$$

so that

$$r = 0.325/1.0400 = 0.314 .$$

The level of significance is then approximately

$$p = P(Q>0.314) = 0.85 ,$$

which does not support rejection of the hypothesis of equal variances. This in fact was to be expected in view of the plots in fig. 13.7, where the lines, fitted by eye, are more or less parallel.

Tabel 13.7. Computation of estimates for μ_i and σ_i^2.

i	n_i	S_i	$\bar{x}_i$	SS_i	SSD_i	s_i^2
1	19	202.457	10.6556	2161.341	4.032	0.224
2	16	174.847	10.9279	1913.266	2.559	0.171
3	8	87.218	10.9023	952.153	1.272	0.182
Total	43	464.522		5026.760	7.862	

The decomposition of the total sum of squares of deviations is shown in table 13.8.

Table 13.8. Decomposition of the total sum of squares of deviations.

Source	Sum of squares of deviations (q)	Degrees of freedom (f)	q/f
Between samples	0.741	2	0.371
Within samples	7.862	40	0.197
Total	8.603	42	0.205

The hypothesis $\mu_1=\mu_2=\mu_3$ is now tested by means of the test statistic (13.27) which has as observed value

$$v = \frac{q_B/2}{q_W/40} = \frac{0.371}{0.197} = 1.89 .$$

The level of significance is

$$p = P(V \geq 1.89) \simeq 0.2,$$

which leads to acceptance of the hypothesis.

In conclusion the analysis reveals that the incomes in each sample can be described by the same logarithmic normal distribution. This means that the income distribution in Elsinore for persons building small houses is the same as for persons building large houses. Estimates of the common mean and variance are

$$\bar{x} = 10.8028 \text{ and } s_0^2 = 0.2048 ,$$

and a 95% confidence interval for the mean μ is given by the limits

$$\begin{cases} \underline{\mu} = 10.8028 - 2.023 \cdot 0.453/\sqrt{43} = 10.663 \\ \overline{\mu} = 10.8028 + 2.023 \cdot 0.453/\sqrt{43} = 10.942 , \end{cases}$$

in accordance with (11.8).

An exponential transformation of these limits provides the 95% confidence interval (42744, 56500) for the mean income. △.

13.8. Distribution free tests

The tests discussed in this and the previous chapter are all based on restrictive distributional assumptions that are often difficult to justify. Attempts have therefore been made to construct test procedures which do not rely on detailed knowledge of the distribution of the observations.

In order to illustrate such procedures, consider the problem of drawing inference for the location parameter of some distribution on the basis of a random sample. Assuming the sample to be normally distributed, the mean is usually taken to represent the location of the distribution. The mean is estimated by the average of the observations and a u-test or a t-test statistic is applied for testing hypotheses concerning the value of the mean. However, if the sample size is small, the assumption of normality is difficult to verify by means of a probability plot for example, and it is then a question of the validity of inference statements if the assumption of normality is violated. In addition, procedures based on the average are often very sensitive to the occurrence of extreme or outlying observations (expecially in small samples), which is why so-called **distribution free** or **non-parametric** methods are considered.

Let $x_1,\ldots,x_n$ be observations of independent continuous random variables $X_1,\ldots,X_n$ with common distribution function F and median μ', so that

$$P(X_i < \mu') = P(X_i > \mu') = 0.5, \quad i=1,\ldots,n,$$

and consider the hypothesis

$$H_0: \mu' = \mu_0'$$

against the alternative

$$H_1: \mu' < \mu_0'.$$

A test statistic whose distribution does not depend on F is to be constructed. Let S_+ be the number of positive differences among $X_1-\mu_0'$, $X_2-\mu_0', \ldots, X_n-\mu_0'$. Under H_0, $P(X_i-\mu_0'>0) = P(X_i-\mu_0'<0) = 0.5$, and since the X_i's are independent, it follows that

$$S_+ \sim b(n, 0.5),$$

which in turn gives that the expected value of S_+ under H_0 is $n/2$. If, however, the median μ' is smaller than μ_0', the number of positive differences can be expected to be less than $n/2$. Hence, a small value of S_+ suggests rejection of H_0. The level of significance is given by

$$(13.32) \quad p = P(S_+ \leq s_+ | H_0) = \sum_{x=0}^{s_+} \binom{n}{x} \left(\tfrac{1}{2}\right)^n,$$

where s_+ is the observed value of S_+.

For the alternative $\mu' > \mu_0'$, a large value of S_+ suggests rejection of H_0, and the level of significance becomes

$$(13.33) \quad p = P(S_+ \geq s_+ | H_0) = \sum_{x=s_+}^{n} \binom{n}{x} \left(\tfrac{1}{2}\right)^n.$$

Of course, in the case of a two-sided alternative, $\mu' \neq \mu_0'$, both small and large values of S_+ suggest rejection of H_0, and the level of significance is computed as

$$(13.34) \quad p = \begin{cases} 2P(S_+ \geq s_+) & \text{for } s_+ > n/2 \\ 2P(S_+ \leq s_+) & \text{for } s_+ < n/2, \end{cases}$$

which is equivalent to

$$p = 2\min\{P(S_+ \geq s_+), P(S_+ \leq s_+)\}.$$

A test based on the test statistic S_+ is called a **sign test**. This is a distribution free test in the sense that the distribution of the test statistic under H_0 is independent of the common distribution function F for the observations. The use of the name non-parametric for such tests stems from the fact that the test is not evaluated within a parametric family of distributions.

For large values of n, a binomial distribution with parameters n and θ can be approximated by a normal distribution so the hypothesis $H_0: \mu' = \mu_0'$ can, in such cases, be tested by

$$U = \frac{S_+ - n/2}{\sqrt{n/4}},$$

which is approximately normally distributed with mean 0 and variance 1.

If X_i is a continuous random variable, the event $\{X_i - \mu_0' = 0\}$ has probability 0, but this does not mean that an observed difference equal to zero is out of the question. In practice, such observations are simply excluded from the analysis.

In the sign test, only the signs of the differences are used. However, if F is symmetric, the information contained in the relative sizes of the differences can also be utilized. Assume that

$$P(X_i - \mu' > c) = P(X_i - \mu' < -c)$$

for any c>0, where μ' is the median of F and $X_1, \ldots, X_n$ are independent. Consider the hypothesis

$$H_0: \mu' = \mu_0'$$

against the alternative

$$H_1: \mu' > \mu_0'.$$

A distribution free test statistic can then be based on the ranks $r_1, \ldots, r_n$ assigned to the differences $x_1 - \mu_0', \ldots, x_n - \mu_0'$ in such a way that $r_1, \ldots, r_n$ is a permutation of the integers from 1 to n, and

$$r_i < r_j \quad \text{if} \quad |x_i - \mu_0'| < |x_j - \mu_0'|.$$

This means that $r_1, \ldots, r_n$ represents the rank order of the numerical values of the differences.

Under H_0, positive and negative differences are equally likely, so the sum r_+ of ranks corresponding to positive differences can be expected to be equal to the sum r_- of ranks corresponding to negative differences. On the other hand, under H_1 r_+ is likely to be larger than

r_-. Therefore, it seems reasonable to employ the random variable R_+ corresponding to r_+ as a test statistic for H_0 against H_1. The level of significance becomes

(13.35) $p = P(R_+ \geq r_+ | H_0)$.

For small values of n, the percentiles of the exact distribution of R_+ can be found in statistical tables and for large values of n, a normal approximation can be used. Combinatorial arguments show that

(13.36) $E[R_+] = \frac{n(n+1)}{4}$

and

(13.37) $\operatorname{var}[R_+] = \frac{n(n+1)(2n+1)}{24}$

so the test statistic

(13.38) $U = \dfrac{R_+ - n(n+1)/4}{\sqrt{n(n+1)(2n+1)/24}}$

approximately follows a standard normal distribution. The approximation can be used for $n \geq 15$. Levels of significance and critical regions are derived from table 13.1.

Likewise, for the alternative

$$H_1: \mu' < \mu_0'$$

the sum R_- of the ranks of the negative differences can be used with the level of significance

(13.39) $p = P(R_- \geq r_-)$,

where r_- is the observed value of R_-. Under H_0, R_+ and R_- are identically distributed and the u-test statistic (13.38) with R_+ replaced by R_- can then be used.

Under the two-sided alternative

$$H_1: \mu' \neq \mu_0' ,$$

the test statistic $R^* = \max(R_+, R_-)$ is used. The larger the value of R^*, the less the data support H_0. Since $r_+ + r_- = n(n+1)/2$, the level of significance can be computed as

(13.40) $p = P(R^* \geq r^*) = 2\min\{P(R_+ \geq r_+), P(R_- \geq r_-)\}$.

If an approximate u-test statistic is used, U is defined as

$$U = \frac{R^* - n(n+1)/4}{\sqrt{n(n+1)(2n+1)/24}}$$

and the level of significance is

$$p = P(U \geq |u|) \, ,$$

where u is the observed value of U.

A test based on R_+, R_- or R^* is called a **one-sample Wilcoxon test**, which is a distribution free alternative to the t-test of section 13.2. The distribution free tests have the advantage that the level of significance is exact regardless of the true form of F as long as F is continuous and symmetric. Their disadvantage is that they are less powerful than the t-tests when the observations in fact follow a normal distribution. Thus, if the normal distribution describes the data, the probability of detecting a departure of a given size from the null hypothesis is smaller for the Wilcoxon test than for the t-test.

Example 13.6 (continued)

In example 13.6, the profits of two bonds were analysed as paired observations assuming that the annual differences between the profits were independent and identically normally distributed. With only ten differences available, the specification of these assumptions is rather tentative. As an alternative to the t-test, it is, therefore, tempting to employ a sign test or a one-sample Wilcoxon test.

If μ' is the median in the distribution of the D_j's, the null hypothesis can be stated as $H_0: \mu' = 0$ and the alternative hypothesis as $H_1: \mu' \neq 0$. From table 13.9 it can be seen that there are $s_+ = 3$ positive differences and $s_- = 7$ negative differences. From (13.34), the level of significance is

$$p = 2P(S_{+-} \leq 3) = 0.344 \, ,$$

and the null hypothesis is strongly supported by the data.

If the distribution of the D_j's is assumed to be symmetric, a Wilcoxon test can be used. The ranks of the numerical differences between the annual profits are shown in table 13.9 together with their signs. The two smallest differences, d_4 and d_6, are assigned ranks 1 and 2. The following three differences, d_2, d_7 and d_8, all have the same numerical value, and are therefore all assigned rank 4, i.e. the average of the ranks 3, 4 and 5. The sums of ranks corresponding to negative and positive differences are $r_-=45$ and $r_+=10$, respectively, and the exact level of significance becomes

$$p = 2P(R_- \geq 45) = 0.084,$$

obtained from a table of the Wilcoxon distribution. The mean and variance of R_- are $E[R_-]=10\cdot 11/4=27.5$ and $\text{var}[R_-]=10\cdot 11\cdot 21/24=96.25$. Hence, the u-statistic (13.38) has the observed value

$$u = (45-27.5)/\sqrt{96.25} = 1.78,$$

and the level of significance can be approximated by

$$p = 2P(U \geq 1.78) = 0.075.$$

The approximation is thus reasonable even for this low value of n.

Table 13.9. Signs and ranks of the numerical differences between the annual profits.

d_j	sign(d_j)	rank$(|d_j|)$	sign$(d_j)\cdot$rank$(|d_j|)$
-0.16	-	9	-9
0.04	+	4	4
-0.10	-	7	-7
-0.02	-	1	-1
-0.23	-	10	-10
0.03	+	2	2
0.04	+	4	4
-0.04	-	4	-4
-0.05	-	6	-6
-0.14	-	8	-8

Both the sign test and the Wilcoxon test lead to an acceptance of H_0 at the level 0.05. But in both cases, the level of significance is higher than for the t-test, and in case of the sign test the difference is considerable. This means that a given null hypothesis will be less often rejected by the distribution free test than by the test based on the assumption of normally distributed random variables. The distribution free test is, on the other hand, a safeguard against wrong conclusions arising from an incorrect assumption of normality.△.

Let $X_{11}, \ldots, X_{1n_1}$ and $X_{21}, \ldots, X_{2n_2}$ be two sets of independent random variables with distribution functions F_1 and F_2, and consider the hypothesis $H_0: F_1 = F_2$ of identical distributions for the two samples. If the actual form of the common distribution function is unimportant, it seems natural to search for a distribution free test statistic. The hypothesis is equivalent to

(13.41) $\qquad H_0: P(X_{1j} > X_{2k}) = 0.5,$

for all j and k. Note that this probability does not depend on j or k.

A test statistic can be based, therefore, on a ranking of all $n_1 + n_2$ observations. Let T_1 be the sum of the ranks corresponding to observations in the first sample, and T_2 the sum of the ranks corresponding to observations in the second sample. Under the alternative

$$H_1: P(X_{1j} > X_{2k}) > 0.5,$$

the observed value t_1 of T_1 will tend to be larger than the observed value t_2 of T_2. The level of significance is then

(13.42) $\qquad p = P(T_1 \geq t_1 | H_0),$

since $t_1 + t_2 = (n_1 + n_2)(n_1 + n_2 + 1)/2$ implies that t_2 is small when t_1 is large. A test based on the test statistic T_1 is called a **Wilcoxon test for two samples**. For small values of n_1 and n_2, the probability (13.42) is given in standard statistical tables. For larger values of n_1 and n_2, a normal distribution approximation can be used. Under H_0,

$$E[T_1] = n_1(n_1 + n_2 + 1)/2$$

and

$$\mathrm{var}[T_1] = n_1 n_2 (n_1 + n_2 + 1)/12,$$

and the level of significance is approximated by

$$p = P(U \geq u_1),$$

where $U \sim N(0,1)$ and

$$u_1 = [t_1 - n_1(n_1 + n_2 + 1)/2]/\sqrt{n_1 n_2 (n_1 + n_2 + 1)/12}.$$

If the alternative is

$$H_1: P(X_{1j} > X_{2k}) < 0.5,$$

the level of significance becomes

$$p = P(T_1 \leq t_1 | H_0),$$

and for large values of n_1 and n_2 the approximation

$$p \simeq P(U \leq u_1)$$

can be used. Finally, against the alternative

$$H_1: P(X_{1j} > X_{2k}) \neq 0.5,$$

the level of significance is given by

$$p = 2\min\{P(T_1 \leq t_1), P(T_1 \geq t_1)\},$$

and for large values of n_1 and n_2, it is approximated by

$$p = 2P(U \geq |u_1|).$$

14. Simple Linear Regression

14.1. Regression analysis

Regression analysis is a method for exploring and analysing the relationship between a response variable and a number of explanatory variables. If the response variable is denoted by y and the explanatory variables by $x_1,\ldots,x_p$, the regression function

$$y = f(x_1,\ldots,x_p)$$

reproduces or describes the response y for given values of the explanatory variables.

The data for a regression analysis consist of n sets of joint observations of the response and the explanatory variables, called the **cases**. The i'th case is denoted by $(y_i, x_{i1},\ldots,x_{ip})$. The aim of the analysis is to describe the relationship between the observed values of the response and the explanatory variables in a simple way, i.e. the regression function must have a simple form and the number of explanatory variables must be limited. The simplicity requirement is met by the linear regression function

(14.1) $y = \beta_0 + \beta_1 x_1 + \ldots + \beta_p x_p$.

It is not possible to obtain an exact reproduction of the observed response by inserting the corresponding values of the explanatory variables in the regression function (14.1) for any set of β_j's, unless the number of explanatory variables is large compared to the number of cases. The regression function must accordingly be regarded as an approximation to the response, so the regression function is satisfactory if

(14.2) $y_i \simeq \beta_0 + \beta_1 x_{i1} + \ldots + \beta_p x_{ip}$

for all cases.

The linear regression model is obtained by adding an error term e to the linear regression function, so (14.2) becomes

(14.3) $\quad y = \beta_0 + \beta_1 x_1 + \ldots + \beta_p x_p + e.$

This error term accounts for that part of the response which cannot be described or reproduced by the linear regression function, and it can be regarded as a random variable which fluctuates from case to case.

If a linear regression function does not give a satisfactory description of the response, it is often possible to describe the relationship between transformations of the variables by a linear function. Consider, for example, the Cobb-Douglas production function

$$y \simeq \beta_0 x_1^{\beta_1} \ldots x_p^{\beta_p}$$

where y is an output variable and $x_1, \ldots, x_p$ are input variables. A logarithmic transformation of both the response and the explanatory variables then yields

$$\ln(y) \simeq \ln(\beta_0) + \beta_1 \ln(x_1) + \ldots + \beta_p \ln(x_p).$$

Hence, the relationship between the logarithms of the response and the explanatory variables can be approximated by a linear function.

14.2. Simple linear regression

In simple linear regression data consist of n cases (y_i, x_i), $i=1, \ldots, n$, which are observations of the response variable y and the explanatory variable x, and the response is approximated by a linear function of x

(14.4) $\quad y \simeq \beta_0 + \beta_1 x.$

It is not usually possible to determine values of β_0 and β_1 such that all pairs of observations fall exactly on a straight line, and an **error term** is therefore added to (14.4), yielding

(14.5) $\quad y = \beta_0 + \beta_1 x + e.$

The error term accounts for that part of the response that cannot be described by the linear regression function $\beta_0 + \beta_1 x$ and may include both random and non-random (so-called systematic) components.

If the true relationship between y and x is non-linear, the error term includes the deviation between the non-linear function and the linear function (14.4), which is a systematic component. Measurement errors in the response enter the error term as a random component and also the aggregated effect of many variables, each with insignificant influence on the response variable, may enter the error term as a random component.

The model is considered satisfactory if the sum of the systematic components in the error term is of minor importance compared to the sum of the random components.

Let y_i be the observed value of a random variable Y_i where

(14.6) $Y_i = \beta_0 + \beta_1 x_i + e_i$, $i=1,\ldots,n$,

and where $x_1, \ldots, x_n$ are regarded as fixed constants. The error terms $e_1, \ldots, e_n$ are random variables for which the following assumptions are made:

(14.7) $E[e_i] = 0$, $i=1,\ldots,n$,

(14.8) $\text{var}[e_i] = \sigma^2$, $i=1,\ldots,n$

and

(14.9) $\text{cov}(e_i, e_j) = 0$, $i \neq j$.

Assumption (14.7) implies that the expected difference between y_i and the expression $\beta_0 + \beta_1 x_i$ must be zero, and assumption (14.8) implies that the variability of the error term must be constant, for example independent of the value of the explanatory variable. Assumption (14.9) means that the value of an error term does not contain information regarding the expected value of any other error term. Assumptions (14.7) to (14.9) may be considered as a set of formal requirements to the effect that the observations scatter randomly around the regression line $y = \beta_0 + \beta_1 x$ in a plot of y_i against x_i, cf. fig. 14.1.

Assumption (14.9) can be replaced by the stronger assumption

(14.10) $e_1, \ldots, e_n$ are independent.

This assumption implies that the value of one error term does not contain any information what so ever about any other error term.

The assumptions (14.6) to (14.9) define the **simple linear regression model**. In this model the random variables $Y_1, \ldots, Y_n$ are uncorrelated with mean values $E[Y_i]=\beta_0+\beta_1 x_i$ and constant variance σ^2. The linear component $\beta_0+\beta_1 x_i$ in (14.6) thus describes the mean of the response variable as a function of the explanatory variable.

14.3. Estimation of the parameters

The regression parameters β_0 and β_1 are estimated by the **method of least squares** or the **LS-method**. According to this method, a line is fitted to the data in such a way that the sum of the squared vertical distances from the cases to the line is minimized. Hence the **least squares (LS) estimates** $\hat{\beta}_0$ and $\hat{\beta}_1$ for β_0 and β_1 minimize the sum of squared deviations

$$(14.11) \quad S(\beta_0,\beta_1) = \sum_{i=1}^{n} (y_i-\beta_0-\beta_1 x_i)^2 .$$

The LS-estimates are derived by setting the partial derivatives of (14.11) with respect to β_0 and β_1 equal to zero and solving the resulting equations.

The solutions to these equations are

$$(14.12) \quad \begin{cases} \hat{\beta}_1 = \Sigma(x_i-\bar{x})(y_i-\bar{y})/\Sigma(x_i-\bar{x})^2 \\ \hat{\beta}_0 = \bar{y}-\hat{\beta}_1\bar{x} . \end{cases}$$

The method of least squares is illustrated in fig. 14.1, where the cases are plotted in a diagram together with a fitted line.

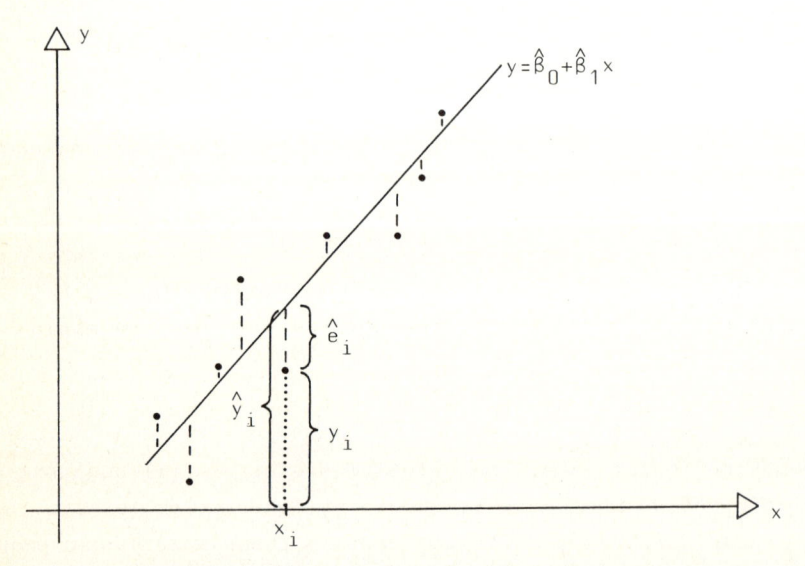

Fig. 14.1. Illustration of the LS-method.

From the estimates $\hat{\beta}_0$ and $\hat{\beta}_1$, the **fitted** or **predicted value** $\hat{y}_i$ of the response for the i'th case is computed as

$$\hat{y}_i = \hat{\beta}_0 + \hat{\beta}_1 x_i.$$

The i'th **residual** $\hat{e}_i$ is defined as the difference between y_i and $\hat{y}_i$,

(14.13) $\qquad \hat{e}_i = y_i - \hat{y}_i = y_i - \hat{\beta}_0 - \hat{\beta}_1 x_i.$

From (14.13)

$$y_i = \hat{y}_i + \hat{e}_i,$$

so the residual represents that part of y_i which cannot be accounted for by the estimated regression line. Alternatively $\hat{e}_i$ can be interpreted as an approximation to the unobservable error term e_i.

Theorem 14.1

If the error terms $e_1,\ldots,e_n$ in the regression model (14.6)-(14.9) are normally distributed, the LS-estimates and the ML-estimates for β_0 and β_1 coincide, while the ML-estimate for σ^2 is

$$\hat{\sigma}^2 = \frac{1}{n} \Sigma \hat{e}_i^2.$$

Proof

If the error terms $e_1,\ldots,e_n$ are normally distributed, the log-likelihood function for $y_1,\ldots,y_n$ becomes

$$l(\beta_0, \beta_1, \sigma^2) = -\frac{1}{2}[n\ln(\sigma^2) + n\ln(2\pi) + \Sigma(y_i - \beta_0 - \beta_1 x_i)^2/\sigma^2].$$

As the log-likelihood function is a decreasing function of

$$\sum_{i=1}^{n} (y_i - \beta_0 - \beta_1 x_i)^2,$$

it follows that the ML-estimates $\hat{\beta}_0$ and $\hat{\beta}_1$ minimize this quantity. Accordingly, the LS-estimates and the ML-estimates for $\hat{\beta}_0$ and $\hat{\beta}_1$ coincide when the error terms are normally distributed.

With $\beta_0 = \hat{\beta}_0$ and $\beta_1 = \hat{\beta}_1$, the log-likelihood function becomes

$$l(\hat{\beta}_0, \hat{\beta}_1, \sigma^2) = -\frac{n}{2}\ln(2\pi) - \frac{n}{2}\ln(\sigma^2) - \frac{1}{2}\Sigma(y_i - \hat{\beta}_0 - \hat{\beta}_1 x_i)^2/\sigma^2.$$

The derivative of this function with respect to σ^2 is

$$\partial l(\hat{\beta}_0,\hat{\beta}_1,\sigma^2)/\partial\sigma^2 = -\frac{n}{2}(\sigma^2)^{-1} + \frac{1}{2}\Sigma(y_i-\hat{\beta}_0-\hat{\beta}_1 x_i)^2/\sigma^4.$$

Solving the equation $\partial l(\hat{\beta}_0,\hat{\beta}_1,\sigma^2)/\partial\sigma^2=0$ then yields the Ml-estimate

$$\hat{\sigma}^2 = \frac{1}{n}\Sigma(y_i-\hat{\beta}_0-\hat{\beta}_1 x_i)^2 = \frac{1}{n}\Sigma\hat{e}_i^2$$

for σ^2. □.

The unbiased estimator

(14.14) $$s^2 = \frac{1}{n-2}\sum_{i=1}^{n}\hat{e}_i^2$$

is usually preferred to the ML-estimator $\hat{\sigma}^2$.

Written in the form

(14.15) $$Y_i = \alpha+\beta_1(x_i-\bar{x})+e_i, \quad i=1,\ldots,n,$$

where $\alpha=\beta_0+\beta_1\bar{x}$, the regression model is said to be **centralized**.

The LS-estimates for the regression parameters in a centralized regression model are given by

$$\hat{\alpha} = \bar{y}$$

and

$$\hat{\beta}_1 = \Sigma(x_i-\bar{x})(y_i-\bar{y})/\Sigma(x_i-\bar{x})^2.$$

In order to simplify the notation, the following quantities are introduced:

$$SSD_x = \sum_{i=1}^{n}(x_i-\bar{x})^2,$$

where SSD stands for Sum of Squared Deviations,

$$SPD_{xy} = \sum_{i=1}^{n}(x_i-\bar{x})(y_i-\bar{y}),$$

where SPD stands for Sum of Products of Deviations, and

$$RSS = (n-2)s^2 = \Sigma\hat{e}_i^2,$$

where RSS stands for Residual Sum of Squares. With this notation, the estimates $\hat{\beta}_1$ and s^2 can be written

$$\hat{\beta}_1 = SPD_{xy}/SSD_x$$

and
$$s^2 = RSS/(n-2).$$

14.4. Properties of the LS-estimator

The LS-estimates $\hat{\beta}_0$ and $\hat{\beta}_1$ can be computed for any set of joint observations of x and y. Under the assumptions (14.6) to (14.9), however, the LS-estimators have a number of distributional properties that may explain the popularity of the LS-method in regression analysis.

Theorem 14.2

Under assumptions (14.6) to (14.9),

$$E[\hat{\beta}_0] = \beta_0$$

and
$$E[\hat{\beta}_1] = \beta_1.$$

Proof

From (14.12), theorem 5.3 and theorem 8.4, it follows that

$$E[\hat{\beta}_0] = E[\overline{Y}] - \bar{x} E[\hat{\beta}_1]$$

and
$$E[\hat{\beta}_1] = \Sigma(x_i - \bar{x}) E[Y_i - \overline{Y}]/SSD_x.$$

Since $E[Y_i] = \beta_0 + \beta_1 x_i$ and consequently $E[\overline{Y}] = \frac{1}{n}\Sigma E[Y_i] = \frac{1}{n}\Sigma(\beta_0 + \beta_1 x_i) = \beta_0 + \beta_1 \bar{x}$,

$$E[Y_i - \overline{Y}] = \beta_1(x_i - \bar{x}).$$

Substituting this expression for $E[Y_i - \overline{Y}]$ in the expression for $E[\hat{\beta}_1]$ yields

$$E[\hat{\beta}_1] = \Sigma(x_i - \bar{x})\beta_1(x_i - \bar{x})/SSD_x = \beta_1.$$

Furthermore, if β_1 is substituted for $E[\hat{\beta}_1]$ and $\beta_0 + \beta_1 \bar{x}$ for $E[\overline{Y}]$ in the expression for $E[\hat{\beta}_0]$, it follows that

$$E[\hat{\beta}_0] = \beta_0 + \beta_1 \bar{x} - \bar{x}\beta_1 = \beta_0. \quad \square.$$

Theorem 14.3

Under assumptions (14.6) to (14.9),

$$(14.16) \quad \begin{cases} \text{var}[\hat{\beta}_0] = \sigma^2(1/n + \bar{x}^2/SSD_x) \\ \text{var}[\hat{\beta}_1] = \sigma^2/SSD_x \\ \text{cov}(\hat{\beta}_0, \hat{\beta}_1) = -\sigma^2\bar{x}/SSD_x. \end{cases}$$

Proof

Since

$$\sum_{i=1}^{n}(x_i-\bar{x})(Y_i-\bar{Y}) = \sum_{i=1}^{n}(x_i-\bar{x})Y_i,$$

(14.12) and theorems 5.3 and 8.5 yield

$$\text{var}[\hat{\beta}_1] = \Sigma(x_i-\bar{x})^2 \text{var}[Y_i]/SSD_x^2 = \sigma^2/SSD_x.$$

The expressions for $\text{var}[\hat{\beta}_0]$ and $\text{cov}(\hat{\beta}_0, \hat{\beta}_1)$ can be derived from (14.12) and (8.28). □.

Theorem 14.3 implies that $\hat{\beta}_0$ and $\hat{\beta}_1$ are correlated. For the LS-estimators of the parameters of the centralized model (14.15), the results corresponding to (14.16) are

$$(14.17) \quad \begin{cases} \text{var}[\hat{\alpha}] = \sigma^2/n \\ \text{var}[\hat{\beta}_1] = \sigma^2/SSD_x \\ \text{cov}(\hat{\alpha}, \hat{\beta}_1) = 0. \end{cases}$$

The LS-estimators for α, β_0 and β_1 are **linear** estimators in the sense that they are linear functions of $Y_1,\ldots,Y_n$. It can be shown that the LS-estimators of α, β_0 and β_1 have the least possible variances among all linear and unbiased estimators. This result, known as the **Gauss-Markov theorem**, is often quoted as a justification for using the LS-method.

If the tails of the error distribution are heavier than the tails of the normal distribution, extreme or outlying observations may occur more frequently than for the normal distribution. In such cases it is possible to derive estimators that are neither unbiased nor linear, but which have a larger precision than the LS-estimators. Furthermore, the LS-method is very sensitive to the occurrence of extreme observations, for example the deletion of an extreme observation may drastically change the values of the LS-estimate. Therefore, the assumption of normality plays a more important role for the application of the LS-method than is immediately apparent from the Gauss-Markov theorem.

Theorem 14.4

If the error terms $e_1,\ldots,e_n$ are normally distributed and satisfy assumptions (14.6) to (14.9), then

$$\hat{\beta}_0 \sim N(\beta_0, \sigma^2[\tfrac{1}{n} + \bar{x}^2/SSD_x]),$$

$$\hat{\beta}_1 \sim N(\beta_1, \sigma^2/SSD_x)$$

and

$$(n-2)S^2/\sigma^2 \sim \chi^2(n-2).$$

Furthermore, $(\hat{\beta}_0, \hat{\beta}_1)$ is independent of S^2.

Proof

Since $\hat{\beta}_0$ and $\hat{\beta}_1$ are linear functions of $Y_1,\ldots,Y_n$, which are normally distributed, $\hat{\beta}_0$ and $\hat{\beta}_1$ are also normally distributed. The means and variances of $\hat{\beta}_0$ and $\hat{\beta}_1$ are given by theorems 14.2 and 14.3. The remaining part of the theorem follows from theorem 9.4. ☐.

Example 14.1

To investigate the effect of organic solvents, the index ISI for the blood flow to the brain was measured on 20 painters. The index is believed to be an indicator of brain activity with low ISI-values indicating low brain activity. Nine of the painters were known to have worked with organic solvents, while the remaining 11 constituted a control group which had had no contact with organic solvents.

In order to study the effect of organic solvents on brain activity, the ISI-measurements for the two groups of painters were compared. Since the ISI-indicator is known to depend on age, it was necessary to adjust for age in the comparison. To make these necessary adjustments, the relationship between age and ISI was accordingly studied.

In this example, the ISI as a function of age is studied for the control group. In a subsequent example, the main problem is considered.

Table 14.1 shows age (x_i) and ISI (y_i) for the 11 painters in the control group. The plot of y_i against x_i, shown in fig. 14.2, indicates that it is reasonable to approximate ISI by a linear function of age. Therefore, y_i is regarded as the observed value of a random variable

$$Y_i = \beta_0 + \beta_1 x_i + e_i,$$

where the error terms $e_1,\ldots,e_n$ satisfy conditions (14.7) to (14.9).

Table 14.1. Age and ISI for eleven painters in a control group.

Case No. i	Age x_i	ISI y_i	Fitted value $\hat{y}_i$	Residual $\hat{e}_i$
1	31	55	52.16	2.84
2	32	51	51.36	-0.36
3	34	44	49.78	-5.78
4	38	45	46.60	-1.60
5	38	48	46.60	1.40
6	38	50	46.60	3.40
7	46	49	40.25	8.75
8	48	34	38.66	-4.66
9	53	31	34.69	-3.69
10	57	33	31.51	1.49
11	39	44	45.80	-1.80

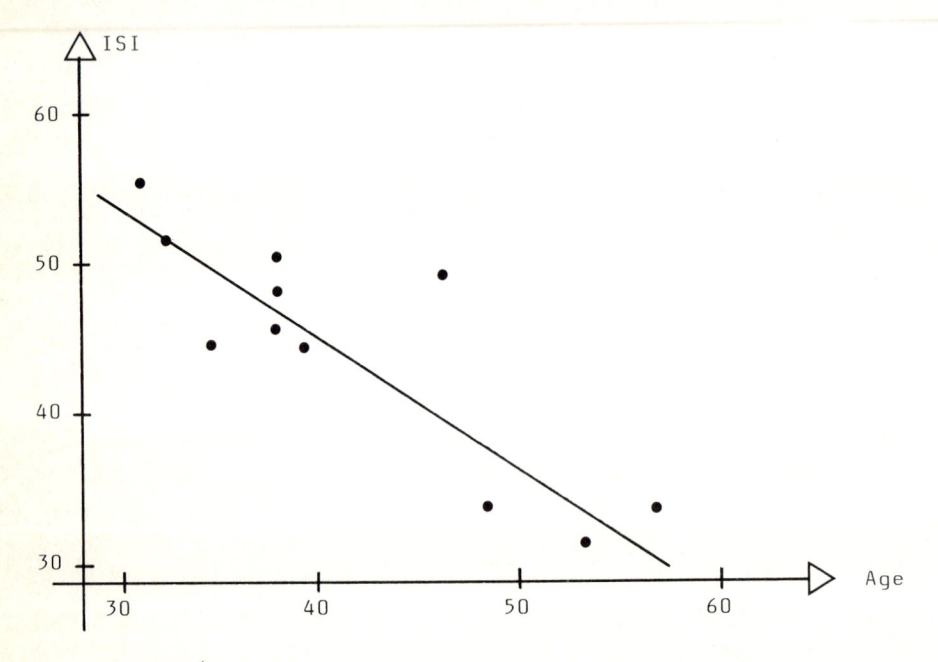

Fig. 14.2. ISI plotted against age for 11 painters.

The regression parameters β_0 and β_1 are estimated by the LS-method and the error variance σ^2 by s^2. The calculations involved are usually performed using a standard computer program. However, the table that follows illustrates how the calculations can be performed using a desk calculator. In the table, as well as in the following, $\hat{var}[.]$ indicates an estimated variance.

The estimated regression line

$$\hat{y} = 76.77 - 0.7941x$$

is shown in fig. 14.2. The 0.95 confidence intervals for β_0 and β_1 are given by

$$\hat{\beta}_0 \pm t_{0.975}(9)\sqrt{\hat{var}[\hat{\beta}_0]}$$

and

$$\hat{\beta}_1 \pm t_{0.975}(9)\sqrt{\hat{var}[\hat{\beta}_1]} \;,$$

according to (11.8) and theorem 14.4, assuming the error terms to be normally distributed. If this assumption is not satisfied, the intervals are only approximations to the 0.95 confidence intervals. $\triangle$.

Computational table for simple linear regression analysis.

$S_x = \sum_{i=1}^{n} x_i = 454$	$S_y = \sum_{i=1}^{n} y_i = 484$
$\bar{x} = S_x/n = 41.27$	$\bar{y} = S_y/n = 44.00$
$SS_x = \sum_{i=1}^{n} x_i^2 = 19472$	$SS_y = \sum_{i=1}^{n} y_i^2 = 21934$
$SSD_x = SS_x - S_x^2/n = 734.18$	$SSD_y = SS_y - S_y^2/n = 638.00$
$SP_{xy} = \sum_{i=1}^{n} x_i y_i = 19393$	$SPD_{xy} = SP_{xy} - S_x S_y/n = -583.00$
$\hat{\beta}_1 = \dfrac{SPD_{xy}}{SSD_x} = -0.7941$	$\hat{\beta}_0 = \bar{y} - \bar{x}\hat{\beta}_1 = 76.77$
$s^2 = \dfrac{1}{n-2} RSS = \dfrac{1}{n-2}\left(SSD_y - \dfrac{SPD_{xy}^2}{SSD_x}\right) = 19.45$	
$\hat{var}[\hat{\beta}_1] = s^2/SSD_x = 0.0265$	
$\hat{var}[\hat{\beta}_0] = s^2(1/n + \bar{x}^2/SSD_x) = 46.89$	

14.5. Analysis of variance

Once the regression parameters have been estimated, it is important that the fit of the estimated model is measured. This can be based on a decomposition of the total variation of the response variable which also forms the basis for the derivation of test statistics for hypotheses concerning the regression parameters or for the comparison of two regression models.

The **total variation** in the response variable is defined as

$$(14.18) \quad SSD_y = \sum_{i=1}^{n} (y_i - \bar{y})^2,$$

which can be decomposed as

$$\Sigma(y_i - \bar{y})^2 = \Sigma(y_i - \hat{y}_i + \hat{y}_i - \bar{y})^2 = \Sigma(y_i - \hat{y}_i)^2 + \Sigma(\hat{y}_i - \bar{y})^2 + 2\Sigma(y_i - \hat{y}_i)(\hat{y}_i - \bar{y}) =$$

$$\Sigma \hat{e}_i^2 + \hat{\beta}_1^2 \Sigma(x_i - \bar{x})^2,$$

since

$$\Sigma(y_i - \hat{y}_i)(\hat{y}_i - \bar{y}) = 0$$

and

$$\Sigma(\hat{y}_i - \bar{y})^2 = \Sigma(\bar{y} + \hat{\beta}_1(x_i - \bar{x}) - \bar{y})^2 = \hat{\beta}_1^2 SSD_x.$$

Using the notation introduced in section 14.3, the decomposition of SSD_y can finally be written as

$$(14.19) \quad SSD_y = RSS + \hat{\beta}_1^2 SSD_x.$$

The quantity RSS can be interpreted as that part of the total variation which cannot be described by the estimated model. The second term on the right hand side of (14.19) is therefore that part of SSD_y, which in fact can be described or explained by the estimated model. Accordingly the quantity

$$(14.20) \quad R^2 = \frac{SSD_y - RSS}{SSD_y} = \frac{\hat{\beta}_1^2 SSD_x}{SSD_y}$$

can be interpreted as the proportion of the variability in the response variable which can be explained by the estimated model. The quantity R^2 is called the **coefficient of determination**. Since R^2 can be shown to be the squared correlation coefficient between the observed and the fitted values of y, or, alternatively, the squared correlation between x and y, it follows that

$$0 \leq R^2 \leq 1.$$

Note that $R^2=1$ corresponds to the case RSS=0, and that the closer R^2 is to 1, the better the fit of the estimated model.

In order to decide whether the explanatory variable x contributes significantly to the description of the variation in the response variable, the residual sum of squares for the model

(14.21) $\quad Y_i = \beta_0 + e_i$

can be compared with RSS for the regression model (14.6).

It is easily shown that $\bar{y}$ is the LS-estimate for β_0 in (14.21), so the residual sum of squares for this model is SSD_y. Hence, the larger the ratio SSD_y/RSS, the larger the contribution from x to the explanation of the variability of y.

Since $(SSD_y-RSS)/RSS$ increases with SSD_y/RSS, the larger the quantity

(14.22) $\quad V = \dfrac{SSD_y - RSS}{RSS/(n-2)} = \dfrac{\hat{\beta}_1^2 SSD_x}{s^2},$

the larger the contribution of x to the description of the variability of y.

Since the model (14.21) is the special case of the regression model with $\beta_1=0$, V can be applied as a test statistic for the hypothesis

$$H_0: \beta_1 = 0$$

against the alternative

$$H_1: \beta_1 \neq 0$$

with small values of V supporting H_0.

If the error terms $e_1,\ldots,e_n$ are normally distributed, it can be shown by an application of definition 9.3 that V under H_0 follows an F-distribution with $(1,n-2)$ degrees of freedom. The level of significance for an observed value v of V is, therefore,

$$p = P(V > v)$$

where $V \sim F(1,n-2)$. The square root of V is

(14.23) $\quad T = \hat{\beta}_1 / \sqrt{s^2/SSD_x}.$

From theorem 14.4 and definition 9.2 it follows that T is t-distributed with n-2 degrees of freedom. Thus, the test of the hypothesis H_0 can also be based on (14.23), which is simply the estimator for β_1 divided by its estimated standard deviation. The advantage of (14.23) over (14.22) is that it allows H_0 to be tested against a one-sided alternative.

The hypothesis

$$H_0: \beta_1 = \beta_{10}$$

can be tested against the alternative

$$H_1: \beta_1 \neq \beta_{10},$$

using the test statistic

(14.24) $$T = \frac{\hat{\beta}_1 - \beta_{10}}{S}\sqrt{SSD_x}.$$

Hypotheses concerning β_0 can also be tested by means of a t-test statistic. According to (14.16), the test statistic for the hypothesis

$$H_0: \beta_0 = \beta_{00}$$

is

$$T = \frac{\hat{\beta}_0 - \beta_{00}}{\sqrt{\hat{var}[\hat{\beta}_0]}}$$

with

$$\hat{var}[\hat{\beta}_0] = S^2\left(\frac{1}{n} + \bar{x}^2/SSD_x\right).$$

The t-tests considered above are against one-sided and two-sided alternatives carried out as described in section 13.2. Confidence limits for β_1 can also be constructed following the guide-lines in section 11.3. Table 14.2 is a review of test statistics and confidence intervals.

A test of the hypothesis $H_0: \beta_0 = 0$ is often interpreted as a test of the hypothesis that "the regression goes through (0,0)". This interpretation is, however, only justified if x=0 is in the domain of variation for the explanatory variable. Otherwise, the correct interpretation is that the fit of a regression model with the intercept β_0 is not significantly better than a fit by a model without an intercept.

Table 14.2. Test statistics and confidence intervals for the parameters of the linear regression model.

Parameter	β_0	β_1
Hypothesis	$\beta_0 = \beta_{00}$	$\beta_1 = \beta_{10}$
Test statistic	$\dfrac{\hat{\beta}_0 - \beta_{00}}{s\sqrt{1/n + \bar{x}^2/SSD_x}}$	$\dfrac{(\hat{\beta}_1 - \beta_{10})\sqrt{SSD_x}}{s}$
Distribution	$t(n-2)$	$t(n-2)$
Confidence interval	$\hat{\beta}_0 \pm t_{1-\alpha/2} s\sqrt{1/n + \bar{x}^2/SSD_x}$	$\hat{\beta}_1 \pm t_{1-\alpha/2} s/\sqrt{SSD_x}$

14.6. Interpretation of the estimated regression parameters and R^2

The simple linear regression model constitutes the formal basis for an analysis of the variation of a response variable as a function of an explanatory variable. Such an analysis may serve various purposes, e.g. the verification of a postulated law governing the relationship between the involved variables or a prediction of the response variable for a given value of the explanatory variable.

If the relationship is actually governed by a law, this law must also be valid for other similar data sets. This means that, apart from random errors, the estimated regression parameters must be the same, independently of the data considered. Such situations are common in the natural sciences, where the parameters usually correspond to physical constants and hypotheses concerning the regression parameters are hypotheses concerning the unknown values of existing quantities.

In the social sciences, however, regression models are not usually considered as law-determined relationships. In many cases, the model only constitutes the formal basis for a description of the covariation between the response variable and the explanatory variable. The parameters of the model are then quantities describing the relationship between variables as they manifest themselves in concrete data sets. Hence, the estimates cannot be expected to attain the same values (even apart from random errors) if the same model is applied to data collected under different circumstances. As an illustration, consider the situation with a response variable y depending on two explanatory variables x and z. Fig. 14.3 shows the relationship between x and y when z takes the values z_1 and z_2, respectively. Suppose that four data sets have been collected. In the first of these $z=z_1$, while x takes values in I_1. In the second $z=z_2$, while x still varies in I_1. In data sets three and four, z again takes the values z_1 and z_2, but x now has I_2 as its domain of variation.

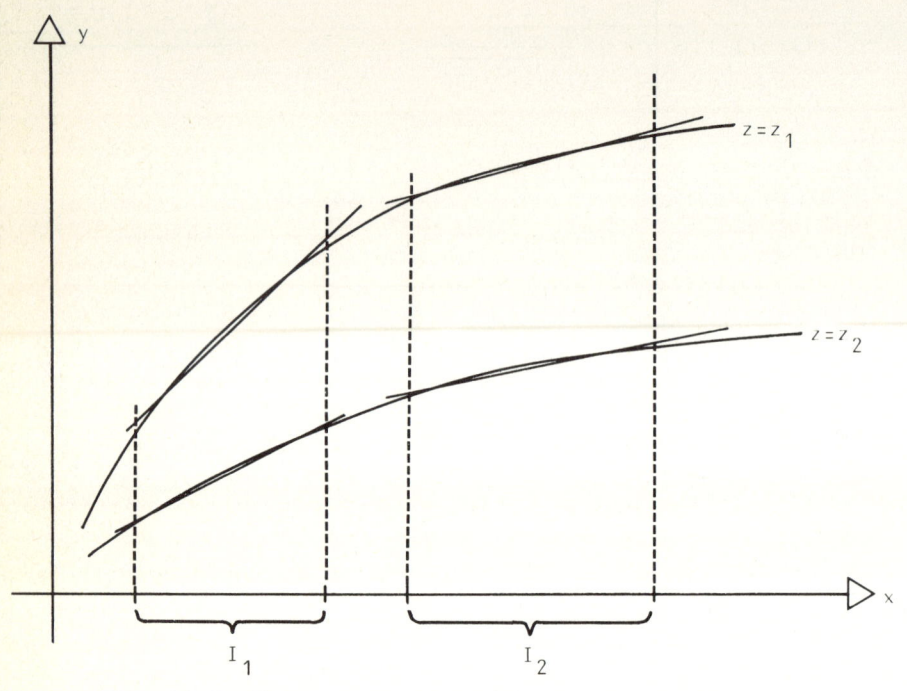

Fig. 14.3. The regression model as an approximation.

In each of the four situations, the relationship between x and y can be approximated by a straight line. Since the approximating lines are different, the slope parameter cannot be regarded as a constant whose unknown value is to be estimated. A test of the hypothesis $\beta_1=0$ can, therefore, only be regarded as an evaluation of the extent to which the explanatory variable contributes to the description of the response variable in the present data.

The coefficient of determination R^2 is a measure of the degree of linear covariation between x and y in the data at hand and should not be used as a measure of covariation between the variables in a more general sense. To illustrate this, consider the data in fig. 14.4, which have been divided into three sections by the dashed vertical lines. Assume that R^2 is computed 1) from all cases with x-values in the middle section, 2) from cases with x-values in the two extreme sections and 3) from all cases.

If these three coefficients are denoted by R_1^2, R_2^2 and R_3^2, one would find that

$$R_1^2 < R_3^2 < R_2^2 .$$

This follows from the relationship

$$R^2 = 1 - \frac{RSS}{SSD_y} .$$

Even though $\hat{\beta}_1$ has approximately the same value in all three cases, the relation between RSS and SSD_y is different as the value of RSS, divided by the number of cases, is approximately constant, while the corresponding value of SSD_y, divided by the number of cases, takes different values. Fig. 14.4 thus shows that R^2 can attain quite different values, even in cases where the same linear relationship is considered.

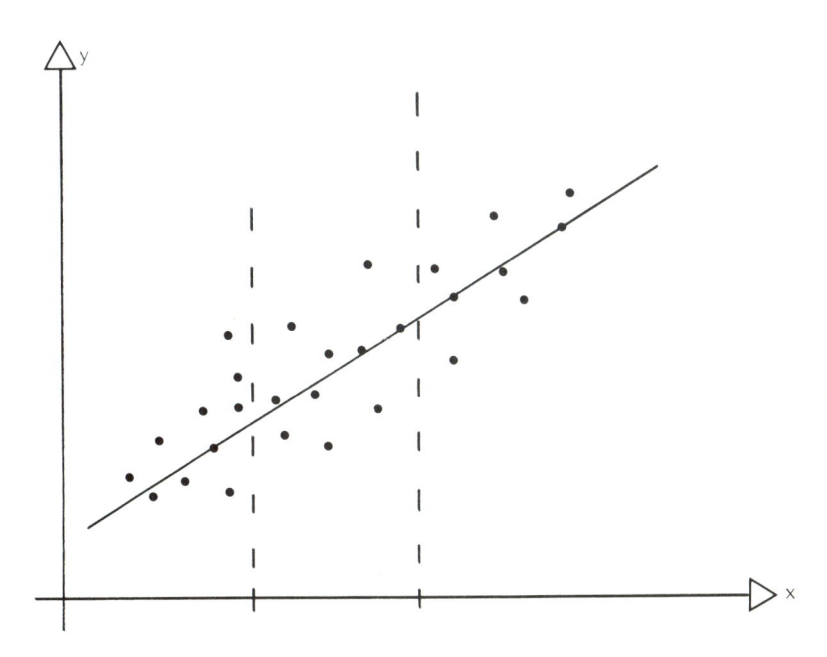

Fig. 14.4. Illustration of the interpretation of R^2.

14.7. Examination of the residuals

The residuals, defined as

(14.25) $\quad \hat{e}_i = y_i - \hat{y}_i = y_i - \hat{\beta}_0 - \hat{\beta}_1 x_i, \quad i=1,\ldots,n,$

are the differences between the observed and the fitted values of the response variable. The residuals are thus in a certain sense estimates of the error terms of the model, and can be used to check the fit of the model, i.e. the agreement between model and data.

It can be shown that

(14.26) $\quad \begin{cases} 1) & E[\hat{e}_i] = 0 \\ 2) & \text{var}[\hat{e}_i] = \sigma^2(1-h_{ii}) \\ 3) & \text{cov}(\hat{e}_i, \hat{e}_j) = -\sigma^2 h_{ij}, \end{cases}$

where

(14.27) $\quad h_{ij} = \frac{1}{n} + \frac{(x_i - \bar{x})(x_j - \bar{x})}{SSD_x}.$

Hence the residuals all have zero means, while the variances and covariances depend on the values of the explanatory variable. It is further seen from (14.26) that the less x_i deviates from $\bar{x}$, the larger the variance of the residual $\hat{e}_i$. This is because cases for which the differences $|x_i - \bar{x}|$ are large, tend to be fitted more closely by the LS-method than cases for which the differences are small. The correlation between the residuals is due to the linear constraints $\Sigma \hat{e}_i = 0$ and $\Sigma \hat{e}_i x_i = 0$. The **standardized residual**, r_i, is defined as

(14.28) $\quad r_i = \frac{\hat{e}_i}{\sqrt{\hat{\text{var}}[\hat{e}_i]}} = \frac{\hat{e}_i}{s\sqrt{1-h_{ii}}}.$

If the error terms are normally distributed, the standardized residuals approximately follow a standardized normal distribution.

Assumptions (14.7) and (14.8) imply that the means and the variances of the errors do not depend on the values of the explanatory variables. These assumptions can be checked in a **residual plot**, where r_i is plotted against x_i.

Fig. 14.5 gives examples of residual plots. Fig. 14.5(a) shows a situation where the variation in the residuals is independent of the explanatory variable, while fig. 14.5(b) shows a situation with systematic variation in the residuals, indicating the existence of a non-linear systematic component in the error terms of the model. If the residuals show a pattern as in fig. 14.5(b), the model should be reformulated, either by transforming the variables or by including more explanatory variables. In fig. 14.5(c), the variability of the residuals tends to increase with the value of x, indicating that the assumption $\text{var}[e_i]=\sigma^2$ may not be satisfied.

It is often difficult to evaluate a residual plot, in particular as regards the assumption that $\text{var}[e_i] = \sigma^2$. This problem may be overcome by plotting $|r_i|$ or r_i^2 against x_i. Such plots may form a better basis for deciding whether to reject the assumption of constant variance for the error terms.

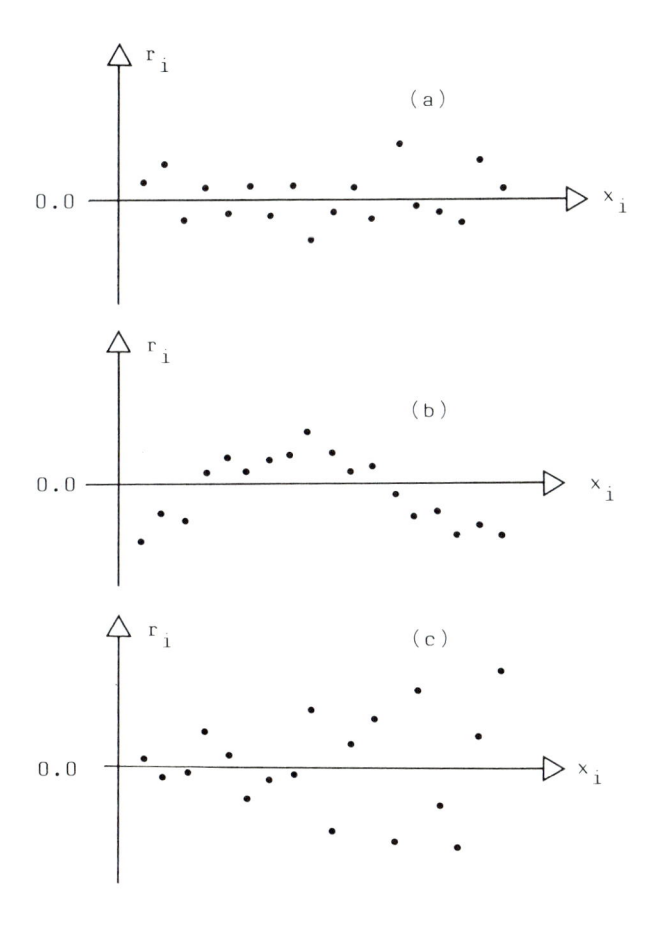

Fig. 14.5. Examples of residual plots.

If the data form a time series, i.e. if the indices i=1,...,n correspond to successive points in time, it is important to check assumption (14.9). Correlation between error terms in time series is called **autocorrelation**. The presence of autocorrelation in data can sometimes be detected by plotting r_i against i. Fig. 14.6 is a situation where residuals which are close in time tend to be more similar to one another than residuals spread over time. The figure thus indicates that the error terms are correlated.

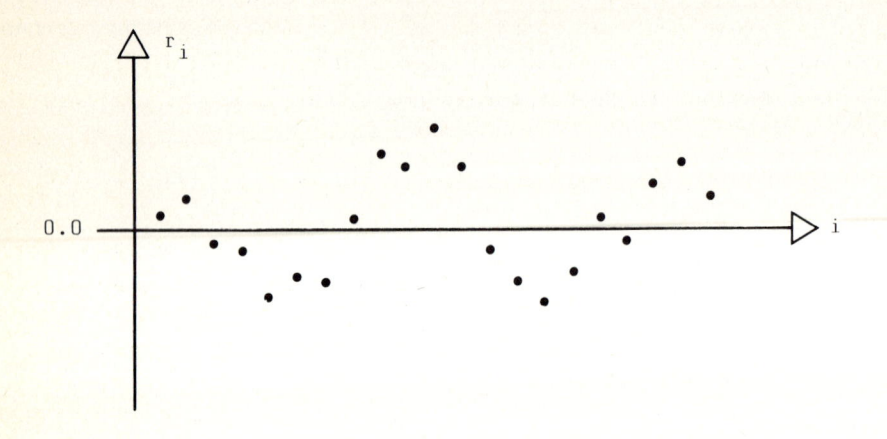

Fig. 14.6. A residual plot indicating autocorrelation.

The assumption of normally distributed error terms is checked by means of a probability plot based on the standardized residuals. If the points of a probability plot cluster around a straight line, it is often concluded that the error terms, and consequently the response variable, are normally distributed. The relationship

(14.29) $$\hat{e}_i = e_i(1-h_{ii}) - \sum_{j \neq i} h_{ij} e_j ,$$

where h_{ij} is defined by (14.27), shows, however, that $\hat{e}_i$ only reflects the distributional properties of the error term e_i if $\sum_{j \neq i} h_{ij} e_j$ is small compared to e_i. If this is not the case, the central limit theorem (theorem 9.11) implies that the distribution of the residuals can be approximated by a normal distribution even in cases where the error terms themselves fail to be normally distributed. Great care must thus be exercised in evaluating the significance of probability plots based on the residuals.

14.8. Predictions

The estimated regression line is often applied to estimate the mean of the response variable for a given value x_0 of the explanatory variable. In the following, such an estimate is called a **prediction** of the response variable. The prediction $\hat{y}_0$ is obtained by substituting x_0 for x in the estimated regression function, i.e.

$$\hat{y}_0 = \hat{\beta}_0 + \hat{\beta}_1 x_0.$$

Since $\hat{\beta}_0$ and $\hat{\beta}_1$ are unbiased estimators for β_0 and β_1, the prediction $\hat{y}_0$ is an unbiased estimator for the mean of the response variable when $x = x_0$.

Applications of (14.16), (8.30) and (8.43) yield

$$\mathrm{var}[\hat{y}_0] = \mathrm{var}[\hat{\beta}_0 + \hat{\beta}_1 x_0] = \mathrm{var}[\hat{\beta}_0] + \mathrm{var}[\hat{\beta}_1 x_0] + 2\mathrm{cov}(\hat{\beta}_0, \hat{\beta}_1 x_0) =$$

$$\sigma^2 \left(\frac{1}{n} + \frac{\bar{x}^2}{SSD_x} \right) + \sigma^2 \frac{x_0^2}{SSD_x} - 2\sigma^2 \frac{x_0 \bar{x}}{SSD_x} = \sigma^2 \left(\frac{1}{n} + \frac{(x_0 - \bar{x})^2}{SSD_x} \right),$$

i.e.

(14.30) $$\mathrm{var}[\hat{y}_0] = \sigma^2 \left[\frac{1}{n} + \frac{(x_0 - \bar{x})^2}{SSD_x} \right].$$

This expression is a measure of the uncertainty about the position of the regression line at $x = x_0$. The further x_0 is from $\bar{x}$, the more uncertain is the position of the regression line.

A confidence interval for the expected value of the response, given that the explanatory variable takes the value x_0, is easily constructed under the assumption of normally distributed error terms. From theorem 14.4, (14.30) and definition 9.2 follows that

$$T = \frac{\hat{y}_0 - \beta_0 - \beta_1 x_0}{s\sqrt{1/n + (x_0 - \bar{x})^2/SSD_x}}$$

is t-distributed with n-2 degrees of freedom and hence a 1-α confidence interval for $\beta_0 + \beta_1 x_0$ becomes

(14.31) $$\hat{y}_0 \pm t_{1-\alpha/2}(n-2) s\sqrt{1/n + (x_0 - \bar{x})^2/SSD_x}$$

A **prediction interval** is an interval which with a fixed probability contains the value of the response for a given value of the explanatory variable. Let Y_0 be the (future) value of the response variable for $x=x_0$. Then Y_0 and $\hat{y}_0$ are independent and

$$\mathrm{var}[Y_0-\hat{y}_0] = \sigma^2 + \mathrm{var}[\hat{y}_0] = \sigma^2(1+\tfrac{1}{n}+(x_0-\bar{x})^2/SSD_x) .$$

Hence $(Y_0-\hat{y}_0)/[s\sqrt{1+\tfrac{1}{n}+(x_0-\bar{x})^2/SSD_x}] \sim t(n-2)$ and a prediction interval, which with probability $1-\alpha$ contains the response when $x=x_0$, is then given by

(14.32) $\quad \hat{y}_0 \pm t_{1-\alpha/2}(n-2) s\sqrt{1+\tfrac{1}{n}+(x_0-\bar{x})^2/SSD_x} .$

The interval (14.32) can also be interpreted as an acceptance region for a test of the hypothesis that a case (y_0,x_0) belongs to the same model as the original data set.

Some caution has to be exercised when an estimated regression line is used for prediction purposes, in particular when x_0 is outside the domain of variation of the original cases. The reason for this is that data do not contain information about the relationship between the response variable and the explanatory variable outside $I=[x_{(1)},x_{(n)}]$, where $x_{(1)}$ denotes the smallest and $x_{(n)}$ the largest observed value of x. This is illustrated in fig. 14.7, where the fully drawn line is the estimated regression line and the dotted curves are hypothetical examples of the "true" model. Predictions of y outside I are called **extrapolations**.

There may be other problems connected with computations of predictions based on an estimated regression model. Often the application of a linear model is based purely on empirical evidence. This will be the case when there is no theory to substantiate a linear relationship. For example, y may depend on variables, which for various reasons have been kept approximately constant in the cases, on which the estimation of the model is based. If one or more of these variables have changed when a prediction is required, an application of the estimated regression model may be erroneous. Obviously, predictions are most realiable if the linear relationship is based on a firmly established theory.

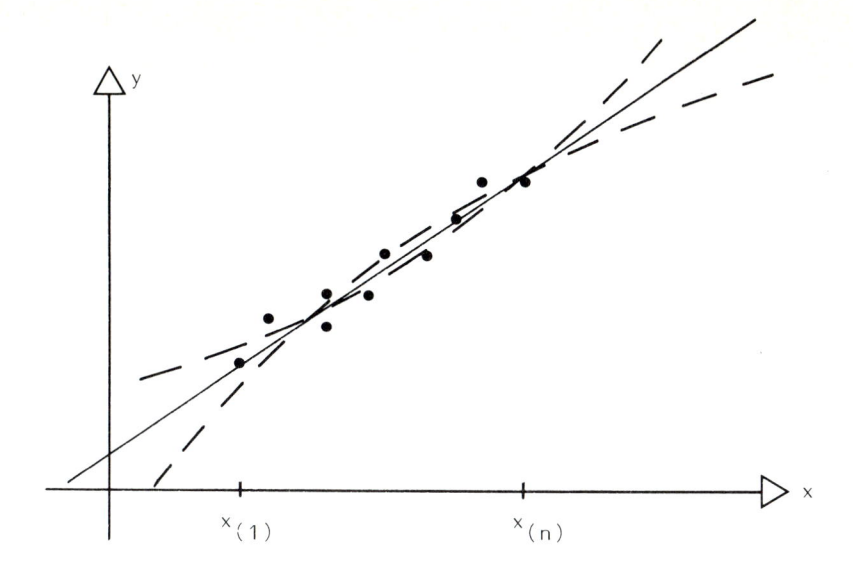

Fig. 14.7. Possible courses of the regression function.

Example 14.2

The Asnæs power plant is owned by the Danish production company Elkraft, which is interested in a description of electricity production as a function of fuel consumption. Therefore, the company in 1982 and 1983 collected monthly data on the electricity production in MegaWatt-hours and the fuel consumption (oil or coal) in Giga Joule. Tabel 14.3 shows the values of these quantities with x=fuel consumption and y=electricity production for one of the units of the power plant. In these figures, fuel consumption is only included for periods in which production has taken place.

For economic reasons, oil is only used when production is low. This is the case just after a production stop due to a technical problem or maintenance. Even a brief production stop entails an extraordinarily high consumption of fuel compared with the amount of electricity produced. For this reason, production is only stopped shortly once a year for maintenance.

Fig. 14.8 shows the relationship between fuel consumption and electricity production.

Table 14.3. Electricity production (y), fuel consumption (x) and standardized residuals (r_i) for a production unit at the Asnæs Power Plant, January 1982 to December 1983.

Year:	1982			1983		
Month	y_i	x_i	r_i	y_i	x_i	r_i
January	150638	1422044	1.13	124743	1178430	1.00
February	139907	1338445	0.26	115333	1078701	1.47
March	127849	1225643	0.18	112994	1086166	0.10
April	117390	1144123	-0.65	123239	1176552	0.42
May	96450	967955	-1.70	58400	561176	0.40
June	113148	1150605	-2.82	17677	192242	-0.48
July	141873	1342686	0.94	3394	39189	0.42
August	177661	1736447	-1.68	136598	1310817	0.08
September	20296	216282	-0.43	69840	692139	-0.64
October	92359	865543	1.24	69941	689855	-0.49
November	92735	879298	0.77	122615	1166354	0.62
December	131728	1267052	-0.03	116869	1129953	0.22

Source: ELKRAFT Production Company.

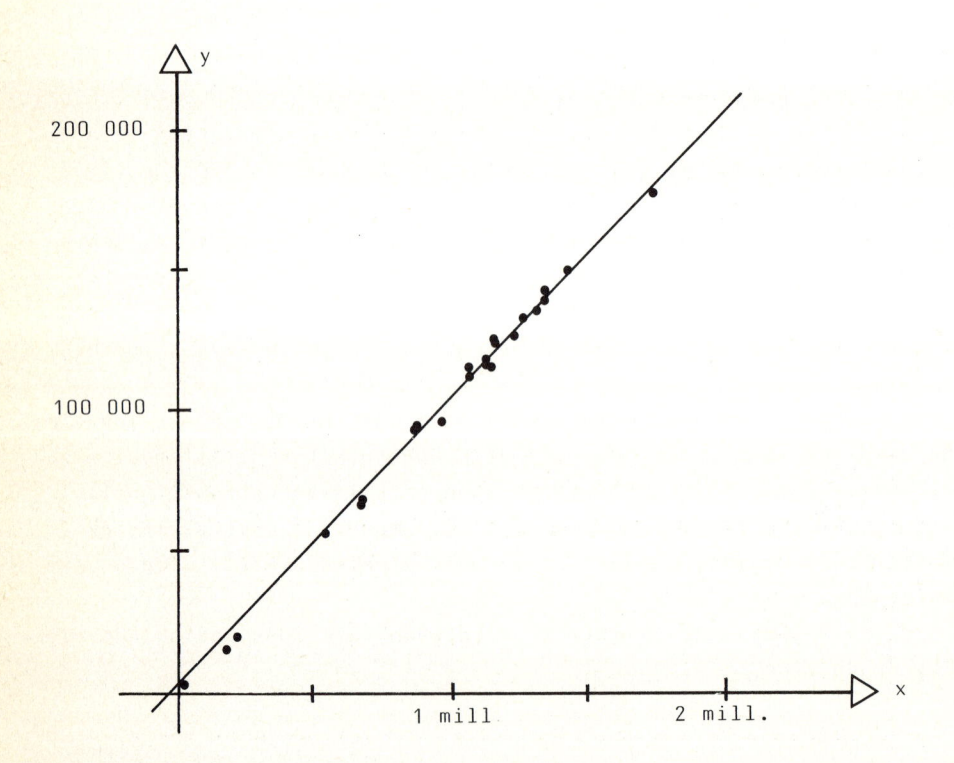

Fig. 14.8. The relationship between the monthly fuel consumption and electricity production, 1982-1983.

From fig. 14.8, it can be concluded that a linear function gives a satisfactory description of the relationship and a linear regression model is fitted to the data with fuel consumption as explanatory variable and electricity production as the response.

Table 14.4 shows the LS-estimates of the parameters of the model together with R^2. The value of R^2 is close to 1, reflecting the fact that the points in fig. 14.8 cluster closely around the regression line. Even when R^2, as here, is very high, it is, however, necessary to check the model by means of residual plots. The standardized residuals are shown in table 14.3 and in fig. 14.9 they are plotted against fuel consumption.

Table 14.4. Summary of a regression analysis of the data in table 14.3.

Parameter	Estimate	Standard deviation	t
β_0	-1569.90	1259.01	-1.24
β_1	0.1052	0.001173	89.75
	s = 2328	R^2 = 0.9973	

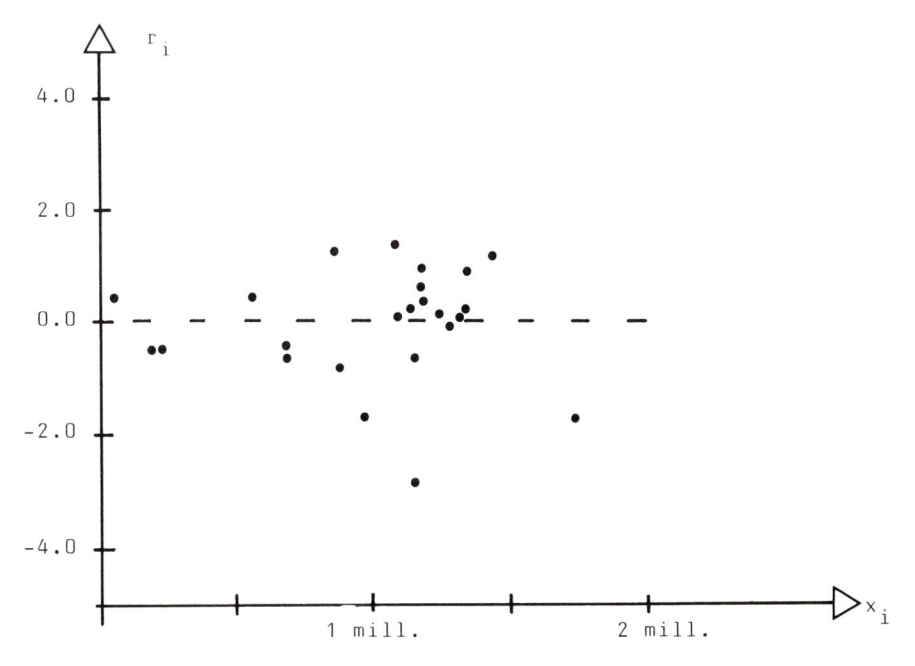

Fig. 14.9. Plot of r_i against x_i.

In fig. 14.9, the numerical values of the residuals tend to increase with fuel consumption. Furthermore, the residual for June 1982 has an exceptionally high numerical value and may be responsible for the impression one gets from the residual plot of an increasing residual variability as fuel consumption increases.

In order to examine the residuals more closely, $|r_i|$ is plotted against x_i in fig. 14.10. This figure seems to confirm that the variability in the residuals increases with x. But apart from the above mentioned residual, the tendency is so weak that it is neglected in the further analysis.

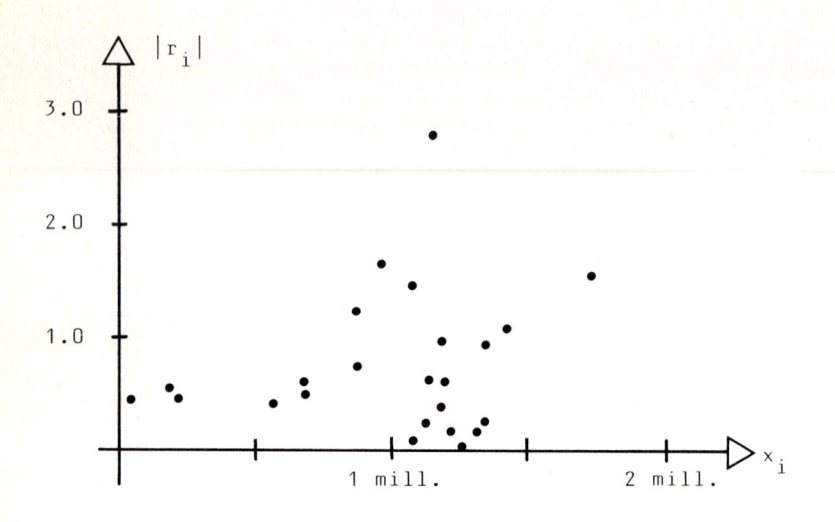

Fig. 14.10. Plot of $|r_i|$ against x_i.

In fig. 14.11, r_i is finally plotted against time. In this plot a clearly systematic variation is present at the beginning of the period. A closer examination reveals that there was in fact a short production stop in June 1982 which no doubt entailed increased fuel consumption in June and possibly also in May 1982. These circumstances may very well explain the systematic variation observed in fig. 14.11.

The aim of the analysis is not only to describe how electricity production depends on fuel consumption, i.e. to estimate β_0 and β_1, but also to describe the deviation of actual electricity production from expected production, i.e. to estimate the variance of the error term. It is, therefore, of interest to evaluate the influence of the observation from June 1982 on the analysis. This is done by reanalysing the data without case 6. The result is shown in table 14.5.

Fig. 14.11. Plot of r_i against time.

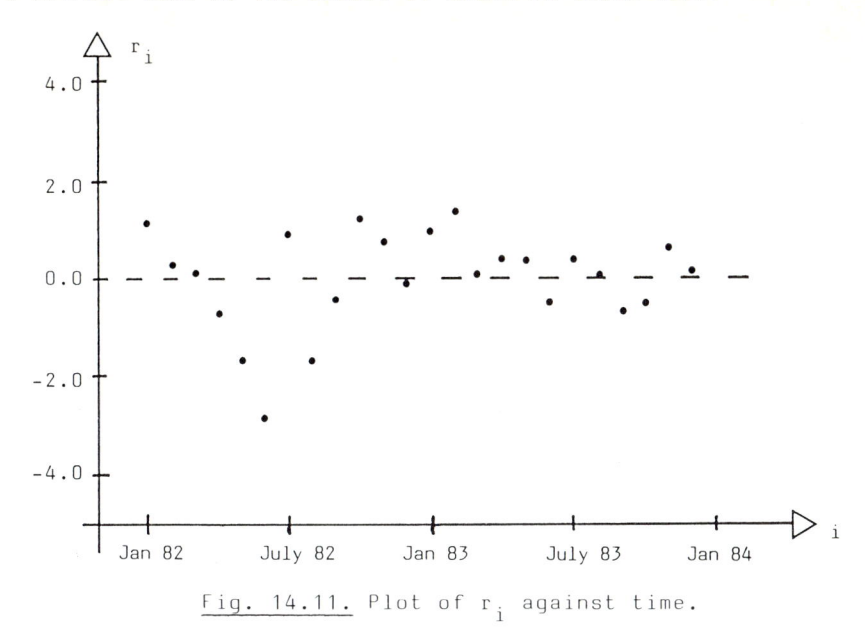

Table 14.5. Comparison of a regression analysis with and without case 6.

	All observations	Without case 6
$\hat{\beta}_0$	-1569.9	-1540.45
$\hat{\beta}_1$	0.1052	0.1055
s	2328.6	1906.1
R^2	.9973	.9983

It is seen that the estimates of β_0 and β_1 by and large are unaffected by the exclusion of case 6. However, the estimate s of the standard deviation of the error term is reduced by 18%, so that case 6 would appear to have considerable influence on the evaluation of the magnitude of the expected deviations from the estimated regression line.

In order to obtain an estimate of the variance of the error term under regular production conditions, the exclusion of case 5 from May 1982 could also be considered.△.

14.9. Experimental and non-experimental data

In the simple linear regression model the values of the response variable y are regarded as realizations of random variables, while the values of the explanatory variable x are regarded as fixed constants. If, for example, $(y_1,x_1),\ldots,(y_n,x_n)$ are jointly observed values of the two variables for n units drawn at random from a population, there is no justification for regarding y as random and x as non-random. But if data are collected as part of a **planned experiment**, where the response variable is observed for a fixed set of x-values, while other potential explanatory variables are kept constant, then only the response should be regarded as random.

In the social sciences, planned experiments are rare. Data usually result either from consecutive joint observations of x and y, for example in case of time series, or from simultaneous observations of two characteristics for the units of a sample.

In order to analyse **non-experimental** data, i.e. data where both x and y can be regarded as random, the linear regression model is interpreted as a description of the conditional distribution of the response variable, given the observed value of the explanatory variable. Thus, let (y_i,x_i), $i=1,\ldots,n$ be independent observations of two-dimensional random variables (Y_i,X_i), $i=1,\ldots,n$. Then the regression model is

$$(14.33) \qquad E(Y_i|X_i=x_i) = \beta_0 + \beta_1 x_i, \quad i=1,\ldots,n,$$

and

$$(14.34) \qquad \mathrm{var}(Y_i|X_i=x_i) = \sigma^2, \quad i=1,\ldots,n.$$

The statistical analysis of data based on the regression model (14.33)-(14.34) is technically the same as for the model in section 14.2, but the interpretation of the results is of course different.

If it is assumed that (y_i,x_i), $i=1,\ldots,n$, are independent observations from the two-dimensional normal distribution, (8.47) and (8.48) imply that (14.33) and (14.34) are satisfied with

$$\beta_0 = \mu_2 - \rho\frac{\sigma_2}{\sigma_1}\mu_1,$$

and

$$\beta_1 = \rho\sigma_2/\sigma_1.$$

Hence, the linear regression model can be obtained through conditioning

in the two-dimensional normal distribution. When non-experimental data
are analysed it is in principle possible to regard y as the response
variable and x as the explanatory variable, as well as to regard y as
the explanatory variable and x as the response variable. These two ways
of analysing the data do not, however, lead to the same results. It is,
for example, impossible to derive the estimates of the regression parameters in one mode of analysis from the estimates obtained from the
second mode. Which model to use will depend on the purpose of the analysis. If the purpose is to predict the value of one variable for a
given value of the other variable, the former is chosen as the response
and the latter as the explanatory variable. If the purpose is to describe one variable as a function of the other, for example in the search
of a causal relationship, the variable to be described should be chosen
as the response.

14.10. Transformations

Applications of linear regression models are primarily based on the
existence of an approximate linear relationship between the explanatory variable x and the response variable y. If such a linear relationship does not exist, it may be possible to find functions h and q, such
that the linear model

$$g(y) = \beta_0 + \beta_1 h(x) + e$$

fits the transformed values of the variables.

The choice of the transformations g and h may be based on prior
knowledge of the relationship between the variables, or may result from
an exploratory graphical analysis. Often logarithmic transformations
linearize the relationship between the variables considered. If, for example, (x_i, y_i), i=1,...,n, scatter around the curve

$$y = \beta_0 + \beta_1 \ln(x),$$

as shown in fig. 14.12(a), and if the variation around the curve does
not depend of x, a linear relationship can be estimated between y and
$\ln(x)$. This is done by simply letting $\ln(x_1),...,\ln(x_n)$ be the values
of the explanatory variable instead of $x_1,...,x_n$.

In other situations, the observations may scatter around a non-
linear function in such a way that the variation around the function
increases with y. In such situations, it is often appropriate to des-

cribe the relationship between x and y by functions of the form

(14.35) $\quad y = \alpha x^{\beta_1}, \quad \alpha > 0, \quad -\infty < \beta_1 < \infty$

or

(14.36) $\quad y = \alpha e^{\beta_1 x}, \quad \alpha > 0, \quad -\infty < \beta_1 < \infty$

as shown in fig. 14.12(b) and (c). Consider first (14.35) and suppose that the error term u is multiplicative, i.e.

(14.37) $\quad y = \alpha x^{\beta_1} \cdot u.$

Taking logarithms on both sides of (14.37) yields

(14.38) $\quad \ln(y) = \ln(\alpha) + \beta_1 \ln(x) + e,$

where $e = \ln(u)$. It follows that the relationship between $\ln(x)$ and $\ln(y)$ can be described by a linear function with parameters $\beta_0 = \ln(\alpha)$ and β_1, which can be estimated by the LS-method.

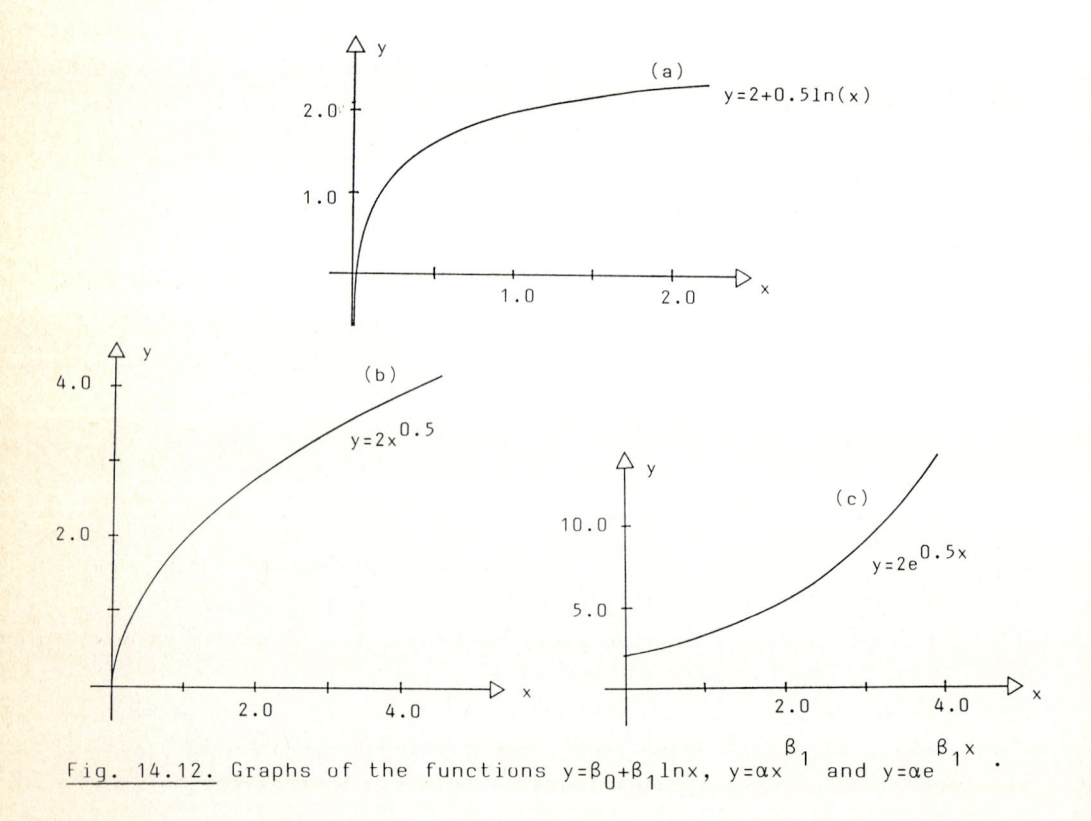

Fig. 14.12. Graphs of the functions $y = \beta_0 + \beta_1 \ln x$, $y = \alpha x^{\beta_1}$ and $y = \alpha e^{\beta_1 x}$.

In the same manner, (14.36) can be transformed to the linear model

$$\ln(y) = \ln(\alpha) + \beta_1 x + e,$$

if the error term is multiplicative.

A multiplicative error term means that the variation around the regression function increases with the level of y, a phenomenon quite common when analysing economic data. It follows that a logarithmic transformation changes not only the mean value structure, but also the variance structure of the data. Note that the impact of a logarithmic transformation on the variance properties of the model is only of importance if there are substantial differences in magnitude between the observed values of y.

Example 14.3

In 1984 the Danish Building Research Institute carried out an investigation of regional productivity differences among Danish manufacturing companies. Companies with at least 20 employees were grouped according to trade, and for each company a measure of the productive efforts of the employees, called value added, and the number of employees were recorded. The annual value added for a company is defined as the turnover (taxes excluded), minus expenditure on raw materials, energy costs and the costs of various services. Within each trade, the companies were ordered according to value added per employee. The value added and the numbers of employees were aggregated over groups of at least three companies.

In economic theory it is assumed that the relationship between the value added y and the number of employees x can be described by the Cobb-Douglas function

$$y = \alpha x^{\beta_1}$$

or on logarithmic form

$$\ln y = \ln \alpha + \beta_1 \ln x = \beta_0 + \beta_1 \ln x.$$

Table 14.6 shows the joint observations y and x for 38 groups of companies within electronics in the Copenhagen Metropolitan area.

Table 14.6. Value added and the numbers of employees for 38 groups of companies.

Case No.	Value added (1000 DKK)	Number of employees
1	80576	141
2	52753	159
3	57479	206
4	31755	121
5	32093	129
6	82269	341
7	230109	1001
8	51260	230
9	196031	895
10	470898	2224
11	45902	222
12	48971	242
13	153189	775
14	176050	930
15	20167	109
16	86289	469
17	47063	262
18	45883	259
19	14876	87
20	67061	398
21	34569	209
22	252896	1540
23	61849	377
24	173950	1082
25	81051	509
26	18078	117
27	9338	62
28	45331	310
29	10434	73
30	21743	158
31	47322	352
32	63406	475
33	2489	19
34	16023	126
35	31635	255
36	23691	194
37	19421	169
38	31831	407

To explore the relationship between x and y, lny is plotted against lnx for the 38 cases as shown in fig. 14.13. This figure confirms that there exists a linear relationship between the logarithms of the variables. Hence, data can be analysed by a linear regression model with the logarithm of the value added as response and the logarithm of the number of employees as the explanatory variable.

Table 14.7 shows the standardized residuals r_i. The residual plot in fig. 14.14 reveals no obvious violations of the assumptions of the linear regression model. The probability plot in fig. 14.15 shows that also the assumption of normally distributed error terms can be maintained.

Table 14.7. Logarithms and residuals for the data in table 14.6.

Case No.	$\ln y_i$	$\ln x_i$	$\hat{y}_i$	$\hat{e}_i$	r_i
1	11.927	4.9487	10.117	1.1798	3.48
2	10.873	5.0689	10.239	0.6339	1.87
3	10.959	5.3278	10.503	0.4561	1.34
4	10.365	4.7957	9.961	0.4044	1.20
5	10.376	4.8598	10.026	0.3498	1.03
6	11.317	5.8318	11.016	0.3015	0.89
7	12.346	6.9087	12.112	0.2337	0.70
8	10.844	5.4380	10.615	0.2294	0.67
9	12.186	6.7968	11.998	0.1874	0.56
10	13.062	7.7070	12.925	0.1370	0.43
11	10.734	5.4026	10.579	0.1550	0.46
12	10.799	5.4889	10.667	0.1319	0.39
13	11.939	6.6528	11.852	0.0874	0.26
14	12.078	6.8351	12.037	0.0408	0.12
15	9.911	4.6913	9.855	0.0568	0.17
16	11.365	6.1506	11.340	0.0247	0.07
17	10.770	5.5683	10.747	0.0227	0.07
18	10.733	5.5568	10.736	-0.0023	-0.01
19	9.607	4.4659	9.625	-0.0180	-0.05
20	11.113	5.9864	11.173	-0.0602	-0.18
21	10.450	5.3423	10.517	-0.0671	-0.20
22	12.440	7.3395	12.551	-0.1104	-0.34
23	11.032	5.9322	11.118	-0.0860	-0.25
24	12.066	6.9865	12.191	-0.1253	-0.38
25	11.302	6.2324	11.424	-0.1212	-0.36
26	9.802	4.7621	9.927	-0.1247	-0.37
27	9.141	4.1271	9.280	-0.1388	-0.42
28	10.721	5.7365	10.919	-0.1974	-0.58
29	9.252	4.2904	9.446	-0.1941	-0.58
30	9.987	5.0626	10.233	-0.2460	-0.72
31	10.764	5.8636	11.048	-0.2838	-0.83
32	11.057	6.1633	11.353	-0.2963	-0.87
33	7.819	2.9444	8.076	-0.2569	-0.85
34	9.681	4.8362	10.002	-0.3208	-0.95
35	10.362	5.5412	10.720	-0.3583	-1.05
36	10.072	5.2678	10.442	-0.3691	-1.08
37	9.874	5.1299	10.301	-0.4274	-1.26
38	10.368	6.0088	11.196	-0.8282	-2.44

Table 14.8 shows the estimates of the regression parameters, their estimated standard deviations, the t-test statistics, the estimate of the standard deviation of the error term and R^2.

Table 14.8. Summary of a regression analysis of the data in table 14.7.

Parameter	Estimate	St.deviation	t
β_0	5.0788	0.3362	15.11
β_1	1.0181	0.0594	17.14
	$R^2=0.8908$	$s=0.3454$	

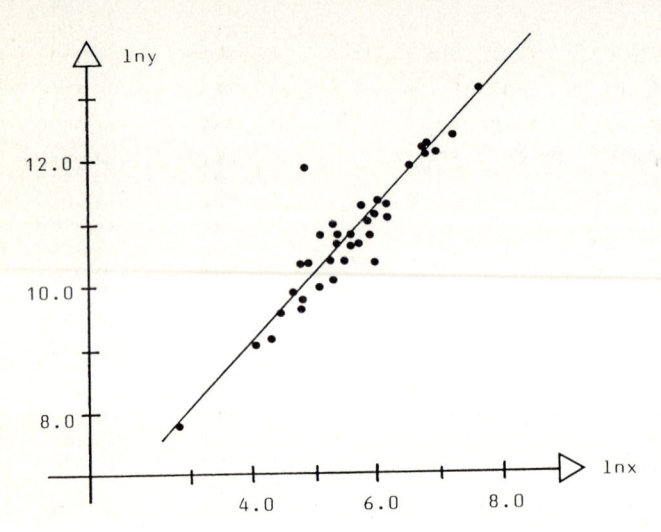

Fig. 14.13. Plot of the logarithms of value added versus the logarithms of the number of employees.

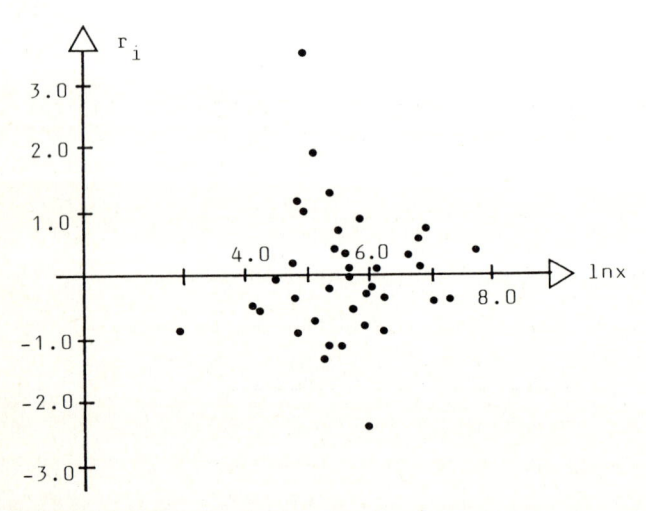

Fig. 14.14. Plot of the standardized residuals versus the logarithms of the number of employees.

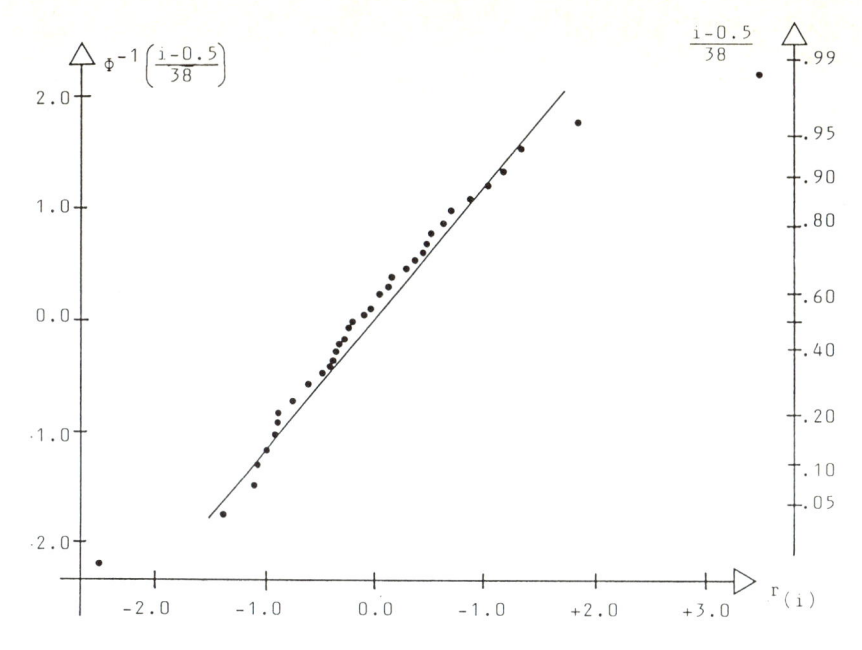

Fig. 14.15. Probability plot for the standardized residuals.

The test statistic for the hypothesis $\beta_1 = 1$ against the alternative $\beta_1 \neq 1$ is, according to (14.24),

$$t = \frac{1.0181 - 1}{0.0594} = 0.305,$$

corresponding to the level of significance $p = P(|T| \geq 0.305) = 0.77$. Hence, it can be concluded that the description by the estimated model is not significantly better than a description by a model with $\beta_1 = 1$.

Consider a company with 500 employees. The expected value of the logarithm of the value added for such a company is

$$\widehat{\ln(y)} = 5.0788 + 1.0181 \ln(500) = 11.4059.$$

From this value a 0.95 confidence interval for the mean of the logarithm of the value added can be computed from (14.31) as

$$11.4059 \pm 2.028 \cdot 0.3454 \sqrt{\frac{1}{38} + (\ln(500) - 5.5803)^2 / 33.8200} =$$

$$\begin{cases} 11.3214 \\ 11.4903 \end{cases}.$$

The 0.95 prediction interval for the logarithm of the value added is computed from (14.32) as

$$11.4059 \pm 2.028 \cdot 0.3454 \sqrt{1 + \frac{1}{38} + (\ln(500) - 5.5803)^2 / 33.8200} =$$

$$\begin{cases} 10.6922 \\ 12.1196 \end{cases}.$$

The actual value of the logarithm of the value added for a company with 500 employees can thus with probability 0.95 be expected to fall between the values of 10.6922 and 12.1196. A transformation back to the value added yields the prediction interval with the limits $\exp\{10.6922\} = 44010$ and $\exp\{12.1196\} = 183438$. Hence, the value added for a company with 500 employees can be expected to fall between 44010 and 183438 DKK. △.

14.11. Comparison of two regression lines

Consider two data sets consisting of joint observations of a response variable y and an explanatory variable x. If y in each of these data sets can be described as a linear function of x, it may be of interest to test whether the two regression lines have identical slopes. Let the first data set consist of n_1 observations (y_{1i}, x_{1i}), $i = 1, \ldots, n_1$, and the second data set of n_2 observations (y_{2i}, x_{2i}), $i = 1, \ldots, n_2$. If Y_{ji} is the random variable corresponding to y_{ji}, it is assumed that the data can be described by the two regression models

$$Y_{1i} = \beta_{01} + \beta_{11} x_{1i} + e_{1i}, \quad i = 1, \ldots, n_1,$$

and

$$Y_{2i} = \beta_{02} + \beta_{12} x_{2i} + e_{2i}, \quad i = 1, \ldots, n_2,$$

where $\operatorname{var}[e_{i1}] = \sigma_1^2$ and $\operatorname{var}[e_{i2}] = \sigma_2^2$. The hypothesis of identical slopes can be tested by a t-test, provided the error terms are independent and normally distributed and that $\sigma_1^2 = \sigma_2^2$.

If the error terms are normally distributed,

$$\frac{(n_1 - 2) S_1^2}{\sigma_1^2} \sim \chi^2(n_1 - 2) \quad \text{and} \quad \frac{(n_2 - 2) S_2^2}{\sigma_2^2} \sim \chi^2(n_2 - 2),$$

where S_1^2 and S_2^2 are the respective estimators of the variances of the error terms in the models for the two data sets. The hypothesis $\sigma_1^2 = \sigma_2^2$

can be tested by the F-test developed in section 13.4. If the hypothesis is not rejected, the estimator of the common variance σ^2 becomes

$$S^2 = \frac{(n_1-2)S_1^2 + (n_2-2)S_2^2}{n_1+n_2-4} .$$

The hypothesis of equal slopes for the regression lines can then be tested by

$$T = \frac{\hat{\beta}_{11}-\hat{\beta}_{12}}{S\sqrt{1/SSD_1 + 1/SSD_2}} ,$$

where $SSD_j = \Sigma(x_{ji}-\bar{x}_j)^2$, $j=1,2$. Under the hypothesis

$$H_0: \beta_{11} = \beta_{12},$$

T follows a t-distribution with n_1+n_2-4 degrees of freedom and the test is carried out as described in section 13.4.

If the hypothesis is not rejected, the common slope is estimated by

$$\hat{\beta}_1 = \frac{SSD_1\hat{\beta}_{11} + SSD_2\hat{\beta}_{12}}{SSD_1 + SSD_2} .$$

If it can be assumed that the regression lines are parallel, the vertical distance between the lines is the expected difference between y-values from the two data sets, corresponding to the same value of x. The situation with two parallel regression lines is illustrated in fig. 14.16.

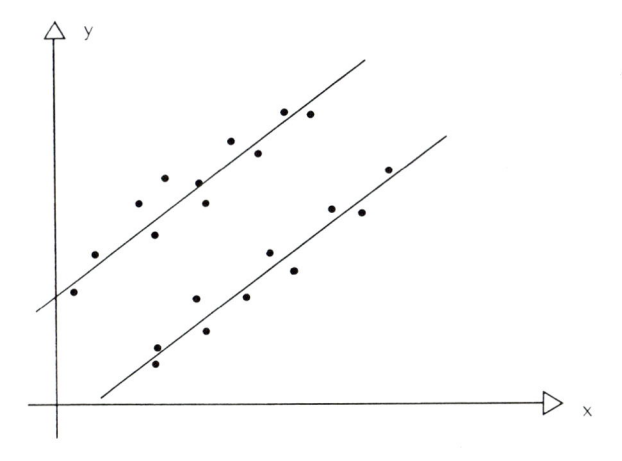

Fig. 14.16. Two parallel regression lines.

The distance between the regression lines is estimated as

$$\hat{\beta}_{01}-\hat{\beta}_{02} = \bar{y}_1-\bar{y}_2-\hat{\beta}_1(\bar{x}_1-\bar{x}_2).$$

Example 14.4

In example 14.1 it was shown that the index of the blood flow, ISI, to the brain could be described by a linear function of age for a control group of 11 painters. Fig. 14.17 shows the corresponding relationship for 9 painters whom in contrast to the members of the control group, have been exposed to organic solvents. From the figure, it follows that for these 9 painters too, ISI can be represented by a linear function of age.

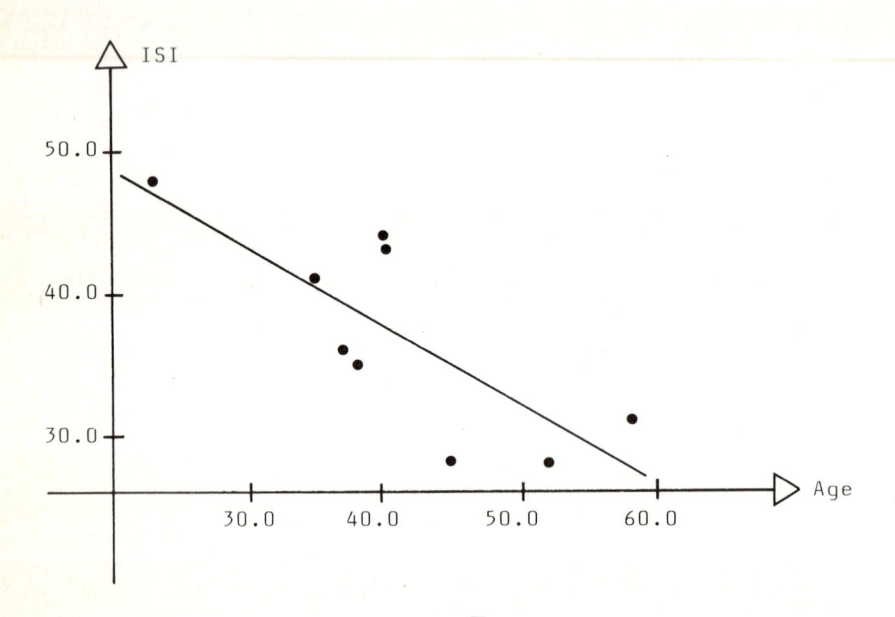

Fig. 14.17. The relationship between ISI and age for 9 exposed painters.

If the two lines describing ISI as a function of age can be assumed to be parallel, the vertical distance between these lines can be interpreted as the effect of organic solvents on the blood flow to the brain.

Estimates of the parameters of the regression models for the two groups of painters are shown in table 14.9.

Table 14.9. Estimates of the parameters of the regression models for two groups of painters.

Group	j	n_j	$\hat{\beta}_{0j}$	$\hat{\beta}_{1j}$	s_j^2	SSD_j
Control	1	11	76.77	-0.7941	19.45	638.00
Exposed	2	9	60.34	-0.5682	23.21	811.89

The value of the test statistic for the hypothesis $\sigma_1^2 = \sigma_2^2$ is

$$v^* = \frac{23.21}{19.45} = 1.19,$$

corresponding to the level of significance

$$p = 2P(V > v^*) = 0.42,$$

where $V \sim F(7,9)$. Hence the hypothesis is not rejected and the common variance is estimated by

$$s^2 = \frac{7 \cdot 23.21 + 9 \cdot 19.45}{16} = 21.10.$$

The value of the test statistic for equal slopes is

$$t = \frac{-0.7941 + 0.5682}{\sqrt{21.10(1/811.89 + 1/638.00)}} = -0.93$$

with the level of significance

$$p = 2P(T > 0.93) = 0.37$$

against the alternative $\beta_{11} \neq \beta_{12}$, since $T \sim t(16)$.

The conclusion is accordingly that the expected difference in ISI between exposed and non-exposed painters for a given age is constant. The common slope of the regression lines is estimated by

$$\hat{\beta}_1 = \frac{SSD_1 \hat{\beta}_{11} + SSD_2 \hat{\beta}_{12}}{SSD_1 + SSD_2} = -0.6676.$$

With parallel regression lines, a hypothesis of no effect on the blood flow to the brain from working with organic solvents becomes

$$H_0: \beta_{01} = \beta_{02}$$

The estimates of β_{01} and β_{02} are

$$\hat{\beta}_{01} = \bar{y}_1 + 0.6676\bar{x}_1 = 71.53$$

and

$$\hat{\beta}_{02} = \bar{y}_2 + 0.6676\bar{x}_2 = 64.41$$

such that the vertical distance between the lines is estimated by

$$\hat{\beta}_{01} - \hat{\beta}_{02} = 7.12.$$

Adjusting for age, the difference in ISI between exposed painters and painters in the control group is accordingly estimated to 7.12.

The variance of $\hat{\beta}_{01} - \hat{\beta}_{02}$ is given by

$$\mathrm{var}[\hat{\beta}_{01} - \hat{\beta}_{02}] = \mathrm{var}[\bar{Y}_1 - \bar{Y}_2 - \hat{\beta}_1(\bar{x}_1 - \bar{x}_2)] =$$
$$\mathrm{var}[\bar{Y}_1] + \mathrm{var}[\bar{Y}_2] + (\bar{x}_1 - \bar{x}_2)^2 \mathrm{var}[\hat{\beta}_1],$$

as $\bar{Y}_1, \bar{Y}_2$ and $\hat{\beta}_1$ are independent.

Since

$$\mathrm{var}[\hat{\beta}_1] = \sigma^2/(SSD_1 + SSD_2)$$

and

$$\mathrm{var}[\bar{Y}_1] = \sigma^2/n_1, \quad \mathrm{var}[\bar{Y}_2] = \sigma^2/n_2,$$

it then follows that

$$\mathrm{var}[\hat{\beta}_{01} - \hat{\beta}_{02}] = \sigma^2 \left[\frac{1}{n_1} + \frac{1}{n_2} + \frac{(\bar{x}_1 - \bar{x}_2)^2}{SSD_1 + SSD_2} \right].$$

For the given data the estimated variance of $\hat{\beta}_{01} - \hat{\beta}_{02}$ is accordingly

$$\widehat{\mathrm{var}}[\hat{\beta}_{01} - \hat{\beta}_{02}] = 21.10(1/11 + 1/9 + (41.27 - 40.89)^2/1449.89) = 4.26.$$

The hypothesis H_0 can thus be tested by

$$t = \frac{\hat{\beta}_{01} - \hat{\beta}_{02}}{\sqrt{\widehat{\mathrm{var}}[\hat{\beta}_{01} - \hat{\beta}_{02}]}} = \frac{7.12}{2.07} = 3.44,$$

which under H_0 is an observation from a t-distribution with 16 degrees of freedom.

The level of significance is

$$P = P(|T| > 3.44) < 0.01,$$

and it is concluded that the ISI-index in fact differs significantly for an exposed and a non-exposed painter of the same age.

The analysis of the given data does not reveal whether this conclusion is valid in general. No information is available regarding exposure times or the physical condition of the painters. It should also be noted that only a limited number of cases are here available for analysis.△.

15. Multiple Linear Regression

15.1. The multiple linear regression model

The multiple linear regression model describes the relationship between a response variable y and a number of explanatory variables $x_1,\ldots,x_p, p \geq 2$. A multiple regression analysis is an analysis of a data set composed of n cases $(y_i, x_{i1}, \ldots x_{ip})$, $i=1,\ldots,n$, where each case consists of joint observations of the response variable and the explanatory variables as displayed in table 15.1.

Table 15.1. Data for a multiple linear regression analysis.

Case No.	y	x_1	...	x_j	...	x_p
1	y_1	x_{11}	...	x_{1j}	...	x_{1p}
⋮	⋮	⋮		⋮		⋮
i	y_i	x_{i1}	...	x_{ij}	...	x_{ip}
⋮	⋮	⋮		⋮		⋮
n	y_n	x_{n1}	...	x_{nj}	...	x_{np}

Each of the rows of table 15.1 corresponds to a case, i.e. simulmultaneously observed values of the response and the explanatory variables, and each column contains the observed values of one of these variables.

The multiple regression model is a straightforward extension of the simple linear regression model. It is assumed that y_i is an observed value of a random variable Y_i for which

(15.1) $\quad Y_i = \beta_0 + \beta_1 x_{i1} + \ldots + \beta_p x_{ip} + e_i, \quad i=1,\ldots,n,$

i.e. Y_i is the sum of the linear regression function $\beta_0 + \beta_1 x_{i1} + \ldots + \beta_p x_{ip}$ and the error term e_i, representing random variation around the regression function. The error terms satisfy the following conditions:

(15.2) $E[e_i] = 0, \quad i=1,\ldots,n,$

(15.3) $\text{var}[e_i] = \sigma^2, \quad i=1,\ldots,n,$

and

(15.4) $\text{cov}(e_i, e_j) = 0, \quad i \neq j.$

These conditions state in a formalized way that the observed values of the response are distributed randomly around the linear regression function.

Since

(15.5) $E[Y_i] = \beta_0 + \beta_1 x_{i1} + \ldots + \beta_p x_{ip},$

the regression function is the mean of the response for given values of the explanatory variables. The error term e_i represents the random part of Y_i and may be composed of measurement errors in the response, effects of variables influencing the response but not explicitly accounted for by the regression function or a component arising from possible non-linearity in $E[Y_i]$.

The error term in (15.1) is of course a random variable, but for convenience the same notation is used for the error term in (15.1) and in the relationship

(15.6) $y_i = \beta_0 + \beta_1 x_{i1} + \ldots + \beta_p x_{ip} + e_i$

for the observed value of the response variable.

The use of matrices facilitates the presentation of multiple regression models so let the vector **Y** and the matrix **X** be given by

$$\mathbf{Y} = \begin{bmatrix} Y_1 \\ \vdots \\ Y_i \\ \vdots \\ Y_n \end{bmatrix} \quad \text{and} \quad \mathbf{X} = \begin{bmatrix} 1 & x_{11} & \cdots & x_{1j} & \cdots & x_{1p} \\ \cdots \\ 1 & x_{i1} & \cdots & x_{ij} & \cdots & x_{ip} \\ \cdots \\ 1 & x_{n1} & \cdots & x_{nj} & \cdots & x_{np} \end{bmatrix},$$

and the vectors **β** and **e** by

$$\boldsymbol{\beta} = \begin{bmatrix} \beta_0 \\ \vdots \\ \beta_j \\ \vdots \\ \beta_p \end{bmatrix} \quad \text{and} \quad \mathbf{e} = \begin{bmatrix} e_1 \\ \vdots \\ e_i \\ \vdots \\ e_n \end{bmatrix}.$$

The regression model (15.1) can then be written as

(15.7) $Y = X\beta + e.$

The first column in **X** allows the intercept β_0 to be treated in the same way as $\beta_1,\ldots,\beta_p$. Arranging the observed values of **Y** in the column vector **y**, (15.6) takes the form

(15.8) $y = X\beta + e,$

where **e** is a column vector with elements e_i defined by (15.6). With the notation introduced in section 8.11, the assumption (15.2) can be written as

(15.9) $E[e] = \begin{bmatrix} 0 \\ 0 \\ \vdots \\ 0 \end{bmatrix} = \mathbf{0},$

and if var[**e**] denotes the variance matrix for **e**, the assumptions (15.3) and (15.4) can be written in closed form as

(15.10) $\text{var}[e] = \begin{bmatrix} \sigma^2 & 0 & \cdots & 0 \\ 0 & \sigma^2 & \cdots & 0 \\ \vdots & \vdots & & \vdots \\ 0 & 0 & \cdots & \sigma^2 \end{bmatrix} = \sigma^2 I_n,$

where I_n is the identity matrix of order n.

Since $E[e]=0$,

(15.11) $E[Y] = X\beta$

and from (15.10) it follows that

(15.12) $\text{var}[Y] = \text{var}[e] = \sigma^2 I_n.$

Often, it is further assumed that the errors are normally distributed. If $N_n(\mu,C)$ denotes the n-dimensional normal distribution with mean value vector μ and variance matrix **C**, the assumption of normally distributed error terms, combined with (15.9) and (15.10), can be written

(15.13) $e \sim N_n(0, \sigma^2 I_n).$

15.2. Estimation of the parameters

The regression parameters $\beta_0, \beta_1, \ldots, \beta_p$ are estimated by the **least squares method**. The **least squares** estimates, or **LS-estimates**, are defined as those values of $\beta_0, \beta_1, \ldots, \beta_p$ for which the sum of squared deviations

$$(15.14) \qquad \sum_{i=1}^n e_i^2 = \sum_{i=1}^n (y_i - \beta_0 - \beta_1 x_{i1} - \ldots - \beta_p x_{ip})^2$$

is minimized. Since $\Sigma e_i^2 = \mathbf{e'e}$, it follows from (15.8) that

$$\sum_{i=1}^n e_i^2 = (\mathbf{y} - \mathbf{X\beta})'(\mathbf{y} - \mathbf{X\beta}).$$

The LS-estimate $\hat{\beta}$ accordingly satisfies

$$(15.15) \qquad (\mathbf{y} - \mathbf{X}\hat{\beta})'(\mathbf{y} - \mathbf{X}\hat{\beta}) = \min_{\beta} (\mathbf{y} - \mathbf{X\beta})'(\mathbf{y} - \mathbf{X\beta}).$$

For p=2, the relation $y = \beta_0 + \beta_1 x_1 + \beta_2 x_2$ for given values of β_0, β_1 and β_2 defines a plane in the three-dimensional Euclidian space. Hence, $e_i = y_i - \beta_0 - \beta_1 x_{i1} - \beta_2 x_{i2}$ is the vertical distance between the i'th case and the plane so the LS-method determines the plane for which the sum of the squared vertical distances from the observed values of the response to the plane is minimized. This is illustrated in fig. 15.1.

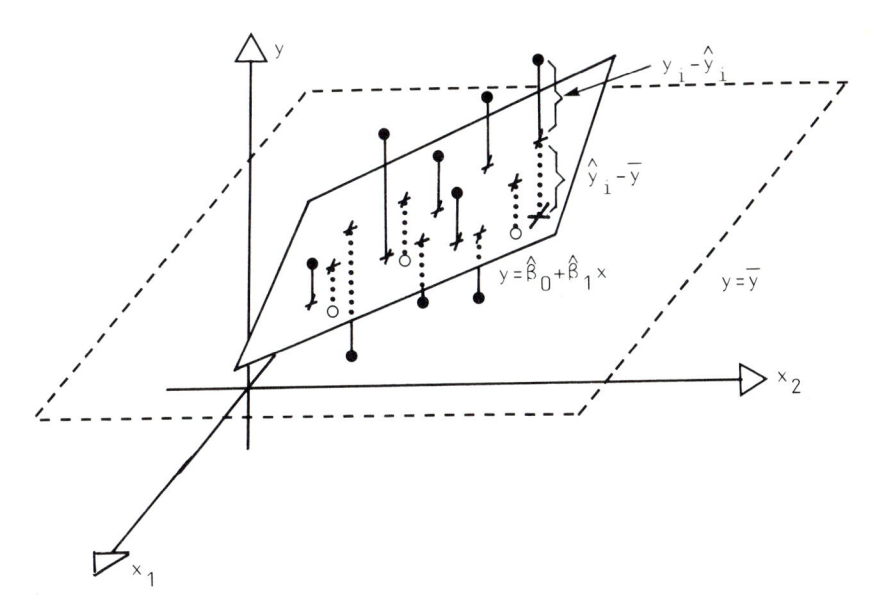

Fig. 15.1. Illustration of the LS-method for p=2.

An explicit expression for the LS-estimates can be derived when the rank of the matrix **X** is $p+1$, i.e. if there are no linear relationships between the columns of **X** and if $n \geq p+1$.

Theorem 15.1

The LS-estimate of β is a solution to the equations

(15.16) $X'y = X'X\beta$.

If X has rank $p+1$, the solution $\hat{\beta}$ to (15.16) is unique and given by

(15.17) $\hat{\beta} = (X'X)^{-1}X'y$.

Proof

Differentiating (15.14) with respect to β_0 and β_j, $j=1,\ldots,p$, yields

$$\partial(\sum_{i=1}^{n} e_i^2)/\partial\beta_0 = -2\sum_{i=1}^{n}(y_i - \beta_0 - \beta_1 x_{i1} - \ldots - \beta_p x_{ip})$$

and

$$\partial(\sum_{i=1}^{n} e_i^2)/\partial\beta_j = -2\sum_{i=1}^{n}(y_i - \beta_0 - \beta_1 x_{i1} - \ldots - \beta_p x_{ip})x_{ij}, \quad j=1,\ldots,p.$$

A necessary condition for (15.14) to attain its minimum at $\hat{\beta}' = (\hat{\beta}_0, \hat{\beta}_1, \ldots, \hat{\beta}_p)$ is that

$$\Sigma y_i = \hat{\beta}_0 n + \hat{\beta}_1 \Sigma x_{i1} + \ldots + \hat{\beta}_p \Sigma x_{ip}$$

and

$$\Sigma y_i x_{ij} = \hat{\beta}_0 \Sigma x_{ij} + \hat{\beta}_1 \Sigma x_{i1} x_{ij} + \ldots + \hat{\beta}_p \Sigma x_{ip} x_{ij}, \quad j=1,\ldots,p,$$

which in matrix notation becomes

$$X'y = X'X\hat{\beta}.$$

Hence, (15.16) is a necessary condition for Σe_i^2 to attain its minimum. If **X** has rank $p+1$, $(X'X)^{-1}$ exists and (15.17) is the unique solution to (15.16). □

If $\hat{\beta}_0, \hat{\beta}_1, \ldots, \hat{\beta}_p$ are the LS-estimates of $\beta_0, \beta_1, \ldots, \beta_p$, then

(15.18) $\hat{e}_i = y_i - \hat{\beta}_0 - \hat{\beta}_1 x_{i1} - \ldots - \hat{\beta}_p x_{ip}, \quad i=1,\ldots,n,$

are called the **residuals**.

It can be shown that

(15.19) $s^2 = RSS/(n-p-1)$

is an unbiased estimator of σ^2, where RSS (Residual Sum of Squares) is given by

$$RSS = \Sigma(Y_i - \hat{\beta}_0 - \hat{\beta}_1 x_{i1} - \ldots - \hat{\beta}_p x_{ip})^2 = (Y - X\hat{\beta})'(Y - X\hat{\beta}) = \hat{e}'\hat{e}.$$

The terms $\hat{e}$ and RSS are used both for the random variables and for the corresponding observed values so

(15.20) $RSS = \Sigma(y_i - \hat{\beta}_0 - \hat{\beta}_1 x_{i1} - \ldots - \hat{\beta}_p x_{ip})^2 = (y - X\hat{\beta})'(y - X\hat{\beta}) = \hat{e}'\hat{e}$.

15.3. Properties of the LS-estimator

The use of matrices also facilitates the derivation of the mean and the variance of the LS-estimator $\hat{\beta}$. From (15.11), (15.17) and the remark after theorem 8.16, it follows that

(15.21) $E[\hat{\beta}] = (X'X)^{-1} X' E[Y] = (X'X)^{-1} X' X \beta = \beta.$

Hence, $\hat{\beta}_j$ is an unbiased estimator of β_j for $j = 0, 1, \ldots, p$.

From (15.12), (15.17) and theorem 8.16, it also follows that

(15.22) $\text{var}[\hat{\beta}] = (X'X)^{-1} X'(\sigma^2 I_n) X (X'X)^{-1} = \sigma^2 (X'X)^{-1}$.

Since $\text{var}[\hat{\beta}_j]$ is the $j+1$'st diagonal element of (15.22), the variance of $\hat{\beta}_j$ is proportional to σ^2, and $\text{cov}(\hat{\beta}_j, \hat{\beta}_l)$ is proportional to σ^2 with the factor of proportionality depending on the values of the explanatory variables. As a rule, $X'X$ is not a diagonal matrix so for $l \neq j$ $\hat{\beta}_j$ and $\hat{\beta}_l$ are in general correlated.

In addition, if it is assumed that the error terms are normally distributed, then $\hat{\beta}$ follows a $(p+1)$-dimensional normal distribution with mean given by (15.21) and variance matrix (15.22). This follows from the fact that $\hat{\beta}$, according to (15.17), is a linear function of $Y_1, \ldots, Y_n$, and according to theorem 8.16 linear combinations of normally distributed random variables are again normally distributed. From (15.1) it follows that Y_i is normally distributed if e_i is normally distributed. What is more, if the error terms are normally distributed it can also be shown that

(15.23) $RSS/\sigma^2 = (n-p-1)S^2/\sigma^2 \sim \chi^2(n-p-1)$.

The results (15.21) to (15.23) can be summarized by the following theorem.

Theorem 15.2

Let $\hat{\beta}$ be the LS-estimator of β in the multiple linear regression model. Then
$$E[\hat{\beta}] = \beta$$
and
$$\text{var}[\hat{\beta}] = \sigma^2(X'X)^{-1}.$$

If in addition $e_1, \ldots, e_n$ are normally distributed,
$$\hat{\beta} \sim N_{p+1}(\beta, \sigma^2(X'X)^{-1}), \quad (n-p-1)S^2/\sigma^2 \sim \chi^2(n-p-1)$$
and $\hat{\beta}$ and S^2 are independent.

The **predicted** or **fitted** value $\hat{y}_i$ of the response for case i is given by
$$\hat{y}_i = \hat{\beta}_0 + \hat{\beta}_1 x_{i1} + \ldots + \hat{\beta}_p x_{ip}.$$

If $\hat{y}$ denotes the column vector with elements $\hat{y}_i$, $i=1, \ldots, n$, then

(15.24) $\hat{y} = X\hat{\beta} = X(X'X)^{-1}X'y = Hy$

where $H = X(X'X)^{-1}X'$ is called the **hat matrix** because it transforms y into $\hat{y}$.

For $\hat{Y} = HY$,

(15.25) $E[\hat{Y}] = X\beta$

and

(15.26) $\text{var}[\hat{Y}] = \sigma^2 X(X'X)^{-1}X' = \sigma^2 H.$

Theorem 15.3

If $e_1, \ldots, e_n$ are normally distributed, then
$$\hat{Y} \sim N_n(X\beta, \sigma^2 H).$$

Proof

Since $\hat{Y}$ is a linear function of Y, which is normally distributed, the theorem follows from theorem 8.16, (15.25) and (15.26). $\square$.

The residual sum of squares can be expressed through the predicted values of the response as

$$RSS = \Sigma(y_i - \hat{y}_i)^2 = (y-\hat{y})'(y-\hat{y}).$$

Substituting s^2 for σ^2 in the expressions for $\text{var}[\hat{\beta}]$ in theorem 15.2 and $\text{var}[\hat{Y}]$ in (15.24) yields the unbiased estimators

(15.27) $\quad \hat{\text{var}}[\hat{\beta}] = s^2(X'X)^{-1}$

and

$$\hat{\text{var}}[\hat{Y}] = s^2 H$$

for $\text{var}[\hat{\beta}]$ and $\text{var}[\hat{Y}]$, respectively.

15.4. Residual analysis

The regression model can be checked by studying the variation of the residuals. According to (15.24), the residuals (15.18) can be written as

(15.28) $\quad \hat{e} = y - X\hat{\beta} = y - X(X'X)^{-1}X'y = (I-H)y,$

where H is the hat matrix.

Inserting $X\beta + e$ for y in (15.28) yields

(15.29) $\quad \hat{e} = (I-H)(X\beta+e) = (I-H)e$

so that the residuals are linear functions of the error terms. From (15.29), it follows by application of (8.21) that

$$E[\hat{e}] = 0$$

and by application of (8.22) that

(15.30) $\quad \text{var}[\hat{e}] = \sigma^2(I-H)$

since $H=HH'$. Consequently, the residuals and the error terms are not identically distributed. While all the residuals have mean 0, the variance of $\hat{e}_i$ is

(15.31) $\qquad \text{var}[\hat{e}_i] = \sigma^2(1-h_{ii})$,

where h_{ii} is the i'th diagonal element of **H**. With non-experimental data, the h_{ii}'s are almost inevitably different, so that even if the error terms have identical variances, this property is not shared by the residuals. In addition, the matrix **I-H** has rank n-p-1, so the fact that the error terms are uncorrelated does not imply that the residuals are uncorrelated. Of the three conditions (15.2)-(15.4) only (15.2) is satisfied by the residuals. The **standardized residuals**

$$r_i = \hat{e}_i / \sqrt{s^2(1-h_{ii})}, \quad i=1,\ldots,n ,$$

however, all have variance 1 and the model is therefore checked by plotting the values of the explanatory variables against the standardized residuals, since these plots are not affected by the residuals having unequal variances. From such **residual plots** the assumption of linearity can be checked, while a plot of the fitted values of the response against the standardized residuals can be used for checking the assumption of the error terms having equal variances. The residual plots are all evaluated in the same way as the corresponding plots for simple linear regression, described in section 14.7.

The assumption of normally distributed error terms can be checked by a probability plot, based on the standardized residuals. However, from (15.28), it follows that

$$\hat{e}_i = (1-h_{ii})e_i - \sum_{j \neq i} h_{ij} e_j$$

so the residual $\hat{e}_i$ comprises e_i and a weighted sum of the error terms e_j, j≠i. If this weighted sum is large compared to e_i, the distribution of the residuals may, according to the central limit theorem, be approximately normally distributed, even if the e_i's are not normally distributed, and it is advisable to exercise some care when evaluating the fit of a normal distribution from probability plot as described above.

15.5. Hypothesis testing

One of the primary purposes of many regression analyses is to describe the observed value of the response by a linear function of a set of explanatory variables. The total variation of the response, defined as

$$SSD_y = \sum_{i=1}^{n} (y_i - \bar{y})^2,$$

where $\bar{y} = \sum y_i / n$, can be decomposed as

(15.32) $$SSD_y = \sum (y_i - \hat{y}_i)^2 + \sum (\hat{y}_i - \bar{y})^2 = RSS + REGSS.$$

The residual sum of squares, RSS, is a measure of that part of SSD_y which cannot be fitted by the estimated regression function, while the regression sum of squares, REGSS, measures the fitted part of SSD_y. To investigate whether the estimated regression function describes a significant part of the variability of the response, it is natural thus to compare RSS with REGSS. Formally, such an investigation amounts to testing the hypothesis

$$H_0: \beta_1 = \beta_2 = \ldots = \beta_p = 0$$

against the alternative H_1 that at least one regression parameter deviates from 0.

Under H_0 and (15.13) the random variables $Y_1, \ldots, Y_n$ are independent and identically normally distributed, so that, according to theorem 9.5,

(15.33) $$\frac{\sum (Y_i - \bar{Y})^2}{\sigma^2} = \frac{SSD_y}{\sigma^2} \sim \chi^2(n-1).$$

With the y_i's replaced by the Y_i's in (15.32) it also follows from theorem 9.4 that RSS and REGSS are independent, with

(15.34) $$\frac{RSS}{\sigma^2} \sim \chi^2(n-p-1)$$

and

(15.35) $$\frac{REGSS}{\sigma^2} = \frac{SSD_y - RSS}{\sigma^2} \sim \chi^2(p).$$

Hence, from definition 9.3

(15.36) $$V = \frac{REGSS/p}{RSS/(n-p-1)} \sim F(p, n-p-1).$$

Large values of V support H_1 and the significance level for a test of

H_0 against H_1 is therefore $P(V \geq v)$, $V \sim F(p, n-p-1)$, where v is the observed value of V.

A summary measure of the proportion of variability of the response described by the estimated regression function is provided by the **coefficient of determination**

$$R^2 = \frac{REGSS}{SSD_y} = 1 - \frac{RSS}{SSD_y}.$$

The larger the value of R^2, the larger the proportion of SSD_y fitted by the estimated regression function. The coefficient of determination can alternatively be computed as the squared correlation coefficient between the observed and fitted values of the response. From the definition, it follows that

$$0 \leq R^2 \leq 1.$$

A value of R^2 close to 1 therefore indicates that the fit is almost perfect, while a value close to 0 is indicative of a poor fit. It must be stressed, however, that a value of R^2 close to 1 does not automatically rule out a check of the distributional assumptions of the regression model as illustrated in example 14.2.

The coefficient of determination is often used to compare the fit of models with different sets of explanatory variables. However, such comparisons are meaningful only when the models considered are applied to the same response and when the intercept, β_0, is included.

Since

$$RSS = (1-R^2)SSD_y,$$

the test statistic (15.36) can be written as

(15.37) $$V = \frac{R^2/p}{(1-R^2)/(n-p-1)}.$$

The importance of an explanatory variable, say x_j, for the description of the response is evaluated by a comparison of the residual sum of of squares RSS from a model with $x_1, \ldots, x_p$ as explanatory variables and the residual sum of squares RSS(j) from a model with $x_1, \ldots, x_{j-1}, x_{j+1}, \ldots, x_p$ as explanatory variables, i.e. by a comparison of the fit of the models with and without x_j. Formally, this means that the hypothesis

$$H_{0j}: \beta_j = 0$$

is tested against the alternative

$$H_{1j}: \beta_j \neq 0.$$

As a test statistic

(15.38) $$V = \frac{RSS(j)-RSS}{RSS/(n-p-1)}$$

is used. Large values of V indicate that the fit can be significantly improved if x_j is included and such values therefore support H_1. It should be pointed out that

$$RSS(j) - RSS \geq 0$$

because $RSS(j)$ is the minimum of $(y-X\beta)'(y-X\beta)$ under the restriction $\beta_j=0$ and RSS is its unrestricted minimum. It can be shown that under H_{0j}, $RSS(j)-RSS$ and RSS are independent and χ^2-distributed with 1 and $n-p-1$ degrees of freedom respectively. Hence, the level of significance for a test of H_{0j} against H_{1j} is computed in the F-distribution with $(1,n-p-1)$ degrees of freedom as

(15.39) $$P(V \geq v)$$

where v is the observed value of V. If the value of (15.39) is sufficiently small, it is concluded that the presence of x_j is significant for the fit. If, on the other hand, (15.39) is large, it can be concluded that x_j can be excluded from the model without significantly worsening the fit. It should be remembered that the conclusions based on such a test are conditional on the other explanatory variables in the model. If the set of explanatory variables is changed, the conclusion concerning the inclusion of x_j in the model may very well be affected.

An alternative expression for the test statistic for the hypothesis H_{0j} is obtained from a comparison of the LS-estimator $\hat{\beta}_j$ with its estimated standard error

(15.40) $$T_j = \hat{\beta}_j / \sqrt{\hat{var}[\hat{\beta}_j]} \quad ,$$

where $\hat{var}[\hat{\beta}_j]$ is given by (15.27). Since $\hat{\beta}_j$ and the residual variance s^2 are independent, $T_j \sim t(n-p-1)$ under H_{0j}. Large values of $|T_j|$ support the alternative H_{1j} and the significance level is

$$2P(T_j \geq |t_j|)$$

where t_j is the observed value of (15.40). The test statistics (15.38) and (15.40) can be shown to be equivalent since $T_j^2 = V$. From (15.40), it follows that a confidence interval for β_j with level $1-\alpha$ is

(15.41) $\quad \hat{\beta}_j \pm t_{1-\alpha/2}(n-p-1)\sqrt{\hat{var}[\hat{\beta}_j]}.$

A test of the hypothesis $\beta_j = \beta_{0j}$ can be based on the test statistic

(15.42) $\quad T = (\hat{\beta}_j - \beta_{0j})/\sqrt{\hat{var}[\hat{\beta}_j]}$

where $T \sim t(n-p-1)$ under the hypothesis.

A hypothesis that a number of regression parameters are equal to 0 can be tested by a test statistic similar to (15.38). For example, consider the hypothesis

$$H_0: \beta_{p-q+1} = \ldots = \beta_p = 0$$

against the alternative that at least one of the parameters $\beta_{p-q+1}, \ldots, \beta_p$ is different from 0, and let $RSS(H_0)$ be the residual sum of squares for the regression model under H_0, i.e. for the model

$$y_i = \beta_0 + \beta_1 x_{i1} + \ldots + \beta_{p-q} x_{ip-q} + e_i.$$

The larger the difference $RSS(H_0) - RSS$, the greater the reduction of the model fit when the last q of the explanatory variables are excluded from the model. Hence,

(15.43) $\quad V = \dfrac{(RSS(H_0) - RSS)/q}{RSS/(n-p-1)}$

can be used as a test statistic for H_0 with small values supporting H_0. Under H_0, it can be shown that $RSS(H_0) - RSS$ and RSS are independent and χ^2-distributed with q and $n-p-1$ degrees of freedom respectively. The level of significance is accordingly $P(V \geq v)$, where $V \sim F(q, n-p-1)$ and v is the observed value of V.

Confidence intervals of the form (15.41) can be used separately for each parameter. If a confidence statement is required for all parameters simultaneously, a so-called confidence region has to be constructed. Since

$$\hat{\boldsymbol{\beta}} \sim N_{p+1}(\boldsymbol{\beta}, \sigma^2 (X'X)^{-1}),$$

it follows that

$$(\hat{\beta}-\beta)'(X'X)(\hat{\beta}-\beta)/\sigma^2 \sim \chi^2(p+1).$$

Hence, according to theorem 15.2 and definition 9.3,

(15.44) $$\frac{(\hat{\beta}-\beta)'(X'X)(\hat{\beta}-\beta)}{S^2(p+1)} \sim F(p+1, n-p-1)$$

and

$$P\{(\hat{\beta}-\beta)'(X'X)(\hat{\beta}-\beta) \leq S^2(p+1)F_{1-\alpha}(p+1, n-p-1)\} = 1-\alpha.$$

Inserting the observed values of $\hat{\beta}$ and s^2 thus yields the confidence region with level $1-\alpha$

(15.45) $$(\hat{\beta}-\beta)'(X'X)(\hat{\beta}-\beta) \leq s^2(p+1)F_{1-\alpha}(p+1, n-p-1)$$

for β. The set of all parameter vectors β satisfying (15.45) forms an ellipsoid in the (p+1)-dimensional Euclidian space and is therefore also called a **1-α confidence ellipsoid**.

Example 15.1

Table 15.2 shows the amount of temporary social security payments per inhabitant aged 18 to 66 years for each of 20 Danish municipalities. The following three socio-demografic variables are also shown in the table:

- x_1: percentage of unmarried persons in the age group 17 to 64 years;
- x_2: percentage of the population aged 18 to 66 years in the age group 18 to 29 years;
- x_3: percentage of the population living in urban areas with more than 5000 inhabitants.

In order to investigate the dependence of temporary social security payments (y) on the variables x_1, x_2 and x_3, a multiple linear regression analysis is carried out with résponse variable y and explanatory variables x_1, x_2 and x_3.

Table 15.3 shows the fitted values of the response variable, the residuals and the standardized residuals, and in figures 15.2 to 15.5 the standardized residuals are plotted against the values of the explanatory variables and the fitted values of the response, respectively. Since no systematic trends are present in the residual plots, it seems reasonable to use a linear model to describe the relationship between the response and the explanatory variables.

Table 15.2. Temporary social security payments y (DKK) and three socio-demografic variables x_1, x_2 and x_3 for 20 Danish municipalities.

Case No.	y	x_1	x_2	x_3
1	508.2	35.9	25.2	85.6
2	877.7	37.8	26.3	67.6
3	1019.4	35.6	23.5	35.2
4	1448.0	43.1	26.0	78.0
5	878.5	39.7	26.5	75.9
6	1945.0	35.8	26.4	90.6
7	1085.0	33.7	25.8	68.4
8	479.2	31.3	21.9	46.6
9	747.9	28.8	25.1	89.1
10	980.0	37.6	26.4	72.4
11	1493.3	44.9	28.4	81.4
12	917.6	37.9	27.7	69.4
13	1872.1	40.8	29.0	70.0
14	1402.9	38.6	26.7	79.4
15	1019.0	37.9	27.0	72.7
16	815.4	42.3	23.8	76.0
17	1248.2	37.6	28.2	59.1
18	840.8	37.8	25.0	52.2
19	1796.6	44.3	29.5	85.0
20	1285.6	38.3	25.8	43.7

Table 15.3. Fitted values $\hat{y}$, residuals $\hat{e}$ and standardized residuals r for the data in table 15.2.

Case No.	$\hat{y}$	$\hat{e}$	r
1	953.6	-445.4	-1.4978
2	1141.5	-263.8	-0.8305
3	744.2	275.2	1.0326
4	1211.0	237.0	0.8209
5	1204.6	-326.1	-1.0351
6	1104.8	840.2	2.8484
7	990.3	94.7	0.3095
8	443.3	35.9	0.1371
9	790.1	-42.2	-0.1812
10	1148.6	-168.6	-0.5311
11	1557.6	-64.3	-0.2225
12	1323.8	-406.2	-1.3207
13	1552.5	319.6	1.0929
14	1206.2	196.7	0.6252
15	1232.3	-213.3	-0.6760
16	910.7	-95.3	-0.3990
17	1385.4	-137.3	-0.4833
18	978.6	-137.8	-0.4521
19	1685.9	110.7	0.3898
20	1095.2	190.4	0.6612

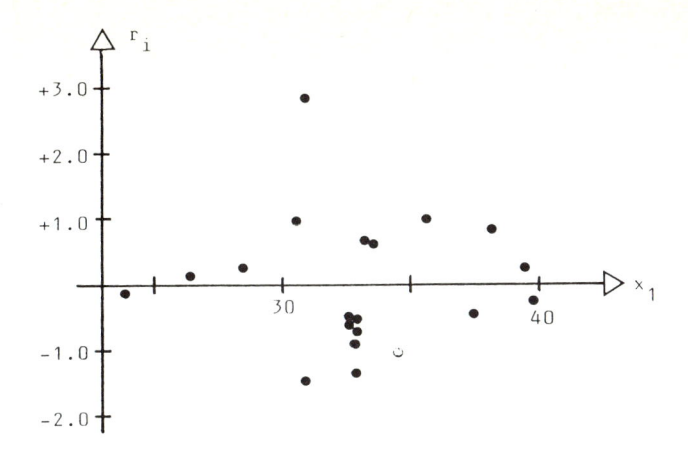

Fig. 15.2. Standardized residuals plotted against x_1.

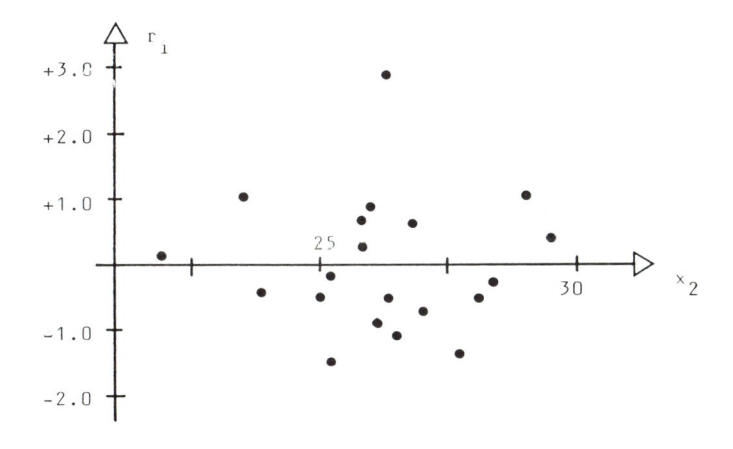

Fig. 15.3. Standardized residuals plotted against x_2.

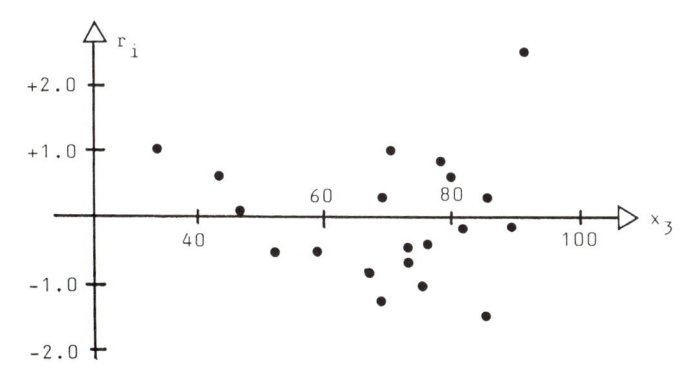

Fig. 15.4. Standardized residuals plotted against x_3.

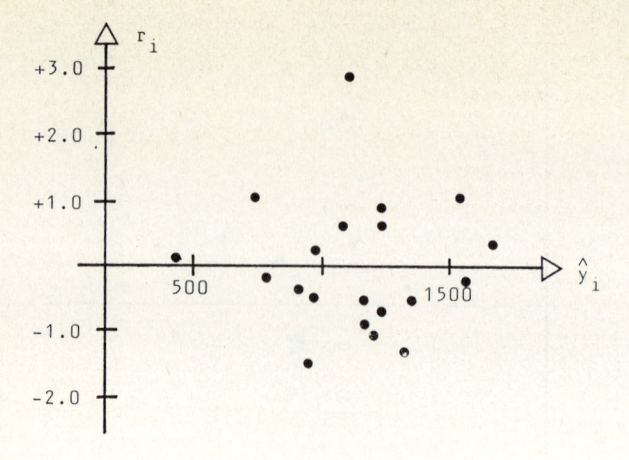

Fig. 15.5. Standardized residuals plotted against fitted values of the response variable.

Fig. 15.6 shows a probability plot for the standardized residuals. Apart from case 6, for which the standardized residual is somewhat larger than residuals of the remaining cases, the probability plot does not imply that the assumption of normally distributed error terms should be rejected.

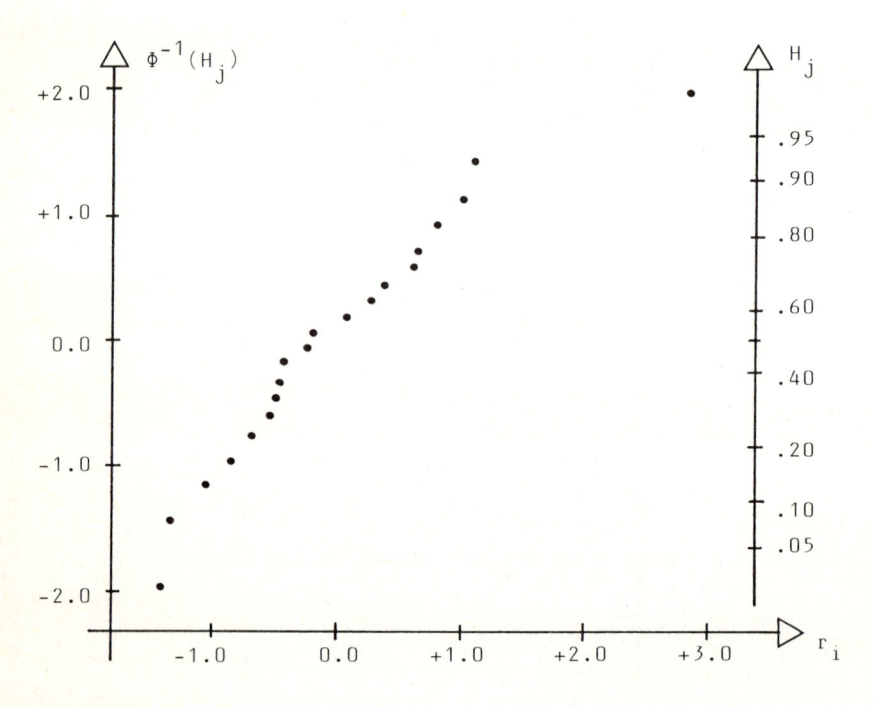

Fig. 15.6. Probability plot for the standardized residuals.

Table 15.4 provides a summary of the regression analysis. Since $R^2=0.49$, 49% of the variability in the response is described by the estimated regression model. The estimates of the regression parameters can be interpreted in the following way: increasing the value of x_1 by one percentage point corresponds on the average to an increase of 21 DKK in temporary social security payments. Similarly, an increase of one percentage point in the variables x_2 and x_3 corresponds to an increase of 129 DKK and a decrease of 0.3 DKK respectively in temporary social security payments. It must be stressed, however, that the estimated relationship is not necessarily causal.

Table 15.4. Summary of the regression analysis of the data in table 15.2.

Variable	Estimate	Stand. deviation	t-value	Significance level
Intercept	-3028.20			
x_1	21.06	22.68	0.93	0.3670
x_2	129.12	52.93	2.44	0.0267
x_3	-0.32	5.40	-0.06	0.9529
$R^2 = 0.49$	s = 326.20			

The estimated standard deviations in table 15.4 reveal that two of the regression parameters are estimated with a low degree of precision. It can be seen from the values of the t-statistics that only x_2 is of significance at the level 0.05 for the description of temporary social security payments. An isolated deletion of either x_1 or x_3 thus only slightly affects the fit of the model.

To test the effect of simultaneously deleting x_1 and x_3, the test statistic (15.43) can be applied. The residual sum of squares under the hypothesis $H_0: \beta_1 = \beta_3 = 0$ obtained from the model

$$y_i = \beta_0 + \beta_2 x_{i2} + e_i, \quad i=1,\ldots,20,$$

becomes $RSS(H_0) = 1\,796\,528.54$ while the residual sum of squares of the model with all three explanatory variables is $RSS = 1\,703\,545.86$. Inserting the values in (15.43) with n=20, p=3 and q=2 yields

$$v = \frac{(1\,796\,528.54 - 1\,703\,545.86)/2}{1\,703\,545.86/(20-3-1)} = 0.44.$$

With $V \sim F(2, 16)$ the corresponding level of significance is 0.65. This means that the simultaneous deletion of x_1 and x_3 has a negligible effect on the fit of the model.△.

15.6. Case analysis

In section 15.4, it was shown how the distributional assumptions behind the application of the LS-method could be checked by various residual plots. These plots must be satisfactory if the conclusions of the analysis are to be reliable. It is, however, preferable that the conclusions are based on the whole sample and not on a few influential cases alone. Since the LS-method is very sensitive to extreme or outlying cases it is therefore important to evaluate the influence of the individual cases on the analysis. To illustrate the problem, consider the situations sketched in fig. 15.7 for simple linear regression. In fig. 15.7(a) it is impossible to change the estimates of the parameters or their precisions substantially simply by deleting a single case. In fig. 15.7(b), the deletion of a single case, denoted by ⊙, changes the estimate of both β_0 and σ^2 and hence also the precision of the LS-estimates of β_0 and β_1, while the deletion of a single case in fig. 15.7(c) only reduces $\hat{\beta}_1$. Finally, the deletion of a single case in fig. 15.7(d) reduces the precision of $\hat{\beta}_1$.

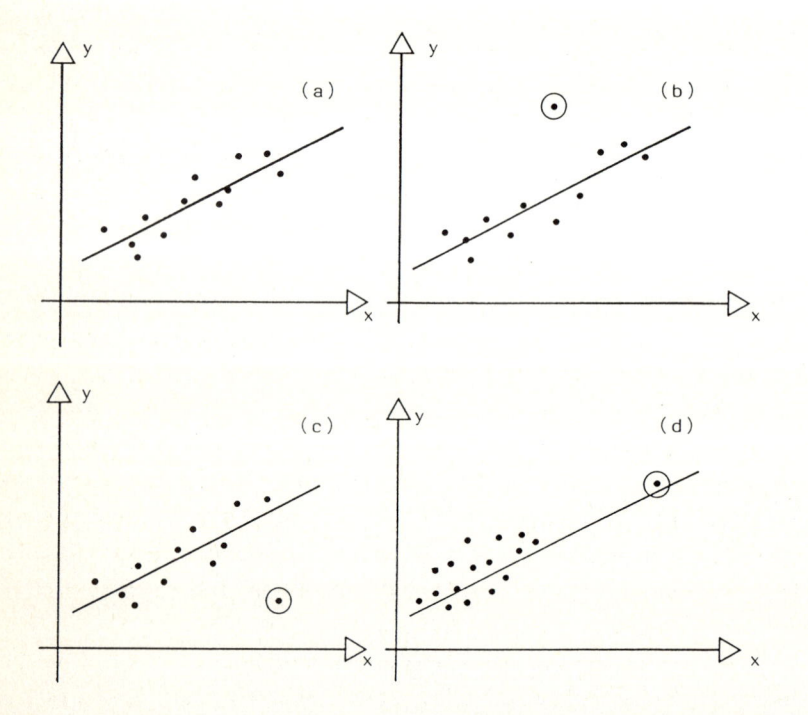

Fig. 15.7. Single influential cases in simple linear regression.

In multiple regression, however, no simple graphic methods exist for the determination of influential cases, so numerical methods have to be applied. Let $\hat{\boldsymbol{\beta}}_{(i)}$ denote the LS-estimate of $\boldsymbol{\beta}$ with case i omitted. The influence of the i'th case upon the LS-estimate can be measured by the difference

$$\hat{\boldsymbol{\beta}} - \hat{\boldsymbol{\beta}}_{(i)}$$

or a standardized version of its individual components $\hat{\beta}_j - \hat{\beta}_{j(i)}$, j=0,1,...,p. Most statistical computer programmes calculate these differences.

The set of p+1 differences can be summarized in **Cook's Distance** defined as

(15.46) $\qquad D_i = \dfrac{(\hat{\boldsymbol{\beta}} - \hat{\boldsymbol{\beta}}_{(i)})'(\mathbf{X}'\mathbf{X})(\hat{\boldsymbol{\beta}} - \hat{\boldsymbol{\beta}}_{(i)})}{s^2(p+1)}$

which can be seen to be a measure of the proximity of $\hat{\boldsymbol{\beta}}_{(i)}$ to $\hat{\boldsymbol{\beta}}$. Thus, the larger the value of D_i, the larger the influence of the i'th case on the LS-estimate of $\boldsymbol{\beta}$.

Since it can be shown that

(15.47) $\qquad D_i = \dfrac{r_i^2}{p+1} \dfrac{h_{ii}}{1-h_{ii}}$,

Cook's Distance is a function of the standardized residual r_i and the i'th diagonal element of the hat matrix, so for D_i to be large, either r_i or h_{ii} (or both) must be large. The standardized residual expresses the influence due to the response, given the values of the explanatory variables, while h_{ii} represents the potential influence of the values of the explanatory variables. The quantity h_{ii} is called the **leverage** of case i. Statistics like r_i, D_i, h_{ii} and $\hat{\beta}_j - \hat{\beta}_{j(i)}$ are called **regression diagnostics**.

Regression diagnostics are important not only because they contain information about the influence from the individual cases but also because they may serve as a means of detecting data errors. Should one or more of the regression diagnostics for a case be considered large, it is advisable to check first of all whether this is due to an error in the recorded values, and if this is so, the error must be corrected whenever possible, otherwise the case must be deleted from the analysis. It is next necessary to investigate whether a simple transformation can change the roles played by one or more cases. Even if a case is regarded as having influence within the framework of one model, it need not necessarily have any significant influence or be extreme within a different model. Extreme cases or cases with significant influence do therefore often have a value in as much as they suggest a change of the model, either by way of transformation of one or more of the variables or by introduction of new explanatory variables. A case regarded as having significant influence should, however, never be deleted from the analysis unless it can be demonstrated that it is in error or has been collected under circumstances which are clearly untypical for the problem considered. If it is clear that a case has extraordinary influence on the conclusions of the analysis, it is advisable to compare the analysis of the complete data set with an analysis which excludes the case in question.

A case is suspected of having significant influence if one or more of its diagnostics are large. If the numerical value of its standardized residual is larger than two it is usually selected for closer examination. For other diagnostics, it is difficult to set limits for when a closer examination is needed, although it has been suggested to investigate more closely cases for which the leverage exceeds $2p/n$ or $3p/n$. It is advisable to examine all cases which have values of a diagnostic clearly distinct from the majority of the cases, which can be revealed, for example, by plotting the diagnostics against the case number.

Example 15.1 (continued)

In table 15.5 various regression diagnostics are shown for an analysis of the data in table 15.2 by a multiple linear regression model: the leverage h_{ii}, the standardized residual r_i and Cook's Distance, D_i. These diagnostics are used partly as a means of detecting errors in the recorded values of the variables and partly as a means of assessing the influence of the individual cases on the analysis.

The largest values of the leverage are found for the cases 9 and 16, both having values between $2p/n=0.4$ and $3p/n=0.6$. As illustrated in fig. 15.6, there is not, however, a substantial difference in the values of the leverage for cases 9 and 16 and the remaining cases, and therefore no further attention is paid to these cases.

As a rule, cases for which $|r_i|>2$ are selected for closer examination. It should be noted, however, that residuals for which $|r_i|>2$ may result from randomness and that the distribution of the largest residual is not the same as the distribution of a randomly selected residual. In table 15.5, the numerically largest residual is $r_6=2.85$. Not only is this value larger than 2, it is also much larger than any of the other residuals.

Table 15.5. Regression diagnostics for the data in table 15.2.

Case No.	Stand. residual r_i	Leverage h_{ii}	Cook's distance D_i
1	-1.50	0.17	0.11
2	-0.83	0.05	0.01
3	1.03	0.33	0.13
4	0.82	0.22	0.05
5	-1.04	0.07	0.02
6	2.85	0.18	0.45
7	0.31	0.12	0.00
8	0.14	0.36	0.00
9	-0.18	0.49	0.01
10	-0.53	0.05	0.00
11	-0.22	0.21	0.00
12	-1.32	0.11	0.06
13	1.09	0.20	0.07
14	0.63	0.07	0.01
15	-0.68	0.06	0.01
16	-0.40	0.46	0.03
17	-0.48	0.24	0.02
18	-0.45	0.13	0.01
19	0.39	0.24	0.01
20	0.66	0.22	0.03

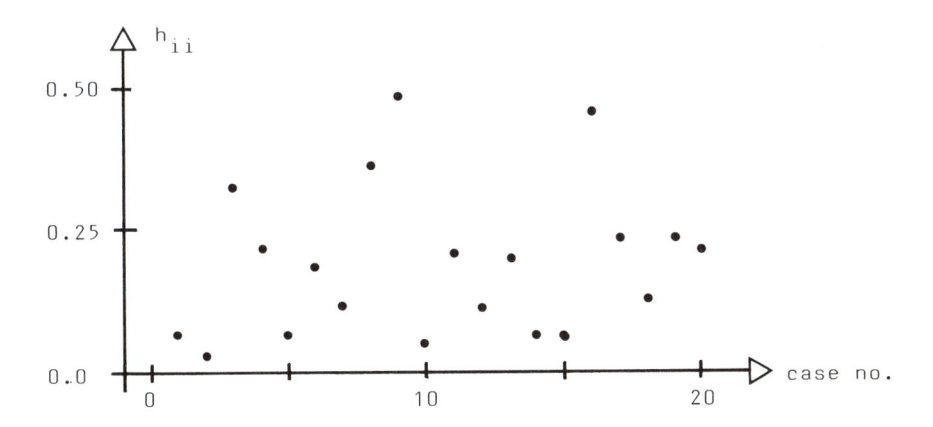

Fig. 15.8. Leverage plotted against case number.

In addition the value $D_6=0.45$ is much larger than the values of Cook's Distance for the other cases, such that the influence of case 6 on the analysis is greater than that of the remaining cases. A check of case 6 revealed no data errors, so it is advisable to repeat the analysis without case 6. Table 15.6 compares the analysis of the complete data set and the analysis after the deletion of case 6. It is apparent that primarily the deletion of case 6 has reduced the estimate of the standard deviation of the error term, but also the evaluation of the influence of x_1 on the response may be different after case 6 has been deleted. △.

Table 15.6. Comparing regression analyses with and without case 6.

Variable	With case 6 Estimate	t	p	Without case 6 Estimate	t	p
Intercept	-3028.20			-3202.20		
x_1	21.06	0.93	0.367	31.87	1.91	0.075
x_2	129.12	2.44	0.027	132.78	3.46	0.004
x_3	-0.32	-0.06	0.953	-5.82	-1.40	0.182
$R^2 = 0.49$	s = 326.30			$R^2 = 0.69$	s = 236.60	

15.7. Collinearity

In the multiple linear regression model, the parameter β_j is often interpreted as the change in the response variable when the j'th explanatory variable is increased by one unit and the remaining explanatory variables are kept fixed. Of course, this interpretation presupposes that it is possible to change an explanatory variable without at the same time inducing a change in one or more of the other explanatory variables.

The question then arises whether the same interpretation applies to the estimated regression parameter $\hat{\beta}_j$. This requires not only that it is possible to change x_j while keeping the other explanatory variables fixed, but also that the observed values of the explanatory variables vary independently of each other. Consider for example the model

$$(15.48) \quad y = \beta_0 + \beta_1 x_1 + \beta_2 x_2 + e$$

and suppose that (x_{i1}, x_{i2}), $i=1,\ldots,n$, cluster around the line $x_1 = a + bx_2$, i.e. that an approximate linear relationship exists between the observed values of the two explanatory variables, as shown in fig. 15.9.

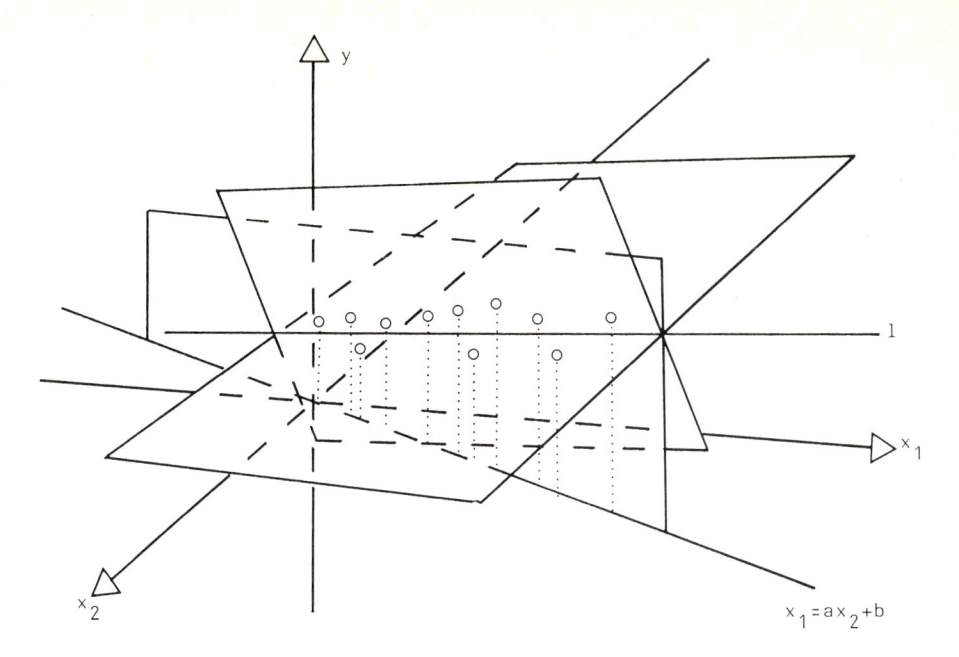

Fig. 15.9. Linear regression with an approximate linear relationship between the explanatory variables.

The figure shows that many different planes fit the data almost equally well. In fact, all planes which cut a vertical plane with base $x_1 = a + bx_2$ at the line l will have more or less the same residual sum of squares. This means, however, that many different combinations of β_1 and β_2 give almost the same fit, a fact that is reflected in unprecise estimates of the regression parameters. The position of the regression line, on the other hand, can be estimated with a high degree of precision in the neighbourhood of l. In spite of the large estimated standard errors of $\hat{\beta}_1$ and $\hat{\beta}_2$, the fit of the model can be relatively good.

In a data set with p explanatory variables, **collinearity** is said to be present if there are one or more approximate linear relationships of the form

$$(15.49) \quad c_0 + c_1 x_{i1} + \ldots + c_p x_{ip} \approx 0, \quad i = 1, \ldots, n,$$

between the observed values of the explanatory variables. If the relationship (15.49) only involves a few of the explanatory variables, then some of the c_j's are 0. Collinearity thus occurs whenever there is an approximate linear relationship between the columns of **X**. Collinearity implies that **X'X** is nearly singular, so the solution to the LS-equations

$$(X'X)\hat{\beta} = X'y$$

becomes unstable, i.e. minor changes in data may cause large changes in the LS-estimate. Furthermore, if **X'X** is close to being singular, $(X'X)^{-1}$ may contain large diagonal elements and hence, according to (15.27), the variance of some of the $\hat{\beta}_j$'s may become large. It is clear from these considerations that collinearity may cause problems regarding the interpretation of the analysis, in particular if it is important to estimate the individual parameters and not just the regression function as a whole.

Collinearities involving only two explanatory variables can be revealed by plotting the variables pairwise against each other, while collinearities involving more than two variables are more difficult to detect. There are, however, a number of symptoms indicative of collinearity of which five are listed below.

a) A high value of R^2 combined with low values of the t-statistics (15.40).

This indicates that the complete set of explanatory variables describes a high proportion of the total variability of the response variables, but the importance of some of the variables is negligible as long as the other variables are present. This means that some of the explanatory variables can be omitted without affecting the fit of the model significantly, but it is not possible to omit all of the variables at the same time. This phenomenon occurs when some of the explanatory variables can be approximated by a linear function of the remaining variables.

b) Omission of an explanatory variable leads to substantial changes in some of the remaining $\hat{\beta}_j$'s.

This implies that linear relationships may exist between the explanatory variables. If one of these variables is omitted its effect on the response is assumed by the remaining variables, thus inducing a change of the estimates of the corresponding parameters.

c) Deletion of a single case implies substantial changes in the estimate of one or more of the regression parameters.

In this case the system of equations, from which the LS-estimates are obtained, is sensitive to marginal changes i **X'X**. This may be the case if this matrix is close to being singular.

d) Occurrence of low values of the t-statistics (15.40) for variables expected to be important for the description of the response, or values of $\hat{\beta}_j$ with signs that are opposite of what was to be expected.

This indicates that the β_j's in question are estimated with large standard errors, which may occur if **X'X** is nearly singular.

e) Large correlations between pairs of explanatory variables.

This means that there are strong linear relationships between pairs of variables.

However, none of these symptoms is conclusive evidence of the exact nature and extent of collinearity in the data and even the absence of large correlations between pairs of explanatory variables is no guarantee that collinearity is not present. Furthermore, the symptoms do not quantify the impact of collinearity on the conclusions of the analysis. If there is a modest number of explanatory variables, such a quantification may be obtained from a comparison of the parameter estimates using different sets of explanatory variables in the regression model.

The main problem caused by collinearity is that it makes the interpretation of the data difficult. It may be impossible to separate the effects of the explanatory variables on the response variable, so the individual parameter estimates cannot be interpreted as measures of the importance of the corresponding variables. Since the problem is that the values of some of the explanatory variables do not vary independently of each other, one may try to apply a model with fewer explanatory variables, having a lesser degree of mutual covariation. But since the problem is also that data are not sufficiently informative for a satisfactory interpretation to be given, this procedure represents no real solution to the problems caused by collinearity. Discarding some of the explanatory variables also has the disadvantage of reducing the information in the data, thereby concealing the problem rather than solving it.

Example 15.1 (continued)

In the first part of example 15.1, the relation between temporary social security payments and three explanatory variables was analyzed by means of a linear multiple regression model. The correlations between the explanatory variables are shown in table 15.7. It is seen that two of the correlations have values around 0.5, indicating the existence of a certain degree of collinearity.

In order to investigate the consequences of these empirical correlations, the estimates of the parameters, their t-values and the value of R^2 are presented in table 15.8 for models with all the possible combinations of the explanatory variables.

Table 15.7. Empirical correlations between the explanatory variables.

	x_2	x_3
x_1	0.57	0.21
x_2		0.44

Table 15.8. Parameter estimates, t-values (in brackets) and R^2 for all possible regression models with one, two and three explanatory variables.

R^2	x_1	Variables x_2	x_3
0.47		153.6(4.0)	
0.28	54.9(2.6)		
0.08			7.7(1.2)
0.49	21.1(1.0)	127.9(2.7)	
0.47		155.7(3.5)	-0.6(-0.1)
0.31	51.0(2.4)		4.9(0.9)
0.49	21.1(0.9)	129.1(2.4)	-0.3(-0.1)

Table 15.8 shows that the estimate of β_2 is relatively stable, while the estimate of β_1 seems to depend on the other explantory variables included in the model. Both x_1 and x_2 are significant in the one-variable models, but when both variables are included, the values of their estimates decrease compared to the one-variable models, and x_1 becomes insignificant. Including the variable x_1 in a model with x_2 as explanatory variable only increases R^2 from 0.47 to 0.49, so it is obvious that the inclusion of x_1 hardly improves the fit at all. The estimate of β_3 fluctuates around 0, and as the t-value is always near 0, this variable is considered to be of no importance for the description of the response. It follows from these considerations that it is impossible to distinguish between the influence of x_1 and that of x_2 on the response in a two-variable model. In fig. 15.10, the observed values of x_1 and x_2 are plotted against each other and it appears from this plot that the two variables are dependent to some extent, indicating a case of collinearity.

This example illustrates that even dependencies between explanatory variables reflected in correlations around 0.5 can make it difficult to isolate the influence of the explanatory variables in question.

Furthermore, the evaluation of the significance of an explanatory variable is seen to be conditional on the explanatory variables retained in the model.△.

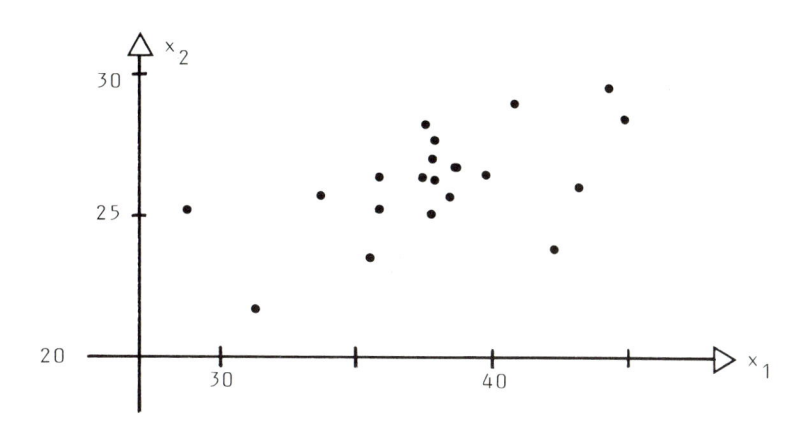

Fig. 15.10. Observed values of the first and second explanatory variable in table 15.2 plotted against each other.

15.8. Predictions

One of the principal aims of fitting a regression model to a set of data is to predict the value of the response variable for given values of the explanatory variables.

If the exact linear relationship between the mean of the response variable and the explanatory variables is known, prediction is straightforward, and the predicted value of the response is calculated as the mean of the response variable simply by inserting the values of the explanatory variables in the regression function.

If, however, the prediction has to be based on an estimated regression function, the predicted value of the response is obtained by inserting the values of the explanatory variables in the estimated regression function. Let $\mathbf{x}_0 = (1, x_{01}, \ldots, x_{0p})$ be a set of values of the explanatory variables. Then the predicted value of the response, $\hat{y}(\mathbf{x}_0)$, is defined by

$$(15.50) \quad \hat{y}(\mathbf{x}_0) = \hat{\beta}_0 + \hat{\beta}_1 x_{01} + \ldots + \hat{\beta}_p x_{0p} = \mathbf{x}_0 \hat{\boldsymbol{\beta}}.$$

Since the regression parameters are estimated, the prediction is subjected to an estimation error which can be assessed by

(15.51) $\text{var}[\hat{y}(x_0)] = \sigma^2 x_0 (X'X)^{-1} x_0' = \sigma^2 h_{00}$

in accordance with theorems 15.2 and 8.16, and inserting s^2 for σ^2 in this expression yields the variance estimator

$$\widehat{\text{var}}[\hat{y}(x_0)] = s^2 h_{00}.$$

Because $\hat{y}(x_0)$ and s^2 are independent,

$$T = \frac{\hat{y}(x_0) - x_0 \beta}{s\sqrt{h_{00}}} \sim t(n-p-1),$$

so a confidence interval for $\hat{y}(x_0)$ with level $1-\alpha$ becomes

(15.52) $\hat{y}(x_0) \pm t_{1-\alpha/2}(n-p-1) s\sqrt{h_{00}}$.

The prediction $\hat{y}(x_0)$ is an estimate of the expected value of the response variable, and (15.52) is a confidence interval for this expected value. In many cases, it is important to compute an interval that contains the value of the response to be observed for given values x_0 of the explanatory variables with a given probability - a so-called **prediction interval**.

Let Y_0 be the response to be observed for a given x_0. Then $Y_0 - \hat{y}(x_0)$ is the difference between the observed and predicted values. The variance of this difference is

$$\text{var}[Y_0 - \hat{y}(x_0)] = \text{var}[Y_0] + \text{var}[\hat{y}(x_0)] = \sigma^2(1+h_{00})$$

since Y_0 and $\hat{y}(x_0)$ are independent. This variance is called the **prediction variance**. If σ^2 is replaced by s^2 in the prediction variance, a prediction interval, which with probability $1-\alpha$ contains the value of the response to be observed, given x_0, is estimated by

(15.53) $\hat{y}(x_0) \pm t_{1-\alpha/2}(n-p-1)\sqrt{s^2(1+h_{00})}$.

By considerations similar to those of section 14.8, this interval can also be interpreted as the acceptance region for a test at level α of the hypothesis that a case (y_0, x_0) can be described by the model used for the description of the n cases from which the regression function was estimated.

The test statistic for the hypothesis $E[Y_0] = x_0 \beta$ can be written as

$$t = \frac{Y_0 - \hat{y}(x_0)}{s\sqrt{1+h_{00}}} \; .$$

If (y_0, x_0) is among the cases used to estimate β, i.e. if x_0 is a row in X, the test statistic can be computed from

$$t = \frac{s}{s_{(0)}} r_0$$

where r_0 is the standardized residual for the case (y_0, x_0) and $s_{(0)}$ is the estimate of σ with the case (y_0, x_0) deleted.

When prediction is based on an estimated regression function, it should be kept in mind that no information concerning the form of the regression function is available outside the range of the explanatory variables for the actual cases. Therefore, only predictions for cases with values of the explanatory variables close to or within this range can be considered as reliable unless supplementary information is available. Predictions within this range are called **interpolations**, while predictions outside the range are called **extrapolations**.

For simple linear regression, the interpolation region is an interval. With two explanatory variables, x_1 and x_2, the region of interpolation can be determined from a plot of the observed values of the variables against each other as shown in fig. 15.11. This figure shows that the region of interpolation should be taken as the interior of the sketched ellipse rather than the intersection of the marginal ranges of the two variables.

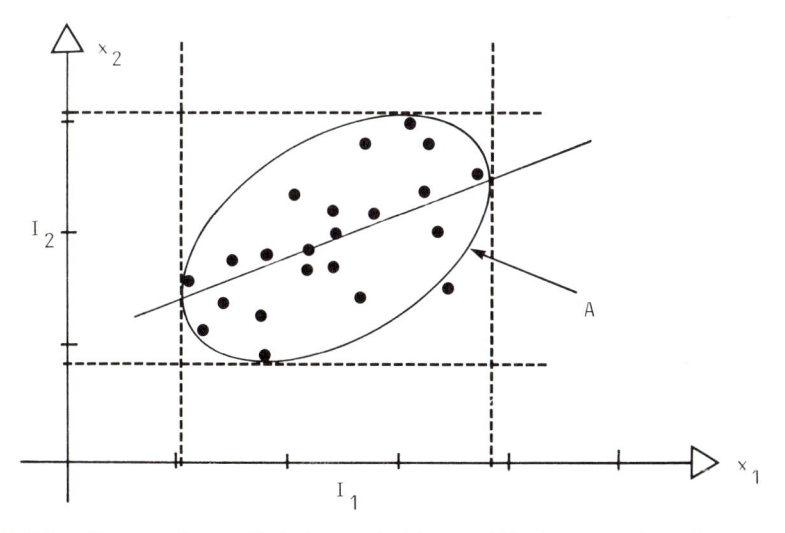

Fig. 15.11. The region of interpolation with two explanatory variables.

With three or more explanatory variables, it is impossible to visualize the interpolation and extrapolation regions. Instead a numerical measure for the distance from a given combination $\mathbf{x}=(x_1,\ldots,x_p)$ of the explanatory variables to the centre $\bar{\mathbf{x}}=(\bar{x}_1,\ldots,\bar{x}_p)$ of the observed values of the explanatory variables has to be used.

Such a measure, called the **Mahalanobis Distance**, is defined by

(15.54) $\quad m(\mathbf{x}) = (n-1)(\mathbf{x}-\bar{\mathbf{x}})(\tilde{\mathbf{X}}'\tilde{\mathbf{X}})(\mathbf{x}-\bar{\mathbf{x}})'$,

where $\tilde{\mathbf{X}}$ is the nxp matrix of the centralized values of the explanatory variables, i.e.

$$\tilde{\mathbf{X}} = \begin{bmatrix} x_{11}-\bar{x}_1 & \cdots & x_{1p}-\bar{x}_p \\ \vdots & & \vdots \\ x_{n1}-\bar{x}_1 & \cdots & x_{np}-\bar{x}_p \end{bmatrix}.$$

Inserting the value $\mathbf{x}_i=(x_{i1},\ldots,x_{ip})$ of the i'th observed explanatory variables for $\mathbf{x}$ in (15.54) yields

$$m(\mathbf{x}_i) = (n-1)(\mathbf{x}_i-\bar{\mathbf{x}})(\tilde{\mathbf{X}}'\tilde{\mathbf{X}})^{-1}(\mathbf{x}_i-\bar{\mathbf{x}})',$$

which reduces to

(15.55) $\quad m(\mathbf{x}_i) = (n-1)(h_{ii}-1/n)$,

where h_{ii} is the i'th diagonal element of the hat matrix. Hence, the set of all values $\mathbf{x}$ of the explanatory variables satisfying

(15.56) $\quad m(\mathbf{x}) \leq \max_{1\leq i\leq n} m(\mathbf{x}_i)$

can be taken as the interpolation region.

16. Heteroscedasticity and Autocorrelation

16.1. Heteroscedasticity

One of the basic assumptions underlying the application of the LS-method is that the variances of the error terms are equal. If this assumption is not satisfied, the LS-method is no longer optimal in the Gauss-Markov sense. Linear and unbiased estimators with a smaller variance than that of the LS-estimator can then be obtained and, furthermore, the expressions (14.16) and (15.22) for the variances of the LS-estimators are not correct.

To improve the precision of the estimators in the case of unequal error variances, also called the case of **heteroscedasticity**, consider the simple linear regression model with

$$(16.1) \qquad \mathrm{var}[e_i] = \sigma_i^2 = \sigma^2/w_i$$

where the weights $w_1, \ldots, w_n$ are assumed to be known and where at least two of the weights are different. Since a large value of σ_i^2 implies that the variability of the response is large, it is intuitively appealling to give cases with small values of σ_i^2 larger weights when estimating the regression parameters than cases with large values of σ_i^2. Therefore, consider the estimates of β_0 and β_1 obtained by minimizing the weighted sum of squared deviations

$$(16.2) \qquad S_w(\beta_0, \beta_1) = \Sigma(y_i - \beta_0 - \beta_1 x_i)^2/\sigma_i^2 = \Sigma w_i(y_i - \beta_0 - \beta_1 x_i)^2/\sigma^2 .$$

It is obvious from (16.2) that the smaller the value of σ_i^2, the larger the influence of the i'th case on the value of S_w. It can be shown that if the error terms are independent and normally distributed with variances given by (16.1), then the values of β_0 and β_1 that minimize S_w are the ML-estimates of β_0 and β_1.

Theorem 16.1
Let
$$Y_i = \beta_0 + \beta_1 x_i + e_i$$
where $e_1, \ldots, e_n$ are independent with $e_i \sim N(0, \sigma_i^2)$ and $\sigma_i^2 = \sigma^2/w_i$. Then

(16.3) $$\hat{\beta}_1^{(w)} = \frac{\Sigma(x_i - \bar{x}_w)(y_i - \bar{y}_w) w_i}{\Sigma(x_i - \bar{x}_w)^2 w_i}$$

and

(16.4) $$\hat{\beta}_0^{(w)} = \bar{y}_w - \hat{\beta}_1^{(w)} \bar{x}_w$$

are the ML-estimates for β_0 and β_1.

In these expressions,
$$\bar{y}_w = \Sigma(y_i w_i)/\Sigma w_i$$
and
$$\bar{x}_w = \Sigma(x_i w_i)/\Sigma w_i .$$

Proof

Under the given assumptions, the log-likelihood function takes the form

$$-\tfrac{1}{2}[n\ln(2\pi) + \Sigma \ln(\sigma^2/w_i) + \Sigma w_i(y_i - \beta_0 - \beta_1 x_i)^2/\sigma^2] .$$

Hence, the log-likelihood function has its maximum and

$$S_w(\beta_0, \beta_1) = \Sigma w_i(y_i - \beta_0 - \beta_1 x_i)^2/\sigma^2$$

has its minimum at the same point $(\hat{\beta}_0^{(w)}, \hat{\beta}_1^{(w)})$.

A necessary condition for S_w to attain its minimum is that

$$\partial S_w/\partial \beta_0 = -2\Sigma(y_i - \beta_0 - \beta_1 x_i) w_i = 0$$

and

$$\partial S_w/\partial \beta_1 = -2\Sigma(y_i - \beta_0 - \beta_1 x_i) x_i w_i = 0$$

or, equivalently,

$$\Sigma y_i w_i = \beta_0 \Sigma w_i + \beta_1 \Sigma w_i x_i$$

and

$$\Sigma y_i x_i w_i = \beta_0 \Sigma w_i x_i + \beta_1 \Sigma w_i x_i^2 .$$

These equations are, however, identical with the equations leading to (14.12), except that all sums are weighted with w_i as weights. Hence,

(16.3) and (16.4) follow from (14.12). $\square$.

The estimates $\beta_0^{(w)}$ and $\beta_1^{(w)}$ are called **weighted least squares** estimates or **WLS-estimates**. For multiple linear regression, the weighted least squares estimates of the regression parameters can be obtained by minimizing the weighted sum of squares

$$\sum w_i(y_i - \beta_0 - \beta_1 x_{i1} - \ldots - \beta_p x_{ip})^2$$

or, equivalently, by minimizing

$$\sum (y_i\sqrt{w_i} - \beta_0\sqrt{w_i} - \beta_1 x_{i1}\sqrt{w_i} - \ldots - \beta_p x_{ip}\sqrt{w_i})^2 .$$

From this last expression it can be seen that by transforming the response and the explanatory variables and adding $\sqrt{w}$ as an explanatory variable, the weighted least squares estimates can be obtained by an application of the LS-method to a linear regression model without intercept.

Assume that y_i is the average of n_i independent observations, all with a common variance σ^2. Then, according to theorem 8.6,

$$\sigma_i^2 = \sigma^2/n_i ,$$

i.e. σ_i^2 has the form (16.1) with $w_i = n_i$, and the parameters of a regression model with y_i as the observed values of the response can be estimated by the WLS-method. If, for example, as in example 15.1 the values of the response variable are computed for a number of geographical regions, the n_i's can be the number of inhabitants in the regions, and the larger the number of inhabitants, the larger the weight of the observation from the particular region is given.

If no information about the variance of the individual error terms is available, the actual form of heteroscedasticity may be deduced from a residual plot where the residuals are plotted either against the fitted values of the response or against one of the explanatory variables. If the residual plot shows that the variability increases linearly with the explanatory variable x, as illustrated in fig. 16.1, it may be assumed that

$$\text{var}[e_i] = x_i^2 \sigma^2$$

and hence WLS-estimation with $w_i = 1/x_i^2$ can be applied. On the other hand if the variability of the residuals is increasing linearly with $\sqrt{x_i}$, as illustrated in fig. 16.2, it can be assumed that

$$\text{var}[e_i] = x_i \sigma^2,$$

provided $x_i > 0$, and WLS-estimation with $w_i = 1/x_i$ can now be applied.

It should be noted that for many economic variables, for example variables measured in current prices, the variability is proportional to the level of the response variable. In such cases, a logarithmic transformation of the response often eliminates the heteroscedasticity and, at the same time, may improve the fit of the normal distribution to the error terms and make the model more plausible from an economic point of view.

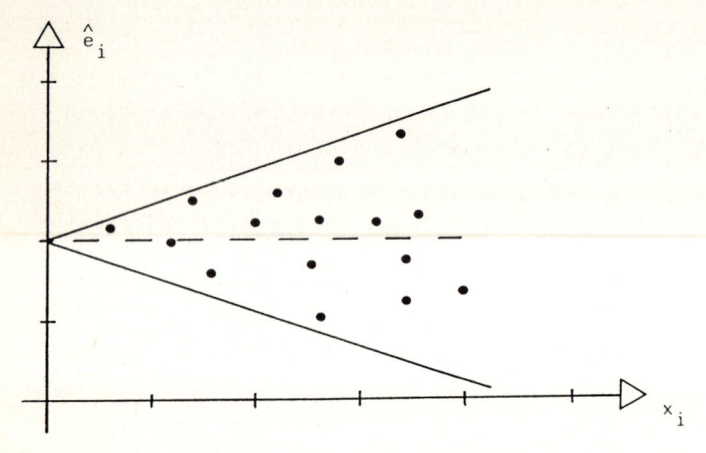

Fig. 16.1. Residual plot, illustrating heteroscedasticity, $\text{var}[e_i] = x_i^2 \sigma^2$.

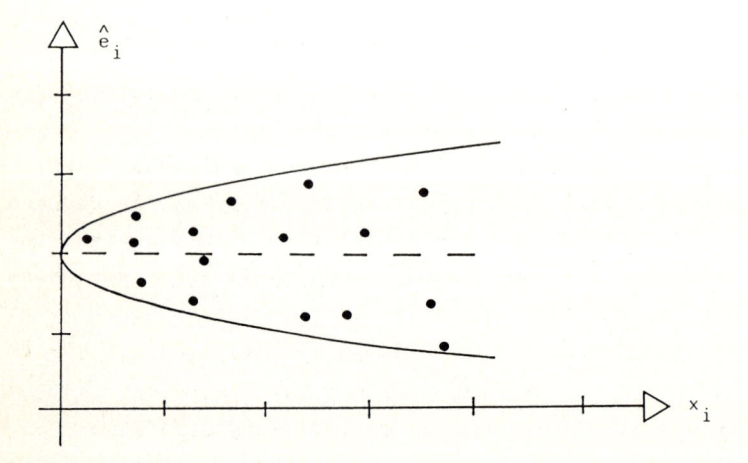

Fig. 16.2. Residual plot, illustrating heteroscedasticity, $\text{var}[e_i] = x_i \sigma^2$.

Example 16.1

The data in table 16.1 originate from the same investigation as the data considered in example 15.1. The variables y, x_1 and x_2 are defined as before. The variable x_3 is now the percentage of dwellings without central heating, erected before 1920, and rented dwellings erected later than 1964. This variable is regarded as a measurement of the need for social security payments among low-income families, since rented dwellings, erected later than 1964, are often owned by non-profit making building societies. The observations in table 16.1 refer to 24 urban municipalities in the Copenhagen area. In addition, the numbers of inhabitants, n, aged 18 to 66 years, are given.

Table 16.1. Average temporary social security payments, y, number of inhabitants, n, and three socio-demographic variables x_1, x_2 and x_3 for 24 urban municipalities in the Copenhagen area.

Case no.	y	n	x_3	x_2	x_1
1	2070.5	315455	30.3	33.6	59.9
2	1317.3	55917	27.5	28.2	57.0
3	1587.9	32305	27.2	27.1	39.7
4	1826.1	24931	32.6	29.0	42.4
5	427.4	8520	13.6	19.6	35.7
6	803.9	13167	17.7	25.0	41.7
7	1516.2	19111	30.0	27.9	39.8
8	2283.5	19316	51.1	31.5	46.1
9	1337.1	34677	25.2	27.3	42.0
10	489.4	5440	9.2	22.6	28.4
11	554.0	33593	12.4	24.1	43.3
12	1138.6	25375	5.4	24.9	41.8
13	920.4	20920	19.5	22.8	40.3
14	1790.6	13301	52.3	34.1	43.0
15	621.0	27867	12.2	22.5	36.3
16	258.8	8289	7.2	25.6	33.9
17	929.5	11795	13.3	20.4	33.6
18	671.4	14327	13.8	24.5	40.9
19	1553.2	10952	37.5	25.2	41.3
20	811.0	11388	22.6	24.6	40.9
21	407.6	14006	24.4	21.0	38.3
22	1901.8	11839	39.4	28.0	39.3
23	940.3	27066	25.1	22.6	31.8
24	779.3	10931	16.8	24.2	32.4

If it is assumed that temporary social security payments for a randomly chosen inhabitant is a random variable with constant variance, the value of y in table 16.1 for the i'th municipality corresponds to the average of n_i observations, so the variance of y_i is inversely proportional to n_i. Therefore the dependence of the payments on the explanatory variables x_1, x_2 and x_3 can be analysed by means of a multiple linear regression model with error variance satisfying (16.1) and $w_i = n_i$.

Fig. 16.3 is a plot of the residuals against $\sqrt{n_i}$ for a regression analysis with $\text{var}[e_i] = \sigma^2$. This plot does not contradict the assumption that the standard deviation of the error term is inversely proportional to $\sqrt{n_i}$.

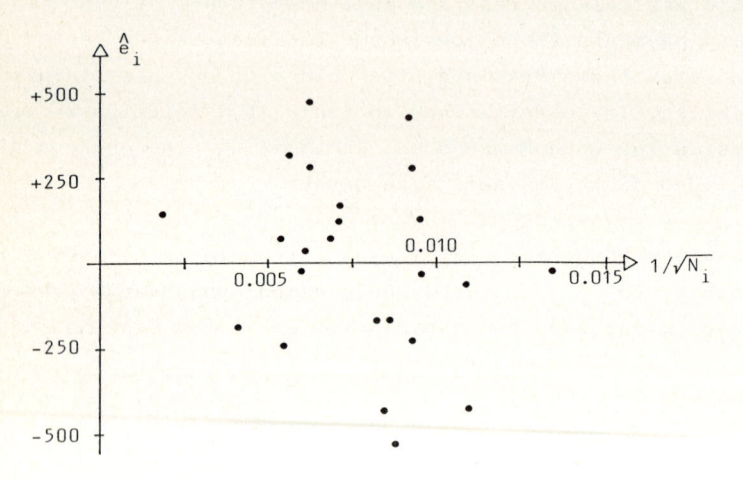

Fig. 16.3. Residuals from a regression analysis with $\text{var}[e_i] = \sigma^2$, plotted against the square root of the number of inhabitants.

Table 16.2 shows the residuals and the standardized residuals from a weighted least squares regression analysis. The model is checked by plotting the standardized residuals against the explanatory variables and the fitted value of the response as exemplified in figures 16.4 and 16.5. From these plots it can be concluded that the linear regression model with x_1, x_2 and x_3 as explanatory variables and with error variances σ^2/n_i gives a satisfactory description of the data.

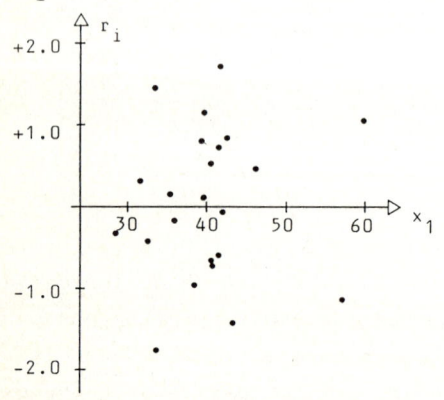

Fig. 16.4. Standardized residuals plotted against x_1.

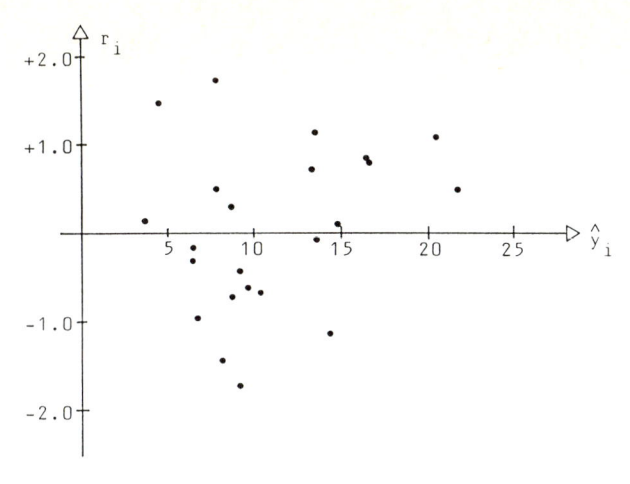

Fig. 16.5. Standardized residuals plotted against the fitted values of the response variable.

Table 16.2. Fitted values and standardized residuals from a regression analysis with $\text{var}[e_i]=\sigma^2$ and a weighted regression analysis with $\text{var}[e_i]=\sigma^2/n_i$.

Case number	$\text{var}[e_i]=\sigma^2$ Fitted values	Stand. residuals	$\text{var}[e_i]=\sigma^2/n_i$ Fitted values	Stand. residuals
1	1922.6	0.71	2048.6	1.05
2	1509.0	-0.85	1446.3	-1.15
3	1284.0	1.12	1363.3	1.17
4	1545.5	1.05	1639.7	0.85
5	487.1	-0.24	377.0	0.13
6	957.8	-0.57	992.8	-0.61
7	1397.1	0.44	1490.0	0.10
8	2152.2	0.54	2178.6	0.47
9	1270.4	0.24	1348.5	-0.06
10	502.0	-0.05	638.9	-0.31
11	796.4	-0.92	813.5	-1.42
12	670.6	1.87	792.6	1.75
13	854.8	0.25	793.2	0.54
14	2308.4	-2.34	2475.9	-2.54
15	634.3	-0.05	657.8	-0.18
16	684.4	-1.81	910.5	-1.78
17	509.8	1.61	460.6	1.46
18	831.4	-0.59	882.1	-0.71
19	1420.3	0.53	1319.6	0.72
20	1039.1	-0.83	1028.1	-0.65
21	841.6	-1.76	684.5	-0.99
22	1614.2	1.10	1646.3	0.80
23	896.5	0.17	876.6	0.31
24	807.4	-0.11	915.0	-0.41

Table 16.3 shows a summary of the weighted regression analysis with $\text{var}[e_i] = \sigma^2/n_i$ and, for comparison, a summary of the regression analysis with $\text{var}[e_i] = \sigma^2$ is also shown.

Table 16.3. Summary of regression analyses with $\text{var}[e_i] = \sigma^2/n_i$ and $\text{var}[e_i] = \sigma^2$.

Variable	$\text{var}[e_i] = \sigma^2$ Estimate	St.dev.	p	$\text{var}[e_i] = \sigma^2/n_i$ Estimate	St.dev.	p
Intercept	-1314.24			-1808.78		
x_1	8.80	11.24	0.4471	- 2.13	9.38	0.8230
x_2	59.98	27.73	0.0428	104.70	26.00	0.0007
x_3	22.93	6.79	0.0030	15.41	6.61	0.0303

Table 16.3 reveals clear differences between the estimates resulting from the two methods of analysis and their significance levels. The evaluation of the importance of the variables thus to some extent depends on the chosen method. There is a slight improvement in the precision of the estimates obtained from the weighted regression analysis as compared with the unweighted analysis. From table 16.2, however, it is obvious that, apart from a few cases, the differences between the estimates of the regression parameters are not reflected in the fitted values and the standardized residuals.

In table 16.3 neither R^2 nor s are given. Most standard computer programmes calculate R^2 in the weighted analysis in such a way that it is not comparable to the value of R^2 in an unweighted analysis. For example, for the present data, the value of R^2 resulting from the weighted analysis is larger than the value resulting from the unweighted analysis. This, however, does not mean that the fit obtained from the weighted analysis is better. The value of s is omitted because the interpretation of σ^2 is different for the two models.△.

16.2. Autocorrelation

Regression models are often applied for the analysis of **time series**. A series of observations of a variable is called a time series if the case number represents the time of observation. In this section, only time series observed with equidistant intervals of time are considered. In time series regression, it is not unusual that the assumption of uncorrelated error terms is violated. This is because many time series are autocorrelated, i.e. knowledge of the series up to time t contains information about the future development of the series.

It is always important to check the assumption of uncorrelated error terms when analysing time series. Graphically this can be done simply by plotting the standardized residuals against time (i.e. case number) to see whether the residuals are scattered randomly around the abscissa. For shorter time series, it may be difficult to decide whether the pattern should be interpreted as a violation of the assumption of uncorrelated error terms or just as a result of randomness, and the graphical check should therefore be supplemented by a numerical test.

The most frequent type of correlation between the error terms manifests itself in the form of **first order autoregression.** Graphically the presence of first order autoregression may give a picture as the one shown in fig. 16.6, where the standardized residuals are plotted against the observation number.

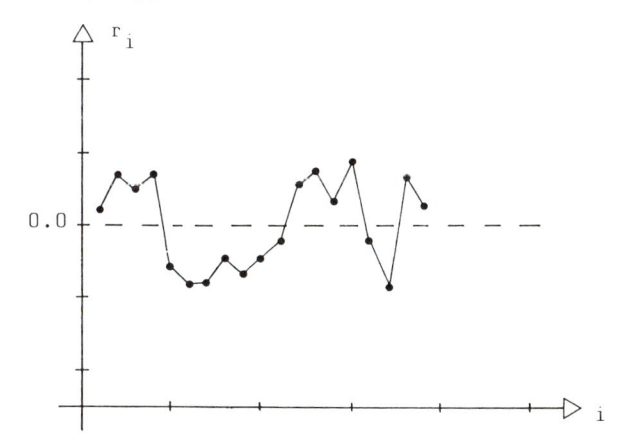

Fig. 16.6. A residual diagram in the presence of first order autoregression.

Formally, the series of error terms is said to follow a stationary **first order autoregressive process** if

(16.5) $e_i = \rho e_{i-1} + u_i,$ $i = 2, \ldots, n$,

where $-1 < \rho < 1$ and $u_2, \ldots, u_n$ are uncorrelated with mean 0 and a common variance. It can be shown that the correlation coefficient between e_{i-1} and e_i does not depend on i and that it is equal to ρ, i.e.

$$\rho = \frac{\text{cov}(e_{i-1}, e_i)}{\text{var}[e_i]}.$$

It follows that the error terms are uncorrelated if $\rho=0$. As an estimate of ρ, the empirical correlation coefficient between $\hat{e}_{i-1}$ and $\hat{e}_i$,

$$r = \sum_{i=2}^{n} \hat{e}_{i-1}\hat{e}_i \Big/ \sqrt{\sum_{i=2}^{n} \hat{e}_{i-1}^2 \sum_{i=2}^{n} \hat{e}_i}$$

can be used.

The hypothesis $\rho=0$ can be tested graphically by plotting $(\hat{e}_{i-1}, \hat{e}_i)$, $i=2,\ldots,n$, in a diagram. If the points scatter at random around a straight line through $(0,0)$ the alternative $\rho\neq 0$ is supported. If the points scatter at random around $(0,0)$ the hypothesis $\rho=0$ is supported.

A numerical test of the hypothesis $H_0: \rho=0$ can be based on the **Durbin-Watson** test statistic

(16.6) $$D = \sum_{i=2}^{n}(\hat{e}_i - \hat{e}_{i-1})^2 \Big/ \sum_{i=1}^{n} \hat{e}_i^2 .$$

Since

$$\sum_{i=2}^{n}(\hat{e}_i - \hat{e}_{i-1})^2 = \sum_{i=2}^{n}\hat{e}_i^2 + \sum_{i=2}^{n}\hat{e}_{i-1}^2 - 2\sum_{i=2}^{n}\hat{e}_i\hat{e}_{i-1}$$

and

$$\sum_{i=2}^{n}\hat{e}_i^2 \approx \sum_{i=2}^{n}\hat{e}_{i-1}^2 \approx \sum_{i=1}^{n}\hat{e}_i^2 ,$$

$D \approx 2(1-r)$ for large values of n. Since r is an estimate of ρ, values of D close to 2 support the hypothesis $\rho=0$. The alternative $\rho>0$ is supported by values of D close to 0, while the alternative $\rho<0$ is supported by values of D close to 4.

The exact distribution of D depends on the number of observations and the values of the explanatory variables. Hence a tabulation of the exact distribution of D is impracticable. For a fixed test level α, however, the upper and lower limits of the α percentile, D_α, of the distribution of D can be determined, given the number of cases and the number of explanatory variables. In other words, it is possible to determine values d_1 and d_2 so that

$$d_1 \leq D_\alpha \leq d_2 ,$$

as illuatrated in fig. 16.7. It can be shown that $D_{1-\alpha}=4-D_\alpha$ such that $d_4=4-d_1$ and $d_3=4-d_2$ are the lower and upper limits respectively for $D_{1-\alpha}$, if $\alpha<0.5$.

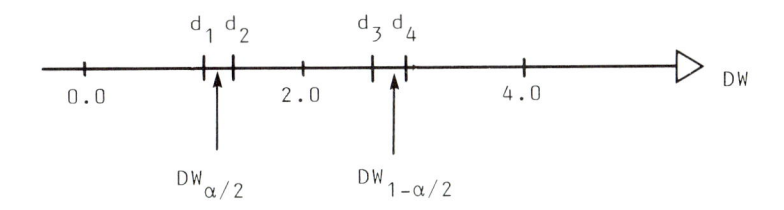

Fig. 16.7. Illustration of the lower and upper bounds for the percentiles of the distribution of D.

If $\rho=0$ is tested against the alternative $\rho>0$, the hypothesis should be rejected at test level α if the value of the test statistic is smaller than d_1 and accepted if the value is larger than d_2. If the value falls between d_1 and d_2 no conclusion can be reached.

The Durbin-Watson test is formally a test for first order autocorrelation in the series of error terms. This type of correlation is often met when analysing yearly observations. If data consist of monthly or quarterly observations, there may be little or no first order autocorrelation present, but observations from the same month or the same quarter in different years may be correlated. Such seasonal variations, however, cannot be detected by the application of a Durbin-Watson test.

When autocorrelation is present in the error terms, the LS-estimators of the regression parameters in a multiple linear regression model are still unbiased, and predictions of the response are therefore also unbiased. The variance of the LS-estimator is, however, no longer given by (15.22) since the variance of

$$\hat{\beta} = (X'X)^{-1}X'y$$

becomes

$$\operatorname{var}[\hat{\beta}] = (X'X)^{-1}X'\operatorname{var}[e]X(X'X)^{-1},$$

If the e_i's are correlated, $\operatorname{var}[e]$ is no longer a diagonal matrix and the variance of $\hat{\beta}$ does not reduce to (15.22). Application of this expression when testing hypotheses concerning the values of the regression parameters may therefore lead to erroneous conclusions. If autoregression is present in data, attempts should be made either to reformulate the model, for example by incorporating more explanatory variables to reduce the degree of autocorrelation, or to apply an estimation method that accounts for the presence of autocorrelation.

When ρ is close to 1, $e_i - e_{i-1} \simeq u_i$, so the differences between successive error terms are approximately uncorrelated. Hence, the LS-method can be applied to the model

$$y_i - y_{i-1} = \beta_1(x_i - x_{i-1}) + (e_i - e_{i-1}) = \beta_1(x_i - x_{i-1}) + u_i .$$

To improve the fit, however, a constant term is usually introduced in models based on the **first order differences** $y_i - y_{i-1}$ and $x_i - x_{i-1}$ between the values of the original variables. Variables like x_{i-1} and y_{i-1} are called **lagged variables**.

Tabel 16.4. The Danish wage index, W, and price index, P, 1957-81.

Case No	Year	W	P	ln(W)	ln(P)
1	1957	6628	251	8.7991	5.5255
2	1958	6867	253	8.8345	5.5334
3	1959	7333	257	8.9001	5.5491
4	1960	7919	260	9.9770	5.5607
5	1961	8882	268	9.0918	5.5910
6	1962	9794	281	9.1895	5.6384
7	1963	10575	297	9.2662	5.6937
8	1964	11487	309	9.3490	5.7333
9	1965	12842	327	9.4605	5.7900
10	1966	14404	352	9.5753	5.8636
11	1967	15759	377	9.6652	5.9323
12	1968	17621	408	9.7768	6.0113
13	1969	19640	420	9.8853	6.0403
14	1970	21841	448	9.9915	6.1048
15	1971	25136	476	10.1321	6.1654
16	1972	28054	507	10.2419	6.2285
17	1973	32365	553	10.3848	6.3154
18	1974	38733	640	10.5644	6.4615
19	1975	46157	698	10.7398	6.5482
20	1976	51445	761	10.8483	6.6346
21	1977	56511	845	10.9422	6.7393
22	1978	62320	929	11.0400	6.8341
23	1979	69392	1019	11.1475	6.9266
24	1980	77206	1145	11.2542	7.0432
25	1981	84031	1278	11.3389	7.1531

Source: S. Gammelgaard: Billeder af dansk macroøkonomi.

Example 16.2

In table 16.4, the values of the Danish wage index (W) and the Danish price index (P) for the years 1957-81 are presented. The linear regression model for the logarithmic transforms,

$$\ln P_i = \beta_0 + \beta_1 \ln W_i + e_i, \quad i=1,\ldots,25,$$

is proposed as a possible model for the description of the price index as a function of the wage index.

A summary of the regression analysis based on this model is given in table 16.5 and the standardized residuals are plotted against time in fig. 16.8.

Tabel 16.5. Summary of the regression analysis of the logarithms of the price and wage indices.

Variable	Estimate	t-value	p
Intercept	-0.034	-0.20	0.8419
ln W	0.619	36.94	0.0001
$R^2 = 0.98$	D = 0.17	r = 0.73	

Both the Durbin-Watson test statistic D and fig. 16.5 clearly show that the assumption of uncorrelated error terms is not satisfied. The value D=0.17 corresponds to a level of significance far below 0.01. In spite of the large value of R^2, the description of the relation between ln(P) and ln(W) is therefore not considered satisfactory.

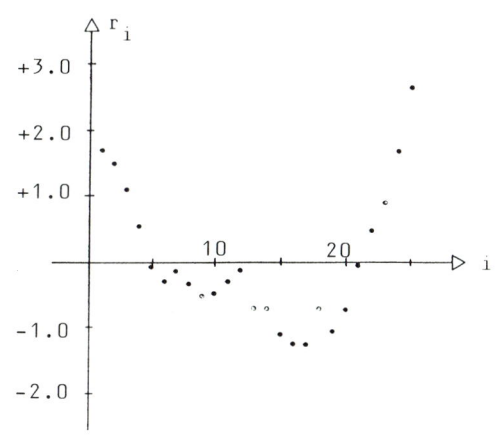

Fig. 16.8. Plot of the standardized residuals against time.

To remove the autocorrelation, consider the variables $x_i = \ln(W_i) - \ln(W_{i-1})$ and $y_i = \ln(P_i) - \ln(P_{i-1})$. These first differences between the logarithms can be regarded as approximations to the relative changes in the variables from year to year.

Table 16.6 summarizes the regression analysis based on the first differences of the logarithmically transformed variables. The value of D still corresponds to a level of significance below 0.01, even though the plot in fig. 16.9 of the standardized residuals against time now exhibits a more irregular pattern than that in fig. 16.8. The plot of r_{i-1} against r_i in fig. 16.10 demonstrates that the correlation is due to a general structure in the residuals and not to a single pair of consecutive residuals.

<u>Table 16.6</u>. Summary of the regression analysis of the first differences of the logarithmically transformed values of the price and wage indices.

Variable	Estimate	t	p
Intercept	-0.0008	-0.04	0.9692
x	0.6486	3.38	0.0027
R^2=0.34	D=0.82		r=0.50

It should be noted that the value of R^2 is much larger in the model for the logarithmically transformed variables than in the model for their first differences. This is due to the existence of a common trend in the two indices. Since most of the trend in the wage index can be described by a linear function of the price index and since the trend is responsible for a substantial part of the total variation in the price index, the value of R^2 becomes large. By taking first differences, the trend in the response variable is, however, eliminated, implying the smaller value of R^2.

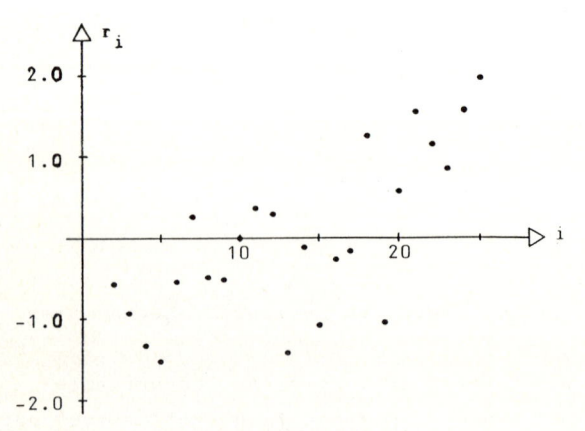

<u>Fig. 16.9</u>. Standardized residuals from the model for the first differences, plotted against time.

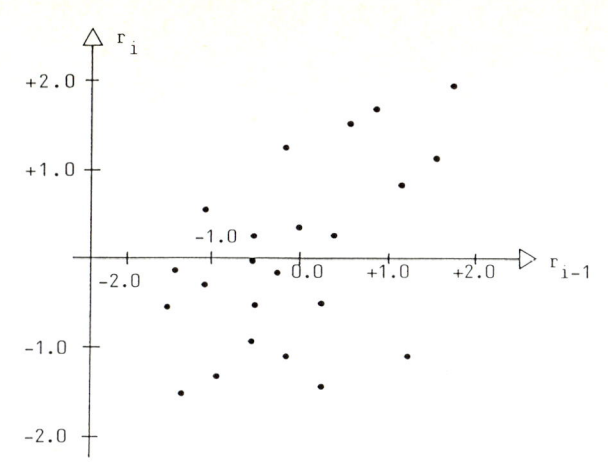

Fig. 16.10. Standardized residuals from the model for the first differences, plotted against their lagged values.

The conclusion is that not even the relation between the first differences of the variables can be described by a linear model with uncorrelated error terms. Therefore it is necessary to apply a model for $\ln(P)$ or y in which the error terms are assumed to follow the first order autoregressive process. $\triangle$.

17. Survey Sampling

17.1. Introduction

The statistical theory of **survey sampling**, often simply called **sampling theory**, is concerned with the selection and analysis of samples selected from finite populations. The purpose of survey sampling is usually to estimate the average (or the sum) of the values of one or more variables for all units in the population.

Survey sampling is employed when it is impractical or impossible, for example because of financial or temporary constraints, to measure the value of the variable, or variables, for all units.

Consider then a population consisting of N units, indexed 1 to N. If the value of a variable μ for unit ν is denoted μ_ν, the **population average** is defined as

$$\bar{\mu} = \frac{1}{N} \sum_{\nu=1}^{N} \mu_\nu ,$$

and the **population total** as

$$N\bar{\mu} = \sum_{\nu=1}^{N} \mu_\nu .$$

Sampling theory deals with methods for selecting the sample and then estimating $\bar{\mu}$ or $N\bar{\mu}$ from the values provided by the sample. When choosing between **sampling procedures**, often called **sampling designs**, the chosen design should provide as precise estimates of $\bar{\mu}$ or $N\bar{\mu}$ as possible, given the financial restrictions set for the sampling, for example in terms of basic costs and cost per sampled unit. The sampling design may also depend on the type of population considered, the nature of the variables in question and prior knowledge of the distribution of the variables in the population.

The basic sampling design is **simple random sampling without replacement**. According to this design, the n units in the sample are drawn one at a time and in each draw all remaining units have the same probability of being selected. In some situations, the population can be divided into strata, such that the variable under consideration has a homogeneous variation within strata, while the different strata are very heterogeneous.

Given proportions of the sample can then be selected from each stratum and the required number of units within each stratum are obtained by simple random sampling without replacement. Such a design is called **stratified sampling**. If the sampling units are clusters of units, the design is called **cluster sampling**, under which either all or no units in a cluster are sampled. Typical examples of clusters are a household or all inhabitants in a building. **Simple random cluster sampling** consists of drawing a number of clusters by simple random sampling without replacement, and the sample then consists of all units belonging to one of the sampled clusters.

Numerous other, often very complicated sampling procedures have been suggested. It should be stressed, however, that the more complicated the sampling procedure, the more complicated the corresponding statistical analysis becomes.

A common feature for all sampling methods under consideration in this book is the randomization element, which entails that the statistical model for the data can be based on probability theory. Thus, if a sample of size n is selected by simple random sampling, each unit in the population of size N is selected with probability n/N.

Accordingly, methods from statistical inference theory can be used to draw conclusions about the population average, for example. In fact, $\bar{\mu}$, can be regarded as the mean value in a discrete distribution with point probabilities equal to the frequencies with which the value of the variable in question occurs in the population. The appropriate estimator for $\bar{\mu}$ and its statistical properties will depend on the sampling design.

Typical examples of sample surveys are political polls, where the units are potential voters and the variable to be measured is the party the voter intends to vote for in the event of an immediate election.

17.2. Simple random sampling

Consider the selection of a sample of size n from a population consisting of N units. The sampling procedure is called **simple random sampling** if all distinct samples of size n have an equal chance of being sampled. Since there are

$$\binom{N}{n}$$

distinct samples, each of these has probability

(17.1) $1/\binom{N}{n}$

of being selected, according to Laplace's formula (3.2). The number of distinct samples which include a given unit is equal to the number of distinct samples of size n-1 with the given unit excluded or

$$\binom{N-1}{n-1}.$$

Hence, the probability of the given unit being included in the sample is

(17.2) $p = \binom{N-1}{n-1} / \binom{N}{n} = n/N.$

One method of drawing a simple random sample without replacement is by drawing the n units one at a time. In the first draw, all units have the same probability, 1/N, of being selected. In the second draw, all remaining units have the probability 1/(N-1) of being selected. In the i'th draw, all remaining units have probability 1/(N-i+1) of being selected and so on.

In practice the selection of one unit at random from among N given units is performed by means of a random number generator after the units have been indexed 1 to N.

Theorem 17.1

The probability $p_i(\nu)$ of selecting unit number ν in the i'th draw is

$$p_i(\nu) = \frac{1}{N},$$

and the probability of selecting unit number ν_1 in the i'th draw and unit number ν_2 in the j'th draw is

$$p_{ij}(\nu_1, \nu_2) = \frac{1}{N(N-1)}.$$

Proof

The proportion of distinct samples containing unit ν is n/N according to (17.2). The units of each of these samples can be rearranged in n! ways of which (n-1)! have unit ν in the i'th place. Hence,

$$p_i(\nu) = \frac{(n-1)!}{n!} \frac{n}{N} = \frac{1}{N}.$$

The number of samples containing both unit number ν_1 and unit number ν_2 is

$$\binom{N-2}{n-2}.$$

The units in the sample can be rearranged in n! different ways of which (n-2)! have unit ν_1 in the i'th place and unit ν_2 in the j'th place. Since there are still $\binom{N}{n}$ possible ways of selecting a sample,

$$p_{ij}(\nu_1,\nu_2) = \frac{(n-2)!}{n!} \frac{\binom{N-2}{n-2}}{\binom{N}{n}} = \frac{1}{N(N-1)} \cdot \square.$$

If the sampled units are drawn one at a time, with the selection in each draw at random from among all units regardless of whether they have already been drawn or not, the procedure is called **simple random sampling with replacement**. In this case, a unit can be included more than once in the sample. The advantage of using simple random sampling with replacement is that the statistical theory is slightly less complicated than for sampling without replacement. However, since the same information may be obtained more than once when sampling with replacement, sampling without replacement is more informative.

17.3. Simple random sampling in the binary case

When the variable to be measured can only take two values, it is called a **binary variable**. The only information to be collected is the proportion of units having one of the values of the binary variable, so the actual values are irrelevant, and as a rule they are coded 1 and 0 for simplicity.

The units having value 1 are called the marked units. It follows that the average θ given by

$$(17.3) \qquad \theta = \frac{1}{N} \sum_{\nu=1}^{N} \mu_\nu$$

is the proportion of marked units in the population. Let the values of the variable for the n units in the sample be $x_1,\ldots,x_n$ and consider the statistic $x = \sum_{i=1}^{n} x_i$, which is the number of marked units in the sample. If the sampling design is simple random sampling without replacement, the corresponding random variable X follows a hypergeometric distribution with parameters $(n,N\theta,N)$, according to the results in section 6.5. Hence, X has point probabilities

$$P(X=x) = \binom{N\theta}{x}\binom{N(1-\theta)}{n-x}\bigg/\binom{N}{n}.$$

The population variance τ^2, defined as

$$\tau^2 = \frac{1}{N-1} \sum_{\nu=1}^{N} (\mu_\nu - \theta)^2,$$

reduces, since μ_ν is either 0 or 1, to

(17.4) $\quad \tau^2 = \frac{1}{N-1}((1-\theta)^2 N\theta + (-\theta)^2 N(1-\theta)) = \frac{N}{N-1}\theta(1-\theta).$

As demonstrated in example 10.8, $\hat{\theta} = \bar{X}$ is an unbiased estimator of θ, and from (6.25) and (17.4) it follows that

(17.5) $\quad \text{var}[\hat{\theta}] = \frac{\theta(1-\theta)}{n} \frac{N-n}{N-1} = \frac{\tau^2}{n}(1-f)$

where $f = n/N$ is called the **sample fraction**.

The accuracy of $\hat{\theta}$ as an estimate for θ thus depends on the population variance, the sample size and the ratio between the sample size and the population size.

An estimate of $\text{var}[\hat{\theta}]$ is obtained by substituting $\hat{\theta}$ for θ in (17.5). Usually, however, the unbiased estimator

(17.6) $\quad \hat{\text{var}}[\hat{\theta}] = \frac{\hat{\theta}(1-\hat{\theta})}{n-1}(1-f)$

is preferred. This is slightly different from the estimate applied in section 11.4, but is directly comparable to the estimate of the variance of the sample mean applied in the general case in the following section.

An unbiased estimator for the population total $N\theta$ is given by $N\hat{\theta}$ and $\text{var}[N\hat{\theta}]$ is estimated by

$$\hat{\text{var}}[N\hat{\theta}] = N^2 \frac{\hat{\theta}(1-\hat{\theta})}{n-1}(1-f).$$

The determination of exact confidence limits for $\hat{\theta}$ under the hypergeometric model is rather complicated, but applying (9.18) the approximate $1-\alpha$ confidence limits become

(17.7) $\quad \hat{\theta} \pm u_{1-\alpha/2}\sqrt{\hat{\text{var}}[\hat{\theta}]}$,

where $\hat{\text{var}}[\hat{\theta}]$ is given by (17.6).

If the sampling design is simple random sampling with replacement, the number of marked units X in the sample follows a binomial distribution with parameters n and θ. To distinguish between the cases with and without replacement, the observed number of marked units in the sample is denoted by x_w when the sampling is with replacement. As a consequence, the estimate of θ is

$$\hat{\theta}_w = x_w/n,$$

and according to theorem 6.1 the variance of $\hat{\theta}_w$ is

$$\text{var}[\hat{\theta}_w] = \frac{\theta(1-\theta)}{n} = \frac{\tau^2}{n} \frac{N-1}{N}.$$

A comparison of this expression and (17.5) reveals that for $n \geq 2$, the estimate of θ is more accurate when the sampling is without than with replacement. This is a consequence of the fact that no additional information is obtained if a unit is selected for a second time, which could happen when the sampling is with replacement. The smaller the ratio n/N, the smaller the difference between the two variances, since the less likely it is, that a unit is selected twice.

The ratio

$$\frac{\text{var}[\hat{\theta}]}{\text{var}[\hat{\theta}_w]} = \frac{N-n}{N-1} \simeq 1 - \frac{n}{N} < 1$$

measures the gain in accuracy of $\hat{\theta}$ over $\hat{\theta}_w$.

Example 17.1

Political sample surveys in Denmark are based on the question "If an election was held tomorrow, what party would you vote for?" The size of the population in Denmark entitled to vote is roughly $N = 3\,700\,000$. From this population a sample of size $n = 1200$ is sampled by simple random sampling without replacement. Let $x_i = 1$ if voter number i in the sample says that he or she intends to vote for the Social Democratic Party and $x_i = 0$ otherwise. Then $x = \Sigma x_i$ is the number of Social Democratic voters in the sample and $\hat{\theta} = x/n$ estimates the proportion θ of potential Social Democratic voters in Denmark. In a concrete poll, $x = 396$ was observed. Then the accuracy of the estimate

$$\hat{\theta} = 396/1200 = 0.330$$

is measured by

$$\hat{\text{var}}[\hat{\theta}] = \frac{(0.33)(0.67)}{1199}\left(1 - \frac{1200}{3700000}\right) = 0.000184.$$

From (17.7) a 0.95 confidence interval can be constructed as

$$0.330 \pm 1.96\sqrt{0.000184} = (0.303, 0.357).$$

At a confidence level of 95%, it can thus be claimed that the proportion of Social Democratic voters in Denmark at the time of the polling was between 30.3% and 35.7%. △.

17.4. Simple random sampling in the general case

Consider a population consisting of N units, indexed 1 to N. The variable under consideration has the value μ_ν for the ν'th unit in the population. The **population mean** is defined as

$$(17.8) \qquad \bar{\mu} = \frac{1}{N} \sum_{\nu=1}^{N} \mu_\nu$$

and the **population variance** as

$$(17.9) \qquad \tau^2 = \frac{1}{N-1} \sum_{\nu=1}^{N} (\mu_\nu - \bar{\mu})^2.$$

Let $x_1, \ldots, x_n$ be the values of the variable for the units of a simple random sample of size n. Then the population mean is estimated by the **sample mean**

$$(17.10) \qquad \bar{x} = \frac{1}{n} \sum_{i=1}^{n} x_i.$$

Let X_i be the random variable of which x_i is the observed value, then $\bar{x}$ is the observed value of

$$(17.11) \qquad \bar{X} = \frac{1}{n} \sum_{i=1}^{n} X_i.$$

Theorem 17.2

For a simple random sample of size n drawn without replacement the sample mean $\bar{X}$ is an unbiased estimator of the population mean $\bar{\mu}$ with variance

$$(17.12) \qquad \mathrm{var}[\bar{X}] = \frac{\tau^2}{n}(1-f),$$

where $f = n/N$ and τ^2 is the population variance.

Proof

According to theorem 17.1, the ν'th unit in the population is with probability $1/N$ selected as unit i in the sample. Hence

$$E[X_i] = \sum_{\nu=1}^{N} \mu_\nu \frac{1}{N} = \bar{\mu}$$

according to (5.1), and

$$E[\overline{X}] = E\left[\frac{1}{n}\Sigma X_i\right] = \overline{\mu},$$

such that $\overline{X}$ is unbiased for μ. Further, theorem 17.1 and (5.5) yield that

$$\text{var}[X_i] = \frac{1}{N}\sum_{\nu=1}^{N}(\mu_\nu-\overline{\mu})^2 = \frac{N-1}{N}\tau^2.$$

From the second formula in theorem 17.1 and (8.26), it follows that

$$\text{cov}(X_i, X_j) = \sum\sum_{\nu_1 \neq \nu_2}(\mu_{\nu_1}-\overline{\mu})(\mu_{\nu_2}-\overline{\mu})\frac{1}{N(N-1)},$$

or, since $\Sigma\Sigma(\mu_{\nu_1}-\overline{\mu})(\mu_{\nu_2}-\overline{\mu})=0$,

$$\text{cov}(X_i, X_j) = \frac{-1}{N(N-1)}\sum_{\nu=1}^{N}(\mu_\nu-\overline{\mu})^2 = -\frac{\tau^2}{N},$$

such that (8.45) yields

$$\text{var}[\overline{X}] = \frac{1}{n^2}\left[\sum_{i=1}^{n}\text{var}[X_i] + \sum\sum_{i \neq j}\text{cov}(X_i, X_j)\right]$$
$$= \frac{\tau^2}{n}\frac{(N-1)}{N} - \frac{n-1}{n}\frac{\tau^2}{N} = \frac{\tau^2}{n}(1-f),$$

which proves (17.12). □.

The somewhat complicated calculations necessary to derive $\text{var}[\overline{X}]$ are due to the fact that $X_1,\ldots,X_n$ are correlated when the sampling is without replacement. When the sampling is with replacement, the X_i's are, however, independent and then according to theorem 8.6

$$\text{var}[\overline{X}] = \frac{1}{n}\text{var}[X_i] = \frac{\tau^2}{n}\frac{N-1}{N}.$$

Since $1-f=1-n/N<(N-1)/N=1-1/N$ for $n\geq 2$, the population mean $\overline{\mu}$ is estimated more accurately for sampling without replacement. The difference in accuracy is negligible if n is small compared to N.

It can be proved that

$$(17.13) \qquad s^2 = \frac{1}{n-1}\sum_{i=1}^{n}(x_i-\overline{x})^2$$

is an unbiased estimate of τ^2, such that

(17.14) $\quad \widehat{\mathrm{var}}[\bar{X}] = \dfrac{s^2}{n}(1-f)$

is an unbiased estimate of $\mathrm{var}[\bar{X}]$. If N is large and if n is not too small, $\bar{X}$ is approximately normally distributed with mean value $\bar{\mu}$ and variance (17.12). Hence, the interval with limits

(17.15) $\quad \bar{x} \pm u_{1-\alpha/2} s\sqrt{(1-f)/n}$

is an approximate $1-\alpha$ confidence interval for $\bar{\mu}$.

An unbiased estimator of $N\bar{\mu}$ is obtained from (17.11) as

(17.16) $\quad N\bar{X} = \dfrac{N}{n} \sum_{i=1}^{n} X_i$.

The variance of this estimator is given by

$$\mathrm{var}[N\bar{X}] = \dfrac{N^2}{n} \tau^2 (1-f),$$

and can be estimated by

$$\widehat{\mathrm{var}}[N\bar{X}] = \dfrac{N^2}{n} s^2 (1-f).$$

For economical or technical reasons it is often necessary to limit the sample size. On the other hand, the parameter of interest, e.g. the population mean $\bar{\mu}$, should be estimated with at least a given precision. This precision can be specified in terms of an interval for $\bar{\mu}$ or in terms of the estimation error. If the estimation error must not exceed, say, σ_0^2, then in the case of simple random sampling without replacement, n must satisfy

$$\dfrac{\tau^2}{n} \dfrac{N-n}{N} \leq \sigma_0^2.$$

Solving this inequality with respect to n yields

(17.17) $\quad n \geq \dfrac{\tau^2}{\sigma_0^2 + \tau^2/N}$.

Hence, the sample must be larger than n_0, where n_0 is the smallest integer larger than or equal to the limit (17.17).

If τ^2 is unknown, past experience may help specify a realistic value for τ^2, or τ^2 can be estimated from other samples believed to be comparable to the sample being planned. Sometimes a small pilot study can be carried out and τ^2 estimated from this.

A specification of the precision can also be given in terms of the maximum length L_0 of an interval, which contains $\bar{\mu}$ with probability $1-\alpha$, i.e.

$$L = 2u_{1-\alpha/2}\tau\sqrt{1-f}/\sqrt{n} \leq L_0.$$

This requirement is met if

$$\frac{\tau^2}{n}\frac{N-n}{N} \leq \frac{L_0^2}{(2u_{1-\alpha/2})^2}$$

or

(17.18) $\quad n \geq \dfrac{\tau^2}{L_0^2/(2u_{1-\alpha/2})^2 + \tau^2/N}.$

The choice of the sample size can be based directly on economic considerations. Suppose that the cost of a given sample survey is specified as basic costs c_0 and a variable cost c_1 per sampled unit, so that the total cost is $c = c_0 + nc_1$. If the survey has a maximum budget of C_0, it is obvious that n cannot be larger than

(17.19) $\quad n_0 = (C_0 - c_0)/c_1.$

Example 17.2

In order to illustrate the various elements of a statistical analysis based on a random sample a fictive population consisting of 5 farms is considered.

The number of pigs on each of the 5 farms respectively is

$$\mu_1 = 30, \; \mu_2 = 30, \; \mu_3 = 20, \; \mu_4 = 10 \text{ and } \mu_5 = 0.$$

A sample of size 2 is drawn from the population of farms by simple random sampling without replacement. The observed numbers of pigs for the two farms of the sample are denoted x_1 and x_2, respectively. If farms 2 and 4 are selected, the observed values are $x_1 = 30$ and $x_2 = 10$. Note that number 1 and 2 in the sample do not correspond to number 1 and 2 in the population. It is possible to select $5(5-1)/2 = 10$ different samples, each of which have probability 1/10 of being selected according to (17.1). All 10 samples are shown in table 17.1.

Table 17.1. Samples of size 2 from a population of 5 farms.

Units selected	Observed number of pigs	$\bar{x}$	s^2
1, 2	30, 30	30	0
1, 3	30, 20	25	50
1, 4	30, 10	20	200
1, 5	30, 0	15	450
2, 3	30, 20	25	50
2, 4	30, 10	20	200
2, 5	30, 0	15	450
3, 4	20, 10	15	50
3, 5	20, 0	10	200
4, 5	10, 0	5	50

Note that the sample consisting of units 1 and 3 is different from the sample consisting of units 2 and 3 even though the observed sets of values are identical. The population mean is the average number of pigs per farm,

$$\bar{\mu} = \frac{1}{5}(30 + 30 + 20 + 10 + 0) = 18,$$

while the population variance is

$$\tau^2 = \frac{1}{5-1}((30-18)^2+(30-18)^2+(20-18)^2+(10-18)^2+(0-18)^2) = 170.$$

The estimates $\bar{x}$ and s^2 for each possible sample of size 2 are also shown in table 17.1.

From the information in table 17.1 the distribution of $\bar{X}$ and S^2 can be computed since each sample has probability 1/10. These distributions are shown in tables 17.2 and 17.3 with f being the point probability.

Table 17.2. The distribution of $\bar{X}$.

$\bar{x}$	5	10	15	20	25	30
$f(\bar{x})$	0.1	0.1	0.3	0.2	0.2	0.1

From table 17.2 it follows that $\bar{X}$ is unbiased, since

$$E[\bar{X}] = 5 \cdot 0.1 + 10 \cdot 0.1 + 15 \cdot 0.3 + 20 \cdot 0.2 + 25 \cdot 0.2 + 30 \cdot 0.1 = 18.$$

Table 17.3. The distribution of S^2.

s^2	0	50	200	450
$f(s^2)$	0.1	0.4	0.3	0.2

In the same way, the mean of S^2 can be computed from table 17.3 as

$$E[S^2] = 0 \cdot 0.1 + 50 \cdot 0.4 + 200 \cdot 0.3 + 450 \cdot 0.2 = 170,$$

showing that S^2 is an unbiased estimator of τ^2. △.

Example 17.1 (continued)

Assume that the sample size be chosen so that the estimated percentage of voters, $\hat{\theta}$, intending to vote for the Social Democratic Party, with probability 0.95 differs less than 2% from the true value θ. In other words, it is required that

$$P(|\hat{\theta}-\theta| \leq 0.02) \geq 0.95.$$

According to (17.5), $\tau^2 = \frac{N}{N-1}\theta(1-\theta)$, so that a lower limit n_0 for the required sample size is given by (17.18), with $L_0 = 0.04$ and $u_{1-\alpha/2} = 1.96$, if θ is known. The voter percentage θ for the Social Democratic Party is usually around 0.35, and since $\theta(1-\theta)$ as a function of θ is relatively stable between 0.3 and 0.4, $\theta = 0.35$ can be used in the expression for τ^2. The total number of voters in Denmark is $N = 3\ 700\ 000$. Hence, the sample size should be at least

$$n \geq \frac{0.35 \cdot 0.65}{(0.04/3.92)^2 + 0.35 \cdot 0.65/3\ 700\ 000} = 2184.$$

The error arising from using $\theta = 0.35$ rather than the unknown true value of θ in the formula of τ^2 can be illustrated by computing n_0 for two neighbouring values of θ. Inserting $\theta = 0.32$ in the expression for τ^2 gives $n_0 = 2092$, and $\theta = 0.38$ gives $n_0 = 2264$. Sample sizes around 1000-1500 are normally used in political polls in Denmark. △.

17.5. Stratified sampling

For simple random sampling the precision of an estimate of $\bar{\mu}$ depends on the sample size n, the population variance τ^2 and the size of the population N. Since N and τ^2 are both fixed quantities, the only way to improve the precision is to increase the sample size. This is often both costly and organizationally complicated. Hence, it is important to improve the precision of the estimate without enlarging the sample, and this can be done if there is some supplementary information on the distribution of the variable to be measured in the population.

Suppose that the population can be divided into m **strata** in such a way that the variation of the variable under consideration is less within a stratum than from stratum to stratum. An estimate with improved precision can then be obtained through **stratified sampling**, i.e. a sample design where the proportion of the sample selected from a given stratum is decided a priori.

A population consisting of N units is divided into m strata. Let the number of units in stratum j be N_j and $\mu_{\nu j}$ be the value of the variable under consideration for the ν'th individual in stratum j. Then

$$\bar{\mu}_j = \frac{1}{N_j} \sum_{\nu=1}^{N_j} \mu_{\nu j}, \quad j=1,\ldots,m,$$

is called the **stratum mean** for stratum j. The population mean can obviously be written

(17.20) $$\bar{\mu} = \frac{1}{N} \sum_{j=1}^{m} N_j \bar{\mu}_j = \sum_{j=1}^{m} W_j \bar{\mu}_j,$$

where the quantities $W_j = N_j/N$, $j=1,\ldots,m$, are called **stratum weights**. For stratum j the **stratum variance** is defined as

(17.21) $$\tau_j^2 = \frac{1}{N_j - 1} \sum_{\nu=1}^{N_j} (\mu_{\nu j} - \bar{\mu}_j)^2$$

A sample design where a sample of size n_j is selected from stratum j by simple random sampling without replacement, and the units from stratum j are selected independently of the selections of the units from the remaining samples is called **stratified random sampling without replacement**. The total sample is composed of the samples of the m strata, and the total sample size is

$$n = n_1 + n_2 + \ldots + n_m.$$

Stratified sampling is illustrated in fig. 17.1.

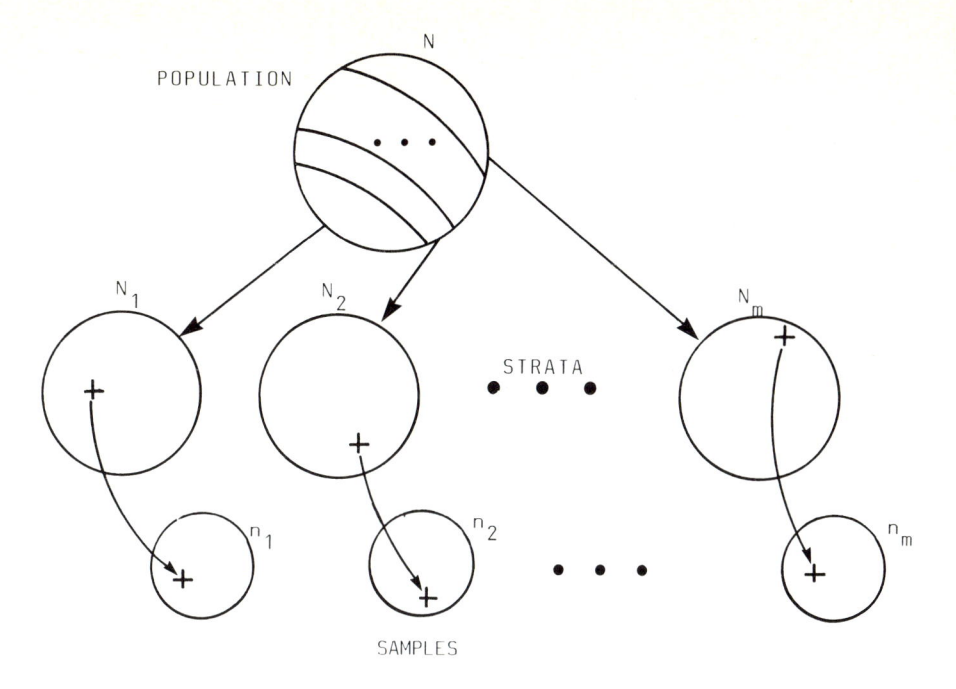

Fig. 17.1. Illustration of stratified sampling.

Let x_{ij} be the observed value for the i'th unit selected from stratum j. The sample mean from stratum j is given by

$$(17.22) \qquad \bar{x}_j = \frac{1}{n_j} \sum_{i=1}^{n_j} x_{ij}$$

and the sample variance from stratum j by

$$(17.23) \qquad s_j^2 = \frac{1}{n_j - 1} \sum_{i=1}^{n_j} (x_{ij} - \bar{x}_j)^2.$$

The population mean $\bar{\mu}$ is estimated by

$$(17.24) \qquad \bar{x}_S = \frac{1}{N} \sum_{j=1}^{m} N_j \bar{x}_j = \sum_{j=1}^{m} W_j \bar{x}_j,$$

and the corresponding estimator is

$$(17.25) \qquad \bar{X}_S = \sum_{j=1}^{m} W_j \bar{X}_j$$

where
$$\bar{X}_j = \frac{1}{n_j} \sum_{i=1}^{n_j} X_{ij},$$

and X_{ij} is the random variable corresponding to x_{ij}.

Theorem 17.3

Under stratified random sampling without replacement, $\bar{X}_S$ is an unbiased estimator of $\bar{\mu}$ with variance

(17.26) $$\text{var}[\bar{X}_S] = \sum_{j=1}^{m} W_j^2 \frac{\tau_j^2}{n_j} (1-f_j),$$

where
$$f_j = n_j/N_j.$$

Proof

The estimator $\bar{X}_S$ is unbiased since

$$E[\bar{X}_S] = E\left[\sum_{j=1}^{m} W_j \bar{X}_j\right] = \sum_{j=1}^{m} W_j \bar{\mu}_j = \bar{\mu}.$$

Furthermore, from theorem 17.2

$$\text{var}[\bar{X}_S] = \text{var}\left[\sum_{j=1}^{m} W_j \bar{X}_j\right] = \sum_{j=1}^{m} W_j^2 \text{var}[\bar{X}_j] = \sum_{j=1}^{m} \frac{W_j^2 \tau_j^2}{n_j}(1-f_j). \quad \square$$

An unbiased estimator of $\text{var}[\bar{X}_S]$ is

(17.27) $$\widehat{\text{var}}[\bar{X}_S] = \sum_{j=1}^{m} \frac{W_j^2 S_j^2}{n_j}(1-f_j),$$

where S_j^2, given by (17.23), is an unbiased estimator of τ_j^2 since the sampling is simple random without replacement within each stratum. If all stratum sizes are large and the sample size n_j for each stratum is also reasonably large but small compared to N_j, $\bar{X}_S$ is approximately normally distributed. An approximate $1-\alpha$ confidence interval is then given by

(17.28) $$\bar{x}_S \pm u_{1-\alpha/2}\sqrt{\widehat{\text{var}}[\bar{X}_S]},$$

where $\widehat{\text{var}}[\bar{X}_S]$ is obtained from (17.27).

It is essential for a successful application of stratified sampling that the stratification, i.e. the distribution of the population over strata, is suitable for the purpose. In many situations, the stratification of the population is given a priori for administrative or other reasons. In other situations, the stratification can be based on statistical considerations, such as the estimates having minimum variance.

Suppose that the stratification is given beforehand and that the problem is to allocate a sample of given size n to the strata. A distribution of a sample over the strata is usually referred to as an **allocation of the sample**. An allocation can be specified by the **selection ratios**

(17.29) $f_j = n_j/N_j, \quad j=1,\ldots,m.$

It follows from theorem 17.3 that the precision of the estimator $\overline{X}_S$ depends on the allocation, so it is possible to improve the precision by choosing a suitable allocation.

Proportional allocation refers to the case where the selection ratios are

$$f_j = n_j/N_j = n/N, \quad j=1,\ldots,m,$$

i.e. the contribution to the sample from stratum j is proportional to the stratum weight W_j, since $n_j/N_j = n/N$ is equivalent to $n_j/n = N_j/N = W_j$.

An allocation for which the variance of $\overline{X}_S$ is minimized is called an **optimal allocation**.

Theorem 17.4

For a given stratification and a given sample size, the optimal allocation is given by

(17.30) $n_j = \dfrac{W_j \tau_j}{\sum\limits_{i=1}^{m} W_i \tau_i} n, \quad j=1,\ldots,m.$

Proof

The variance (17.26) is to be minimized with respect to $n_1,\ldots,n_m$ under the constraint $\Sigma n_j = n$. This can be done by minimizing (17.26) with respect to $n_1,\ldots,n_{m-1}$ and n_m replaced by $n-n_1-\ldots-n_{m-1}$. If the n_j's are assumed technically to have a continuous variation, partial differentiation yields

$$\frac{\partial \mathrm{var}[\overline{X}_S]}{\partial n_j} = -W_j^2 \tau_j^2/n_j^2 + W_m^2 \tau_m^2/n_m^2, \quad j=1,\ldots,m-1.$$

The solution to the equations

$$\text{var}[\overline{X}] \simeq \frac{1-f}{n}\left(\sum_j W_j \tau_j^2 + \sum_j W_j(\overline{\mu}_j - \overline{\mu})^2\right),$$

and (17.26) gives

(17.32) $\quad \text{var}[\overline{X}] - \text{var}[\overline{X}_S] \simeq \frac{1-f}{n}\sum_j W_j(\overline{\mu}_j - \overline{\mu})^2 + \sum_j \left(\frac{1}{n} - \frac{W_j}{n_j}\right) W_j \tau_j^2.$

The difference (17.32) may under unfavourable circumstances be negative, making the estimates under stratified sampling less precise than under simple random sampling. The first term on the right hand side in (17.32) is always non-negative, but the second may be negative and larger in magnitude than the first, depending on the values of n_j. For example, this would be the case if $\overline{\mu}_j = \overline{\mu}$ for all j, $n_j/n < W_j$ for strata where τ_j^2 is large and $n_j/n > W_j$ when τ_j^2 is small. This result suggests the need for care in the allocation of the sample over the strata.

Given the validity of the approximation (17.32), proportional allocation is at least as good as simple random sampling. In fact, the difference (17.32) between $\text{var}[\overline{X}]$ and $\text{var}[\overline{X}_S]$ is

(17.33) $\quad \text{var}[\overline{X}] - \text{var}[\overline{X}_p] \simeq \frac{1-f}{n} \sum_j W_j (\overline{\mu}_j - \overline{\mu})^2$

for proportional allocation where the subscript P indicates proportional allocation. This expression shows that the larger the differences between the stratum means, the more is gained by using stratified sampling with a proportional allocation rather than simple random sampling.

By definition, $\text{var}[\overline{X}_S]$ is less for optimal allocation than for proportional allocation. The gain in precision with stratified sampling and optimal allocation over simple random sampling is derived from (17.32) by inserting the n_j's given by (17.30). This yields

(17.34) $\quad \text{var}[\overline{X}] - \text{var}[\overline{X}_0] \simeq \frac{1-f}{n}\sum_j W_j(\overline{\mu}_j - \overline{\mu})^2 + \frac{1}{n}\sum_j W_j(\tau_j - \overline{\tau})^2$

where $\overline{\tau} = \sum_j W_j \tau_j$ and the subscript O indicates optimal allocation. Equation (17.34) shows that stratified sampling with an optimal allocation improves the precision of the estimate both when, as for proportional allocation, the stratum means are different, and when the stratum variances $\tau_1^2, \ldots, \tau_m^2$ are different. The stratification depends, however, on the τ_j's, so that at least approximations to the τ_j's must be available when the allocation is determined. In most cases, estimates of the stratum variances based on earlier sample surveys or pilot studies are used. It must be stressed, however, that if for some reason the estimates of the τ_j's used in the allocation formula (17.30) are

$$\frac{\partial \text{var}[\overline{X}_S]}{\partial n_j} = 0, \quad j=1,\ldots,m-1,$$

must accordingly satisfy

$$W_j^2 \tau_j^2 / n_j^2 = K,$$

where K is a certain constant, or

$$n_j = W_j \tau_j / \sqrt{K}, \quad j=1,\ldots,m-1.$$

From the condition $n = \Sigma n_j$ it then follows that

$$n_j = n W_j \tau_j / (\sum_{i=1}^{m} W_i \tau_i), \quad j=1,\ldots,m,$$

and it can be shown that these values in fact minimize (17.26). □.

It follows from (17.30) that proportional and optimal allocation are identical if all stratum variances are equal. The larger the differences between the stratum variances the larger the gain in precision obtained by optimal allocation compared to proportional allocation. For more precise comparisons of the variances of the various estimators of the population mean, consider the following decomposition of the total variation in the population:

$$(17.31) \quad (N-1)\tau^2 = \sum_{j\nu}\sum(\mu_{\nu j} - \overline{\mu})^2 = \sum_{j\nu}\sum(\mu_{\nu j} - \overline{\mu}_j)^2 + \sum_j N_j(\overline{\mu}_j - \overline{\mu})^2$$

$$= \sum_j (N_j - 1)\tau_j^2 + \sum_j N_j(\overline{\mu}_j - \overline{\mu})^2,$$

where $\sum_{j\nu}\sum(\mu_{\nu j} - \overline{\mu}_j)^2$ is called the **variation within strata** and $\sum_j N_j(\overline{\mu}_j - \overline{\mu})^2$ the **variation between strata**. In most applications all stratum sizes are large, so the approximations

$$(N_j - 1)/N_j \simeq 1, \quad j=1,2,\ldots,m,$$

and

$$(N-1)/N \simeq 1,$$

allow the decomposition above to be written

$$\tau^2 \simeq \sum_j W_j \tau_j^2 + \sum_j W_j (\overline{\mu}_j - \overline{\mu})^2.$$

Inserting this expression in (17.12) yields

clearly different from the true τ_j's, then the allocation is no longer optimal, and the improvement arising from use of an optimal rather than a proportional allocation may disappear.

In many sample surveys, more than one variable is considered and it must be noted that an allocation which is optimal with respect to the estimation of the population mean for one variable need not be optimal for the estimation of the population mean of another variable. In such situations, a proportional allocation is often a satisfactory compromise.

For a given allocation, assume that the sample size must be chosen so large that $\text{var}[\bar{X}_S] \leq \sigma_0^2$. In other words, according to (17.26) n should with $w_j = n_j/n$ satisfy

$$\sum_{j=1}^{m} \frac{W_j^2 \tau_j^2}{w_j n} (1 - w_j n/N_j) = \Sigma W_j^2 \tau_j^2 / (w_j n) - \Sigma W_j \tau_j^2 / N \leq \sigma_0^2.$$

Solving this inequality with respect to n yields

(17.35) $\qquad n \geq n_0 = \dfrac{\Sigma W_j^2 \tau_j^2 / w_j}{\sigma_0^2 + \Sigma W_j \tau_j^2 / N}.$

Alternatively, it could be required that $\bar{X}_S$ with probability $1-\alpha$ must not differ more than ε from $\bar{\mu}$. This requirement can also be stated as

(17.36) $\qquad P(|\bar{X}_S - \bar{\mu}| \geq \varepsilon) \leq \alpha,$

or equivalently

$$P\left(\frac{|\bar{X}_S - \bar{\mu}|}{\sigma_S} \geq \frac{\varepsilon}{\sigma_S}\right) \leq \alpha,$$

where $\sigma_S^2 = \text{var}[\bar{X}_S]$.

Hence, if the conditions for an approximate normal distribution of $\bar{X}_S$ are satisfied, the requirement is satisfied if

$$\frac{\varepsilon}{\sigma_S} \geq u_{1-\alpha/2},$$

or

(17.37) $\qquad \text{var}[\bar{X}_S] \leq (\varepsilon/u_{1-\alpha/2})^2.$

It follows that the sample size must satisfy inequality (17.35) with σ_0^2 replaced by $(\varepsilon/u_{1-\alpha/2})^2$.

Example 17.3

Consider the problem of estimating the number of inhabitants $\bar{\mu}$ per household in Denmark based on a sample survey. It is required that the estimate of $\bar{\mu}$ with probability 0.95 differs less than 0.1 from the true value of $\bar{\mu}$. If stratified sampling is used, this corresponds to putting $\alpha=0.05$ and $\varepsilon=0.1$ in (17.36). It follows then from (17.37) that $\text{var}[\bar{X}_S]$ must be less than or equal to

(17.38) $\sigma_0^2 = (0.1)^2/(1.96)^2 = 0.002603$.

Also with simple random sampling the requirement is met if (17.38) is an upper limit for $\text{var}[\bar{X}]$.

The actual distribution of households in Denmark on January 1st 1981 according to number of rooms and number of inhabitants is shown in table 17.4.

Table 17.4. Households in Denmark in 1981 distributed according to number of rooms and number of inhabitants.

Number of inhabitants	1	2	3	4	5	6	7	Total
1	87560	217074	143995	87145	31283	11886	8370	587313
2	9688	101649	198572	186578	82262	33912	24947	638008
3	1837	17301	73707	119407	62327	26327	20522	322068
4	878	6470	43257	120493	86273	40867	30696	328934
5	357	1695	10319	30898	31316	18963	19593	113141
6	153	415	2487	6578	6134	4453	6973	27193
7	51	106	554	1568	1312	1002	2204	6837
≥ 8	167	59	314	758	674	464	1824	4260
Total	100691	344769	473645	553425	301581	138514	115129	2027754

Source: The Household Count 1981. Danmarks Statistik.

From table 17.4 a number of quantities of importance for the planning of a sample survey can be computed. The population mean and variance are given by

$$\bar{\mu} = 2.4441$$

and

$$\tau^2 = 1.7767$$

if it is assumed that no households have more than 8 inhabitants. With simple random sampling, the smallest number n_0 satisfying the above requirement is according to (17.17)

$$n_0 \approx \frac{\tau^2}{\sigma_0^2 + \tau^2/N} = \frac{1.7767}{0.002603 + 1.7767/2027754}.$$

With simple random sampling without replacement and sample size $n_0 = 683$, the average number of rooms can be estimated with the required precision provided that the population variance τ^2 at the time of the sampling is still approximately equal to 1.7767.

Not surprisingly, table 17.4 shows that the number of inhabitants varies with the number of rooms. A stratification according to number of rooms, therefore, implies that the stratum means of the number of inhabitants can also be expected to vary from stratum to stratum. This is one of the conditions for a stratification to be successful. Let the population be divided into seven strata according to the number of rooms of the household. The proportional and the optimal allocations for this stratification are shown in table 17.5, still assuming that no household has more than 8 inhabitants.

Table 17.5. The proportional and the optimal allocation for a stratification according to rooms.

Stratum/ number of rooms	$\bar{\mu}_j$	W_j	τ_j^2	τ_j	$n_j = 683 W_j$	$n_j = 683 W_j \tau_j / \Sigma W_i \tau_i$
j=1	1.195	0.0497	0.4038	0.6354	34	19
2	1.480	0.1700	0.5621	0.7497	116	78
3	2.131	0.2336	1.1431	1.0692	159	153
4	2.731	0.2729	1.5223	1.2338	186	206
5	3.103	0.1487	1.6870	1.2989	102	118
6	3.295	0.0683	1.8328	1.3538	47	56
7	3.581	0.0568	2.3824	1.5373	39	53
Sum	2.444[1]	1.0000	1.3083[1]	1.1184[1]	683	683

1) Weighted sum.

A comparison of the proportional and the optimal allocations shows that under an optimal allocation relatively fewer households are selected from strata with small stratum variances and relatively more households from strata with large variances. The variance of the estimate of $\bar{\mu}$ for various sample designs and allocations can be computed from (17.12) and (17.26). For simple random sampling

$$\text{var}[\bar{X}] = 0.002601$$

and for stratified sampling

$$\text{var}[\bar{X}_S] = \begin{cases} 0.001916 & \text{for proportional allocation} \\ 0.001831 & \text{for optimal allocation} \end{cases}$$

The variance is thus reduced by 36.8% if proportional allocation is chosen instead of simple random sampling. If optimal instead of proportional allocation is chosen, the gain in precision is only 4.4%. These results are quite typical. A considerable gain is often achieved by choosing proportional sampling instead of simple random sampling when the variable under consideration varies from stratum to stratum. The gain in precision obtained from optimal instead of proportional allocation is often moderate. △.

The formulas for stratified sampling are somewhat simpler in the binary case. According to (17.4)

$$\tau_j^2 = \frac{N_j}{N_j - 1} \theta_j (1 - \theta_j)$$

where θ_j is the proportion of marked units in the j'th stratum. It can also be seen that the sample mean $\bar{x}_j$ in stratum j is equal to the observed proportion $\hat{\theta}_j$ of marked units in stratum j. From (17.6) and (17.14), the sample variance in the j'th stratum is given by

$$s_j^2 = \frac{n_j}{n_j - 1} \hat{\theta}_j (1 - \hat{\theta}_j).$$

One of the features that characterizes the binary case is the dependency between the stratum mean θ_j and the stratum variance, which often implies that only little is gained using optimal rather than proportional allocation.

Example 17.4

The aim of a political poll in Denmark is to estimate the proportion of voters who would vote for the Liberal Party if there were an election on the following day. Combining various counties and voting districts, the 8 strata listed in table 17.6 can be formed. If the budget allows for a total sample size of n=2000, the optimal and the proportional allocation over strata are shown in table 17.7. Since the Danish electorate is large, $\tau_j^2 = \sqrt{\theta_j(1-\theta_j)}$ has been used in (17.30) to compute the optimal allocation, where the θ_j's, shown in table 17.6, are the results of the last election in February, 1977. The quantities τ_j, $j=1,\ldots,8$, are also shown in table 17.7. It follows from this table that with an optimal allocation, fewer units are selected from strata where τ_j is small, i.e. where the percentage of liberal voters is small.

Table 17.6. Liberal voters distributed over 8 regional strata. General Election 1977.

	Number of voters	Proportion of Liberal voters
City of Copenhagen	413249	2.9
Copenhagen County	385567	4.8
Zealand (outside Copenhagen)	622242	12.0
Bornholm	28828	23.4
Funen	274938	13.0
Mid- and West Jutland	411641	21.2
South and East Jutland	684358	13.5
Northern Jutland	285474	15.6
Total	3106297	12.0

Source: Statistical Yearbook. Danmarks Statistik. 1978.

Table 17.7. Proportional and optimal allocation for the estimation of Liberal voters in Denmark.

Stratum	Proportional allocation	τ_j	Optimal allocation
City of Copenhagen	266	0.1678	144
Copenhagen County	248	0.2138	171
Zealand (outside Copenhagen)	401	0.3250	419
Bornholm	19	0.4234	25
Funen	177	0.3360	192
Mid- and West Jutland	265	0.4087	349
South and East Jutland	440	0.3417	485
Northern Jutland	184	0.3629	215
Total	2000		2000

The variance of $\overline{X}_S$, computed from the figures in tables 17.6 and 17.7, is

$$\text{var}[\overline{X}_S] = \begin{cases} 0.0000510 & \text{for proportional allocation} \\ 0.0000482 & \text{for optimal allocation.} \end{cases}$$

It may be rather surprising, though not unusual, that there are substantial differences between the optimal and the proportional allocation, but that the estimates of θ have approximately the same precision.

For simple random sampling, the variance is

$$\text{var}[\hat{\theta}] = 0.0000528$$

according to (17.5) with n=2000 and θ=0.12. Thus little is gained in this case by using stratified sampling rather than simple random sampling.

As noted earlier, an allocation which is optimal for one variable is not necessarily optimal for other variables. This can be illustrated by deriving the optimal allocation for the estimation of the proportion of voters intending to vote for the Socialist Peoples Party. The results from the General Election in February, 1977, are used. Table 17.8 shows the number voting for the Socialist Peoples Party (SF) in the election, together with the optimal and the proportional allocation. It is striking that in order to measure the strength of a socialist party with an optimal allocation fewer individuals need to be selected in Jutland and more in the Copenhagen area, compared to proportional allocation. △.

Table 17.8. Optimal and proportional allocation for the estimation of the percentage of Socialist Peoples Party (SF) voters in 1977.

Stratum	The percentage of SF votes	Optimal allocation	Proportional allocation
City of Copenhagen	5.4	328	266
Copenhagen County	4.1	269	248
Zealand (outside Copenhagen)	3.3	391	401
Bornholm	2.3	15	19
Funen	4.0	189	177
Mid- and West Jutland	2.0	203	265
South and East Jutland	3.6	448	440
Northern Jutland	2.5	157	184
Total		2000	2000

18. Applications of the Multinomial Distribution

18.1. Hypothesis testing in the multinomial distribution

A discrete random variable $(X_1, \ldots, X_m)$ is multinomially distributed if its point probabilities are

$$f(x_1, \ldots, x_m) = \binom{n}{x_1, \ldots, x_m} p_1^{x_1} \cdots p_m^{x_m}$$

where $x_1 + \ldots + x_m = n$ and $p_1 + \ldots + p_m = 1$. Conditions for $(X_1, \ldots, X_m)$ to be multinomially distributed were given in sections 6.4 and 8.9.

The statistical analysis of data $x_1, \ldots, x_m$, which can be described by a multinomial distribution, often takes as its starting point a comparison of the observed frequencies $x_1/n, \ldots, x_m/n$ of the m categories with a set of probability parameters $p_1, \ldots, p_m$, or, equivalently, a comparison of the observed numbers $x_1, \ldots, x_m$ with their expected values $np_1, \ldots, np_m$. If the agreement between the observed and expected numbers is satisfactory in a statistical sense, the multinomial distribution with parameters $(n, p_1, \ldots, p_m)$ is assumed to describe the data. A measure of the degree of agreement is provided by the quantity

$$(18.1) \qquad q = \sum_{i=1}^{m} (x_i - np_i)^2 / np_i \ .$$

The random variable corresponding to (18.1) is

$$(18.2) \qquad Q = \sum_{i=1}^{m} (X_i - np_i)^2 / np_i \ ,$$

whose exact distribution in general is difficult to derive. If n is sufficiently large and none of the p_i's are too small, this distribution can, however, be approximated by a χ^2-distribution.

Theorem 18.1
Suppose $(X_1, \ldots, X_m)$ follows a multinomial distribution with parameters $(n, p_1, \ldots, p_m)$. Then with Q given by (18.2)

$$P(Q \leq q) \to F(q) \quad \text{for } n \to \infty,$$

for all q>0, where F is the distribution function of a χ^2-distribution with m-1 degrees of freedom.

From theorem 18.1, it follows that the distribution of Q can be approximated by a χ^2-distribution with m-1 degrees of freedom if n is sufficiently large. The actual requirement to be met by n depends on the p_i's. The closer some of these are to zero, the larger a value of n is required to guarantee a satisfactory approximation by the χ^2-distribution. Usually the approximation is considered valid if $np_i \geq 5$ for i=1,...,m. In many situations, the condition $np_i \geq 5$ can, however, be relaxed to allow expected numbers np_i as low as one, as long as this only occurs for a small proportion of the categories.

The quantities $x_i - np_i$, i=1,...,m, measure the agreement between the data and the multinomial distribution with parameters $(n, p_1, ..., p_m)$. The larger the differences, the less satisfactory the agreement. Hence, q can be used as a summary measure of agreement between data and model. If $x_1, ..., x_m$ are assumed to be observations of multinomially distributed random variables $X_1, ..., X_m$ with parameters $(n, p_1, ..., p_m)$,

$$Q = \sum_{i=1}^{m} (X_i - np_{i0})^2 / np_{i0}$$

can accordingly be used as a test statistic for the hypothesis

(18.3) $\quad p_i = p_{i0}, \quad i=1,...,m,$

with approximate level of significance

(18.4) $\quad p = P(Q \geq q)$

where $Q \sim \chi^2(m-1)$.

Example 18.1

Table 18.1 shows the observed number of traffic accidents involving pedestrians in Denmark in 1981 distributed according to the day of the week. The hypothesis under consideration is that traffic accidents involving pedestrians are uniformly distributed over the 7 days of the week. Let $x_1, ..., x_7$ be the observed number of accidents on each of the days of the week. If the 1739 accidents can be regarded as independent events, the hypothesis of a uniform distribution of accidents over the

7 days of the week can be expressed as

$$(X_1,\ldots,X_m) \sim M(1739, 1/7, \ldots, 1/7)$$

where X_i is the random variable corresponding to x_i. The expected numbers np_{i0} are shown in table 18.1 together with the differences $x_i - np_{i0}$ and the individual terms in (18.1). As can be seen, the condition $np_{i0} \geq 5$ is satisfied.

Table 18.1. Comparison of observed and expected numbers of accidents involving pedestrians.

Week day	x_i	np_{i0}	$x_i - np_{i0}$	$(x_i - np_{i0})^2/np_{i0}$
Monday	279	248.4	30.6	3.8
Tuesday	256	248.4	7.6	0.2
Wednesday	230	248.4	-18.4	1.4
Thursday	304	248.4	55.6	12.4
Friday	330	248.4	81.6	26.8
Saturday	210	248.4	-38.4	5.9
Sunday	130	248.4	-118.4	54.4
Sum	1739	1738.8	0.2	104.9

Source: Road traffic accidents 1981. Danmarks Statistik.

The large deviations between observed and expected numbers are reflected in q=104.9. With 7-1=6 degrees of freedom the level of significance is approximately

$$p = (Q \geq 104.9) \ll 0.0005 ,$$

where the symbol "$\ll$" means that p is much smaller than 0.0005. Thus, a multinomial distribution with $p_i = 1/7$, $i=1,\ldots,7$ does not fit the data, and accidents involving pedestrians cannot be assumed to occur with the same expected frequency on each day of the week. Note from table 18.1 that expected values and the value of q are usually computed with one decimal point. $\triangle$.

The result of theorem 18.1 is used whenever the data are compared with a multinomial distribution with known values of the probability parameters. In practice, however, problems frequently occur in which these parameters depend on k<m-1 unknown parameters $\theta_1,\ldots,\theta_k$, whereby

the hypothesis of interest is

(18.5) $H_0: p_i = p_i(\theta_1,\ldots,\theta_k)$, $i=1,\ldots,m$,

where p_i is a known function of $\theta_1,\ldots,\theta_k$. In order to compare observed and expected numbers by a test statistic similar to (18.2), it is necessary to estimate $\theta_1,\ldots,\theta_k$ from the data. The likelihood function for the observations $x_1,\ldots,x_m$ is given by

$$L(\theta_1,\ldots,\theta_k) = K \prod_{i=1}^{m} p_i(\theta_1,\ldots,\theta_k)^{x_i}$$

where K is the multinomial coefficient (6.21). Differentiation of $\ln L$ yields the likelihood equations

(18.6) $\dfrac{\partial \ln L(\theta_1,\ldots,\theta_k)}{\partial \theta_j} = \sum_{i=1}^{m} x_i \dfrac{\partial \ln p_i(\theta_1,\ldots,\theta_k)}{\partial \theta_j} = 0$, $j=1,\ldots,k$.

Usually these equations have a unique solution which can be shown to be the ML-estimate $\hat{\theta}_1,\ldots,\hat{\theta}_k$ for $\theta_1,\ldots,\theta_k$, and the fit of the model under the hypothesis (18.5) can then be evaluated by the quantity

(18.7) $q = \sum_{i=1}^{m} (x_i - n\hat{p}_i)^2/n\hat{p}_i$,

where $\hat{p}_i = p_i(\hat{\theta}_1,\ldots,\hat{\theta}_k)$.

Theorem 18.2
Suppose $X_1,\ldots,X_m$ follow a multinomial distribution with parameters $(n, p_1,\ldots,p_m)$ where $p_i = p_i(\theta_1,\ldots,\theta_k)$ and let $\hat{\theta}_1,\ldots,\hat{\theta}_k$ be the ML-estimators for $\theta_1,\ldots,\theta_k$. Then with

(18.8) $Q = \sum_{i=1}^{m} (X_i - n\hat{p}_i)^2/(n\hat{p}_i)$

and $\hat{p}_i = p_i(\hat{\theta}_1,\ldots,\hat{\theta}_k)$, $i=1,\ldots,m$,

$$P(Q \leq q) \to F(q) \quad \text{for } n \to \infty$$

for all $q > 0$, where F is the distribution function of a χ^2-distribution with $m-k-1$ degrees of freedom.

This theorem implies that the distribution of Q can be approximated by a χ^2-distribution for n sufficiently large. The approximation is usually considered to be valid if $np_i \geq 5$ for $i=1,\ldots,m$. If the data are multinomially distributed, Q can be used as a test statistic for the hypothesis (18.5) since the larger the value of q, defined by (18.7), the less the hypothesis is supported by the data. The level of significance can be approximated by

(18.9) $\qquad p = P(Q \geq q)$

where $Q \sim \chi^2(m-k-1)$. For a fixed level α, the critical region consists of values q for which $q > \chi^2_{1-\alpha}(m-k-1)$.

Example 18.2

Suppose it is postulated that the accidents considered in example 18.1 occur with the same frequency on the five first days of the week and with the same (but presumably lower) frequency on Saturdays and Sundays. This means that $p_1 = p_2 = p_3 = p_4 = p_5$ and $p_6 = p_7$. Let θ be the probability that a randomly chosen accident occurs on a Monday. The hypothesis to be tested is then

(18.10) $\qquad p_i = \begin{cases} \theta & , i=1,\ldots,5 \\ (1-5\theta)/2, & i=6,7 \end{cases}$

As is easily seen, (18.10) is a special case of (18.5) for k=1 and m=7. The derivatives of $\ln p_i(\theta)$ with respect to θ are

$$\frac{\partial \ln p_i(\theta)}{\partial \theta} = \frac{1}{\theta} \quad \text{for } i=1,\ldots,5 ,$$

and

$$\frac{\partial \ln p_i(\theta)}{\partial \theta} = \frac{-5}{1-5\theta} \quad \text{for } i=6,7 .$$

Inserting these expressions in (18.6) yields

$$\frac{\partial \ln L(\theta)}{\partial \theta} = \frac{x_1 + \ldots + x_5}{\theta} - \frac{5(x_6 + x_7)}{1-5\theta} = 0$$

with the solution

(18.11) $\qquad \hat{\theta} = (x_1 + \ldots + x_5)/5n ,$

since $x_1 + \ldots + x_7 = n$. With the observed values of n and $x_1, \ldots, x_7$, the ML-estimate of θ is thus $\hat{\theta} = 0.1609$. The expected values for the week days and the individual terms of q are shown in table 18.2. The observed value q=40.8 corresponds approximately to the level of significance

$$p = P(Q \geq 40.8) < 0.0005 .$$

The agreement between the model (18.10) and the data is still unsatisfactory, although the fit has improved considerably by introducing two levels of accident frequency.

Table 18.2. Comparison of observed and expected numbers of traffic accidents under the model (18.10).

Week day	x_i	$n\hat{p}_i$	$x_i - n\hat{p}_i$	$(x_i - n\hat{p}_i)^2 / n\hat{p}_i$
Monday	279	279.8	- 0.8	0.0
Tuesday	256	279.8	-23.8	2.0
Wednesday	230	279.8	-49.8	8.9
Thursday	304	279.8	24.2	2.1
Friday	330	279.8	50.2	9.0
Saturday	210	170.0	40.0	9.4
Sunday	130	170.0	-40.0	9.4
Sum	1739	1739.0	0.0	40.8

The column $x_i - n\hat{p}_i$ shows that Tuesday and Wednesday have less accidents than expected under the model and Thursday and Friday more accidents than expected. △.

A test of a hypothesis concerning the structure of the parameters of a multinomial distribution based on (18.1) or (18.7) is called a **Q-test**. The Q-tests are so-called **goodness-of-fit tests** since they evaluate the agreement between data and a model. It is essential for the application of Q-tests that $x_1, \ldots, x_m$ can indeed be regarded as an observation from a multinomial distribution. The number of degrees of freedom, f, of the χ^2-distribution, which approximates the distribution of Q, is given as

   f = number of categories minus 1 minus the number of
       estimated parameters.

This way of calculating the degrees of freedom can be justified intuitively. Firstly, it is reasonable to reduce the number of degrees of freedom when more parameters are introduced. In fact, the larger the number of estimated parameters, the better the expected numbers can be fitted to the observed numbers and the smaller the expected value of Q, i.e. the smaller the number of degrees of freedom. If no parameters are estimated, i.e. when the parameters $p_1,\ldots,p_m$ are fully specified, the number of degrees of freedom is equal to the number of terms of Q minus 1, which accounts for the linear constraint

$$\sum_{i=1}^{m} (x_i - np_i) = 0.$$

If a number of parameters are estimated, a new set of linear constraints are imposed corresponding to the likelihood equations (18.6). In a sense, it can be said, therefore, that a multinomial model has m-1 degrees of freedom which are reduced by the number of estimated parameters in the model under a hypothesis like (18.5). The remaining number of degrees of freedom, m-1-k, are then available for testing the goodness-of-fit of the model.

18.2. Goodness-of-fit tests of discrete distributions

Let $y_1,\ldots,y_n$ be independent observations from a discrete distribution. A common statistical problem is then to test the hypothesis that the distribution in question belongs to a given class of distributions, for example the class of Poisson distributions. Such hypotheses can be tested by a Q-test.

Consider first the situation where the class only contains one distribution with point probabilities $f(i)$, $i=0,1,\ldots,m$. It follows then from the independence of the y's that the m+1 counts

$$x_i = \text{number of observations equal to } i, \quad i=0,1,\ldots,m,$$

can be regarded as observations of multinomially distributed random variables $X_0,\ldots,X_m$ with parameters $(n,p_0,\ldots,p_m)$, where

(18.12) $p_i = f(i), \quad i=0,1,\ldots,m$.

The hypothesis (18.12) that the common distribution of the y's have point probabilities $f(0),\ldots,f(m)$ can accordingly be tested by means of the Q-test statistic

(18.13) $Q = \sum_{i=0}^{m} (X_i - np_i)^2 / (np_i)$.

Under (18.12), the distribution of Q can be approximated by a χ^2-distribution with m+1-1=m degrees of freedom. The larger the observed value of Q, the larger the disagreements between the observed values of the X's and the corresponding expected values under the hypothesis. Hence, the distribution with parameters given by (18.12) is rejected as a description of the data if the level of significance

$$p = P(Q \geq q)$$

is sufficiently small.

In most situations, the class of distributions assumed to have generated the y's is indexed by a set of parameters $\theta_1,\ldots,\theta_k$. The point probabilities thus have the form $p_i = f(i|\theta_1,\ldots,\theta_k)$, $i=0,1,\ldots,m$. The counts $(x_0,\ldots,x_m)$ can then be regarded as observed values of a multinomially distributed random variable $(X_0,\ldots,X_m)$ with parameters $(n,p_0,\ldots,p_m)$ where

(18.14) $\quad p_i = f(i|\theta_1,\ldots,\theta_k)$, $i=0,\ldots,m$.

A test of the hypothesis that $y_1,\ldots,y_n$ are independent observations from a discrete distribution with point probabilities $f(i|\theta_1,\ldots,\theta_k)$, $i=0,\ldots,m$, can, therefore, be based on the test statistic (18.8). Let thus $\hat{\theta}_1,\ldots,\hat{\theta}_k$ be the ML-estimators of the unknown parameters and let

(18.15) $\quad \hat{p}_i = f(i|\hat{\theta}_1,\ldots,\hat{\theta}_k)$, $i=0,\ldots,m$.

From theorem 18.2, it then follows that

(18.16) $\quad Q = \sum_{i=0}^{m} (X_i - n\hat{p}_i)^2/(n\hat{p}_i)$,

under the hypothesis (18.14), is approximately χ^2-distributed with $(m+1)-1-k = m-k$ degrees of freedom. The larger the observed value q of (18.16), the less likely it is that the y's are independent observations from a discrete distribution with point probabilities $f(i|\theta_1,\ldots,\theta_k)$, $i=0,\ldots,m$. The level of significance is given approximately by

(18.17) $\quad p = P(Q \geq q)$,

where $Q \sim \chi^2(m-k)$ and q is the observed value of Q.

If the sample space of the y's is countable, for example $S = \{0,1,2,\ldots\}$, the method above does not apply directly. Suppose, however, that the counts $x_0,\ldots,x_m$ are defined as

x_i = number of observations with value i, $i=0,\ldots,m-1$,

and

x_m = number of observations with values larger than or equal to m.

Then $(x_0,\ldots,x_m)$ can be regarded as an observation of the random variable

$$(X_0, X_1, \ldots, X_m) \sim M(n, p_0, p_1, \ldots, p_m) ,$$

where

(18.18) $\quad p_i = \begin{cases} f(i|\theta_1,\ldots,\theta_k) , & i=0,\ldots,m-1 , \\ \sum_{j=m}^{\infty} f(j|\theta_1,\ldots,\theta_k), & i=m. \end{cases}$

If $\hat{\theta}_1,\ldots,\hat{\theta}_k$ are the ML-estimates of $\theta_1,\ldots,\theta_k$ and if

$$\hat{p}_i = \begin{cases} f(i|\hat{\theta}_1,\ldots,\hat{\theta}_k) , & i=0,\ldots,m-1, \\ \sum_{j=m}^{\infty} f(j|\hat{\theta}_1,\ldots,\hat{\theta}_k), & i=m, \end{cases}$$

then the hypothesis that the y's are independent observations from a distribution with point probabilities $f(i|\theta_1,\ldots,\theta_k)$, $i=0,1,\ldots$ can be tested by the Q-test statistic (18.16). The asymptotic distribution of this test statistic can in principle be deduced from theorem 18.2. But for theorem 18.2 to apply, $\hat{p}_0,\ldots,\hat{p}_m$ must be based on the ML-estimates of $\theta_1,\ldots,\theta_k$ and it is often complicated to derive these ML-estimates because of the form of p_m. Fortunately, it can be shown that theorem 18.2 is still valid if the estimates $\hat{\theta}_1,\ldots,\hat{\theta}_k$ are derived as ML-estimates based on the log-likelihood function of the y's

$$\ln L(\theta_1,\ldots,\theta_k) = \sum_{j=1}^{n} \ln f(y_j|\theta_1,\ldots,\theta_k).$$

Hence, the Q-test statistic given by (18.16) is also approximately χ^2-distributed with m-k degrees of freedom when the sample space is countable. As for the other cases discussed above, the approximation is valid if $n\hat{p}_i \geq 5$ for $i=0,\ldots,m$. This requirement can be used to determine a convenient value of m in (18.18). But also when the sample space is finite, it may be necessary to group neighbouring categories to obtain estimated expected numbers larger than 5. The fact that the distribution of the test statistic can be approximated by a χ^2-distribution is not affected by a grouping of categories, but of course the number of degrees of freedom is affected. It is important to note, therefore, that the number of degrees of freedom is the number of actual terms in Q, minus 1, minus the number of estimated parameters.

When using the Q-test statistic to test the fit of a discrete distribution to a given data set, not only the magnitude of the observed value of Q, but also the sign variation of the differences between observed and expected numbers is of importance. For example, positive differences observed for low and high values of i, i.e. in the tails of the distribution, indicates that a better description of the data could be obtained by a class of distributions with heavier tails than the one under consideration. Likewise, positive differences for small values of i and negative differences for larger values of i, imply that an alternative class of more right skewed distributions should be considered. Attention must be paid to the sign pattern because the ordering of the outcomes in the sample space is usually of importance for the characterization of a discrete distribution. Such an ordering is not reflected in the observed value of the Q-test statistic.

Example 18.3

The distribution of the number of arrivals per time unit to the checkout at a supermarket was discussed in example 6.3. The observed distribution of arrivals per 2 minutes over a time period of 90 minutes is shown again in table 18.3. To test the fit of a Poisson distribution to these data, a Q-test is well suited.

The hypothesis to be tested is that the 45 observed numbers of arrivals are independent observations from a common Poisson distribution with unknown intensity λ. The point probabilities are thus given by

$$f(i|\lambda) = e^{-\lambda} \frac{\lambda^i}{i!}, \quad i = 0, 1, 2, \ldots .$$

Based on the observed numbers in table 18.3, the ML-estimate for λ is

$$\hat{\lambda} = \bar{x} = 1.76 .$$

Table 18.3. Q-test for the fit of a Poisson model.

Number of arrivals	x_i	$45\hat{p}_i$	$x_i - 45\hat{p}_i$	$(x_i - 45\hat{p}_i)^2 / 45\hat{p}_i$
0	6	7.7	-1.7	0.4
1	18	13.6	4.4	1.4
2	9	12.0	-3.0	0.8
3	7	7.0	0.0	0.0
4	4 ⎫ 5	3.1 ⎫ 4.7	0.3	0.0
≥ 5	1 ⎭	1.6 ⎭		
Sum	45	45.0	0.0	2.6

Under the hypothesis, the observed counts $(x_0,\ldots,x_5)=(6,18,9,7,4,1)$ are observations from a multinomial distribution with parameters

$$p_i = \begin{cases} e^{-\lambda}\dfrac{\lambda^i}{i!} , & i=0,1,\ldots,4, \\ \sum_{j=5}^{\infty} e^{-\lambda}\dfrac{\lambda^j}{j!} , & i=5. \end{cases}$$

From these expressions, the expected numbers $45\hat{p}_i$ in table 18.3 are computed with $\hat{\lambda}=1.76$. Table 18.3 also shows the differences $x_i - n\hat{p}_i$ and the individual terms of q. Since the estimated expected numbers are below 5 in the last two categories, these are grouped.

With only one category now having an expected number slightly below 5, the approximation to a χ^2-distribution can be considered satisfactory. The observed value of Q is q=2.6. This corresponds to the approximate level of significance

$$p = P(Q \geq 2.6) \simeq 0.4 .$$

Accordingly, it can be concluded that the Poisson distribution describes the data. △.

18.3. Goodness-of-fit tests of continuous distributions

The Q-test can also be used to check the agreement between continuous data and a continuous distribution. Let $y_1,\ldots,y_n$ be independent observations of a continuous random variable Y with density function

(18.19) $f(y|\theta_1,\ldots,\theta_k)$,

where $\theta_1,\ldots,\theta_k$ are unknown, real-valued parameters. In order to develop a Q-test statistic, the y-axis is split up into intervals by the points $t_0, t_1,\ldots,t_m$ with, if necessary, $t_0=-\infty$ and $t_m=+\infty$. These points define a grouped distribution $(x_0,\ldots,x_m)$ where x_i is the number of observations in the i'th interval $(t_{i-1}, t_i]$, $i=1,\ldots,m$. If $(X_1,\ldots,X_m)$ is the random variable corresponding to $(x_1,\ldots,x_m)$, then under the model (18.19), $(X_1,\ldots,X_m)$ follows a multinomial distribution with parameters $(n,p_1,\ldots,p_m)$, where p_i is the probability

(18.20) $p_i(\theta_1,\ldots,\theta_k) = \int_{t_{i-1}}^{t_i} f(y|\theta_1,\ldots,\theta_k)dy$

that an observation falls in the interval $(t_{i-1}, t_i]$. The hypothesis that the y's are independent observations with common density (18.19) can, therefore, be tested by the Q-test statistic

(18.21) $\quad Q = \sum_{i=1}^{m} (X_i - n\hat{p}_i)^2 / (n\hat{p}_i)$,

where

$$\hat{p}_i = \int_{t_{i-1}}^{t_i} f(y|\hat{\theta}_1, \ldots, \hat{\theta}_k) dy, \quad i=1, \ldots, m,$$

and $\hat{\theta}_1, \ldots, \hat{\theta}_k$ are the ML-estimates of $\theta_1, \ldots, \theta_k$. According to theorem 18.2, Q is approximately χ^2-distributed with m-1-k degrees of freedom, provided the ML-estimates are derived from the likelihood function

$$L(\theta_1, \ldots, \theta_k) = K \prod_{i=1}^{m} p_i(\theta_1, \ldots, \theta_k)^{X_i}$$

of the multinomial distribution of $(X_1, \ldots, X_m)$. The relationship between the p_i's and the θ_j's, as given by (18.20), is often of such a character that it is not feasible to solve the derived likelihood equations. Approximations to the $\hat{\theta}_j$'s can, however, be obtained from more simple equations which still lead to an asymptotic χ^2-distribution of the Q-test statistic. Instead of maximizing the likelihood equation $L(\theta_1, \ldots, \theta_k)$, it is possible to consider the approximate likelihood equation

(18.22) $\quad L_1(\theta_1, \ldots, \theta_k) = \prod_{i=1}^{m} f(t_i^* | \theta_1, \ldots, \theta_k)^{Z_i}$,

formed from the likelihood function of the original sample

$$\prod_{i=1}^{n} f(y_i | \theta_1, \ldots, \theta_k) ,$$

by locating all observations in the i'th interval at the interval midpoint $t_i^* = (t_i + t_{i-1})/2$. It can be shown also when $\hat{\theta}_1, \ldots, \hat{\theta}_k$ are obtained by maximizing (18.22) that the Q-test statistic (18.21) is asymptotically χ^2-distributed with m-1-k degrees of freedom. In most cases, it is straightforward to maximize (18.22).

Example 18.4

The Danish Ministry of Housing conducts regular checks of the Credit Associations in Denmark, in particular whether they comply with the law as regards the maximum level of mortgage as a percentage of the property value. The actual percentages, called credit percentages, were collected from 228 houses given credit in the third quarter 1981 by the credit association "Byggeriets Realkreditfond". The observed percentages are shown in table 18.4 with a convenient grouping. It is claimed that observed credit percentages follow a normal distribution. In order to check that the 228 observed credit percentages can be regarded as independent observations from a common normal distribution, a Q-test with test statistic (18.21) is performed. The estimates of $\theta_1=\mu$ and $\theta_2=\sigma^2$, when $f(x|\theta_1,\theta_2)$ is a normal density function, are obtained from (5.20) and (5.21) as

$$\bar{t} = \frac{1}{228} \sum_{i=1}^{12} t_i^* x_i \quad \text{and} \quad s^2 = \frac{1}{227} \sum_{i=1}^{12} (t_i^* - \bar{t})^2 x_i$$

where t_i^* is the midpoint of the i'th interval and x_i the number of observations in the interval.

Table 18.4. Q-test for normality of 228 credit percentages.

$t_{i-1}-t_i$	x_i	$228\hat{p}_i$	$x_i - 228\hat{p}_i$	$(x_i - 228\hat{p}_i)^2/228\hat{p}_i$
- 70	2	1.3	} 3.8	} 3.5
70 - 72	6	2.9		
72 - 74	6	7.1	- 1.1	0.2
74 - 76	8	14.5	- 6.5	2.9
76 - 78	21	24.5	- 3.5	0.5
78 - 80	38	35.1	2.9	0.2
80 - 82	50	39.5	10.5	2.8
82 - 84	40	37.5	2.5	0.2
84 - 86	18	29.4	-11.4	4.4
86 - 88	16	19.4	- 3.4	0.7
88 - 90	17	10.1	6.9	4.8
90 -	6	6.7	- 0.7	0.1
Sum	228	228.0	0.0	20.2

Source: Byggeriets Realkreditfond.

With $t_0=60.0$ and $t_{12}=100.0$, $\bar{t}=81.46$ and $s=4.52$. Based on these estimates, the estimated interval probabilities are obtained as

$$\hat{p}_i = \Phi\left(\frac{t_i-\bar{t}}{s}\right) - \Phi\left(\frac{t_{i-1}-\bar{t}}{s}\right).$$

The estimated expected values, the differences between the observed and expected numbers and the individual q-terms are shown in table 18.4.

Since the expected numbers are small in the first two intervals, these are grouped. The number of degrees of freedom for the approximating χ^2-distribution is, therefore, 11-1-2=8. With q=20.2, the level of significance is then 0.01, and the fit to the normal distribution is not satisfactory. The departures form normality are illustrated by the differences $x_i - 228\hat{p}_i$ in table 18.4. The observed distribution is flatter in the middle and has heavier tails than the normal distribution. △.

18.4. Comparison of k Poisson distributions

Suppose that the numbers of traffic accidents with serious personal injuries have been observed for the month of January in two consecutive years. As these numbers inevitably are different, it is of interest to evaluate whether the difference is due to a real change in the intensity of accidents or whether the difference is attributable to purely random variation within a certain statistical model. If the two observed numbers of accidents are assumed to be Poisson distributed and independent, the method of section 12.5 applies. This method can be generalized to cover the case of k distributions.

Theorem 18.3
Let $X_1,\ldots,X_k$ be independent Poisson distributed random variables with parameters $\lambda_1,\ldots,\lambda_k$. Then

$$(18.23) \quad (X_1,\ldots,X_k | X_. = x_.) \sim M(x_., \lambda_1/\lambda_., \ldots, \lambda_k/\lambda_.),$$

where $\lambda_. = \lambda_1 + \ldots + \lambda_k$, $X_. = X_1 + \ldots + X_k$ and $x_. = x_1 + \ldots + x_k$.

Proof
From theorem 8.11, it follows that $X_.$ is Poisson distributed with parameter $\lambda_.$. Hence the definition (3.10) of a conditional probability yields

$$P(X_1 = x_1, \ldots, X_k = x_k | X_. = x_.) = \frac{P(X_1 = x_1, \ldots, X_k = x_k)}{P(X_. = x_.)} =$$

$$\frac{\Pi e^{-\lambda_i} \dfrac{\lambda_i^{x_i}}{x_i!}}{e^{-\lambda_.} \dfrac{\lambda_.^{x_.}}{x_.!}} = \frac{x_.!}{x_1!\cdots x_k!} \left(\frac{\lambda_1}{\lambda_.}\right)^{x_1} \cdots \left(\frac{\lambda_k}{\lambda_.}\right)^{x_k},$$

from which the theorem follows. □.

Suppose $x_1,\ldots,x_k$ are the observed values of k independent Poisson distributed random variables $X_1,\ldots,X_k$ with parameters $\lambda_1,\ldots,\lambda_k$, and consider the hypothesis

$$(18.24) \quad \lambda_i = \alpha_i \lambda, \quad i=1,\ldots,k,$$

where $\alpha_1,\ldots,\alpha_k$ are known constants.

Under the hypothesis (18.24), the distribution (18.23) becomes

(18.25) $\quad (X_1,\ldots,X_k | X_. = x_.) \sim M(x_., \alpha_1/\alpha_., \ldots, \alpha_k/\alpha_.)$,

i.e. the conditional distribution of $X_1,\ldots,X_k$ given their sum is multinomial with known probability parameters

$$p_i = \alpha_i/\alpha_. \quad, \quad i=1,\ldots,k.$$

Consequently, hypothesis (18.24) can be tested by the Q-test statistic

(18.26) $\quad Q = \sum_{i=1}^{k} (X_i - x_. p_i)^2/(x_. p_i)$,

which according to theorem 18.1 approximately follows a χ^2-distribution with k-1 degrees of freedom.

Example 18.5

In example 18.1, a multinomial model of the daily distribution of accidents was formulated and the hypothesis of a uniform distribution of the accidents was tested by a Q-test. This choice of test statistic can be motivated in the following way. Assume that the number of accidents on day number i is Poisson distributed with parameter λ_i. A uniform distribution of accidents over the week days will then entail that the expected values $\lambda_1,\ldots,\lambda_7$ are equal, i.e. the hypothesis to be tested is

$$H_0: \lambda_1 = \ldots = \lambda_7 = \lambda.$$

Under H_0, the conditional distribution of $X_1,\ldots,X_7$ given $X_.=1739$ is according to theorem 18.3 multinomial with probability parameters

$$p_i = 1/7, \quad i=1,\ldots,7.$$

The test of H_0 is thus the Q-test applied in example 18.1. Conditioning on the sum of all observed accidents means that the information contained in this sum is disregarded. This information is, however, only of interest when the total accident level is discussed. For a discussion of how the accidents are distributed over the week days it is of no importance. △.

Example 18.6

The mobility on the Danish labour market has been studied by the Danish National Institute for Social Research. In the beginning of 1974, a random sample of 1335 employees were asked how often they had changed employer within the last 4 months. Towards the end of 1974, a second independent random sample of 1392 employees were asked how often they had changed employer within the last 8 months. The resulting answers are summarized in table 18.5.

Table 18.5. The number of changes of employer for two samples of employees.

	First sample	Second sample
Number of changes	83	142
Sample size	1335	1392

The question is whether the mobility on the labour market, measured as the expected number of changes of employer, has changed from 1973 to 1974. Suppose the number of changes for a given employee in a time interval of length t is Poisson distributed with parameter λt. One way of arguing for the validity of this assumption would be to check assumptions (i) to (iii) for a Poisson process. If the employees act independently of each other, then it follows from theorem 8.11 that the number of changes for a group of n employees is Poisson distributed with parameter $n\lambda t$. Let now X_1 and X_2 be the number of changes in the two periods in 1973 and 1974. Then $X_1 \sim Ps(1335 \cdot 4\delta_1)$ and $X_2 \sim Ps(1392 \cdot 8\delta_2)$, where δ_1 and δ_2 are the intensities of mobility in the two considered periods. The hypothesis of identical mobilities in 1973 and 1974 can, therefore, be tested through the hypothesis $H_0: \delta_1 = \delta_2$. If $\lambda_1 = E[X_1]$ and $\lambda_2 = E[X_2]$ are the parameters of the Poisson distributions for X_1 and X_2, H_0 is equivalent to

$$H_0: \begin{cases} \lambda_1 = 5340\delta \\ \lambda_2 = 11136\delta \end{cases}$$

which is a hypothesis of the form (18.24). Hence, H_0 can be tested by the test statistic (18.26) with

$$p_1 = \frac{5340}{5340+11136} = 0.324 \ .$$

and $p_2 = 0.676$. The observed value of the test statistic is

$$q = \frac{(83-72.9)^2}{72.9} + \frac{(142-152.1)^2}{152.1} = 2.1.$$

The level of significance is

$$P \simeq P(\chi^2(1) \geq 2.1) \simeq 0.17.$$

It follows that the data do not support a hypothesis of a change in mobility from 1973 to 1974. △.

19. Analysis of Contingency Tables

19.1. The test of independence

A table showing the distribution of n units according to two or more criteria, each with a finite number of categories, is called a **contingency table**. If there are two criteria with I and J categories respectively, the contingency table can be presented in the form of a matrix

$$(19.1) \quad \begin{bmatrix} x_{11} & \cdots & x_{1j} & \cdots & x_{1J} \\ \vdots & & \vdots & & \vdots \\ x_{i1} & \cdots & x_{ij} & \cdots & x_{iJ} \\ \vdots & & \vdots & & \vdots \\ x_{I1} & \cdots & x_{Ij} & \cdots & x_{IJ} \end{bmatrix}$$

where x_{ij} is the number of units belonging to both category i of criterion 1 and category j of criterion 2. With reference to the matrix representation, the two criteria are called respectively the **row criterion** and the **column criterion**. If a unit belongs to row category i and column category j, it is said to be in cell (i,j) of the table.

Many contingency tables are formed by sampling from a finite population. Let the population consist of N units of which the proportion p_{ij} belongs to cell (i,j). If a random sample of size n is drawn with replacement from the population, then $(x_{11}, \ldots, x_{IJ})$ can be regarded as an observation of a multinomially distributed random vector $(X_{11}, \ldots, X_{IJ})$, with parameters n and $p_{11}, \ldots, p_{IJ}$ i.e.

$$(19.2) \quad (X_{11}, \ldots, X_{IJ}) \sim M(n, p_{11}, \ldots, p_{IJ}).$$

If the sample has been drawn without replacement, the distribution of $(X_{11}, \ldots, X_{IJ})$ is a multivariate version of the hypergeometric distribution, which can, however, be approximated by the multinomial distribution (19.2) in the same way as a hypergeometric distribution according to theorem 6.7 can be approximated by the binomial distribution.

Under the model (19.2), the marginal probability that a unit belongs to row category i is

$$(19.3) \quad p_{i.} = \sum_{j=1}^{J} p_{ij}, \quad i=1,\ldots,I,$$

and the corresponding marginal probability for column category j is

$$(19.4) \quad p_{.j} = \sum_{i=1}^{I} p_{ij}, \quad j=1,\ldots,J.$$

The row and column criteria are said to be independent if

$$(19.5) \quad p_{ij} = p_{i.}p_{.j} \quad \text{for all i and j},$$

i.e. if the events "belongs to row category i" and "belongs to column category j" are independent. Independence between the row and column criteria implies that the conditional probability that a randomly selected unit belongs to row category i, given that it belongs to column category j, has the same value for all column categories. Under the **hypothesis of independence** (19.5), the distribution of the units over the row categories is thus not influenced by the column category in question.

Under hypothesis (19.5), the model (19.2) is parameterized by $p_{1.},\ldots,p_{I.}$ and $p_{.1},\ldots p_{.J}$ with the constraints

$$\sum_{i=1}^{I} p_{i.} = \sum_{j=1}^{J} p_{.j} = 1,$$

so that the p_{ij}'s only depend on $(I-1)+(J-1)$ parameters with free variation.

The ML-estimates of the marginal probabilities (19.3) and (19.4) are

$$(19.6) \quad \begin{cases} \hat{p}_{i.} = \sum_{j=1}^{J} x_{ij}/n = x_{i.}/n, & i=1,\ldots,I, \\ \hat{p}_{.j} = \sum_{i=1}^{I} x_{ij}/n = x_{.j}/n, & j=1,\ldots,J, \end{cases}$$

and the ML-estimate of p_{ij} under (19.5) becomes

$$(19.7) \quad \hat{p}_{ij} = \hat{p}_{i.}\hat{p}_{.j} = x_{i.}x_{.j}/n^2.$$

Since the expected value of X_{ij} under the hypothesis of independence is estimated by

$$n\hat{p}_{i.}\hat{p}_{.j} = x_{i.}x_{.j}/n ,$$

the hypothesis can be tested by the test statistic

(19.8) $$Q = \sum_{i=1}^{I} \sum_{j=1}^{J} (X_{ij} - X_{i.}X_{.j}/n)^2 / (X_{i.}X_{.j}/n).$$

From theorem 18.2, it follows that Q is approximately χ^2-distributed with IJ-1-(I-1)-(J-1) = (I-1)(J-1) degrees of freedom. This number of degrees of freedom arises from the fact that the number of categories of the multinomial distribution is I·J, and there are (I-1)+(J-1) free parameters estimated under the hypothesis.

The fit of the model under the hypothesis is evaluated by the value of

(19.9) $$q = \sum_{j=1}^{J} \sum_{i=1}^{I} (x_{ij} - x_{i.}x_{.j}/n)^2 (x_{i.}x_{.j}/n).$$

A large value of q indicates that there are substantial differences between the observed numbers and the estimated expected numbers under the hypothesis for at least one cell of the table. Hence, (19.5) is rejected for large values of q.

The level of significance is

(19.10) $$p \simeq (Q \geq q),$$

where $Q \sim \chi^2((I-1)(J-1))$. With test level α, (19.5) is rejected if

(19.11) $$q \geq \chi^2_{1-\alpha}((I-1)(J-1)).$$

With a low level of significance, the cells of the table contributing significantly to the value of q should be identified. This is done by means of the **residuals**

$$r_{ij} = (x_{ij} - e_{ij})/\sqrt{e_{ij}} ,$$

where $e_{ij} = x_{i.}x_{.j}/n$. As a rule of thumb, the (i,j)'th cell is said to contribute significantly to the value of q if

(19.12) $$|r_{ij}| > 2\sqrt{(I-1)(J-1)}/\sqrt{IJ} .$$

In fact if all the residuals are equal to this limit, the observed value of Q will be just above $\chi^2_{0.95}((I-1)(J-1)) = (1.96)^2$.

If there exists a natural ordering of the categories of one or both criteria, it is often helpful to study the sign pattern of the residuals. This may suggest alternative models for describing the data structure.

Example 19.1

Table 19.1 is based on a random sample of 2610 married Danish women below the age of 60. The sample is distributed according to employment status and degree of urbanization in 1964.

Table 19.1. Married women in Denmark in 1964, according to employment and degree of urbanization.

Degree of urbanization	House-wife	Part time work outside the home	Full time work outside the home	Assisting in family business	Total
I	188	66	139	16	409
II	145	32	98	14	289
III	401	114	239	65	819
IV	81	24	53	25	183
V	364	118	164	264	910
Total	1179	354	693	384	2610

Source: Married Women, Family and Work. Publication No.37. Table 4.3. Danish National Institute of Social Research. 1969.

The urbanization levels in table 19.1 are
  I: Copenhagen
 II: Suburbs of Copenhagen
III: Provincial Towns
 IV: Urban districts in rural areas
  V: Rural districts

The purpose of the analysis of table 19.1 is to determine any dependency between degree of urbanization and the employment status of married women.

The planned sample size was in fact 3000, so the proportion of nonrespondents was 13%. Nevertheless, the sample size is here regarded as fixed.

Under the additional assumption of random selection of women to be interviewed and independence between individual interviews, the data in table 19.1 may be assumed to follow a multinomial distribution (19.2) with $I=5$ and $J=4$.

The hypothesis of independence, (19.5), is tested by the Q-test statistic (19.8). Table 19.2 shows the expected values in the 20 cells of the table under the hypothesis.

Table 19.2. Estimated expected values for the data of table 19.1 under the hypothesis of independence between employment status and degree of urbanization.

	\multicolumn{4}{c}{Employment}			
Degree of urbanization	House-wife	Part time work outside the home	Full time work outside the home	Assisting in family business
I	184.8	55.5	108.6	60.2
II	130.5	39.2	76.7	42.5
III	370.0	111.1	217.5	120.5
IV	82.7	24.8	48.6	26.9
V	411.1	123.4	241.6	133.9

The observed value of q is 258.9, which, under the hypothesis of independence, can be regarded as an observation from a χ^2- distribution with (5-1)(4-1)=12 degrees of freedom. The level of significance is then $p \approx P(Q>258.9)$, which is less than 0.0001.

Table 19.3. The residuals under the hypothesis of independence for the data in table 19.1.

Degree of urbanization	House-wife	Part time work outside the home	Full time work outside the home	Assisting in family business
I	+0.24	+1.41	+2.92	-5.69
II	+1.27	-1.15	+2.43	-4.37
III	+1.61	+0.28	+1.46	-5.06
IV	-0.19	-0.16	+0.63	-0.37
V	-2.32	-0.49	-4.99	+11.24

The residuals shown in table 19.3 exhibit a clear sign pattern. In particular, the difference between urbanization levels I - III and level V is striking. The numerical values of the residuals suggest that the data may be described by a model with independence between the row and column criteria if all women in rural areas, i.e. the last two rows, are omitted. For this part of the table the residuals under the hypothesis of independence are shown in table 19.4.

If the contingency table only consists of the first three rows of table 19.1, the Q-test statistic for the hypothesis of independence is approximately χ^2-distributed with $(3-1)(4-1)=6$ degrees of freedom. The observed value of Q is 14.8 and the level of significance is

$$p \simeq P(Q \geq 14.8) = 0.023.$$

Even when attention is restricted to married women living in urbanized areas, there is still a covariation between employment status and degree of urbanization.

An inspection of the residuals of table 19.4, based on the limit 1.414 computed from (19.12), reveals that the large value of q is primarily due to the fact that more women assist in family business in the larger cities than in the capital. For the other three employment categories, the observed differences in employment patterns between Copenhagen and the larger cities may well be due to randomness.

Table 19.4. Residuals for the data in table 19.1 with the last two rows omitted.

Degree of urbanization	House-wife	Part time work outside the home	Full time work outside the home	Assisting in family business
I	-0.70	1.16	0.94	-1.90
II	0.44	-1.32	0.77	-0.96
III	0.24	-0.04	-1.12	1.91

Alltogether, the result of the analysis of the data in table 19.1 is not at all satisfactory. The two criteria considered are seen to be dependent, but the exact nature of this dependency and its probable causes are still unknown. $\triangle$.

It is not unusual that contingency tables are based on large samples as in example 19.1. For such tables, with a moderate number of cells, the hypothesis of independence is often rejected at a test level of 0.05, in cases where the residuals exhibit a random sign pattern and those cells which contribute significantly to q have residuals close to the limit (19.12). This is due to the fact that a large sample carries a large amount of information. Hence, a simple model like (19.2) is almost certain to be rejected by the data. Large samples are not, however, needed for the purpose of testing simple hypotheses, but they are necessary for the study of complex relationships. Therefore, if large samples are used for testing simple hypotheses, the null hypothesis should only be rejected at low test levels such as 0.01 or 0.001. In this way, models, which for all practical purposes are quite acceptable are not rejected so easily.

The sample from which the data in table 19.1 is extracted is not a simple random sample but results from a complex two-stage stratified sampling scheme. Hence, the assumptions underlying the multinomial distribution of (19.2) are not satisfied, and the use of the χ^2-approximation to the distribution of the test statistic (19.8) cannot be justified by theorem 18.2. It has been shown, however, that the χ^2-approximation is often valid, even when it is not a case of a simple random sample. On the other hand, if the sampling is complex, as in the case of stratified sampling with many strata (section 17.5), the χ^2-approximation may be too coarse. Problems arise in particular if the variation within strata is very homogeneous. The variance of the estimators of the parameters may then be considerably smaller than the variance obtained from the multinomial distribution. This means that the denominators of the individual terms in q become too large and as a result q becomes too small. A small value of q may thus be due to the complexity of the sampling procedure rather than to a good fit of the model.

19.2. The test of homogeneity

Assume that a population is divided into J subpopulations and the distribution of the units according to a criterion with I categories within each of the subpopulations is to be compared. This comparison can be based on the following sample: From the j'th population a simple random sample of n_j units is drawn and its distribution over the I categories of the criterion is observed. If x_{ij} is the observed number in category i within the sample drawn from subpopulation j, the x_{ij}'s form a contingency table similar to the one discussed in section 19.1. The statistical model for the table is, however, different from the one discussed there, since the column sums $n_1,\ldots,n_j$ are given in advance.

One of the reasons for sampling within subpopulations with given sample sizes may be a particular interest in a small subgroup of units. With simple random sampling this group may be poorly represented in the sample with the result that little information is obtained about the group. A sampling design which preassigns the numbers of selected units from each subpopulation guarantees a certain amount of information about the subgroup in question.

If the units from the subpopulations are selected independently of each other and by means of simple random sampling without replacement, and if the total sample is small compared with the population size, then the distribution of the random variables $X_{11},\ldots,X_{IJ}$ corresponding to the cells of the contingency table can be described by J independent multinomial distributions,

(19.13) $\quad (X_{1j},\ldots,X_{Ij}) \sim M(n_j, p_{1j},\ldots,p_{Ij}), \qquad j=1,\ldots,J.$

The hypothesis of interest is usually that the distribution over the categories of the row criterion is the same for all subpopulations. As p_{ij} is the frequency of individuals in subpopulation j belonging to category i, the parametric form of the hypothesis is

(19.14) $\quad p_{i1} = \ldots = p_{iJ} = p_i, \qquad i=1,\ldots,I,$

which is termed the **hypothesis of homogeneity.**

In order to derive a test statistic for (19.14), it is first assumed that $p_1,\ldots,p_I$ are known quantities. Theorem 18.1 then implies that for each j

(19.15) $\quad Q_j = \sum_{i=1}^{I} (X_{ij} - n_j p_i)^2 / (n_j p_i)$

is approximately χ^2-distributed with I−1 degrees of freedom. Since, by assumption, $Q_1,\ldots,Q_J$ are independent, it follows from theorem 9.2 that

(19.16) $\quad Q = \sum_{j=1}^{J} Q_j = \sum_{j=1}^{J} \sum_{i=1}^{I} (X_{ij} - n_j p_i)^2 / (n_j p_i)$

is approximately χ^2-distributed with J(I−1) degrees of freedom. For known values of $p_1,\ldots,p_I$, the hypothesis (19.14) can thus be tested by (19.16).

If, as is usually the case, $p_1,\ldots,p_I$ are unknown they need to be estimated. The likelihood function under the hypothesis is

(19.17) $\quad L(p_1,\ldots,p_I) = \prod_{j=1}^{J} \frac{n_j!}{x_{1j}! \cdots x_{Ij}!} p_1^{x_{1j}} \cdots p_I^{x_{Ij}},$

from which the ML-estimator under the constraint $p_1 + \ldots + p_I = 1$ can be derived as

(19.18) $\quad \hat{p}_i = X_{i.}/n, \qquad i=1,\ldots,I,$

with $n = n_1 + \ldots + n_J$ and $X_{i.} = X_{i1} + \ldots + X_{iJ}$. Substituting $\hat{p}_i$ for p_i in (19.16), the test statistic becomes

(19.19) $\quad Q = \sum_{j=1}^{J} \sum_{i=1}^{I} (X_{ij} - n_j \hat{p}_i)^2 / (n_j \hat{p}_i).$

Under the hypothesis of homogeneity, it can be shown that (19.19) is approximately χ^2-distributed with $(I-1)(J-1)$ degrees of freedom. An intuitive argument for the number of degrees of freedom is that Q has $(I-1)J$ degrees of freedom for known values of $p_1,\ldots,p_I$, and if the p_i's are unknown, $I-1$ parameters are estimated since $p_1+\ldots+p_I=1$. Hence, the number of degrees of freedom is reduced by $I-1$, giving

$$J(I-1)-(I-1) = (J-1)(I-1).$$

The approximation to the χ^2-distribution can be regarded as satisfactory if all estimated, expected values $n_j\hat{p}_i$ are larger than 5.

The observed value

(19.20) $$q = \sum_{j=1}^{J} \sum_{i=1}^{I} (x_{ij}-n_j\hat{p}_i)^2/(n_j\hat{p}_i)$$

of Q can then be compared with the percentiles of a χ^2-distribution with $(I-1)(J-1)$ degrees of freedom, and the hypothesis of homogeneity is rejected if q is large. The level of significance is given by (19.10) and a test with approximate level α has critical region (19.11).

It should be noted that the quantities (19.9) and (19.20), since $n_j=x_{.j}$ and $\hat{p}_i=x_{i.}/n$, are numerically identical, and that the asymptotic distributions of the corresponding test statistics are identical. The hypotheses (19.5) and (19.14) are, however, different as they refer to different statistical models. The connection between the models and the test statistic of sections 19.1 and 19.2 is discussed in section 19.5.

19.3. Comparison of binomial distributions

For $I=2$, the test of homogeneity reduces to a comparison of the probability parameters of J binomial distributions, in which case it is more convenient to use the notation

$$X_{1j} = X_j \text{ and } p_{1j} = p_j,$$

so that

$$X_{2j} = n_j - X_j \text{ and } p_{2j} = 1-p_j.$$

The hypothesis of homogeneity then becomes

(19.21) $$H_0: p_1=\ldots p_J = p,$$

and the test statistic (19.19) can with $\hat{p}=(X_1+\ldots+X_J)/n$ be written as

(19.22) $$Q = \sum_{j=1}^{J} (X_j - n_j\hat{p})^2 / (n_j\hat{p}(1-\hat{p})),$$

since

$$\frac{(X_j-n_j\hat{p})^2}{n_j\hat{p}} + \frac{((n_j-X_j)-n_j(1-\hat{p}))^2}{n_j(1-\hat{p})} = \frac{(X_j-n_j\hat{p})^2}{n_j\hat{p}(1-\hat{p})}.$$

The case $I=J=2$ was treated in sections 12.5 and 12.6 where the probability parameters of two independent binomial distributions were compared. The test statistics in section 12.6 and in this section are equivalent since the square of the u-test statistic (12.18) equals the Q-test statistic (19.22) for $I=J=2$.

Note, however, that one-sided alternatives cannot be tested on the basis of a Q-test, since the Q-test statistic attains large values both when the data support $p_1 > p_2$ and when they support $p_1 < p_2$.

19.4. The multiplicative Poisson model

The analysis of contingency tables in which neither the total nor any of the marginals are fixed in advance is usually based on the Poisson distribution, so let X_{ij} be the random variable corresponding to the observed number x_{ij} in cell (i,j), and assume that

(19.23) $$\begin{cases} X_{ij}, \quad i=1,\ldots I, \quad j=1,\ldots,J, \text{ are independent} \\ X_{ij} \sim Ps(\lambda_{ij}). \end{cases}$$

If the parameters of the Poisson distributions (19.23) satisfy

(19.24) $$\lambda_{ij} = \gamma \epsilon_i \delta_j, \quad i=1,\ldots,I, \text{ and } j=1,\ldots,J,$$

where

$$\sum_{i=1}^{I} \epsilon_i = 1 \quad \text{and} \quad \sum_{j=1}^{J} \delta_j = 1,$$

the model is called the **multiplicative Poisson model**.

The linear constraints are necessary in order for the parameters to be uniquely determined, but if the parameter γ is omitted, then one of the constraints becomes superfluous. From theorem 18.3, it follows that

(19.25) $$(X_{i1},\ldots,X_{iJ} | X_{i.} = x_{i.}) \sim M(x_{i.}, \delta_1, \ldots, \delta_J)$$

since
$$\gamma \varepsilon_i \delta_j / \sum_{j=1}^{J} \gamma \varepsilon_i \delta_j = \delta_j,$$

and the expected value of X_{ij} given $X_{i.} = x_{i.}$ is then

$$E[X_{ij} | X_{i.} = x_{i.}] = x_{i.} \delta_j.$$

This implies that the relative distribution over the J columns under assumption (19.24) does not depend on the row considered, and that $\delta_1, \ldots, \delta_J$ characterize this relative distribution. Likewise $\varepsilon_1, \ldots, \varepsilon_I$ characterize the relative distribution over the row categories, which is the same for all columns under (19.24).

Consider finally the conditional distribution of all the X_{ij}'s given the value of

$$X_{..} = \sum_{i=1}^{I} \sum_{j=1}^{J} X_{ij}.$$

Theorem 18.3 yields

(19.26) $\quad (X_{11}, \ldots, X_{IJ} | X_{..} = x_{..}) \sim M(x_{..}, \lambda_{11}/\lambda_{..}, \ldots, \lambda_{IJ}/\lambda_{..})$

where $\lambda_{..} = \Sigma\Sigma\lambda_{ij}$.

It is easy to verify that the hypothesis of multiplicativity (19.24) in this conditional model is equivalent to the hypothesis of independence (19.5). If $p_{ij} = \lambda_{ij}/\lambda_{..}$, then under (19.24)

$$p_{i.} = \varepsilon_i, \quad i=1,\ldots,I,$$

and

$$p_{.j} = \delta_j, \quad j=1,\ldots,J,$$

in which case

$$p_{ij} = \varepsilon_i \delta_j$$

and (19.5) is satisfied. If, on the other hand, (19.5) is satisfied, then $p_{ij} = \lambda_{ij}/\lambda_{..}$ has the multiplicative form (19.24). Since

$$E[X_{ij} | X_{..} = x_{..}] = x_{..} \varepsilon_i \delta_j,$$

the sample size n in model (19.2) has in (19.24) been replaced by the parameter γ. In the multiplicative Poisson model, γ thus represents a general level of no importance for testing a multiplicative structure, so a test of the hypothesis (19.24) can justifiably be based on the conditional distribution (19.26), which is independent of γ. Since (19.24) is equivalent to the hypothesis of independence (19.5), the test statistic is

$$(19.27) \quad Q = \sum_{i=1}^{I} \sum_{j=1}^{J} \left(x_{ij} - \frac{x_{i.} x_{.j}}{x_{..}} \right)^2 / \left(\frac{x_{i.} x_{.j}}{x_{..}} \right),$$

which is approximately χ^2-distributed with $(I-1)(J-1)$ degrees of freedom. The level of significance and the critical region for a level α test are given by (19.10) and (19.11) respectively. If hypothesis (19.24) is rejected, the sign pattern of the residuals should be studied to identify the cells responsible for the poor fit.

The ML-estimates of the ε's and the δ's are, according to (19.6), given by

$$\hat{\varepsilon}_i = x_{i.}/x_{..}, \quad i=1,\ldots,I,$$

and

$$\hat{\delta}_j = x_{.j}/x_{..}, \quad j=1,\ldots,J,$$

since $p_{ij} = \varepsilon_i \delta_j$ implies $p_{i.} = \varepsilon_i$ and $p_{.j} = \delta_j$.

Example 19.2

To investigate the effect of speed limits on the number of traffic accidents in Sweden, limits were imposed during the summer of 1962 and the number of accidents in this period was compared to the number of accidents in a similar period without limits. The number of accidents can, however, be influenced by other factors such as weather conditions and traffic volume so a direct comparison of the number of accidents in the two periods would not be satisfactory. Since it was expected that the impact of the speed limits on the number of accidents would be larger on trunk roads than elsewhere, it was decided to compare the relative distribution of the accidents on three road types: trunk roads, major roads and minor roads in the two periods. A decrease in the relative frequency of accidents on the trunk roads from the period without limits to the period with limits can then be interpreted as a positive effect of the speed limits. However, this comparison is only meaningful if the relative distribution over the road types is stable in both periods. It was decided that the first step of the analysis should be to check the fit of the multiplicative Poisson model to the distribution of the accidents in a two-way table, where the accidents are distributed according to day number and road type.

Table 19.5 shows the distribution of accidents with serious personal injuries over road types for 15 Sundays in the period without speed limits. Under the assumption of multiplicativity the percentage distribution of the accidents should, approximately, be the same for all 15 days.

Table 19.5. Traffic accidents with serious personal injuries distributed according to day number and road type.

Day number	Trunk roads	Major roads	Minor roads	Total
1	2	7	4	13
2	8	8	4	20
3	7	9	9	25
4	7	4	8	19
5	3	5	7	15
6	5	4	4	13
7	4	5	7	16
8	4	4	12	20
9	7	3	8	18
10	3	8	12	23
11	4	12	15	31
12	4	5	14	23
13	9	12	10	31
14	10	9	17	36
15	10	9	14	33
Total	87	104	145	336

Let x_{ij} be the observed number of accidents on day number i and for road type j, and let X_{ij} be the corresponding random variable. It is assumed that X_{ij}, i=1,...,15, j=1,2,3, is distributed in accordance with the model (19.23). A discussion of the feasibility of the assumption of independence between the observed cell counts is left to the reader. An assumption of a stable distribution of accidents over the road types for the fifteen days entails that the expected numbers of accidents have the multiplictive structure (19.24) since this implies that

$$E[X_{ij}]/E[X_{i\cdot}] = \delta_j, \quad j=1,2,3,$$

independent of i. This relationship again implies that δ_1, δ_2 and δ_3 can be interpreted as the expected accident frequencies for the three road types. Hypothesis (19.24) is tested by the test statistic (19.27). The estimated expected values $x_{i..}x_{.j.}/x_{..}$ are shown in table 19.6 and the residuals

$$r_{ij} = \frac{x_{ij} - x_{i..}x_{.j.}/x_{..}}{\sqrt{x_{i..}x_{.j.}/x_{..}}}$$

in table 19.7.

Table 19.6. Expected number of accidents under a multiplicative Poisson model.

Day number	Trunk roads	Major roads	Minor roads
1	3.4	4.0	5.6
2	5.2	6.2	8.6
3	6.5	7.7	10.8
4	4.9	5.9	8.2
5	3.9	4.6	6.5
6	3.4	4.0	5.6
7	4.1	5.0	6.9
8	5.2	6.2	8.6
9	4.7	5.6	7.8
10	6.0	7.2	9.9
11	8.0	9.6	13.4
12	6.0	7.1	9.9
13	8.0	9.6	13.4
14	9.3	11.1	15.5
15	8.5	10.2	14.2

Table 19.7. Residuals under the multiplicative Poisson model.

Day number	Trunk roads	Major roads	Minor roads
1	-0.75	1.50	-0.68
2	1.23	0.72	-1.57
3	0.20	0.45	-0.55
4	0.94	-0.78	-0.07
5	-0.45	0.19	0.20
6	0.89	0.01	-0.68
7	-0.07	0.02	0.04
8	-0.52	-0.88	1.15
9	1.06	-1.10	0.08
10	-1.21	0.30	0.66
11	-1.42	0.77	0.44
12	-0.80	-0.79	1.29
13	0.34	0.77	-0.92
14	0.22	-0.63	0.37
15	0.50	-0.38	-0.06

No systematic structure seems to be present in the sign pattern of table 19.7. Under the assumption of multiplicativity the observed value q=26.5 of (19.27) can be compared with a χ^2-distribution with (15-1)(3-1)=28 degrees of freedom and hence the level of significance is approximately $P(Q \geq 26.5)=0.46$.

The hypothesis of multiplicativity is thus supported strongly by the data. This means in particular that the frequency distribution over road types, apart from random variations, can be regarded as constant over the period considered. This distribution is estimated by

$$(\hat{\delta}_1, \hat{\delta}_2, \hat{\delta}_3) = (0.259, 0.310, 0.431).$$

In this example, the χ^2-approximation is used even though the estimated expected numbers are less than 5 in several of the cells. Some investigations, however, indicate that the χ^2-approximation can be used if 80% of the cells have expected numbers above 5 and none of the expected numbers are less than 1. If these results can be trusted, the χ^2-approximation to the distribution of Q should be reliable in the present case. △.

19.5. The effect of the sampling procedure

The various contingency tables analysed in the previous sections have had similar data structures although the data have been collected by different sampling schemes. In each case a large population has been sampled, so it is of no significance whether the sampling is with or without replacement. The sampling schemes considered can be distinguished in the following way:

(i)   There are no constraints on the numbers in the cells of the table (section 19.4).

(ii) The total number of observations is fixed prior to the collection of the data (section 19.1).

(iii) The column totals are fixed prior to the collection of the data (section 19.2).

Scheme (i) is the most general of the schemes discussed and corresponds to the multiplicative Poisson model, where no constraints are imposed on the observed numbers. By conditioning the multiplicative Poisson model can, however, be reduced to the multinomial model of section 19.1 since the conditional distribution of $X_{11},\ldots,X_{IJ}$, given $X_{..}=x_{..}$, corresponds to (19.2) with $p_{ij}=\lambda_{ij}/\lambda_{..}$, according to theorem 18.3.

Conditioning with respect to $X_{..}$ in a contingency table means that the statistical information contained in the observed total $x_{..}$ is excluded from the analysis, i.e. sampling scheme (ii) is applied. This information is, on the other hand, of no importance as long as only the interaction between the row and the column criteria is of interest. The total $x_{..}$ contains information about the general level of the observed numbers, not about the relative distribution over the cells of the contingency table. It follows that the tests in sections 19.1 and 19.4 are concerned with the same hypothesis, whether expressed as independence in the multinomial model (19.2) or as multiplicativity in the Poisson model (19.23). In both cases, acceptance of the hypothesis under consideration is interpreted as "independence between the row criterion and the column criterion".

Sampling schemes (i) and (ii) can be reduced to (iii) by considering the column totals as fixed. The conditional distribution of $X_{11}, \ldots, X_{IJ}$, given the column totals $X_{.1}, \ldots, X_{.J}$, in the multiplicative Poisson model is a product of k independent multinomial distributions. In fact an application of theorem 18.3 yields that

$$(X_{1j}, \ldots, X_{Ij} | X_{.j} = x_{.j}) \sim M(x_{.j}, \lambda_{1j}/\lambda_{.j}, \ldots, \lambda_{Ij}/\lambda_{.j}).$$

This means that hypothesis (19.24) in the Poisson model is transformed by conditioning to a hypothesis of homogeneity in the model (19.13) since $\lambda_{ij}/\lambda_{..} = \varepsilon_i$ under (19.24). Conditioning on the column totals means that the information contained in these totals is excluded from the analysis. This information is, however, of no significance as long as only the interaction between the column and the row criteria is of interest. This interaction can be studied by means of the relative distribution over the row categories within a given column. The more these distributions differ, the more the row and column categories interact. Thus, the evaluation of the degree of interaction does not depend on how the individuals in the various column categories are sampled. Therefore, if only the degree of interaction is of interest, the column totals can be fixed at given values as part of the sampling scheme. If the data are sampled with pre-set column totals, there will of course be no information about the distribution of the population on the categories of the column criterion.

19.6. Analysis of the marginals of a two-way table

A test of multiplicativity in a two-way table may only be the first step in the statistical analysis of the table. If, for example, the hypothesis (19.24) has been accepted the next step could be to test hypotheses concerning the values of the row parameters $\varepsilon_1, \ldots, \varepsilon_I$ or of the column parameters $\delta_1,\ldots,\delta_J$. Assume that the X_{ij}'s are independent and Poisson distributed with

$$E[X_{ij}] = \gamma\epsilon_i\delta_j$$

and consider the hypothesis

(19.28) $\quad \epsilon_i = c_i, \quad i=1,\ldots,I,$

where $c_1,\ldots,c_I$ are given constants. A test statistic can then be derived from the conditional distribution of the row totals $X_{1.},\ldots,X_{I.}$, given $X_{..}=x_{..}$. The row totals are independent and, by theorem 8.11, Poisson distributed with

$$E[X_{i.}] = \gamma\epsilon_i$$

since $\Sigma\delta_j=1$. From theorem 18.3 it then follows that $X_{1.},\ldots,X_{I.}$, given $X_{..}=x_{..}$, has a multinomial distribution with parameters $x_{..}$ and

(19.29) $\quad p_i = \gamma\epsilon_i/\gamma = \epsilon_i, \quad i=1,\ldots,I.$

Hypothesis (19.28) can accordingly be tested by

(19.30) $\quad Q = \sum_{i=1}^{I}(X_{i.}-x_{..}c_i)^2/(x_{..}c_i),$

which under (19.28) is approximately χ^2-distributed with $I-1$ degrees of freedom, according to theorem 18.1. When

(19.31) $\quad \epsilon_1=\ldots=\epsilon_I=1/I,$

the test statistic becomes

(19.32) $\quad Q_r = \sum_{i=1}^{I}(X_{i.}-x_{..}/I)^2/(x_{..}/I).$

Tests concerning the column parameters are analogous to those with test statistics of the form of (19.30) and (19.32). For example, the hypothesis

(19.33) $\quad \delta_1=\ldots=\delta_J=1/J$

can be tested by

$$(19.34) \quad Q_c = \sum_{j=1}^{J} (X_{.j} - x_{..}/J)^2 / (x_{..}/J),$$

which under (19.33) is approximately χ^2-distributed with J-1 degrees of freedom.

Under the hypothesis of independence (19.5) in the multinomial model (19.2), tests for hypotheses concerning the values of $p_{1.},\ldots p_{I.}$ or $p_{.1},\ldots,p_{.J}$ are analogous to the tests concerning the values of the ε_i's and the δ_j's in the multiplicative Poisson model. The hypothesis

$$p_{.1} = \ldots = p_{.J} = 1/J$$

can thus be tested by the test statistic (19.34) and the hypothesis

$$p_{1.} = \ldots = p_{I.} = 1/I$$

by (19.32).

For the multinomial model in section 19.2, the test statistic (19.32) corresponds to the hypothesis

$$p_1 = \ldots = p_I = 1/I ,$$

while it does not make sense to test hypotheses concerning the distribution of the population over column categories.

The test for interaction between row and column criteria and the tests for hypotheses (19.31) and (19.33) can be combined in a **table of variation** as shown in table 19.8.

Table 19.8. Table of variation for a two-way contingency table.

Variation	Hypothesis	Test statistic	Degrees of freedom
Interaction	$\lambda_{ij} = \gamma \varepsilon_i \delta_j$	Q	$(J-1)(I-1)$
Between rows	$\varepsilon_1 = \ldots \varepsilon_I = 1/I$	Q_r	$I-1$
Between columns	$\delta_1 = \ldots = \delta_J = 1/J$	Q_c	$J-1$
Total	$\dfrac{\lambda_{ij}}{\lambda_{..}} = \dfrac{1}{IJ}$	Q_0	$IJ-1$

The test in the last line of table 19.8 is seldom used. It corresponds to the unrealistic assumption that the population is uniformly distributed over all IJ cells, or that all λ_{ij}'s are equal so that

$$\lambda_{ij}/\lambda_{..} = 1/IJ.$$

The Q-test statistic for this hypothesis is

$$Q_0 = \sum_{j=1}^{J} \sum_{i=1}^{I} (X_{ij} - X_{..}/IJ)^2/(X_{..}/IJ)$$

which according to theorem 18.1 is approximately χ^2-distributed with IJ-1 degrees of freedom. Note that Q_0 is not the sum of Q, Q_r and Q_c.

Table 19.8 demonstrates the use of the IJ-1 degrees of freedom in the multinomial model (19.2), or in the conditional multinomial distribution of $X_{11},\ldots,X_{IJ}$ given $X_{..}=x_{..}$ for the Poisson model (19.23), to test various hypothesis. Of the IJ-1 degrees of freedom available, (I-1)(J-1) are used to test the hypothesis of no interaction by means of Q, (J-1) are used to test the hypothesis of uniform distribution over columns by means of Q_c and I-1 are used to test the hypothesis of uniform distribution over rows by means of Q_r.

Example 19.3

Table 19.9 shows the number of recognized cases of lung cancer, distributed according to age, in four Danish cities: Fredericia, Horsens, Kolding and Vejle. The data were collected in order to study whether the rate of occurrence of lung cancer was higher in Fredericia than in the other three cities.

Let x_{ij} and n_{ij} denote the numbers of lung cancer cases and the number of inhabitants in age group i and city j. It is assumed that x_{ij} is an observation from a Poisson distribution with mean value $\lambda_{ij}=\theta_{ij}n_{ij}$ where θ_{ij} is the rate of occurrence of lung cancer in age group i and city j. If it is assumed that the age distribution is the same in all four cities, λ_{ij} can be written as

$$\lambda_{ij} = \theta_{ij} n_{.j} f_i$$

where $n_{.j}$ is the number of inhabitants in city j and f_i the proportion of inhabitants in age group i. If there exists a multiplicative structure so that $\theta_{ij}=\alpha_i\beta_j$, then λ_{ij} can be written as

$$\lambda_{ij} = \alpha_i \beta_j n_{.j} f_i = \gamma \epsilon_i \delta_j ,$$

where $\epsilon_i = \alpha_i f_i$, $\delta_j = \beta_j n_{.j}/n_{..}$ and $\gamma = n_{..}$.

Under the assumption of a multiplicative structure in the rates of occurrence of lung cancer, the model for the observed number of lung cancer cases is accordingly a multiplicative Poisson model.

The value of the test statistic (19.27) is 19.3, giving a level of significance $p \approx P(Q \geq 19.3) = 0.80$, where $Q \sim \chi^2(15)$. It is, therefore, reasonable to assume that the data can be described by a multiplicative Poisson model. Table 19.10 shows the residuals. The hypothesis of equal rates of occurrence of lung cancer in the four cities, i.e. $H_0: \beta_1 = \ldots = \beta_4 = \beta$, corresponds under the multiplicative Poisson model to the hypothesis $\delta_j = n_{.j}/n_{..}$, $j=1,\ldots,4$. Hence the test statistic for H_0 is

$$Q = \sum_{j=1}^{4} (x_{.j} - x_{..} n_{.j}/n_{..})^2 / (x_{..} n_{.j}/n_{..}).$$

The observed value of Q is $q=3.5$ with level of significance $p \approx P(Q \geq 3.5) = 0.68$ where $Q \sim \chi^2(3)$, and the hypothesis of equal rates of occurrence of lung cancer cannot be rejected.

Table 19.9. Recognized number of cases of lung cancer, distributed according to age and city.

Age	Fredericia	Horsens	Kolding	Vejle	Total
40-54	11	13	4	5	33
55-59	11	6	8	7	32
60-64	11	15	7	10	43
65-69	10	10	11	14	45
70-74	11	12	9	8	40
75-	10	2	12	7	31
Total	64	58	51	51	224

Table 19.10. Residuals under the assumption of multiplicativity in the distribution of the number of cases of lung cancer.

Age	Fredericia	Horsens	Kolding	Vejle
40-54	+0.51	+1.52	-1.28	-0.92
55-59	+0.61	-0.79	+0.26	-0.11
60-64	-0.37	+1.16	-0.89	+0.07
65-69	-0.80	-0.48	+0.24	+1.17
70-74	-0.13	+0.51	-0.04	-0.37
75-	+0.38	-2.13	+1.86	-0.01

It should be noted that the analysis can be improved slightly if the actual age distributions within each of the four cities is used, but this improvement complicates the analysis at the same time. △.

19.7. Three-way contingency tables

The distribution of n units according to three criteria, each with a finite number of categories, is called a **three-way contingency table**. If the criteria have I, J and K categories respectively the table is also called an (I×J×K)-contingency table. A unit belonging simultaneously to the categories i, j and k of the first, second and third criterion respectively is said to belong to cell (i,j,k) of the table. This terminology refers to a visualization of the table as a block with I rows, J columns and K layers.

The number of units in the (i,j,k)'th cell is denoted x_{ijk}. If a given number of units, n, are drawn from a large population by simple random sampling, the observed numbers in the cells of the table can be described by a multinomial distribution, i.e. the x_{ijk}'s are observed values of an (I×K×J)-dimensional random variable

$$(19.35) \quad (X_{111},\ldots,X_{IJK}) \sim M(n, p_{111},\ldots,p_{IJK}),$$

where p_{ijk} is the proportion of units in the population belonging simultaneously to the categories i, j and k of the three criteria.

Three-way contingency tables can be analysed by means of so-called **log-linear models**. In a log-linear model, the expected values of the X_{ijk}'s are reparameterized as

$$(19.36) \quad \ln E[X_{ijk}] = \ln(np_{ijk}) = \theta + \theta_i^{(1)} + \theta_j^{(2)} + \theta_k^{(3)} + \theta_{ij}^{(12)} + \theta_{ik}^{(13)}$$
$$+ \theta_{jk}^{(23)} + \theta_{ijk}^{(123)}.$$

The parameter θ is called the **overall mean**, $\theta_i^{(1)}$, $\theta_j^{(2)}$ and $\theta_k^{(3)}$ are called **main effects** and the remaining parameters are called **interactions**. Constraints of the form $\sum_i \theta_i^{(1)} = 0$, $\sum_i \sum_j \theta_{ij}^{(12)} = 0$ and so on are imposed on (19.36) such that it is a true reparameterization of the multinomial model in the sense that to each set of p_{ijk}'s, there exists a unique set of θ's satisfying (19.36). Any hypothesis expressed in terms of the p_{ijk}'s can be expressed uniquely in terms of the log-linear parameters. By means of the log-linear representation (19.36), most hypotheses of interest can be expressed in particularly simple ways. Consider the following hypotheses, where a dot indicates summation over the index replaced by the dot:

(19.37) $$H_1: \frac{p_{ijk}}{p_{..k}} = \frac{p_{i.k}}{p_{..k}} \frac{p_{.jk}}{p_{..k}},$$

(19.38) $$H_2: \begin{cases} p_{ij.} = p_{i..} p_{.j.} \\ p_{i.k} = p_{i..} p_{..k} \end{cases}$$

(19.39) $$H_3: p_{ijk} = p_{i..} p_{.j.} p_{..k}.$$

In order to interpret these hypotheses, define the events

A_i = {a sampled unit belongs to category i of criterion 1},

B_j = {a sampled unit belongs to category j of criterion 2}

and

C_k = {a sampled unit belongs to category k of criterion 3}.

The hypothesis H_1 is then equivalent to

$$P(A_i \cap B_j | C_k) = P(A_i | C_k) P(B_j | C_k),$$

i.e. given the observed category of criterion 3, the distribution over the categories of criteria 1 and 2 are independent. Under H_1, an observed interaction or lack of independence between criteria 1 and 2 can thus be explained by a common dependency on criterion 3. Accordingly, H_1 is called the hypothesis of **conditional independence**. Conditional independence in a three-way contingency table is illustrated in fig. 19.1 (a) where a line indicates that the criteria in question interact.

Hypothesis H_2 can be written

$$P(A_i \cap B_j) = P(A_i) P(B_j)$$

and

$$P(A_i \cap C_k) = P(A_i) P(C_k)$$

The interpretation of H_2 is thus that the distribution over the categories of criterion 1 is independent of the distribution over the categories of criterion 2 as well as over the categories of criterion 3. This is illustrated in fig. 19.1(b). Finally, H_3 can be expressed as

$$P(A_i \cap B_j \cap C_k) = P(A_i) P(B_j) P(C_k),$$

implying that the distribution over the categories of all three criteria are independent, as illustrated in fig. 19.1(c).

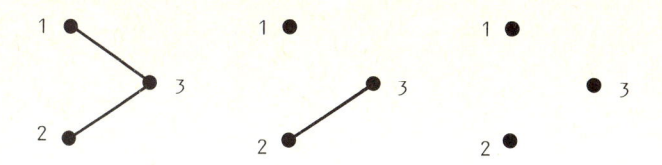

Fig. 19.1. Graphical illustration of the hypotheses H_1, H_2 and H_3.

Theorem 19.1

The hypothesis H_1 is equivalent to

(19.40) $\theta_{ijk}^{(123)} = \theta_{ij}^{(12)} = 0$ for all i, j and k,

H_2 is equivalent to

(19.41) $\theta_{ijk}^{(123)} = \theta_{ij}^{(12)} = \theta_{ik}^{(13)} = 0$ for all i, j and k,

and H_3 is equivalent to

(19.42) $\theta_{ijk}^{(123)} = \theta_{ij}^{(12)} = \theta_{ik}^{(13)} = \theta_{jk}^{(23)} = 0$ for all i, j and k.

The hypotheses H_1, H_2 and H_3 are **hierarchical** in the sense that if H_2 is satisfied then H_1 is also satisfied, and if H_3 is satisfied then H_2 and hence H_1 are also satisfied. The three hypotheses can, therefore, be tested successively. First H_1 is tested, and if H_1 is accepted, then H_2 can be tested, and if H_2 is accepted, H_3 can be tested.

If the parametric formulations of H_1, H_2 and H_3 in theorem 19.1 are related to the interpretation of the hypotheses in terms of independence and conditional independence, it is seen that the interaction parameters represent dependencies between the criteria. Thus, in order for criteria 1 and 2 to be independent, given criterion 3, all interactions involving criteria 1 and 2 must be zero, i.e. $\theta_{ijk}^{(123)}=0$ and $\theta_{ij}^{(12)}=0$ for all i, j and k. If, in addition, criteria 1 and 3 are independent, then $\theta_{ik}^{(13)}$ must be zero for all i and k. Under H_3, all three criteria are independent, corresponding to all interactions being zero, such that the model only contains the over-all mean θ and the main effects $\theta_i^{(1)}$, $\theta_j^{(2)}$ and $\theta_k^{(3)}$.

Under H_1, the expected numbers np_{ijk} in the cells of the contingency table are

(19.43) $$n\hat{p}_{ijk} = x_{i.k} x_{.jk} / x_{..k},$$

under H_2,

(19.44) $$n\hat{p}_{ijk} = x_{i..} x_{.jk} / n,$$

and under H_3,

(19.45) $$n\hat{p}_{ijk} = x_{i..} x_{.j.} x_{..k} / n^2.$$

All hypotheses are tested by a test statistic of the form

(19.46) $$Q = \sum_{i=1}^{I} \sum_{j=1}^{J} \sum_{k=1}^{K} (X_{ijk} - n\hat{p}_{ijk})^2 / (n\hat{p}_{ijk}),$$

the distribution of which can be approximated by a χ^2-distribution. The number of degrees of freedom is equal to the number of log-linear parameters with free variation assumed to be zero under the hypothesis in question.

Under H_1, the number of parameters with free variation assumed to be zero is $(I-1)(J-1)(K-1)+(I-1)(J-1)$, under H_2 $(I-1)(K-1)$ additional θ's are assumed to be zero; and under H_3 $(I-1)(J-1)(K-1)+(I-1)(J-1)+(I-1)(K-1)+(J-1)(K-1)$ parameters are assumed to be zero.

In many applications, H_1 is the hypothesis of greatest interest. An apparent dependency between two criteria can then be explained by the influence of a third criterion. An analysis of the marginal two-way contingency table of criteria 1 and 2 may show that the two criteria are dependent. By including criterion 3, however, it is revealed that this dependency is in fact due to the influence of criterion 3.

Example 19.4

The data considered in this example originate from a study carried out in 1968 of the job satisfaction of blue collar workers. Three criteria are considered: (1) the job satisfaction of the worker, (2) the job satisfaction of his supervisor and (3) the quality of the management at his factory. Criteria (1) and (2) were measured by the number of positive answers to a set of questions concerning the satisfaction with various aspects of working life. Criterion 3 was measured by external evaluation. For all three criteria, two categories were used to form the three-way contingency table shown as table 19.11.

Table 19.11. The distribution of 715 workers according to two measures of satisfaction and the quality of the management.

Quality of management	Job satisfaction of supervisor	Job satisfaction of worker Low	High
Bad	Low	103	87
	High	32	42
Good	Low	59	109
	High	78	205

Source: Eggert Petersen: Job Satisfaction in 15 Factories.
Copenhagen Institute for Mental Health. 1968.
Table M/7.

Assuming that the 715 workers comprise a simple random sample of blue collar workers in Denmark in 1968, the model (19.35) can be used to explore the dependencies between the three criteria in question. First the hypothesis

(19.47) $\quad H_1: \theta_{ijk}^{(123)} = \theta_{ij}^{(12)} = 0, \quad i,j,k = 1,2,$

is tested by (19.46) with (19.43) inserted for $n\hat{p}_{ijk}$. The interpretation of (19.47), as illustrated in fig.19.2, is that an interaction between the job satisfaction of a worker and that of his supervisor can be explained by the common dependency on the quality of the management.

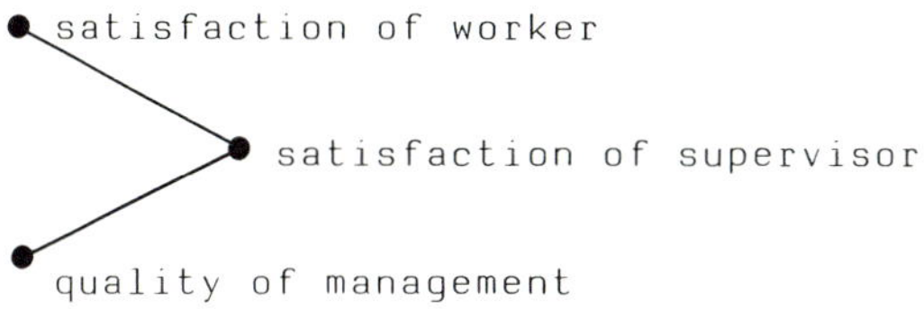

Fig. 19.2. Graphical illustration of hypothesis (19.47).

The level of significance can be computed approximately from a χ^2-distribution with 2 degrees of freedom since $(2-1)(2-1)(2-1)+(2-1)(2-1)=2$ log-linear parameters with free variation are zero under H_1. With q=5.4, the level of significance is

$$p \simeq P(Q \geq 5.4) = 0.067.$$

Accepting H_1, further tests show that neither $\theta_{ik}^{(13)}$ nor $\theta_{jk}^{(23)}$ can be assumed to be zero. Hence it can be concluded that the quality of the management seems to be a more important factor for the job satisfaction of the worker than the job satisfaction of the supervisor. The conditional independence between criteria 1 and 2 illustrated in fig. 19.2 does not manifest itself as independence in the marginal two-way contingency table between the two criteria shown in table 19.12. In

Table 19.12. Two-way contingency table for the job satisfaction of 715 workers and the job satisfaction of their supervisors.

Job satisfaction of supervisor	Job satisfaction of worker	
	Low	High
Low	162	196
High	110	247

fact, the value of the test statistic (19.8) for independence in table 19.12 is q=15.8 with approximate level of significance p=0.0001 computed in a χ^2-distribution with 1 degree of freedom. △.

It is illustrative to consider a decomposition of (19.46) according to the value of k. When K=2, (19.46) can be written

$$(19.48) \quad Q = \sum\sum_{ij}(X_{ij1}-n\hat{p}_{ij1})^2/(n\hat{p}_{ij1}) + \sum\sum_{ij}(X_{ij2}-n\hat{p}_{ij2})^2/(n\hat{p}_{ij2}).$$

Under (19.40), the expected number in cell (i,j,k) is given by (19.43), which for k=1 becomes

$$n\hat{p}_{ij1} = x_{i.1} x_{.j1}/x_{..1}.$$

The first term in (19.48) is thus the observed value of the Q-test statistic for independence between criteria 1 and 2, if only cells with k=1 are considered, while the second term in a similar way is the observed test statistic for independence between criteria 1 and 2 if only cells with k=2 are considered. Under H_1, both terms are approximately χ^2-distributed with one degree of freedom. It follows that the test statistic for H_1 is obtained by adding the two test statistics for tests of independence between criteria 1 and 2 given the category of criteria 3.

Example 19.5

As a final example a set of data from the investigation referred to in example 19.2 is considered. Table 19.13 shows the number of traffic accidents with personal injury in Sweden in two periods in 1961 and in two periods in 1962. In each of the years, one period was without speed limits and in the other a speed limit of 90 km/hour was imposed. All accidents were counted for main roads and secondary roads separately.

Table 19.13. Observed number of traffic accidents with personal injuries in Sweden distributed according to periods with and without speed limits and road type.

Year	Speed limit	Road type Main road	Secondary road
1961	90 km/hour	8	42
	None	57	106
1962	90 km/hour	11	37
	None	45	69

In order to study the dependencies between the criteria (1) "Year", (2) "Speed limit" and (3) "Road type", a log-linear model can be applied.

The analysis of the data shows that all three versions of the hypothesis (19.37) are accepted, and that also

(19.49) $\quad \theta_{ijk}^{(123)} = \theta_{ij}^{(12)} = \theta_{ik}^{(13)} = 0$

is accepted. The only dependency in the table is thus between the "Speed limit" criterion and the "Road type" criterion, so the data can be described by the log-linear model

$$\ln E[X_{ijk}] = \theta + \theta_i^{(1)} + \theta_j^{(2)} + \theta_k^{(3)} + \theta_{jk}^{(23)},$$

as illustrated in fig. 19.3.

● year

● road type

● speed limit

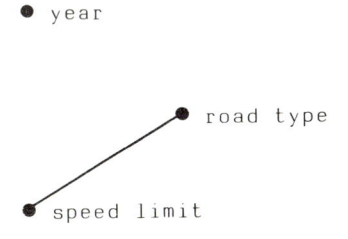

Fig. 19.3. Graphical illustration of the model selected for table 19.13.

The conclusion of the analysis is that the effect of speed limits depends on the road type considered. The distribution of accidents on road types and the categories "Speed limit" and "No speed limit" does not seem to depend on the year considered. △.

Appendix Table

Upper and lower bounds for the percentiles of the distribution of the Durbin-Watson test statistic.

Number of cases	Percentile	\multicolumn{2}{c}{1}	\multicolumn{2}{c}{2}	\multicolumn{2}{c}{3}	\multicolumn{2}{c}{4}	\multicolumn{2}{c}{5}
		d_1	d_2	d_1	d_2	d_1	d_2	d_1	d_2	d_1	d_2
15	.01	.81	1.07	.70	1.25	.59	1.46	.49	1.70	.39	1.96
	.025	.95	1.23	.83	1.40	.71	1.61	.59	1.84	.48	2.09
	.05	1.08	1.36	.95	1.54	.82	1.75	.69	1.97	.56	2.21
20	.01	.95	1.15	.86	1.27	.77	1.41	.68	1.57	.60	1.74
	.025	1.08	1.28	.99	1.41	.89	1.55	.79	1.70	.70	1.87
	.05	1.20	1.41	1.10	1.54	1.00	1.68	.90	1.83	.79	1.99
25	.01	1.05	1.21	.98	1.30	.90	1.41	.83	1.52	.75	1.65
	.025	1.18	1.34	1.10	1.43	1.01	1.54	.94	1.65	.86	1.77
	.05	1.29	1.45	1.21	1.55	1.12	1.66	1.04	1.77	.95	1.89
30	.01	1.13	1.26	1.07	1.34	1.01	1.42	.94	1.51	.88	1.61
	.025	1.25	1.38	1.18	1.46	1.12	1.54	1.05	1.63	.98	1.73
	.05	1.35	1.49	1.28	1.57	1.21	1.65	1.14	1.74	1.07	1.83
40	.01	1.25	1.34	1.20	1.40	1.15	1.46	1.10	1.52	1.05	1.58
	.025	1.35	1.45	1.30	1.51	1.25	1.57	1.20	1.63	1.15	1.69
	.05	1.44	1.54	1.39	1.60	1.34	1.66	1.29	1.72	1.23	1.79
50	.01	1.32	1.40	1.28	1.45	1.24	1.49	1.20	1.54	1.16	1.59
	.025	1.42	1.50	1.38	1.54	1.34	1.59	1.30	1.64	1.26	1.69
	.05	1.50	1.59	1.46	1.63	1.42	1.67	1.38	1.72	1.34	1.77
60	.01	1.38	1.45	1.35	1.48	1.32	1.52	1.28	1.56	1.25	1.60
	.025	1.47	1.54	1.44	1.57	1.40	1.61	1.37	1.65	1.33	1.69
	.05	1.55	1.62	1.51	1.65	1.48	1.69	1.44	1.73	1.41	1.77
80	.01	1.47	1.52	1.44	1.54	1.42	1.57	1.39	1.60	1.36	1.62
	.025	1.54	1.59	1.52	1.62	1.49	1.65	1.47	1.67	1.44	1.70
	.05	1.61	1.66	1.59	1.69	1.56	1.72	1.53	1.74	1.51	1.77
100	.01	1.52	1.56	1.50	1.58	1.48	1.60	1.46	1.63	1.44	1.65
	.025	1.59	1.63	1.57	1.65	1.55	1.67	1.53	1.70	1.51	1.72
	.05	1.65	1.69	1.63	1.72	1.61	1.74	1.59	1.76	1.57	1.78

Index

A

acceptance region, 216
additive structure, 22
additivity theorem, binomial distribution, 163
additivity theorem, χ^2-distribution, 172
additivity theorem, exponential distribution, 163
additivity theorem, mean values, 149
additivity theorem, normal distribution, 164
additivity theorem, Poisson distribution, 162
additivity theorem, probabilities, 36, 37
additivity theorem, variances, 149
allocation of a sample, 377
allocation, optimal, 377
allocation, proportional, 377
alternative hypothesis, 210
analysis of variance, 258
analysis of variance, regression model, 286
approximate confidence interval, 211
approximate test, 228
asymptotic distribution, 179
asymptotic distribution of ML-estimator, 200
asymptotically unbiased estimator, 199
autocorrelation, 294, 354
autoregression, first order, 355
autoregressive process, 355
average, 80
average, distribution of, 170, 173
average, grouped distribution, 85
average, mean value and variance of, 150
average, population, 362
axioms for probabilities, 34

B

Bartlett's test, 260
Bayes' theorem, 41
bias, 196
binomial coefficient, 90
binomial distribution, 89, 136
binomial distribution, additivity theorem, 163
binomial distribution, asymptotic limit, 179
binomial distributions, comparison of, 411
binomial distribution, conditional, 223, 225
binomial distribution, confidence interval, 202, 209
binomial distribution, estimation, 190, 195
binomial probability, 53
binomial process, 135
binary case, sampling, 365
block diagram, 9
box plot, 15

C

case, 275
case analysis, 334
categorical variable, 7
Cauchy distribution, 175
centralized regression model, 280
central limit theorem, 181
central moment, 76
check of additive structure, 22
check of multiplicative structure, 22
chi-square distribution, 170
chi-square distribution, limiting, 287, 289
classification, 40
cluster sampling, 363
Cochran-Fisher theorem, 173
coefficient of determination, 286, 326
collinearity, 338
column criterion, 403
comparison of two independent samples, 246
complementary event, 26, 35

composite hypothesis, 240
conditional density function, 145
conditional distribution, 145
conditional independence, 424
conditional mean value, 146
conditional point probability, 145
conditional probability, 39
conditional test, 222
conditional variance, 146
confidence level, 203
confidence ellipsoid, 329
confidence interval, 202, 233
confidence intervals, normal distribution, 204
confidence intervals, regression analysis, 285
confidence intervals, sampling theory, 366, 370, 376
consistency, 198
contingency table, two-way, 2, 402
contingency table, three-way, 423
continuous random variable, 51, 56
Cook's distance, 335
correlation coefficient, 153
correlation coefficient, empirical, 155
covariance, empirical, 155
covariance matrix, 166
criterions, in contingency table, 403
critical region, 216
critical region, t-test, 241
critical region, u-test, 236
cumulative frequency function, 17

D

data set, 7
decision procedure, 262
decomposition theorem, 173
degrees of freedom, 171
degrees of freedom, computation, 391, 405, 410, 426
de Moivre-Laplace theorem, 179
density function, 56
density function, conditional, 145
density function, multi-dimensional, 140
density, marginal, 144
descriptive statistics, 7
design, sampling, 362
diagnostics, regression analysis, 335
disjoint events, 29
discrete random variable, 51, 52
dispersion measure, 72, 80
distribution function, 47, 50
distribution function, multi-dimensional, 140
distribution free test, 267
Durbin-Watson test, 356

E

empirical correlation coefficient, 155
empirical covariance, 155
empirical distribution, 8
empirical variance, 80
empirical variance, distribution, 170, 173
empirical variance, grouped distribution, 85
empty event, 27, 35
equally likely events, 32
Erlang distribution, 133, 136, 163
error of type I, 231
error of type II, 232
error term, 276, 316
estimation error, 193
estimation, survey sampling, 366, 368, 375
estimation theory, 185
estimator, 186
elementary event, 26
event, 26
expectation, 66
experimental data, 302
explanatory variable, 275
exponential distribution, 60, 125, 136
exponential distribution, additivity theorem, 163
exponential distribution, mean value, 70
exponential distribution, variance and third moment, 78
extrapolation, 296, 345
extremes, 15

D

factorial moment, 75
F-distribution, 175
first order difference, 358
Fisher distribution, 175
fitted value, 279, 322
frequency distribution, 8
F-test, comparison of two variances, 248
F-test, analysis of variance, 261

G

gamma distribution, 132
Gauss-Markov theorem, 282
geometric distribution, 105, 136
goodness-of-fit test, 391
goodness-of-fit test, continuous distribution, 396
goodness-of-fit test, discrete distribution, 392
grouped distribution, 16
grouped variable, 7

H

hat matrix, 322
heteroscedasticity, 347
hierachical hypothesis, 425
histogram, 9, 16, 64
homogeneity, hypothesis of, 410
homogeneity, test of, 409
hypergeometric distribution, 108, 184
hypergeometric distribution, asymptotic limit, 182
hypergeometric distribution, confidence interval, 209
hypergeometric distribution, conditional, 226
hypergeometric distribution, estimation, 185, 192
hypergeometric distribution, survey sampling, 365
hypothesis, 214
hypothesis of homogeneity, 410
hypothesis of independence, 404

I

independence, conditional, 424
independence hypothesis, 404
independence of random variables, 147, 148
independence, stochastic, 44
inference theory, 169, 184
intensity, 100
interaction, 423
interquartile distance, 15, 79
interpolation, 345
intersection of events, 29
interval estimation, 233
interval estimate, 202

J

joint density function, 140
joint distribution function, 140

L

lagged variable, 358
Laplace's formula, 32
law of large numbers, 176, 178
law of total probability, 40
least squares estimator, 278, 320
level of significance, 215
level of significance, t-test, 241
level of significance, u-test, 236
leverage, 347, 335
likelihood equation, 188, 190
likelihood function, 187
likelihood ratio, 219
likelihood ratio test, 219
limit theorems, 169, 179
linear dependence between random variables, 154
linear estimator, 282
linear regression, 275
linear regression, simple, 276
linear relationship, 20
linear transformation, 62
linear transformation, mean and variance, 75
linear transformation, normal distribution, 113
location measure, 15, 80
location parameter, 71
logarithmic transformation, 72
log-likelihood function, 188, 190
log-linear model, 423
log-normal distribution, 122
lower confidence limit, 203
lower quartile, 15
LS-method, 278, 319

M

Mahalanobis distance, 346
main effect, 423
marginal analysis in two-way table, 418
marginal density, 114
marginal distribution, 143
marginal point probability, 143
maximum likelihood, 187
mean, binomial distribution, 94
mean, χ^2-distribution, 171
mean, exponential distribution, 126
mean, gamma distribution, 133
mean, hypergeometric distribution, 109
mean, normal distribution, 112
mean, normal distribution, confidence interval for, 204
mean, Pareto distribution, 130
mean, Pascal distribution, 104
mean, Poisson distribution, 98
mean squared error, 193
mean value, 66
mean value, conditional, 146
mean value, linear transformation, 75
mean value, transformed random variable, 74
mean value vector, 166
median, 15, 78
method of least squares, 278, 319
minimum variance unbiased estimator, 193
ML-estimate, 187, 191
ML-estimate, contingency tables, 404, 410, 414
ML-estimates, parametric multinomial distribution, 389, 394, 397
ML-estimates, weighted regression, 348
ML-estimation, 187

ML-estimator, 188, 191
ML-estimator, asymptotic distribution, 200
mode, 79
multicollinearity, 339
multi-dimensional random variable, 107, 137
multinomial coefficient, 108
multinomial distribution, 107, 159, 386, 399, 420, 423
multinomial distribution, parametric, 399, 403, 410, 412
multiple comparisons, 262
multiple decision procedure, 262
multiple linear regression, 316
multiplication rule for probabilities, 39, 47
multiplicative Poissonmodel, 412
multiplicative structure, 22
multi-variate normal distribution, 165

N

negative binomial distribution, 103
non-experimental data, 302
non-parametric tests, 267
normal distribution, 112, 185
normal distribution, additivity theorem, 164
normal distribution, estimation, 191, 194, 199
normal distribution, multi-variate, 165
normal distribution, standardized, 114

O

observation, 26
optimal allocation, 377
order statistics, 14
outcome, 26
over-all mean, 423

P

pairwise observations, model for, 253, 256
parametric multinomial distribution, 389, 403, 410, 412
Pareto distribution, 64, 129
Pareto distribution, mean value, 70
Pascal distribution, 102, 136
percentile, 14, 79
pie chart, 9
planned experiment 302
point estimate, 185
point probability, 52
point probability, conditional, 145
point probability, joint, 137
point probability, marginal, 143
Poisson distribution, 95, 136, 395, 399, 412

Poisson distribution, additivity theorem, 162
Poisson distribution, asymptotic limit, 182
Poisson distribution, conditional, 223
Poisson distributions, comparison of, 399
Poisson distribution, estimation, 189, 196, 199, 200
Poisson model, multiplicative, 412
Poisson process, 99, 135
population average, 362
population mean, 368
population total, 362
population variance, 368
power function, 232
power function, u-test, 237
power of test, 232
precision of estimator, 193
predicted value, 279, 322
prediction, 295, 343
prediction interval, 296, 344
prediction variance, 344
probability, 34
probability distribution, 47
probability paper, 118
probability parameter, 90
probability plot, exponential distribution, 127
probability plot, normal distribution, 118
probability selection in sampling, 364
proportional allocation, 377

Q

quadratic form, 172
qualitative observation, 26
quantitative observation, 26
quantitative variable, 7
quartile, 15, 79
quartile distance, 15, 79
Q-test, 391
Q-test, check of continuous distribution, 396
Q-test, check of discrete distribution, 392
Q-test statistic, 387, 390, 392, 397, 400, 405, 410, 412, 414, 419, 426
Q-test, the variance in a normal distribution, 241

R

R^2, 286, 326
random variable, 50
random variable, m-dimensional, 137
regression analysis, 5, 275
regression diagnostics, 335
regression model, 277

regression model, centralized, 280
regression model, multiple, 316
regression model, simple linear, 277
relative frequency, 31
replacement, sampling with, 362
replacement, sampling without, 362, 374
residual, 279, 292, 321
residual analysis, 323
residual, contingency tables, 405
residual plot, 292, 324
residual standardized, 292, 324
residual sum of squares, 280, 321
response variable, 275
row criterion, 403
RSS, 280, 321

S

sample fraction, 366
sample function, 169
sample mean, 368, 375
sample variance, 26, 369, 375
sampling, binary case, 365
sampling, cluster, 363
sampling design, 362
sampling procedure, 362
sampling procedure, effect of, 417
sampling, simple random, 363, 368
sampling, stratified, 363, 373
sampling theory, 362
sampling with replacement, 46, 110, 365
sampling without replacement, 46, 108, 362, 274,
scale invariance, exponential distribution, 126
scale invariance, gamma distribution, 133
scale parameter, 133
Sct. Petersburg paradox, 67
selection probability, 364
selection ratio, 379
shape parameter, 133
skew distribution, 77
significance level, 215
significance test, 215
sign test, 269
simple linear regression, 276
simple random sampling, 362, 368
standard deviation, 72
standardized normal distribution, 114
standardized random variable, 76
standardized residual, 292, 324
statistic, 169
statistical model, 140, 184
statistical test, 214
stem and leaf diagram, 11
stochastic independence, 44
stochastic process, 99, 135
stratified sampling, 135, 363

stratum mean, 374
stratum variance, 374
stratum weight, 374
sufficient statistic, 190
survey sampling, 3, 361
symmetric distribution, 76

T

table of variation, two-way contingency table, 420
Tchebychev's inequality, 177
t-distribution, 174
test, 214
test level, 216
test statistic, 215
time series, 354
total, population, 362
total variation, 286
transformation, 62, 303
true value, 186
truncation, 130
t-test, 240
t-test, analysis of variance, 262
t-test, comparison of two mean values, 250
t-test, pairwise observations, 250
t-test, regression analysis, 287, 327
two independent samples, comparison, 246, 256
two regression lines, comparison, 310
two-sided confidence interval, 203
two-way table, 22
type I error, 231
type II error, 232

U

upper confidence limit, 203
upper quartile, 15
unbiased estimator, 192
unbiased estimator, asymptotically, 199
uncorrelated random variables, 150, 154
uniform distribution, 59
uniform distribution, mean value, 69
uniform distribution, variance, 72
unimodal distribution, 79
union of events, 28
u-test, 218, 235
u-test, comparison of two mean values, 251

V

variance, 71
variance, binomial distribution, 94

variance, exponential distribution, 126
variance, χ^2-distribution, 171
variance, conditional, 146
variance, gamma distribution, 133
variance, hypergeometric distribution, 109
variance of linear transformation, 75
variance, normal distribution, 112
variance in normal distribution, confidence interval for, 208
variance, Pareto distribution, 130
variance, Pascal distribution, 104
variance, Poisson distribution, 98
variation between samples, 260
variation between strata, 386
variation within samples, 260
variation within strata, 386

W

waiting time distribution, 126, 134, 136
weighted least squares estimate, 349
Wilcoxon test, one sample, 271
Wilcoxon test, two samples, 273
WLS-estimate, 249

Index of Examples with Real Data

Age of wife and husband at time of divorce, 157

Alcohol content in human blood, 236, 251

American aptitude test, 92

Annual profits for two bonds, 253, 271

Apartments in Denmark according to number of residents, 67

Arrivals to check-out in supermarket, 64, 87, 100, 214, 232, 395

Beer bottling, 243

Cars passing a counting station, 102, 105

Consumer price index and land value, 21

Content of cholesterol in blood, 123

Credit percentages on houses in Denmark, 392

Danish population distributed according to sex and geographical region, 27, 38

Danish wage index and price index 1957-81, 358

Effect of organic solvents on ISI-index for painters, 283, 312

Electricity production and fuel consumption, 5, 297

Examinations at the Copenhagen School of Business Administration, 230

Farms distributed according to size, 18

Fluctuations of the exchange rate between US$ and Danish Kroner, 120

Gross income distribution in Denmark 1981, 131

Heights of American men, 116

Households in Denmark distributed according to number of rooms and number of inhabitants, 381

Incomes for families in Elsinore, 81, 85, 263

Income and number of children, 19

Income and type of holiday, 8

Indoor climate at the University of Copenhagen, 226

Job satisfaction of blue collar workers, 426

Live birth in Greater Copenhagen distributed according to sex, 196

Lung cancer cases in four Danish cities, 421

Marital status for Danish population, 159

Married women according to employment and degree of urbanization, 2, 406

Mobility on Danish labour market, 401

Monthly exchange rate of US$ 1983 to 1984, 7, 12, 14, 16

Number of inhabitants per apartment, 54

Party affiliation and employment, 42

Political sample surveys, 367, 383

Social group and employment status, 30, 33

Speed limits and traffic accidents, 24, 224, 414, 429

Temporary social security payment and three socio-demografic variables, 329, 336, 341, 351

Test of psychic vulnerability, 138, 144, 146, 147, 154, 157

Traffic accidents in Sweden according to road type, 23, 224, 414, 429

Traffic accidents involving pedestrians, 387, 390, 400

Value added and number of employmee's for Danish manifacturing companies, 305

Waiting time in a queue, 127

Wild cat oil well discoveries in Canada, 97